One-Stop Internet Resources

Log on to

marketingessentials.glencoe.com

Online Learning Center

- Math Review and Practice
- Annotated Marketing Plan
- DECA Resources
- Marketing Internship Guidelines and Rubrics
- Online Action Enrichment
- Online Student Edition

Student Resources

- Student Activity Workbook
- Marketing Math Workbook
- Competitive Events Workbook
- *BusinessWeek* Reader With Case Studies
- Marketing Research Activity Workbook
- School-to-Work Activity Workbook

Marketing Education Resources

- Business Plan Project Workbook
- Marketing Education Web Site at glencoe.com/sec/marketingeducation
- *Virtual Business*®

Marketing Essentials

Lois Schneider Farese

Grady Kimbrell

Carl A. Woloszyk, Ph.D.

New York, New York Columbus, Ohio Chicago, Illinois Peoria, Illinois Woodland Hills, California

Glencoe

The McGraw-Hill Companies

Printed in the United States of America.

Send all inquiries to:
Glencoe/McGraw-Hill
21600 Oxnard Street, Suite 500
Woodland Hills, CA 91367

ISBN 0-07-861257-8 (Student Edition)
ISBN 0-07-868914-7 (Teacher Wraparound Edition)

2 3 4 5 6 7 8 9 079 10 09 08 07 06 05

About the Authors

Lois Schneider Farese is a nationally recognized secondary marketing educator and DECA advisor from New Jersey. She has been involved in organizing and running New Jersey regional and state DECA conferences and has also participated as series director and event manager at state and national DECA conferences. The State Officer Action Team presented Farese with the Outstanding Service Award for her dedication, professionalism, and commitment to New Jersey DECA in 1993, 1996, and 1999, as well as with the Honorary Life Membership Award in 1990 for setting a new level of professionalism for local advisors. She was inducted into the DECA Hall of Fame in 1996.

Farese was named "Teacher of the Year" in 1981 by the Marketing Education Association of New Jersey. In 1993 and 1999, the University of Richmond recognized Farese for her contributions to the intellectual growth and achievement of students who graduated from her marketing program. In 2000, Farese was the nominee from Northern Highlands Regional High School for the Princeton Prize for Distinguished Secondary School Teaching.

Farese holds a bachelor's degree in business and distributive education and two master's degrees from Montclair State University in New Jersey.

Grady Kimbrell, a nationally recognized author and consultant on career education, began his career in education teaching high school business in Kansas. After relocating to Southern California, Kimbrell taught business courses and coordinated students' in-class activities with their on-the-job experience. He later directed the work experience program for the high schools of Santa Barbara, California.

A pioneer in the use of computers as a tool for educational research, Kimbrell has assisted school districts with a wide variety of research and evaluation activities. His research into on-the-job work activities led to the development of a new type of career interest inventory used in career guidance. In addition, Kimbrell has served on numerous state instructional program committees and writing teams, designed educational computer programs, and produced educational films.

Kimbrell holds degrees in business administration, educational psychology, and business education.

Carl A. Woloszyk is a professor emeritus from Western Michigan University with an extensive background in marketing education. He has served as a state department of education consultant for marketing and cooperative education, DECA and Delta Epsilon Chi state advisor, a career and technical administrator for a regional education service agency, and a secondary marketing teacher-coordinator. As a secondary marketing teacher-coordinator, he taught beginning and advanced marketing courses. His students have received numerous awards at district, state, and national DECA conferences. Woloszyk has served on the board of directors for DECA; he has been president of the Marketing Education Foundation and of the Cooperative Work Experience Education Association of ACTE. He is a board member of the Michigan Marketing Educators' Association. He has received the Marketing Education Professional Award from the national Marketing Education Association for Exemplary Service to Marketing Education.

Woloszyk holds a master's degree from Eastern Michigan University and an educational specialist degree in occupational education from the University of Michigan. He received his doctorate in business and distributive education from Michigan State University.

Reviewers

Dennis Bristow
Professor of Marketing
St. Cloud State University
St. Cloud, Minnesota

Monica Caillouet
East Ascension High School
Gonzales, Louisiana

Deborah Deacon
Stoneham High School
Stoneham, Massachusetts

Jennifer Killingsworth
West Hall High School
Oakwood, Georgia

Liberty A. Lacy
Woodland High School
Woodland, Washington

Atkins D. Trey Michael, III
Marketing Education Consultant
North Carolina Department of Public Instruction

Tom Scharine
Oregon High School
Oregon, Wisconsin

Michael T. Seltzer
Oxford Academy
Cypress, California

James W. Todd
Mac Arthur High School
San Antonio, Texas

Michelle Totra
Lindbergh High School
St. Louis, Missouri

Dana Young
Yuma High School
Yuma, Colorado

Contributing Writer

Priscilla McCalla
Professional and Program Development Director
DECA
Reston, Virginia

CONTENTS

CONTENTS

CONTENTS

CONTENTS

CONTENTS

CONTENTS

CONTENTS

CONTENTS

CONTENTS

CONTENTS

CONTENTS

CONTENTS

CONTENTS

Understanding the Unit

Unit Opener

Marketing Essentials has 12 units that group the 38 chapters by theme. Each unit opens with an advertisement that shows marketing in action.

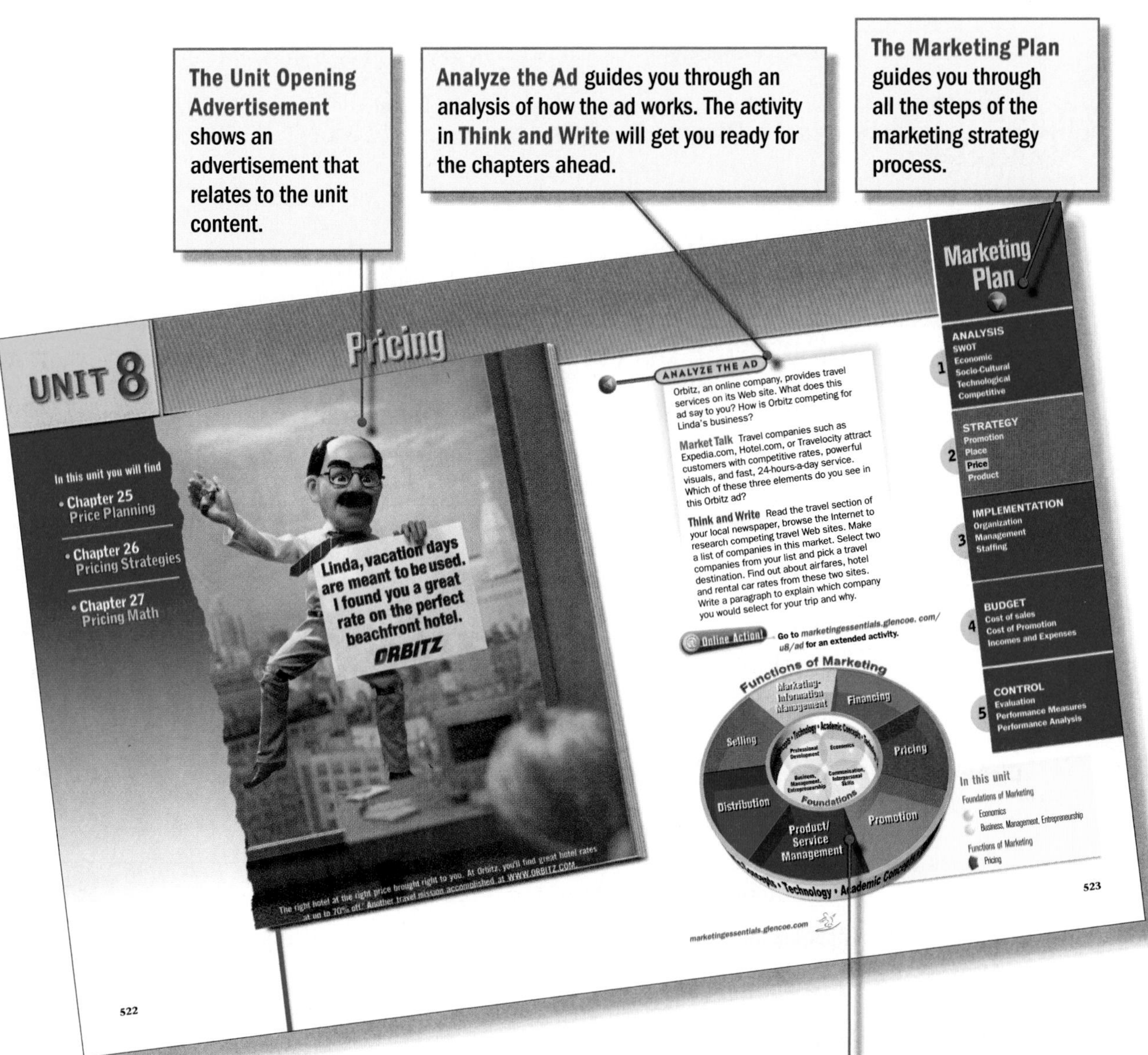

The Marketing Wheel illustrates basic marketing concepts. The four marketing foundations are important building blocks: Business, Management, and Entrepreneurship; Communication and Interpersonal Skills; Economics; and Professional Development. The marketing functions are what marketers do: Distribution, Financing, Marketing-Information Management, Pricing, Product/Service Management, Promotion, and Selling.

The Marketing Internship

Each unit closes with a simulated DECA event called **Marketing Internship.** Each internship gives you a background scenario, an assignment, and a suggested strategy. After that, you make all the decisions—you're the marketer!

Build Your Portfolio helps you collect your reports, charts, and plans from each Marketing Internship to create a portfolio of your best work. You can use the portfolio when you apply for real internships and jobs.

MARKETING INTERNSHIP

A SIMULATED DECA PRODUCT AND SERVICE MANAGEMENT EVENT

Pricing Toys

BASIC BACKGROUND

Tri-Star Toys is introducing two new products influenced by Japanese pop culture. One is a trading card game called Laszot. The other is a line of 12-inch stuffed animals called Mie Dolls. Each doll is supposed to have a unique trait, such as being friendly or mischievous.

Setting a Price Tri-Star Toys wants your firm's help deciding how to price these two new products. The biggest cost factor with the trading card games is creating the stories and characters. Assume a cost of \$.25 per card for the initial production. For the dolls, assume an initial cost of \$4.50. Marketing expenses are \$0.05 per trading card and \$1.00 per doll. Demand for both items depends on conditions in the marketplace, which you will need to determine.

YOUR OBJECTIVE

Your objective is to prepare an effective pricing and retail strategy for Tri-Star's two new products. The company wants to make a 15 percent profit off the products in the first year. You will need to identify a price for sale to wholesalers, retailers, and e-commerce sites, as well as a suggested retail price for those businesses to charge their customers. Base your conclusions on research and analysis of current market conditions.

ASSIGNMENT AND STRATEGY

- **Get the background** To get started you will need to conduct a situation analysis and competitive assessment for these two new products made by the Tri-Star Toy Company. Learn all you can about the markets for trading card games and dolls, some of which may be collectibles.

  You may want to look at the introductions of other trading card games, including Pokemon and Yu-Gi-Oh, and other dolls, such as Ugly Dolls and Beanie Babies.

- **Write the pricing proposal** Begin your proposal by reviewing the reason the client hired your firm.

  Then, provide background information you learned from your situation analysis and competitive assessment.

  Use your research to justify your assumptions as you go through the six steps of pricing a product.

  The six steps are: (1) establish pricing objectives; (2) determine costs; (3) estimate demand; (4) study competition; (5) decide on a pricing strategy; and (6) set prices.

- **What your project should include** Show the math you used to arrive at suggested prices for wholesalers, retailers, and e-commerce sites, as well as the suggested prices for retail customers. Also create a table that depicts your competitive price analysis. Create other tables and figures as needed to show relationships among data.

YOUR REPORT

Use a word processing program and presentation software to prepare a double-spaced report and an oral presentation for Tri-Star Toys. See a suggested outline and key evaluation points at *marketingessentials.glencoe.com/internship*

BUILD YOUR PORTFOLIO

Option 1 Internship Report Once you have completed your Marketing Internship project and presentation, include your written report and a few printouts of key slides from your oral presentation in your Marketing Portfolio.

Option 2 Multi-tiered Pricing Strategies A designer of high-priced apparel is thinking of also designing moderate-priced fashions. After doing some research, including a situation analysis, create a pricing plan for this designer. It should include a suggested target market and customer profile, distribution, and pricing strategies. Prepare a written report and an oral presentation using word processing and presentation software. See a suggested outline and key evaluation points at *marketingessentials.glencoe.com/portfolio*

Online Action!

Go to *marketingessentials.glencoe.com/Unit/8/DECA* to review pricing concepts that relate to DECA events.

marketingessentials.glencoe.com

586 UNIT 8 - PRICING

Marketing Internship 587

Online Action sends you to marketingessentials.glencoe.com, to find more information about DECA events.

TO THE STUDENT

Understanding the Chapter

Each *Marketing Essentials* chapter opens with a list of chapter objectives, a photo related to the chapter content, and information about DECA events.

Chapter Objectives preview the most important things to remember about each chapter.

The DECA Connection lists the DECA competitive events that relate to the chapter and explains how you will be evaluated in these competitions.

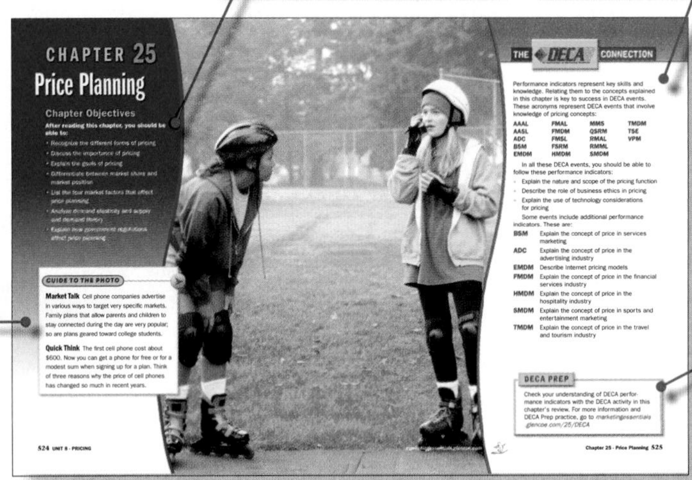
CHAPTER 25

Price Planning

Chapter Objectives

GUIDE TO THE PHOTO

Market Talk Cell phone companies advertise in various ways to target very specific markets. Family plans that allow parents and children to stay connected during the day are very popular; so are plans geared toward college students.

Quick Think The first cell phone cost about $500. Now you can get a phone for free or for a modest sum when signing up for a plan. Think of three reasons why the price of cell phones has changed so much in recent years.

THE DECA CONNECTION

DECA PREP

Guide to the Photo has two parts: **Market Talk** tells you how the photograph relates to the chapter, then **Quick Think** asks a question you can answer based on your own experience.

DECA Prep directs you to the DECA activity that closes every chapter.

Understanding the Section

Each chapter is divided into two or three sections that group the chapter material by topic.

Objectives lists the concepts you will cover in the section.

Key Terms lists the vocabulary words you will learn in the section. Look for them in the text—they will be highlighted and in boldface type.

Read and Study makes your reading and studying more productive. It has three sections:

- **Before You Read** encourages you to think about what you might already know about the subject.
- **The Main Idea** tells you the primary concept you will be learning.
- **Study Organizer** gives you ideas for taking notes as you read.

While You Read connects the material you are reading with something you already know.

After You Read is a self-check of what you have read. You can check your answers on the Internet, at marketingessentials.glencoe.com.

Chapter Review

Each chapter closes with a variety of exercises and activities to assess how well you have absorbed the material. It will help you remember, apply, and use what you have learned.

Focus on Key Points reviews the chapter highlights. Read them to make sure you have not missed an important concept.

Review Vocabulary helps you memorize the definitions of the vocabulary words in the chapter.

Review Facts and Ideas asks questions to test your recall and understanding of chapter material.

Build Skills gives you a chance to practice workplace skills, technology applications, and math. Each activity is based on the world of marketing.

Apply Concepts asks you to take what you have learned and apply it to a realistic situation.

The DECA Connection asks you to role-play a marketing scenario, just like you would in a real DECA competition.

Develop Critical Thinking are questions to help you interpret, analyze, compare, or make judgments based on what you learned in the chapter.

Net Savvy focuses on sharpening your Internet research skills.

Understanding the Features

Each chapter has features that demonstrate how the marketing concepts work in the real world. A question and an activity follow each feature.

Case Study

Case Study offers a real-world story about a marketing decision or a situation facing a company.

GLOBAL MARKET

Global Market tells a story of a real-world, international business scenario. Largely because of the Internet and increased global access, marketing horizons have expanded, and many businesses now operate in multiple countries.

MARKET TECH

Market Tech goes beyond the Internet and tells you about other creative uses of technology. Each Market Tech feature briefly explains how the technology works, notes the strategy, and evaluates the success of the technology.

NET MARKETING

Net Marketing highlights a new or innovative Internet marketing technique that uses original ideas.

A MATTER OF ETHICS

A Matter of Ethics lets you ponder a situation that challenges you to pick the right thing to do.

CAREERS IN MARKETING

Careers in Marketing is an interview with someone who works in one of the many jobs in marketing. You will learn how people chose their careers, what education they have, what skills are most important in their jobs, and what they do to succeed.

Reading Strategies

Use this menu for reading strategies to get the most from your reading.

Before You Read . . .

SET A PURPOSE
- Why are you reading the textbook?
- How does the subject relate to your life?
- How might you be able to use what you learn in your own life?

PREVIEW
- Read the chapter title to preview the topic.
- Read the subtitles to see what you will learn about the topic.
- Skim the photos, charts, graphs, or maps. How do they support the topic?
- Look for key terms that are boldfaced. How are they defined?

DRAW FROM YOUR BACKGROUND
- What have you read or heard concerning new information on the topic?
- How is the new information different from what you already know?
- How will the information that you already know help you understand the new information?

While You Read . . .

PREDICT
- Predict events or outcomes by using clues and information that you already know.
- Change your predictions as you read and gather new information.

CONNECT
- Think about people, places, and events in your own life. Are there any similarities with those in your textbook?
- Can you relate the textbook information to other areas of your life?

QUESTION
- What is the main idea?
- How do the photos, charts, graphs, and maps support the main idea?

VISUALIZE
- Pay careful attention to details and descriptions.
- Create graphic organizers to show relationships that you find in the information.

NOTICE COMPARE AND CONTRAST SENTENCES
- Look for clue words and phrases that signal comparison, such as *similarly*, *just as*, *both*, *in common*, *also*, and *too*.
- Look for clue words and phrases that signal contrast, such as *on the other hand*, *in contrast to*, *however*, *different*, *instead of*, *rather than*, *but*, and *unlike*.

NOTICE CAUSE-AND-EFFECT SENTENCES
- Look for clue words and phrases, such as *because*, *as a result*, *therefore*, *that is why*, *since*, *so*, *for this reason*, and *consequently*.

NOTICE CHRONOLOGICAL SENTENCES
- Look for clue words and phrases, such as *after*, *before*, *first*, *next*, *last*, *during*, *finally*, *earlier*, *later*, *since*, and *then*.

After You Read . . .

SUMMARIZE
- Describe the main idea and how the details support it.
- Use your own words to explain what you have read.

ASSESS
- What was the main idea?
- Did the text clearly support the main idea?
- Did you learn anything new from the material?
- Can you use this new information in other school subjects or at home?
- What other sources could you use to find more information about the topic?

TO THE STUDENT

What is DECA?

DECA is a national association for students of marketing. It was formed in 1946 to improve the education of students in business subject areas, in particular marketing, entrepreneurship, and management.

DECA, which stands for the Distributive Education Clubs of America, offers students the opportunity to develop their leadership and professional skills. This is done through on-the-job experience, activities and projects sponsored by individual schools or chapters, and a series of competitive events in specific occupational areas. All activities apply the concepts of marketing to real-life situations. It is likely that DECA will be an integral part of your learning experience as you explore the world of marketing.

What is DECA's mission statement?

The mission of DECA is to enhance the co-curricular education of students with interests in marketing, management, and entrepreneurship. DECA helps students develop skills and competence for marketing careers, build self-esteem, experience leadership, and practice community service. DECA is committed to the advocacy of marketing education and the growth of business and education partnerships.

How can DECA help me?

Even though some activities may take time outside of school, DECA should be considered a co-curricular activity instead of an after-school activity. The basis for the projects and events will come from your classroom learning. Information from events that you take back to the classroom will enhance not only your learning experience, but that of your classmates as well.

DECA also offers scholarships and other recognition awards to exceptional students. In general, success in DECA events is a positive addition to your résumé or portfolio.

DECA can help you:

- Develop strong leadership abilities
- Understand the importance of making ethical decisions in your personal life and future career
- Focus on enhancing effective public speaking and presentation skills
- Understand the need for diversity in the global marketplace
- Enhance those skills that are necessary for a career in marketing or as an entrepreneur
- Increase your self-confidence, especially when presenting or speaking in public
- Investigate different career opportunities available in the marketing field
- Develop good social and business etiquette

How are DECA activities related to my marketing class?

Marketing Essentials is designed to prepare you for a career or further study of marketing. It is also helpful in preparing for DECA activities. You will notice that the DECA logo and DECA approved activities are prominently featured throughout your book. The DECA Connection feature is modeled after DECA individual or team projects. It will let you practice applying the knowledge that you have gained from your marketing class. DECA activities can also enhance your classroom learning, because they help you develop stronger communication and analytical skills.

DECA sponsors competitive events in approximately 30 occupational areas. These areas include:

- Advertising and Visual Merchandising Services Series
- Apparel and Accessories Marketing Series
- Finance and Credit Services Series
- Food Marketing Series
- General Marketing Series
- Hospitality and Tourism Marketing Series
- Retail Merchandising Series
- Quick Serve Restaurant Management Series
- Full Service Restaurant Management Series
- Vehicles and Petroleum Marketing Series
- Sports and Entertainment Marketing Management Team Decision Making Pilot Event
- Travel and Tourism Marketing Management Team Decision Making Pilot Event

UNIT 1 The World of

In this unit you will find

- **Chapter 1** Marketing Is All Around Us
- **Chapter 2** The Marketing Plan

Marketing

Marketing Plan

1 ANALYSIS
- SWOT
- Economic
- Socio-Cultural
- Technological
- Competitive

2 STRATEGY
- Promotion
- Place
- Price
- Product

3 IMPLEMENTATION
- Organization
- Management
- Staffing

4 BUDGET
- Cost of Sales
- Cost of Promotion
- Income and Expenses

5 CONTROL
- Evaluation
- Performance Measures
- Performance Analysis

ANALYZE THE AD

This ad invites readers to visit the state of West Virginia for a vacation. What is the main theme? How does the picture work with the words?

Market Talk Marketing promotes and sells products such as food and clothing, or services such as a haircut or a vacation in West Virginia. Do you think marketing promotes ideas, as well?

Think and Write Print ads use powerful visual components and interesting, catchy writing to draw in the reader. Read the slogans in this ad. Do you think they work? Why or why not? Look through magazines or newspapers and write down three slogans you think are effective. Next, select a state or a country that interests you and write a slogan for it that would encourage tourism.

@ Online Action! Go to *marketingessentials.glencoe.com/u1/ad* for an extended activity.

In this unit

Foundations of Marketing
- Economics

Functions of Marketing
- Pricing
- Promotion
- Selling

CHAPTER 1

Marketing Is All Around Us

Chapter Objectives

After reading this chapter, you should be able to:

- Define marketing
- Explain the four foundations of marketing
- List the seven functions of marketing
- Understand the marketing concept
- Analyze the benefits of marketing
- Apply the concept of utility
- Describe the concept of market
- Differentiate consumer and industrial markets
- Describe market share
- Define target market
- List the components of the marketing mix

GUIDE TO THE PHOTO

Market Talk In the United States, it is rare to be far from an ad of some sort. A passing hiker in a national park might be wearing a T-shirt with a corporate logo. A sign on the side of a country road could announce fresh eggs for sale. In a mall or a major city, the marketing is much more intense. Everywhere you look, you see signs, brands, and ads.

Quick Think Promotion is only one aspect of marketing. How would you define marketing and all the activities that fall under its umbrella?

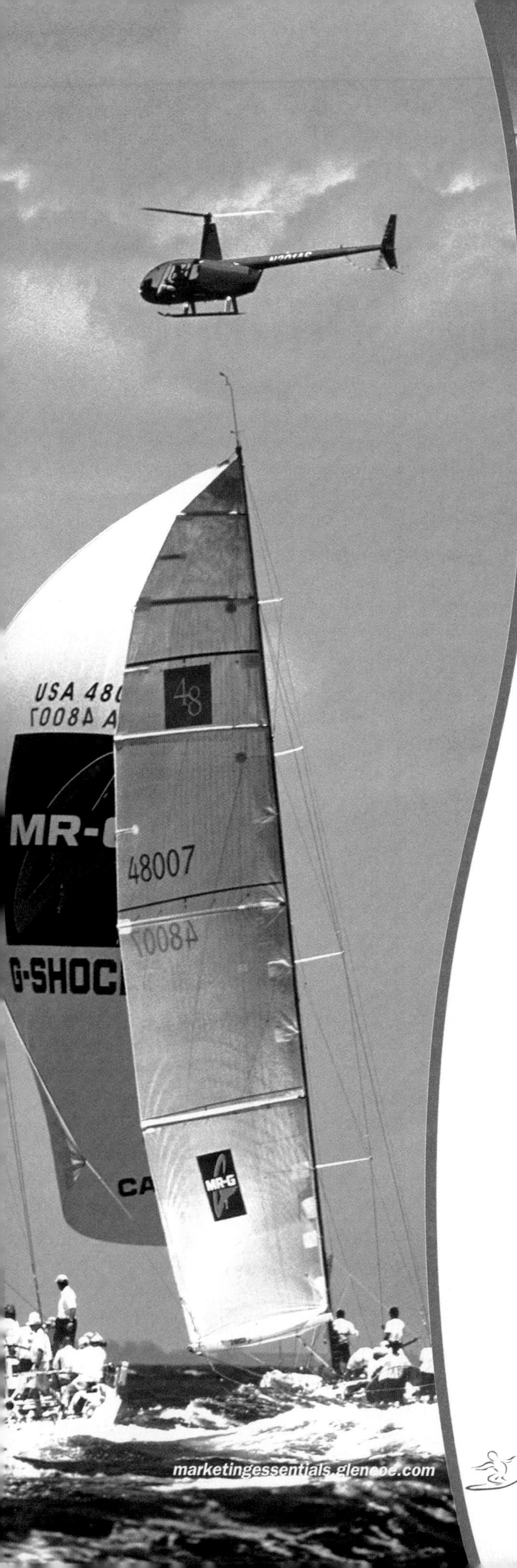

THE DECA CONNECTION

An Association of Marketing Students

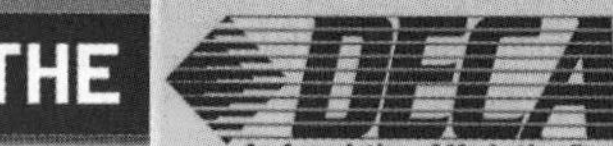

Performance indicators represent key skills and knowledge. Relating them to the concepts explained in this chapter is your key to success in DECA events. These acronyms represent DECA events that involve knowledge of concepts in this chapter.

AAAL	**FMAL**	**MMS**	**TMDM**
AAML	**FMDM***	**QSRM**	**TSE***
ADC*	**FMML**	**RMAL**	**VPM**
BSM	**FSRM**	**RMML**	
EMDM	**HMDM***	**SMDM***	

In all these DECA events, you should be able to follow these performance indicators:

- Distinguish between economic goods and services
- Determine the forms of economic utility that marketing creates
- Explain the concept of marketing strategies
- Explain the concept of market and market identification
- Select target market

All the events with an asterisk (*) also include this performance indicator:

- Describe the nature of target marketing in a specific industry

Some events include additional performance indicators. These are:

FMDM	Target financial products for specific markets
SMDM	Identify target markets for a sports/ entertainment event
ADC	Develop a customer/client profile
HMDM	Determine potential lodging markets
EMDM	Identify online target market
TSE	Design a customer/client profile

DECA PREP

Check your understanding of DECA performance indicators with the DECA activity in this chapter's review. For more information and DECA Prep practice, go to *marketingessentials .glencoe.com/1/DECA*

SECTION 1.1

OBJECTIVES

- Define marketing
- Explain the four foundations of marketing
- List the seven functions of marketing
- Understand the marketing concept

KEY TERMS

- marketing
- goods
- services
- marketing concept

Marketing and the Marketing Concept

READ and STUDY

BEFORE YOU READ

Connect Do you think you have ever been influenced by marketing? Explain why or why not and give examples if necessary.

THE MAIN IDEA

Marketing is an umbrella term that includes many activities and has many functions. To be a successful marketer, you need to understand the foundations, functions, and basic tools of marketing.

STUDY ORGANIZER

Draw an umbrella shape like the one below to organize the marketing concepts you will read about in this section.

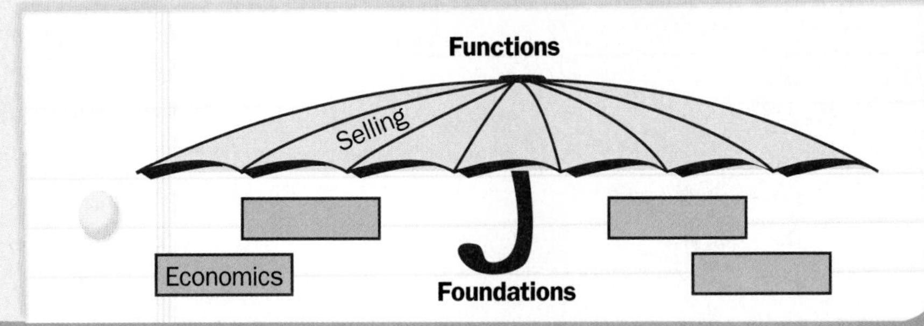

WHILE YOU READ

Connect Relate the definition of marketing to the functions of marketing and to the marketing concept.

The Scope of Marketing

You already know a lot about marketing because it is all around you. You have been a consumer for many years and you have made decisions about products you liked and did not like. As you study marketing, you will analyze what businesses do to influence consumers' buying decisions. That practice will help you make the transition from thinking like a consumer to thinking like a marketer.

• **MARKETING IDEAS** The definition of marketing includes marketing ideas, such as eating healthful foods.

What other ideas have you seen marketed?

Marketing is a broad term that includes many activities and requires many skills. **Marketing** is the process of planning, pricing, promoting, selling, and distributing ideas, goods, or services to create exchanges that satisfy customers. Note that marketing is a process. This means it is ongoing and it changes. As a marketer, you need to keep up with trends and consumer attitudes. The products, ideas, or services you develop and the way you price, promote, and distribute them should reflect these trends and attitudes. All functions of marketing support this effort. Current marketing practices focus on customers and maintaining a close relationship with them.

Ideas, Goods, and Services

Marketing promotes ideas, goods, and services. Politicians, for example, use marketing techniques to promote their platform, or ideas. **Goods** are tangible items that have monetary value and satisfy your needs and wants such as cars, toys, furniture, televisions, clothing, and candy. Intangible items that have monetary value and satisfy your needs and wants are **services**. Intangible means you cannot physically touch them. In most cases, services involve a task, such as cooking a hamburger or cutting hair. Banks, dry cleaners, amusement parks, movie theaters, and accounting offices all provide economic services.

Every time someone sells or buys something, an exchange takes place in the marketplace. The marketplace is the commercial environment where such trades happen. It is the world of shops, Internet stores, financial institutions, catalogs, and much more.

Foundations of Marketing

The practice of marketing depends on four key areas of knowledge. These are the four foundations of marketing. The marketing wheel on page 1 includes these four foundations.

The topics you will study in *Marketing Essentials* are based on these four foundations of marketing:

1. **Business, management, entrepreneurship** Understanding the basics of business, management, and entrepreneurial concepts that affect business decision making
2. **Communication and interpersonal skills** Understanding concepts, strategies, and systems needed to interact effectively with others
3. **Economics** Understanding the economic principles and concepts that are basic to marketing
4. **Professional development** Understanding concepts and strategies needed for career exploration, development, and growth

Seven Functions of Marketing

The seven functions include distribution, financing, marketing information management, pricing, product/service management, promotion, and selling. The marketing wheel on page 1 also includes these functions. These functions define all the aspects that are part of the practice of marketing.

Distribution

Distribution is the process of deciding how to get goods in customers' hands. Physically moving and storing goods is part of distribution planning. The main methods of transportation are by truck, rail, ship, or air. Some large retail chains store products in central warehouses for later distribution. Distribution also involves the systems that track products so that they can be located at any time.

Financing

Financing is getting the money that is necessary to pay for setting up and running a business. Business owners often obtain bank loans to start a new business. Some also form corporations and may sell shares (or stock) of the business. Financing also involves decisions such as whether to offer credit to customers. Most retailers offer customers payment options such as MasterCard or Visa, while other stores offer their own credit services.

Marketing Information Management

Good business and marketing decisions rely on good information about customers, trends, and competing products. Gathering this information, storing it, and analyzing it are all part of marketing information management. Collecting information is done on a continual basis and through special marketing research studies. This is what marketers do to find out about customers, their habits and attitudes, where they live, and trends in the marketplace. Have you ever been asked to complete a questionnaire about the service at a restaurant or other type of business? If so, you have participated in marketing research. Companies conduct research so they can be successful at marketing and selling their products.

Pricing

Pricing decisions dictate how much to charge for goods and services in order to make a profit. Pricing decisions are based on costs and on what competitors charge for the same product or service. To determine a price, marketers must also determine how much customers are willing to pay.

Product/Service Management

Product/service management is obtaining, developing, maintaining, and improving a product or a product mix in response to market opportunities. Marketing research guides product/service management toward what the consumer needs and wants.

Promotion

Promotion is the effort to inform, persuade, or remind potential customers about a business's products or services. Television and radio commercials are forms of promotion. This type of promotion is called advertising. Promotion is also used to improve a company's public image. A company can show that it is socially responsible by recycling materials or cleaning up the environment. Promotion concepts and strategies are used to achieve success in the marketplace.

Selling

Selling provides customers with the goods and services they want. This includes selling in the retail market to you, the customer, and selling in the business-to-business market to wholesalers, retailers, or manufacturers.

Selling techniques and activities include determining client needs and wants and responding through planned, personalized communication. The selling process influences purchasing decisions and enhances future business opportunities.

The Marketing Concept

The **marketing concept** is the idea that a business should strive to satisfy customers' needs and wants while generating a profit for the firm. The focus is on the customer. For an organization to be successful, all seven functions of marketing need to support this idea.

The personnel responsible for those functions must understand the marketing concept and reach for the same goal in order to send a consistent message to the customer. The message is that the customer satisfaction is most important. Everyone in an organization needs to recognize that repeat customers keep a company in business. For example, the switchboard operator in a large corporation or the pizza delivery person must understand the marketing concept and be mindful of the company's goals. Everyone in an organization is an extension of that firm and must provide the best possible service to its customers. Businesses that stress the marketing concept with all employees are successful.

Customer Relationship Management (CRM)

In today's marketplace, customer relationship is most important. Customer relationship management (CRM) is an aspect of marketing that combines customer information (through database and computer technology) with customer service and marketing communications. Marketers who specialize in CRM try to create more meaningful one-on-one communications with the customer by applying customer data (demographic, industry, buying history, etc.) to every communication.

1.1 AFTER YOU READ

Reviewing Key Terms and Concepts

1. Name two ideas that can be marketed.
2. Where do exchanges take place?
3. What is the main difference between consumers and industrial users?

Integrating Academic Skills

Math

4. A customer purchases two tables at $149.99 each and would like them to be delivered. Your company charges customers $50 for delivery and the state imposes a 5 percent sales tax on furniture, but not on the delivery charge. What is the total amount due from the customer?

Economics

5. List at least three ways the Internet has changed marketing functions.

@ Online Action!

Check your answers at *marketingessentials.glencoe.com/1/read*

SECTION 1.2

OBJECTIVES

- Analyze the benefits of marketing
- Apply the concept of utility

KEY TERM

- utility

The Importance of Marketing

READ and STUDY

BEFORE YOU READ

Use Prior Knowledge When did you last shop at a mall? Did you witness any promotion effort? Did you compare prices? What role did this play in your decision to buy?

THE MAIN IDEA

Marketing is a key part of our economy because it supports competition and offers benefits to consumers.

STUDY ORGANIZER

Reproduce the figure below. As you read this section, note the benefits of marketing and list the five utilities on lines jutting out from one of the ovals.

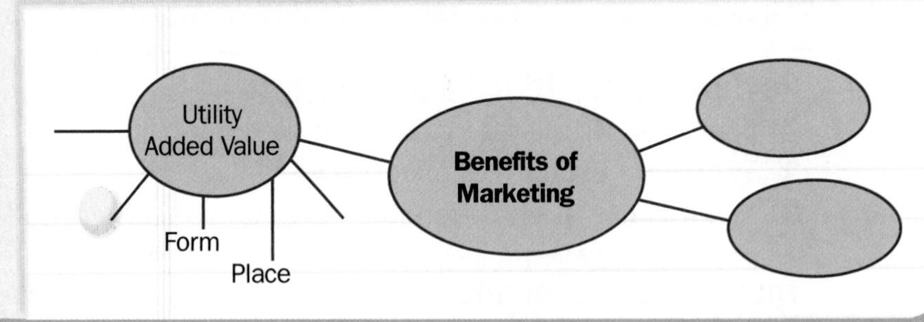

WHILE YOU READ

Connect List your own experiences and observations about how marketing benefits you personally.

Economic Benefits of Marketing

Through the study of marketing you will realize just how important marketing is and how much it affects your life and the lives of other consumers. Its impact is even more dramatic when you consider how it affects our economy and standard of living.

Marketing plays an important role in an economy because it provides the means for competition to take place. In a competitive marketplace, businesses try to create new or improved products at lower prices than their competitors. Those efforts force

• NEW PRODUCTS One of the major economic benefits of marketing is the proliferation of new and improved products.

List three new and improved products you have seen marketed lately.

them to be efficient and responsive to consumers. In addition, businesses look for ways to add value to a consumer's shopping experience. Let's look at the economic benefits of marketing to the economy and to consumers.

New and Improved Products

Marketing generates competition, which in turn fosters new and improved products. Businesses always look for ways to satisfy customers' wants and needs and to keep customers interested. This creates a larger variety of goods and services. For example, personal computers have gotten smaller, lighter, more powerful, and less expensive. As more people use computers, this market continues to grow.

Lower Prices

Marketing activities increase demand, and this helps to lower prices. When demand is high, manufacturers can produce products in larger quantities. This reduces the unit cost of each product. This is because the fixed costs (such as the rent on a building) remain the same whether the company produces 10 units or 10,000 units. When a company produces a larger quantity of a product, it spends less per unit on fixed costs. The company can charge a lower price per unit, sell more units, and make more money. Here is an example using a fixed cost of $20,000.

Quantity Produced	Fixed Cost Per Unit
10,000	$2.00
	($20,000 ÷ 10,000)
200,000	.10
	($20,000 ÷ 200,000)

As you can see, the increased quantity significantly reduces the fixed cost per unit.

In addition, when products become popular, more competitors enter the marketplace. To remain competitive, marketers find ways to lower their prices. Look at the DVD market for some examples of this phenomenon. DVD players were introduced in 1997. Since then, there has been an explosion in the sales and rentals of DVDs and DVD players. Combination DVD/CD/MP3 players were very costly products when they were introduced on the market, but now they can be purchased for less than $100.

Added Value and Utility

The functions of marketing add value to a product. This added value in economic terms is called **utility**. Utilities are the attributes of a product or service that make it capable of satisfying consumers' wants and needs.

There are five economic utilities involved with all products: form, place, time, possession, and information. Although form utility is not directly related to marketing, much of what goes into creating new products, such as marketing research and product design, makes it an integral part of the marketing process.

MARKET TECH

Supermarket Personal Shopper

Albertsons introduced its Shop 'n' Scan technology by testing it—first in a handful of stores in Chicago, then expanding the test to more than 100 stores in the Dallas area. The tests started in October 2002. By October 2004 the company was planning to roll out the system in other cities.

The system enables customers to use handheld scanners to scan and bag their purchases as they shop at several Jewel-Osco stores.

Focus on the Shopper

The technology has some other customer-friendly features. A portable computer keeps a running total of the prices of the items in the cart. Customers can also use an express pay station to ring up their purchases.

Company Goals

These customer-focused developments are in keeping with the overall policies and objectives of the company:

- Focusing on customers
- Building efficiency
- Capitalizing on technology

The company has had success with Shop 'n' Scan. According to the *Wall Street Journal*, shoppers using the technology bought, on average, twice as many groceries as shoppers using regular carts.

THINK LIKE A MARKETER

How does this technology add value (utility) to a customer's shopping experience?

Online Action!

Go to *marketingessentials.glencoe.com/1/tech* to find a project on technology as added value.

Form Utility

Form utility involves changing raw materials or putting parts together to make them more useful. In other words, it deals with making or producing things. The manufacturing of products involves taking things of little value by themselves and putting them together to create more value. If you consider the value of a zipper, a spool of thread, and several yards of cloth, each would have some value, but not as much as when you put all three together by making a jacket.

Form utility involves making products that consumers need and want. Special features or ingredients in a product add value and increase its form utility. For example, electronic controls on the steering wheel of an automobile add value to the final product.

Place Utility

Place utility involves having a product where customers can buy it. Businesses study consumer shopping habits to determine the most convenient and efficient locations to sell products.

Some businesses use a direct approach by selling their products through catalogs, and other businesses rely on retailers to sell their products. The Internet offers even more options to businesses that want to sell their products directly to their customers without the use of any intermediaries.

Time Utility

Time utility is having a product available at a certain time of year or a convenient time of day. For example, supermarkets and other food stores offer convenient shopping hours or they are open 24-hours a day. Retailers often have extended shopping hours during the busiest shopping season of the year, from Thanksgiving till Christmas. Marketers increase the value of products by having them available when consumers want them.

Possession Utility

How do you come into possession of the items you want? You generally buy them for

a price. The exchange of a product for money is possession utility. Retailers may accept alternatives to cash, such as personal checks, debit or credit cards, in exchange for their merchandise. They may even offer installment or layaway plans (delayed possession in return for gradual payment). Every one of these options adds value to the product being purchased. In fact, without these options, some customers would not be able to buy the items they want. In business-to-business situations, companies also grant their customers credit. They may give them a certain period (for example, 30 days) to pay a bill. This adds value to the products they sell.

Possession utility is involved every time legal ownership of a product changes hands. Possession utility increases as purchase options increase. The Internet also provides consumers with options to pay by providing secure sites where credit cards are accepted.

Information Utility

Information utility involves communication with the consumer. Salespeople provide information to customers by explaining the features and benefits of products. Displays communicate information, too. Packaging and labeling inform consumers about qualities and uses of a product. The label on a frozen food entrée will tell you the ingredients, nutritional information, directions for preparation, and any safety precautions needed.

Advertising informs consumers about products, tells where to buy products, and sometimes tells how much products cost.

Many manufacturers provide owners' manuals that explain how to use their products. Businesses have Web sites on the Internet where they provide detailed information about their companies and their products.

1.2 AFTER YOU READ

Reviewing Key Terms and Concepts

1. How does marketing help to lower prices?
2. In what way is marketing related to form utility?
3. Which utility is added by drive-through windows at fast-food restaurants?

Integrating Academic Skills

Math

4. In a business-to-business transaction, the seller offers the buyer a 2 percent discount for paying a bill early. Assuming the buyer took advantage of this offer, how much would be discounted on a $10,000 invoice?

Writing

5. Write a brief story (two to three paragraphs) about a young person shopping at the local mall that incorporates all the benefits of marketing.

Check your answers at *marketingessentials.glencoe.com/1/read*

Fundamentals of Marketing

OBJECTIVES

- Describe the concept of market
- Differentiate consumer and industrial markets
- Describe market share
- Define target market
- List the components of the marketing mix

KEY TERMS

- market
- consumer market
- industrial market
- market share
- target market
- customer profile
- marketing mix

READ and STUDY

BEFORE YOU READ

Predict How do you think marketers decide where to advertise their products?

THE MAIN IDEA

The term *market* refers to all the people who might buy a product or service. The marketing mix is a set of four tools or strategies the marketer uses to influence buying decisions.

STUDY ORGANIZER

Draw two diagrams like the ones below. In the first diagram, record four terms about the concept of market. In the second diagram, record the four Ps of the marketing mix.

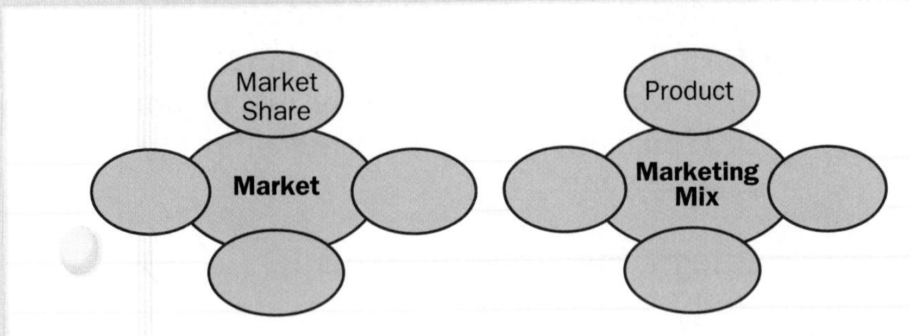

WHILE YOU READ

Connect Jot down examples of ads you have seen or heard and how they relate to your reading.

Market and Market Identification

The terminology found in this section is the foundation for future work and study in marketing. You need to commit these terms to memory so you can use them correctly when discussing marketing principles and practices. You will find that these terms are used throughout this textbook. So let's begin your journey into becoming a marketer.

Marketers know that their product or service cannot appeal to everyone. To do their job, they look for people who might have an interest in or a need for their product. They also look at people who have the ability to pay for their product. These people often share other similar needs and wants. All people who share similar needs and wants and who have the ability to purchase a given product are called a **market**.

You could be part of the market for video games, but not be part of the market for an expensive car. Even though you may want an expensive car, you may not have the means to buy one. If you liked video games and had the resources to buy or rent them, you would be part of the video game market.

Consumer Versus Industrial Markets

There are different types of markets. A market can be described as a consumer market or an industrial market.

The **consumer market** consists of consumers who purchase goods and services for personal use. Consumers' needs and wants generally fall into a few categories that address their lifestyles. For the most part, consumers are interested in products that will save them money, make their life easier, improve their appearance, create status in the community, or provide satisfaction related to some other personal motivation.

The **industrial market** or business-to-business (B-to-B) market includes all businesses that buy products for use in their operations. The goals and objectives of business firms are somewhat different from those in the consumer market. Most relate to improving profits. Companies want to improve productivity, increase sales, decrease expenses, or in some other way make their work more efficient.

Companies that produce products for sale in the consumer market consider the reseller of their products to be part of the industrial

• ADVERTISING in the INDUSTRIAL MARKET
This ad, published in *Supermarket News*, highlights advantages to businesses who sell chicken to customers.

How do the objectives for purchases in the industrial market differ from those in the consumer market?

Market Share

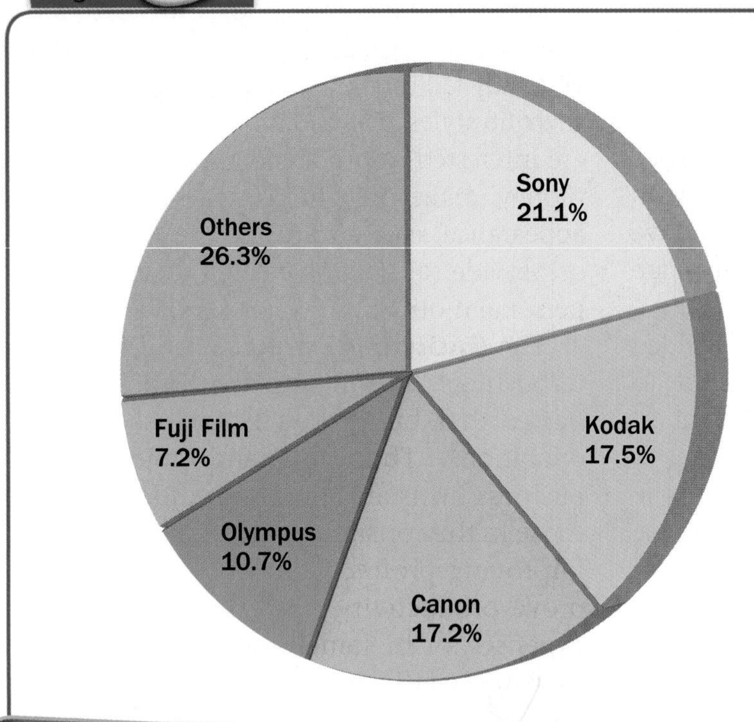

• **Who Leads in the Camera Market?** A company's percentage of total sales in a given market is its market share.

How do you think businesses use the concept of market share in their marketing programs?

@ Online Action! Go to ***marketingessentials.glencoe.com/1/figure/1*** to find a project on market share.

market. Therefore, they require two distinct marketing plans to reach each market.

Market Share

A market is further described by the total sales in a product category. Examples of categories are video games, fax machines, cameras, ice cream, or soft drinks. For example, everyone who bought digital still cameras in February 2004 from photo specialty, electronic/appliance stores, computer/office superstores, mass merchandisers, the Internet, and through mail order were part of the $211,464,600 digital still camera market.

A company's **market share** is its percentage of the total sales volume generated by all companies that compete in a given market. Knowing one's market share helps marketers analyze their competition and their status in a given market. (See Figure 1.1.) Market shares change all the time as new competitors enter the market and as the size of the market increases or decreases in volume.

Target Market and Market Segmentation

Businesses know they cannot convince everybody to buy their product or service. They look for ways to offer their product or service to the people who are most likely to be interested. This involves segmenting, or breaking down the market into smaller groups that have similar needs. Market segmentation is the process of classifying customers by needs and wants.

You already know that a market can be segmented into a consumer and an industrial market. Within those markets, further segmentation is possible. You will learn about market segmentation in Chapter 2. The goal of market segmentation is to identify the group of people most likely to become customers. The group that is identified for a specific

• **MARKET SEGMENTATION** A professional photographer shops for a top-performance camera to use as a work tool while an amateur would look for a basic, easy-to-use model.

How would marketing efforts differ for these two types of cameras and customers?

marketing program is the **target market**. Target markets are very important because all marketing strategies are directed to them. When a business does not identify a target market, its marketing plan has no focus. Identifying the target market correctly is a key to success.

Consumers Versus Customers

A product may have more than one target market. For example, manufacturers of children's cereal know that they need to target children and parents differently. They have two target markets: one is the children (consumers) who will be asking for the cereal and eating it. The other is the parents (customers) who need to approve of it and will be buying it. To reach the children, marketers might advertise on Saturday morning television programs specifically designed for children. The advertising message might be how much fun it is to eat this cereal. To reach parents, print advertising in magazines such as *Family Circle* or *Parenting* might be used, and the ad message might stress health benefits.

To develop a clear picture of their target market, businesses create a **customer profile**. A customer profile lists information about the target market, such as age, income level, ethnic background, occupation, attitudes, lifestyle, and geographic residence. Chapter 2 focuses on this aspect of marketing. Marketers spend a lot of money and time on research to collect data so that they understand the characteristics of their target market's customer profile. This information helps them make intelligent marketing decisions.

An easy and fun way to understand customer profiles is to look at magazines. If you thumb through a magazine's articles and advertisements, you will know who reads the publication. According to *Seventeen* magazine's

A MATTER OF ETHICS

Targeting Children

You may have observed young children mesmerized by television commercials or seen children crying when a parent refuses to buy a product that a child had seen advertised on television.

Messages to Children

Businesses that target young children generally create images that their products are fun and enjoyable.

Messages to Parents

Some of these same companies target parents and send a different message about their products—stressing qualities that parents deem important, such as education, safety, or health.

THINKING ETHICALLY

Do you think targeting children with food products and toys is ethical? Should advertising to children be restricted? Why or why not?

Online Action!

Go to *marketingessentials.glencoe.com/1/ethics* to find a project on ethical marketing techniques.

Web site, the magazine targets teen girls and young women who are interested in beauty, fashion, and entertainment. It is larger than any competitor in the 12- to 17-year-old market and 97.9 percent of its readers have accessed the Internet regularly.

Marketing Mix

The **marketing mix** includes four basic marketing strategies called the four Ps: **p**roduct, **p**lace, **p**rice, and **p**romotion. These are tools marketing professionals or businesses use and control in order to influence potential customers. Marketers control decisions about each of the four Ps and base their decisions on the people they want to win over and make into customers. Because of the importance of customers, some would add a fifth P to the list: people. Marketers must first clearly define each target market before they can develop marketing strategies.

The four elements of the marketing mix are interconnected. Actions in one area affect decisions in another. Each strategy involves making decisions about the best way to reach, satisfy, and keep customers and the best way to achieve the company's goals.

Let's look at what each marketing mix component involves. Follow Figure 1.2 to see each of the four Ps illustrated and explained for Tropicana's Light 'n Healthy® brand orange juice.

Product

Product decisions begin with choosing what products to make and sell. Much research goes into product design. A product's features, brand name, packaging, service, and warranty are all part of the development. Companies also need to decide what to do with products they currently sell. In some cases, those products require updating or improvements to be competitive. By developing new uses and identifying new target markets, a company can extend the life of a product. In the orange juice example illustrated in Figure 1.2, Tropicana chose health conscious men and women as the target market for a new juice. It produced a lower-calorie, lower-carbohydrate orange juice and it selected a name—Light 'n Healthy—that would appeal to its target market.

Place

The means of getting the product into the consumer's hands is the place factor of the marketing mix. Knowing where one's customers shop helps marketers make the

Figure 1.2 Marketing Mix for a New Juice

• **Light 'n Healthy's Four Ps** Tropicana's marketing department develops strategies for each brand of orange juice in its product line. The four Ps of the marketing mix focus on the customer profile for a specific target market. The Light 'n Healthy brand targets men and women who are health conscious and want to stay physically fit.

Would you have made different choices about the four Ps to introduce this product? If so, what would you have done differently?

PRODUCT

Product decisions include naming the product and deciding how to match the target market's needs. Tropicana's Light 'n Healthy brand has a third less sugar and a third fewer calories than regular orange juice.

PLACE

Since most people shop in supermarkets for orange juice, the place decision was an easy one.

Target Market

PROMOTION

Tropicana decided to run humorous ads in *Health* magazine and on television that showed oranges exercising. This reinforced the image it wanted for its Light 'n Healthy brand.

PRICE

To be competitive, Tropicana priced its Light 'n Healthy brand in line with other premium orange juices.

Online Action! Go to *marketingessentials.glencoe.com/1/figure/2* to find a project on the marketing mix.

Case Study

Pay as You Go Wireless Phones

The Roxy i90c phone from Boost is created for active young women. The Roxy brand represents freedom, fun, and individual expression, all of which are reflected in the design and custom features of the Roxy phone.

The Right Ring Tones

The Roxy wireless phone features ring tones such as *Funky Town, Girls Just Wanna Have Fun,* and *California Dreamin'*. The phone is preloaded with Java™ games, including Tetris® and Snood® from THQ and Blazing Boards™ by Cybiko. As with all Boost Mobile's models, the Roxy wireless phone comes with Boost 2WAY™, the long-range walkie-talkie feature.

Price and Place

Advertisements for the Roxy phone focus on girls involved in sports. The suggested retail price is $199, which includes $25 in wireless service credits that are loaded on activation. The limited edition Roxy phone is available at select Quiksilver Boardrider Club stores, select Surf & Specialty stores that carry the Quiksilver and Roxy brands, as well as Best Buy, Good Guys, Wherehouse Music, and Nextel Retail Stores. Boost Mobile customers pay for the minutes only as they need them through the purchase of Re-Boost™ cards, which are available in $20, $30, and $50 denominations and may be purchased as needed at all authorized Boost Mobile retailers (such as Nextel and Target) and 7-Eleven stores.

THINK STRATEGICALLY

Identify the target market and provide a customer profile for the Roxy brand wireless phone. Explain Boost Mobile's marketing mix decision (four Ps) for the Roxy phone and its Mobile service.

@ Online Action!

Go to *marketingessentials.glencoe.com/1/case* to find a project on customer profiles.

place decision. Place strategies determine how and where a product will be distributed. For global companies, it may mean making decisions about which products will be sold in which countries and which retail outlets or other means of selling the product will best reach the customer. Can the product be sold directly to the consumer, or are intermediaries necessary? Other place decisions include deciding which transportation methods and what stock levels are most effective.

In the Tropicana orange juice example, the place decision was to sell 64-fluid-ounce containers of the Light 'n Healthy brand in food stores that have refrigerated cases. You see these products primarily in supermarkets, convenience stores, and mass merchandise retailers with food departments, such as Smart & Final, Wal-Mart, or Costco.

Price

Price is what is exchanged for the product. Price strategies should reflect what customers are willing and able to pay. To that end, marketers must consider the price they will charge their industrial customers, including resellers. Pricing decisions also take into account prices the competition charges for comparable products.

Pricing Strategies

Price strategies therefore include arriving at the list price or manufacturer's suggested retail price, as well as discounts, allowances, credit terms, and payment period for industrial customers.

On occasion, a company may use special promotional pricing that would adjust the suggested retail price. A manufacturer may decide to use a promotional price for a fixed period of time, for example. This technique is frequently used to launch new products.

Promotion

Promotion refers to decisions about advertising, personal selling, sales promotion, and publicity.

Promotional Strategies

Promotional strategies deal with how potential customers will be told about a company's products, including the message, the media selected, special offers, and the timing of the promotional campaigns. Figure 1.2 highlights the Tropicana Light 'n Healthy ad campaign. In that campaign, images were carefully created to match a key feature of the product. Ads for orange juice with added calcium or vitamins might have different graphics and might run in different magazines.

1.3 AFTER YOU READ

Reviewing Key Terms and Concepts

1. What is the difference between consumer and industrial markets?
2. What is the relationship among market segmentation, target markets, and customer profiles?
3. Name the four Ps of the marketing mix and explain the importance of a target market for each of them.

Integrating Academic Skills

Math

4. If total sales in the ice cream category were $4.4 billion and Breyers's sales were $650,417,792, what would be its market share? Round your answer to the tenth decimal place.

Language Arts

5. Write a customer profile for a magazine of your choice. Support your description by describing sample articles and advertisements from the magazine.

@ Online Action! Check your answers at *marketingessentials.glencoe.com/1/read*

CAREERS IN MARKETING

CHARLES SPIVEY
ARTIST DEVELOPMENT

What do you do at work?

Artist development is all about helping my client take the next step, depending on where he or she is in his or her career. Some already have a couple albums under their belt, while others are looking to record a first demo. Fundamentally, I am a people broker. If a client needs a new Web site, I connect her to the best Web people I know. If a singer needs a new headshot, I hand him over to my best photographer. If a band needs 200 people at a show, I talk to every newspaper and radio person I know and get them to push the band.

What skills are most important to you?

People skills, without a doubt, are the most important aspects of my job. I know that PR means public relations but I think it means people relations. Know your clients, know your friends, and know your business partners. They're all people and want to be treated like people, not profit centers. My undergraduate education had nothing to do with music, PR, or management, but my MBA course load of marketing classes has certainly paid big dividends. The best lessons I've learned have come from other people in the business—people I admire and look up to.

What is your key to success?

It's important to set high goals and be tenacious, but also have the ability to accept failure and see it as an opportunity to grow. Sure I want to succeed every time I pick up the phone to market my clients, but I have to be willing to accept the rejection that often comes in the music business; I just dust myself off and come back for more.

Aptitudes, Abilities, and Skills

Strong interpersonal skills, resourcefulness, creativity, contact management, and organization

Education and Training

MBA degrees provide core-level skills that are valuable in a variety of careers.

Career Path

Entry-level opportunities abound for MBA graduates in virtually every field you can imagine.

THINKING CRITICALLY

Why might MBA-level marketing courses be helpful, even in a career that was not specifically the focus of those courses?

@ Online Action!

Go to *marketingessentials.glencoe.com/1/careers* to find a career-related activity.

FOCUS on KEY POINTS

SECTION 1.1

- Marketing is defined as the process of planning and executing the conception, pricing, promotion, and distribution of ideas, goods, and services to create exchanges that satisfy individual and organizational objectives.
- There are four foundations and seven functions of marketing. The marketing concept is a focus on customers' needs and wants while generating a profit.

SECTION 1.2

- Three benefits of marketing are new and improved products, lower prices, and added value (utility). Five economic utilities are form, place, time, possession, and information.

SECTION 1.3

- A market is defined as all people who share similar needs and wants and who have the ability to purchase given products.
- Market share is a firm's percentage of total sales of all competitors in a given market.
- The four Ps of the marketing mix are product, place, price, and promotion. Marketing decisions and strategies for the four Ps are based on the target market.

REVIEW VOCABULARY

Define each of the following terms in writing.

1. marketing (p. 5)
2. goods and services (p. 5)
3. marketing concept (p. 7)
4. utility (p. 9)
5. market (p. 13)
6. consumer and industrial markets (p. 13)
7. market share (p. 14)
8. target market (p. 15)
9. customer profile (p. 15)
10. marketing mix (p. 16)

REVIEW FACTS and IDEAS

11. Define marketing. (1.1)
12. Identify and explain the four foundations of marketing. (1.1)
13. List the seven functions of marketing. (1.1)
14. Explain the marketing concept. (1.1)
15. What is meant by *utility* and what are the five economic utilities? (1.2)
16. What is a market and in what ways can a market be identified? (1.3)
17. What is market share? (1.3)
18. Define a target market. (1.3)
19. What are the four components of the marketing mix? (1.3)

BUILD SKILLS

20. **Workplace Skills**

The Right Choice Assume you are a salesperson in a computer store. A customer is hesitant about buying a mid-priced laptop computer you are showing. The customer's objection is that it will sell for much less in a year. Do you think the customer is correct? What would you say?

21. **Technology Applications**

Understanding Market Functions With two or three classmates, use a word processing program to write a short report about a new fruit beverage that you believe will be popular with teenagers. Assume your team develops this new product and wants to start selling it. Consider all seven marketing functions (distribution, financing, information management, pricing, product/service management, promotion, and selling) in your report and explain for each function how it applies to the marketing of your new product.

22. **Math Practice**

Figure the Market Share Calculate Nikon's market share if total sales in the digital camera market are $211,464,600 and Nikon's sales are $120,305,671? Round your answer to the tenth decimal place.

DEVELOP CRITICAL THINKING

23. **The Cost of Marketing**

It is often said that marketing costs represent about 50 percent of the selling price of an item. Select a product that you have recently purchased or a product that interests you and research (on the Internet, in magazines and newspapers, etc.) what type of marketing has been done for this product. List all the examples you can find. Do you think all the items on the list were good marketing ideas? Why or why not?

24. **Explain the Marketing Concept**

Write a 200-word essay to convince a friend that maketing is more than just merchandising—displaying products in stores. Include how important consumers are to marketers by explaining the marketing concept.

APPLY CONCEPTS

25. Understand Target Markets and the Marketing Mix

Select an existing product that interests you. Look at how it is advertised in print or on television and the Internet. Research your product's price and where it is sold. Identify its target market and the four Ps of its marketing mix. Then change the target market for the product.

Activity Show how the four Ps of the marketing mix must be revised to focus on your newly defined target market. Prepare a written report and an oral presentation using presentation software.

26. Research Customer Relationship Management

Use magazine articles, Internet sources, and your own observations to research efforts made by companies to develop close relationships with customers. Analyze the effectiveness of customer relationship management (CRM). What pitfalls have been experienced by companies and what successes have been reported?

Activity Prepare a three-page written report, complete with citations from appropriate sources, to document the research you have done on the topic of CRM.

NET SAVVY

27. Check an Online Dictionary

Visit the American Marketing Association's (AMA) Web site and use its online dictionary to review its definition of marketing, as well as other key marketing terms covered in this chapter.

THE DECA CONNECTION

An Association of Marketing Students

Role Play: Benefits of Marketing

Situation You are to assume the role of a marketing student at your local high school. Your marketing teacher (judge) has asked you to put together a presentation about the importance of marketing in our society. This presentation will be made to a group of incoming freshmen that have little knowledge of marketing or of its importance.

Activity You are to prepare an outline of your presentation on the importance of marketing and present it to your marketing teacher (judge) for approval.

Evaluation You will be evaluated on how well you meet the following performance indicators:

- Explain marketing and its importance in a global economy
- Describe marketing functions and related activities
- Determine forms of economic utility created by marketing activities
- Explain types of business activities
- Prepare simple written reports

For more information and DECA Prep practice, go to *marketingessentials.glencoe .com/1/DECA*

CHAPTER 2

The Marketing Plan

Chapter Objectives

After reading this chapter, you should be able to:

- Conduct a SWOT analysis
- List the three key areas of an internal company analysis
- Identify the factors in an environmental scan
- Explain the basic elements of a marketing plan
- Explain the concept of market segmentation
- Analyze a target market
- Differentiate between mass marketing and market segmentation

GUIDE TO THE PHOTO

Market Talk Marketers understand that for a product or service to be successful, they first have to find out who needs it or has an interest in it. Marketers must determine their potential customers among diverse groups of people.

Quick Think There are 24.3 million teenagers in the U.S. They spend $120 billion each year. Many have regular jobs and weekly income. List three ways you would research this market.

THE   CONNECTION

Performance indicators represent key skills and knowledge. Relating them to the concepts explained in this chapter is your key to success in DECA events. Keep this in mind as you read this chapter and write some notes each time you encounter material that helps you master a key concept.

These acronyms represent DECA events that involve knowledge of concepts in this chapter.

AAAL	**FSRM***	**TSE**	**FMAL**
FMML	**VPM**	**TMDM**	**RMAL**
RMML	**SMDM**	**BSM**	**FMDM**
HMDM*	**ADC**	**QSRM***	
AAML	**MMS**	**EMDM**	

In all these DECA events you should be able to follow these performance indicators:

- Explain the nature of marketing plans
- Explain the role of situational analysis in the marketing-planning process
- Conduct a SWOT analysis for use in the marketing-planning process
- Conduct an environmental scan to obtain marketing information
- Forecast sales
- Develop a marketing plan
- Describe measures used to control marketing planning
- Evaluate a marketing plan
- Conduct marketing audits

All the events with an asterisk (*) also include this performance indicator:

- Forecast servings of each food item

DECA PREP

Check your understanding of DECA performance indicators with the DECA activity in this chapter's review. For more information and DECA Prep practice, go to *marketingessentials .glencoe.com/2/DECA*

SECTION 2.1

Marketing Planning

OBJECTIVES

- Conduct a SWOT analysis
- List the three key areas of an internal company analysis
- Identify the factors in an environmental scan
- Explain the basic elements of a marketing plan

KEY TERMS

- SWOT analysis
- environmental scan
- marketing plan
- executive summary
- situation analysis
- marketing strategy
- sales forecasts
- performance standard

READ and STUDY

BEFORE YOU READ

Connect Suppose you are organizing a magazine sale for a school fund-raiser. Your goal is to raise $500 in one month. How would you organize the task and plan to meet your goal?

THE MAIN IDEA

A company starts its marketing planning with a look at itself and at the world around it. Marketers use this information to create a marketing plan to reach their goals.

STUDY ORGANIZER

Follow the outline below to identify the steps of a marketing plan.

Elements of a Marketing Plan

I. Executive summary
II. Situation analysis
III.
IV.
V.

WHILE YOU READ

Connect Conduct a SWOT analysis on yourself. What are your strengths and weaknesses? What outside opportunities and threats may impact your personal goals?

SWOT Analysis

Good marketing relies on good plans. A company's planning efforts begin with a critical look at itself and its business environment, or the market in which it operates. This assessment lists and analyzes the company's strengths and its weaknesses. It also includes the opportunities and the threats that surround it. In other words, this analysis lists everything that can foster the business's success and what could make it fail. The acronym for strengths, weaknesses, opportunities, threats is also the name of this process: **SWOT analysis**.

This internal and external awareness will help a business deal with weaknesses and prepare it to handle threats such as competition or a changing marketplace. An accurate analysis also will help a company be more competitive because it provides guidance and direction. The company will develop strategies around the SWOT analysis.

Internal Strengths and Weaknesses

Strengths and weaknesses are internal factors that affect a business operation. The internal analysis centers around three Cs: company, customers, and competition. It is important to review these factors objectively and fairly. For this reason, some firms bring in outside consultants to conduct this phase of the analysis.

Company Analysis

Questions that are part of a company's internal analysis are about what a company does well and what areas are weak. This includes a review of the staff (both management and other personnel), the company's financial situation, its production capabilities, and each aspect of the marketing mix (product, promotion, place, and pricing). Here are a few sample questions that could be used as part of a company analysis:

Staff-Related Questions

- What is the company's mission statement? Does everyone know it? Is everyone on staff following it?
- How experienced are the company executives? What have they accomplished?
- Does the company have too much or not enough staff in each area to provide the quality of service it should? Should staff be re-assigned?
- What is the quality of the staff? Are there formal training and assessment programs?
- How effective is its sales force?

Financial Questions

- Has the company been profitable? In which areas and why?
- Are there enough financial resources to achieve the company's goals?
- What is the company's sales history? Are sales increasing or decreasing?

Production Capability Questions

- How are adjustments made in production due to an increase or decrease in sales orders?
- Has the research and development (R & D) department created successful new products?
- What percentage of sales come from products that are five years or older?
- What changes in technology are required to remain competitive?

Marketing Mix (Four Ps) Questions

Product

- What new products have been successful and why?
- Does the company own a patent on any of those products?
- Are any patents expiring in the future?

Price

- What are the present pricing strategies?
- Are the pricing strategies working?

Promotion

- How is the company positioned in the marketplace?
- What are the promotional strategies and have they been successful?
- What is the company's reputation and image among consumers?

Place

- Do products easily reach customers?
- Who helps the company with distribution?

The answers to these questions might reveal such strengths (or core competencies) as talented and well-trained employees, quality workmanship, and an excellent service record.

Case Study

Amazon.com

Amazon.com was one of the first online discount book retailers, and it enjoys a positive reputation and excellent name recognition. After being in business for seven years, it finally made a profit in 2001. Some of its strengths at that time included an increase in sales outside North America. In mid-2004, sales at sites outside the United States rose 50 percent to $595 million. They climbed 13 percent to $792 million in the United States. In 2004, Amazon agreed to buy Joyo.com, China's largest online retailer of books, music, and videos, to gain access to the world's second-biggest Internet market in terms of users. Amazon expects sales from foreign sites in China, Canada, France, Germany, and Great Britain to surpass U.S. sales in the future.

Amazon's Other Strengths

Other strengths were: expanded product selections (electronics, apparel, toys, and more) and successful pricing strategies, which included discounted prices and free shipping for orders over $25. However, this very same pricing strategy was also considered a weakness because it produced low gross profit margins. (Gross profit margin is the percentage of sales revenue left after paying for the cost of the goods or services sold.)

THINK STRATEGICALLY

What strategies do you think Amazon.com should adopt to capitalize on its new strengths?

Online Action! **Go to *marketingessentials.glencoe.com/2/case* to find a research project on companies' strengths and weaknesses.**

Customer Analysis

Customers are a great source of information. Studying their buying habits may reveal patterns that offer insights into product offerings and pricing strategies. Here are a few questions that help in the analysis of customers.

- Who are the customers?
- How do groups of customers differ from one another?
- What, when, where, and how much do they buy?
- How do customers rate the company on quality, service, and value?
- How satisfied is each customer segment?
- What customer segments are not having their needs met?
- Is your customer base increasing or decreasing? Why?

Catalog companies use database technology to see buying patterns, which allow them to produce interest-specific catalogs. Companies with this technology and know-how

have a major advantage over their competitors because they can structure their product selection, pricing, and promotional messages to very specific targeted audiences.

To monitor customer satisfaction, many firms ask customers to complete a questionnaire or some form of survey after making a purchase. Data from this research helps companies pinpoint areas that need improvement.

Monitoring customer satisfaction reveals both strengths and weaknesses. Take, for example, the case of an eye doctor. Suppose that a strength is the amount of personal attention the doctor gives each patient. Patients report that the doctor spends a lot of time answering their questions. This strength also creates a weakness: complaints about the time patients spend in the eye doctor's waiting room. The solution seems simple: schedule fewer patients in a given time period so there is less overlap. This poses another problem that may generate complaints from patients wishing to make appointments. Under that new policy, patients might have to wait two weeks or more before they can get an appointment. So, what appeared to be a quick and easy solution is not so simple.

Competitive Position

A company may find that it has certain strengths and weaknesses when compared to its competitors. A company's market share may be greater than its competitors', which would be a major strength. If a company loses market share to its competitors, it would be a weakness. Questions that help a company analyze its internal competitive position are:

•COMPARE and CONTRAST **UPS, the United States Postal Service, and DHL all compete in the same market and provide similar services.**

What do they do to keep or increase their market share?

- What market share does the company have?
- What advantages does the company have over its competitors?
- What core competencies does the company possess? Does it have a better reputation, own a patent, have special resources, or better distribution capabilities?
- Are competitors taking business away from the company? How? New products? Better promotion?

External Opportunities and Threats

Companies must always look for opportunities to create competitive advantage due to external factors.

Competition

To stay competitive, companies need to know what their competitors are doing at all times. Changes in a competitor's financial situation and problems in the marketplace can provide opportunities. For example, Smart & Final, a discount supermarket chain based in the western United States, enjoyed increased customer traffic and increased sales when a labor strike crippled three competitors (Vons, Ralphs, and Albertsons) in 2004. The obvious weakness of Vons, Ralphs, and Albertsons (their inability to end the strike quickly) opened the door for competitors to take business away from them.

Companies that conduct a SWOT analysis on an ongoing basis are in a better position to react and make adjustments to their marketing mix. To assist in this process, companies must continually scan the external environment.

Environmental Scan

An **environmental scan** is an analysis of outside influences that may have an impact on an organization. This is a methodical look at the world that typically includes four areas: political, economic, socio-cultural, and technological (sometimes referred to with the acronym PEST). Understanding how each of these areas is changing or is likely to change in the future can lead to a better appreciation of potential opportunities or threats for the firm. An alert business owner may use a change in one of these four aspects as an opportunity to be first to market products customers want.

Political

Political issues center around government involvement in business operations. Companies must be alert to changes in laws and regulations that affect their industries. Global companies need to understand the political structure and regulations of each foreign country in which they conduct business. To assess potential political risks and new opportunities, it is important to see what changes are likely in the laws governing your business operation, as they will have an impact on marketing plans. Here are a few examples of issues and current regulations that may affect certain industries in a positive way (opportunity) or in a negative way (threat):

- **Do Not Call Registry** The U.S. government passed this legislation in 2003. It gives people the ability to demand that telemarketers not call their phone numbers. This regulation forced many businesses to rethink part of their marketing strategies. Telemarketing companies had to adjust their data files to comply with the law.
- **Downloading Music from the Internet** The problem of illegal downloading of music created a whole industry with online companies that now provide legal downloading of music for a fee. This new industry may hurt music stores but has become an opportunity for companies like Apple's iTunes, RealNetworks' RealRhapsody, and Roxio's Napster.

Economic

The current state of the economy is of interest to all businesses: If the economy is robust, businesses are more likely to invest in new products and markets. An economy that is in a recession or slowing down sends a completely different message to the company's

• KNOWING YOUR MARKET

General Motors, one of the largest auto manufacturers in the United States, has added a navigation and emergency assistance system to some of its cars.

How may this technology affect auto companies?

decision makers. Upcoming marketing programs may be altered or scrapped altogether in a weak economy. Factors, such as the unemployment rate, inflation, retail sales figures, productivity, and consumer confidence, are tools to estimate the current status of the economy. The value of the dollar in relation to foreign currencies affects imports and exports. Here are some economic factors marketers would consider opportunities or threats:

- An economy in recession poses a threat to nearly all companies. Most companies slow or stop plans for new facilities and often reduce research and development (R&D) efforts.
- If unemployment figures decrease and consumer confidence increases, companies may see an opportunity to grow their business.
- Changes in foreign currency rates could be seen as a threat or an opportunity depending on whether this makes the company's products or services cheaper or more expensive in their foreign target market.
- Illegal dumping (selling imported products at a very low price) in a given market is a threat to all businesses in that industry.
- Changes in trade restrictions, such as lowering or raising tariffs (taxes) on imported goods, could be considered a threat or an opportunity, depending on where a company does business.

Socio-Cultural

A socio-cultural analysis is based on customers and potential customers. Changes in their attitudes, lifestyles, and opinions provide a multitude of opportunities and threats. Socio-cultural analysis covers changes in all demographic factors, such as age, income, occupation, education level, and marital status. Here are two examples.

- The United States is becoming a more ethnically and racially diverse country. Marketing plans need to meet this change. For example, in the area of home buying, minority consumers are expected to account for nearly two-thirds of all new home purchases by 2010.
- Obesity is an issue in the United States, as it causes many health problems. Consumer advocates for healthier eating habits have criticized fast-food chains.

Technological

Changing technology may be a threat for one industry or company, but an opportunity for others. A perfect example is digital photography. To be competitive, traditional photo companies like Kodak are looking for ways to adapt to this new technology. Camera companies are making more digital cameras. Other companies are seizing the opportunity to capitalize on this new technology by developing products to support it. Printer companies like Epson and Hewlett-Packard have developed products to make it easy for consumers to print their own digital photographs. Companies that keep abreast of the newest technological breakthroughs can use that knowledge to be more competitive. Here are a few examples:

- **Computer Automation** The home of the future may be completely automated. You may be able to call from your cell phone to change your thermostat so your home is warm when you arrive.
- **Satellite Technology** Cars now offer satellite radio and navigation systems that direct you to your destinations, as well as SOS systems such as OnStar that help you in an emergency.

Writing a Marketing Plan

Marketing is a complicated activity that relies on many different tasks. For this reason, marketers create a marketing plan. A **marketing plan** is a formal, written document that directs a company's activities for a specific period of time. It details analysis

NET MARKETING

Take Me Out to the Webcast

Major League Baseball (MLB) is betting that fans will pay to see games on their PCs. Distribution deals worth a combined $49 million were announced in March 2004 with Internet service providers AOL and MSN to stream live games and highlights over the Web. The league also signed marketing deals with three cable operators (Charter, Cablevision, and Comcast) to attract cable customers to the MLB Webcasts of more than 240 games a month. Fans can also access archived games for later replay. There's a big potential market. Broadband subscribers in the United States will grow from 27 million in 2004 to 46 million in 2008, says Jupiter Research. Plus, the recent success of streamed college basketball games on AOL suggests that people might finally be ready to log on rather than tune in to sports.

THINK LIKE A MARKETER

Which age group is most likely to be interested in this new way of viewing games? Why?

Online Action!

Go to *marketingessentials.glencoe.com/2/net* to find a research project on technology and growth opportunities.

GLOBAL MARKET

The Tesco Strategy

The British supermarket chain Tesco is aiming for long-term growth. It is best known as a grocery store, but it sees its future as something much bigger than the four food groups.

Expand and Diversify According to the company's Web site, Tesco is expanding even more into international markets, such as Japan, Turkey, Poland, Hungary, and the Czech Republic. At the end of the 2003/2004 fiscal year, about half of its stores were outside the United Kingdom. The company says it is now the world's biggest online grocery store.

Tesco has also started stocking non-food products, including consumer electronics and housewares. It sells financial services, such as mortgages, insurance, and even do-it-yourself wills. Its online services include music downloads, DVD rentals, and a flower delivery service.

The Company's Mission Tesco claims its core purpose is "creating value for customers, to earn their lifetime loyalty." The company says it has two values that drive the way it does business: "No one tries harder for customers;" and "Treat people how we like to be treated."

In what way are Tesco's core purpose and values related to its marketing objectives and strategies?

@ Online Action!

Go to *marketingessentials.glencoe.com/2/global* to find a research project on global marketing.

and research efforts and provides a roadmap for how a product will enter the market, be advertised, and sold. A marketing plan also communicates the goals, objectives, and strategies of a company to members of the management team. The specifics in the plan let managers know their responsibilities, budget, and timelines for completion. A marketing plan helps a company monitor a company's performance. A small retail business may develop a simple marketing plan for a year, but a large manufacturer with global sales would prepare a marketing plan that covers five years.

Elements of a Marketing Plan

Marketing plans may differ from company to company. However, there are some basic elements that will be found in all marketing plans. Those elements include an executive summary, a situation analysis, marketing goals/objectives, marketing strategies, and implementation, as well as a system for evaluation and control. See Figure 2.1 for a complete outline of a marketing plan. Follow the annotations on the figure to see how a plan can be built.

Executive Summary

An **executive summary** is a brief overview of the entire marketing plan. It briefly addresses each topic in the plan and gives an explanation of the costs involved in implementing the plan. The executive summary may also be used to provide information to people outside the organization, especially those who may be investing in the company or organization.

Figure 2.1 Elements of a Marketing Plan

- **How to Build a Marketing Plan** A marketing plan is an essential planning tool for a company. This document defines the company's overall goals, determines strategies for achieving those goals, and, at the end of a predetermined period of time, assesses how well those goals were achieved. Below are the basic elements found in a marketing plan.

How can a small company benefit from writing a marketing plan?

This is the introduction to the marketing plan. Its clarity and brevity sell the plan to readers.

This part provides a snapshot of the company's present position. It often reports the results of a SWOT analysis and an environmental scan.

I. Executive summary

II. Situation analysis
   A. SWOT analysis
   B. Environmental scan

III. Objectives
   A. Company's mission
   B. Marketing objectives
   C. Financial objectives

This section defines specific goals to be met. To be effective, objectives must be single-minded, specific, realistic, and measurable, and must contain a time frame.

IV. Marketing strategies
   A. Positioning and points of difference
   B. Marketing mix (four Ps)
      1. Product
      2. Promotion
      3. Price
      4. Place (distribution)

This is where the company defines how it is going to meet its objectives with a marketing mix: the four Ps.

V. Implementation
   A. Organization
   B. Activities and responsibilities
   C. Timetables

This part outlines how the company will put its plans into effect.

VI. Evaluation and control
   A. Performance standards and measurements
      1. Marketing objectives
      2. Financial objectives
      3. Marketing mix strategies
   B. Corrective action

This part tells how the marketing plan will be evaluated and what measures might be necessary if objectives are not met.

VII. Appendix

Supplemental materials are included in the appendix.

Online Action! Go to ***marketingessentials.glencoe.com/2/figure/1*** to find a project on marketing plans.

Situation Analysis

Situation analysis is the study of the internal and external factors that affect marketing strategies. The information from a company's SWOT analysis and from the environmental scan becomes the basis for this portion of the marketing plan.

Goals and Objectives

Objectives let everyone know what the marketing plan will accomplish. To be useful, an objective must be single-minded (have only one topic for each objective), specific, realistic, measurable, and have a time frame. For example, you cannot include increasing sales and increasing profits in the same objective. Each topic needs to be a separate objective.

Specific means that the objective provides enough detail that there can be no misunderstanding. You cannot use, "to be better than a competitor" as an objective because what is "better" to one person may not be to another.

Measurable means that the objective includes a way to evaluate it. For example, you cannot simply say you want to increase sales. You need to identify the percentage increase in dollar or unit sales to make that objective measurable. Thus, you could use, "to increase dollar sales by 15 percent as compared to the same time last year."

Finally, you must include a time frame, such as in six months, or as compared to last year's sales. Without a time frame, you would not know if an objective was actually reached.

Marketing objectives must be in line with the organization's goals and mission. If an organization's goal is to double its business in five years, marketing objectives must coincide with that goal and provide the means to reach it.

A company's mission statement provides the focus for a firm's goals with its explanation of the company's core competencies, values, expectations, and vision for the future.

Marketing Strategies

A **marketing strategy** identifies target markets and sets marketing mix choices that focus on those markets. All strategies need to take the customer's needs and wants into account, as well as the objectives of the marketing plan.

A company's or product's position in the marketplace determines the appropriate marketing strategy. The positioning of the product or service will drive decisions for each of the four Ps.

An effective marketing strategy should be focused on the key points of difference. The key point of difference is the advantage a company, a product, or service has over its competition. The point of difference could be the quality of the product, a superior distribution system, a more creative ad campaign, or a more competitive pricing structure.

This competitive advantage is what will make the company successful. The marketing mix elements can help create points of difference with respect to competition.

The results of the SWOT analysis should provide enough information to identify the specific target market and suggest ideas to create the necessary point(s) of difference to be competitive.

Implementation: Make the Plan, Work the Plan

Implementation is putting the marketing plan into action and managing it. This means obtaining the financial resources, management, and staffing necessary to put the plan into action. A timetable shows when each part goes into play.

This part of the marketing plan outlines a schedule of activities, job assignments, **sales forecasts** (the projection of probable, future sales in units or dollars), budgets, details of each activity, and who will be responsible for each activity.

This phase of the plan requires excellent communication among members of the management team so that tasks are completed on a timely basis.

Evaluation and Control

In the evaluation section of the marketing plan, measures that will be used to evaluate the plan are discussed. It is important to explain exactly how a specific objective will be measured and who will be responsible for providing that evaluation.

Performance Standards and Evaluation

Performance standards are the measuring stick. A **performance standard** is an expectation for performance that reflects the plan's objectives. As part of the planning process, the control section suggests actions that should be considered if objectives are not met. In the control phase, the company's goal is to reduce the gap between planned performance standards and actual performance.

Let's say sales did not reach the sales forecast numbers. One reason for this discrepancy could be recent changes in economic conditions. In such a situation, a company may revise its sales forecast to make it more realistic.

Appendix

The appendix is the section of the marketing plan that includes supplemental materials such as detailed financial statements, sample ads, and other materials that support the plan.

Conclusion

The marketing process is ongoing. Think of it as a circular pattern that keeps going through the three phases of the marketing process of planning, implementation, and control. The key question at the end of the process is "Did we accomplish the objectives listed in the marketing plan within the boundaries of the plan?"

A marketing audit evaluates a company's marketing objectives, strategies, budgets, organization, and performance. It identifies problem areas in marketing operations. A marketing audit happens on a formal basis once a year and informally on a continuous basis.

2.1 AFTER YOU READ

Reviewing Key Terms and Concepts

1. What is a SWOT analysis and why is it helpful?
2. How can a business use a SWOT analysis and an environmental scan to create a marketing plan?
3. Why are evaluation and control important elements of a marketing plan?

Integrating Academic Skills

Math

4. If a company's current sales revenue is $1,386,000 and its marketing objective is to increase sales by 10 percent in the next year, what is the dollar sales goal for the following year?

Economics

5. How can a country's current economic situation impact a business's marketing plan?

Check your answers at *marketingessentials.glencoe.com/2/read*

Market Segmentation

OBJECTIVES

- **Explain the concept of market segmentation**
- **Analyze a target market**
- **Differentiate between mass marketing and market segmentation**

KEY TERMS

- **market segmentation**
- **demographics**
- **disposable income**
- **discretionary income**
- **geographics**
- **psychographics**
- **mass marketing**

READ and STUDY

BEFORE YOU READ

Predict How do marketers find out who their customers are?

THE MAIN IDEA

The key to marketing and selling goods, services, or ideas is to know who your customer or audience is. This is called a target market and the process to find that specific market is called market segmentation. The factors that define a particular market are demographic, geographic, psychographic, and behavioral.

STUDY ORGANIZER

Use a chart like the one below to list differences between mass marketing and market segmentation.

Mass Market Versus Market Segmentation

Mass Market	Market Segmentation
Definition	Ways to segment 1. Demographics 2. 3. 4.

Identifying and Analyzing Markets

Businesses look for ways to connect with current and potential customers. The surest way to make that connection is to know them well. This means knowing where they live, their income level, age, ethnic background, activities, values, and what interests them. When a company looks at its customers this way, it can identify groups of people who have many things in common.

WHILE YOU READ

Connect Think of yourself as a consumer. What are your key characteristics?

• PEPSI for EVERYBODY PepsiCo, Inc. does extensive market research as do many other large corporations. This research reveals how the market for a given product is segmented. This information plays an important role in determining where and how a product is advertised.

Which market is PepsiCo trying to reach with this ad? How?

Marketers analyze groups of customers to see if any of them can be further broken down into smaller, more precise clusters. The process of classifying people who form a given market into even smaller groups is called **market segmentation**. Let's look at the market for jeans. A marketer might ask, "Who buys jeans? At what price? What special features do they want?" Depending on the answers to these questions, the market for jeans could be segmented:

- **By age** jeans for kids, teens, and adults.
- **By price** marketers need to reach different income levels (often referred to as socio-economic groups).
- **By desired features** tight fit, comfortable fit, newest fashion, or a unique design.

To meet the needs of these different market segments, jeans manufacturers develop a unique marketing mix, including different products, promotions, stores for distribution, [illegible]ce points. For example, Levi's jeans are available in relaxed fit, regular fit, 501 original, loose straight, loose boot cut, low rise straight, and low rise boot cut.

The next question marketers ask is, "Which of these segments should we target?" It is usually too costly to target all the potential target markets. So, it is very important to identify those markets in which the company has an advantage that enables it to survive against its competition over a long period of time. This is what marketers call a sustainable competitive advantage.

Companies study data generated by governments, private research firms, trade associations, and their own research to determine if a given target market is large enough to justify the expense. For example, United States census data might reveal that there are enough teenagers to justify making jeans for that segment of the market. To get a handle on the jeans market, additional research would reveal more about this market segment: their buying behavior, interests, activities, opinions about fashion, values, status, household income levels, ethnic background, and any other factor that might help marketers create a customer profile. The more specific the information is, the easier it is to design the jeans, price them, create the appropriate promotions, and sell them in the right outlets. The same factors that help segment a market are used to describe a target market. They are: demographics, geographics, psychographics, and behavioral factors.

Demographics

Demographics refer to statistics that describe a population in terms of personal characteristics such as age, gender, income, marital status, ethnic background, education, and occupation.

Age

Marketers can easily use age to segment the market by creating age ranges. The United States census provides information that might help in deciding on the age categories. Here are common labels used to segment the population by generation:

Baby Boom Generation

The 76 million babies born in the United States between 1946 and 1964 are known as the baby boomers. As baby boomers get older, their income and spending power increase. Therefore, they are prime targets for all types of products.

Generation X (or the Baby Bust Generation)

They followed the Baby Boom Generation. Most members of Generation X are children of dual-career households or divorced parents. They have been bombarded with media from an early age, and they are savvy purchasers and skeptical consumers. To reach this group, marketers must use sharp images, music, a sense of humor, and meet them on their own terms.

Generation Y

They are the sons and daughters of the later baby boomers. Generation Y is also known as the Echo Boomers or Millennium Generation. According to the United States census, this group is more racially and ethnically diverse with a lot of spending power. Fashions and information about products get passed along via the Internet, as almost all of the members of this generation have e-mail and surf the Web.

Gender

Gender helps to create market segments as well. Jockey, at one time a men's underwear company, doubled its sales when it entered the women's market with Jockey underwear for women.

Income

Marketers want to know how much money they have to spend on different products. For this reason, they look at two types of income measurement: disposable income and discretionary income. **Disposable income** is the money left after taking out taxes. Marketers who produce and distribute products that are necessities are interested in changes in consumers' disposable income. **Discretionary income** is the money left after paying for basic living necessities such as food, shelter, and clothing. Marketers who sell luxury and premium products are interested in changes in consumers' discretionary income.

Marital Status

The U.S. Census indicates that married couples have slipped to 50.7 percent of total households, compared with 80 percent in the 1950s. Reasons for this reduction in married couples can be attributed to several factors. People are older when they get married for the first time, divorcing more, living longer, and remarrying less. Married couples with kids represent 25 percent of the population.

Ethnic Background

The U.S. population is becoming more multicultural and ethnically diverse, mainly as a result of increased immigration. The Caucasian population is declining, relative to other ethnic populations. African American, Hispanic, and Asian American populations make up 28 percent of the U.S. population. By 2025 these ethnic groups will represent 37.2 percent of all Americans.

Geographics

The term **geographics** refers to segmentation of the market based on where people live. Geographics relate closely to demographics because of the similarity among people who live in a certain area. To segment a market geographically, you can refer to local, regional, national, or even global markets. For example, a small, independent restaurant generally caters to people who live in its vicinity. Some products, such as Coca-Cola and Pepsi, are marketed nationally and internationally.

- If you were interested in marketing to Latinos, it would be good to know the top Hispanic markets, which are Los Angeles, New York, Miami, Chicago, and Houston. If you were to introduce a new line of Hispanic products, the best place to market test them would be in these geographic areas.
- Fifty-five percent of the African American population live in the South. However, the city with the largest number of people identified as African American is New York City with 2.3 million. Chicago is second with 1.1 million, followed by Detroit, Philadelphia, Houston, Los Angeles, Baltimore, Memphis, Washington, D.C., and New Orleans. Any company that wants to reach African Americans would want to make sure it has distribution outlets in those key cities.
- If you were interested in marketing to children, it would be good to know where a large number of them live. According to the U.S. Census, Utah and Alaska had the highest proportion of their populations in the 5-to-13 age group (15 percent each). States with 14 percent were Texas, Arizona, California, and Idaho.
- In 2003, the population 65 years of age and older could be found in the greatest numbers in California (3.8 million), Florida (2.9 million), New York (2.5 million), Texas (2.2 million), and Pennsylvania (1.9 million).
- The states with a median household income of at least $50,000 in 2002 were Maryland ($55,912), Alaska ($55,412), Minnesota ($54,931), New Hampshire ($53,549), Connecticut ($53,325), New Jersey ($53,266), Delaware ($50,878), and Massachusetts ($50,587). Banks and other financial institutions would be interested in these geographic areas, as many of these states' residents would be prime candidates for investments and insurance. Makers of luxury items would also target these geographical areas.

Psychographics

Psychographics involves grouping people with similar lifestyles, as well as shared attitudes, values, and opinions. Consumer lifestyles include how people spend their time and money. Attitudes, values, and opinions require special research to learn more about a group's personality traits and motivation.

Activities

If you made a list of all of your present activities, you would come to realize just how many market segments can be identified by psychographics. A good way to get a feel for market segmentation by activities is to visit the magazine section of a bookstore. For each interest group and activity, you will find at least one related magazine, which represents a market segment.

Attitudes

Consumers' attitudes, such as taking responsibility for one's health, eating healthier, and becoming physically fit, are trend-setting issues for marketers in the twenty-first century.

Personality & Values

More advanced study of psychographics includes the study of personality characteristics and values.

Behavioral

Segmenting the market based on product-related behavior involves looking at the benefits desired by consumers, shopping patterns, and usage rate. For example, many people, regardless of their socio-economic status, desire luxury and premium merchandise. The luxury market is a growing consumer trend as individuals define themselves more and more through the products and brands they buy.

For example, MasterCard research revealed five groups of online consumers: confident core users, cautious shoppers, mainstream users, curious but not convinced, and technology skeptics. The overriding finding was that enhanced security measures influenced a shopper's online purchase decision. Each group had different levels of concern about security.

How Marketers Use Consumers' Behavioral Patterns

Astute marketers study shopping patterns to determine usage rates. Jupiter Research, a market research company, has determined that most teenagers spend less than $50 a month on entertainment and that teenage girls spend 15 percent more on music than teenage boys.

Companies classify their customers according to the percentage of sales each group generates. Many businesses find that the 80/20 rule applies. The 80/20 rule means that 80 percent of a company's sales are generated by 20 percent of its loyal customers.

Mass Marketing Versus Segmentation

When products have universal appeal and few features to differentiate them from competitors, mass marketing is used. **Mass marketing** involves using a single marketing strategy to reach all customers.

A New Marketing Trend

Since most products can be segmented by demographics, psychographics, geographics, or buying behavior, mass marketing is not as popular as it once was. The current trend is niche marketing, which means that markets are narrowed down and defined with extreme precision. Even products that use one slogan in their advertising, such as *Got Milk?* ads, will use different models or themes to reach different segments of the market.

2.2 AFTER YOU READ

Reviewing Key Terms and Concepts

1. Which type of income, disposable or discretionary, is more important to businesses that sell expensive watches, second homes, and financial services?
2. Of what significance are the combined African American, Hispanic, and Asian-American populations to marketers?
3. A recent study shows that teens are drinking more bottled water and reducing the amount of carbonated beverages they drink. Which psychographic or lifestyle trend does this study support?

Integrating Academic Skills

Math

4. If 93 percent of the U.S. population of 290,890,777 (2003 estimate) snacks at least once a day, how large is the market for snack food?

Civics and Government

5. Why does the United States conduct a census of its residents every ten years?

Check your answers at *marketingessentials.glencoe.com/2/read*

CAREERS IN MARKETING

ROBERT MARCUM
MARKETING COORDINATOR
ARGOS, KLEIN AND HAMMERSMITH

What do you do at work?
I'm an employee of a consulting firm that focuses on using all types of marketing disciplines to help organizations achieve their goals. These include media relations, grassroots marketing, Internet communications, lobbying, investor relations, and advertising. My job mostly entails three things: leading and executing the communications programs for various clients, handling operations issues such as managing local staff, and pursuing new business.

What skills are most important to you?
A lot of what marketing people do is apply a measurable goal to creative pursuits: writing, oration, design, etc. Therefore, if you want to succeed in marketing, you'd better have an eye for design, write well, or be a persuasive conversationalist.

What kind of training do you recommend?
Read, read, read. Observe, observe, observe. Read everything. Read books on marketing. Read magazines to figure out how journalists craft stories. The best marketers are generally very observant people. Study psychology and learn to empathize with others. Marketing and communications are about evaluating an audience, and then communicating to that audience according to what you know about them in order to inspire the audience to do or think something so that you can further an organization's goals.

Aptitudes, Abilities, and Skills

Strong and outgoing personality, creativity, writing and communication skills

Education and Training

Degrees in marketing, communication, and psychology

Career Path

Marketing and communications positions range from entry-level assistant to upper-level executives. Entry-level positions provide real-world experience and a first step on the ladder upward.

THINKING CRITICALLY

Why is it valuable for marketing professionals to study psychology?

Online Action!

Go to *marketingessentials.glencoe.com/2/careers* to find a career-related activity.

CHAPTER 2 REVIEW

FOCUS on KEY POINTS

SECTION 2.1

- A SWOT analysis identifies a company's internal strengths and weaknesses, as well as external opportunities and threats. Internal strengths and weaknesses involve analysis of the company, its customers, and its competitive position. External opportunities and threats include political, economic, socio-cultural, and technological factors.

- A marketing plan is a written document that directs the marketing activities of a company for a specific period of time. The elements of a marketing plan are an executive summary, a situation analysis, marketing goals/objectives, marketing strategies, implementation, as well as evaluation and control, and appendix.

SECTION 2.2

- Market segmentation classifies people in a given market into smaller groups. Four methods of segmenting a market are demographics, geographics, psychographics, and buying behavior.

- Demographics can be broken down into age, gender, income, marital status, and ethnic background. Geographics relates to similarities among people who live in a certain area. Psychographics groups people with similar lifestyles, attitudes, values, and opinions.

REVIEW VOCABULARY

Review the definition of each key term and explain where each term belongs in the marketing plan.

1. SWOT analysis (p. 27)
2. environmental scan (p. 30)
3. executive summary (p. 33)
4. situation analysis (p. 35)
- market segmentation (p. 38)
- demographics (p. 39)
- disposable income (p. 39)
- discretionary income (p. 39)
5. marketing strategy (p. 35)
6. sales forecast (p. 35)
7. performance standard (p. 36)
- geographics (p. 40)
- psychographics (p. 40)
- mass marketing (p. 41)

REVIEW FACTS and IDEAS

8. Explain the purpose of a SWOT analysis. (2.1)
9. List the three key areas involved in an internal company analysis. (2.1)
10. Identify the factors in an external environmental scan. (2.1)
11. What are the basic elements found in all marketing plans? (2.1)
12. Explain market segmentation. (2.2)
13. How can a market be analyzed using demographics? Using geographics? (2.2)
14. What factors are involved in analyzing a market according to psychographics? (2.2)
15. Differentiate between mass marketing and market segmentation. (2.2)

BUILD SKILLS

16. Workplace Skills

Customer Service Skills Try to recall a businessperson or a salesperson who was able to establish a bond with you or one of your friends or family members during a business transaction at a store or a business office. List three things the person did to accomplish this.

17. Technology Applications

Age Groups Use spreadsheet software to create a chart that depicts the age groups reported by the U.S. Census Bureau's estimates as of July 2003:

Total population 290,808,777

Under 5 years 19,769,279

5 to 13 years 36,752,056

14 to 17 years 16,522,171

18 to 24 years 28,899,571

Include the 25 and older age group in your chart.

18. Math Practice

The 80/20 Rule Here are the sales figures for ten customers (1) $75,000; (2) $700,000; (3) $815,000; (4) $70,000; (5) $60,000; (6) $30,000; (7) $25,000; (8) $53,750; (9) $40,000; and (10) $25,000. Explain the 80/20 rule using the above ten sales figures.

DEVELOP CRITICAL THINKING

19. Analyze the Marketing Mix

Select two competing companies that target teens. Evaluate the effectiveness of their efforts with regard to the four Ps of the marketing mix. Which one is doing a better job and why?

20. Prepare a SWOT Analysis

Select a company that interests you and on which you can find information (on the Web, through observations at different stores, or in business publications). Prepare a SWOT analysis. Then, prepare a chart that depicts the company's internal strengths and weaknesses, as well as its external opportunities and threats. Be prepared to discuss your analysis with classmates.

APPLY CONCEPTS

21. Compare and Contrast the Effects of Marketing Activities

Research and list teen fashions and fads in clothing, footwear, electronics, or personal grooming products. Name factors that influence teen fashions and fads, as well as companies that are doing a good job of addressing them in the products they sell and the way they market those products to teens. Also cite companies that have been ineffective in their marketing efforts to teens. Consider all four Ps of the marketing mix in your analysis (product, place, price, and promotion).

Activity Prepare a written report and use presentation software to prepare an oral report on your research and your findings.

22. Segment a Market

Research the nutritional value of almonds and FDA approval of claims that can be used to market these products. Suggest trends that help segment the nut market. Choose and describe the most viable target market (segment). Suggest a promotional campaign for an organization (such as the Almond Board of California) that will use your proposal to increase sales. What would be the key message? What media would you choose?

Activity Prepare a written report and a visual presentation of your ideas using computer presentation software.

NET SAVVY

23. Learn From the Census

Visit the Web site for the United States Census Bureau and select one of its reports from its Facts for Features series. Share the report you selected with your class.

THE DECA CONNECTION

DECA — An Association of Marketing Students

Role Play: Marketing Intern

Situation You are to assume the role of intern for a marketing consulting firm. A customer (judge) is considering turning his/her hobby of making special occasion chocolate candies into a full time career. The customer (judge) is fairly inexperienced in business matters and has come to your company for help and advice in developing a marketing plan for the proposed business.

Activity You must explain to the customer (judge) the importance and function of a good marketing plan.

Evaluation You will be evaluated on how well you meet the following performance indicators:

- Explain the nature of marketing plans
- Conduct SWOT analysis for use in a marketing planning process
- Explain the concept of a market and market identification
- Explain the nature of sales forecasts
- Select a target market

@ Online Action!

For more information and DECA Prep practice, go to *marketingessentials.glencoe .com/2/DECA*

MARKETING INTERNSHIP

A SIMULATED DECA SPORTS AND ENTERTAINMENT MARKETING EVENT

Conduct a SWOT Analysis for NASCAR

BASIC BACKGROUND

NASCAR wants to begin holding races in the New York City area and attract teenagers as new fans. It would also like to sign sponsorship deals with high-tech and financial services companies. A few of your clients fit that description. You work with a large bank, an Internet company, a mobile phone service provider, and a teen apparel retailer.

Which Company Is the Right Sponsor? Before suggesting a sponsorship to any of these clients, you need to conduct a complete analysis of NASCAR. Official sponsors have exclusive rights, which means a competing company could not be a sponsor in that category. For example, if McDonald's is the sponsor for fast food at an event, no other fast food company would be permitted to sponsor that event.

YOUR OBJECTIVE

Once you know more about NASCAR, you will be in a better position to suggest a client for a sponsorship deal. The bank has branches in four states. The Internet company is a small auction site specializing in sports memorabilia. The cell phone company sells phones and plans with walkie-talkie and messaging features. The apparel retailer is a chain found in major shopping malls around the country.

ASSIGNMENT AND STRATEGY

- **Conduct research** Research NASCAR and its marketing activities. How successful is NASCAR as a business entity? How well does it follow the marketing concept? Who are NASCAR's official sponsors? Do any of them compete with your clients? What is the customer profile of NASCAR's target market?

  Do the demographic, psychographic, geographic, and behavior factors that describe a fan match the target markets of any of your clients? You will need to conduct research at a library and on the Internet. You could review news coverage of NASCAR to learn more about its operations.

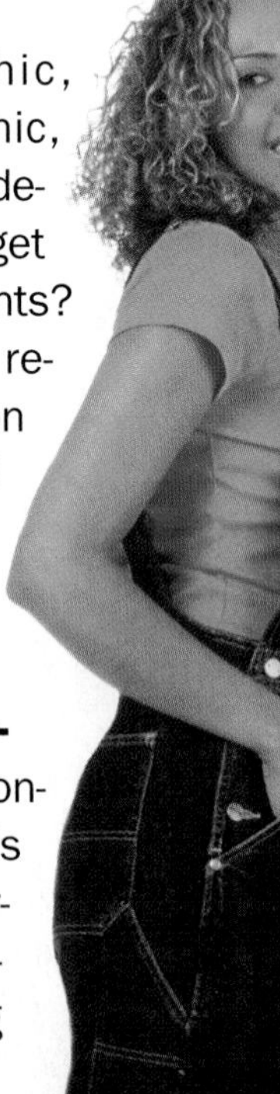

- **Develop a SWOT analysis** Use the format for conducting a SWOT analysis to analyze NASCAR's current situation. How effective are its marketing mix strategies (product, place, price, promotion)? Are there any external threats or opportunities that might impact NASCAR now or in the future?

- **What your project should include** Select a client for NASCAR sponsorship and a specific type of sponsorship. Note the benefits of sponsorship for the client.

  Develop other creative marketing strategies the client could use to make the investment worthwhile.

  Conclude with a strong argument as to why your ideas are feasible and how your company can make it happen for the client you selected.

YOUR REPORT

Use a word processing program and presentation software to prepare a double-spaced report and an oral presentation for the client you selected. See a suggested outline and key evaluation points at *marketingessentials.glencoe.com/internship*

BUILD YOUR PORTFOLIO

Option 1 Internship Report
Once you have completed your Marketing Internship project and presentation, put your written report and a few printouts of key slides from your oral presentation in your Marketing Portfolio.

Option 2 Analyzing a Company
Analyze a company of your choice. Research how the company follows the marketing concept. What does a SWOT analysis reveal? What is the company's market share and who are its competitors? Who are its target markets? What would you suggest to improve its marketing mix strategies? Prepare a written report and an oral presentation using word processing and presentation software. See a suggested outline and key evaluation points at *marketingessentials.glencoe.com/portfolio*

@ Online Action!

Go to *marketingessentials.glencoe.com/Unit/1/DECA* to review the SWOT analysis concepts that relate to DECA events.

UNIT 2 Economics

In this unit you will find

- **Chapter 3** Political and Economic Analysis
- **Chapter 4** Global Analysis

What keeps beautiful things beautiful?

All those water words borrowed from the beauty world.
Dewy, moisture, shiny, hydrated.
Those things that promise to keep you young and beautiful.
What's in them? Water, mostly. Water is the original beauty product.
It makes you, and everything on earth, look and feel alive.
So which is the fairest water of them all?
Every drop of Evian comes from a spring, deep in the heart of the Alps.
It's naturally filtered for over fifteen years through pristine
glacial rock formations. So it has a neutral pH balance
and a unique blend of minerals, including calcium, magnesium and silica.
No water is better than Evian to help you feel young,
fresh and beautiful.
So when you choose a bottled water to believe in, consider the source.

evian. your natural source of youth.™

Marketing Plan

ANALYSIS
1
SWOT
Economic
Socio-Cultural
Political
Technological

STRATEGY
2
Promotion
Place
Price
Product

IMPLEMENTATION
3
Organization
Management
Staffing

BUDGET
4
Cost of Sales
Cost of Promotion
Incomes and Expenses

CONTROL
5
Evaluation
Performance Measures
Performance Analysis

ANALYZE THE AD

Evian is drinking water bottled from a spring in the French Alps. The French food producer Danone sells Evian as a high-quality, healthful drink, and beauty aid. How does this relate to this ad's visual component?

Market Talk The market for bottled water is expanding. Many consumers are willing to pay more for bottled water. Not all bottled water originates from natural springs. Would you choose bottled spring water? Why or why not?

Think and Write Grocery shelves stock bottled water from the United States and from springs around the world. Visit the Web sites of four major bottled water brands. Note their slogans or other marketing messages, then write a paragraph comparing and contrasting how the brands try to appeal to consumers.

Online Action! Go to *marketingessentials.glencoe.com/u2/ad* for an extended activity.

In this unit

Foundations of Marketing

Economics

CHAPTER 3
Political and Economic Analysis

Chapter Objectives

After reading this chapter, you should be able to:

- Define the concept of an economy
- List the factors of production
- Explain the concept of scarcity
- Discuss how traditional, market, command, and mixed economies answer the three basic economic questions
- Cite examples of various economic systems
- List the goals of a healthy economy
- Explain how an economy is measured
- Analyze the key phases of the business cycle

GUIDE TO THE PHOTO

Market Talk The stock exchange is one place to take an economy's pulse. When investors are optimistic about the economy, they may buy more stocks. This is a way to own a small part of a company and share in its profits. Investors and consumers usually react to economic and political news and adjust their spending or investing accordingly.

Quick Think Why would a weak economy in some countries affect other countries' economies?

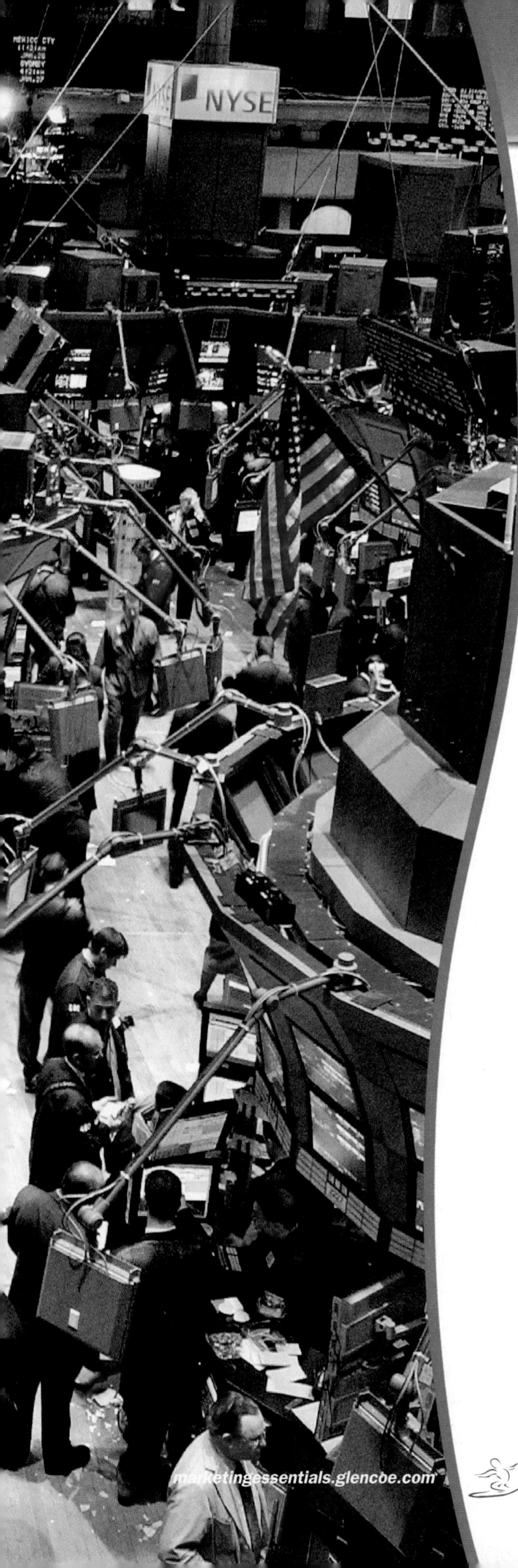

THE DECA CONNECTION

Performance indicators represent key skills and knowledge. Relating them to the concepts explained in this chapter is your key to success in DECA events. Keep this in mind as you read this chapter and write some notes each time you encounter material that helps you master a key concept.

These acronyms represent DECA events that involve knowledge of concepts in this chapter.

AAAL	**FMAL**	**MMS**	**TMDM**
AAML	**FMDM**	**QSRM**	**TSE**
ADC	**FMML**	**RMAL**	**VPM**
BSM	**FSRM**	**RMML**	
EMDM	**HMDM**	**SMDM**	

In all these DECA events you should be able to follow these performance indicators:

- Explain the concept of economic resources
- Describe the nature of economics and economic activities
- Explain the types of economic systems
- Determine the relationship between government and business
- Explain the concept of productivity
- Analyze the impact of specialization/division of labor on productivity
- Explain measures used to analyze economic conditions
- Explain the consumer price index
- Explain the concept of gross domestic product
- Determine the impact of business cycles on business activities
- Describe the nature of current economic problems

DECA PREP

Check your understanding of DECA performance indicators with the DECA activity in this chapter's review. For more information and DECA Prep practice, go to *marketingessentials.glencoe.com/3/DECA*

What Is an Economy?

OBJECTIVES

- **Define the concept of an economy**
- **List the factors of production**
- **Explain the concept of scarcity**
- **Discuss how traditional, market, command, and mixed economies answer the three basic economic questions**
- **Cite examples of various economic systems**

KEY TERMS

- **economy**
- **resources**
- **factors of production**
- **infrastructure**
- **entrepreneurship**
- **scarcity**
- **traditional economy**
- **market economy**
- **command economy**

BEFORE YOU READ

Connect Do you think economic decisions affect your daily life? How?

THE MAIN IDEA

An economy is how a nation makes economic choices that involve how the nation will use its resources to produce and distribute goods and services to meet the needs of its population.

STUDY ORGANIZER

Create a diagram like the one below to record information about market economies and command economies.

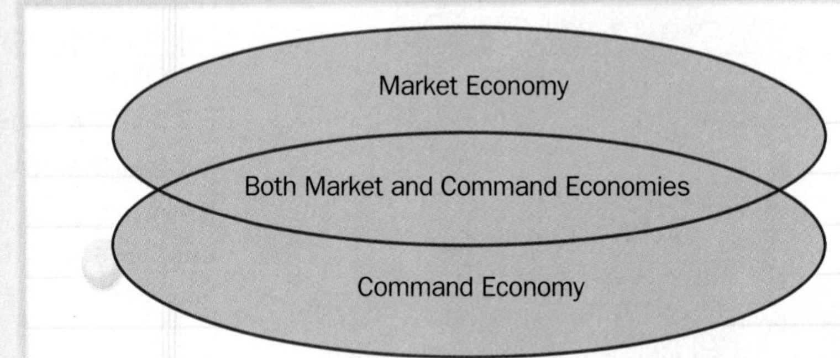

Connect Choose a country that interests you and note how its economy works as you study this chapter.

Economic Systems

An **economy**, or economic system, is the organized way a nation provides for the needs and wants of its people. A nation chooses how to use its resources to produce and distribute goods and services. Countries with different economic systems have different approaches when making these choices. A country's resources determine economic activities such as manufacturing, buying, selling, transporting, and investing. Broad categories of resources that are common to all nations affect how business is done across the world.

Resources

Resources are all the things used in producing goods and services. Economists use the term **factors of production** when they talk about resources. Factors of production comprise four categories: land, labor, capital, and entrepreneurship.

Land

Land includes everything contained in the earth or found in the seas. Coal and crude oil are natural resources, and so is a lake and all of the living things in the lake. Trees and plants, as well as the soil in which they grow, are natural resources. These natural resources are used as the raw material for making goods and creating services that are marketed to customers. Some countries' climate and geography are perfect for attracting tourists. Switzerland is a choice destination for skiing and enjoying mountain landscapes. For this country, the tourist trade is a viable industry that helps to support the economy.

Labor

Labor refers to all the people who work. Labor includes full- and part-time workers, managers, and professional people in both the private and public sectors. Companies may spend a lot of money training employees because a well-trained labor force is an asset to a company. Economies with well-educated and well-trained labor have an advantage over other nations in attracting business.

Capital

Capital includes money to start and operate a business. It also includes the goods used in the production process. Factories, office buildings, computers, and tools are all considered capital resources. Raw materials that have been processed into a more useful form (such as lumber or steel) are also considered capital. Without the capital to run a business, marketers would not have the funds or the resources needed to develop, to advertise, and to transport goods. Capital includes **infrastructure**, which is the physical development of a country. This includes its roads, ports, sanitation facilities, and utilities, especially telecommunications. These things are necessary for the production and distribution of goods and services in an economy. Think of the challenges of trying to run an international business without dependable phone service.

Entrepreneurship

Entrepreneurship refers to the skills of people who are willing to invest their time and money to run a business. Entrepreneurs organize factors of production to create the goods and services that are part of an economy. They are the employers of a population.

• ECONOMICS and the SHOPPING MALL

Your local shopping mall is a good place to observe economic principles. Labor is represented by salespeople employed in stores and also by all the people who manufactured the products for sale. Capital is at work here, too, as money was invested in manufacturing products and selling them.

Do you think there are examples of the other two factors of production (land and entrepreneurship) in a shopping mall? Explain your answer.

•SPAIN Tourism contributes greatly to Spain's economy. Spain wants to attract tourists.

What resources or factors of production make Spain a good vacation spot?

Scarcity

Different economies have different amounts of resources. The United States has an educated labor force, a great deal of capital, an abundance of entrepreneurs, and many natural resources. Most underdeveloped nations are not that fortunate. They might have natural resources to spare but not the capital or the skilled labor to develop them.

Even the United States, with its wealth of resources, cannot meet the needs and wants of all its citizens. Many citizens live below poverty level. Businesses go bankrupt on a regular basis. It is apparent that nations have unlimited wants and needs for growth and development but limited resources to meet them. The difference between wants and needs and available resources is called **scarcity**. Scarcity forces nations to make economic choices.

How Does an Economy Work?

Nations must answer three basic questions when deciding how to use their limited resources. The way nations answer these questions defines their economic system.

1. Which goods and services should be produced?
2. How should the goods and services be produced?
3. For whom should the goods and services be produced?

Economists have studied the way nations answer the three basic economic questions and have classified economic systems into three broad categories: traditional, market, and command economies.

However, no economy is purely traditional, purely market, or purely command. Elements of all three systems are found in all economies.

Traditional Economies

In a **traditional economy**, traditions and rituals answer the basic questions of what, how, and for whom. The answers are often based on cultural or religious practices and ideals

•A TRADITIONAL ECONOMY Bhutan, one of the world's smallest and least developed countries, has a traditional economic system based on agriculture and forestry. However, lately it has expanded its tourism industry which brings in elements of a market economy.

What benefits would this change provide for Bhutanese people?

that have been passed from one generation to the next. Typically, these activities are assigned through tradition rather than by choice.

1. What? In a traditional economy there is little choice as to what to produce. If people belong to a community of farmers, they farm for generations.
2. How? Again, this is bound by traditions. The potter whose family has made clay pots for generations will continue to follow the practices of his or her ancestors.
3. For whom? Tradition regulates who buys and sells and where and how the exchange takes place.

Market Economies

In a pure **market economy**, there is no government involvement in economic decisions. Individuals and companies own the means of production and businesses compete for consumers. The government lets the market answer the three basic economic questions.

1. What? Consumers decide what should be produced in a market economy through the purchases that they make in the marketplace. Products that do not satisfy consumers' needs are not purchased and therefore will not achieve success.
2. How? Businesses in a market economy decide how to produce goods and services. Businesses must be competitive and produce quality products at lower prices than their competitors. It is necessary for them to find the most efficient way to produce their goods and services and the best way to encourage customers to buy these products.
3. For whom? In a market economy, the people who have more money are able to buy more goods and services. To obtain money, people are motivated to work and invest the money they make.

Command Economies

A **command economy** is a system in which a country's government makes economic decisions and decides what, when, and how much will be produced and distributed. Under this system, the government controls the factors of production and makes all decisions about their use. In a command economy, the

NET MARKETING

E-Commerce Readiness

International e-commerce is flourishing because even small businesses find that having a Web site can generate sales from around the country and abroad. Amazon.com has gone international and has Web sites in Canada, the United Kingdom, Germany, Japan, and France. If a business is interested in reaching out to the global marketplace, it needs to review the Internet readiness of the countries where it wishes to expand. Most European countries have access to the Internet, but in developing countries the number of Internet hosts is significantly lower. Canada, the United States, and the United Kingdom top the charts with regard to Internet providers. You can check a country's Internet readiness by visiting the CIA *World Fact Book* Web site and selecting Communications from the menu. It lists the number of Internet providers and Internet users for each country. For example, in 2002, Angola had one Internet service provider and an estimated 60,000 users. By comparison, the United States had 7,000 Internet service providers and 165.75 million users in 2002.

How could a developing country, such as Angola, use the Internet to improve its economy?

@ Online Action!

Go to *marketingessentials.glencoe.com/3/net* to find a project on e-commerce.

government is responsible for answering the three basic economic questions.

1. What? One person (often a dictator) or a group of government officials (a central planning committee) decides what products are needed based on what they believe is important.
2. How? Since the government owns all means of production, it runs all businesses. It decides how goods and services will be produced. It controls all employment opportunities and workers' benefits. In the most extreme command economy, the government tells people where they will work and how much they will get paid.
3. For whom? The government decides who will receive what is produced. In principle, wealth is shared equally among all people to ensure that everyone's basic needs are met. The idea is that all people are equal and are offered the same opportunities. The government provides subsidies for housing and food for everyone, as well as medical care, education, and jobs for everyone who wants to work.

Mixed Economies

No economy is purely a traditional, market, or command economy. Every economy has influences that make it at least somewhat mixed. The United States is considered a mixed economy with leanings toward a market economy. In a pure market economy, there is no government interference at all. However, there is some government involvement in the U.S. economy through the laws and regulations that businesses must follow. There are also regulations to protect our food, air, and water supplies, and to protect consumers from unsafe products. There are labor laws that determine at what age people can start working, and the minimum wage they earn. The U.S. government provides social programs for those who need help, such as welfare and Medicaid

for the poor and Medicare for the elderly. Because of these characteristics, the U.S. economy is technically a mixed economy.

Since all economies in the world today are mixed, a meaningful economic classification depends on how much a government interferes with the free market. The three political philosophies that have shaped world economies are capitalism, socialism, and communism.

Capitalism

Capitalism is a political and economic philosophy characterized by marketplace competition and private ownership of businesses. It is the same as free enterprise. Government in a capitalist society is also concerned about its people and cares for those who cannot care for themselves. The number of social services, however, does not match that of a socialist country.

Political Foundations of Capitalism

The political system most frequently associated with capitalism is democracy. Nations that practice democracy believe that political power should be in the hands of the people. There is usually more than one political party from which to choose representatives to run the government in a democratic country. People in a democracy are free to elect those candidates who agree with their philosophy on how the government and the economy should be run. The United States and Japan are two examples of countries that are classified as capitalist and have a democratic form of government.

Communism

Communism is a social, political, and economic philosophy in which the government, usually authoritarian, controls the factors of production. There is no private ownership of property or capital. The theory behind these practices is that goods owned in common (by the government representing the community as a whole) are available to all as needed and society is classless.

Characteristics of a Communist Country

In a communist country all people who are able to work are assigned jobs. Theoretically, there is no unemployment. Employees who do not go to work continue to get paid under this system. The government decides the type of schooling people will receive and also tells them where to live. Housing accommodations are assigned according to need. Food and housing subsidies keep prices low, so everyone has a place to live and food to eat. Medical care is free. However, there is a little or no economic freedom associated with communism. In this system there is no financial incentive for people to increase their productivity.

There are very few communist countries left in the world today. The economies of such countries have collapsed in recent years. The few countries that can still be classified as communist include Cuba and North Korea. China, which is still politically dominated by a communist party, is allowing more and more free enterprise practices. Vietnam and Laos are also following that path.

Socialism

Socialism is a term that originally referred to a system on its way to the communist ideal of a classless society. Today, most countries that are defined as socialist have democratic political institutions. They differ from capitalist nations in the increased amount of government involvement in the economy. The main goal is to meet basic needs for all and to provide employment for many.

Characteristics of Socialist Countries

Socialist countries tend to have more social services to ensure a certain standard of living for everyone. Medical care is free or low cost, as is education. These countries have systems for pensions and elderly care. Businesses and individuals pay much higher taxes than those in capitalist countries, so all contribute to financing government services.

The Role of Government in Socialist Countries

The government runs key industries and makes economic decisions. State-controlled, noncompetitive companies are often found in industries such as telecommunications, natural resources (such as gas, water, and power),

Case Study

Transforming an Economic System: The Reunification of Germany

East Germany was a country of 18 million people whose standard of living, technology, and productivity had fallen far behind that of its western counterpart during more than four decades of Soviet Union-imposed command economics. After the reunification, wages in eastern Germany quickly rose to near the western levels. Western Germany's welfare and pension systems and its business regulations were extended to the east, despite warnings that they were too demanding for the east's lower level of economic development.

A Tough Road to the West

Nearly 20 percent of eastern Germans are still officially unemployed, compared with about nine percent in western Germany. Rethinking eastern Germany's economy became urgent when the European Union (EU) included ten former Soviet satellite countries that had also converted to a market economy. Many Germans fear that vigorous, cheap competition from Poles, Czechs, and other new EU citizens will further harm eastern Germany's economy, increase its reliance on government handouts, and weigh down the overall German economy. About four percent of western Germany's gross domestic product is transferred to the east every year, a massive drain on the nation's finances.

THINK STRATEGICALLY

What can the German government do to fight competition from other new members of the EU?

@ Online Action! **Go to *marketingessentials.glencoe.com/3/case* to find a project on German reunification.**

transportation, and banking. Canada, Germany, and Sweden are generally characterized as having socialist elements in their economies.

Economies in Transition

The breakup of the former Soviet Union probably provides the best example of societies making the difficult change from command to market economies. Most Eastern European countries that were once communist satellites have moved toward global market economies and more democratic forms of government. This means that the state-owned industries have been privatized in many of these nations. Privatization refers to the process of selling government-owned businesses to private individuals.

This process generates much-needed revenue for the governments involved. It also demonstrates a high level of commitment to making the transition to a market system.

A Move Toward Privatization

Today, many socialist countries are selling some of their state-run businesses to help balance their budgets as the costs of national health care, unemployment, and retirement programs soar.

Great Britain has sold its national phone company, national steel company, national sugar company, and several others. Another example of such a transfer, also called privatization, is British Airways. Since its privatization in 1987, the company has been increasing exponentially and has become Europe's number-one airline. These sales generated approximately $63 billion for Great Britain.

Developing Economies

Developing economies are mostly poor countries with little industrialization that are trying to become more prosperous and develop their infrastructure. Much of their success depends on improving the education levels of their labor force and on directing and using foreign investment efficiently.

Chad, a country in central Africa, is a good example of this situation. It is a traditional economy based on agriculture and farming. Cotton, cattle, and gum arabic are its primary exports. However, with an oil field and pipeline project paid for by foreign investors, Chad has begun to develop its oil reserves for export. This investment will help generate much-needed funds for this poor nation to use to improve its infrastructure and its labor resources.

3.1 AFTER YOU READ

Reviewing Key Terms and Concepts

1. Explain how the infrastructure of a country is related to the factors of production.
2. What three broad categories do economists use to classify all economic systems?
3. In which economic system does the government let the market answer the three basic economic questions?

Integrating Academic Skills

Math

4. In a country with a population of 290,342,554, how many people would be considered below the poverty line if the percentage in that category was 12.7 percent?

Civics and Government

5. Write a letter to a pen pal in a socialist country to learn more about that country's economic and political system. Be sure to include pertinent questions about taxes, as well as social services for its residents.

Check your answers at *marketingessentials.glencoe.com/3/read*

Understanding the Economy

OBJECTIVES

- List the goals of a healthy economy
- Explain how an economy is measured
- Analyze the key phases of the business cycle

KEY TERMS

- productivity
- gross domestic product (GDP)
- gross national product (GNP)
- inflation
- consumer price index (CPI)
- producer price index (PPI)
- business cycle
- expansion
- recession
- depression
- recovery

BEFORE YOU READ

Predict What do you think constitutes a healthy economy?

THE MAIN IDEA

Aspects of an economy such as consumers, businesses, and governments affect each other and the economy in general. Companies need current economic information to make good marketing decisions.

STUDY ORGANIZER

Draw a chart like the one below and use it to take notes about economic measurements.

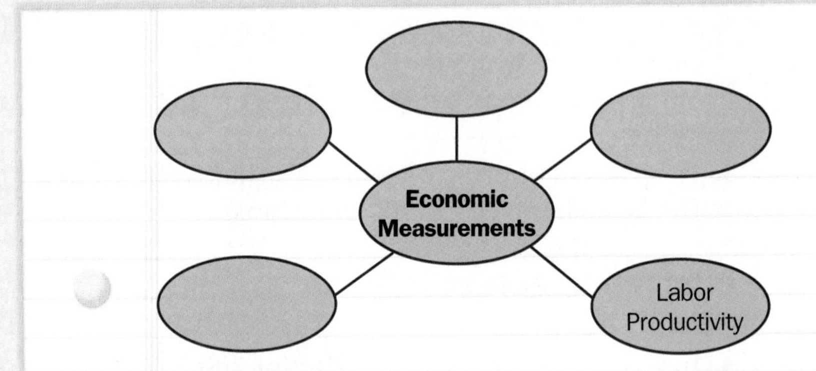

WHILE YOU READ

Cause and Effect
Note how economic measurements affect each other and how all of them influence business cycles.

The Economy and Marketing

If you are a marketer and you want to perform a useful SWOT analysis (see Chapter 2), you need to consider the economic factors that will influence your marketing planning. An understanding of how to measure an economy and what factors contribute to economic strength or weakness is essential. It is only then that you can appreciate how the economy, consumers, businesses, and government influence each other.

When Is an Economy Successful?

A healthy economy has three goals: increase productivity, decrease unemployment, and maintain stable prices. All nations analyze their economies to keep track of how well they are doing. This analysis allows businesses, consumers, and governments to make appropriate economic decisions.

Economic Measurements

Accurate information about an economy is essential to the whole process. The key economic measurements that nations routinely use to determine their economic strength are labor productivity, gross domestic product, gross national product, standard of living, inflation rate, and unemployment rate.

Labor Productivity

Productivity is output per worker hour that is measured over a defined period of time, such as a week, month, or year. Businesses can increase their productivity in a number of ways. They can invest in new equipment or facilities that allow their employees to work more efficiently. Providing additional training or financial incentives can also boost staff productivity. Businesses can also reduce their work force and increase the responsibilities of the workers who remain. This makes an organization more financially efficient and more effective. Higher productivity improves a company's profit.

Specialization and division of labor are key concepts related to increasing productivity. An assembly line is an example of specialization and division of labor whereby each part of a finished product is completed by a person who specializes in one aspect of its manufacturing. The theory behind this method of production is that the work can be completed faster and more efficiently when people specialize in their respective areas.

Gross Domestic Product

Most governments study productivity by keeping track of an entire nation's production

• **WHAT IS PRODUCED WHERE** Toyota, a Japanese car manufacturer, produces cars in Japan that are exported and sold in the United States. Toyota has also built factories in North America.

If you buy a car manufactured by Toyota in Alabama, is this car part of the U.S. GDP? Is the same car also part of the U.S. GNP?

output. Today the principal way of measuring that output in the United States is gross domestic product. **Gross domestic product (GDP)** is the output of goods and services produced by labor and property located within a country. The U.S. Bureau of Economic Analysis publishes a report on the United States' GDP. According to its 2003 report, the GDP grew 3.1 percent that year, which was its best showing since 2000. Total output was $11 trillion, which was $1 trillion more than in 2001.

The GDP is made up of private investment, government spending, personal spending, net exports of goods and services, and change in business inventories (see Figure 3.1). Private investment includes spending by businesses for things like equipment and software, as well as home construction. Government spending includes money spent by local, state, and federal governments. Personal spending includes all consumer expenditures for goods and services. Expanding inventories show that businesses are producing goods that are being stored in their warehouses—that adds to the GDP. Inventories that are shrinking indicate that people are buying more than what was actually produced, so you subtract that figure from the GDP.

As a review, here is the calculation for GDP: Add private investment, government spending, and personal spending, then you either add a trade surplus or subtract a trade deficit and you either add expanding inventories or subtract shrinking inventories.

Since 1991, the United States has been using GDP as its primary measurement of productivity. Before 1991, it used a measurement called gross national product. **Gross national product (GNP)** is the total dollar value of goods and services produced by a nation, including goods and services produced abroad by U.S. citizens and companies. Note the difference between GNP and GDP: With the GNP, it is not where the production takes place but who is responsible for it. For example, Ford is a U.S. corporation that has a plant in England. The portion of Ford's production that occurs in England is included in the U.S. GNP, but not in its GDP.

Standard of Living

A country's standard of living is a measurement of the amount and quality of goods and services that a nation's people have. It is a figure that reflects their quality of life. To calculate the standard of living, you divide the GDP or GNP of a country by its population to get the per capita GDP or GNP. Most industrialized nations enjoy a high standard of living because they have a high level of production.

Some marketers also look at additional factors to get a broader picture of a nation's standard of living. Since some countries provide more in terms of social services for their citizens, social benefits, such as free education and health care provided by the government may be reviewed. Number of households per 1,000 inhabitants with durable goods, such as washing machines, refrigerators, dishwashers, and autos, can be included in the analysis.

Inflation Rate

Inflation refers to rising prices. A low inflation rate (one to five percent each year) is good because it shows that an economy is stable. Double-digit inflation (10 percent or higher), on the other hand, devastates an economy. When inflation gets that high, money does not have the same value it did with lower inflation. The period from the mid-1960s to the early 1980s was a highly inflationary period. Prices tripled in the United States during that time. People who live on a fixed income such as a monthly Social Security check are especially hurt by high inflation.

Controlling inflation is one of a government's major goals. When inflation starts to go up, many governments raise interest rates to discourage borrowing money. The result is a slowdown in economic growth, which helps to bring inflation down.

Two measures of inflation used in the United States are the consumer price index and the producer price index. The **consumer price index (CPI)** measures the change in price over a period of time of some 400 specific retail goods and services used by the average urban household. It is also called the cost of living index. Food, housing, utilities,

Figure 3.1 The Gross Domestic Product

• **The United States GDP** GDP, or gross domestic product, is the output of goods and services produced by labor and property located within a country. Here is a look at what made up the U.S. economy in 2003.

Why is consumer confidence so important to the United States' GDP?

15.7% Private Investment is the smallest of the three segments. Investment by businesses is critical to the overall health of the economy.

18.6% Government Spending includes everything the government spends money on: entitlements (Social Security, Medicare, veterans' benefits), defense (weapons, military operations), discretionary spending (NASA, Park Service), and interest payments on the national debt (the deficit).

The deficit: The federal government usually has to borrow money to pay its bills. For example, during the 2003 calendar year, it borrowed $395 billion, which amounts to 2.8 percent of the GDP.

70.4% Personal Spending is the foundation of the economy. Consumer spending includes almost everything people purchase (from a cup of coffee to medical insurance). This is why consumer confidence is so important. Confident consumers spend more money.

Note

If you are saying, "But this adds up to more than 100 percent," you are correct. Two items can shrink the economy's total production: imports and diminishing inventories. When we import more than we export, the resulting trade deficit is subtracted from the GDP. Expanding inventories add to the GDP. Shrinking inventories subtract from the GDP.

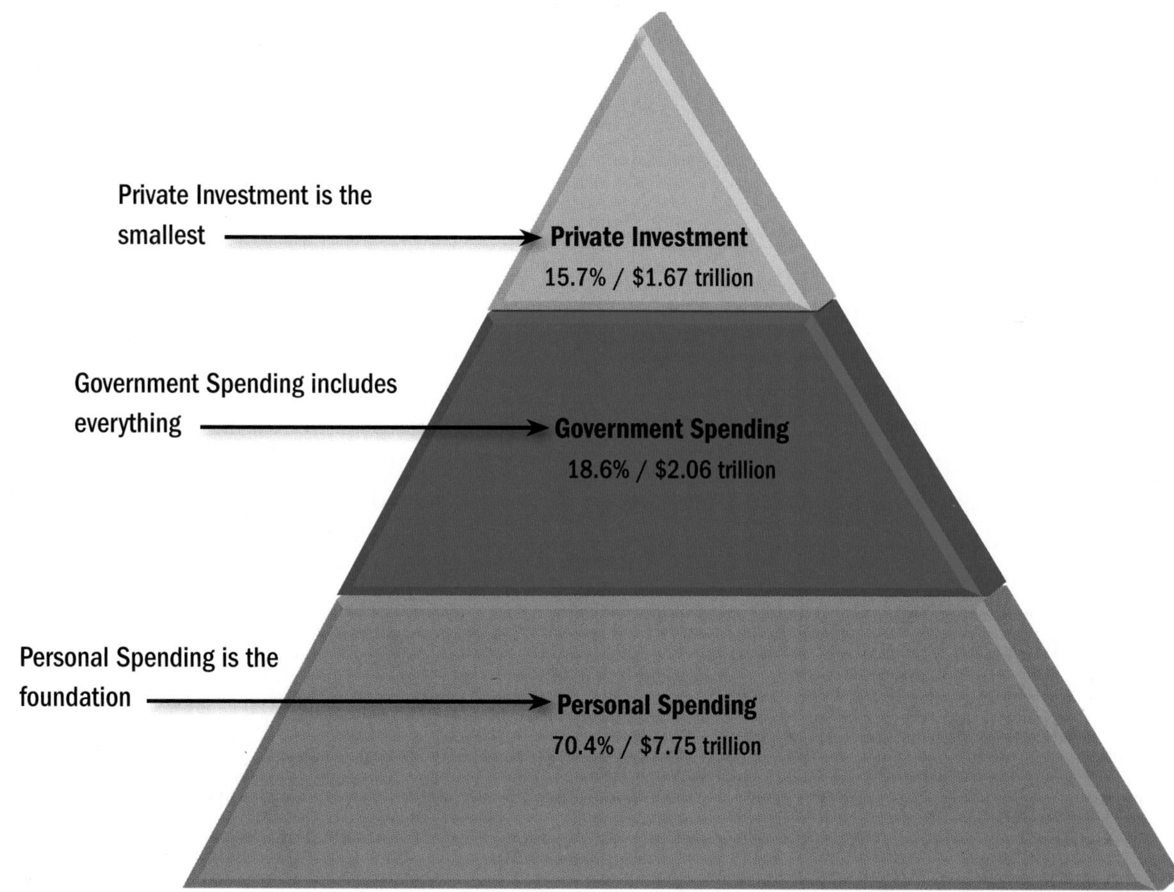

Go to *marketingessentials.glencoe.com/3/figure/1* to find a project on the GDP.

transportation, and medical care are a few of its components. The core CPI excludes food and energy prices, which tend to be unpredictable. The **producer price index (PPI)** measures wholesale price levels in the economy. It is often a trendsetter, as producer prices generally get passed along to the consumer. When there is a drop in the PPI, it is generally followed by a drop in the CPI.

Unemployment Rate

All nations chart unemployment, or jobless rates. The higher the unemployment rate, the greater the chances of an economic slowdown. The lower the unemployment rate, the greater the chances of an economic expansion. This is true because when more people work, there are more people spending money and paying taxes. Businesses and government both take in more money, and the government does not have to provide as many social services.

Other Economic Indicators and Trends

The Conference Board provides additional indicators to help economists evaluate the performance of the U.S. economy. The Conference Board is a private business research organization that is made up of businesses and individuals who work together to assess the state of the economy. Three Conference Board indicators are the consumer confidence index, the consumer expectations index, and the jobs index, which measures consumers' perceptions regarding the number of jobs available. Consumers are polled to see how they feel about personal finance, economic conditions, and buying conditions. Retail sales are studied to see if consumer confidence polls match consumer actions in the marketplace. Along those same lines, the rate of housing starts is reviewed, as are sales of trucks and autos. These are big expenditures that tend to be affected by the economy and interest rates.

Wages and new payroll jobs provide additional information about the strength of the economy at any given point in time. When everyone is employed, supply and demand theory predicts that wages should increase due to the shortage of workers. Economists study these factors, because they may affect inflation and other economic indicators.

The Business Cycle

History shows that sometimes an economy grows, which is called expansion, and at other times it slows down (contraction). These recurring changes in economic activity are called the **business cycle** (see Figure 3.2).

The business cycle includes the following key phases: expansion, recession, trough, and recovery, at which time expansion begins again. **Expansion** is a time when the economy is flourishing, sometimes referred to as a period of prosperity. Nationwide there is low unemployment, an increase in the output of goods and services, and high consumer spending. This is a good time for new businesses to start up or expand their operations. Expansion continues until it reaches a peak. A peak signifies the end of expansion and the beginning of a recession.

A **recession** is a period of economic slowdown that lasts for at least two quarters, or six months, according to financial experts. The National Bureau of Economic Research (NBER) defines a recession as a significant decline in activity spread across the economy, lasting more than a few months. During a recession, companies reduce their workforces and consumers have less money to spend. Since consumers are spending less, producers make fewer goods and services. Research and development (R&D) is cut back, and future plans for expanding business operations are generally put on hold. Recessions can end relatively quickly or last for a long time. According to the NBER, a recession begins immediately after the economy reaches a peak of activity and ends as the economy reaches its trough. A trough is when the economy reaches its lowest point in a recession, after which economic activity begins to rise.

A **depression** is a period of prolonged recession. During a depression, it becomes nearly impossible to find a job, and many businesses are forced to shut down. During a depression, consumer spending is very low,

Figure 3.2 The Business Cycle

• **The Four Key Phases of the Cycle** Throughout history, economies have followed a pattern of expansion and contraction called the business cycle. There are four phases in the business cycle: expansion (ended by a peak), recession, trough, and recovery. The length and intensity of each of the phases depends on many factors such as wars, natural disasters, and industrial innovation.

Which phase do you think the United States is in now?

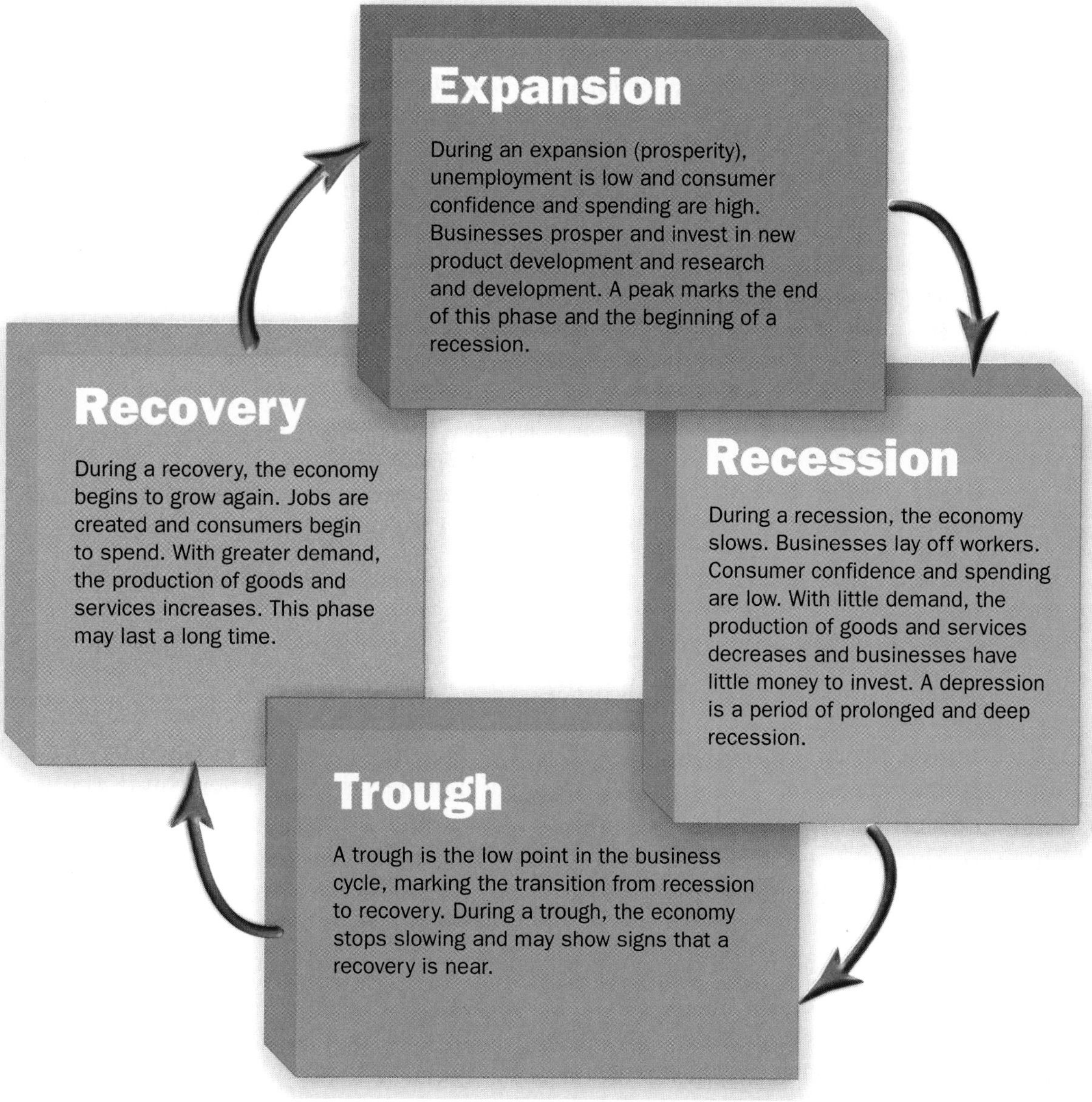

Expansion

During an expansion (prosperity), unemployment is low and consumer confidence and spending are high. Businesses prosper and invest in new product development and research and development. A peak marks the end of this phase and the beginning of a recession.

Recession

During a recession, the economy slows. Businesses lay off workers. Consumer confidence and spending are low. With little demand, the production of goods and services decreases and businesses have little money to invest. A depression is a period of prolonged and deep recession.

Trough

A trough is the low point in the business cycle, marking the transition from recession to recovery. During a trough, the economy stops slowing and may show signs that a recovery is near.

Recovery

During a recovery, the economy begins to grow again. Jobs are created and consumers begin to spend. With greater demand, the production of goods and services increases. This phase may last a long time.

Go to *marketingessentials.glencoe.com/3/figure/2* for a project on the business cycle.

GLOBAL MARKET

China Anxiously Seeks a Soft Economic Landing

After a decade with the economic throttle wide open, China is overheating, and the country's leaders are grappling with ways to slow the breakneck growth without choking it off. This is difficult for China's leaders, who are fairly new to the market economy game and who lack many of the finely tuned policy tools available to central bankers in the West and in Japan. Prime Minister Wen Jiabao has sought to assure foreign investors that China is taking significant steps to achieve a soft landing. The global recovery now depends on China as one of its twin engines, along with the United States. A hard landing—a steep decline in economic growth leading to higher urban unemployment and a sharp drop in imports—would rattle economies across Asia and the world.

Many Asian nations now depend heavily on selling to China, especially after China's overall imports jumped 40 percent in 2003. The Chinese accounted for a third of all the growth in Japan's exports, and a similar share of South Korea's, and they took two-thirds of the growth in Taiwan's exports. A sharp slowing of growth in China would hit those economies hard.

CRITICAL THINKING

How do you classify China politically and economically? What is its new role in the global economy?

@ Online Action!

Go to *marketingessentials.glencoe.com/3/global* to find a project on China's economy.

unemployment is very high, and production of goods and services is down significantly. Poverty results because so many people are out of work and cannot afford to buy food, clothing, or shelter. The Great Depression of the early 1930s best illustrates this phase of the business cycle.

Recovery is the term used to signify a period of renewed economic growth following a recession or depression. This is where the cycle begins again with economic expansion. The GDP begins to increase. During this stage, business picks up, people find jobs, and the demand for goods increases. Thus, recovery is characterized by reduced unemployment, increased consumer spending, and moderate expansion by businesses. Periods of recovery differ in length and strength.

Factors That Affect Business Cycles

Business cycles are affected by the actions of businesses, consumers, and the government. In turn, businesses, consumers, and the government are affected by business cycles.

Businesses tend to react to business cycles by expanding their operations during periods of recovery or expansion and curtailing their operations during periods of recession. During an expansion they may invest in new properties, equipment, and inventories, as well as hire more employees. When the economy moves into a recession, one of the first things a business does is lay off workers. Businesses also cut back on inventories to match lowered demand for goods and services in a recession or depression. This has a ripple effect in the economy as business suppliers feel the effects of lost revenues.

During a period of recession, consumers' biggest fear is losing their jobs; the other big fear is a decrease in wages. These fears result in a loss of consumer confidence in the economy, which reduces consumer spending. Reduced consumer spending causes businesses to reduce their operations in response to lower demand. The opposite is true during periods of prosperity and recovery. During those periods, consumers are more optimistic. They spend more money on material goods and luxury items. Businesses will also respond by producing more goods. This cycle shows how important consumers are to an economy—consumer spending accounts for more than two-thirds of the U.S. GDP.

Government's Influence Over Business Cycles

A government influences business cycles through its policies and programs. Taxation has a strong bearing on what happens in an economy. As the government requires more money to run programs, higher taxes are needed. When taxes are raised, businesses and consumers have less money with which to fuel the economy. When the economy needs a boost, the government may reduce interest rates, cut taxes, or institute federally funded programs to spark a depressed economy. When an economy worsens, the Federal Reserve generally responds by lowering interest rates to encourage businesses and consumers to spend. Mortgage rates are low because the commercial banks' prime lending rate reflects the Fed's funding rate. For example, when the Federal Fund rate was at one percent, the prime lending rate was around four percent and mortgage rates were between five and six percent. If inflation becomes a problem, interest rates might be increased to discourage buying on credit.

Another action a government can take to spur economic growth is illustrated by Japan's decision to hand out free shopping coupons to its citizens. In 1999, Japan slashed income tax rates and distributed nearly $6 billion in shopping coupons to encourage people to spend. The government took these dramatic actions to spur consumption and revive an economy that was in its worst recession in 50 years.

3.2 AFTER YOU READ

Reviewing Key Terms and Concepts

1. How can businesses increase productivity?
2. Explain the difference between GNP and GDP.
3. What three factors affect business cycles?

Integrating Academic Skills

Math

4. If a country's GDP is $10 billion and its population is 250,000, what is its per capita GDP?

Civics and Government

5. Write a short newspaper article for the school newspaper regarding the current economy of the United States and why it is important for teenagers to understand economic indicators.

Check your answers at *marketingessentials.glencoe.com/3/read*

CAREERS IN MARKETING

OLIVIER TRAVERS
INTERNET MARKETING CONSULTANT
PUBLISHER, THEENDOFFREE.COM

What do you do at work?
I typically act as the hub of communication between team members and contractors who handle marketing, development, and design. Most clients already have an Internet presence they want to grow or improve. I help clients determine what types of technical services they require, and in many cases, which vendors will be able to provide the best and most efficient services. I have a background in sales and channel marketing so I'm always interested in helping companies set up partnerships and affiliate programs, as well as launch and grow outbound sales efforts.

What skills are most important to you?
Salesmanship, listening skills, empathy, self-motivation and autonomy, and the ability to keep learning on the fly. Nothing beats working as a sales rep before getting into marketing and consulting. It gives you a firm grasp of how customers think, what a sales cycle is, how to close a sale, and it forces you to be pragmatic and realistic.

What is your key to success?
Personal networking, providing value to people who will partner with me or will send me leads in the future. Also, the ability to connect the dots between various disciplines: marketing, sales, business operations, and online technology.

Aptitudes, Abilities, and Skills

Creativity, sales ability, tenacity, personal organization, and time and project management skills

Education and Training

Advanced degrees in marketing and general business are helpful.

Career Path

Marketing careers often begin with entry-level sales positions in companies of all types and sizes.

THINKING CRITICALLY

How does working as a sales representative prepare you for a career in marketing?

@ Online Action!

Go to *marketingessentials.glencoe.com/3/careers* to find a career-related activity.

CHAPTER 3 REVIEW

FOCUS on KEY POINTS

SECTION 3.1

- An economy is how a nation chooses to use its resources to produce and distribute goods and services to provide for the needs and wants of its people.
- The four factors of production are land, labor, capital, and entrepreneurship. Due to the possibility of scarcity, all nations must answer three fundamental economic questions: what will be produced, how will it be produced, and who should get what is produced. These questions are answered differently in traditional, market, command, and mixed economies.
- Economic/political philosophies of capitalism, socialism, and communism tend to encourage different types of economic systems.

SECTION 3.2

- The characteristics of a healthy economy are high productivity, stable prices, and low unemployment. Economic indicators such as productivity, gross domestic product (GDP), standard of living, CPI, consumer confidence, and unemployment rates can measure an economy.
- The key phases of the business cycle are expansion, recession, trough, and recovery. Economic business cycles affect businesses, consumers, and governments and they in turn affect business cycles, both domestically and globally.

REVIEW VOCABULARY

List a synonym or a brief definition for each key term.

1. economy (p. 52)
2. resources (p. 53)
3. factors of production (p. 53)
4. infrastructure (p. 53)
5. entrepreneurship (p. 53)
6. scarcity (p. 54)
7. traditional economy (p. 54)
8. market economy (p. 55)
9. command economy (p. 55)
10. productivity (p. 61)
11. gross domestic product (GDP) (p. 62)
12. gross national product (GNP) (p. 62)
13. inflation (p. 62)
14. consumer price index (CPI) (p. 62)
15. producer price index (PPI) (p. 64)
16. business cycle (p. 64)
17. expansion (p. 64)
18. recession (p. 64)
19. depression (p. 64)
20. recovery (p. 66)

REVIEW FACTS and IDEAS

21. What is an economy? (3.1)
22. Name the factors of production necessary to create goods and services in an economy. (3.1)
23. Explain the concept of scarcity. (3.1)
24. What are the three goals of a healthy economy? (3.2)
25. Describe the key phases of a business cycle. (3.2)

BUILD SKILLS

26. Workplace Skills

Human Relations Assume you work in a bank and an elderly couple on a fixed income asks you why the interest rate is so low on their savings account. How would you explain the basis for fluctuations in interest rates?

27. Technology Applications

Compare Two Economic Systems Select a foreign country and compare its economic system with that of the United States. Use the Internet to research all economic aspects of this country. If you lived in that country, how different would your life be? Why? Be prepared to share your insights with classmates. Use a word processing program and presentation software to prepare an oral report for your class.

28. Math Practice

Fixed Income Madeline, a retiree, lives on a fixed income of $1,200 a month. Each month she spends $450 for rent, and she budgets $150 for food, $50 for clothing, and $40 for various needs. She deposits the money that is left over into her savings account. How much money does she put into her savings each month? If her rent is increased by ten percent, how much money does she have left to put into her savings?

DEVELOP CRITICAL THINKING

29. What Is Your Role in the Economy?

Consider the part you play in the U.S. economy. Consider the following questions:

- What goods and services do you consume?
- What labor do you provide?
- What are some of your rights as a citizen and consumer?
- What are some of your responsibilities?

30. Evaluate the Impact of Economics on Marketing

How is the current economy affecting the way businesses market their goods and services? Select two specific examples that interest you and examine these businesses in relation to the economy. Are they part of an industry that is expanding? Are there any new laws that affect them? Do they face global competition? How do these factors influence the marketing strategies of these companies?

APPLY CONCEPTS

31. Researching Different Economic Systems

Select a foreign country that either has gone through a major transformation from a command economy to a market-oriented economy or is an emerging country that is trying to become more industrialized. What obstacles did the nation have to overcome? What is its current economic situation? What is the future of this nation's economy?

Activity Write a three-page report using a word processing program. Cite your sources in a written bibliography. Be prepared to share your findings with classmates in an oral presentation.

32. Analyzing the Current U.S. Economy

Using government Internet sites and other sources, research the current U.S. productivity, GDP, standard of living, inflation, CPI, interest rates, and unemployment rates. Use the figures you gather to determine the business cycle phase of the U.S. economy at the present time.

Activity Using presentation software, create an oral report based on your findings. For all facts presented, cite the source of that data directly on the presentation slide and in a written bibliography.

NET SAVVY

33. What Is the Current State of the Economy?

Visit the Web site for the United States Department of Commerce to find current information on economic indicators. Prepare a list of the economic indicators that are provided at this Web site.

THE DECA CONNECTION

An Association of Marketing Students

Role Play: Assistant Manager

Situation Assume the role of assistant manager of an online business that specializes in antique prints, matting, and custom framing. Your customers can call your toll-free phone line or communicate by e-mail. You do business through the business's Web site. The business's owner (judge) has just received an e-mail from one of your best customers requesting that you look for a special print.

Activity You are to compose an e-mail to assure the customer that you will make every effort to obtain the print and that regular communication will be maintained about the progress of the search.

Evaluation You will be evaluated on how well you meet the following performance indicators:

- Write business letters
- Use communications technologies/systems (e.g., e-mail, faxes, voice mail, cell phones, etc.)
- Explain the nature of written communications
- Handle customer inquiries
- Demonstrate a customer-service mindset

@ Online Action!

For more information and DECA Prep practice, go to *marketingessentials.glencoe.com/3/DECA*

CHAPTER 4
Global Analysis

Chapter Objectives

After reading this chapter, you should be able to:

- Explain the interdependence of nations
- Explain the nature of international trade
- Discuss the balance of trade
- List three types of trade barriers
- List three significant trade agreements and alliances that foster worldwide free trade
- List forms of international trade
- Identify political, economic, socio-cultural, and technological factors that affect international business
- Suggest global marketing strategies

GUIDE TO THE PHOTO

Market Talk How many products that you use are made in foreign countries? How many products made in the United States are sold in foreign countries? When you answer those two questions you will realize that the world is now a global marketplace.

Quick Think What factors should a company consider when deciding if it should get involved in international trade?

THE DECA CONNECTION

An Association of Marketing Students

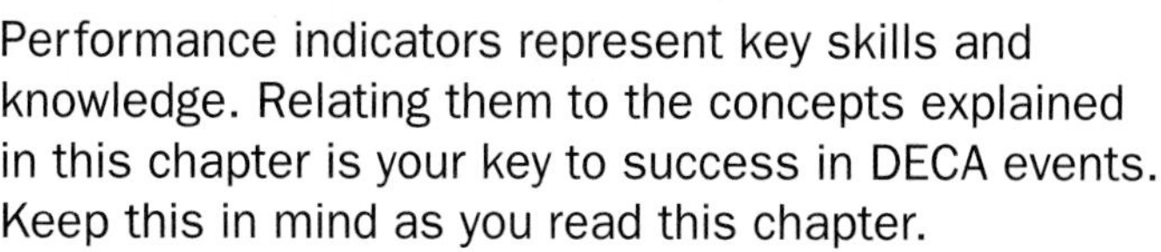

Performance indicators represent key skills and knowledge. Relating them to the concepts explained in this chapter is your key to success in DECA events. Keep this in mind as you read this chapter.

These acronyms represent DECA events that involve knowledge of concepts in this chapter.

AAAL	**FMAL**	**MMS***	**TMDM***
AAML*	**FMDM***	**QSRM***	**TSE***
ADC*	**FMML***	**RMAL**	**VPM**
BSM	**FSRM***	**RMML***	
EMDM*	**HMDM***	**SMDM***	

In all these DECA events you should be able to follow these performance indicators:

- Explain the nature of international trade
- Identify the impact of cultural and social environments on world trade
- Explain marketing and its importance in a global economy

Events with an asterisk (*) include:

- Evaluate influences on a nation's ability to trade

Some events include other indicators:

EMDM Describe the impact of e-commerce on international trade

SMDM Describe the impact of international policies on sports and entertainment marketing

FMDM Identify global exchange services

RMAL Explain the effect of international trade on retailing

AAAL Explain the effect of international trade on retailing

VPM Explain the effect of international trade on retailing

FMAL Explain the effect of international trade on food marketing

DECA PREP

Check your understanding of DECA performance indicators with the DECA activity in this chapter's review. For more information and DECA Prep practice, go to *marketingessentials.glencoe .com/4/DECA*

SECTION 4.1

International Trade

OBJECTIVES

- Explain the interdependence of nations
- Explain the nature of international trade
- Discuss the balance of trade
- List three types of trade barriers
- List three significant trade agreements and alliances that foster worldwide free trade

KEY TERMS

- international trade
- imports
- exports
- balance of trade
- free trade
- tariff
- quota
- embargo
- protectionism
- World Trade Organization (WTO)
- North American Free Trade Agreement (NAFTA)
- European Union (EU)

BEFORE YOU READ

Connect Consider all the reasons why international trade is flourishing around the world.

THE MAIN IDEA

Since no country has all the resources it needs, nations rely on each other to provide goods and services that they do not have. This interdependence, along with trade agreements among countries, creates a global marketplace.

STUDY ORGANIZER

On a chart like the one below, organize the key concepts related to international trade.

International Trade

Balance of Trade	Trade Barriers	Trade Agreements

WHILE YOU READ

Connect Observe signs of global trade as you shop for groceries, clothes, and other items.

Nature of International Trade

The global marketplace exists because countries need to trade with one another. It continues to expand because of the reduction of trade restrictions throughout the world. This new global marketplace makes all people and businesses in the world both potential customers and potential employees or employers.

•VERIZON GLOBAL Companies do not necessarily have to establish a business abroad to cash in on the global market. Verizon, a U.S. leading wireless communication company, tries to fulfill business travelers' needs.

Why do you think Verizon decided to market global phone service?

International trade is the exchange of goods and services among nations. **Imports** are goods and services purchased from other countries. Conversely, **exports** are goods and services sold to other countries. These exchanges occur among businesses, but they are controlled by the governments of the countries involved.

Interdependence of Nations

Most countries do not produce or manufacture all the goods and services they need. They get some of their goods and services from other nations. This economic interdependence happens because each country possesses unique resources and capabilities. The principle of economic interdependence is fundamental to marketing in a global environment.

Absolute Advantage and Comparative Advantage

Any nation that takes part in international trade may have an economic advantage over its trading partners. There are two types of advantages in international trade—absolute and comparative.

Absolute advantage occurs when a country has natural resources or talents that allow it to

MARKET TECH

Wi-Fi in Europe: Not So Hot

The Starbucks coffee shop in London has a high-speed Wi-Fi (wireless fidelity) network that its customers can use to surf the Web at a price of 5.50 pounds (about $10.31 or €8.25) an hour. The Starbucks shop is one of thousands of coffee shops, airport lounges, hotels, and other public places worldwide where consumers can use laptops or personal organizers with Wi-Fi connections to surf the Internet.

Prices Influence Interest

Analysts say high prices in Europe are putting off many potential users. By comparison, Wi-Fi spots in the United States are a lot less expensive and are aimed at a wide audience. For example, McDonald's offers Wi-Fi access for less than $5 (€4) an hour in the United States. One of the reasons given for the high price in Europe is that Wi-Fi services are aimed at business travelers who are not concerned about price.

Europe is adding more Wi-Fi hot spots in airports and hotels, where business travelers spend much of their time. The average price in European hotels for business travelers was about $20 per day in 2004.

THINK LIKE A MARKETER

Assume you work for a U.S. company, such as Verizon or T-Mobile, both of which offer Wi-Fi service. How would you recommend they price their service in foreign countries?

@ Online Action!

Go to *marketingessentials.glencoe.com/4/tech* for an activity on technology and international business.

produce an item at the lowest cost possible. China produces 80 percent of all the silk in the world, which gives it absolute advantage in the silk market.

Comparative advantage is the value that a nation gains by selling what it produces most efficiently. When countries specialize in products or services well suited to their capabilities, they may gain a comparative advantage in international trade. Businesses in those countries produce these goods and services to satisfy economic needs in an international economy.

The United States has a comparative advantage in producing high-tech goods and services because of this country's infrastructure, raw materials, and educated labor force. These products include airplanes, computers, high-tech machinery, entertainment, and telecommunications.

Some emerging nations have large, unskilled labor forces available at a low cost. Labor-intensive industries—ones that rely on labor as opposed to machinery—do well in such an environment. Emerging nations can produce labor-intensive products such as toys, clothing, and shoes at a lower cost than most industrialized nations. They have a comparative advantage when manufacturing these goods. It is more cost effective for high-wage countries like the United States to buy those items from emerging nations rather than making them themselves.

Benefits of International Trade

Consumers, producers, workers, and nations benefit from international trade in different ways. Consumers benefit from the competition that the foreign companies offer. This competition encourages the production of high-quality goods with lower prices. The variety of goods increases as more producers market their goods in other countries.

Many producers expand their business by conducting operations in other countries. Almost one-third of the profits of U.S. businesses come from international trade and foreign investment.

Workers also benefit from international trade. Increased trade can lead to higher employment rates both at home and abroad. For example, according to the U.S. Chamber of Commerce, Toyota, a Japanese company, has generated 500,000 jobs in the United States.

Nations as a whole benefit from international trade. Increased foreign investment in a country often improves the standard of living for that country's people. Individuals have more options to choose from when making purchasing decisions.

Government Involvement in International Trade

All nations control and monitor their trade with foreign businesses. The U.S. government monitors imports through the customs division of the U.S. Treasury Department. All goods that enter the United States from a foreign country are subject to search and review by U.S. customs officials. Other countries also check incoming goods. All U.S. citizens and firms must meet the customs requirements of foreign countries when visiting or when exporting goods.

Balance of Trade

Nations must keep track of their international trade to be aware of their economic status. The difference in value between exports and imports of a nation is called its **balance of trade**. A positive balance of trade, or trade surplus, occurs when a nation exports more than it imports. A negative balance of trade, or trade deficit, occurs when a nation imports more than it exports.

Trade Deficit

The large U.S. trade deficit may seem surprising because the United States is the world's biggest exporter. Some analysts believe this situation exists because Americans purchase more goods and services than people of other nations. Others believe that the United States is now focusing more on providing services than on manufacturing and farming, making it more economical to import goods that were once domestically manufactured.

Negative Consequences of a Trade Deficit

An unfavorable balance of trade reduces a nation's revenue. When more money leaves a country than comes in, that country is in debt, or is a debtor nation. To survive as a debtor nation, the United States relies on foreign investors who buy U.S. securities. Another effect of a negative balance of trade can be increased unemployment. People may lose their jobs as foreign competitors take business away from domestic firms. If domestic businesses do not become competitive, they will fail.

Trade Barriers

Many countries around the world favor and practice **free trade**, or commercial exchange between nations that is conducted on free market principles, without restrictive regulations. However, nations sometimes impose trade barriers or restrictions when they want to limit trade. These controls restrict the flow of goods and services among nations. The three main types of trade barriers are tariffs, quotas, and embargoes.

Tariffs

A **tariff** (sometimes called a duty) is a tax on imports. Tariffs may be used to produce revenue for a country. Revenue-producing tariffs were used in the United States as a primary source of income for the government before income taxes were established in 1913. These tariffs exist today, but they are as low as 25 cents or less per item or pound.

Another type of tariff is protective. A protective tariff is generally high. Its purpose is to increase the price of imported goods so that domestic products can compete with them. Protective tariffs can prevent foreign businesses from trading with the United States. This would protect domestic jobs and new domestic industries from foreign competition.

Case Study

The New Calcutta

Rapid changes are taking place in Calcutta (Kolkata), which shows how the outsourcing of jobs from the United States is helping to transform India. Long neglected by investors, Calcutta is attracting technology companies ranging from International Business Machines Corp. (IBM) to India's Wipro Ltd., thanks to its educated workforce and low costs. Software engineers who had gone abroad for opportunity are returning. Even though Calcutta is still poverty stricken, changes around the city are encouraging. The changes include brand new offices springing up on vacant land outside the city, huge housing developments, and new malls complete with cinemas and cafés.

Stressing the Positives

In the past, Calcutta suffered from a reputation for labor unrest. So, the city stressed the positive. Unlike many parts of India, Calcutta's power supply is fairly reliable. Costs are even lower than in Bangalore or Bombay (Mumbai). There is a huge supply of talent from nearby engineering schools such as the prestigious Indian Institute of Technology. To ease apprehensions about possible labor stoppages, the government made software and office services legally equivalent to a public utility so that in the event of a general strike, the government will ensure their work goes on as usual.

THINK STRATEGICALLY

Evaluate Calcutta as a site for a U.S. tech company by conducting an environmental scan.

@ Online Action!

Go to *marketingessentials.glencoe.com/4/case* for an activity on international business and economic development.

Quotas

An import **quota** limits either the quantity or the monetary value of a product that may be imported. For example, the U.S. government could place a quota on foreign automobiles, limiting the number that may be imported. This would control the number of cars that could enter the U.S. market from other countries. In theory, such a measure would give U.S. auto manufacturers a better chance to sell their own cars.

Sometimes one trading partner voluntarily puts quotas on exports to improve its relations with another country. In the 1980s, Japan placed quotas on its auto exports to the United States to improve trade relations between the two nations.

Embargoes

An **embargo** is a total ban on specific goods coming into and leaving a country. A government can impose an embargo for health reasons. The U.S. government embargoed Chilean grapes in 1989 as a precaution after inspectors found poisoned fruit in a shipment. That embargo was lifted within a week.

Embargoes are also used for political reasons. Such embargoes based on political differences can last for a very long time. The United States lifted its 30-year embargo on Vietnam in 1994 so that trade relations could start again between the two nations. The U.S. embargo against Cuba—imposed in 1960 when Fidel Castro created a communist state—still remains in effect. In 2000, President Clinton signed a law that relaxed restrictions on food sales to Cuba. As a result, U.S. exports to Cuba were $1 million a day in January 2004.

Protectionism

Trade regulations can have many political and economic consequences. **Protectionism** is a government's establishment of economic policies that systematically restrict imports in order to protect domestic industries. Protectionism is the opposite of free trade. Imposing tariffs and quotas is one method of practicing protectionism.

Protectionism and Subsidies

A government can accomplish the same goal by subsidizing domestic industries, thus allowing them to be more competitive against foreign competition.

For example, the United States and Europe subsidize their farmers. Those subsidies allow farmers to overproduce products that they can sell or donate overseas. All excess output can then be sold internationally at very low prices. Naturally this displeases the foreign competitors who cannot compete with those low prices in the global marketplace.

Sometimes, when one country imposes a tariff or quota, the other country retaliates. For example, in November 2003, the United States imposed new import quotas on Chinese dressing gowns, knitwear, and bras in order to protect domestic textile firms that produce those products. After those quotas were announced, China cancelled a trade mission to the United States to buy farm products such as cotton, wheat, and soybeans.

Trade Agreements and Alliances

Governments make agreements with each other to establish guidelines for international trade and to set up trade alliances. Some milestones in the movement toward worldwide free trade are the formation of the World Trade Organization, the North American Free Trade Agreement, and the creation of the European Union.

The World Trade Organization

The **World Trade Organization (WTO)** is a coalition of nations that makes rules governing international trade. The WTO had 148 members as of October 2004.

The WTO was formed in 1995 as the successor to the General Agreement on Tariffs and Trade (GATT). GATT was an international trade agreement designed to open markets and promote global free trade. It reduced tariffs and created a common set of trading rules. GATT had no enforcement power, so it created the WTO to police the agreement and resolve disputes among nations. For example, in 2004, the WTO ruled in favor of Brazil, which had alleged that U.S. cotton subsidies violated international trade rules and hurt Brazilian farmers by depressing global prices.

The WTO also manages world trade by studying important trade issues and evaluating the health of the world economy. It deals with activities that GATT was unable to address, including intellectual property rights, investment, and services.

The WTO, For or Against?

Supporters of the WTO and free trade stress that globalization and the expansion of trade have created enormous wealth in both rich and previously poor countries.

Free trade supporters believe global prosperity can be maintained and expanded only through a borderless economy. This requires a set of rules that is universally accepted. Advocates argue that such a system is the only way to ensure fairness and avoid damaging trade wars.

Critics of the WTO raise concerns about democracy, labor rights, and the environment. They charge that the WTO makes decisions affecting all of society on a commercial basis. They do not like giving a nonelected body the power to overrule governments on issues of environmental protection and labor rights. Some of the more radical critics want the organization disbanded. Others want to transform it into a body that addresses social and environmental concerns as well as economic ones.

North American Free Trade Agreement

The **North American Free Trade Agreement (NAFTA)** is an international trade agreement among the United States, Canada, and Mexico. It went into effect on January 1, 1994.

The main goal of NAFTA is to get rid of all trade barriers and investment restrictions among the three countries by 2009. Tariffs were eliminated immediately on thousands of goods traded between Mexico and the United States, including food, clothing, and automobiles.

European Union

The **European Union (EU)** is Europe's trading bloc. In 1992, the Maastricht Treaty created the EU to establish free trade among the member nations, as well as a single European currency (the euro) and a central bank. Other treaty provisions relate to fair competitive practices, environmental and safety standards, and security matters.

In 2004, the EU added ten new members, including Poland, Hungary, the Czech Republic, and the Slovak Republic. To be considered part of the EU, these countries had to conform to the EU's political, economic, and legal standards.

4.1 AFTER YOU READ

Reviewing Key Terms and Concepts

1. Explain the nature of international trade.
2. What are two key reasons why embargoes are imposed?
3. What is the common goal or purpose of the WTO, NAFTA, and the EU trade agreements?

Integrating Academic Skills

Math

4. If a Japanese company reported an 8.8 percent increase in net profit from last year's 426 billion yen, what would be this year's net profit in yen?

History

5. Why does the United States have an embargo against Cuba?

Check your answers at *marketingessentials.glencoe.com/4/read*

SECTION 4.2

The Global Marketplace

OBJECTIVES

- List forms of international trade
- Identify political, economic, socio-cultural, and technological factors that affect international business
- Suggest global marketing strategies

KEY TERMS

- licensing
- contract manufacturing
- joint venture
- foreign direct investment (FDI)
- multinationals
- mini-nationals
- globalization
- adaptation
- customization

READ and STUDY

BEFORE YOU READ

Connect Suppose you have manufactured a new product and you want to sell it in a foreign country. List three things you would need to know to accomplish your goal.

THE MAIN IDEA

Doing business in a foreign country can be very different from doing business in the United States. Besides language barriers, there are many other factors that must be considered in international business. Without this understanding, costly problems may arise.

STUDY ORGANIZER

Create a chart like the one below to list factors that affect international business.

International Business	Global Environment	Market Strategies
______	______	______
______	______	______
______	______	______

Doing Business Internationally

The global marketplace has been growing with the increasing acceptance of capitalism around the world, advances in technology such as Internet connections, and the reduction of trade barriers. Global news coverage is instantaneous, connecting people throughout the world. These factors have encouraged businesses to venture into foreign countries. In this section, you will see what it takes for a business to become a global player.

Connect Think of one example for each type of international business transaction this section describes.

Trade agreements by governments set the guidelines for businesses to operate in the global marketplace. Getting involved in international trade can mean importing, exporting, licensing, contract manufacturing, joint ventures, or foreign direct investment. Each option offers a different level of risk and control. Figure 4.1 shows how the profit potential increases as the levels of financial commitment, risk, and marketing control increase with the different market entry options.

Importing

Importing involves purchasing goods from a foreign country. Products imported for the U.S. market must meet the same standards as domestic products, including those imposed by the Food and Drug Administration. If these standards are met, most products can be imported without prior government approval.

A quota can limit entry of certain goods into the country. Quotas exist on cotton, peanuts, and sugar. Once a quota is reached for a certain item, no more of that item may enter the country. Any shipment in excess of the quota is quarantined by U.S. Customs. Knowing the details of importing is difficult and U.S. businesses usually hire customs brokers—specialists licensed by the U.S. Treasury Department. Customs brokers know the laws, procedures, and tariffs governing imports. They handle over 90 percent of imports because of the complex procedures involved.

Exporting

A domestic company that wishes to enter into the global marketplace with minimal risk and control might consider exporting. Domestic companies that want to export their goods and services can get help from the United States government, through its Internet export portal and at its BuyUSA site.

Licensing

Licensing involves letting another company (licensee) use a trademark, patent, special formula, company name, or some other intellectual property for a fee or royalty. This type of market entry has its pros and cons. With licensing, a foreign company makes the

Figure 4.1 **Doing Business Internationally**

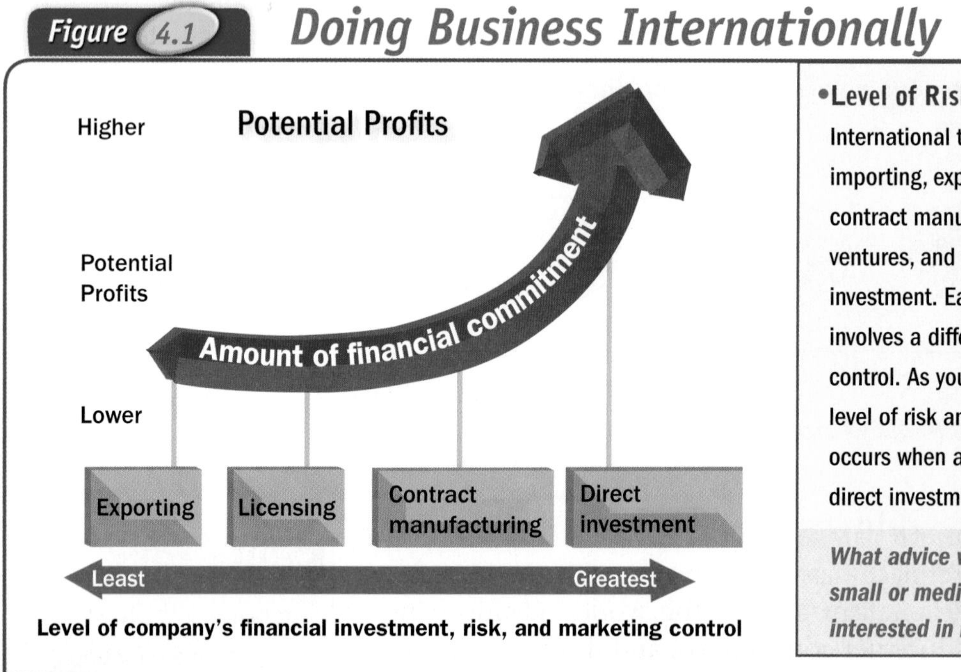

•Level of Risk and Control
International trade includes importing, exporting, licensing, contract manufacturing, joint ventures, and foreign direct investment. Each of these options involves a different level of risk and control. As you can see, the greatest level of risk and marketing control occurs when a company makes a direct investment in a foreign country.

What advice would you give to a small or medium-sized company interested in international trade?

Online Action! Go to *marketingessentials.glencoe.com/4/figure/1* to find a project on international trade.

•OPENING a GLOBAL BUSINESS Starting an import-export business is one way to capitalize on the global marketplace.

What might you need to know before starting such a business with Japan?

product using the information or guidelines provided by the licensor. If the product is a success in the foreign country, the licensor has gained entry with minimal risk. If the product fails, the licensor's name is tarnished.

A special type of licensing is franchising. In a franchise agreement, a franchisor grants the franchisee the rights to operate under the company name. The agreement involves following specific guidelines for operation to foster a unified image of the franchisor. Many fast-food chains, like McDonald's, Wendy's and Burger King, have franchised operations in foreign countries.

Contract Manufacturing

Contract manufacturing has become popular as emerging countries offer facilities, know-how, and inexpensive labor. **Contract manufacturing** involves hiring a foreign manufacturer to make your products, according to your specifications. The finished goods are either sold in that country or exported. Many U.S. companies that sell clothing, toys, golf clubs, and computers use contract manufacturers in emerging countries to manufacture their products.

The major benefit is lower wages, which allow companies to be more competitive in their pricing. One of the pitfalls of contract manufacturing is that proprietary information must be given to these companies. Golf clubs are an example. In China, molds of new golf club heads have been stolen by workers and sold to counterfeiters. The counterfeit clubs are then sold as copies or knockoffs in the United States and abroad for much less than the brand-name clubs.

Joint Ventures

A **joint venture** is a business enterprise that companies set up together. In some countries, foreign investors are not permitted to own 100 percent of a business. If you want to conduct business in those countries, you must find a local business partner, thus creating a joint venture. This is often a good idea even when it is not mandated by law. Domestic business partners know the market and procedures for conducting business in their own country.

For example, Viacom Inc., which owns CBS, Nickelodeon, and MTV, has a minority share in a joint venture with Shanghai Media Group.

Foreign Direct Investment

All the joint ventures described above are considered foreign direct investments. A **foreign direct investment (FDI)** is the establishment of a business in a foreign country.

Sometimes that may involve no more than setting up an office with a staff to maintain a presence in that country. Higher levels of direct investment involve acquisitions of existing foreign companies and construction of facilities such as manufacturing plants and retail stores. Sony, a Japanese company, has invested in several countries. It has direct foreign investment of approximately $8 billion in China. In the United States, Sony has 11 manufacturing facilities. Honda, another Japanese company, has a manufacturing plant in Alabama.

Multinationals and Mini-Nationals

Multinationals are large corporations that have operations in several countries. About one-third of the world's private-sector assets are controlled by some 37,000 transnational corporations with over 170,000 foreign affiliates. Gillette, Procter & Gamble, Unilever, Nike, PepsiCo, and Coca-Cola are multinational firms. Gillette has manufacturing operations in 14 countries. The products from these operations are distributed in more than 200 countries.

Mini-nationals are midsize or smaller companies that have operations in foreign countries. The key characteristic that sets multinationals and mini-nationals apart from domestic businesses is foreign investments in factories, offices, and other facilities abroad that are used for operations. All these investments are referred to as FDIs.

Global Environmental Scan

Recall the factors involved in an environmental scan (see Chapter 2). How would you use those factors to evaluate a country's marketing opportunities and threats?

A global environmental scan is in order. This includes analysis of political and economic factors, sociocultural differences, and technological levels.

Political Factors

Political factors include a government's stability, its trade regulations and agreements, and any other laws that impact a company's operation.

Government Stability

A government's stability is an important factor when considering international business operations. If there are changes in the government, investors become wary. For example, when Luiz Inácio Lula da Silva, a left-wing politician, won Brazil's presidential election in 2002, stock prices in Brazil plunged. Stocks regained strength when businesses saw that President da Silva supported continued economic reform.

Trade Regulations and Laws

A business must keep abreast of new trade regulations, which can force companies to reconsider doing business in a country. Changes in trade regulations include reduced tariffs, laws to protect intellectual property, and an increase in the percentage of business ownership allowed by foreign investors. For example, on January 1, 2004, the United States-Chile Free Trade Agreement went into force. Under this agreement, Chile must have stronger standards for the protection of intellectual property rights. This means that Chile will need to adopt rules similar to those in the United States for copyrights, trademarks, patents, and trade secrets.

Domestic laws must be followed by foreign marketers. For example, toys cannot be advertised in Greece. These regulations are important for retailers like Toys "R" Us.

Economic Factors

Key economic factors relevant to doing business in another country include infrastructure, the quality and cost of labor, employee benefits, taxes, the standard of living, and foreign exchange rates.

Infrastructure

Things like undependable telephone service or inadequate roads would rule out a location for some businesses. Yet these same infrastructure factors would be an opportunity for companies involved in building roads, energy plants, and telecommunications systems. For example, Poland and the Czech Republic had to carry out environmental cleanup to meet the entry requirements for membership in the European Union. U.S. companies that have expertise in that area could partner with companies in Poland and the Czech Republic to help them with these projects.

Labor Force

If you are establishing a business in another country, you must consider the quality and cost of the labor force available there. You need to know the educational and skill levels of the workers, as well as the customary wages and employment laws. For example, India has been supporting technology education and now has a pool of highly qualified workers whose wages are lower than those for similar workers in the United States. U.S. companies like AOL, Yahoo, and Google have recognized this opportunity and now look to India for computer programming and other computer-related expertise.

Employee Benefits

In most countries, employers are responsible for paying for mandated employee benefits above and beyond wages. Many companies shy away from investing in France because of labor policies. France restricts the work week to 35 hours and requires companies to consult with employees before downsizing or restructuring. Payroll taxes and employee benefits are high, so that the cost of the total employee package is higher in France than in other European countries.

Taxes

Other costs include taxes on property and profits. Countries that want to attract foreign investment may offer reduced taxes for a period of time as an incentive. Switzerland offered corporate tax breaks in 1997 and since

A MATTER OF ETHICS

Is the Price Right?

Suppose an international company is a direct purchaser of many products it sells. Because of its size, it is also able to negotiate great prices from suppliers. For example, it has been able to get low prices on raw materials for its suppliers.

Economies of Scale

In the case of clothing, this large international company visits mills around the world to get the best deal it can on fabric. Its supplier of jeans, for example, benefits because it is able to get a great price on the fabric.

Lower Than Low Prices

As a result, jeans that used to sell for $30 are now selling for under $10. The company's competitors cannot keep up with such low prices for jeans because their manufacturers pay regular prices for the fabric.

THINKING ETHICALLY

Is it ethical for a large business to use its clout to secure low prices on raw materials for its suppliers too?

@ Online Action!

Go to *marketingessentials.glencoe.com/4/ethics* for an activity on ethics and international business.

then has experienced a growth in foreign direct investment. Some large companies, like Procter & Gamble, Starbucks, and Google, have their European headquarters in Switzerland.

Standard of Living

Standard of living can be a consideration if a business is eyeing a country as a market rather than a manufacturing site. When Honda entered China's consumer market, it recognized that most Chinese people could not afford cars. The company targeted the motorcycle market instead and was very successful.

The number of middle-income workers is increasing in poorer nations. This increases the demand for all types of ordinary consumer goods. U.S. products like soaps, detergents, breakfast cereals, snack foods, and soft drinks are gaining popularity among consumers in emerging nations.

Foreign Exchange Rate

The foreign exchange rate is the price of one country's currency if you were to buy it with another country's currency. Exchange rates vary every business day. The exchange rate for a nation's currency based on the U.S. dollar is an important factor to consider. Changes in an exchange rate affect businesses that sell abroad. If the dollar strengthens in value against other currencies, that means it costs more yen, euros, or pesos to buy one dollar. It also means it costs more yen, euros, or pesos to buy one dollar's worth of U.S.-made products. International sales of U.S.-made products are likely to fall. If the reverse happens—if the U.S. dollar is devalued—U.S. products are more attractive in the global marketplace. The devaluation of the dollar in 2004 affected the profits of many international companies that do business in the United States. For example, Honda Motor Co. reported a drop in net income in April 2004, which it attributed to lower sales, rising costs, and the effects of a stronger yen against the U.S. dollar.

Socio-Cultural Factors

Marketers must be savvy with cultural diversity and a foreign society's value system. Before conducting business in a foreign country, a cross-cultural analysis should be performed. This analysis should include socio-cultural factors such as language and symbols, holidays and religious observances, and social and business etiquette.

Language and Symbols

Differences in language and customs make international trade more challenging than doing business at home. Cultural symbols are often different. In the United States, the number 13 is considered unlucky. Many hotels do not include a 13th floor. In China and Japan, the number four is unpopular because it relates to death. Marketers in these countries who sell multiple units of a product should consider groups of six or eight, never four.

Holidays and Religious Observances

Holidays and religious observances are part of a country's culture too. In India, the cow is sacred, so little beef is sold there. Fast-food companies like McDonald's adapt to India's culture by selling chicken, fish, and vegetarian burgers. Marketers must heed these cultural differences when creating, naming, and packaging products, as well as when designing ad campaigns for them.

Social and Business Etiquette

Social and business etiquette is important when doing business abroad. A common practice in one country may take on a different meaning elsewhere. Gift giving is one area of concern. A gift may be considered part of business etiquette in the Far East; however, it might be considered an illegal bribe in the United States or Canada.

Technological Factors

Technology is changing the ways that businesses can get involved in international trade. Studying a country's technology means taking into consideration even the most basic factors such as measurement systems and electric voltage standards. A thorough look at the use of computers, faxes, voice mail, cellular phones, and the Internet is important. A

• A NEW FORM of CUSTOMIZATION: TRANSCREATION Marvel Enterprises, Inc. and Gotham Entertainment Group, an Indian publishing licensee of Marvel Comics, launched *Spider-Man India*, the first-ever comics transcreation: They re-invented the origin of Spider-Man so that he is an Indian boy in Bombay (Mumbai), dealing with local challenges and problems.

Why do you think the Spider-Man story was re-invented instead of translated?

visit to the CIA's *World Fact Book* Web site provides information about the number of telephones (main lines and mobile), radio and television broadcast stations, Internet service providers, and Internet users in a given country. These facts can help you decide if setting up a Web site in a specific country would be worthwhile.

Global Marketing Strategies

In planning and making decisions about the four Ps (see Chapter 1) of the marketing mix, global marketers need to consider all the factors analyzed for the environmental scan. The possibilities for marketing strategies that involve product and promotion decisions range from complete standardization, called globalization, to new product development, which is complete customization. Figure 4.2 shows examples of the global marketing strategies for product and promotion decisions.

Globalization

Globalization is selling the same product and using the same promotion methods in all countries. Only a small portion of products that are common to all global customers can use this marketing strategy. Coca-Cola and other soft drink companies can use a globalization marketing strategy by offering the same version of its products with the same advertising message in countries around the world.

How Globalization Works

The reason these companies are able to use the same product and same promotion is that they have uncovered a common need that transcends different cultures. They are able to identify a global consumer. One of the benefits of globalization is global brand recognition. An example of a company that answers common needs across the globe is Microsoft. While users do need computer programs to function in different languages, the basic applications remain the same; likewise Internet search engines such as Yahoo and Google. The success of e-commerce has increased the power of globalization in some instances, particularly where technology is involved.

Adaptation

Companies study the characteristics of a country and find ways to target consumers with similar needs and wants. That often requires adapting their products or promotions to each country where they do business. Sometimes, only the product is changed, while in other cases, only the promotion is changed.

Global Marketing Strategies

• **Marketing Abroad** When marketing products in foreign countries, companies must make product and promotion decisions. Some create completely new products for specific countries (customization), while others use the same products and promotions for every country (globalization). Between these two extremes are companies that keep their products' brand names but vary their products and/or promotions enough to meet local tastes. Here are some examples of each strategy.

How do companies reach customers around the world?

Customization Customization is creating entirely new products and promotions for a specific country or region. The Coca-Cola Company developed the Smart brand specifically for the Chinese market. This carbonated soft drink comes in flavors such as apple, watermelon, grape, and mandarin orange. The company also developed a ready-to-drink carbonated tea called Ice Lemon Tea. Product packaging uses Chinese icons, and ads show young people having fun drinking Smart.

Globalization Pringles Potato Chips are marketed with the same product packaging and promotional message around the world. The company's slogan in Germany is *"Einmal Gepoppt, Nie Mehr Gestoppt!"* In Italy it is *"Se Fai Pop, Divertimento Non Stop!"* In Brazil it is *"Fale de boca cheia!"* They all mean, "Once you pop, you can't stop!"

Product Adaptation The Campbell Soup Company uses product adaptation to sell its soups internationally. With product adaptation, the company keeps the brand name but changes the product to meet local needs and tastes. In Australia you can get Campbell's pumpkin soup, and in Mexico, you will see chile poblano and squash flower (*flor de calabaza*) soups.

Promotion Adaptation Promotion adaptation involves changing some part of the promotional message or visuals used in the promotional campaigns for different markets. Advertisements for Kellogg's cereals use the same message (in different languages) and format but different models to appeal to customers from different countries.

Go to *marketingessentials.glencoe.com/4/figure/2* to find a project on global marketing strategies.

Adaptation is a company's use of an existing product and/or promotion to which changes are made to better suit the characteristics of a country or region.

Product Adaptation

Changing a product to meet different consumer needs and/or to reflect the cultural differences in a foreign market is product adaptation. In some cases, a product's brand name is changed. For example, Unilever's Sunsilk hair products are called *Seda* (which means silk) in Latin America. In addition, Sunsilk's ingredients are formulated to match consumers' needs (prevalent hair types) in different countries.

Promotion Adaptation

A promotion adaptation strategy involves changing the advertising message to reflect the values, familiar images, and cultural differences in a foreign market. In some cases, the advertising is changed to adhere to government regulations. For example, McDonald's is careful to use only adults in its advertising in Sweden, where advertising to children is prohibited.

Another facet of adaptation is the use of adaptation pricing policy. This pricing technique requires a careful competitive analysis so that a product's price can be accurately set to match and compete with the prices of comparable local products.

Customization

Customization involves creating specially designed products or promotions for certain countries or regions. Each geographical area where a product is sold or a service is offered becomes a unique market segment.

4.2 AFTER YOU READ

Reviewing Key Terms and Concepts

1. Give an example of a political factor that could discourage a business from engaging in international trade with a given country.
2. Give an example of how a country's poor infrastructure can create opportunities for foreign companies.
3. Which socio-cultural factors make doing business abroad difficult?

Integrating Academic Skills

Math

4. Assume the currency exchange rate between the United States and Canada is 1.25, which means US$1 dollar is equal to CN$1.25 in Canadian currency. If a T-shirt costs $20 at a Gap store in Montréal, how much should it cost at a Gap in Detroit?

Foreign Language

5. Translate a magazine ad or advertising slogan into a foreign language you are studying. Then, translate back into English. Note any problems and suggest any changes as necessary.

Check your answers at *marketingessentials.glencoe.com/4/read*

CAREERS IN MARKETING

LEE DULANEY
SENIOR ACCOUNT EXECUTIVE
CREATIVE ALLIANCE

What do you do at work?
My job is to coordinate all of Creative Alliance's advertising account services for Yum! Brands' KFC franchisees in the Caribbean and Central and South America. Creative Alliance handles all the TV, radio and in-store POP (point of purchase) advertising for this diverse region. I also act as agency producer for TV and radio, because of my background in broadcast/video production.

What skills are most important to you?
A willingness to learn and the ability to think on your feet are just two of the skills that I believe are the basis for everything. In a marketing capacity, be it national or international, you need to be able to listen and learn about your client, and the consumer your client is trying to reach. In an international marketing capacity, it's crucial that you try your best to understand the culture of your target audience. What motivates them? How do they spend their disposable income? Organizational skills and the ability to prioritize are also critical, because you can often have three or four campaigns in production at any given time.

What is your key to success?
Being able to communicate, listen and follow-through are three very important keys. You also have to make the effort to understand cultural nuances and customs. A marketing idea that works in the United States may not work in, say, the Caribbean or Latin America.

Aptitudes, Abilities, and Skills

International marketers must be able to step inside the mindset of other cultures. Research skills are a must.

Education and Training

Degrees in marketing, advertising, foreign languages, and general business are helpful.

Career Path

Entry-level marketing positions can lead to global careers like this one, particularly if the person has foreign language skills.

THINKING CRITICALLY

Why is spending time abroad prior to launching a career in international marketing helpful?

Online Action!

Go to *marketingessentials.glencoe.com/4/careers* to find a career-related activity.

CHAPTER 4 REVIEW

FOCUS on KEY POINTS

SECTION 4.1

- International trade is necessary because of the interdependence of nations. It benefits consumers, producers, workers, and nations in different ways.
- Governments are involved in international trade through monitoring trade between countries and establishing trade regulations. Currently, the United States has a negative balance of trade, also called a trade deficit.
- Three types of trade barriers are tariffs, quotas, and embargoes.
- Three significant trade agreements and alliances that foster free trade are the World Trade Organization (WTO), the North American Free Trade Agreement (NAFTA), and the European Union (EU).

SECTION 4.2

- Businesses can get involved in international trade through importing, exporting, licensing, contract manufacturing, joint ventures, and foreign direct investments.
- A global environmental scan analyzes political, economic, socio-cultural, and technological factors.
- Global marketing strategy options include globalization, adaptations of product and promotion, and customization.

REVIEW VOCABULARY

The groups of words below involve international trade and free trade. Explain how the words in each group relate to each other.

1. imports (p. 75)/exports (p. 75)/balance of trade (p. 77)
2. tariff (p. 77)/quota (p. 78)/embargo (p. 78)/protectionism (p. 79)
3. World Trade Organization (WTO) (p. 79)/ North American Free Trade Agreement (NAFTA) (p. 80)/European Union (EU) (p. 80)
4. licensing (p. 82)/contract manufacturing (p. 83)/joint venture (p. 83)/foreign direct investment (FDI) (p. 84)/multinationals/mini-nationals (p. 84)
5. globalization/adaptation/customization (p. 89)

REVIEW FACTS and IDEAS

6. Explain the concept of economic interdependence of nations. (4.1)
7. How are governments involved in international trade? (4.1)
8. Explain the U.S. balance of trade. (4.1)
9. What are three basic types of trade barriers? (4.1)
10. List three significant trade agreements and alliances. (4.1)
11. What is a global environmental scan? (4.2)

BUILD SKILLS

12. **Workplace Skills**

Teamwork and Presentation Skills Work in a group to prepare a three-minute presentation that addresses the impact and value of diversity, as well as how diversity affects marketing in a global marketplace. Include specific examples in your oral presentation.

13. **Technology Applications**

Global Crisis Look up information on the Internet about the global recession of the late 1990s. Using word processing software, charts, and graphs, prepare a short report on your findings.

14. **Math Practice**

Prices in Japan Suppose you are going to Japan and plan to bring $2,000 in spending money. If the exchange rate is 118 yen to the U.S. dollar, how many yen would you have? Research prices for items such as food and lodging (hotels) in Japan. How many days could you afford to stay in a major Japanese city such as Tokyo or Kyoto? Use a spreadsheet program to present a report on the daily costs of your trip.

DEVELOP CRITICAL THINKING

15. **Trading With the World**

Why does the global economy have an impact on marketing? Give three examples of foreign products that are imported and explain how they are marketed in the United States.

16. **Analyze the Consequences of Outsourcing**

What impact does outsourcing have on a country's economy and on business? Explain how it affects:

- Employment
- Standard of living
- Consumer prices
- Direct foreign investment
- Business operations and profits

Make sure you consider consequences for both the country that outsources and the country that receives the work.

APPLY CONCEPTS

17. Benefiting from International Trade

Work in groups to prepare an oral presentation that explains international trade to a group of teenagers. Include why it is important, how we benefit from it, what government measures affect or regulate it, and what business ventures foster it. Make sure you find and present several examples of companies that are involved in international trade.

Activity Use presentation software and lots of current examples to make your points come alive.

18. Researching Global Marketing Strategies

Search the Internet to find examples of globalization, customization, and product and promotion adaptations used by multinational companies. Possible key words for your search include: *international products* or *American products abroad.* You may also access the Web site of a well-known company, such as Nike or PepsiCo.

Activity Present your findings in a written report, using word processing software, and create an oral presentation, using presentation software. Cite the Web sites and other sources you used in your written report.

NET SAVVY

19. Global Scan

Visit the Web site for the CIA's *World Fact Book* to conduct a global environmental scan for a country of your choice.

THE 

CONNECTION

Role Play: Assistant Buyer

Situation Assume the role of assistant to a buyer for a gift shop. Your shop imports gift items from South America that are then sold from your retail shop, catalog, and Web site. A newly hired sales associate (judge) has many questions about importing and the countries your company imports its merchandise from.

Activity The store's buyer has asked you to help orient the new sales associate (judge) by answering some of the sales associate's (judge's) questions about importing in general and about the merchandise your company imports.

Evaluation You will be evaluated on how well you meet the following performance indicators:

- Explain the nature of international trade
- Identify the impact of cultural and social environments on world trade
- Explain the principles of supply and demand
- Orient new employees
- Address people properly

@ Online Action!

For more information and DECA Prep practice, go to *marketingessentials.glencoe.com/4/DECA*

MARKETING INTERNSHIP

A SIMULATED DECA PRODUCT AND SERVICE MANAGEMENT EVENT

Conduct a Global Environmental Scan

BASIC BACKGROUND

Friendly Supermarkets is looking to expand its operations globally. An article in *Supermarket News* (May 31, 2004) identified four countries that have potential for growth in this area: Russia, China, India, and Japan. Multinational competitors include Wal-Mart (United States), Carrefour (France), Tesco (United Kingdom), and Metro (Germany).

The Ideal Destination The marketing director has indicated that Friendly is not interested in countries where the market is saturated, such as Brazil, Poland, Hungary, and South Africa. It is also not interested in areas where there are aggressive price promotions, such as western Europe, or where there is political unrest, such as the Persian Gulf region. For its first venture, it wants the location to be one that has the greatest potential with the least risk.

YOUR OBJECTIVE

You will be working in a team. Your objective is to give Friendly Supermarkets well-researched advice on how to proceed. The company needs to know which country to pick, how to set up its business there, and how to give the local customers what they want. There is a good chance Friendly's marketing plan for the United States will not apply overseas.

ASSIGNMENT AND STRATEGY

- **Get the background** Research the four countries and the competition. Consider the stability of the governments and their attitudes toward foreign investors. Look at the countries' economic philosophies (traditional, market, command), economic health, factors of production, infrastructure, and technology. Consider Friendly's potential customers. What sociocultural factors, such as languages, customs, and religion, would affect the four Ps of the marketing mix? Consider the competition. Local and multinational competitors may already be growing in these countries. What are the successful competitors doing differently?

- **Conduct an analysis** Use your research to conduct an environmental scan for each country. Look for opportunities and threats.

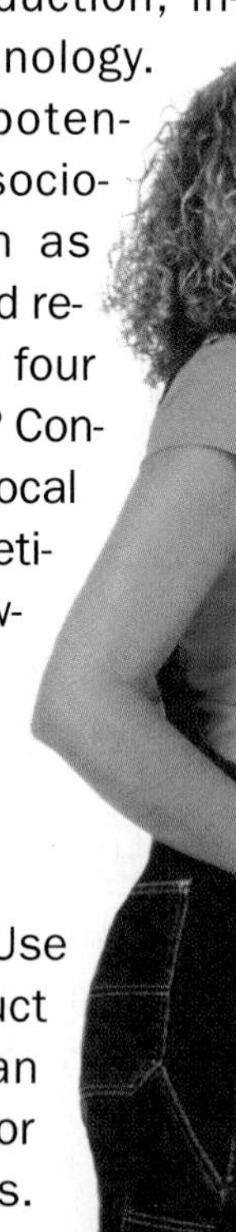

Come to a consensus as a team about which country Friendly Supermarkets should invest in first. Rank the second, third, and fourth choices. Support your recommendations with facts.

- **What your project should include** Choose a country for Friendly Supermarkets' international expansion and explain why it is the best choice. Which city or region should Friendly try first? Should the company go it alone or work with a local partner? Should Friendly use its existing products and promotions, adapt them somewhat, or customize them for the local population? How should it answer the other P questions: place, price, and promotion?

YOUR REPORT

Use a word processing program and presentation software to prepare a double-spaced report and an oral presentation for Friendly Supermarkets. See a suggested outline and key evaluation points at *marketingessentials.glencoe.com/internship*

BUILD YOUR PORTFOLIO

Option 1 Internship Report Once you have completed your Marketing Internship project and presentation, include your written report and a few printouts of key slides from your oral presentation in your Marketing Portfolio.

Option 2 Searching the Globe Select a special product, such as a locally made soft drink or handcrafted jewelry, to market in a foreign country. Conduct environmental scans (PEST) of several countries before choosing the best one for the product. Investigate competitors and target markets. Conduct a SWOT analysis. Prepare a written report and an oral presentation using word processing and presentation software. See a suggested outline and key evaluation points at *marketingessentials.glencoe.com/portfolio*

@ Online Action!

Go to *marketingessentials.glencoe.com/Unit/2/DECA* to review global environmental scan concepts that relate to DECA events.

UNIT 3 Business and

In this unit you will find

- **Chapter 5** The Free Enterprise System
- **Chapter 6** Legal and Ethical Issues

THE BAYOU IS NO ORDINARY FOOTBALL GAME.

STATE FARM® IS PROUD TO BE THE TITLE SPONSOR OF THE BAYOU CLASSIC.

Honor. Pride. Tradition. Things that matter long after the season ends. The State Farm Bayou Classic® is a time-honored battle on the gridiron. It's a symbol of pride that we're excited to bring to the community. From kick-off to the thrilling finish, everyone knows this is more than just a football game. WE LIVE WHERE YOU LIVE.®

LIKE A GOOD NEIGHBOR  STATE FARM IS THERE.®

Providing Insurance and Financial Services

statefarm.com®

State Farm Insurance Companies • Home Offices: Bloomington, IL

Society

Marketing Plan

1 **ANALYSIS**
- SWOT
- Economic
- Socio-Cultural
- Technological
- Competitive

2 **STRATEGY**
- Promotion
- Place
- Price
- Product

3 **IMPLEMENTATION**
- Organization
- Management
- Staffing

4 **BUDGET**
- Cost of Sales
- Cost of Promotion
- Incomes and Expenses

5 **CONTROL**
- Evaluation
- Performance Measures
- Performance Analysis

ANALYZE THE AD

Is this ad promoting a football game or an insurance company? Both! Why would State Farm sponsor this annual matchup between two Louisiana football teams?

Market Talk All insurance companies sell similar products and services, so each one has to find a way to differentiate itself from the others. What statement is State Farm making about itself in this ad?

Think and Write Insurance companies have to compete in a free enterprise system. Some try to appeal to customers with their prices, others emphasize their services. Research three large insurance companies and note their slogans and messages to consumers. List two ways the companies you selected try to set themselves apart.

Online Action! Go to *marketingessentials.glencoe.com/u3/ad* for an extended activity.

In this unit

Foundations of Marketing
- Economics
- Business, Management, Entrepreneurship

CHAPTER 5

The Free Enterprise System

Chapter Objectives

After reading this chapter, you should be able to:

- Explain the characteristics of a free enterprise system
- Distinguish between price and nonprice competition
- Explain the theory of supply and demand
- Recognize the difference between for-profit and nonprofit organizations
- Distinguish between the public and private sectors
- List the types of businesses in the industrial market

GUIDE TO THE PHOTO

Market Talk A new company's marketing strategies for its product, pricing, promotion, and place all focus on showing how it can be better than its competitors. Why? To convince customers to buy its products instead of those of a competitor. The free enterprise system allows competition. It also implies the risk of failure. That's free enterprise.

Quick Think List three benefits of the free enterprise system.

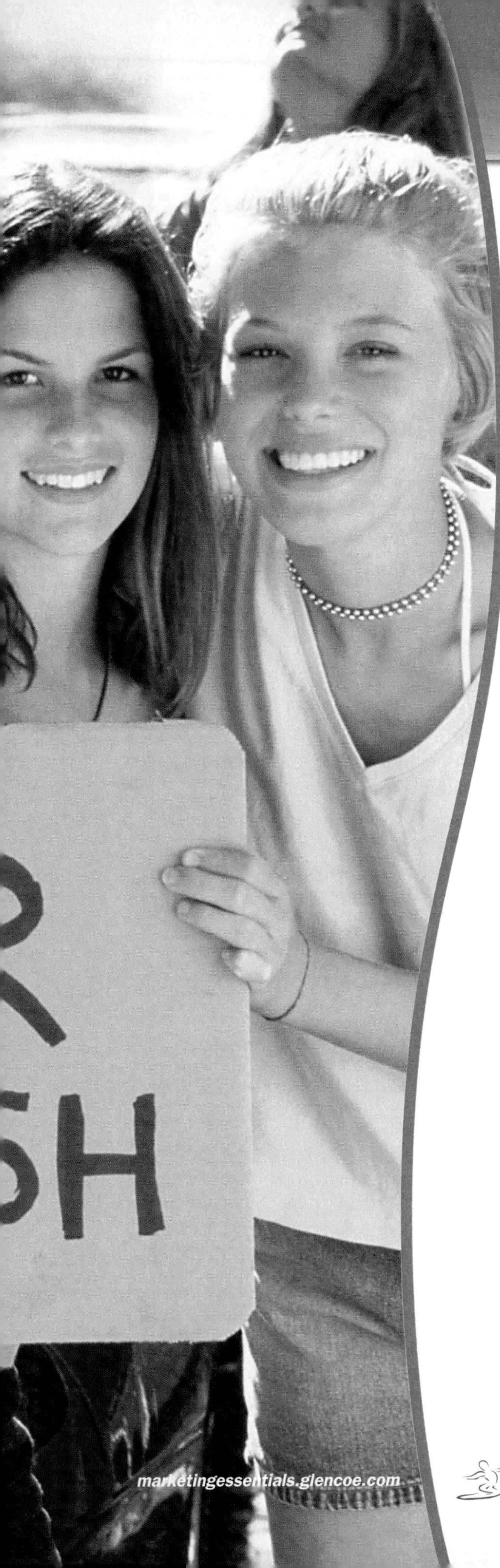

THE   CONNECTION

Performance indicators represent key skills and knowledge. Relating them to the concepts explained in this chapter is your key to success in DECA events. Keep this in mind as you read this chapter and write some notes each time you encounter material that helps you master a key concept.

These acronyms represent DECA events that involve knowledge of concepts in this chapter.

AAAL	**FMAL**	**MMS**	**TMDM**
AAML	**FMDM**	**QSRM**	**TSE**
ADC	**FMML**	**RMAL**	**VPM**
BSM	**FSRM**	**RMML**	
EMDM	**HMDM**	**SMDM**	

In all these DECA events you should be able to follow these performance indicators:

- Explain the concept of private enterprise
- Identify factors affecting a business's profit
- Determine factors affecting business risk
- Explain the concept of competition
- Explain the principles of supply and demand
- Describe the concept of price
- Determine the relationship between government and business
- Explain the concept of organized labor and business
- Describe types of business activities

Some events include additional performance indicators. These are:

BSM Describe factors that influence the demand for services

SMDM Describe factors that influence the demand for services

DECA PREP

Check your understanding of DECA performance indicators with the DECA activity in this chapter's review. For more information and DECA Prep practice, go to *marketingessentials.glencoe.com/5/DECA*

SECTION 5.1

Market-Oriented Economic Systems

OBJECTIVES

- Explain the characteristics of a free enterprise system
- Distinguish between price and nonprice competition
- Explain the theory of supply and demand

KEY TERMS

- free enterprise system
- patent
- trademark
- copyright
- competition
- price competition
- nonprice competition
- monopoly
- business risk
- profit
- supply
- demand

READ and STUDY

BEFORE YOU READ

Connect Why do you think the free enterprise system is called "free"?

THE MAIN IDEA

Countries that are active in the global marketplace have market-oriented economic systems and follow the principles of the free enterprise system: competition, property ownership, risk, and the profit motive. Pricing in a free enterprise system is determined primarily by supply and demand theory.

STUDY ORGANIZER

Use a chart like the one below to take notes about the characteristics of a free enterprise system.

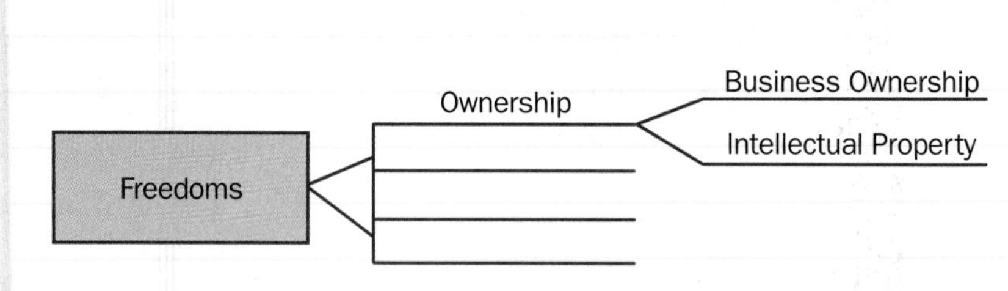

WHILE YOU READ

Connect List two everyday examples of business life in a free enterprise system.

Basic Principles

Our nation's founders believed that individuals should have freedom of choice. They defined rights that are central to our society. For example, in the United States, we have the freedom to elect the people who represent us in our government. We have the freedom to make decisions about where we work and how we spend our money. Workers have the freedom to organize and negotiate with business, as part of a labor union. Consumers

•**CHOOSING WHERE YOU WORK** In a free enterprise system, some people choose not to work in an office environment. They create their own businesses and sometimes work out of their homes.

Why is this flexibility an important part of our system?

have the freedom to purchase goods and services and to invest their money in banks or businesses.

The basis of the free enterprise system is the freedom to own personal property, to compete, to take risks, and to make a profit. A **free enterprise system** encourages individuals to start and operate their own businesses in a competitive system, without government involvement. The marketplace determines prices through the interaction of supply and demand. The free enterprise system we have today in the United States is modified because the government does intervene in business on a limited basis. It does this to protect citizens, while supporting the basic principles of free enterprise.

Freedom of Ownership

Individuals in our free enterprise system are free to own personal property, such as cars, computers, and homes, as well as natural resources such as oil and land. You can buy anything you want as long as it is not prohibited by law. You can also do what you want with your property in a free enterprise system. You can give it away, lease it, sell it, or use it yourself.

Business Ownership

The free enterprise system encourages individuals to own businesses. There are all types of business, as you will see in Section 5.2. You may have heard of people who have started and run their own businesses. These individuals are called entrepreneurs. Others may not want to be involved in running a business, but they support business by investing their money in parts or shares of business. These shares of a business are called stocks, and the investors are called stockholders. Company stocks are bought and sold daily.

• CREATING YOUR OWN BUSINESS
Another way to be your own boss is to open a store.

What are the pros and cons of opening a business?

When a company is doing well, stock prices generally increase because more people want to buy that stock.

There are, however, some restrictions on how and where businesses may operate. Businesses may be restricted in where they can locate. Most kinds of businesses are zoned out of areas intended for private housing. Manufacturers may be forced to comply with certain environmental and safety measures.

Intellectual Property Rights

Intellectual property rights are protected in a free enterprise system. Patents, trademarks, copyrights, and trade secrets are intellectual property rights. If you get a **patent** on an invention, you alone own the rights to that item or idea. To ensure that protection, you would apply for a patent in the U.S. Patent and Trademark Office. If granted, you would have the exclusive rights to make, use, or sell that invention for up to 20 years. During this time, anyone who wanted to manufacture your product would have to pay you for its use through a licensing agreement. A **trademark** is a word, name, symbol, sound, or color that identifies a good or service and that cannot be used by anyone but the owner. Unlike a patent, a trademark can be renewed forever, if it is being used by a business. A **copyright** involves anything that is authored by an individual, such as writings (books, magazine articles, etc.), music, and artwork. It gives the author the exclusive right to reproduce or sell the work. A copyright is usually valid for the life of the author plus 70 years. A trade secret is information that a company keeps and protects for its use only, but it is not patented. Coca-Cola's formula for Coke is a trade secret.

When a company wants to use another's name, symbol, creative work, or product, it must get permission to do so and pay a fee for the use. A licensing agreement protects the originator's name and products. A T-shirt manufacturer might be granted a licensing agreement with the National Football League (NFL) so that it can produce T-shirts with NFL logos on them. The company will have to pay NFL Properties a fee for this privilege. It will also have to agree to certain standards to protect the NFL's reputation. In addition, the NFL has control over all team logos and how the teams can use them.

Competition

Businesses that operate in a free enterprise system try to attract new customers and keep old ones. Other businesses try to take those same customers away. This struggle for customers is called **competition**.

Competition is an essential part of a free enterprise system. It is one of the means by which the free enterprise system functions to benefit consumers. Competition forces businesses to produce better-quality goods and services at reasonable prices.

Businesses constantly look for ways to develop new products and improve old ones to attract new customers. Competition results in a wider selection of products from which to choose. The results of these efforts is an

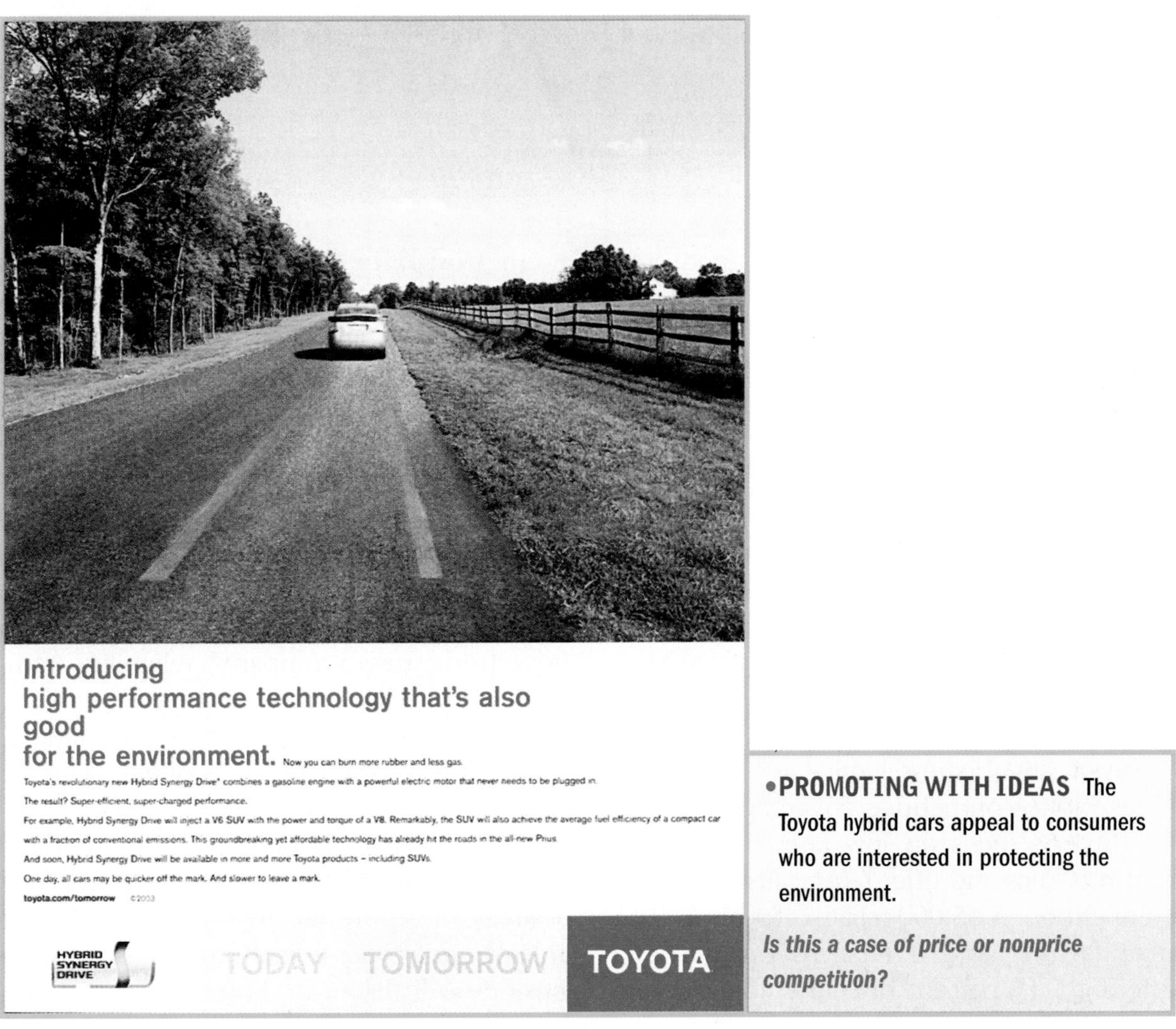

• PROMOTING WITH IDEAS The Toyota hybrid cars appeal to consumers who are interested in protecting the environment.

Is this a case of price or nonprice competition?

• **THE MARKET DETERMINES SUCCESS** In the 1980s, Coca-Cola changed the formula of its leading soda and launched New Coke in a highly publicized effort. The resulting flop of New Coke remains a classic example of product failure.

What do you think is a common cause of product failure?

increase in the nation's output of goods and services, as well as in its standard of living.

There are two basic ways businesses compete: price competition and nonprice competition.

Price and Nonprice Competition

Price competition focuses on the sale price of a product. The assumption is that, all other things being equal, consumers will buy the products that are lowest in price.

The marketing strategies used by Wal-Mart and Southwest Airlines are examples of price competition. Wal-Mart's "Always Low Prices. Always." slogan stresses price as the primary focus of its competitive advantage, as does Southwest's focus on low fares. Companies that run sales and offer rebates also use price competition. A $5,000 rebate offer by an auto manufacturer and a retailer's one-day sale offering a 15 percent discount storewide are examples of price competition.

In **nonprice competition**, businesses choose to compete on the basis of factors that are not related to price. These factors include the quality of the products, service, financing, business location, and reputation. Some nonprice competitors also stress the qualifications or expertise of their personnel. Businesses that use nonprice competition may charge more for products than their competitors do.

Examples of nonprice competition in advertising stress a company's reliability, tradition, superior know-how, and special services. An example of nonprice competition among dot-com companies are offers of free shipping and same-day delivery.

These examples of price and nonprice competition suggest that businesses adopt one strategy or the other. In our value-oriented society, however, it is not uncommon for businesses to try to do both. As competition increases, you may see more price-oriented competitors offering services they never offered in the past.

Monopolies

When there is no competition and one firm controls the market for a given product, a monopoly exists. A **monopoly** is exclusive control over a product or the means of producing it.

Monopolies are not permitted in a free enterprise system because they prevent competition. A company can charge whatever it wants without competition. It can also control the quality of a product and who gets it. Without competition, there is nothing to stop a company from acting without regard to customer wants and needs.

One of the most publicized monopoly cases in recent history involved Microsoft, the computer software company. A federal judge declared Microsoft's Windows operating system was a monopoly. Its technology dominance was said to have stifled innovation and hurt consumers.

The U.S. government has allowed a few monopolies to exist, mainly in industries where it would be wasteful to have more than one firm. These regulated monopolies, however, are on the decline.

Currently, utility companies are being deregulated. This will allow customers to choose their own electric and natural gas suppliers. In order for this deregulation to work, the government will still control natural gas and electric companies by imposing price restrictions, preventing the formerly regulated monopolies from charging excessive prices.

Risk

Along with the benefits that come from competition and private ownership of property, businesses also face risk. **Business risk** is the potential for loss or failure. As the potential for earnings gets greater, so does the risk. For example, putting money in the bank with guaranteed interest rates is less risky than investing in the stock market where the value of shares of stocks fluctuates. Simply starting a company is a risk. If you wanted to open your own business, you would probably put your savings into the enterprise. You make money if the business is successful; but if the business fails, you lose all your savings. One out of every three businesses in the United States fails after one year of operation.

Businesses also run the risk of being sued or having their name tarnished by bad publicity (warranted or not). Natural disasters could also ruin a business. You will learn more about business risks and how to manage them in Chapter 34.

When an industry develops and profits are great, more people enter that industry. This increases competition and the risk of failure for individual firms. You may have read of businesses closing operations in an effort to reduce losses and become more competitive. For example, Levi Strauss & Co. closed its manufacturing plants in North America and now contracts with foreign manufacturers to make its garments.

Risk is also involved in the development of new products. Product introductions are costly and risky; up to 85 percent of new products fail in the first year.

Profit

Profit is the money earned from conducting business after all costs and expenses have been paid. Profit is often misunderstood. Some people think the money a business earns from sales is its profit. That is not true. The range of profit for most businesses is one percent to five percent of sales; the remaining 95 to 99 percent goes to pay costs, expenses, and business taxes.

Profit is the motivation for taking the risk of starting a business. It is the potential reward for taking that risk. It is also the reward for satisfying the needs and wants of customers and consumers. Businesses may use their profits to pay owners or stockholders, or they may elect to reinvest those profits in their businesses.

Profits are good for our economy in many ways. The concept of profit is the driving force in our free enterprise system. It encourages people to develop new products and services in the hope of making a profit. Without profit, few new products would be introduced.

Profit remains high when sales are high and costs are kept low. This encourages companies to work in an efficient way that helps to conserve precious human and natural resources. Profits provide money for a company to keep its facilities and machinery up-to-date. Then the business can produce goods more efficiently.

Economic Cost of Unprofitable Firms

An unprofitable business faces many problems. One of the first things businesses do when their profits decline is lay off employees. Investors in publicly traded companies can lose money if the stock value falls below what they paid for it.

Government also suffers when business profits decline. Poorly performing businesses pay less money to the government in taxes. When businesses lay off workers, there is a rise in unemployment. This causes an increase in the cost of social services and puts more stress on such agencies.

Economic Benefits of Successful Firms

Profitable businesses hire more people. Employees may have higher incomes, better benefits and higher morale. Investors earn money from their investments, which they spend or reinvest. Vendors and suppliers make more money, too. As employment and profits climb, the government makes more money from taxation of individuals and businesses. Companies and individuals are also more likely to donate to charities when they are doing well.

Remember that profitable companies attract competition, which is beneficial to the consumer. To satisfy consumer wants and needs, they try to offer new products, the lowest prices, the highest quality, and the best service.

When people earn higher incomes, they have more money to spend. There is increased demand not only for expensive products such as cars and homes, but also for services provided by a variety of businesses, from hair salons to travel agencies.

Supply and Demand

In a market-oriented economy, supply and demand determine the prices and quantities of goods and services produced. To understand how prices are determined, you have to look at supply and at demand and at how they interact. See Figure 5.1.

Supply is the amount of goods producers are willing to make and sell. The law of supply is the economic rule that price and quantity supplied move in the same direction. This means that as prices rise for a good, the quantity supplied generally rises, and as the price falls, the quantity supplied by sellers also falls. Thus, suppliers want to supply a larger quantity of goods at higher prices so their businesses can be more profitable.

Demand refers to consumer willingness and ability to buy products. The law of demand is the economic principle that price and demand move in opposite directions. As the price of a good increases, the quantity of the good demanded falls. And as the price falls, demand for the good increases.

When supply and demand interact in the marketplace, conditions of surplus, shortage, or equilibrium are created. These conditions often determine whether prices will go down, go up, or stay the same.

Surpluses

Surpluses of goods occur when supply exceeds demand. If the price of a product is too high or seems unreasonable to customers, they may decide not to buy it. Their decisions will affect the market. When this happens, businesses respond by lowering their prices in order to encourage people to buy more of the product. To do so, they may run sales or special promotions.

One of the best examples of surpluses can be found in the produce section of a supermarket. Peaches, apples, broccoli, or other produce may be priced very low one week due to supply. When a given crop is in season, there is often an excess supply, and farmers lower their prices to sell large quantities. Supermarkets that buy large quantities of the crop at the low price do the same. The surplus affects the price all the

Figure 5.1 Supply and Demand Theory

• **Supply and Demand** Supply and demand interact to determine the price customers are willing to pay for the goods producers are willing to make.

How do supply and demand work?

DEMAND

Demand refers to consumer willingness and ability to buy products. According to the law of demand, if the price drops, demand for a product usually increases. This is reflected in the demand schedule. It provides the points to plot a demand curve.

Demand Schedule for Athletic Shoes Sold at Retail	
Price per Pair	Number Demanded
$155	600
140	800
125	1,100
110	1,500
95	2,000
80	3,000
65	3,400
50	4,600
35	6,200

SUPPLY

Supply is the amount of goods producers are willing to make and sell. The law of supply states that at a higher price, producers will offer a larger quantity of products for sale. At a lower price, they will offer fewer products. This is reflected in the supply schedule. It provides the points to plot a supply curve.

Supply Schedule for Athletic Shoes Sold at Retail	
Price per Pair	Number Supplied
$155	6,000
140	5,800
125	5,600
110	5,400
95	5,000
80	4,400
65	3,400
50	2,000
35	1,000

EQUILIBRIUM

Equilibrium exists when the amount of product supplied is equal to the amount of product demanded. On the graph, this is the point where the supply and demand curves meet. It is also the point where both producer and consumer are satisfied with the price. The equilibrium price, therefore, is the price at which customers are willing to buy and producers are willing to sell.

Go to *marketingessentials.glencoe.com/5/figure/1* to find a project on supply and demand theory.

way down the line. You can see how a produce shortage affects produce prices. When there is a poor season for oranges, you will find that the price of oranges is higher. For produce, extreme weather conditions such as drought or flood can affect supply. However, if the product in question is a necessity, customers will pay the price determined by the market.

Shortages

When demand exceeds supply, shortages of products occur. When shortages occur, businesses can raise prices and still sell their merchandise. An oil shortage increases the price of gasoline, so consumers who want to drive their vehicles pay the higher price. Price increases also raise the cost of doing business, which in turn affects profits. For example, in 2004, rubber prices increased significantly due to strong demand from China. The increased prices affected all types of companies, such as surgical-glove makers, producers of hoses and conveyor belts, and tire manufacturers.

Equilibrium

When the amount of a product being supplied is equal to the amount being demanded, equilibrium exists. When supply and demand are balanced, everyone wins. Customers are able to purchase goods and services at a fair price, and retailers experience a steady flow of business. Customers buy the entire stock of the product that is available. Retailers clear their shelves of merchandise. Everyone's needs and wants are satisfied in the most efficient manner possible.

There are exceptions to the rules of supply and demand, which you will learn about in Chapter 25 on price planning. There, you will see how demand elasticity and the law of diminishing returns affect supply and demand theory.

5.1 AFTER YOU READ

Reviewing Key Terms and Concepts

1. Provide an example of how freedom of ownership may be limited by government.
2. What are intellectual property rights and how does the law protect these rights?
3. In supply and demand theory, when is equilibrium achieved?

Integrating Academic Skills

Math

4. A discount retailer reported a profit of $93 million on sales of $4.6 billion. What percentage of sales was its profit?

Economics

5. If the local hair salon increased its price for a hair cut from $25 to $50, what might happen to demand for that service? What should happen if the opposite occurred—if the price was reduced from $50 to $25? What other factors could influence consumer demand in these situations?

Check your answers at *marketingessentials.glencoe.com/5/read*

SECTION 5.2

Business Opportunities

OBJECTIVES

- **Recognize the difference between for-profit and nonprofit organizations**
- **Distinguish between the public and private sectors**
- **List the major types of businesses in the industrial market**

KEY TERMS

- **domestic business**
- **global business**
- **for-profit business**
- **nonprofit organization**
- **public sector**
- **private sector**
- **industry**
- **derived demand**
- **wholesalers**
- **retailers**
- **production**
- **management**
- **finance**
- **accounting**

READ and STUDY

BEFORE YOU READ

Connect Can you think of some businesses that are not interested in making a profit?

THE MAIN IDEA

The major functions of a business are production or procurement, marketing, management, and finance. The analysis of these key functions is an excellent basis for determining the strengths and weaknesses of a company as part of a SWOT analysis.

STUDY ORGANIZER

In charts like the one below, record the various ways to classify businesses and the major functions of business.

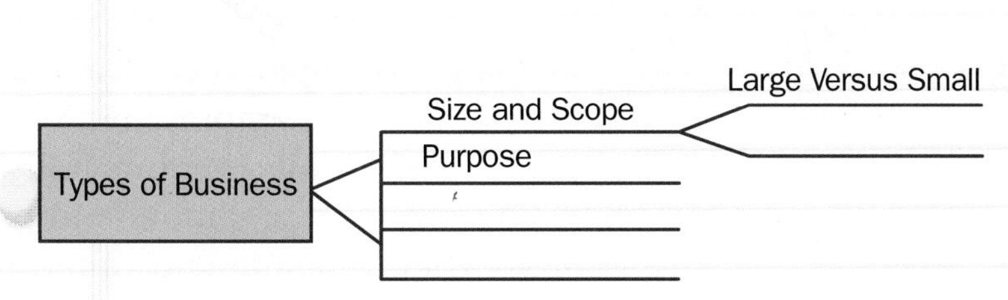

Types of Business

In a free enterprise system, there are many opportunities to invest or work in many different types of businesses. In order to view those opportunities, it is a good idea to start by classifying businesses. To understand their differences, you will need to know the terminology associated with business classification. Keep in mind that a business may be classified in more than one

WHILE YOU READ

Connect List four businesses in your community. How would you classify each one?

•CLASSIFYING BUSINESSES Qantas Airlines flies many routes around the globe as well as in Australia.

What type of company is Qantas, domestic or global?

category. A business can be classified by its size and scope, by its purpose, and by its place within the industry.

Size and Scope

One of the easiest ways to describe a business is by its size. It is large or small? The scope of a business refers to the extent of its business operation. Some businesses serve a small neighborhood, while others do business globally. Now we will look at these two ways to categorize businesses.

Large Versus Small Businesses

A small business is one that is operated by only one or a few individuals. It generally has fewer than 100 employees. A large business is usually one that employs more than 1,000 people. Nationwide, there are millions of small businesses, or "mom-and-pop" operations. They include neighborhood grocery stores, florists, gift shops, photocopy and print shops, and secretarial services. This category also contains many Internet start-up companies and dot-com businesses that often start off with small budgets and staffs. About 95 percent of all U.S. businesses are classified as small businesses. These types of businesses employ more than half of the private-sector (nongovernment) workforce.

NET MARKETING

Web Sites Created by Kids

A 14-year old entrepreneur designs Web sites for other small businesses and has four clients. Other teenagers who are building Web sites are doing so to promote a cause or provide help for others. Peter Grunwald of the Internet research firm Grunwald Associates estimates there are about two million sites created by kids aged 6 to 17.

Getting Started

Terra Lycos is a company that promotes site building. People start with its free service and then can upgrade for a charge. The company offers two sites—Angelfire.com and Tripod.com—that host personal sites.

Kids do not have to know computer code—software programs make site building easy.

THINK LIKE A MARKETER

List three reasons why teenagers would use Terra Lycos's service.

Online Action!

Go to *marketingessentials.glencoe.com/5/net* to find an activity on Internet marketing and the free enterprise system.

Domestic Versus Global

A business that sells its products only in its own country is considered a **domestic business**. Because a domestic business limits its scope of operation to one country, its opportunities for growth are limited to customers within that country. A **global business** sells its products in more than one country. The advent of the Internet, along with faster transportation and financial transfers, makes it easier to do business globally. Products produced in one country are now finding greater acceptance around the world. The trend among large and small businesses is toward a more global market.

Purpose

A business firm serves the needs of its customers in order to make a profit. However, there are other organizations that function like a business but have a different purpose. To understand this difference, we need to distinguish between for-profit and nonprofit organizations, and between public and private enterprise.

For-Profit Versus Nonprofit Organizations

A **for-profit business** seeks to make a profit from its operations. A **nonprofit organization** functions like a business but uses the money it makes to fund the cause identified in its charter. Nonprofit organizations generate revenue through gifts and donations. Some even sell goods or services, which generate income. They usually do not have to pay taxes on their income. They also have expenses. They pay employees and rent for their office space. Other expenses may include supplies, printing, and postage for letters sent requesting donations. The Red Cross, the Boy Scouts of America, DECA, and other nonprofit organizations strive to generate more income than expenses, just like a for-profit business. However, unlike profit-oriented businesses, nonprofit organizations use that extra money to fund their respective causes. Thus, their organizational goal is not to make a profit but rather to use that money for their cause. Many people who feel strongly about helping others seek to start or work for a nonprofit organization. Although there are many unpaid volunteers, a staff of paid workers is often also needed to manage the operation of a nonprofit organization.

Public Versus Private

In addition to charitable institutions, other organizations operate like businesses but are not intended to earn a profit. Most local, state, and federal government agencies and services, such as public schools and public libraries, fall into this category. Their main purpose is to provide service to the people in the country or community in which they operate. At the federal level, there are military agencies, like the Army and the Air Force; social agencies, like Social Security and Medicare; and regulatory agencies, like the Food and Drug Administration and the Environmental Protection Agency. Government-financed agencies like

Case Study

Entrepreneurship and Science

The Wisconsin Alumni Research Foundation (WARF) is a little-known nonprofit organization that was founded in 1925 by Harry Steenbock and eight other alumni of the University of Wisconsin-Madison. Each of the nine founders contributed $100 to hold patents developed by the university. Today, patent royalties and investment income have piled up a $1.3 billion endowment, which returns $40 million a year to the university for scientific research.

A 1923 Discovery

This all came about after Steenbock discovered, in 1923, that irradiating food increased its vitamin D content, which would eliminate rickets, a crippling bone disease. The Quaker Oats Company offered $1 million ($10.8 million in today's dollars) to purchase the rights to this process. But Steenbock reckoned the university could reap far more if the foundation held on to the patent and licensed the technology to Quaker Oats. Vitamin D still accounted for 70 percent of the $38.7 million in patent royalties earned in 2003. Today, inventors get 20 percent of the royalties generated by their invention. WARF collects the remaining 80 percent but agrees to defend the patent against challenges (which can cost $1 million or more).

THINK STRATEGICALLY

How can WARF be helpful to a scientist who has an idea for curing cancer or another life-threatening disease?

@ Online Action!

Go to *marketingessentials.glencoe.com/5/case* to find an activity about scientific research and the free enterprise system.

• ZAPPOS'S ADVANTAGE
This ad advertises Converse sport shoes. But it also advertises Zappos.com, a shoe e-tailer.

Would you shop at Zappos.com? Why or why not?

these are part of the **public sector**. Businesses not associated with government agencies are part of the **private sector**.

Public-sector organizations purchase one-third of all goods and services sold in the United States each year. Just think about all the products and supplies purchased in the operation of your public school system and you will see why businesses seek out customers in the public sector.

Industry and Markets

Businesses are often classified according to the industry they represent, the products they sell, and the markets they target. The government provides a system for classifying types of business by industry and sector. Products and markets are classified according to intended use. All of these classifications are interrelated based on the customers served.

NAICS

According to the U.S. Department of Labor, an **industry** consists of a group of establishments primarily engaged in producing or handling the same product or group of products or in rendering the same services. For 60 years, the U.S. government used the Standard Industrial Classification (SIC) system to collect data on businesses and analyze the U.S. economy. However, rapid changes in services and technology made a new system necessary. The United States, Canada, and Mexico jointly developed the North American Industry Classification System (NAICS). In a nutshell, it states that "establishments that do similar things in similar ways are classified together." NAICS uses a six-digit hierarchical coding system to classify all economic activity into 20 industry sectors. For example, the information sector includes the industries involved in communications, publishing, and motion pictures, as well as Internet companies. Some of the subcategories of the Internet industry are Web search portals, Internet publishing and broadcasting, electronic shopping, and electronic auctions. The information in the NAICS can be helpful to businesses looking for new marketing opportunities and to individuals who may want to find employment or invest in those sectors.

Consumer, Industrial, and Service Markets

As you read in Chapter 2, the consumer market consists of customers who buy goods for personal use. The industrial market consists of business customers who buy goods for use in their operations. The two are interrelated because of the economic concept of derived demand. For example, when consumers decide to buy more automobiles, dealers need more cars, so auto manufacturers will need an increased supply of auto components, such as tires, radios, batteries, and electronic parts. Companies that make such parts experience an increased demand as a result of consumer decisions to buy more cars. This is called derived demand. **Derived demand** in the industrial market is based on, or derived from, the demand for consumer goods and services. Because of this relationship between consumer and industrial demand, industrial companies look for opportunities to increase their business by studying consumer trends. Service-related businesses function in both consumer and industrial markets.

Businesses that are involved in the industrial market include extractors, construction and manufacturing businesses, wholesalers, retailers, and service-related firms.

Extractors are businesses that take something from the earth or sea. They include agriculture, forestry, fishing, and mining. The products are sold primarily to other businesses.

Construction companies build structures such as houses, office buildings, and manufacturing plants. Manufacturing involves producing goods to sell to other manufacturers or to wholesalers and retailers. **Wholesalers** obtain goods from manufacturers and resell them to industrial users, other wholesalers, and retailers. Wholesalers are also called distributors. **Retailers** buy goods from wholesalers or directly from manufacturers and resell them to the consumer. For the most part, retailers cater to the consumer market.

Service-related businesses are companies that provide intangible products to satisfy needs and wants of consumers and/or businesses. Consumer services include such things as dry cleaning, hair styling, entertainment, transportation, insurance, and personal needs, such as lawn-cutting, child care, and housekeeping. Business services follow the same concept. That is why you have firms that specialize in accounting, marketing, management, insurance, shipping, and finance. There are also professional services—those provided by professionals such as doctors, dentists, and lawyers.

Internet-related services, such as Web portals, Web casting, Web site design, and Web advertising have created opportunities that did not exist many years ago. For example, e-commerce (short for "electronic commerce") is the buying and selling of products through the use of electronic networks, usually the Internet. Even traditional retailers are adapting their marketing to e-commerce, creating e-tailing.

The Functions of Business

Regardless of the type of business, there are four main functions involved in an organization's operation. They are production or procurement, marketing, management, and finance. The ways each business performs these activities may differ. However, all four are essential for running a business or organization. The success of a business is dependent on how well these activities are coordinated, managed, and performed.

A company that has a great product but is poorly managed will not succeed. A company will also fail if it lacks the resources to pay for experienced personnel or to maintain inventory levels so products are available for sale. Poor financial record keeping can lead to poor management decisions, which may result in poor performance. If inaccurate accounting causes investors to believe that a company is more profitable than it really is, a corporation's reputation may be damaged. That in turn can lead to bad publicity and lower stock prices. Thus, the four business functions must be viewed in relation to one another. As you evaluate strengths and weaknesses during a SWOT analysis, review all four activities. For now, we will look at the role each plays in a firm's operation. Keep in mind that all these functions must be performed well for a company to be successful.

Production and Procurement

The process of creating, expanding, manufacturing, or improving on goods and services

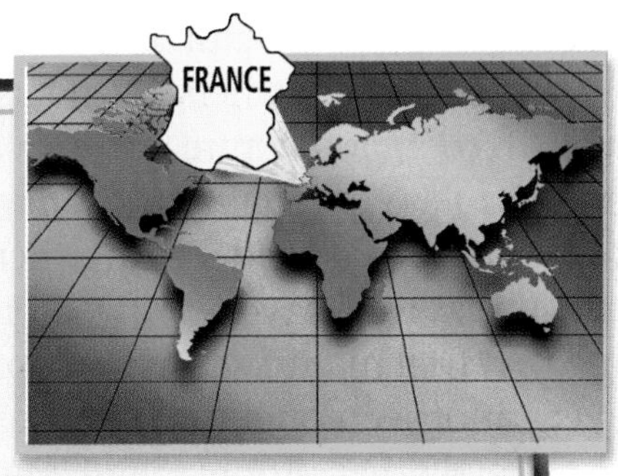

A Hidden Champion

Hidden champions is a term that was coined by a German business consultant, Hermann Simon. A hidden champion is a small to medium-sized company that is narrowly focused on a small, highly specialized market. Such companies are usually not well known, yet are very profitable. One example of a hidden champion is the French company Essilor.

Staying the Course Essilor manufactures ophthalmic lenses, which is the formal name for contact lenses and lenses for eyeglasses. Over the years, Essilor has reinforced its single focus and avoided branching out into eyeglass retailing. Instead, the company concentrated its efforts on going global. Today, Essilor is the industry's leader. Besides staying specialized and having a clear strategy, Essilor kept innovations coming. For example, Essilor invented progressive lenses. These alternatives to bifocal lenses have a gradual change in correction power from top to bottom. Like most other hidden champions, Essilor invests a notable four to five percent of its annual sales on research and development. Other characteristics of hidden champions include tight financial management, superior customer service, and foresight.

CRITICAL THINKING

How would you evaluate this hidden champion based on the functions of business?

Online Action!

Go to *marketingessentials.glencoe.com/5/global* to find an activity on global marketing and free enterprise.

is called **production**. A songwriter creates a song. A farmer grows wheat. Ford Motor Company manufactures cars. Van conversion companies improve new vans to make them more suitable for a disabled driver, or for camping and travel. Thus, production, as a function of business, is found in industries such as farming, mining, forestry, manufacturing, and service-related operations.

When evaluating this function of business in a SWOT analysis, look for innovation, speed to market, efficiency, and level of success with products. Companies that want to be leaders in an industry produce the most innovative products and do so before their competitors do. Efficiency helps to keep prices down and sales up, which makes for a profitable company.

Hewlett-Packard is a good example of an industry leader in printers. The computer equipment maker has 9,000 patents, and anything that is not patented is protected by trade secrets. As a result, it is the industry leader in printers. In 2004, the printer division accounted for 80 percent of Hewlett-Packard's earnings.

Procurement

Procurement involves buying and reselling goods that have already been produced. Retail and wholesale businesses function in this capacity. A supermarket (retailer) buys cans of soup, fresh produce, frozen foods, dairy products, and the other nonfood items for resale. Most of these products were purchased from manufacturers, while a few may have been purchased from wholesalers. Wholesalers buy goods from manufacturers for resale to other wholesalers and retailers. Even businesses that appear to manufacture their own products may actually be buying those products from other companies and putting their names on the labels. You may buy a Dell printer thinking that Dell manufactured that printer. However, another company like Lexmark may have made that product with minor changes and re-branded it a Dell.

SWOT Analysis, Wholesalers, and Retailers

In a SWOT analysis, you would evaluate wholesalers and retailers on their merchandising ability.

The five "rights" of merchandising are having:

- the right goods
- at the right time
- in the right place
- at the right price
- in the right amount.

Predicting customer demand and product preferences is a difficult task, as is determining the price at which those products will sell.

Marketing

All activities from the time a product leaves the producer or manufacturer until it reaches the final consumer are considered marketing activities.

All types of business, regardless of size, scope, intended purpose, and products sold use marketing activities in their operations. Manufacturers, service operations, wholesalers, and retailers buy goods for use in their operations and sell their finished products to customers.

The Role of Marketing Activities

All related marketing activities support the buying and selling functions. For example, research helps to determine what products to make and/or purchase, as well as how to price and promote them. Promotion helps to educate potential customers about a company's products and is used to stimulate sales.

Aeropostale, a New York-based chain of retail apparel stores, spends heavily for consumer research. Since it is a teen-oriented company, it must keep up with teens' changing tastes in clothing. To do so, it runs high school focus groups, in-store product tests, and an online research program. The Internet-based research is conducted with 100,000 online shoppers who are asked for their input in creating new styles. It runs this program 20 times a year and averages 3,500 participants.

In a SWOT analysis, you would evaluate the four Ps of the marketing mix and how well they focus on the intended market(s). They should also be reviewed in relation to the company's objectives and sales performance.

Management

Management is the process of achieving company goals by effective use of resources through planning, organizing, and controlling.

Planning involves establishing company objectives and forming strategies to meet those objectives. Management will determine the corporate culture and mission or vision for a firm.

Organizing involves specific operations, such as scheduling employees, delegating responsibilities, and maintaining records.

Controlling has to do with overseeing and analyzing operating budgets to suggest the most cost-effective measures for a company to follow. Analysis of financial reports, such as cash flow and profit and loss statements, is part of its controlling function.

A SWOT analysis would evaluate the personnel who run a company. The CEO or owner in a smaller operation, as well as the key managers and their expertise, are important indicators.

Finance and Accounting

Finance is the function of business that involves money management. **Accounting** is the discipline that keeps track of a company's financial situation. If you want to analyze a company's finances, you would study its balance sheet, profit and loss statement, and possibly its cash flow statement.

Balance Sheet

A balance sheet reports a company's assets, liabilities, and owner's equity. Assets are things a company owns. Liabilities represent money owed by a business to its creditors.

If most of a company's liabilities have not been paid for yet, a company's financial situation would not be positive. For example, if a company had assets of $100,000 and liabilities of $75,000, its owner's equity would be only $25,000. In this case, creditors own more of the company than the owners.

Profit and Loss Statements

Profit and loss statements reflect the ongoing operations of a firm. They include income from sales revenue and investments, as well as costs and expenses of doing business. A profitable company generates more income than it pays out for costs of goods and expenses to run the business. When a business suffers a loss, its costs and expenses exceed its revenue.

Financial Statements and the SWOT Analysis

In a SWOT analysis, both financial statements provide important information regarding how well a business is doing financially.

A profitable business with high owner's equity allows a company to grow. It can invest in more research and development. It can expand its operations by building new facilities or acquiring other business. Why? Because it has the money to do so.

5.2 AFTER YOU READ

Reviewing Key Terms and Concepts

1. Of what significance are small businesses to the U.S. economy?
2. Why would DECA, an international association of marketing students, be classified as a nonprofit organization?
3. What information is reported in a company's balance sheet? In its profit and loss statement?

Integrating Academic Skills

Math

4. Determine the net worth (owner's equity) of a company that has assets of $500,000 and liabilities of $200,000.

History

5. Research how the Red Cross, a nonprofit organization, began internationally and in the United States, and identify its fundamental principles and any interesting historical facts about its operations. Prepare a written report on your findings.

Check your answers at *marketingessentials.glencoe.com/5/read*

CAREERS IN MARKETING

MICHAEL SARAY
DIRECTOR, HISPANIC COUNCIL, DIRECT MARKETING ASSOCIATION

What do you do at work?
Many direct marketers realize the importance of the Hispanic market and MSHM helps them get started. Typically, we do not do primary research, but instead we look for the relevant information regarding market size and consumer attitudes. With the relevant information in hand, we develop a strategic plan that considers strengths and weaknesses, consumer awareness, and media options. Once the communication platform is developed, we create the actual message. This involves integrating the words and the images so that the consumer is motivated to act. We do this with mail pieces, the Internet, and television and print advertising.

What skills are most important to you?
I have a good education with a bachelor of commerce degree and an MBA. This has taught me to be analytic and consider the whole picture. Make sure that you take every opportunity you can to improve your technical and computer skills. The most important training is informal and on the job. There is always something to be learned from those around you.

What is your key to success?
Be passionate about your work. Listen and understand what people are telling you. Be an expert in your area. Never stop learning.

Aptitudes, Abilities, and Skills

Strong research, communication, and writing skills, creativity, organization, and time management skills

Education and Training

Degrees in marketing, communication, or general business; MBAs are also helpful.

Career Path

Entry-level marketing positions often deal with the basics of the field and might be thought of as apprenticeships of sorts. Higher-level marketing positions are often filled from this pool of talent.

THINKING CRITICALLY

How can specialized knowledge of a particular market—in this case, the Hispanic consumer—be an asset?

Online Action!

Go to *marketingessentials.glencoe.com/5/careers* to find a career-related activity.

CHAPTER 5 REVIEW

FOCUS on KEY POINTS

SECTION 5.1

- The characteristics of a free enterprise system are freedom of ownership, freedom to compete, freedom to make a profit, and freedom to take risks. Price competition involves competing with a lower price, while nonprice competition involves factors other than price, such as special services and an excellent reputation.
- The economic cost of unprofitable businesses includes loss of jobs, loss of revenue to investors and to the government, and increased government costs for social services. The possible benefits of successful firms include increased employment, better returns for investors, more sales revenue for supporting companies, more tax revenue for the government, higher charitable donations, and more competition.
- Supply and demand interact to create price. Theory suggests that as prices rise, demand drops. As prices increase, supply increases. The equilibrium point is where the supply and demand curves meet. At that point, consumers are willing to buy and suppliers are willing to sell.

SECTION 5.2

- Businesses can be classified on the basis of size and scope, purpose, and place within industry.
- Unlike profit-oriented businesses, which keep their profits, nonprofit organizations use the money they make (profit) to fund the causes identified in their charters. The public sector consists of all organizations and agencies funded by the government. The private sector consists of all nongovernmental organizations and businesses. The major types of businesses that comprise the industrial market are extractors, construction companies, manufacturers, wholesalers, retailers, and service-related companies.

REVIEW VOCABULARY

Explain how the terms in the groups below relate to each other.

1. free enterprise system (p. 101) business risk and profit (p. 105)
2. patents, trademarks, and copyrights (p. 102)
3. competition (p. 103), monopoly (p. 105), price, and nonprice competition (p. 104)
4. supply and demand (p. 106)
5. domestic and global business (p. 111)
6. for-profit and nonprofit organizations (p. 111)
7. public sector and private sector (p. 113)
8. industry (p. 113) and derived demand (p. 114)
9. retailers and wholesalers (p. 114)
10. production (p. 115), management, finance, and accounting (p. 116)

REVIEW FACTS and IDEAS

11. What are the key characteristics of a free enterprise system? (5.1)
12. Provide examples of price and nonprice competition. (5.1)
13. Explain the basic theory of supply and demand. (5.1)
14. What are three major categories for classifying businesses? (5.2)
15. How do for-profit businesses and nonprofit organizations differ? (5.2)
16. What are the differences between the public and private sectors? (5.2)

CHAPTER 5 REVIEW

BUILD SKILLS

17. **Workplace Skills**

Communication Conduct a telephone interview with a representative of your local chamber of commerce. Ask what new businesses have joined the organization in the past year. Also, ask about the economic, political, and other conditions facing businesses in your community. Write about your findings in a one-page report.

18. **Technology Applications**

Creating Charts Using a spreadsheet program like Excel, create a chart to depict supply and demand curves for a jeans jacket. When graphing your chart, select an equilibrium point and note it in ink on the completed chart. The price range is from $50 to $250. The range for the amount demanded/supplied is from 0 to 5,000 jackets.

19. **Math Skills**

How Much Profit? Determine the profit a company makes with sales of $2,456,700, costs of $1,246,100, and expenses of $1,112,332. What percentage of sales does the profit represent?

DEVELOP CRITICAL THINKING

20. **Supply and Demand**

Provide examples of supply and demand theory at work. Think of products or services that interest you. For example, you may select music-related products such as MP3 players, or music-related services such as music download sites. Other possibilities include sports or fashion apparel, cars, or tutoring services. Then, try to think of one example each to illustrate surplus, shortage, and equilibrium.

21. **SWOT Analysis and Free Enterprise**

Select a business of your choice and review its four major functions: production or procurement, marketing, management, and finance. Identify the company's strengths and weaknesses for each of those functions as part of a SWOT analysis. Why is this an important process to follow in a free enterprise system?

APPLY CONCEPTS

22. Designing a Plan

A small, family-owned paint and wallpaper store that has been in existence for three generations is facing stiff competition from some retail giants. Within 15 miles of the store are five Home Depots, five Sherwin-Williams paint stores, three Sears, and a newly opened Lowe's store. The owners know they cannot compete on price, so they need a cost-effective plan to compete on some other basis.

Activity Your job is to develop that plan and present it to the owners in a written document and an oral presentation, complete with examples and visuals to support your ideas.

23. Researching Intellectual Property Rights

Conduct research on the nature of patents, copyrights, and trademarks in the United States. Since 1790, how many patents have been issued? Which industries and companies hold the most patents? How long does it take to get a patent approved? What are some of the current issues with patents, copyrights, and trademarks? What can a business do if its patent, copyrighted material, or trademark has been copied by a competitor? Provide examples.

Activity Prepare a written report using a word processing program. Cite all your sources.

NET SAVVY

24. Industry Classification

Visit the Bureau of Labor Statistics Web site, which provides background information on NAICS. Select an industry of your choice to review. Report your findings.

THE

CONNECTION

Role Play: The Free Enterprise System

Situation You are to assume the role of sales associate for a locally owned sporting goods store located in a small, but rapidly growing community. Your store sells a limited line of sporting goods that concentrates on items of interest and use to local athletes. Your store has enjoyed the unique position of having no competing stores within your immediate trading area. You have learned that another local merchant plans to add a limited line of sporting goods to its merchandise offerings.

Activity You are to respond to another sales associate (judge) who questions why the other merchant would want to compete with your store.

Evaluation You will be evaluated on how well you meet the following performance indicators:

- Explain the concept of private enterprise
- Explain the concept of competition
- Explain the types of economic systems
- Describe current business trends
- Demonstrate a customer-service mindset

@ Online Action!

For more information and DECA Prep practice, go to *marketingessentials.glencoe .com/5/DECA*

CHAPTER 6
Legal and Ethical Issues

Chapter Objectives

After reading this chapter, you should be able to:

- Explain the role of government in a free enterprise system
- Identify federal regulatory agencies and laws that protect consumers, workers, investors, and the environment
- Provide examples of the impact of government on business
- Provide examples of business's social responsibilities
- Explain the concept of business ethics
- Apply guidelines for ethical behavior

GUIDE TO THE PHOTO

Market Talk There are no laws requiring businesses to go above and beyond government agency mandates. However, some businesses choose to establish programs to benefit employees, the community, and the environment. Such programs include volunteering for community actions.

Quick Think How do government and socially responsible businesses affect the lives of people in the United States?

THE DECA CONNECTION

Performance indicators represent key skills and knowledge. Relating them to the concepts explained in this chapter is your key to success in DECA events.

These acronyms represent DECA events that involve knowledge of concepts in this chapter.

AAAL	**FMAL**	**MMS***	**TMDM***
AAML*	**FMDM***	**QSRM***	**TSE***
ADC*	**FMML***	**RMAL**	**VPM**
BSM	**FSRM***	**RMML***	
EMDM*	**HMDM***	**SMDM***	

In all these DECA events you should be able to follow these performance indicators.

- Determine the relationship between government and business
- Explain the role of business in society
- Describe current business trends
- Describe legal issues affecting businesses

All the events with an asterisk (*) also include these performance indicators:

- Explain the nature of personnel regulations
- Explain the nature of workplace regulations (including OSHA, ADA)
- Explain the nature of trade regulations
- Explain the nature of environmental regulations
- Explain the nature of businesses' reporting requirements

Some events include additional performance indicators. These are:

FMML Explain the nature of health and sanitation laws affecting food marketing

FSRM Explain the nature of health and sanitation laws

QSRM Explain the nature of health and sanitation laws

DECA PREP

Check your understanding of DECA performance indicators with the DECA activity in this chapter's review. For more information and DECA Prep practice, go to *marketingessentials.glencoe.com/6/DECA*

SECTION 6.1

Government and Laws

OBJECTIVES

- Explain the role of government in a free enterprise system
- Identify federal regulatory agencies and laws that protect consumers, workers, investors, and the environment
- Provide examples of the impact of government on business

KEY TERMS

- Food and Drug Administration (FDA)
- Consumer Product Safety Commission (CPSC)
- Equal Employment Opportunity Commission (EEOC)
- Occupational Safety and Health Administration (OSHA)
- Securities and Exchange Commission (SEC)
- Environmental Protection Agency (EPA)
- Federal Trade Commission (FTC)

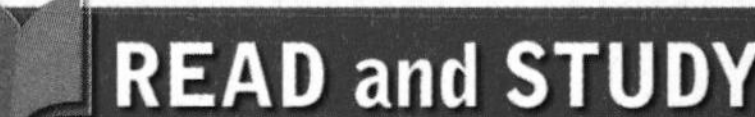

BEFORE YOU READ

Predict What are two ways government can affect business?

THE MAIN IDEA

In a free enterprise system, the government plays a role in safeguarding its own principles and providing for the health, general welfare, and safety of its citizens.

STUDY ORGANIZER

Use a chart like the one below to take notes about the U.S. government and its role in the free enterprise system.

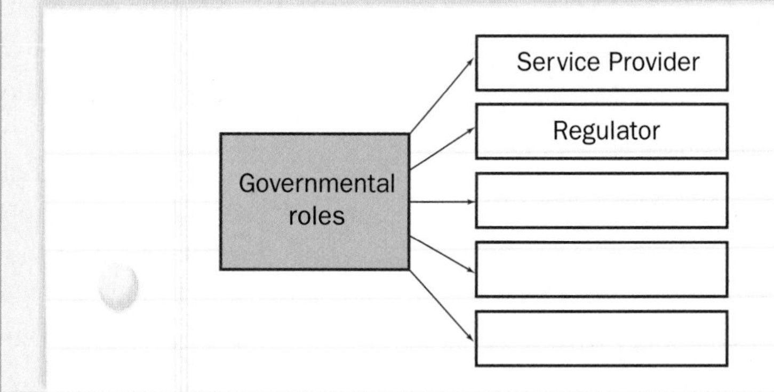

WHILE YOU READ

Connect List three ways local, state, and national governments serve and protect businesses.

The Roles of Government

The stability of a government and its policies shape the political climate of a country. Government actions have a great impact on business and its operations. Thus, it is important to understand how government functions and how it affects businesses.

The stability of a government, of its structure, and of its legal system is always part of the analysis of a business (the environmental scan). The government plays the roles of a provider of services, a customer, a regulator, an enforcer of free enterprise, and a monitor of the economy. All these roles involve laws and regulations that have consequences for business.

Structure of the United States Government

In the United States, each of the three branches of government—executive, legislative, and judicial—limits the power of the other two. This provides a system of checks and balances that prevents any one branch of government from becoming too powerful. Comparable branches of government exist at the state and local levels. Business owners and trade groups must follow the actions of all branches and levels of government, because they all affect business operations.

Executive Branch

The executive branch of the federal government includes the Office of the President; Executive Departments (for example, Interior, Commerce, Defense), as well as independent agencies and corporations, boards, commissions, and committees; and quasi-official agencies. Each administration tends to have different initiatives and issues that impact business due to economic times and political agendas.

The U.S. Department of Agriculture (USDA) is an agency that is part of the executive branch. It provides the inspection, grading, and certification of beef, lamb, pork, and veal, for example. The meat grades are used as a marketing tool by retailers and restaurants to distinguish the better cuts from less expensive ones. The USDA also provides a grading service for dairy products. States may contract with the USDA to have grading and inspection carried out by inspectors who are trained and licensed by the USDA.

Legislative Branch

The legislative branch of the U.S. government is the U.S. Congress. It is made up of the Senate and the House of Representatives. Members of Congress debate and vote on laws and regulations. Lobbyists try to influence the way legislators vote on bills that affect their interests.

• USDA INSPECTORS at WORK The USDA, a government agency founded in 1862 by President Abraham Lincoln, controls the safety and quality of meat, poultry, and egg products.

Why do you think a USDA grade could be used in marketing?

For example, even before the appearance of mad cow disease in the United States, some politicians, farm groups, and the Consumer Federation of America lobbied for mandatory country of origin labeling (COOL) on meat products. Lobbyists for the food industry asked Congress to at least postpone COOL for a few years. In 2004, Congress granted the meat, produce, and peanut industries a two-year reprieve in the implementation of the mandatory labels.

Judicial Branch

The judicial branch of government is responsible for interpreting, applying, and administering the laws of the United States. The judicial system consists of a network of courts at all levels of government.

When the legislative or executive branches of government enact laws or regulations that negatively affect businesses, those businesses may appeal to the judicial branch of government. Any court decision may create opportunities for some and threats to others. In 2004, four regional telephone companies (Verizon, BellSouth, Qwest Communications, and SBC Communications) appealed the part of the Telecommunications Act of 1996 that required them to make their phone networks available to competitors at heavy discounts. This provision was originally established to combat the near-monopoly the regional companies had in local telephone service.

The Role of Service Provider and Customer

The government must spend a lot of money to carry out its responsibility to ensure the safety and general welfare of people in the United States. As a matter of fact, approximately one-third of the country's gross domestic product is generated by government expenditures.

To keep the country safe, the Department of Homeland Security spends money on border protection, disaster recovery, and on other measures such as airport security. For example, to improve the country's infrastructure, federal, state, and local governments fund the construction of roads and bridges.

Businesses that provide products and services for any government installation, project, or institution must adhere to certain guidelines. Why? Because it is taxpayers' money that the government is spending.

The Role of Regulator

In the United States, most laws are designed to protect the safety, health, and welfare of individuals. At the federal, state, and local levels, these laws are carried out by government agencies. The government acts as a regulator to protect consumers, employees, investors, and the environment and this affects businesses. (See Figure 6.1.) Note that businesses must comply or suffer the legal consequences.

Protecting Consumers

At the state and local levels, government agencies are involved with consumer protection. People who perform certain services, such as hairstylists, manicurists, and electricians, must be licensed. Local zoning laws about where homes, businesses, and farms can be located protect real estate investments and quality of life for residents. Health departments inspect restaurants and other food-handling businesses to protect consumers. If a business fails these inspections, it is cited and required to correct the problems identified. Failure to do so can result in closure of the business.

The Food and Drug Administration and the Consumer Product Safety Commission are two federal agencies that protect consumers.

The **Food and Drug Administration (FDA)** regulates the labeling and safety of food, drugs, and cosmetics sold in the United States.

The FDA approves new products and reviews products already on the market. For example, in 2004 the FDA banned a dietary supplement, ephedra, because of health risks associated with products that contain that ingredient. The government first issued a warning telling consumers to stop taking ephedra products immediately and asking companies to voluntarily stop selling products that contained ephedra and ephedrine alkaloids. The actual ban became effective 60 days after issuance. Obviously, this ruling had a negative impact on manufacturers of products that contained ephedra.

The FDA also responds to petitions for action. For example, the Grocery Manufacturers of America asked the FDA to provide definitions for low-carb food items.

The **Consumer Product Safety Commission (CPSC)** is responsible for overseeing the safety of products such as toys, electronics, and household furniture. The CPSC is not responsible for oversight of food, drugs, cosmetics, medical devices, tobacco products, firearms and ammunition, motor vehicles, pesticides, aircraft, boats, and fixed site amusement rides. The CPSC was established under the Consumer Product Safety Act of 1972. That act gives the commission the authority to set standards for products that are

Figure 6.1 The Government's Regulatory Role

• The Music Industry Versus Copyright Violators **The music industry's struggle to protect copyrighted music—and the right of musicians to make a living—illustrates the regulatory roles of the different branches of the federal government.**

If it's legal is it ethical?

The law U.S. copyright law gives ownership and the right to reproduce, distribute, or license an original work to the creator of that work. Originally written to protect authors, the law now covers software, sound recordings, and motion pictures.

◀ **The infringement** The development of the Internet and file-sharing software made it possible for music lovers to download their favorite recordings for free.

The cases: Mitch Bainwol, Chairman, CEO, RIAA, testifies before the Senate The recording industry fought back, filing suit in federal court. The Recording Industry Association of America (RIAA), a trade group, has sued more than 4,000 individuals for illegally downloading music from popular music Web sites. In 2001, it won a case against Napster for its role in the music downloads and succeeded in shutting down the popular site. ▶

◀ **File-sharing software** Since the ruling against Napster, the computer industry has developed new peer-to-peer file-sharing software which enables files to be shared without the use of a central computer. It was Napster's use of a central computer that led to the guilty verdict. Now, free music Web sites, such as Kazaa, advertise that because the sites do not actually host the file sharing, they are legal. Congress is attempting to pass legislation that will provide additional protection for musicians and for the music industry.

@ Online Action!

Go to *marketingessentials.glencoe.com/6/figure/1* to find a research project on the government's regulatory process.

•ALMONDS: GOOD for YOUR HEALTH This ad uses a health claim to promote a food product.

Which government agency had to approve this health claim before it could be used in this advertisement?

considered hazardous and to recall dangerous products. Product recalls are published at the CPSC Web site.

The Consumer Product Safety Commission covers many areas. It also enforces the Federal Hazardous Substances Act, the Flammable Fabrics Act, the Poison Prevention Packaging Act, and the Refrigerator Safety Act. Of prime concern with all these acts is the safety of children. It is a good idea for businesses to test their products before marketing them to the public. Businesses should also keep up with new guidelines in the labeling of their products, especially with regard to directions for their safe use.

Protecting Workers

The Equal Employment Opportunity Commission and the Occupational Safety and Health Administration are among the groups responsible for protecting employees at the federal level. Companies also must comply with minimum wage standards and other laws and regulations established by state and federal governments, such as the Family and Medical Leave Act. There are also laws to protect employees who report illegal practices by their employers. These laws protecting whistle-blowers are covered later in this section.

The **Equal Employment Opportunity Commission (EEOC)** is responsible for the fair and equitable treatment of employees with regard to hiring, firing, and promotions. Some of the laws it enforces are Title VII of the Civil Rights Act, the Equal Pay Act of 1963, the Age Discrimination in Employment Act of 1967 (ADEA), Sections 501 and 505 of the Rehabilitation Act of 1973, Titles I and V of the Americans with Disabilities Act of 1990 (ADA), and the Civil Rights Act of 1991.

Businesses must adhere to the policies established by the United States Department of Labor. The **Occupational Safety and Health Administration (OSHA)** provides guidelines for workplace safety and enforces those regulations. For example, construction workers must wear hard hats for protection.

The Family and Medical Leave Act (FMLA) of 1993 requires employers that qualify to grant eligible employees up to a total of 12 workweeks of unpaid leave during any 12-month period for one or more of the following reasons: the birth and care of the newborn child of the employee; placement with the employee of a son or daughter for adoption or foster care; to care for an immediate family member (spouse, child, or parent) with a serious health condition; or to take medical leave when the employee is unable to work because of a serious health condition.

Protecting Investors

The **Securities and Exchange Commission (SEC)** regulates the sale of securities (stocks and bonds). It is responsible for licensing brokerage firms and financial advisers. It also investigates any dealings among corporations, such as mergers, that affect the value of stocks.

This type of regulation helps protect investors from deceptive practices. The SEC requires that all information about the corporation that is given to investors be truthful. This requirement protects both the investor and the corporation. Companies whose shares are traded on the stock exchange must publish a company's prospectus and an annual report. A prospectus is a document offered to potential investors for their review when they are making a decision about whether to invest in a company. Corporations must prepare an annual report at least once a year to show its investors how the company has performed. On a more frequent basis, such corporations report their profits and stock dividends for publication in the media.

Protecting the Environment

The **Environmental Protection Agency (EPA)** was established in 1970 to protect human health and our environment. Its responsibilities include monitoring and reducing air and water pollution, as well as overseeing hazardous waste disposal and recycling.

For example, the 1970 Clean Air Act was amended in 1990, making it more effective. In 2004, new rules to improve air quality were added. One of those rules involves stringent pollution controls on diesel engines used in industries such as construction, agriculture, and mining. Two other industries that will have similar emission standards are diesel locomotives and marine diesel engines.

Environmental laws cover problem areas such as acid rain, asbestos, lead poisoning, mercury, mold, ozone depletion, pesticides, and radon. They also address littering. For example, new laws regarding distribution of advertising materials went into effect on April 1, 2001. A company can be fined if it distributes advertising materials inappropriately. For example, businesses are no longer allowed to place advertising leaflets on vehicles.

Enforcer of the Free Enterprise System

The **Federal Trade Commission (FTC)** has the responsibility of enforcing the principles of a free enterprise system and protecting consumers from unfair or deceptive business practices. As an independent agency, it reports to Congress on its actions. Its commissioners are nominated by the President and confirmed by the Senate. The FTC runs three bureaus: the Bureau of Consumer Protection; the Bureau of Competition; and the Bureau of Economics.

Bureau of Consumer Protection

The Bureau of Consumer Protection is responsible for enforcing consumer protection laws and trade regulation rules. It investigates individual companies and industry-wide operations and initiates lawsuits against companies that violate these laws and regulations.

There are six divisions with special responsibilities: advertising, enforcement, financial, marketing, international, and planning and information.

• **FMLA** The Family and Medical Leave Act is making it possible to have flexible work arrangements and encourages work/home life balance.

What consequence does FMLA have on employees? On business?

- The Advertising Division enforces truth-in-advertising laws.
- The Enforcement Division ensures compliance with the laws involving the Internet; the U.S. Postal Service; textile, wool, fur, and care labeling; and energy use. For example, clothing labels must identify the fabric content, country of origin, and care instructions.
- The Financial Practices Division covers the Truth-In-Lending Act, as well as leasing and privacy issues.
- The Marketing Practices Division is responsible for responding to fraudulent activities and scams. The Telemarketing Sales Rule, the 900-Number Rule, the Funeral Rule, and the Magnuson-Moss Act are a few of the laws enforced by the Marketing Practices Division.
- The International Division of Consumer Protection promotes consumer confidence in the international marketplace through cross-border cooperation and information sharing.

Case Study

Car Emissions

California's plan for sharp cuts in automotive emissions of global warming gases could eventually lead much of the coastal United States to turn to vehicles that are substantially cleaner, and also probably more fuel efficient, than those in the rest of the nation.

New Jersey, Rhode Island, and Connecticut have said they intend to start following California's rules instead of the federal government's. New York, Massachusetts, Vermont, and Maine already do so. Other states are also considering doing so in order to comply with federal ozone emission regulations.

Regulation's Cost

"It would be a logistical and engineering challenge, and a costly problem to make different vehicles for different states," said Dave Barthmuss, a spokesman for General Motors. "It is more cost effective for us to have one set of emissions everywhere."

The California plan would require auto manufacturers to reduce global warming emissions from their new vehicles by 29.2 percent over the next decade, phasing in from the 2009 to the 2015 model years. The California Air Resources Board has estimated that the cost for these changes would run around $1,047 per vehicle.

The California regulators are adamant that the plan is not a fuel economy measure because the federal government has authority over that issue.

THINK STRATEGICALLY

Use this proposed legislation to explain how government functions and its impact on business. How does this affect marketing?

Online Action!

Go to *marketingessentials.glencoe.com/6/case* to find an activity on ethics, consumption, and consumerism.

- The Division of Planning and Information helps consumers get information. There are help lines where consumers can report identity theft and other fraud-related complaints.

Bureau of Competition

The FTC's antitrust responsibilities involve prevention of anti-competitive mergers and business practices. Some of the acts that the bureau enforces include the following:

- The Federal Trade Commission Act, which prohibits unfair methods of competition.
- The Sherman Antitrust Act (1890), which outlawed all contracts and agreements that would limit trade or competition in interstate commerce. It also prevents one company from undercharging for an item or service in order to put the competition out of business. This practice is known as predatory pricing.
- The Clayton Antitrust Act (1914), which reduced loopholes in the Sherman Antitrust Act and covered mergers and acquisitions.
- The Hart-Scott-Rodino Amendment to the Clayton Act (1976), which requires companies to notify antitrust agencies before planning a merger.
- The Robinson-Patman Act (1936), which prohibits price discrimination.

Distribution laws also fall under the FTC's jurisdiction. Several states have similar laws, which may be challenged in the future, especially with the growth of the Internet and e-commerce.

Another example of distribution law is the sale of tobacco products to minors. It is illegal to sell tobacco products or distribute samples to underage customers. On July 1, 2004, a new state law went into effect that requires California retailers to obtain a state license to sell tobacco products. Retailers that do not comply are subject to fines and may even be arrested.

MARKET TECH

Item Pricing

New technology now makes it possible for digital bar code scanners to apply an adhesive price sticker to a product at the point-of-purchase station. This technology makes it possible for retailers to give consumers the proper price label by unit for each product they buy, no matter how small.

Legal Roots for Technology

Several large chains, such as Wal-Mart and Home Depot, have gotten into legal tangles in the past few years over the lack of consistent unit price labeling for all items on their shelves.

In Wal-Mart's case, Massachusetts resident Colman Herman won a multimillion-dollar legal settlement in a class-action suit with Wal-Mart Corp. over the chain's alleged failure to comply with the state's item-pricing regulation. The settlement agreement says Wal-Mart will spend $5.6 million over the next three years to bring its Massachusetts stores into compliance with the regulation.

The legal victory in the Wal-Mart case and the ensuing outcry from retailers about the high costs associated with item pricing prompted revisions to the original regulation that forced retailers to label items on the shelves. Retailers are now allowed to stop marking prices on individual items if they install the new bar code scanners. Then, the choice is the consumers'.

THINK LIKE A MARKETER

In what way did technology help to change the item-pricing regulation?

Online Action!

Go to *marketingessentials.glencoe.com/6/tech* to find an activity on ethics and technology.

Bureau of Economics

The Bureau of Economics studies the impact of its actions on consumers and reports its findings to Congress, to the executive branch, and to the public. Its reports cover antitrust, consumer protection, and regulation. In certain instances, it may also provide information on pending bills to help policy makers in the legislative branch.

Monitor of Our Economy

To ensure economic stability of the United States, the government monitors our economy and controls our monetary supply through the Federal Reserve System. This is our nation's central bank. When the Federal Reserve Board of Governors thinks that the economy is moving too fast or too slowly, it reacts to correct the problem. When prices are going up too fast, the board may increase interest rates to slow economic activity. Higher interest rates generally make it more difficult to borrow money and therefore discourage expansion by businesses.

Business Supporter

The role of the Small Business Administration (SBA) is to support business and encourage our free enterprise system. The SBA provides counseling and educational materials to prospective business owners. Additional support comes in the form of loan guarantees for some business owners who cannot get conventional loans.

International Issues

Foreign governments may not provide the legal protection or the framework necessary to ensure that business operations are conducted in a safe and secure manner. Thus, it is important to analyze U.S. government's role in promoting free enterprise and its ability to enforce those principles in the context of international business. For example, limited intellectual property protection in China and a challenging legal system make it a tough place for U.S. companies to do business.

6.1 AFTER YOU READ

Reviewing Key Terms and Concepts

1. How does the role of government influence marketing?
2. Name some of the responsibilities and functions of the Food and Drug Administration.
3. What are the three bureaus of the Federal Trade Commission?

Integrating Academic Skills

Math

4. The Truth in Lending legislation requires banks and other lending institutions to clearly disclose their annual interest rates. If the monthly interest rate on an outstanding credit card is 1.5 percent, what is the annual interest rate?

Government and Civics

5. Research the current status of the country-of-origin labeling (COOL) legislation and write a one-page report on it.

Check your answers at *marketingessentials.glencoe.com/6/read*

SECTION 6.2

Social Responsibility and Ethics

OBJECTIVES

- Provide examples of business's social responsibilities
- Explain the concept of business ethics
- Apply guidelines for ethical behavior

KEY TERMS

- flextime
- telecommuting
- Ad Council
- green marketing
- ethics
- Better Business Bureau
- price gouging
- whistle-blowing

READ and STUDY

BEFORE YOU READ

Predict Why do you think it is a good idea for companies to be civic-minded and ethical?

THE MAIN IDEA

Socially responsible businesses see their role extending into community issues. Civic-minded companies are concerned with their workers, customers, communities, and the environment. Business ethics are part of social responsibility and play a role in decisions made by businesses that affect the same stakeholders.

STUDY ORGANIZER

As you read, jot down an outline of the concept of social responsibility, ethics in business, and the guidelines for ethical behavior.

Connect List two business practices that demonstrate social responsibility and ethics.

Business and Social Responsibility

Social responsibility and ethics have become important business topics as trust has deteriorated due to corporate scandals. Corporate scandals and unethical behavior have a very negative effect on consumer confidence and the image of a company. It is essential to see the role of business in society not only as a provider of goods and services but also as an integral part of the society at large.

Anyone can choose to go into business in a free enterprise system, but everyone must abide by local, state, and federal laws that apply to businesses. Some of those laws encourage fair business practices, while others protect consumers, workers, investors, and the environment.

Apart from following the law, should businesses have any further social responsibility? Some businesses feel they should. They believe their role in society includes actions affecting employees, consumers, the communities in which they operate, and the environment. These civic-minded businesses set themselves apart from others on the basis of management's vision of their role in the workplace, marketplace, community, and environment.

In the Workplace

Many businesses recognize their employees' needs outside the workplace and try to accommodate them. In so doing, they create a user-friendly workplace environment. Some employee benefits offered by socially responsible companies include flextime, telecommuting, extended family leave, on-site child care, health care benefits, and time off with pay.

Flextime

Flextime allows workers to choose their work hours. Possible arrangements include early start/early finish (e.g. 7 A.M.–3 P.M.), late start/late finish (e.g. 10 A.M.–6 P.M.), and even four-day workweeks (often four 9- or 10-hour days followed by a three-day weekend).

Telecommuting

Telecommuting involves working at home, usually on a computer. Completed jobs are transmitted by e-mail or mail-in disk. For working parents this benefit provides some flexibility in their child care arrangements. For the company, it helps reduce office space requirements. Because telecommuting employees do not have to travel to work, this arrangement is also good for the environment.

Extended Family Leave

Some companies offer employees family leave without pay beyond the time required by the Family and Medical Leave Act. In some professions and under some employee contracts, the time off could be for as long as one year. Such a policy allows companies to retain valued employees who are encouraged to stay with a company that allows such flexibility.

On-Site Child Care

On-site child care is a benefit that has grown in popularity with the increase in two-income families. Some employers have expanded it to include on-site schools and on-site clinics for children who are ill. Any form of the benefit tends to reduce employee absenteeism and employee turnover.

Health Care Benefits

With rising health costs, health care insurance paid for by employers is a major employee benefit. Some health care benefits cover employees and their dependents and even extend into retirement. Employee health care is often a major issue during contract negotiations with employee unions.

Time Off With Pay

Time off with pay includes vacations, sick days, and personal days. Paid vacations are generally part of an employee's contract. The time allotted for the paid vacation is generally based on the length of time an employee has been with the company.

In the Marketplace

Consumers are the focal point of a company that follows the marketing concept. Such businesses are concerned about consumers' perceptions of a company, as well as issues that impact consumers.

Providing Information

Socially responsible companies cooperate with the government and consumer groups to provide important information to consumers. For example, the National Consumers League and the Food and Drug Administration created a public education campaign about the safe and proper use of over-the-counter pain relievers.

The **Ad Council** is a nonprofit organization that helps produce public service advertising campaigns for government agencies and other qualifying groups.

Employing Self-Censorship

In the broadcast industry, standards are established by the Federal Communications Commission (FCC). Beyond those regulations, network executives establish their own policies for self-regulation. For example, many broadcast networks (CBS, ABC, NBC, Fox) and cable channels (like CNN and MTV) have no-advocacy policies. Each station reviews commercials that might be considered controversial. If the commercial is not socially acceptable, is inaccurate, or poses a legal liability, it is rejected.

Anything that is broadcast comes under FCC scrutiny. This includes radio as well.

Responding to Consumer Concerns

Socially responsible companies look for ways to respond to consumers' concerns. As an example, a United States government report identified obesity as a major consumer problem. That prompted many companies to seek solutions.

In the Community

Businesses in the United States have many means of providing community support. Multinational companies view their role in the global community as well.

Local Businesses

Socially responsible local businesses support community efforts. You may know of a local business that funds a Little League team or that sponsors a holiday food drive for the needy. Local companies will act as drop-off

• McDONALD'S and FITNESS McDonald's is making a very publicized effort to offer healthier menus at its fast-food restaurants.

Why do you think the company logo is so small in this ad?

• PETROLEUM ADDRESSES THE ISSUES
British Petroleum is one of the largest energy companies in the world. They are working to meet the challenges of balancing the world's growing demand for energy with the need for a cleaner environment.

How does BP handle this issue and the competition from alternative energy?

centers for a Community Food Bank or for the Marine Corps Toys for Tots Program.

Large Companies

Many large companies have guidelines and initiatives that clearly define how they see their role in supporting community causes. Ben & Jerry's, the ice cream manufacturer, donates 7.5 percent of its pretax earnings to the disadvantaged and the needy. The company also contributes to groups that strive for social change and environmental protection.

Paul Newman started his own company, Newman's Own. Newman's Own donates its profits and royalties after taxes to educational and charitable causes.

International Businesses

The United Nations has a Division of Economic and Social Affairs. An outgrowth of that division is the World Business Council for Sustainable Development (WBCSD), which is a coalition of international companies with a mission "to provide business leadership as a catalyst for change toward sustainable development, and to promote the role of eco-efficiency, innovation, and corporate social responsibility." Some international companies that are members of the WBCSD include Time Warner, AT&T, Bayer, BP, Coca-Cola, Unilever, Dow Chemical, and Shell.

In the Environment

Socially responsible companies are concerned about our environment and have programs to work toward saving the earth for future generations. Two major issues involve cleaner fuel and green marketing.

Cleaner Fuel

Alternatives to the traditional transportation fuels of gasoline and diesel fuel are currently being developed. Some vehicle fuels, because

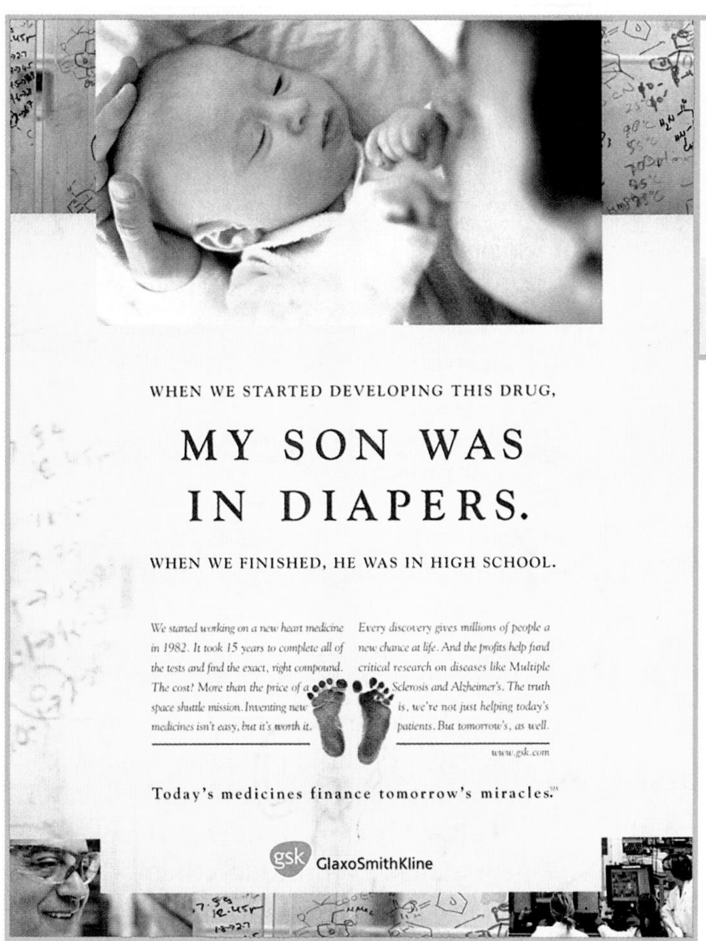

•PRICE GOUGING Pharmaceutical companies have been accused of price gouging for prescription drugs. To counter those attacks, GlaxoSmithKline ran this ad. The company claims the high prices reflect the upfront cost in the development of life-saving drugs.

What do you think? Are pharmaceutical companies price gouging?

of physical or chemical properties, create less pollution than do today's gasolines. These are called clean fuels. They include certain types of alcohol, electricity, natural gas, and propane.

Green Marketing

Consumer concern over the environment is increasing, and marketers are paying attention. The growing importance of ecological issues has brought about green marketing. In **green marketing**, companies make an effort to produce and promote environmentally safe products. Such products are often labeled as ozone-safe, recyclable, environmentally friendly, or biodegradable. Green marketing strategies have become an increasingly important way for companies to build consumer loyalty. A significant number of consumers are willing to pay more for products that are environmentally friendly.

Business Ethics

A major aspect of social responsibility is business ethics. **Ethics** are guidelines for good behavior. Ethical behavior is based on knowing the difference between right and wrong—and doing what is right. Ethical behavior is truthful and fair and takes into account the well-being of everyone. There is often a fine line between legal issues and ethical issues, especially when cultural differences are involved. Ethical businesses follow the laws established for their operations.

Ethics and Consumerism

Consumerism involves the relationship of marketing to those who buy a company's goods or services. Consumerism is the societal effort to protect consumer rights by putting legal, moral, and economic pressure on business. Individual consumers, consumer groups, government, and socially responsible business leaders share this effort.

The greatest growth in consumerism took place from the early 1960s until about 1980. It involved all areas of marketing. President John F. Kennedy's Consumer Bill of Rights dominated the beginning of this consumer period. It stated that consumers have four basic rights:

- To be informed and protected against fraud, deceit, and misleading statements, and to be educated in the wise use of financial resources
- To be protected from unsafe products
- To have a choice of goods and services
- To have a voice in product and marketing decisions made by government and business

Ethics in Marketing

Consumerism and corporate scandals have prompted businesses to address the many ethical issues and topics that involve marketing in general, as well as specific functions and activities. It is important to study ethics because you may be faced with ethical dilemmas as an employee or business owner. Whether you choose the right course of action may affect your career and company. Ethical principles are important in business because they reflect the management of the company and the trust between a company and its stakeholders.

Self-Regulation

Ethical companies are proactive. They join organizations that help to create an ethical business environment. The **Better Business Bureau** (BBB), established in 1912, is one of the oldest nonprofit organizations to set up self-regulation among businesses. To be a member of the BBB, a business must "agree to follow the highest principles of business ethics and voluntary self-regulation, and have a proven record of marketplace honesty and integrity." The BBB has a strict Code of Advertising as well as one for online businesses that defines what is acceptable and not acceptable with regard to truth in advertising.

Another comprehensive guide for marketing ethics is the Code of Ethics adopted by the American Marketing Association (AMA). Ethical companies subscribe to the AMA's Code of Ethics which is a guideline for ethical professional conduct. Its basic rule is "not knowingly to do harm," and it includes "all relevant publics: customers, organizations, and society." The Code addresses honesty and fairness, rights and duties in all areas of marketing, and organizational relationships. Let's look at two examples of how ethical businesses comply with the AMA's Code of Ethics in the areas of marketing exchange and product development.

- **Marketing exchange** "products and services offered are safe and fit for their intended uses." In 2002, General Mills recalled 4,080 cans of Old El Paso Traditional Variety Refried Beans in five states. They did so because they discovered that one batch of those products may have been underprocessed and could have contained bacteria that would make people sick. Even though there were no reports of illness, General Mills acted ethically and removed those products from retailers' shelves.

- **Product Development and Management** "disclosure of all substantial risks associated with product or service usage." Some people are highly allergic to certain products, especially nuts. As a result, food companies have been diligent in product labeling that provides allergy warnings. For example, the Morning Start brand Apple Crisp breakfast bar includes the following warning on its packages: "Allergy Information: This product is manufactured in a facility that uses peanuts and other nuts and seeds."

Ethical Issues Related to Marketing Functions

Ethical issues can always arise when doing business. Let us look at a few ethical issues that involve specific marketing functions, such as pricing, distribution, promotion, management of marketing information, and selling.

Price gouging is not covered in the AMA's Code of Ethics; however, it is a major concern in the pharmaceutical industry, as well as when a natural disaster creates a need for products such as bottled water or flashlights. **Price gouging** is pricing products unreasonably high when the need is great or when consumers do not have other choices.

In the pharmaceutical industry, patented prescription drugs are granted monopoly status for a period of time. How companies price their patented product during that time is an area of dispute. Pharmaceutical companies argue that high prices are due to the time and money spent on research and development to come up with the medicine. Many consumer groups think price gouging exists when consumers must pay extraordinarily high prices for drugs they need to stay alive.

Some states have laws that govern price gouging during disasters, like hurricanes or tornadoes. Products in high demand, such as hotel rooms, bottled water, flashlights, food, and fuel, are often priced higher due to the unusual demand created by the catastrophe.

Management of marketing information involves issues of privacy. Industries that maintain customer databases containing your personal information have a responsibility to keep that information private. Banking, finance companies, medical practices, marketing research companies, and any other industry that collects personal data must not share that information with anyone unless you give them permission to do so. For years, it was unethical; now, it is also against the law.

Product research and marketing research must report findings honestly by disclosing all the facts involved in the research design and results.

Selling practices that come under scrutiny because of ethical issues often involve bribes,

• **PLAYING a SOCIAL ROLE** In this ad Sodexho USA, the leading food and facilities management company, is presenting its positive role in society.

Do the pictures in this ad convey yet another message?

A MATTER OF ETHICS

Gouging or Marketing Tactics?

In June 2004, an investigation revealed price gouging affecting a federally funded program called the Special Supplemental Nutrition Program for Women, Infants, and Children (WIC). This program provides government vouchers to needy families to buy specific foods that meet the program's nutritional guidelines.

Higher Prices

Specialty WIC stores have been pricing their products 10 to 20 percent higher than regular supermarkets have priced them. Some WIC stores sent sales representatives to hospitals to sign up new mothers as customers. At that time, gifts could be offered such as baby strollers, diapers, and baby clothes, as well as free transportation.

THINKING ETHICALLY

Should the government step in to regulate WIC stores, or would that go against the principles of the free enterprise system?

@ Online Action!

Go to *marketingessentials.glencoe.com/6/ethics* to find a research activity on ethics and marketing.

kickbacks, favors, and high-pressure tactics used to close a sale. Cultural differences complicate those issues.

For example, in some Asian countries, businesspeople expect to receive a gift as part of customary practice. The same gift given in the United States might be considered a bribe and thus be illegal.

Another issue involving bribes and kickbacks is defining what they are. Is taking a client out to dinner a bribe? Is giving a customer a free gift for buying a product considered a kickback? Some companies avoid these ethical issues by imposing strict rules against offering any type of gift to customers. Their buyers are also not permitted to accept any gifts, no matter how inexpensive they are.

High-pressure selling tactics and failure to follow through on promises made to close a sale are examples of unethical selling practices. One of the reasons for this unethical behavior can be undue pressure to meet sales quotas established by high-level management. Sales representatives feel pressured to produce, so they hound customers and make promises they cannot keep, just to make a sale.

Managerial and Personnel Issues

Management ultimately makes the decisions about major ethical issues that confront a business. From the top level right on down to the supervisory level, managers must take responsibility for establishing and creating a role model for ethical practices within a firm. Their decisions impact how customers view the company, as well.

Proper Accounting and Reporting

The Sarbanes-Oxley Act of 2002 was passed in response to the corporate scandals that involved misuse of company funds and unethical corporate governance. Accounting and proper reporting of a corporation's financial situation are addressed by this new legislation. Company executives and their consulting firms can be held accountable for misinformation.

Whistle-Blowing

Provisions in the Sarbanes-Oxley Act of 2002, as well as many other laws involving management and personnel issues, include whistle-blowing protection. **Whistle-blowing** involves reporting an illegal action of one's employer. If you discovered that financial records were being altered in order to cover up extravagant personal purchases made by the top executives, would you report it? If you did, you would be a whistle-blower. If you got fired for your whistle-blowing, you would have recourse under several federal laws governing whistle-blowing.

Making a decision to be a whistle-blower involves personal ethics. Employees and managers who face such decisions find it easier to report offenses when a company has specific guidelines for making ethical decisions and a way to report offenses.

Guidelines for Ethical Behavior

Companies with an interest in ethical business behavior have or are developing guidelines to help employees make ethical decisions. It is important to remember that people make the decisions and that business ethics are closely related to personal ethics for that reason.

To make the right ethical choices, employees at all levels should follow a decision-making process that includes the following:

1. Get the facts.
2. Identify all parties concerned.
3. Think of all your alternatives.
4. Evaluate your alternatives by asking yourself the following questions:
   - Is it in compliance with the law?
   - Does it go against company policy?
   - How does it affect everyone involved?
   - Is it right, fair, and honest?
   - Will it build good will for the company?
   - Am I comfortable with it? Can I live with my decision?
   - How will it hold up to public scrutiny?

6.2 AFTER YOU READ

Reviewing Key Terms and Concepts

1. Name six employee benefits that demonstrate social responsibility in the workplace.
2. What can businesses do in the marketplace to demonstrate social responsibility?
3. What things can a local business do to support the community?

Integrating Academic Skills

Math

4. If an employee took a $1.79 candy bar from her employer every day and worked five days a week for 50 weeks of the year, how much would that pilfering cost the company? If 20 employees did the same thing, how would that affect the company's profits?

Civics and Government

5. Research the legal and ethical issues about what can and cannot be said when advertising and promoting products. Prepare a one-page written report on your findings.

Check your answers at *marketingessentials.glencoe.com/6/read*

CAREERS IN MARKETING

KARL HAMPE
DIRECTOR, LITIGATION & INVESTIGATIVE SERVICES
BDO SEIDMAN, LLP

? What do you do at work?
I identify new opportunities to provide accounting and economic consulting services to assist attorneys involved in complex business litigation. I also manage large-scale engagements and provide testimony on specialized topics relating to the accounting and economic aspects of litigation.

? What skills are most important to you?
Listening and writing skills are the foundation of the ability to identify new opportunities, secure new business, and deliver high quality work. Both listening and writing skills require ongoing sharpening and, frankly, humility—because everyone needs to recognize that he or she can always improve in these areas. Listening and writing skills are also catalysts for creative and critical thinking, which enables us to provide innovative responses to complex problems in litigation matters.

? What is your key to success?
Exceed the client's expectations while adhering to strict integrity. To do that, you must understand the client's expectations, develop a response that is creative, accurate, well presented, and delivered on time, and then make sure to take credit for a job well done.

Aptitudes, Abilities, and Skills

Writing, communication, and listening skills are essential in this career

Education and Training

Degrees in business, communication, and psychology, with at least some focus on the liberal arts.

Career Path

Most litigation and investigative specialists have a background in law and in business.

THINKING CRITICALLY

What are some of the benefits of identifying a mentor in your chosen field and working to emulate that person's skills?

@ Online Action!

Go to *marketingessentials.glencoe.com/6/careers* to find a career-related activity.

CHAPTER 6 REVIEW

FOCUS on KEY POINTS

SECTION 6.1

- The government plays a critical role in enforcing the free enterprise system and providing for the health, safety, and welfare of its citizens. The three branches of the U.S. government are the executive, legislative, and judicial branches. The Food and Drug Administration (FDA) and the Consumer Product Safety Commission (CPSC) are two federal agencies that protect consumers. Employment protection at the federal level includes the Equal Employment Opportunity Commission (EEOC) and the Occupational Safety and Health Administration (OSHA). The Securities and Exchange Commission (SEC) protects investors and the Environmental Protection Agency (EPA) protects the environment. The Federal Trade Commission (FTC) has the responsibility of enforcing the principles of a free enterprise system and protecting consumers from unfair or deceptive business practices.

SECTION 6.2

- Socially responsible businesses have policies and programs that address issues in the workplace, marketplace, community, and environment. Business ethics are guidelines for good behavior. Ethical businesses are community-conscious.

REVIEW VOCABULARY

For each of the following terms, define its meaning or explain its function in one sentence.

1. Food and Drug Administration (FDA) (p. 126)
2. Consumer Product Safety Commission (CPSC) (p. 126)
3. Equal Employment Opportunity Commission (EEOC) (p. 128)
4. Occupational Safety and Health Administration (OSHA) (p. 128)
5. Securities and Exchange Commission (SEC) (p. 128)
6. Environmental Protection Agency (EPA) (p. 129)
7. Federal Trade Commission (FTC) (p. 129)
8. flextime (p. 134)
9. telecommuting (p. 134)
10. Ad Council (p. 135)
11. green marketing (p. 137)
12. ethics (p. 137)
13. Better Business Bureau (BBB) (p. 138)
14. price gouging (p. 139)
15. whistle-blowing (p. 140)

REVIEW FACTS and IDEAS

16. Explain the role of government in a free enterprise system. (6.1)
17. How is the U.S. government structured? (6.1)
18. Name the federal regulatory agencies that have been established to protect consumers, workers, investors, and the environment, as well as the one that enforces the free enterprise system. (6.1)
19. What are business ethics, and how are they related to the law? (6.2)
20. Provide examples of ethical issues in marketing, management, and personnel. (6.2)

CHAPTER 6 REVIEW

BUILD SKILLS

21. **Workplace Skills**

Writing Write a letter to the appropriate federal regulatory agency to complain about an unfair business practice, an ethical issue, or another topic of concern to you, such as identity theft.

22. **Technology Applications**

Examining the Benefits of Recycling Visit the Web site for the Environmental Protection Agency and conduct additional research to examine the benefits of recycling on the environment. Work in groups to create a promotional plan to educate the public about those benefits. Use presentation software to share your promotional plan and the sources you used with classmates.

23. **Math Practice**

The Price of Recycling If the local recycling plant pays $.06 per pound for aluminum cans, how many pounds of cans would it take to get $10?

DEVELOP CRITICAL THINKING

24. **Considering the Use of a Law Degree**

Review this chapter's main points. Research the type of courses a law student would take to study for a law degree or J.D. (juris doctor). An efficient way to perform this research is to key the words *juris doctor courses* on an Internet search engine. Be sure to compare several programs and course listings before forming an opinion about which courses are typically required. From your research and your review, make a list of all the ways a law degree could be useful for business and marketing employment. Compare your list with your classmates'.

25. **Summarizing Key Concepts**

Summarize an article that demonstrates any of the key concepts in this chapter. In the summary, identify the specific key concepts in parenthesis. Use business publications, such as *BusinessWeek, Fortune, Forbes,* and *Nation's Business,* to find an applicable article.

APPLY CONCEPTS

26. Investigating the Price for Medicine

Many U.S. citizens are visiting Canada to buy their prescription drugs at greatly reduced prices. Investigate the issues surrounding the prices of prescription drugs in the United States. Present all sides of the issue—the consumer's side, the pharmaceutical firm's side, and the role of government.

Activity Use word processing to prepare a three-page written report on this issue.

27. Developing a Socially Responsible Company

Work in groups to research the code of ethics established by organizations such as the BBB and AMA, as well as by socially responsible businesses. Use those examples to develop a code of ethics for your school store, a local business, or a hypothetical business. Begin with a paragraph on the importance of ethics in business. Include ethical issues and scenarios to help guide employees into taking the ethical course of action.

Activity Prepare your code of ethics in writing for publication. Share your work with classmates in an oral presentation.

NET SAVVY

28. Product Recalls

Visit the Consumer Product Safety Commission Web site. List and explain five current product recalls from that Web site.

THE DECA CONNECTION

Role Play: Legal and Ethical Issues

Situation You are to assume the role of an experienced sales associate for a men's clothing store. You have been assigned the duty of orienting a new sales associate (judge) about the types of clothing the store carries and the importance of reading the labels attached to them. The new sales associate (judge) wonders why clothing labels are so important.

Activity You are to explain to the new sales associate (judge) the importance of the care labels and fiber content labels in the garments that your store sells.

Evaluation You will be evaluated on how well you meet the following performance indicators:

- Describe the nature of selling regulations
- Explain business ethics in selling
- Determine the relationship between government and business
- Explain the role of business in society
- Orient new employees

@ Online Action!

For more information and DECA Prep practice, go to *marketingessentials.glencoe.com/6/DECA*

MARKETING INTERNSHIP

A SIMULATED DECA CIVIC CONSCIOUSNESS PROJECT EVENT

Write a Proposal for a Civic-Minded Project

BASIC BACKGROUND

Your firm is a member of the American Association of Advertising Agencies. One of your firm's responsibilities as a member is to donate its time and resources to create public service ads when assigned them by the Ad Council. Now your firm would like to submit its own idea to the Ad Council for a public service ad on behalf of a government agency or a nonprofit organization.

Marketing for Social Change As part of the initiative, your firm is asking every employee to submit proposals for consideration by management. According to the Ad Council, "The objectives of these ads are education and awareness of significant social issues in an effort to change the public's attitudes and behaviors and stimulate positive social change."

YOUR OBJECTIVE

Your objective is to complete a proposal for a project that would meet the Ad Council's criteria and the criteria of the firm's civic-minded initiative. The firm wants its public service ads to be just as well planned and interesting as its work for a paying customer. Your idea will need a design element as well as an effective message.

ASSIGNMENT AND STRATEGY

- **Conduct research** Research the Ad Council. Learn more about its purpose, mission, and past campaigns. Review the acceptable topics, which include educational issues and community health and safety. Review possible clients. They may be government agencies or nonprofit organizations.

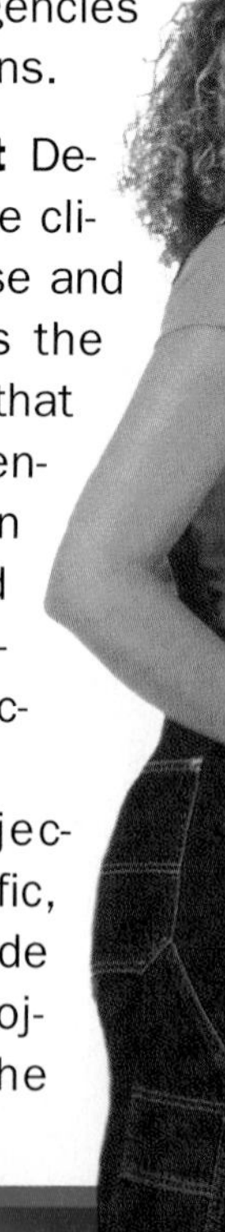

- **Develop your concept** Develop a plan to help the client. Include the purpose and objectives, as well as the rationale for selecting that particular topic and beneficiary. Explain the main purpose of the proposed project and specific objectives you expect to accomplish.

  Be sure your objectives are simple, specific, and measurable. Include a time line for the project, as well as all the organizational details required for its completion. Explain how the project will be evaluated.

- **What your project should include** Describe the project that you are proposing and its potential benefits. Include samples of proposed marketing materials. For example, include a sample advertisement, complete with headline, illustration(s), and a slogan, or a Web page design and site map of what would be included on a Web site. Conclude with a persuasive argument why the firm should select your proposal as its submission to the Ad Council.

YOUR REPORT

Use a word processing program and presentation software to prepare a double-spaced report and an oral presentation for your supervisors. See a suggested outline and key evaluation points at *marketingessentials.glencoe.com/internship*

BUILD YOUR PORTFOLIO

Option 1 Internship Report Once you have completed your Marketing Internship project and presentation, include your written report and a few printouts of key slides from your oral presentation in your Marketing Portfolio.

Option 2 Promoting Free Enterprise Evaluate advertisements by states or local areas that attempt to attract businesses and/or tourists. Research other ways local communities try to promote economic growth, such as hosting golf tournaments or a state fair. Select a state or community that needs economic help. Then design a marketing strategy around specific objectives, including ways to evaluate the effectiveness of the plan. See a suggested outline and key evaluation points at *marketingessentials.glencoe.com/portfolio*

@ Online Action!

Go to *marketingessentials.glencoe.com/Unit/3/DECA* to review public service concepts that relate to DECA events.

UNIT 4 Skills for

In this unit you will find

OCCUPY THE EXECUTIVE SUITE.

Advertise locally in the nation's best business magazines in your priority markets with one simple media buy exclusively through MNI. In 48 top local markets, the MNI Executive Network delivers an exclusive group of business leaders who invest for success. If you want your message to reach business decision-makers, call your MNI representative or Robert Reif, National Ad Director at 877.ASK.4MNI.

LOCAL ADS. NATIONAL MAGS.

www.mni.com

Marketing

Marketing Plan

ANALYZE THE AD

One of the goals of marketing is getting a message to a specific audience. Media Networks, Inc. sells ad space in business magazines. What does it promise?

Market Talk Ad placement firms specialize in newspaper, magazine, broadcast, or Internet advertising. They can advise clients on the best places to feature their messages and the most efficient way to spend their advertising budgets.

Think and Write Just like communication between people, advertising is more effective if it says exactly what it means. List three ways Media Networks, Inc. gets its message across to potential customers.

Online Action! Go to *marketingessentials.glencoe.com/u4/ad* for an extended activity.

Functions of Marketing

- Marketing-Information Management
- Financing
- Pricing
- Promotion
- Product/Service Management
- Distribution
- Selling

Foundations

- Professional Development
- Economics
- Business, Management, Entrepreneurship
- Communication, Interpersonal Skills

Technology • Academic Concepts

1 **ANALYSIS**
- SWOT
- Economic
- Socio-Cultural
- Technological
- Competitive

2 **STRATEGY**
- Promotion
- Place
- Price
- Product

3 **IMPLEMENTATION**
- Organization
- Management
- Staffing

4 **BUDGET**
- Cost of Sales
- Cost of Promotion
- Incomes and Expenses

5 **CONTROL**
- Evaluation
- Performance Measures
- Performance Analysis

In this unit

Foundations of Marketing

- Communication, Interpersonal Skills
- Professional Development
- Business, Management, Entrepreneurship

CHAPTER 7
Basic Math Skills

Chapter Objectives

After reading this chapter, you should be able to:

- Write numbers in words, using commas and hyphens correctly
- Understand fractions
- Perform basic math operations with decimal numbers and round answers
- Convert fractions to decimal equivalents
- Use a calculator to solve math problems
- Convert percentages to decimals and decimals to percentages
- Read graphs used to present mathematical data

GUIDE TO THE PHOTO

Market Talk Everyday tasks, even figuring out the odds of winning a prize at a fair, relate to math concepts. Marketers use basic math skills in every phase of marketing, including purchasing, advertising and promotion, distribution, pricing, selling, entrepreneurship, and finance.

Quick Think If you are working with a calculator, what is the point of estimating the answer to a math problem?

 THE  CONNECTION

Performance indicators represent key skills and knowledge. Relating them to the concepts explained in this chapter is your key to success in DECA events. Keep this in mind as you read this chapter and write some notes each time you encounter material that helps you master a key concept.

These acronyms represent DECA events that involve knowledge of concepts in this chapter.

AAAL	**FMAL**	**MMS***	**TMDM***
AAML*	**FMDM***	**QSRM***	**TSE***
ADC*	**FMML***	**RMAL**	**VPM**
BSM	**FSRM***	**RMML***	
EMDM*	**HMDM***	**SMDM***	

In all these DECA events you should be able to follow these performance indicators:

- Calculate net sales
- Interpret descriptive statistics for marketing decision making
- Calculate media costs
- Calculate miscellaneous charges

All the events with an asterisk (*) also include these performance indicators:

- Calculate financial ratios
- Forecast sales
- Determine discounts and allowances that can be used to adjust base prices
- Analyze cost/benefits of company participation in community activities
- Prepare a promotional budget
- Analyze sales reports
- Analyze operating results in relation to budget/industry

DECA PREP

Check your understanding of DECA performance indicators with the DECA activity in this chapter's review. For more information and DECA Prep practice, go to *marketingessentials.glencoe.com/7/DECA*

SECTION 7.1

Math Fundamentals

OBJECTIVES

- Write numbers in words, using commas and hyphens correctly
- Understand fractions
- Perform basic math operations with decimal numbers and round answers
- Convert fractions to decimal equivalents

KEY TERMS

- digit
- fractions
- numerator
- denominator
- mixed number
- decimal number

BEFORE YOU READ

Predict Why do you think math skills relate to the study of marketing?

THE MAIN IDEA

Virtually every job in marketing and business requires a good understanding of math fundamentals; the sharper your math skills, the more successful you will be.

STUDY ORGANIZER

Use a chart like the one below to write down examples of rounding from three decimal places to the nearest tenth, converting a fraction to a decimal, and calculating the area of a rectangular room.

Rounding From Three Decimal Places to the Nearest Tenth	Converting a Fraction to a Decimal	Calculating the Area of a Rectangular Room
4.888 = 4.9		

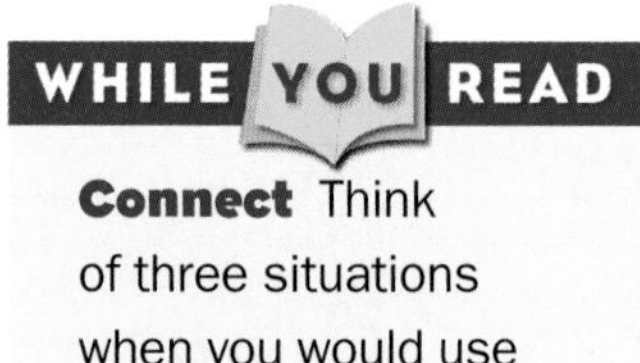

Connect Think of three situations when you would use fractions.

Writing Whole Numbers

A company needs to know exactly how many of each product remains in its warehouse, so it takes inventory. When taking inventory, count using whole numbers.

The numbering system we use is composed of ten basic symbols called digits: 0, 1, 2, 3, 4, 5, 6, 7, 8, and 9. Each **digit** represents a number and can be combined to represent larger numbers, such as 14; 215; 7,901; and 36,852.

These numbers are all whole numbers because they can be written without fractions or decimals. Each digit in a whole number represents *how many* of something. The digit on the far right represents the number of ones. The next digit to the left represents the number of tens. So, in the number 25, there are five ones and two tens.

Knowing the place name for each digit and for groups of digits is necessary for reading numbers and writing them in words. You use this skill, for example, when you write a check. The check format requires that amounts be written in both figures and words. Follow these five steps when you read whole numbers or write them in words:

1. Separate the number into groups of three digits: units, thousands, and millions. Very large numbers may include groups of digits for billions, trillions, and so on.

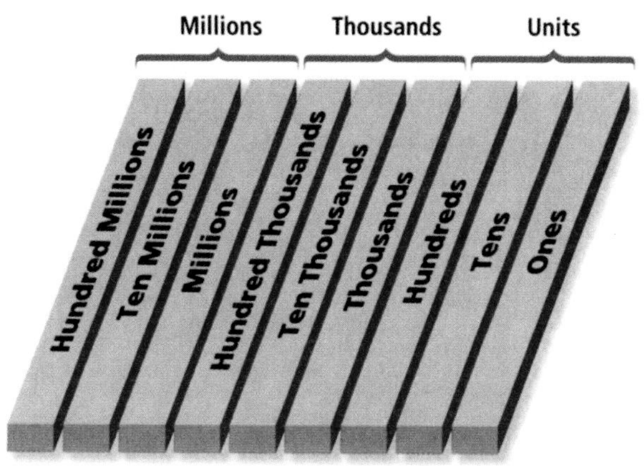

2. Separate the groups with commas.

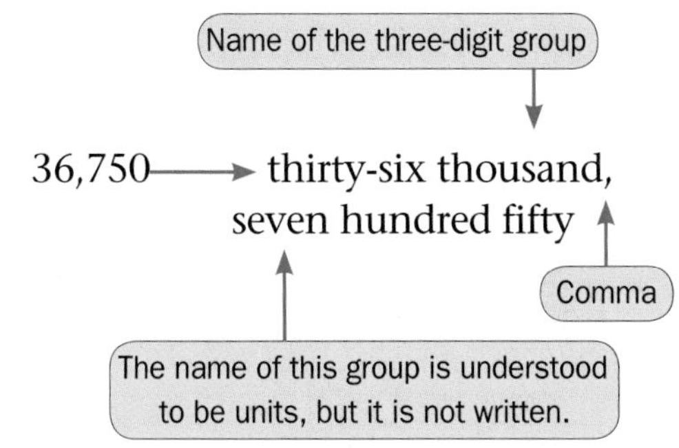

3. When writing the names of whole numbers, never use the word *and.*

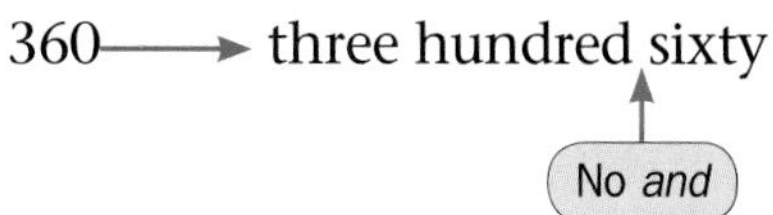

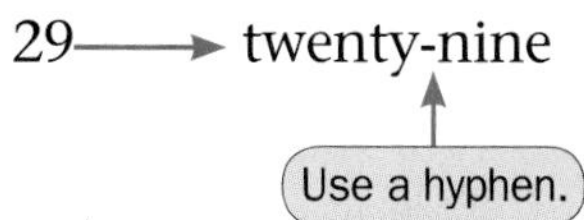

4. Use hyphens in numbers less than 100 that are written as two words.

29 → twenty-nine

Use a hyphen.

5. When a three-digit group is made up of only zeros, do not write the name of the group.

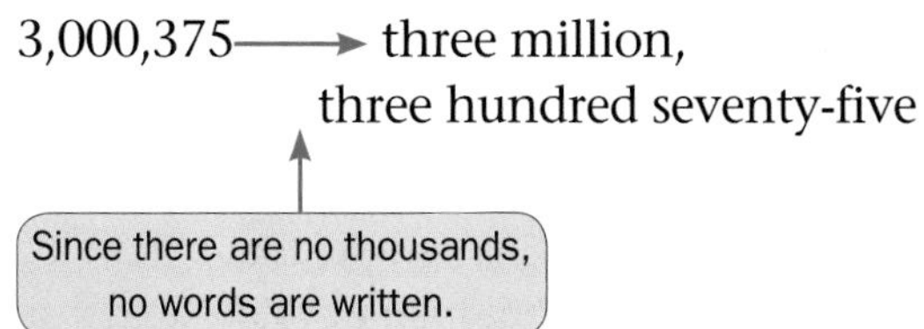

Fractions

The marketing research department of a soap company did a survey and found that two-thirds of the people who bought its new dish detergent thought it did a better job than the competition. This means that, for every three people surveyed, two were pleased with the new product, and one was not. Many jobs in business, especially in marketing, require a good understanding of fractions.

Fractions are numbers used to describe or compare parts of a whole. The top number, the **numerator**, represents the number of parts being considered. The bottom number, the **denominator**, represents how many parts in a whole. For example, the shaded area in the rectangle below is 3⁄5 (three-fifths) of the total rectangle.

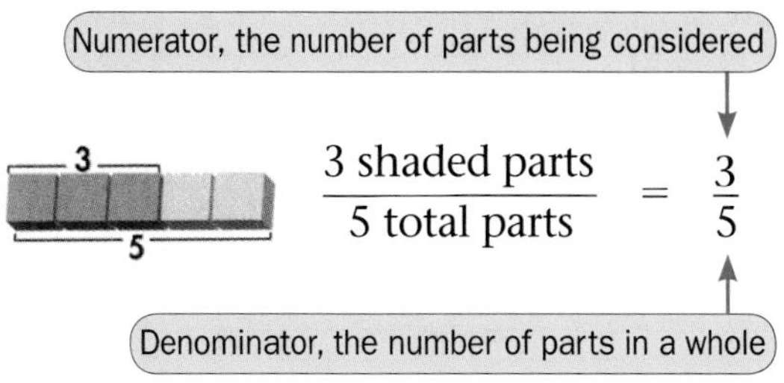

NET MARKETING

Micropurchases for Microprices

Web purchases of more than a few dollars go through traditional credit-card-based billing systems. But what if you sell something that only costs 25 cents? Credit charges and fees cost more than that.

Micropayment carriers offer billing services to Web marketers including writers, artists, and musicians who want to offer very low-cost products online. Consumers open an account with an initial payment of $20 or more, and purchases are then deducted from the account. Obstacles to success include convincing Web surfers to open accounts to pay for such tiny purchases and keeping costs low to make a profit. But the market is potentially huge.

Micropayments for Words

RedPaper.com is a membership Web site that operates like an eBay for words; members buy articles, poems, and stories for less than $1. RedPaper developed its own micropayment system rather than contracting for the service. With 26,000 members, that makes sense.

THINK LIKE A MARKETER

Name one disadvantage of micropayments.

Online Action!

Go to *marketingessentials.glencoe.com/7/net* to find a project on Internet pricing.

In the example below, the number of circles is $2/7$ (two-sevenths) of the total number of shapes.

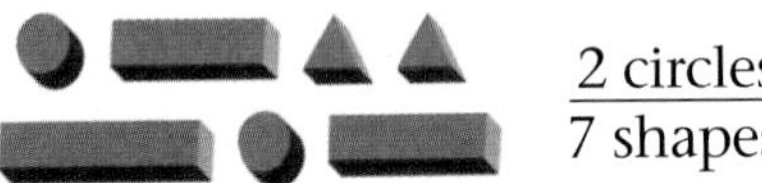

$$\frac{\text{2 circles}}{\text{7 shapes}} = \frac{2}{7}$$

Here are more examples illustrating the same principle.

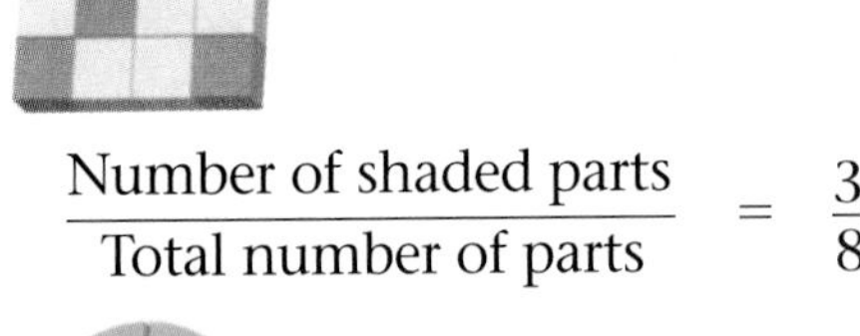

$$\frac{\text{Number of shaded parts}}{\text{Total number of parts}} = \frac{3}{8}$$

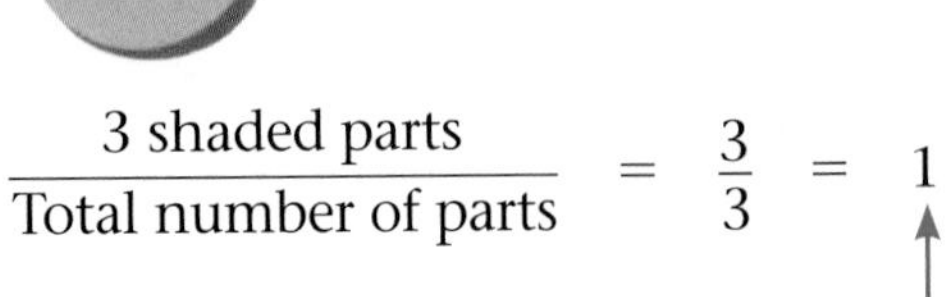

$$\frac{\text{3 shaded parts}}{\text{Total number of parts}} = \frac{3}{3} = 1$$

One whole circle is shaded.

$$\frac{\text{5 shaded triangles}}{\text{4 triangles in a square}} = \frac{5}{4} \text{ of a square}$$

A fraction can describe a number greater than 1.

When the numerator is greater than the denominator, the fraction describes a number greater than 1. It can be written as a **mixed number**, which is a whole number and fraction together.

$$\frac{6}{5} = 1\frac{1}{5}$$

Mixed number

Numerator is greater than denominator.

Decimal Numbers

A **decimal number** is another way to write a fraction or mixed number whose denominator is a power of 10 (10, 100,

PRACTICE 1

What fraction of each shape is shaded?

1. 2. 3.

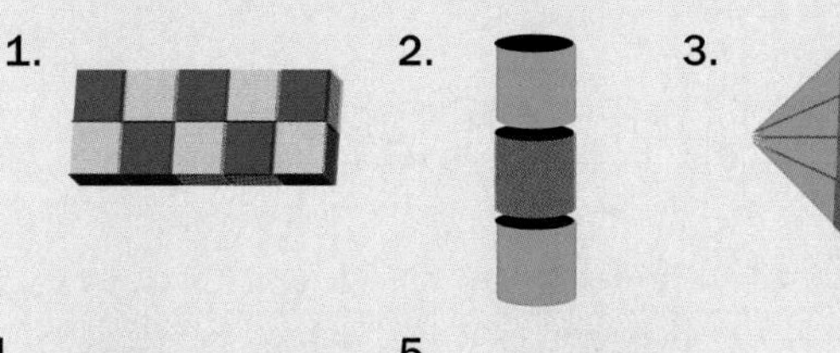

4. 5.

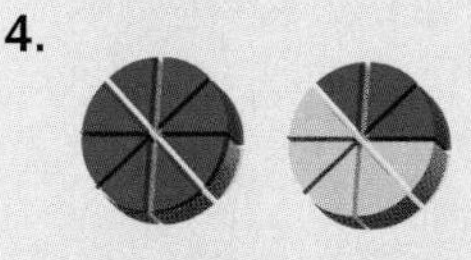

Answer each question with a fraction:

6. If you spend seven hours a day sleeping, what fraction of the day are you asleep?
7. You have saved $69 of the $159 you need to buy a new printer. What fraction of the money do you still need to save?
8. Your class has 14 male and 17 female students. What fraction of your class is female?
9. If one-third of your family's income is spent on housing, what fraction is left for other expenses?
10. Seventy-five cents represents what fraction of one dollar?

Note: Answers to all practice sets at *marketingessentials.glencoe.com*

1000, etc). The decimal number 5.3 means $5 + 0.3$ or $5 + \frac{3}{10}$ or $5\frac{3}{10}$. The decimal number 935.47 can be broken down as $900 + 30 + 5 + \frac{4}{10} + \frac{7}{100}$.

Knowing place names is necessary for reading decimals and writing them in words. Decimal place names apply to digits to the right of the decimal point.

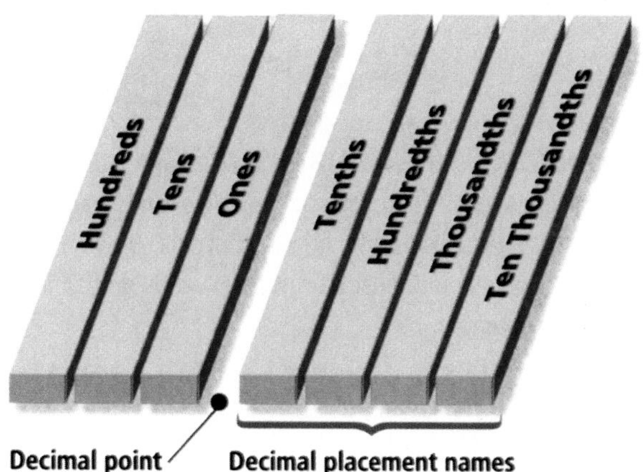

To read a decimal number or write it in words, follow the steps below. Use 15.083 as an example.

1. Begin with the whole number to the left of the decimal point (*fifteen*).
2. Read or write *and* for the decimal point.
3. Read or write the number to the right of the decimal point as a whole number (*eighty-three*).
4. Use the name of the decimal place of the final digit (*thousandths*).

The result is *fifteen and eighty-three thousandths.*

There is another way to read numbers with decimal points. You may hear decimal numbers read using the whole number and only the names of the digits in the decimal places, with *point* for the decimal point. For example, 9.7 could also be read as *nine point seven*; 15.083 might be read as *fifteen point zero eight three.*

Why You Should Know How to Write Numbers

Why is it important for you to know how to write decimals and fractions, and to understand the relationship between the two?

Understanding the relationship between decimal numbers and fractions is important when you are writing a check. After writing the amount in decimal form, you must write it again, using words for the dollars and a fraction for the cents. (See example on page 156.)

PRACTICE 2

Write the decimals as words. Write the money amounts as words and fractions. Write the words as decimals.

1. 9.8
2. 0.3
3. 23.67
4. 0.056
5. $67.40
6. $457.89
7. $112.07
8. Two thousand, one hundred sixty-four and eight tenths
9. Three hundred four and seven hundredths
10. Four hundred twenty-one dollars and thirty-seven cents

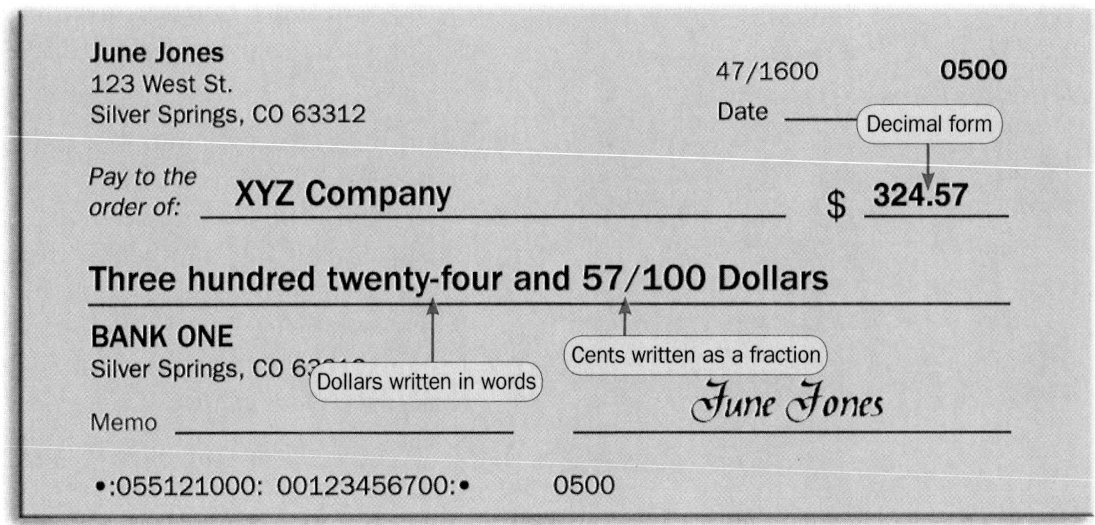

Adding and Subtracting Decimal Numbers

To add or subtract decimal numbers, first list the numbers vertically, keeping the decimal points in line with each other. Then add or subtract as you would with whole numbers. Sometimes you may need to write zeros to fill a column.

1.45 + 3.4 = ?

Align decimal points vertically.

```
  1.45
+ 3.40   <— Write 0s as needed.
  4.85   <— Add as with whole numbers.
```

13.4 − 7.56 = ?

Align decimal points vertically.

```
 13.40   <— Write 0s as needed.
− 7.56
  5.84   <— Subtract as with whole numbers.
```

• **REPRESENTING NUMBERS** More and more people pay bills online or use electronic funds transfer, but writing checks is still an essential skill. On a check, the amount must be written in words and as a decimal number.

What other math skills are required to manage a checking account?

Multiplying Decimal Numbers

The Carpet Store was having a sale on carpeting priced by the square yard. What is the area of carpeting for a room that is 9.6 yards long and 4.25 yards wide?

To multiply decimal numbers, use the following two-step process.

PRACTICE 3

Complete the following addition and subtraction problems with decimal numbers.

1. 7.3 + 8.2 =
2. 6.7 + 9 =
3. 9.8 + 7.05 =
4. 20.04 + 7.7 =
5. 0.08 + 4.075 =
6. 0.04 + 0.25 =
7. 3.71 + 0.6 + 1.89 + 11 =
8. 7.6 − 3.6 =
9. 54.9 − 27 =
10. \$10 − \$3.99 =
11. 7.5 − 2.11 + 26.045 =
12. 33.4 − 9.428 =
13. Maps To Go paid the following shipping charges in the first week of April: FedEx—\$14.75, \$28.00, \$14.75; UPS—\$23.69, \$84.27, \$47.88, \$119.57, \$63.74. What was their total shipping charge for that week?
14. Luis was given a roll of paper 35 yards long. He was asked to make four banners for the upcoming student elections. Two banners need to be 13.75 yards in length, one banner is to be 7.5 yards, and the final banner is to be 2 yards in length. How much more paper will he need?

1. Multiply the two numbers as if they were whole numbers. Pay no attention to the decimal points yet.
2. Add the number of decimal places in the two numbers being multiplied. Then, working from the right, count off the same number of decimal places in the product and insert the decimal point. Note: When counting off places from the right, you may have to add a zero in order to place the decimal point.

$9.6 \times 4.25 = ?$

```
   4.25  ← 4.25 has two decimal places.
 × 9.6   ← 9.6 has one decimal place.
 ------
   2550
  3825
 ------
 40.800
 ↑ Place the decimal three places to the left.
```

Since 40.800 = 40.8, the answer is 40.8 square yards.

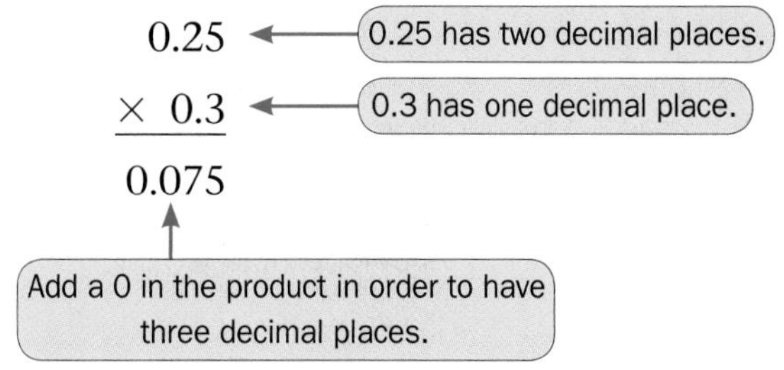

Multiply amounts of money as you would other decimal numbers. Remember to include the dollar sign in your answer.

```
  $4.98
 ×    2
 ------
  $9.96
  ↑ Write the dollar sign.
```

Rounding Decimal Numbers

Sometimes you may have to round a decimal number. This is especially common when multiplying with amounts of money, as when figuring tax amounts, discounts, and so on.

Use the following steps to round decimal amounts.

Round 16.842, 16.852, and 16.892 to the nearest tenth.

1. Find the decimal place you are rounding to.

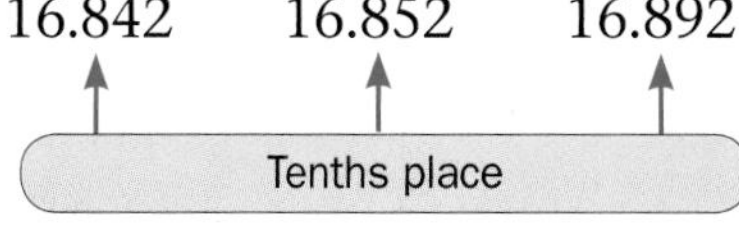

2. Look at the digit to the right of that place.

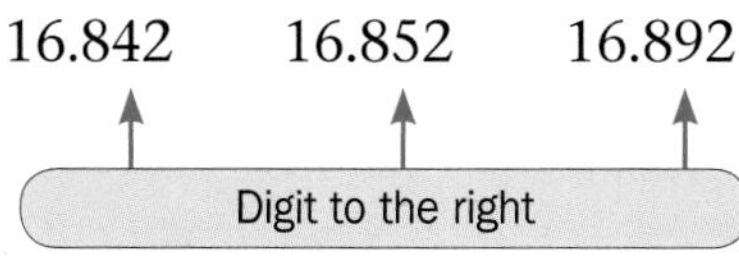

3. If the digit to the right is less than 5, leave the first digit as is. If the digit is 5 or greater, round up.

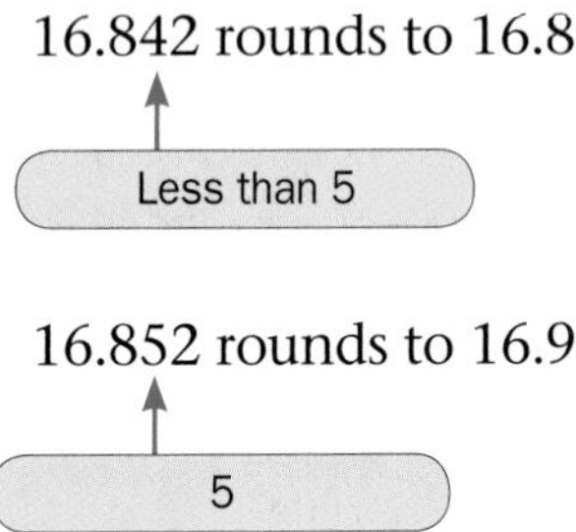

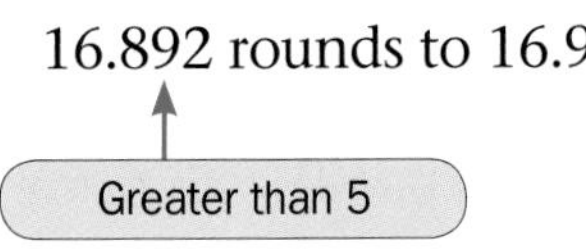

When you are working with amounts of money, use the same steps to round your answer to the nearest cent (the nearest hundredth).

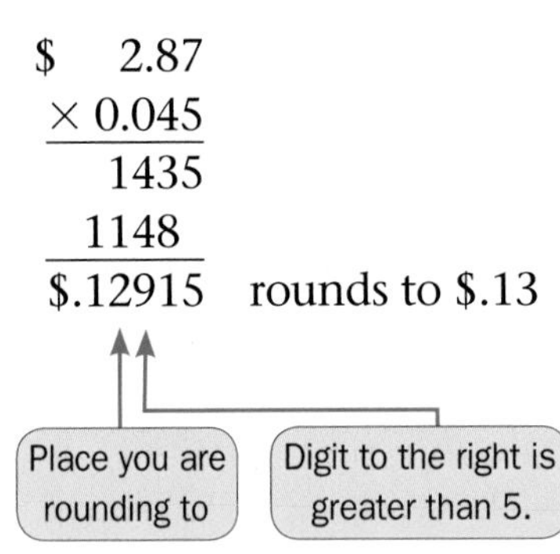

Dividing Decimal Numbers

Division of decimal numbers is similar to division of whole numbers. Follow the steps below to divide decimal numbers.

1. Set up the division problem as you would with whole numbers.

   69.7 divided by $1.724 = 1.724\overline{)\,69.7}$

2. Shift the decimal point in the divisor so that the divisor becomes a whole number. The divisor is the number you are dividing by. Then shift the decimal point in the dividend the same number of decimal places. The dividend is the number to be divided. Write zeros in the dividend, if necessary, in order to place the decimal point.

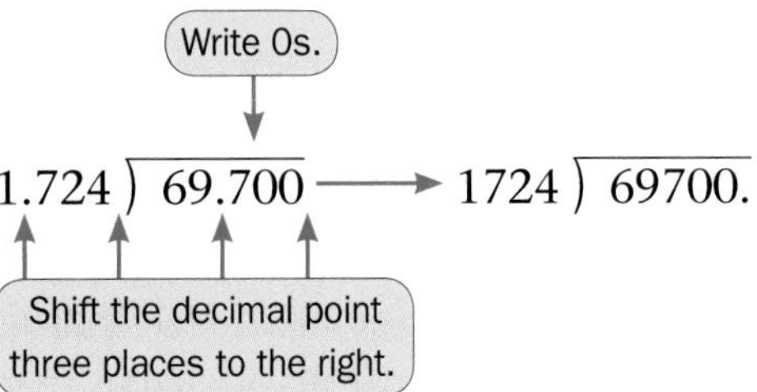

PRACTICE 4

Complete the following multiplication problems with decimal numbers. Round any money amounts to the nearest cent.

1. 4.8 × 9
2. 27.3 × 2.04
3. 3.14 × .5
4. 29.26 × 0.49
5. 8.2 × .0001

6. 2.76 × 10 =
7. 0.687 × 100 =
8. 12.345 × 1,000 =

9. Gasoline costs $2.02 per gallon when you pay with a credit card, but $1.94 when you pay with cash. How much do you save on a 12-gallon purchase if you pay with cash?
10. Every month you deposit $75 into a savings account for insurance costs. Your insurance expenses for this year were four equal payments of $219.50. How much remained in your savings account after the last payment?
11. Your phone company charges a $3.95 monthly long distance service fee plus $0.07 per minute for long distance phone calls. How much will you pay if you have 646 minutes of long distance calls for the month?

3. Place a decimal point in the answer space directly above its new position in the dividend. Then divide as with whole numbers.

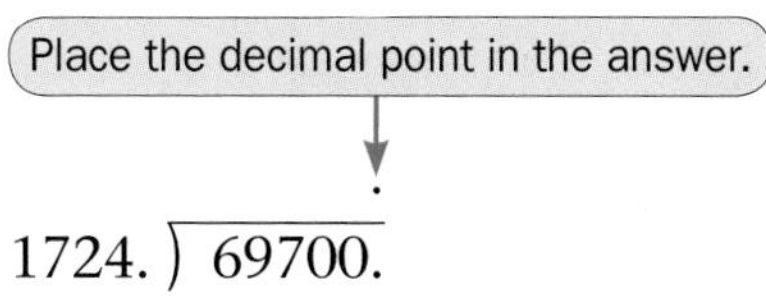

Sometimes you may need to write extra zeros after the decimal point in order to complete the division.

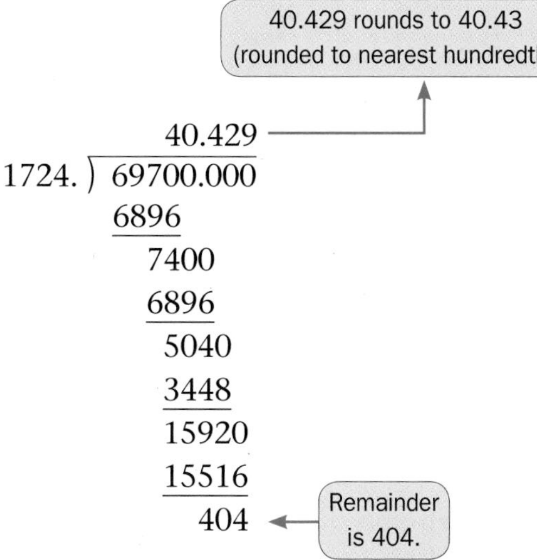

Some decimal answers will continue infinitely as you write zeros to the right of the decimal point. *Repeating decimals* will repeat a number or pattern of numbers.

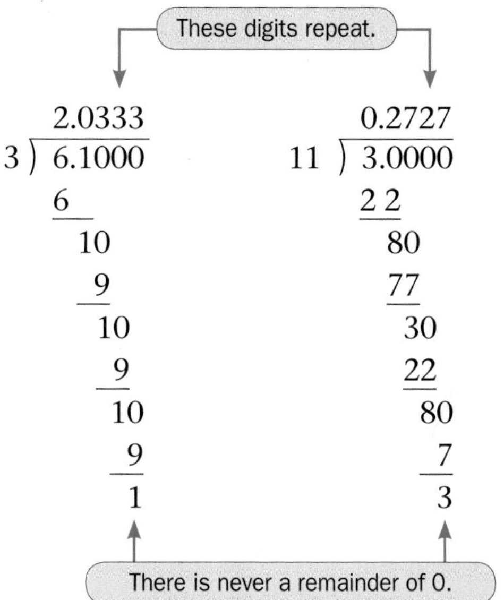

PRACTICE 5

Complete the following division problems. Round answers to the nearest thousandth.

1. 438 ÷ 15 =
2. 40.7 ÷ 3.7 =
3. 2.685 ÷ 8.25 =
4. 7.8 ÷ 0.035 =
5. 0.01 ÷ 2 =
6. 4.002 ÷ 0.75 =
7. If you are paid $11.02 per hour, how many hours must you work to pay for a computer that is priced at $495.90?
8. Compare the cost of Brand X and Brand Y laundry detergent. Which is the better buy? Brand X is $6.59 for 64 ounces. Brand Y is $10.79 for 96 ounces.

Converting Fractions to Decimals

Decimals are easier than fractions to add, subtract, multiply, and divide. To convert any fraction to a decimal, simply divide the numerator by the denominator.

Numerator → 1; Denominator → 4

$\frac{1}{4} = 1 \div 4 = 4\overline{)1.00}$ = 0.25

```
   0.25
4) 1.00
    8
    20
    20
     0
```

$\frac{2}{3} = 2 \div 3 = 3\overline{)2.000}$ = 0.666

```
   0.666
3) 2.000
   18
    20
    18
     20
     18
      2
```

There is never a remainder of 0.

In its decimal form, 2⁄3 is a repeating decimal. When working with repeating decimals, you may round to the nearest hundredth in most cases. Thus, 2⁄3 = 0.67.

Case Study

Selling Music and Style

When Apple Computer introduced the first iPod in late 2001, music lovers rejoiced. About the size of a deck of cards and weighing only 6.5 ounces, it could store a thousand songs in the form of digital sound files, and the sound reproduction quality was excellent. The iPod was perfectly placed to ride the wave of popularity of downloading music from the Internet. The company sold almost 3 million iPods by 2004, contributing to a turnaround in profits for the company. That same year, Apple released a model with 40 GB of memory. It could store up to 10,000 songs.

iPod and iTunes: Two Peas in a Pod

Apple also developed iTunes, a Web service for low-cost downloading of music that pays a royalty to musicians and music producers. Fifty million songs had been sold on the service by March of 2004. iTunes gained the support of popular musicians, who were happy to encourage use of a service that provides legal paid downloads. In return, close association with hip rock musicians gave a big boost to iPod's and iTunes' market appeal.

In early 2004, Apple brought out the iPod mini, weighing only 3.6 ounces, which came on the market with prerelease orders of over 100,000. With 4GB of memory, the mini still stores a thousand songs. Sleekly designed and available in five colors, it quickly became a fashion accessory. Again, the hipness angle paid off for Apple.

THINK STRATEGICALLY

Apple has benefited from the free publicity generated by having famous people praise and use its product and service. Can you think of a situation in which having a celebrity endorse your product might harm your sales?

Go to *marketingessentials.glencoe.com/7/case* to find a project on the use of celebrities in advertising.

Calculating Surface Measurements

When planning the installation of new carpeting or the use of space in an office, warehouse, or retail store, you will need to calculate the area of floor surface.

The area of a surface is the number of squares of a certain measure that the surface covers. If you measure the length and width in feet, the area will be expressed in square feet. If you measure in inches, the area will be expressed in square inches.

To compute the area of a rectangle or square, multiply the length of one side by the length of the side next to it. The shorter length is commonly called the width. The formula for the area of a rectangle is

$$A = l \times w$$

where A stands for area, l for length, and w for width.

The formula for the area of a square is really the same, but because there is no difference in the length and width, it may be written

$$A = s^2$$

where A stands for area and s for side.

Business Applications of Surface Measurements

Calculating surface is a business skill that is useful for retailers to figure out the floor space they need or how this space can be rearranged. It is also necessary for fabric retailers and wholesalers, contractors, and anybody who sells, distributes, or manufactures products that need to have an exact area measurement. For example, how would you go about deciding how much fabric you would need to re-upholster a sofa? You would carefully measure each area that needs to be covered. You would then have several geometric shapes with perimeter measurements. With that information you would be able to calculate the area measurement of each shape, add them up to know what amount of fabric you would need.

PRACTICE 6

The owner of a retail store wishes to replace the carpeting. The store measures 86 feet long and 50 feet wide. The store also includes two fitting rooms measuring each two feet wide by three feet long. The new carpet is priced at $35 per square yard and sales tax is 7 percent. Calculate the total surface area of the floor, and estimate the cost of material to replace the carpet, including sales tax. (Remember that 9 square feet are equivalent to 1 square yard.)

7.1 AFTER YOU READ

Reviewing Key Terms and Concepts

1. Write the whole number 3,010,049 in words, using commas and hyphens correctly.
2. Round $6.875 to the nearest cent and to the nearest dollar.
3. Convert the fraction 1/8 to its decimal equivalent.

Integrating Academic Skills

Math

4. Create a place value chart ranging from the thousands place to the thousandths place. Why is there no "ones" place to the right of the decimal point?
5. Prepare a lesson explaining why the decimal number 2.25 correctly represents $2.25 when talking about money, but does not correctly represent 2 hours and 25 minutes when talking about time. What other examples can you give where this occurs?

Check your answers at *marketingessentials.glencoe.com/7/read*

SECTION 7.2

Interpreting Numbers

OBJECTIVES

- Use a calculator to solve math problems
- Convert percentages to decimals and decimals to percentages
- Read graphs used to present mathematical data

KEY TERMS

- percentage
- bar graph
- line graph
- circle graph
- pie chart

READ and STUDY

BEFORE YOU READ

Predict What marketing situations might require the use of charts and graphs?

THE MAIN IDEA

Today's marketing jobs require the use of various tools to analyze information and make decisions. Calculators, computers to create graphic displays, algebraic thinking, and statistics are all important tools of the marketing professional.

STUDY ORGANIZER

In a chart like the one below, write in your own example of calculating tax on a sale, estimating for a gratuity, and a simple chart or graph to illustrate and compare data.

Calculating Tax on a Sale	Estimating for a Gratuity	A Simple Chart or Graph to Illustrate and Compare Data

Analyze List five situations in which you would use a calculator to solve a problem.

Using a Calculator

Calculators simplify the computation that is common in both the business world and in people's personal lives. Many people find calculators vital when paying bills, creating budgets, and balancing their checkbooks. There are two basic types of calculators. The most widely used type employs the algebraic entry system. This is the type of calculator used in the problems that follow. The other type uses the reverse-entry system.

The basic difference is that with the reverse-entry system, you enter the first amount and press the enter key, then the second amount, and then the operation (added to, subtracted from, multiplied by, or divided into the first amount). If you have a calculator that uses the reverse-entry system, read the instruction book that accompanies your calculator very carefully. You will get a very different answer if you enter numbers as if using algebraic entry.

If you expect to be hired in sales or any other marketing job, you will almost certainly use a calculator. Besides simply knowing which buttons to press, you will be expected to work with accuracy, know how to work with fractions and amounts of money, and have an understanding of how the calculator computes with multiple operations.

Estimate, Then Operate

When using a calculator, many people follow the guess-and-check method. They estimate first, then enter the problem in the calculator. Finally, they check the displayed answer against the estimate.

$$388 + 995 = ?$$

Estimate: 400 + 1,000 = 1,400
Enter the problem:
3 8 8 + 9 9 5 = 1,383

Displayed answer

Check: 1,383 is reasonably close to the estimate of 1,400.

$$480 \times 112 = ?$$

Estimate: 500 × 100 = 50,000
Enter the problem:
4 8 0 × 1 1 2 = 53,760

Displayed answer

Check: 53,760 is reasonably close to the estimate of 50,000.

It is important to estimate your answers when you use a calculator because you may make errors when entering numbers or even press the wrong operation key. It is a good idea to have an estimate of the answer in mind. For example, if you are expecting an answer of about 300, you will know something is wrong if the displayed answer on your calculator is 3,300.

Another way to ensure accuracy when using a calculator is to check the display after you enter each number and before you press the operation key. If you have made an error, press the Clear Entry key CE to remove the last entry. Suppose you want to multiply 5.8 × 7.2, but you enter 5 . 8 × 7 2. Press CE to delete the last two keystrokes. Then you can reenter the second number correctly. The first number will remain in the calculator. Press the Equals key =, and the answer will be displayed: 41.76.

How to Make Entries

Keep in mind as you enter digits that you can disregard leading zeros to the left of the decimal point (as in 0.6 or 0.375) and final zeros after the decimal point (as in 9.250 or 41.500). You do not need to enter these zeros. The calculator will display all the digits needed.

Number	Keystrokes Entered	Display
0.785	. 7 8 5	0.785
5.10	5 . 1	5.1

When dealing with mixed numbers or fractions, you must first convert the fractions to decimal form. Do this by dividing the numerator by the denominator. For example, to enter 5¼, first enter 1 ÷ 4. Then add the whole number by entering + 5.

When solving problems dealing with money, remember to write the dollar sign in the answer. You may also have to round the displayed answer to the nearest cent.

Display	Answer Written as Money Amount
5.25	$5.25
25.368216	$25.37 (Round to nearest cent)
46.0194	$46.02 (Round to nearest cent)
76514.1	$76,514.10

A calculator can operate on only two numbers at a time. However, you can perform a string of involved calculations on more than two numbers if you are very careful. When only addition and subtraction are involved, the calculator will perform these operations as they are entered.

8 . 6 + . 2 5 + 1 1 . 9
− 3 . 6 2 = 17.13

When only multiplication and division are involved, the calculator will also perform these operations as they are entered.

7 7 5 × . 9 6 ÷ 5 ×
1 . 9 6 = 291.648

However, when a calculation involves a combination of addition or subtraction with multiplication or division, not all calculators work the same way. You will need to check how your calculator performs the operations in this type of problem. Most calculators will do the operations as they are entered.

$6 + 4 \times 6$ will be calculated as

$6 + 4 \times 6 =$

$10 \times 6 = 60.$

$6 \times 4 + 6$ will be calculated as

$6 \times 4 + 6 =$

$24 + 6 = 30.$

$9 - 5 \times 2 + 6 \div 7$ will be calculated as

$9 - 5 \times 2 + 6 \div 7 =$

4×2

$8 + 6$

$14 \div 7 = 2.$

Ten-Key by Sight or Touch

Ten-key calculators have been popular for many years. They use algebraic entry. Most computer keyboards have a 10-key keypad along the right side of the board. (There are actually more than 10 keys; the 10-key designation refers to the digits 0 through 9.) With practice, you can learn to operate a 10-key keypad by touch, just as you learned to type the alpha characters on a keyboard by touch. This allows very fast operation and is a valuable skill for online point-of-sale entries, accounting, using spreadsheet programs, and other computer-related applications.

While learning to use a 10-key keypad, keep your fingers close to the home row of keys—the 4, 5, and 6 keys. Try to keep your arm, wrist, and hand in a straight line; do not rest your wrist on your desk. Relax your fingers, and press the keys lightly. Frequent,

•CHECKING the CHECKER To be sure that the amount they are charged for a multi-purchase sale is accurate, some people take a calculator when they go shopping.

What math skills are required to check the checker?

short periods of practice are most effective in developing speed with accuracy. Courses for developing skill on a 10-key keypad are available at many community colleges and on the Internet.

Percentages

Two percent of a company's revenue goes to pay for insurance. This means that $2 of every $100 that comes in goes to pay for insurance. **Percentage** means parts per 100. Thus, a number expressed as a percentage represents the number of parts per 100.

To write a whole number or a decimal number as a percentage, multiply it by 100. A simple way to do this is to move the decimal point two places to the right.

Move the decimal point two places to the right.

0.705 = 0.7 × 100 = 70% or 0.70 = 70%
0.05 = 0.05 × 100 = 5% or 0.05 = 5%
2.5 = 2.5 × 100 = 250% or 2.50 = 250%

Write 0s as needed.

You can use a calculator to do this operation.

[.] [7] [×] [1] [0] [0] [=] 70 = 70%
[2] [.] [5] [×] [1] [0] [0] [=] 250 = 250%

Converting Fractions to Percentages

To write a fraction or mixed number as a percentage, first convert the fraction to decimal form. Do this by dividing the numerator by the denominator. If there is a whole number, add it to the converted fraction. Then multiply by 100. You can use a calculator to do this operation.

$1/2$ = [1] [÷] [2] [×] [1] [0] [0] [=] 50 = 50%

$3/8$ = [3] [÷] [8] [×] [1] [0] [0] [=]
37.5 = 37.5%

$4\,2/5$ = [2] [÷] [5] [+] [4] [×] [1] [0] [0] [=]
440 = 440%

Converting Percentages to Decimals

Sometimes it may be easier to complete a math problem by changing a percentage to a decimal. You can change a percentage to a decimal number by dividing by 100. A simple way to do this is to move the decimal point two places to the left.

Move the decimal point two places to the left.

24.8% = 24.8 ÷ 100 = .248
or 24.8% = 0.248
0.5% = 0.5 ÷ 100 = 0.005
or 0.5% = 0.005

Write 0s as needed.

You can use a calculator to do this operation.

12.6% = [1] [2] [.] [6] [÷] [1] [0] [0] [=] 0.126
1.4% = [1] [.] [4] [÷] [1] [0] [0] [=] 0.014

You can also convert a percentage with a fraction or mixed number to a decimal by using a calculator.

$7\,1/4$% = [1] [÷] [4] [+] [7] [÷] [1] [0] [0] [=]
0.0725

Percentage Problems

Percentage problems are often encountered on a marketing job. For example, you may be asked to figure a tip, a discount amount, or the amount of sales tax. You may have to figure the total selling price, including the tax. Maybe you will be asked to figure the percentage of commission on your total sales.

Most percentage problems will involve finding a percentage of a number. To do that, multiply the decimal equivalent of the percentage by the number.

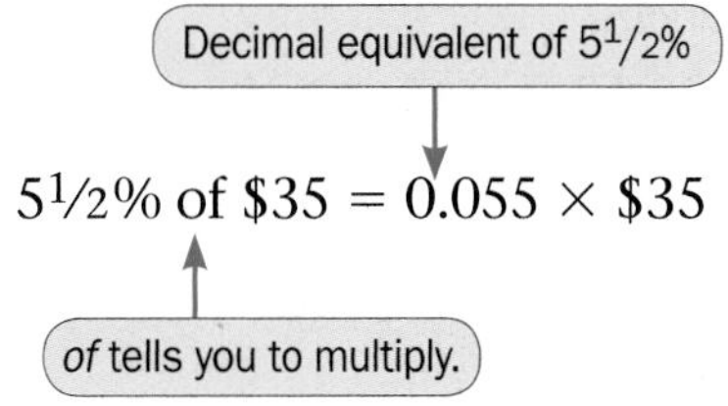

Follow these steps to solve percentage problems.

1. Estimate the answer.
2. Translate the problem into a math statement.
3. Do the calculations.
4. If necessary, round money amounts to the nearest cent.
5. Check your answer.

Read the instructions for your calculator to find out how to use its percent key.

Three types of percentage problems are explained below. Solve the first problem by estimating the answers. The other problems can be solved with a calculator without the use of a percent key.

1. Suppose you and three friends have enjoyed a delicious dinner at a restaurant. When the waiter brings the check, you decide to treat your friends and pay for dinner. To figure the gratuity (tip), you will not need to dig out a calculator because you know how to estimate. The total on the check is $93.58, including tax. You know that a 15 percent gratuity is usual, so you round the total to $100. You know that 10 percent of $100 is $10, and 15 percent is 1½ times 10 percent. Your estimate for the gratuity is $15, and a good estimate is all that is needed. You leave $115.
2. Suppose you have sold a set of golf clubs listed at $395.99 to someone eligible for a 15% discount. How much in dollars and cents will you allow as a discount on the golf clubs?
   - *First: Estimate the answer.* Round the list price to $400. Figure that 10% of $400 is $40. Since 15% is 1½ times 10%, estimate the discount at about $60 (1½ times $40).
   - *Second: Translate the problem into a math statement.*

     15% of $395.99 = 0.15 × $395.99
   - *Third: Do the calculations.*

     0.15 × $395.99 = $59.3985
   - *Fourth: Round the answer to the nearest cent, if necessary.*

     $59.3985 rounds to $59.40
   - *Finally: Check the answer against your estimate.* The amount $59.40 is reasonably close to the estimate of $60. The discount is $59.40.
3. If sales tax is 6½%, how much tax should you collect on the sale of the golf clubs? Before you can figure the tax, you have to find out the net selling price.

   List price − discount = net price
$395.99 − $59.40 = $336.59
Now you can proceed, following the guidelines given above.
   - *Estimate:* Round 6½% to 7% and $336.59 to $300. A 7% sales tax means that $7 tax is collected on every $100 in sales. So you can estimate the tax to be $21 (3 × $7).
   - *Translate:* 6½% of $336.59 = 0.065 × $336.59
   - *Calculate:* 0.065 × $336.59 = $21.8784
   - *Round:* $21.8784 rounds to $21.88
   - *Check:* $21.88 is reasonably close to the estimate of $21. The sales tax to be collected is $21.88.

Reading Charts and Graphs

Often in marketing, people need to use numbers to describe market trends, growth of sales, and other data. Graphs are a way of presenting such information that is easier to understand. It is easier to tell that one bar is longer than another, or that a line is going up or down, than it is to try to understand data by reading lists of numbers. Usually a graph shows the relationship between two kinds of data, or statistical information.

Bar Graphs

A **bar graph** is a drawing made up of parallel bars whose lengths are proportional to the qualities being measured. The bar graph in Figure 7.1 shows cell phone ownership by

GLOBAL MARKET

Foreign Exchange

Selling products abroad is a long-range goal for many marketers in the United States. One factor that makes doing business in another country complicated is the currency exchange rate, or the amount in dollars that another country's money is worth.

The world's major currencies change in value in relation to each other every day. When the euro (the European currency) was introduced in 1999, it was worth 89¢ U.S. But the euro's value has crept up since its introduction. In late 2003, the euro was worth $1.23, an increase of 38 percent.

When the value of the U.S. dollar is low against the euro, as it was in late 2004, American goods are cheaper for buyers using the euro. This helps increase American exports.

Sometimes, governments keep the value of their currencies low so their products are cheaper for others to buy. The Chinese government often does this. The practice makes Chinese goods very cheap for Americans, but makes American goods expensive in China.

Manufacturers selling abroad must be good predictors of trends in the exchange rate. If a sports shoe maker believes the dollar's value is declining, he or she may want to ship more shoes to Europe. But if the dollar's value rises instead, the company may earn a lower profit than expected.

CRITICAL THINKING

You manufacture snowboards and you want to sell in foreign countries. How will you choose in which country to start?

@ Online Action!

Go to *marketingessentials.glencoe.com/7/global* to find a project on foreign exchange.

different age groups. The bottom of the graph lists the age groups. Each group is represented by a bar of a certain height. There is a vertical line along the left side of the graph indicating the percentage of individuals in each age group who own cell phones.

To discover what percentage of 18- to 24-year-olds own cell phones, simply draw an imaginary line across the top of the bar that represents that age group. Then note where that line intersects the left side of the graph. As you can see, 66 percent of 18- to 24-year-olds own cell phones.

Look at the bar representing cell phone ownership for 30- to 39-year-olds. Compare it to the bar for 40- to 49-year-olds. They are the same, at 76 percent, representing the highest percentage on the chart. The relative heights of the bars gives an instant picture of the cell phone ownership of various age groups.

Line Graphs

Another kind of graph you have probably seen often in magazines and newspapers is a line graph. A **line graph** uses a line that joins points representing changes in a variable quantity, usually over a specific period of time. It is very useful for charting sales, prices, profits, output, and things that people expect to change over time. The information is useful in predicting future trends so that businesses can make plans to prepare for them.

The line graph shown in Figure 7.1 charts the changes in cell phone ownership for

Figure 7.1 Charts and Graphs

• How to Use Charts and Graphs
Bar graphs, line graphs, and circle, or pie graphs are used to display different kinds of data. Here's how to choose the best type of graph to show your results.

How are graphs used?

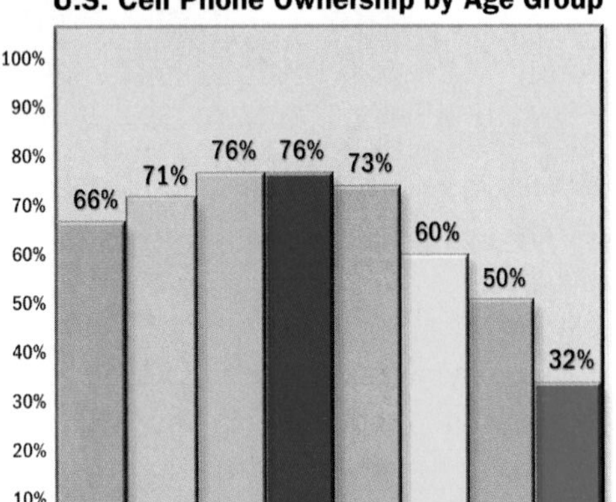

Bar Graphs

Bar graphs are best for comparing groups. The groups or items being compared do not need to affect each other. They are also a fast way to show big differences. Notice how easy it is to see which age groups own the most cell phones.

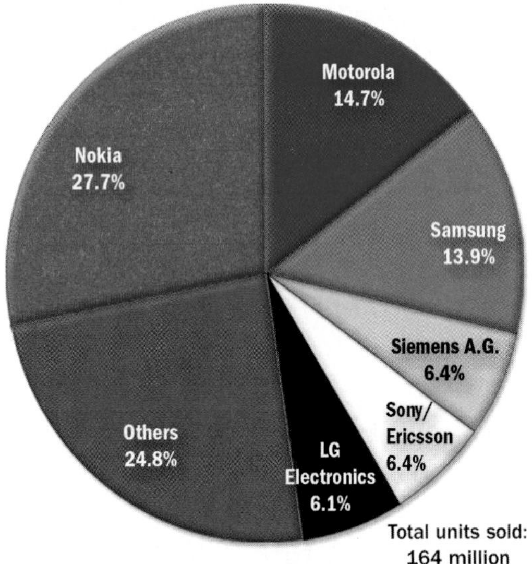

Circle Graphs

A circle, or pie, graph is used to show how a part of something relates to the whole. This kind of graph shows percentages effectively. It's easy to see from this circle graph that Nokia has the largest market share of the cell phone market.

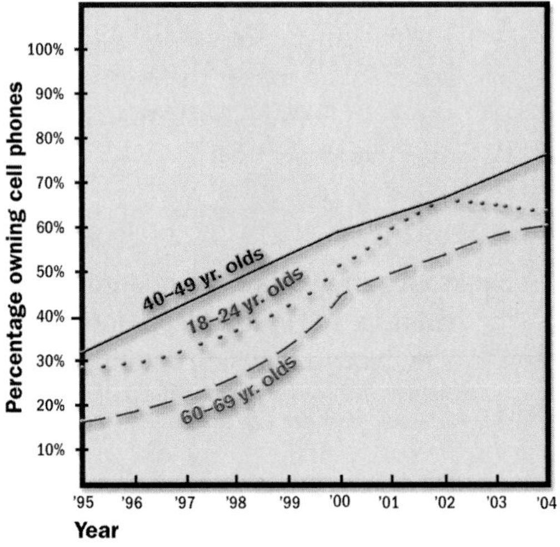

Line Graphs

Line graphs are used to show how one thing is influenced by another. They are especially useful in showing how things change over time. Line graphs are helpful when predicting future trends because they clearly show patterns from the past. This line graph shows that sales of cell phones are increasing for all but one age group.

Go to *marketingessentials.glencoe.com/7/figure/1* for a project on graphs.

different age groups over a nine-year period. Along the bottom of the graph are the years. Along the left side are the percentages of cell phone ownership. As you can see by following the lines, cell phone ownership increased steadily during that time period for all but 18- to 24-year-olds. This kind of information can help marketers determine how to market their product and help stores decide how much merchandise to order for the following year.

Circle Graphs

A **circle graph** is a geometric representation of the relative sizes of the parts of a whole. Businesses often choose such a graph to compare things like the cost of different aspects of manufacturing, the expenditures of one specific department, or the way income from sales is used by a company.

Circle graphs offer a visual that is easy to understand when considering how a large figure is broken down into several parts. A circle graph is better known as a **pie chart**, because it looks like a pie cut into slices of different sizes. The proportions of the different slices are sometimes expressed as percentages of the whole circle and sometimes as dollar amounts.

The pie chart in Figure 7.1 shows a percentage breakdown of cell phone sales among the major cell phone manufacturers. Even without reading the numbers, you can easily see which company accounted for the largest share of the cell phone market. You can also see that the second- and third-largest market shares were very close to each other, but not very close to the market leader.

This kind of chart enables companies to see at a glance how successful they were compared to other companies. The companies can then determine whether the current market position meets their goals. If not, they can institute new marketing strategies to help them reach their goals.

Frequency Tables

A frequency table lists numbers, fractions, or percentages observed for different intervals. In practical terms, a frequency table can reveal information for things like consumer buying behavior. For example, the frequency table shown in Figure 7.2 was constructed from survey information about the primary uses of the Web. Information in a frequency table can be presented in graphic form to make it easier to understand.

PRACTICE 7 (PROJECT)

The information in the following frequency table is data from a survey by age group on the uses of the Web. Based on this information, create a bar graph for the age ranges of 11–20 and 21–25.

PRIMARY USE OF THE INTERNET

	Percentage of Responses	
	Ages 11–20	Ages 21–25
Education	17%	16%
Shopping	8%	12%
Entertainment	19%	17%
Work	8%	15%
Communication	12%	10%
Personal information	16%	17%
Time-wasting	16%	11%
Other	4%	2%
Total responses:	100%	100%

Algebraic Thinking

Charts and graphs are used to organize information so we can analyze it and make decisions. But how do we analyze numbers to make sense of them? Using algebraic thinking, we look for patterns and relationships, which are called functions in mathematics. We also use symbols to represent variables, numbers we are not sure of or those that will change. For example, Sheila, a marketing analyst, does a study and finds that 30 percent of those who buy a new car will purchase four new tires after two years. Sheila's company needs to plan ahead, so she wants to know how many tires this group will purchase three years from now. Sheila lets n stand for the number of new cars purchased next year, and t stand for the number of tires purchased in three years. Then, she writes an equation: $t = n \times 30\% \times 4$. So if she estimates that 1 million new cars are sold next year, she knows that this group will purchase $1{,}000{,}000 \times 0.30 \times 4 = 1.2$ million tires in three years.

Descriptive Statistics

Statistics are used to describe and summarize data, thus making the data more meaningful and easier to understand. If you ever read the sports page of your local newspaper, you know something about statistics. Professional baseball, basketball, and football standings indicate the ranking of teams by games won and lost. They also show the percentage of wins for each team. Box scores for a baseball game include statistics on each team member's times at bat, hits, runs batted in, and runs scored.

Business Applications of Descriptive Statistics

In business, statistics are used in analyzing data. For example, Sam is doing a study to track how many people use the Internet to make purchases. He collects data on thousands of people and uses statistics to find:

- The distribution
- The central tendency
- The dispersion

The distribution is a summary of the frequency of values for a variable such as age. This may be presented in a frequency distribution table listing the percentage of customers making Internet purchases by age group.

Customers by Age	Percentage
18–28	12%
29–38	23%
39–48	28%
49–58	16%
59–68	11%
69 and up	10%

The central tendency of a distribution is an estimate of the center of a distribution of

Figure 7.2 **Main Reasons for Using the Web**

Purpose for Use	Count, or Frequency, of Uses	Percent of Responses
Education	2,020	16%
Shopping	1,725	13%
Entertainment	1,977	15%
Work	2,168	17%
Communication	1,165	9%
Personal information	2,421	19%
Time-wasting	1,219	9%
Other	286	2%
Total responses:	**12,981**	**100%**

- **Frequency Tables Display Counts** Frequency tables are used to show counts for particular categories or intervals. This frequency table shows the number of Web site uses, or hits, by purpose of visit.

What was the most frequent purpose for using the Web? How might marketers use this information?

Online Action! **Go to *marketingessentials.glencoe.com/7/figure/2* for a project on frequency tables.**

values. Here are the three main types of estimates of central tendency:

- Mean
- Median
- Mode

The mean, sometimes called the arithmetic mean, is the most common way of describing central tendency. Most people know this as the average. The mean is computed by adding up all the values and dividing by the number of values. Thus, the average of the values 4, 8, 13, 28, 35, 44, and 56 is 188 divided by 7 = 26.86, rounded to 27.

The median is the exact middle of a set of values. The median in the set of values above is 28. Notice that it is very close to the mean of 27.

The mode is the most frequently occurring value. You would not look for a mode in a set of only seven values, but it can be useful when there is a large number of values. For example, suppose you take a final exam in your marketing class. When the exams are corrected and graded, the scores range from 65 to 95. No more than two students receive the same score, except that 5 students scored 81. Thus, 81 is the most frequently occurring value and is the mode.

Dispersion is the spread of values around the central tendency. The simplest way to measure the dispersion is with the range. The range is the highest value minus the lowest value. With final exam scores between 65 and 95, the range is 30. This is how far the scores are dispersed from the center of the scores.

7.2 AFTER YOU READ

Reviewing Key Terms and Concepts

1. Use a calculator to find the decimal equivalent of ⅓. Round to the nearest thousandth.
2. What is the decimal equivalent of 40%? What is the percentage equivalent of 1?
3. Why are graphs used to represent numerical data? What are three common forms of graphic representation?

Integrating Academic Skills

Mathematics

4. Employees who work overtime are often paid time-and-a-half. How do you write time-and-a-half as a percentage? If your regular pay rate is $13.50 per hour, how much will you receive for overtime?

History

5. Use the Internet to learn about the prime rate. Define the prime rate. Using historical information about the prime rate for the last 10 years, create a line graph.

Check your answers at *marketingessentials.glencoe.com/7/read*

CAREERS IN MARKETING

RAY LINDLE
CPA
KOSSE AND LINDLE

What do you do at work?

I have 34 years of accounting experience. My CPA practice focus is in the construction, wholesale, manufacturing, and service industries. I supervise and perform audit field work, reviews, and prepare financial reports and business income tax returns. I also provide succession planning, tax planning for business owners, and litigation support services. I hold NASD Series 6 & 63 securities licenses.

What skills are most important to you?

Being able to analyze the numbers beyond the profit statement. It is important to be able to visualize options to achieve a goal. Of course an in-depth knowledge of tax laws is mandatory to planning. When I can help a client achieve profitability by exploring the past and coming up with options for the future, then I can feel satisfied. It is also important to understand an owner's long-term objectives, so that I can help plan for the future, such as retirement or succession.

Also, a CPA is now mandated 150 hours of college before he or she can sit for the licensing exam, but this is just the start. I continually take professional education courses in excess of the annual requirement of 40 hours. Tax classes are a must, and audit and financial planning requirements are constantly changing.

What is your key to success?

Providing your clients not only what they think they need, but also ideas and suggestions which they may not have thought of yet. My clients are my friends and I need to remember that my goal is to know their long-term business and personal goals and help them achieve both.

Aptitudes, Abilities, and Skills

Analytical and research skills, attention to detail, proficiency in mathematics

Education and Training

Bachelor's and Master's degrees in accounting and general business help pave the way for the CPA exam.

Career Path

Most accountants begin entry-level work with a CPA firm; occasionally, entrepreneurial students can set up shop quickly as a bookkeeper, doing basic work while studying for the CPA exam.

THINKING CRITICALLY

Why do you think this career requires such extensive on-going training?

@ Online Action!

Go to *marketingessentials.glencoe.com/7/careers* for a career-related activity.

CHAPTER 7 REVIEW

FOCUS on KEY POINTS

SECTION 7.1

- The placement name for each digit and for groups of digits is necessary for reading numbers, writing numbers, and for writing a check. A fraction is a number used to describe a part of a whole amount.
- A decimal number is a fraction or mixed number whose denominator is a power of 10. Rounding decimal numbers is common when multiplying with amounts of money, as when figuring tax, discounts, and gratuities. Decimal equivalents of fractions are used in many marketing jobs. To convert a fraction to a decimal, divide the numerator by the denominator.

SECTION 7.2

- Nearly everyone in marketing uses a calculator, and there are two basic types. The most commonly used calculator uses the algebraic entry system. The other type uses the reverse-entry system.
- Charts and graphs present data in a way that is easier to understand than a long series of numbers. They are used to describe market trends, growth of sales, and other data.

REVIEW VOCABULARY

1. What is the name for the ten basic symbols used in our numbering system? (p. 152)
2. Name the numbers at the top and bottom of a fraction. (p. 153)
3. What is another way to write a fraction with a denominator that is a power of 10? (p. 154)
4. Representing a number as parts per 100 is representing it as a what? (p. 165)
5. Name four ways to present numbers graphically. (pp. 166–169)

REVIEW FACTS and IDEAS

6. How are commas used to write numbers in words? When are hyphens used in writing numbers in words? (7.1)
7. What are fractions? What does the denominator tell you? The numerator? (7.1)
8. What rule must you follow when adding or subtracting decimal numbers? Multiplying decimal numbers? Dividing decimal numbers? (7.1)
9. List the steps for rounding decimal numbers. To what place do you usually round money? (7.1)
10. Explain how to convert $^2/_5$ to its decimal equivalent. (7.1)
11. The use of a calculator increases accuracy and efficiency. Why is it important to estimate your answer when using a calculator? (7.2)
12. How do you convert a percentage to a decimal? A decimal to a percentage? (7.2)
13. Graphs are used to illustrate data. Give an example of how each of the following types of graphs might be used in business: Bar graph, line graph, circle graph. (7.2)

BUILD SKILLS

14. Workplace Skills

Human Relations You work for a small company. Hourly wages at the company range from $11 per hour to $55 per hour. Lately, the company has experienced financial difficulty. A task force has been set up to provide possible solutions to avoid layoffs. One suggestion from management is that each employee take a voluntary cut in wages of 3 percent. Is this a fair solution? Why or why not?

15. Technology Applications

Math Software Prepare a short oral report on software programs for math applications in daily business life. Make sure you consider many different kinds of job situations. Include information about which type of job makes use of each type of software you list.

16. Math Practice

Working With a Calculator Use a calculator to solve the following problem: Your store is advertising pencils at three for $1.00. What is the cost per pencil if you round to the nearest cent? If a customer wanted to buy just one pencil, what would you charge? Why?

DEVELOP CRITICAL THINKING

17. How Are the Different Graphs and Charts Used?

Using business magazines and newspapers, locate and make copies of a bar graph, a line graph, and a circle graph. Briefly summarize the information that each graph communicates in a few written paragraphs.

Bring your examples to class and be ready to discuss and share them with your classmates.

18. What Is the Difference Among Calculators?

Research graphing calculators and financial calculators at a local retailer or on the Internet. You might also consider asking your math teacher about the various functions available for calculators. Use a word processing program to prepare a one-page report summarizing the features of each type of calculator.

APPLY CONCEPTS

19. Using Circle Graphs

Assume that you are accepting a full-time job in your locality that pays $2,600 after taxes per month. Using your local newspaper, determine what it will cost you to rent a one-bedroom apartment. Estimate your other living costs for one month such as food, clothing, transportation, utilities, insurance, miscellaneous.

Activity Use a computer program to create a circle graph representing this data.

20. Research Refrigerator Offers

Assume that you are looking for a new refrigerator for your apartment. Using newspaper and magazine ads or searching on the Internet, find the same refrigerator offered by two different stores in your area. Compare the offers on the two refrigerators, including rebates, discounts, and other sales promotions to determine which is the better offer.

Activity Write a short, one-page report comparing and contrasting the offers and defend your decision to buy one refrigerator over the other.

NET SAVVY

21. Inflation

Use a search engine to locate an inflation calculator that is based on the consumer price index (CPI). Begin with a basket of items costing $100 in 1950. Compute the inflated cost for 1960, 1970, 1980, 1990, and 2000. Enter your data into a spreadsheet program such as Excel. Create both a bar graph and a line graph based on your data. Which graph do you think is most effective in presenting your data? Why?

THE 

CONNECTION

Role Play: Sales Associate

Situation You work at a large department store. You are preparing for the school year and want to purchase some new clothes. One of the employee benefits your store offers is a 20 percent discount on store purchases. You want to purchase a pair of jeans that cost $65.00, a pair of shoes that cost $95.00, 2 tops that cost $40.00 each, and a jacket that costs $125.00. You must also add the sales tax of 7.5 percent to your total purchase.

Activity You must determine the amount of money you will spend and save by taking advantage of your employee discount to make your back-to-school purchases.

Evaluation You will be evaluated on how well you meet the following performance indicators:

- Explain the nature of personnel regulations
- Explain the nature of wage and benefit programs
- Calculate miscellaneous charges
- Make decisions
- Prepare simple written reports

@ Online Action!

For more information and DECA Prep practice, go to *marketingessentials.glencoe.com/7/DECA*

CHAPTER 8
Communication Skills

Chapter Objectives

After reading this chapter, you should be able to:

- Define effective verbal and nonverbal communication
- Explain the role of listening in communication
- Explain why awareness of cultural differences is important
- Define reading for meaning
- Explain how to organize and present your ideas
- Demonstrate professional telephone communication skills
- Explain how to write effective business letters and persuasive messages

GUIDE TO THE PHOTO

Market Talk Communicating clearly is necessary for success in school or in business. The ability to send a message that is easily understood by the market, or by an audience, is critical to all aspects of marketing—from advertising to sales to customer service.

Quick Think Business communication via e-mail has increased in recent years. How has this affected formal letter writing?

THE  CONNECTION

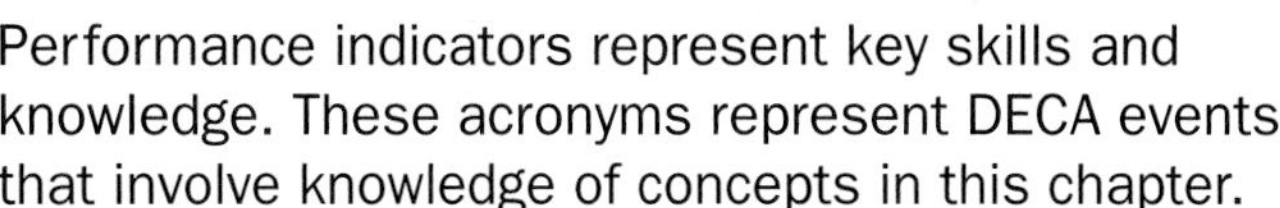

Performance indicators represent key skills and knowledge. These acronyms represent DECA events that involve knowledge of concepts in this chapter.

AAAL	**FMAL**	**MMS***	**TMDM***
AAML*	**FMDM***	**QSRM***	**TSE***
ADC*	**FMML***	**RMAL**	**VPM**
BSM	**FSRM***	**RMML***	
EMDM*	**HMDM***	**SMDM***	

In all these DECA events you should be able to follow these performance indicators:

- Explain the nature of effective communication
- Apply effective listening skills
- Use proper grammar and vocabulary
- Explain the nature of effective verbal communications
- Address people properly
- Handle telephone calls in a businesslike manner
- Persuade others
- Make oral presentations
- Explain the nature of written communications
- Write business letters
- Prepare simple reports
- Follow directions
- Explain the nature of staff communication
- Explain the use of interdepartmental/company communications
- Describe ethical considerations in providing information

All the events with an asterisk (*) also include these performance indicators:

- Give directions for completing job tasks
- Conduct staff meetings

DECA PREP

Check your understanding of DECA performance indicators with the DECA activity in this chapter's review. For more information and DECA Prep practice, go to *marketingessentials .glencoe.com/8/DECA*

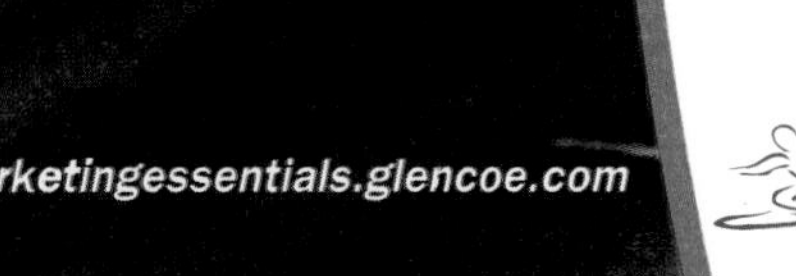

SECTION 8.1

Defining Communication

OBJECTIVES

- Define effective verbal and nonverbal communication
- Explain the role of listening in communication
- Explain why awareness of cultural differences is important
- Define reading for meaning

KEY TERMS

- communication
- channels/media
- feedback
- barriers
- setting
- distractions
- emotional barriers
- jargon

READ and STUDY

BEFORE YOU READ

Predict Write two words that you associate with the word *communicate*. Add to or change the list as you read.

THE MAIN IDEA

Effective communication—sending and receiving messages that are understood in the same way by both sender and receiver—is a key component of marketing. Understanding the communication process and improving listening and reading skills will lead to greater success on the job and in the marketplace.

STUDY ORGANIZER

Copy the chart below and use it to take notes about the listening process.

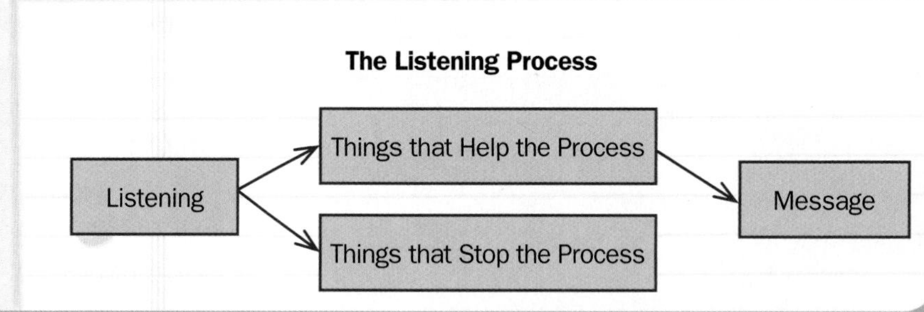

WHILE YOU READ

Connect Do you prefer writing, speaking, or some other method of communication?

The Communication Process

Communication is the process of exchanging messages between a sender and a receiver. These messages can be about information, ideas, or feelings. The skills used to send and receive these messages are called communication skills. They include listening, reading, speaking, and writing. Good communication skills are key to effective communication, in which the speaker or writer presents the message clearly and concisely so that the listener or reader can understand it easily. Effective communication is vital in every aspect of business, including developing job skills, training employees, working as a team, networking, and marketing products.

Businesses now compete around the globe, which means they must make their messages understood by people of different cultural backgrounds.

Channels or Media

Channels, or **media**, are the avenues through which messages are delivered. Examples include face-to-face conversations, telephone calls, written memos, letters, reports, and e-mail. Advertising channels include television, radio, print media, and the Internet. Channels differ in terms of message-carrying capacity (how much content they can carry), the speed with which the message is delivered, cost of the message, and its accuracy, or quality of content. The choice of medium depends on the relative importance of these factors in the delivery of the message.

Feedback

A receiver's response to a message is known as **feedback**. For example, if your boss asks you to post a report on the company Web site, you will probably ask some questions about what to include, when to post it, and so on. Your questions are feedback to your boss. Feedback in communication allows participants to clarify the message and make sure that all parties gave the message the same meaning.

Barriers

Barriers to communication are obstacles that interfere with the understanding of a message. They can be verbal barriers, such as using vague or unclear language or using a language or dialect that is unfamiliar to the receiver of the message. For example, what do you call a carbonated, sugary beverage that comes in cans and bottles? Depending on where you live, you might call this drink *soda, pop, soda pop,* or even something else. Marketing professionals need to make sure the language that they are using is appropriate for and able to be understood by their audience. This applies to cross-cultural marketing as well. For example, the Spanish language has many dialects, and people from different Spanish-speaking countries, such as Cuba, Mexico, Spain, and the Dominican Republic often use different Spanish words to express the same concept. So when businesses are trying to target the Hispanic market, it is important for them to know something about the cultural backgrounds of potential customers.

•CULTURAL NORMS Different cultures have different gestures to show respect or greeting.

What are some gestures that you use to demonstrate greeting or respect?

Setting

The **setting** is the circumstance under which communication takes place. These circumstances include place, time, sights, and sounds. The setting can help or hinder the ability to exchange messages. For example, a salesperson at an electronics store may find it difficult to explain the features of a video camera to a customer if the music department across the aisle has a stereo playing at full volume.

Listening

Listening for understanding is one of the most valuable communication skills. Listening is the active mental process by which a person recognizes, assimilates, assesses, and evaluates what is heard. (See Figure 8.1 for a list of barriers to listening.) Situations in which listening plays an important role include handling customer complaints, understanding feedback, recognizing clients' needs, following directions, and resolving conflicts with coworkers.

Techniques for Effective Listening

Listening, like all skills, must be learned. The following techniques will improve your listening skills and help you to be an effective listener.

Identify the Purpose

Prepare to listen by learning and reviewing the purpose of the communication. Managers planning a group meeting, for example, send out an agenda in advance so everyone will know the meeting's purpose. When a customer sets up a meeting, it is especially important to understand the meeting's purpose so that you will be prepared to respond to the customer's questions.

Look for a Plan

When you listen to a structured speech, think about how the speaker has organized the presentation. Be alert at the beginning of the speech, because the speaker may give an outline of the main ideas of the talk. If you see a structure or pattern, it will be easier to see how the different parts of the message fit together.

Face-to-face conversations are often informal and unplanned, so just stay focused on the message instead of thinking about structure.

Give Feedback

When you are conversing about business, listen carefully and then give feedback to show whether you have understood the message. Without interrupting, you can nod your head, raise an eyebrow, smile, or frown. Look for an opportunity to ask questions when the speaker pauses or completes his or her point. Think through what has been said and summarize your understanding of the message. Acknowledge your understanding respectfully or ask the speaker for clarification if you are uncertain.

When a speaker is giving instructions, it may be better to interrupt with questions than to wait for a pause. In that way, a confusing point can be clarified, and you can follow the remainder of the directions. However, before interrupting, you should be sure that the speaker is comfortable with this approach.

Search for a Common Interest

Effective listening is easier when you are interested in the ideas being discussed. If you find the subject boring and are tempted to tune out, resist the temptation. Try to find something that interests you or that you can use. Tuning out can become a bad habit and can cause you to miss some important information.

Evaluate the Message

It is important to know how to respond appropriately to a message. To do so, you must evaluate it. For example, if a customer shares a personal point of view with you, even if you disagree, it would be inappropriate to make a sudden judgment. Doing so could be destructive to your relationship. Instead, try to view the message from the speaker's point of view. Listen carefully and try to understand the new information even if it conflicts with what you believe. Relax and do not become defensive. Recognize that your customer's experience may be unlike yours. Different experiences may cause differences in perception. Ask polite but probing questions to understand the message better. Try to identify any parts of the speaker's message with which you do agree.

Listen for More Than Verbal Content

Listen for more than just words in the speaker's message. What is communicated by the speaker's rate of speech, pitch, volume, and voice quality?

Awareness of cultural differences will help in the understanding of vocal cues. In the United States and other Western countries, including Canada, Australia, and Great Britain, speakers are expected to look at and speak directly to listeners. In many Asian countries, however, speakers show respect by averting their eyes, speaking in soft tones, and approaching their subject indirectly. A speaker

Figure 8.1 Barriers to Listening

• **How Listening Can Fail** Barriers to listening stop the communication process. They prevent the listener from receiving and understanding the messages sent to them.

How can you be a good listener?

Distractions Distractions interfere with the ability to listen well. You may be distracted by thoughts about another subject. Focus your attention on the speaker's words.

Emotional Barriers When you have a negative emotional reaction to something someone says, it prevents you from concentrating on what is being said. To overcome this barrier, try to keep an open mind.

Planning a Response This is a very common block to listening. If you are trying to figure out what to say when other people are still speaking, you will not take in all that they are saying. To overcome this barrier, listen carefully until the other person has finished, then respond.

Online Action! Go to *marketingessentials.glencoe.com/8/figure/1* to find a project on listening skills.

in Canada who wants to say "No" will simply say "No." In Korea, a person who wants to communicate the same message may say, "That might be very difficult." Both statements mean "No," but the messages reflect cultural differences.

Listen for a Conclusion

Listen carefully for the speaker's conclusion. You may want to take action based on it. Do not jump to your own conclusion before the speaker has finished presenting the facts that support his or her conclusion. Be prepared to check your understanding by asking well-thought-out questions. If the situation is a formal one, wait to ask questions at the right time. Intelligent questions indicate not only interest but also respect for the speaker's work.

Take Notes

Try to identify a plan in the presentation of formal meetings. Then structure your notes according to the plan. Take notes on the main points presented at business meetings. Important points are often preceded by signal words such as *first, second, next, then, another, therefore,* and *thus.* If there is a summary or a recap at the end of the meeting, listen carefully and check your notes to make sure you understood the main ideas.

Barriers to Listening for Understanding

A barrier to receiving a message can be environmental, such as a plane flying overhead, or it may involve attitudes and characteristics of the listener. Common barriers to listening include the following:

- **Distractions** **Distractions** are things that compete with the message for the listener's attention. These can include noises, conversations, and competing thoughts. One way to overcome this barrier is to move away from the distractions—to change the setting.
- **Emotional barriers** **Emotional barriers** are biases against the sender's opinions that prevent a listener from understanding. Poor listeners close their minds to things with which they disagree. Good listeners always listen with an open mind, even when they do not agree with the speaker's ideas.
- **Planning a response** Planning a response occurs when the receiver of the message stops listening and instead begins to think about what to say next. A person cannot focus on the message and plan a response at the same time.

Listeners must be aware of and actively avoid or overcome any barriers in order to concentrate on the message.

Reading

Reading, like listening, is an active mental process of receiving and understanding a message. Reading skills are essential on any job; in fact, they are usually needed to get a job in the first place. Applicants must read help-wanted ads or search online for job postings. In the workplace, reading skills are needed to interpret information in schedules, graphs, training manuals, e-mails, and reports.

Know the Purpose of Your Reading

Many of the techniques for effective listening also apply to reading. For instance, it is helpful when reading to look for a plan, search for an interest, and evaluate the message. A technique that is especially valuable in building good reading skills is to keep in mind the purpose for your reading. Good readers know why they are reading. This awareness determines how they read.

Reading for Meaning

Reading for meaning requires that a person read carefully, figure out the meaning of new words, search for answers, and analyze and evaluate information—often in a short period of time. Most job-related reading assignments involve reading for meaning. For example, you may be required to search for sources online or read through a large report to find information about marketing trends. Another job-related reading task is checking facts. There are five strategies that can improve the ability to read for meaning:

1. **Focus your mind** The mind does not focus on a subject automatically. It must be trained. Monitoring your thoughts when you read can keep you focused. Think about how each paragraph relates to your purpose for reading.
2. **Summarize as you read** As you finish each paragraph and section of the text, mentally review what you have just read and summarize it. If you do not understand the text, go over it again. If it is still unclear, jot down a question so that you can follow up on it later.
3. **Make connections** Think about how the material relates to ideas or information with which you are familiar.
4. **Form mental pictures** Try to form pictures of the people, places, things, and situations described. This can help you remember the material in a form that is meaningful to you.
5. **Build your vocabulary** You may come across words that are unfamiliar when reading. Skipping over these words may cause you to miss key points in the message. Try to figure out the meaning by the way the word is used in the sentence. Always keep a dictionary nearby and learn how to use both the thesaurus and dictionary included in office computer software. Looking up words will improve your vocabulary and your understanding of what you are reading.

In job-related reading, you may come across **jargon**, specialized vocabulary used by members of a particular group. Because these words or meanings are not commonly used, they are often not listed in standard dictionaries. For example, the word *market* as used by marketing professionals is jargon because it has a specific meaning for marketers. A market, to marketers, is a group of people or organizations that share a need for a particular product and have the willingness and ability to pay for it. Learning the jargon used in your field will make it easier for you to do job-related reading.

8.1 AFTER YOU READ

Reviewing Key Terms and Concepts

1. What listening techniques can help you better understand messages you receive?
2. What are two barriers that could interfere with receiving a message?
3. List three ways to improve reading for meaning.

Integrating Academic Skills

Math

4. Assume that the average number of waking hours per day is 16. If we spend 70 percent of our waking hours communicating, how many hours do we spend communicating each day?

Language Arts

5. Listen to a news report. Apply two techniques for effective listening, such as listening for a conclusion and taking notes. Summarize the report in a short paragraph.

Check your answers at *marketingessentials.glencoe.com/8/read*

SECTION 8.2

Elements of Speech and Writing

OBJECTIVES

- Explain how to organize and present your ideas
- Demonstrate professional telephone communication skills
- Explain how to write effective business letters and persuasive messages

KEY TERMS

- persuade
- enumeration
- generalization

READ and STUDY

BEFORE YOU READ

Predict List three ways businesspeople communicate.

THE MAIN IDEA

Speaking and writing are ways to send messages—a key component of marketing. Building professional speaking and writing skills will help to ensure that your business messages are communicated successfully.

STUDY ORGANIZER

Use a chart like the one below to write tips for effective speaking in one circle, and tips for effective writing in the other circle. Write all the tips that apply to both in the space that overlaps.

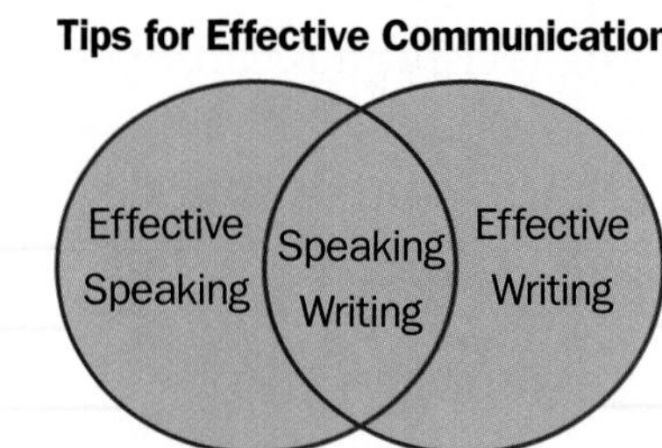

Connect As you read, list ideas about how you could improve your speaking and writing skills.

Speaking

Speaking is an important part of most jobs. People use speech to ask questions at meetings, to answer the telephone, and to discuss plans at a meeting. In marketing, speaking has applications in customer relations, presenting marketing plans, and television advertising. Because speaking is an important part of most business and marketing, it is important to know how to speak effectively.

Show Respect

In most business situations, the most important rule is to show courtesy and respect for others. Whether handling a customer complaint or addressing a coworker at a meeting, you should maintain a cordial tone.

Know the Purpose

As with listening and reading, it is helpful when speaking to know your purpose. In most business situations, speaking is done to inform, persuade, or entertain.

- **Inform** Conversations with customers and general business meetings are often held to inform others—to pass on information. When speaking to inform, be clear and concise—get to the point.
- **Persuade** Marketing involves sending messages that persuade others to change how they think or what they do. To **persuade** someone is to convince that person to change a perception in order to get him or her to do what you want. As you prepare an oral presentation, determine what your listeners' needs are. Then, talk about how you, your company, or your product can satisfy those needs. Persuasive speaking is also important in conflict resolution, when there is a need to present a point of view or suggest a solution.
- **Entertain** Sometimes the purpose of speaking is to entertain others. Salespeople frequently need to entertain clients or customers. It is not necessary to be a comedian to joke and tell stories. This kind of informal speaking helps create a comfortable atmosphere, build friendships, and improve customer relations.

Using Your Voice and Nonverbal Cues

Good communicators use their voices effectively, modulating tone and pace to improve delivery. Some people, such as news or sports commentators, have a natural talent for delivery. With practice, you too can improve communication by better controlling your voice.

•TELEPHONE SKILLS Many of today's marketing jobs require the ability to communicate clearly over the telephone.

What are some advantages and disadvantages of telephone communication?

Nonverbal cues that can enhance presentation are body language and eye contact. When speaking, maintain eye contact with your listeners as much as possible.

Speaking Formally

The general rules for effective speaking apply to all professional speaking. Whether the speech is used to present a marketing plan to the department or to give a speech to an audience of 500 people, the guidelines are the same. A good speech has a formal structure, or organization. It begins with an opening statement, which summarizes the topics to be covered. It ends with a concluding statement that reviews the main points. In between, four basic patterns can be used to structure the message.

Enumeration

Enumeration is listing items in order. This strategy is often used when giving directions or explaining a process with steps. Use signal words, such as *first, second, third,* or *next,* to help the listener. These signal words show the relationship between what you have already said and what you will say next.

Generalization With Examples

Many speakers use generalizations to make a point. A **generalization** is a statement that is accepted as true by most people. Speakers support generalizations with evidence and examples; this creates confidence in the listener. For example, when you make a general statement such as, "People agree that high definition television (HDTV) has great picture quality that's worth the added cost," you could support the claim with evidence such as, "In a Sony survey conducted in 2002, 80 percent of the HDTV owners surveyed said picture clarity is worth the higher price." Using evidence to support your generalizations also helps your listeners remember the main points. Signal words, such as *for instance* and *for example,* will help get your point across.

Case Study

Talking About Price

Selling successfully requires persuasive, informative, and entertaining speech. You must keep the purpose of your communication in mind, and organize your presentation to serve that purpose. It is essential to read the customer's body language and listen carefully to his or her needs.

The Five Ws and H

Prices for many goods and services are negotiable. A salesperson's communication skills are tested when it comes to negotiating price. Michelle Nichols, a well-known consultant on selling, reminds salespeople to remember the five Ws and H: who, what, when, where, why, and how.

- **Who** mentions price? Conventional wisdom is that the first person to mention price loses, but there are times when you have to break the ice. Practice different ways of broaching the topic.
- **What** is the price? Read your customer to decide at what price to begin negotiations. Start too high and he or she may lose interest. Too low, and you cut off potential profit.
- **When** is price mentioned? Mention price before the customer is sufficiently interested and he or she may walk away. Too late, and you may find he or she cannot afford it. You will have wasted your time. If the customer asks, it's the right time to begin discussing it.
- **Where** to talk about it? Where a sale can be completed. If you're selling cars, for example, wait until you're back in the office.
- **Why** mention it? Clearly, if you don't, there can be no sale.
- **How** to talk about it? Lightly, even with humor. If the customer is spending a significant amount, it will not help you to make him or her feel heavy or unhappy about it.

THINK STRATEGICALLY

Which of the five Ws and H is the most difficult and why?

Online Action!

Go to *marketingessentials.glencoe.com/8/case* to find a research project on sales communication skills.

Cause and Effect

When you present an issue in terms of cause and effect, you attempt to demonstrate that one event or situation is the cause of another. For example, you can show how implementing your marketing plan will allow the client to meet a sales goal. This pattern can be used effectively to persuade the listener. Use signal words or phrases, such as *therefore, consequently,* and *as a result* to help the listener understand the sequence.

Compare and Contrast

Another pattern often used to persuade a listener is compare and contrast. In this pattern, new concepts are explained by showing how they are similar to or unlike those listeners already know. This approach is particularly useful when working in cross-cultural situations. Signal words or phrases such as *similarly, however, nevertheless,* and *on the other hand,* help to make the differences and similarities clear.

Speaking on the Telephone

In most telephone conversations, your listener cannot see you, so you cannot rely on facial expressions and body language to help get your message across. The message is communicated solely by voice, so a pleasant voice is very important.

Whether answering or initiating the call, greet the other person in a cheerful but formal way. For example, you might say, "Customer Relations, this is Maria. How may I help you?" This greeting signals to the caller that he or she has reached the right number. Use a pleasant tone, enunciate clearly, and speak directly into the mouthpiece. Speak loudly enough for the other person to hear, but do not shout. Be courteous and respectful, and never interrupt when the other person is speaking.

It is also necessary that you convey all the necessary information. It may be a good idea to write down key points before a phone call. Telephone customer service representatives and telemarketers use scripts.

Be prepared to take a message. Note the time of the call, the caller's name and message, and the return phone number. Repeat the telephone number to the caller to make sure it is correct. Most companies make use of voice mail so that callers may leave a message when the person is unavailable.

Writing

Much business and marketing communication is in written form. A written message is necessary when there is a large volume of material and presenting it verbally would be impractical. Writing is also necessary when a permanent record of the communication is required. For instance, legal documents, manuals describing company policy, and letters confirming the terms of a deal are all written.

Writing takes more time and thought than a conversation. One advantage of writing a message rather than speaking it is that there is more time to organize the message. There are different forms of business writing—e-mail, letters, reports—each with specific uses and conventions. Marketing writing takes many forms, including print ads, scripts, and packaging.

Basic Considerations in Writing

As with listening, reading, and speaking, it is important when writing to know the precise reason for the message. The three basic considerations in writing are:

1. **Know your audience** Before you begin writing, think about who will receive your message. What do you know about them? Do they have the same experiences as you? Why will they read your message? What do they know about the subject? Answering these questions will help you to write a meaningful message.
2. **Know your purpose** Why are you writing? Most of your marketing writing is done to inform, confirm, inquire, answer, or persuade. Marketing messages are often written to persuade. Some messages, of course, combine two or more of these purposes.
3. **Know your subject** To write effective messages, you need in-depth knowledge and you must know how to relate what

MARKET TECH

Push-to-Talk Marketing

Following the popularity of push-to-talk buttons on cell phones, another push-to-talk technology is now in use in marketing.

Technology company eStara offers VoIP (Voice over Internet Protocol) service, allowing users to respond verbally to printed communication. A customer can click on a button on a Web page and initiate a live conversation using his or her Internet connection.

On-Demand Live Service

Another option is for the user to key in his or her phone number and click the same button to receive a call back from a customer service employee. The technology is gaining popularity with marketers who can no longer make unsolicited calls to consumers as a result of legislation restricting telemarketing.

Testing Banner Ads

The VoIP service also allows advertisers to test the effectiveness of Web banner ads, based on how many calls they generate. In one survey of customers using the technology to buy something online, 25 percent said they would have quit the transaction if they hadn't had the push-to-talk option.

THINK LIKE A MARKETER

Why is it a plus for marketers to be able to move from a written communication like Web advertising or e-mail to an actual conversation?

@ Online Action!

Go to *marketingessentials.glencoe.com/8/tech* to find a project on VoIP technology.

you know to what the customer wants to know. You may be well educated on certain subjects, but almost every new assignment will require further research.

Developing a Writing Style

Writing style differs from industry to industry. The executives of a company generally establish the company's writing style, which usually includes guidelines on when to use formal and informal communication. You can read company letters, official e-mail, memos, and reports to gain a feel for how the firm wishes to present itself to its clients.

In business writing, it is generally best to use a direct yet respectful conversational style. Whether writing to inquire, inform, or persuade, your writing should be crisp, clear, and easy to read. Be professional in tone, but do not use big words to impress others. Use a word processing program with spelling and grammar checkers to eliminate common errors. Always review your writing one final time to ensure that all errors are corrected. If you have a tendency to overlook minor mistakes, ask a colleague to proofread your work.

Personalize your message by using the name of the person who will receive it. The receiver will have a warmer feeling toward you if you do. When writing to someone outside your company, be formal until you have permission to be more informal and personal in your writing.

You may want to use jargon in your messages to people in your professional field. However, when writing to a mixed audience, it is best to avoid jargon. If jargon is necessary, clearly define any technical words.

Use Language Effectively

Pay attention to the words and phrases used by your clients, vendors, and associates. If they are different from the ones you generally use, translate your ideas and feelings into language that makes sense to them. Using the words and phrases familiar to your audience in your communications can be a powerful persuasive technique.

Organize Your Thoughts

Construct your persuasive message in three parts: an opening paragraph, a persuasive body, and a concluding paragraph. In the opening paragraph, grab your readers' attention. State clearly why you are writing and involve them in some way, perhaps addressing them as *you* if appropriate.

Begin each body paragraph with a topic sentence. Follow with three to five sentences in which you develop a single point. Use connectives, such as *therefore* and *so you see*. Ethical writing requires honesty, so be sure to acknowledge any significant point of view that may differ from your own. There is nothing wrong with presenting evidence showing that your view is more likely to result in the desired outcome. If you can, quote a recognized expert or survey to add support for your case. Try to create a vivid image to help your reader see your point of view.

Your concluding paragraph should be positive and interesting and should strongly support the message outlined in your introduction. Restate the points made in the body, citing the evidence in support of each point. Emphasize the overall reason your position, product, or service is worth considering. Finally, state exactly what action should be taken next to achieve the mutually acceptable outcome.

Forms of Written Communication

Most business writing takes the form of letters, e-mail, memos, and reports. Each of these formats follows its own very specific rules of style and format.

Letters

Communication with people outside the company is usually done with business letters or e-mail. Letters are the more formal of the two. They are used for purposes such as official announcements, thank yous, and confirmations of business transactions. In direct-mail marketing, targeted letters are often written addressing the needs or interests of specific groups.

E-Mail

E-mail has become the method of choice for fast, informal communication with those inside and outside the company. Marketers often use e-mail for informal contacts between the firm and the client. E-mail has the advantage of speed over other forms of written communication. With e-mail, documents can be attached to, or sent along with, the message.

A MATTER OF ETHICS

Ethics in Communication

In cases where others are affected, the writer or speaker has an ethical responsibility to make sure the message is clear and understood.

Suppose you supervise a large car manufacturing company with many different departments. You ask the engineering department to send you a memo evaluating recent complaints about a possible manufacturing defect in one model. You also ask for a recommendation for action.

Targeting Questions and Answers

The engineering department sends you a detailed report with a lot of objective data on the different components of the car but no recommendation for action. Three weeks later, you receive several reports of fatal injuries in accidents involving the same car model and the same car parts.

THINKING ETHICALLY

Does this engineering department bear any responsibility in this lack of communication? Why or why not?

@ Online Action!

Go to *marketingessentials.glencoe.com/8/ethics* to find a project on communication and ethics.

While e-mail norms differ from company to company, a typical interoffice e-mail contains the following:

- An informative subject title
- A traditional (not personal) greeting
- A concise, clearly stated body
- A statement regarding the type of response needed
- A formal closing and signature (for the signature, type your name, company, address, phone and fax number, and e-mail address)

Although e-mail has a reputation for speed and informality, it is important to remember that, like all written communication, it leaves a permanent record. Business e-mails are official documents. They are the property of the company or firm.

Many companies now have strict e-mail policies. The following rules are found in most e-mail policies:

- Save only essential e-mail.
- Do not forward e-mail without the sender's express permission.
- Seek permission and then use extreme care when forwarding confidential e-mails.
- Use only copyrighted materials that you have permission, or have paid, to use.

When writing business e-mail, follow the guidelines for business writing described above. Compose your messages carefully. Use conventional business language and style. Use the company computer only for business communication, not for private messages.

Memos

A memorandum, or memo, is a written message to someone in the company. It is usually brief and covers only one subject. Most memos are written in a simple format that has a standard set of headings. The standard headings include the sender's and receiver's names, the date, the subject, and a message in paragraph form. In many businesses, e-mail has taken the place of memos.

Business Reports

Business reports usually cover lengthy topics, such as yearly sales, survey results, or problems that need attention. Some, called in-house reports, are meant to be read only by company employees. Others, such as reports to stockholders, are written for a wider audience and are more formal. An in-house report can be written by a company department to let management know the results of a project, or a report might move from one department to another. For example, the sales department may produce a report to tell the design department how customers like a product. Several people may give input to produce the report, but one person is usually responsible for writing the final document.

Many of the techniques used in preparing a speech are also appropriate in preparing a report. Enumeration, generalization with example, cause and effect, and compare and contrast are patterns of organization that work well for reports. A simple report can be brief, perhaps as short as one page. Complex reports include more data and may use a variety of charts and graphs.

Company Publications

Many companies produce internal publications for their employees. These might be newsletters or employee handbooks that outline policies and procedures. Some companies produce external publications, such as promotional brochures about the company or individual products. A communications department usually writes internal publications, while a marketing department writes external publications.

Meetings and Parliamentary Procedure

Parliamentary procedure is a structure for holding group meetings (such as DECA's) and making decisions. Parliamentary procedure favors the opinion of the majority of a group, but the viewpoint of the minority is not overlooked. Parliamentary procedure has a specific structure.

A Quorum

A quorum is a proportion of the membership needed to conduct official business. It may be a set number of members, like 20, or a percentage of members, like 51 percent.

Order of Business

The meeting follows a standard order of business, which is called an agenda. The standard format for a meeting is as follows

1. **Call to order** This statement alerts all members that the meeting is beginning and that they should be quiet.
2. **Minutes of the meeting** The secretary reads the minutes, which are a written record that outlines the decisions made at the last meeting.
3. **Treasurer's report** The treasurer reports the money that the organization received since the last meeting and the money it spent, as well as the current balance.
4. **Committee reports** Each committee presents a report to let the entire membership know what they have done and what they plan to do.
5. **Old business** Any issues that were discussed but were not decided on become old business.
6. **New business** New ideas are brought up at the end of the meeting.
7. **Adjournment** This is the official end of the meeting. The secretary records the time of adjournment in the minutes.

The Motion

After being allowed to speak by the chairperson, one member makes a motion, or a proposal. Another member must second the motion. A period of discussion follows.

8.2 AFTER YOU READ

Reviewing Key Terms and Concepts

1. Name the three most common purposes for speaking, and give an example of how each can be applied in a business situation.
2. What are three basic considerations in writing an effective message?
3. What is the difference between persuading and influencing?

Integrating Academic Skills

Mathematics

4. Communication on the Internet travels at the speed of light—186,000 miles per second. The Earth is approximately 8,000 miles in diameter. How long would it take an e-mail to circle the Earth one time? Round your answer to the nearest one-thousandth of a second.

Social Studies

5. Identify a political issue that is being debated at the local, state, or national level. Write a letter to persuade your government representative to vote for or against the issue. Construct your letter using the three parts outlined in your text.

Check your answers at *marketingessentials.glencoe.com/8/read*

CAREERS IN MARKETING

MARIAN DOUGLAS PEARCE, APR, CCC
ACCOUNT EXECUTIVE
SEMAPHORE, INC.

What do you do at work?
I spend a considerable amount of my time talking to clients on the phone, in meetings, or via e-mail. After determining their needs, I develop a marketing plan to achieve their goals and objectives. I collaborate with the creative team (an art director and copywriter) to develop the product (ad, billboard, etc.) that best suits their needs. I also am responsible for creating project and annual marketing budgets and account administration tasks such as billing, filing, and supplier coordination.

What skills are most important to you?
Time management skills, organization, and diplomacy. If I were not organized, I could not keep up with all the projects we have in the agency at one time. An account executive must be diplomatic when it comes to giving the clients what they want but giving them what they need to accomplish their goals. I recommend learning the basics of all integrated marketing communications. I received my undergraduate degree in advertising and public relations management and minored in marketing. Training in business administration basics such as accounting will help you understand the budgeting and billing processes that are a daily part of an account executive's routine. And training in presentation skills is a must.

What is your key to success?
I treat my clients the way that I would like to be treated. I respect them and their ideas because they intrinsically know their business better than I can ever know.

Aptitudes, Abilities, and Skills

Organization, strong interpersonal skills, diplomacy, the ability to manage and wisely use resources

Education and Training

Degrees in marketing, communication, and general business courses

Career Path

Account executives can be recruited from within. As an entry-level sales position, account executive jobs are usually paid on a commission-only basis. Established account executives are often in high demand.

THINKING CRITICALLY

Why is diplomacy such an important skill in this career?

Go to *marketingessentials.glencoe.com/8/careers* to find a career-related activity.

CHAPTER 8 REVIEW

FOCUS on KEY POINTS

SECTION 8.1

- The global economy has brought new pressures on companies to communicate with customers and vendors around the world. Overcoming cultural barriers to listening with understanding is now more important than ever.
- As the volume of information to be absorbed increases, reading for meaning—the ability to differentiate what is important from what is not—is becoming an important business skill.

SECTION 8.2

- Most business and marketing jobs require the ability to communicate a message clearly, concisely, and courteously by speaking and writing.
- Persuasion is used to convince others of the value or importance of an idea or thing—an essential skill in marketing. The simplest and often most effective way to persuade others is to learn their needs and propose a way to fulfill them.

REVIEW VOCABULARY

Define each of the following terms in a short sentence.

1. communication (p. 178)
2. channels/media (p. 179)
3. feedback (p. 179)
4. barriers (p. 179)
5. setting (p. 179)
6. distractions (p. 182)
7. emotional barriers (p. 182)
8. jargon (p. 183)
9. persuade (p. 185)
10. enumeration (p. 185)
11. generalization (p. 186)

REVIEW FACTS and IDEAS

12. List three examples of barriers to listening (8.1)
13. Explain three ways to improve listening skills. (8.1)
14. Why is it important for businesspeople to be aware of cultural differences? (8.1)
15. What five techniques will help you read for understanding? (8.1)
16. List three professional telephone skills. (8.2)
17. Explain the different uses of letters, e-mail, memos, and reports. (8.2)
18. What are the three basic considerations in business writing? (8.2)
19. Describe a method of organizing and presenting your ideas. (8.2)

BUILD SKILLS

20. Workplace Skills

Public Speaking Using presentation software or visual aids, prepare a five-to-ten-minute presentation on how body language, tone, and mannerisms affect communication.

21. Technology Applications

Writing Effective E-Mails Imagine that employees at your work have been using company e-mail to send personal or social messages.

Use an e-mail or word processing program to compose an e-mail memo that instructs employees on the appropriate use of interoffice e-mail.

22. Math Practice

Determine Costs You have been asked to make the arrangements for a conference meeting for your company. A local conference center charges $150 to rent a room for a half day and $200 to rent a room for a full day. They charge $15.00 per person for each lunch served and $30.00 per person for each dinner served.

How much will it cost to rent the facility for one and one-half days and to provide lunch for 46 conference attendees on the first day?

DEVELOP CRITICAL THINKING

23. Following Directions

Describe a situation where you have had to follow directions to complete a task. Explain how you listened to the instructions (or read them) and how you made sure to follow each step.

List three ways improving your listening skills could help you accomplish tasks at school or at work?

24. Communicating in Person

Even though high-tech communication channels are available, many businesspeople still prefer face-to-face meetings for important transactions. Explain why you think businesspeople in your culture and other cultures might sometimes prefer to communicate in person.

APPLY CONCEPTS

25. Prepare a Business Letter

Your high school debate team is having a raffle. The money from the raffle will be used to send your team to district, state, and national debate tournaments.

Activity Use a word processing program to write a business letter from your high school debate club to local business owners soliciting donations for your annual raffle.

26. Research Public Speaking

Use the Internet to research Toastmasters International, an organization for public speakers. Describe how its logo communicates its goals. Lists the four skills this organization will help you develop or strengthen.

Activity Use a graphic-design or word processing program to create a brochure to persuade your classmates that membership in this organization will benefit them.

NET SAVVY

27. The Internet and Government

Do an Internet search to discover what the U.S. government is doing to fight spam, or unwanted e-mail, on the Internet. Write a brief report on your findings. Then use the Web to find the e-mail addresses of the senators from your state. Send them an e-mail expressing your view on the issue.

THE 

CONNECTION

Role Play: Customer Service

Situation You are to assume the role of assistant manager of an online business that specializes in antique prints, matting, and custom framing. Your customers have the choice of using your toll-free phone line or communicating by e-mail. You do business through the business's Web site. The business's owner (judge) has just received an e-mail from one of your best customers requesting that you look for a special print to add to an existing collection.

Activity Compose an e-mail response to the customer for the owner's (judge's) approval.

Evaluation You will be evaluated on how well you meet the following performance indicators:

- Write business letters
- Use communications technologies/systems (e.g., e-mail, faxes, voice mail, cell phones, etc.)
- Explain the nature of written communications
- Handle customer inquiries
- Demonstrate a customer-service mindset

@ Online Action!

For more information and DECA Prep practice, go to *marketingessentials.glencoe.com/8/DECA*

CHAPTER 9
Technology Applications for Marketing

Chapter Objectives

After reading this chapter, you should be able to:

- Identify eight types of computer applications and explain how these are used in business and marketing
- Describe the types of computer software that are influencing and reshaping the world of marketing
- Explain how the Internet and the World Wide Web can increase business productivity

GUIDE TO THE PHOTO

Market Talk Continuing advances in technology have brought about the most productive period in U.S. and world history. Technology has also hastened the arrival of the global economy.

Quick Think The widespread use of computers has made it easy to communicate with people all over the world. Name a few advantages of fast, around-the-globe communication. Name a few disadvantages.

THE DECA CONNECTION

Performance indicators represent key skills and knowledge. Relating them to the concepts explained in this chapter is your key to success in DECA events.

These acronyms represent DECA events that involve knowledge of concepts in this chapter.

AAAL	**FMAL**	**MMS**	**TMDM***
AAML	**FMDM**	**QSRM**	**TSE**
ADC	**FMML**	**RMAL**	**VPM**
BSM*	**FSRM**	**RMML**	
EMDM	**HMDM***	**SMDM***	

In all these DECA events you should be able to follow these performance indicators:

- Use communication technologies/systems
- Describe ethical considerations in providing information
- Identify ways that technology impacts business
- Demonstrate basic word processing skills
- Demonstrate basic presentation software skills
- Demonstrate basic database skills
- Demonstrate basic spreadsheet skills
- Demonstrate basic search skills on the Web
- Explain how technology impacts the industry

Events with an asterisk (*) also include:

- Use check authorization system

Some events include other indicators:

EMDM Explain the nature of the Internet
Use e-mail functions
Demonstrate basic desktop publishing
Integrate software applications
Create and post a Web page
Describe tools used in Web site creation
Explain basic programming languages
Select a Web host

DECA PREP

Check your understanding of DECA performance indicators with the DECA activity in this chapter's review. For more information and DECA Prep practice, go to *marketingessentials .glencoe.com/9/DECA*

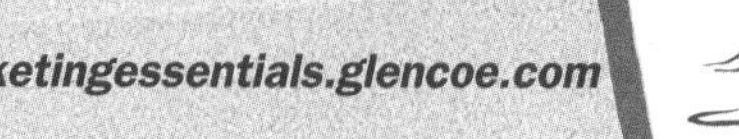

SECTION 9.1

Computer Applications

OBJECTIVES

- **Identify eight types of computer applications and explain how these are used in business and marketing**

KEY TERMS

- **word processing programs**
- **database programs**
- **spreadsheet programs**
- **desktop publishing programs**
- **graphics and design programs**
- **presentation software**
- **home page**
- **hypertext markup language (HTML)**
- **communications programs**

READ and STUDY

BEFORE YOU READ

Predict Are computers necessary for a marketing project to be successful?

THE MAIN IDEA

Your career success will probably require an understanding and skillful use of computers and of certain key software applications.

STUDY ORGANIZER

In a chart like the one below, note the eight types of software discussed in this section.

Computer Program	Uses
Word processing program	Letters and memos

Connect Name three computer applications you use often.

Types of Applications

There is a computer application for just about every purpose you can imagine. For personal use, daily planner and calendar applications manage time, and financial software manages money. Some applications serve as address books, while others help manage photos. Virtually all businesses use computer applications. Medical practices use programs to schedule patients and track billing. Hotels use applications to manage room assignments and generate bills.

Software is constantly being written, tested, and marketed to meet every conceivable business need.

Word Processing Programs

Word processing programs are software applications designed to create documents that are primarily text but that may contain a few graphics. The benefits of a word processing program include being able to determine the format of a document and see on screen exactly how the document will look when printed out. This is called WYSIWYG, for "What You See Is What You Get." Word processing programs also help correct mistakes in spelling and grammar, give accurate word counts, and add design elements, among dozens of other features. The most common word processing program is Microsoft Word. Others include WordPerfect, Nisus Writer Express, and Mariner Write. Businesses use word processing programs to

- Write letters and memos
- Produce research papers and reports
- Develop business and marketing plans
- Write contracts
- Take notes and record meeting minutes
- Create announcements

Database Programs

Database programs are applications that store and organize information. They are like filing cabinets, but with much greater flexibility. Database programs allow users to sort, find, choose (or filter), and organize information. A single database can hold information about the products a company sells, the orders the company has received, shipments of those products, and its customers. The power of a database is its ability to link that information together. Database software ranks among the most popular business applications. Common database software includes Filemaker Pro, Microsoft Access, 4D, and Oracle. Marketers use database programs to

- Maintain customer lists for automated mass mailings
- Keep information about guests and vendors for parties and events
- Catalog furniture and assets for insurance records
- Manage time and track billable hours
- Catalog personnel records
- Scan the Internet to find suppliers and customers
- Track the searches and purchases of clients visiting Web sites

Suppose you are using a database of your company's mailing list. That mailing list contains the names and addresses of more than 3,000 customers. With one keystroke, the database can alphabetize the list by last name, group the addresses by zip code, or display only those customers who use post office boxes. Including purchase histories in the database would allow you to quickly pull up a list of all customers who made purchases during a certain month or who purchased a certain dollar amount of merchandise.

Spreadsheet Programs

Spreadsheet programs are used to organize, calculate, and analyze numerical data. With spreadsheets, you can perform financial and scientific calculations, organize numeric information, illustrate data with charts and graphs, and create professional-looking reports. Spreadsheets also graphically display the relationship of data in the form of charts and graphs that are often easier for people to understand than tables of raw data. Microsoft Excel is one of the most popular spreadsheet programs. Others include Quattro Pro and XESS. Businesspeople use spreadsheets for many purposes:

- Develop a budget
- Analyze financial performance
- Track loans or mortgages
- Track stock and bond performance
- Schedule projects
- Manage business assets

• **FAST RESULTS** This ad is for one of many software applications for business. It makes financial management easier and faster.

Why would a travel planning site like Expedia.com need such software?

- Produce profit and loss statements
- Calculate and produce a payroll
- Track client/customer responses to marketing promotions
- Build relationship marketing based on customer value profiles
- Track sales and service
- Conduct marketing research

A spreadsheet consists of a grid of rows and columns. Users enter data and formulas into cells on the grid, and the program performs calculations with speed and accuracy not possible by hand or with a calculator. When you change one piece of information, the spreadsheet will automatically update all related numbers. This allows users to test different scenarios. For example, you can see how adjusting the price of a product would affect projected sales, taxes, and the overall budget.

Desktop Publishing Programs

The invention and rapid development of **desktop publishing programs** illustrate both the computer's creative potential and its usefulness for business. Part word processor and part graphics application, desktop publishing programs enable users to edit and manipulate both text and graphics in one document. This is how books, magazines, and flyers are designed and produced. Desktop publishing software can produce documents that are creative, eye-catching, attractive, professional, and easy to read. The two most popular commercial desktop publishing programs are Adobe InDesign and QuarkXPress. Marketing uses desktop publishing to

- Create layouts for newsletters, books, brochures, and advertisements
- Create professional-looking forms, such as invoices and project planning sheets

Businesses can save money by using desktop publishing programs in-house to produce printed materials.

Graphics and Design Programs

Graphics and design programs are software applications for creating and modifying images, including drawings, designs, and photographs. Designers can create all graphic elements themselves with the drawing tools provided by the software, or they can use photos and ready-made artwork, often called clip art. These images are usually grouped together in categories like business, food, sports, people, places, animals, cartoons, and holidays.

There are thousands of graphics programs, with some of the most common being Adobe Photoshop, Adobe Illustrator, CorelDRAW, Flash, and Macromedia Freehand. Graphics programs can be used by marketers and businesses to

- Design marketing promotion materials
- Create logos and letterheads
- Illustrate floor plans and furniture arrangements
- Create professional-looking illustrations and photographic prints
- Create images for presentations or for Web pages and Internet ads

Presentation Software

Presentation software produces slide shows or multimedia presentations. This software helps users organize ideas and concepts to be presented in a meeting. Presentation software can be used by businesses and marketers to

- Prepare verbal and visual copy for meetings

•SHOW and TELL Presentation software has become an indispensable tool in many business meetings.

How could you use such software in your schoolwork?

GLOBAL MARKET

Growing E-Clout of China

With 1.3 billion people, China has the largest population in the world, a huge potential e-commerce market. The Chinese economy is expanding, and computer sales are increasing. In 2003, 80 million Chinese were online, and that number is expected to almost double by 2006 as 800,000 Chinese become Internet users each week. International Data Corporation (IDC) estimated that there would be 84.2 million Web-enabled PCs in China by the end of 2004. Investment in Chinese Web portals is increasing dramatically. U.S. Web titans Yahoo and eBay have both entered the Chinese market, and Google opened a Chinese-language site in early 2004.

Governmental Help The Chinese government gives help to companies developing Web technologies. This provides a competitive advantage over businesses from free market economies like the United States. Web portals in the United States get most of their income from advertising. Chinese portals take advantage of the high rate of cellular phone use to sell services like messaging, games, even video greeting cards—all displayed on cell phones. Retailing and business-to-business sales lag far behind such services in the United States because of credit card and delivery obstacles.

CRITICAL THINKING

Do you think the U.S. government should make grants to technology companies to help them compete? Why or why not?

@ Online Action!

Go to *marketingessentials.glencoe.com/9/global* for an activity on international marketing and computer technology.

- Present and discuss ideas interactively via the Internet with clients in other cities or countries
- Create slide shows using pictures or Web pages
- Add voice narration to accompany visual material

Presentation software can incorporate a series of slides, film clips, and streaming video. Presentations can include text, bulleted lists, graphs, photos, screen shots from the company Web page, and even interactive problem and decision situations. Colorful graphics and concise text can be used in marketing promotions and sales presentations to persuade clients and close sales. Voice narration can create the feeling of attending a conference, even when participants are thousands of miles apart.

As global interaction in the business world increases, programs like this simplify communication and cut down on travel time. Some examples of presentation software programs are Microsoft PowerPoint and Apple Keynote.

Web Page Editors

The Web has become an integral part of our world. Many businesses use their Web sites to promote their companies and products and to stay connected to their customers. Web sites generally contain an initial **home page** which is the entry point for a Web site. It gives general information to introduce the company, person, or product. The home page has links to other pages containing additional information, such as product details and contact information.

The home page can also link to an online store or other interactive resources such as online questionnaires.

At first, creating a Web page meant writing very specific, detailed, and complicated code, called **hypertext markup language (HTML)**. Today, Web editing programs enable people to create Web pages as if they were using a word processor or a desktop publishing program. Some of the most popular of these applications are Macromedia Dreamweaver, Adobe GoLive, and Microsoft FrontPage.

Communications Programs

Communications programs enable users to electronically communicate with

Case Study

Online Radio

Radioparadise is an online radio station run out of the home of Bill and Rebecca Goldsmith. A 30-year veteran of FM radio, Bill Goldsmith loves his new career. He uses a laptop computer to program the station to play an eclectic mix of musical styles. There is no advertising, but satisfied listeners contributed $120,000 in 2003, enough to cover all the station's costs and still give the Goldsmiths a comfortable lifestyle. As sound and Internet technology continue to become more powerful and less expensive, opportunities for online radio entrepreneurs are likely to expand.

A New trend

Internet radio is gaining in popularity. Not long ago, online sound quality was poor and it often dropped out due to connection problems. But digital audio file quality has improved, and broadband technology makes connections more stable. Most new computers have built-in sound capability, so no new equipment is required. You can sit at your computer, do your homework, and listen to your favorite band. Online listening is growing at an average rate of 43 percent a year. Yahoo's music site and radio network, Launchcast, gets one million listeners a week. Nineteen million people tune in to Internet radio each week.

Just like other broadcasters, Internet radio stations are legally required to pay music companies for the copyrighted music they play.

Global Reach

More than 6,500 stations are available online from more than 130 countries. They are an easy and inexpensive way for immigrants to stay in touch with their home countries. They can also help students learn the language and music of the cultures they are studying.

THINK STRATEGICALLY

If you were the owner of an online radio station, how would you plan to earn money from your site?

@ Online Action!

Go to *marketingessentials.glencoe/9/case* to find an activity about online technology and marketing.

others around the world through their computers. The key to any communication software is connecting to some kind of network.

Broadband Technology

Broadband technology is a high-speed connection that transmits information through special phone or TV cable lines. It dramatically reduces the time it takes for a computer to send and receive data over a network. This extra bandwidth can be used to send files attached to e-mails and can turn text-based instant messaging sessions into audio chats or even video conference calls where participants use small cameras and can see and hear each other in real time.

Videoconferencing

Videoconferencing has many practical advantages. Perhaps the greatest professional advantage to videoconferencing is that it can reduce the need for expensive business travel. Travel time and expenses can be dramatically reduced by holding videoconferences rather than meeting in person.

Communications Programs

Communications programs include e-mail software such as Microsoft Outlook and Qualcomm Eudora; instant messaging software such as AOL Instant Messenger; and videoconference software, including Apple iChat and Microsoft NetMeeting.

9.1 AFTER YOU READ

Reviewing Key Terms and Concepts

1. List eight types of software applications commonly used by businesses.
2. What is a database program? What advantage does such a program offer a business that gathers a large quantity of data?
3. When might a business use presentation software? Name two examples of this type of software.

Integrating Academic Skills

Mathematics

4. You are comparing the cost of two high-speed Internet services. The cable company charges a $59.95 one-time connection fee, plus $34.95 per month. It provides free connection hardware if you keep the service for one year. The phone company charges $89.95 for the connection fee and hardware, plus $29.95 per month. What is the difference in the cost of the two plans for a 12-month period?

Geography

5. Using the Internet or reference materials in a library, research the geography and culture of a country you know little about but would like to visit. Then use word processing software to write a tourism advertisement describing the points of interest that a visitor should not miss.

@ Online Action!

Check your answers at *marketingessentials.glencoe.com/9/read*

Computer Technology and Marketing

OBJECTIVES

- Describe the types of computer software that are influencing and reshaping the world of marketing
- Explain how the Internet and the World Wide Web can increase business productivity

KEY TERMS

- enterprise resource planning (ERP)
- Internet
- Internet service providers (ISPs)
- Wi-Fi
- World Wide Web
- hypertext transfer protocol (HTTP)
- uniform resource locator (URL)
- firewall
- site map

READ and STUDY

BEFORE YOU READ

Connect How do you think computer technology will change marketing and business in the future?

THE MAIN IDEA

Technological advances are changing the scope of marketing. With innovations that speed up the transfer of information and increase the use of the Internet, businesses are finding new marketing opportunities and can offer better service to customers.

STUDY ORGANIZER

In a chart like the one below, list the five types of specialized computer technology marketers use.

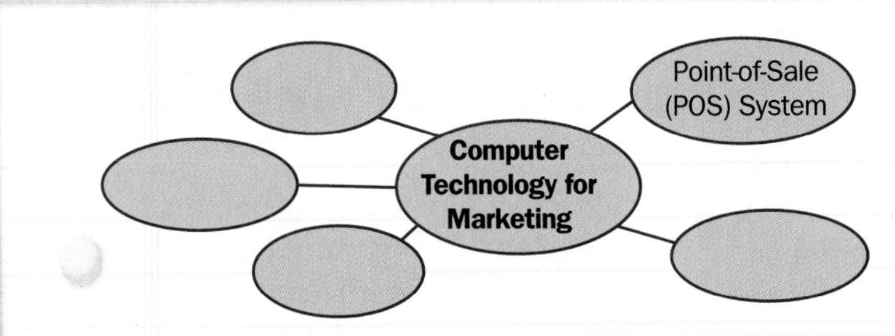

Interactive Technology for Marketing

Marketing applications for computer technology appear endless. In addition to the software applications discussed in Section 9.1, many other computer applications are shaping the way we conduct business. These include point-of-sale systems, interactive touch-screen computers, interactive TV, just-in-time schedulers, customer relationship management and enterprise resource planning systems, and the Internet.

Analyze Think of the ways you have used the Internet.

Point-of-Sale Systems

A common use of computers in retailing is the point-of-sale (POS) system. This system consists of cash registers and peripherals, such as scanners, touch screens, handheld checkout devices, printers, and electronic kiosks. Scanners feed information directly from merchandise tags or product labels into a computer to update inventory. See Chapter 16 for more information on POS systems.

Integrated Marketing Software

Capturing customer information, viewing customers' sales histories, and customizing promotions are the core of customer relationship management (CRM). New CRM applications are Internet-enabled, fully integrated Web service applications. A customer can place an order online and check the progress of the order on the Web or by telephone. In addition to tracking the business the customer is doing with the firm, CRM can also track the customer's satisfaction level at each step in the sales process.

Enterprise Resource Planning (ERP)

Enterprise resource planning (ERP) software is even more sophisticated. Using new ERP software, all parts of a company's business management are integrated, including planning, manufacturing, sales, marketing, invoicing, and payroll. Applications are now available to help management with such activities as inventory control, order tracking, customer service, finance, and human resources. ERP vendors are now integrating CRM software into their ERP suites. Both CRM and ERP applications can help generate marketing reports and solve marketing problems.

Interactive Touch-Screen Computers

A touch screen is a computer display screen that responds to human touch. This allows the user to interact with the computer by touching words or pictures on the screen. (See Figure 9.1.) In retail marketing, there is a strong move toward the greater use of this kind of interactive technology. Interactive computers are on shelves in retail stores and in stand-alone kiosks at malls and airports. The customer reads and responds to questions on the touch-sensitive screen. In this way, the "computerized salesperson" directs the customer to the correct product.

Customers like touch screens, and the maintenance costs to business are very low. However, it would be a mistake to think all sales can be made via touch-screen technology. The computer-assisted transactions discussed here are used for products, goods, and services that are fairly standard and receptive to programmable decision making. Costly or complex products need a degree of personal contact that is not possible without a real person.

Interactive TV

Interactive TV marries television with Internet-style interactivity. Such systems combine satellite dishes, DVD players, and television set-top boxes equipped with modems, microprocessors, hard drives, operating systems, and software, including browsers to make the TV behave more like a computer.

Advertisers like the idea of interactive television because consumers can instantly get more information about products through their TVs. Viewers can actually interact with the programming. For example, when a viewer sees an ad for pizza and decides he is hungry he can click a link to have that company's pizza delivered right to the door.

The Click Stream

Interactive TV also benefits marketers because of the click stream. Every click of the remote control goes into a database for later analysis. From this data, a picture of individual viewers and what motivates them emerges. TV programmers can use this data to check viewers' reaction to content and use that information in deciding what to show in the future. Over time, psychological profiles of individual viewers can be developed, providing an enormous amount of information. Today, companies are developing and testing ways in which interactive television can be used for advertising and promotion.

Figure 9.1 Marketing With Interactive Technology

• Conversing With a Computer Interactive technology, in which a customer interacts with a computer to get a desired result, is dramatically changing the way products and services are marketed. Applications of this technology are making sales and ordering more streamlined and efficient. They allow market research to capture an enormous amount of data, and, by using these data, advertisers are able to more effectively reach their markets. Let's look at some of the ways interactive technology is being put to use in marketing.

What's the importance of interactive technology to marketers?

Touch-Screen Computers, Computerized Salespeople
Touch-screen computers allow customers to locate product information without the help of salespeople. The computers can check inventory and prices, suggest other merchandise a customer might like, and even connect to a wedding gift registry created in another state.

Interactive TV
With interactive TV, viewers can vote for their favorite TV character, access information related to a program, download reality show contestant biographies, or link to an online store. Sports fans can use interactive TV to get up-to-the-minute results for their favorite teams or athletes.

E-Commerce
E-commerce allows customers to view products, compare prices, and order—all at the click of a mouse. This young man can compare prices and styles at hundreds of hip-hop "stores" in a matter of minutes without leaving his home. Information he supplies when placing his order is captured in a database and used by a marketer to generate future sales.

@ Online Action! Go to *marketingessentials.glencoe.com/9/figure/1* to find a research project on marketing with technology.

Internet Connectivity

The **Internet** appears to be the world's biggest computer network, but it is actually a network of networks, across which information flows freely.

The Internet began life as a research project for the U.S. Defense Department. Over time, it became popular among researchers at universities. Then it took on a life of its own, growing slowly at first and then exploding in popularity in the 1990s. Telephone companies provided connectivity to the first commercial Internet service providers. During this time, most people connected to the Internet using a dial-up modem connected to telephone lines. The first modems were quite slow, but improved technology brought faster modems and more reliable service.

Broadband Connection

In the 1990s, high-speed connectivity became affordable for home users. This service, called broadband, uses technology that moves much more data per second along a phone line. Two types of broadband technology were introduced: the digital subscriber line (DSL) and Internet access via cable TV. Both are provided by **Internet service providers (ISPs)**, which are companies that provide Internet access for businesses, organizations, and individuals. Estimates in 2004 showed that 48 million Americans have broadband connections in their homes.

Yet another technology is being developed for faster Internet access. New modems transmit data across the power grid. Introduced in 2004 by the publicly owned electric power utility in Manassas, Virginia, this new service is known as broadband-over-power-lines (BPL). All you have to do to connect is plug into any electric outlet. Because the power lines are already in place, the cost of BPL connection is expected to remain lower than DSL or cable connections. With 40 million people still using dial-up connections, there may be a sizable market for BPL.

Wireless Connectivity

Wireless routers provide Internet connectivity without a physical connection. This technology, called **Wi-Fi**, (short for wireless fidelity) establishes a wireless Internet connection using radio frequencies.

Hundreds of millions of people around the world are expected to join the online community over the next few years. As of 2004, 945 million people used the Internet, according to the *Computer Industry Almanac.* That figure is expected to hit 1.1 billion by 2005, 1.3 billion by 2006, and close to 1.5 billion by 2007.

The World Wide Web

Although the terms are often used synonymously, the **World Wide Web** and the Internet are actually two different things. The Web is a subset of the Internet and is a collection of interlinked electronic documents. These pages are viewed with a browser. A browser is any piece of software that tells the computer what Web content to display. Web pages contain links that prompt the browser to load a new page.

Researcher Tim Berners-Lee invented the technology behind the Web. He developed the **hypertext transfer protocol (HTTP)** that links documents together and the **uniform resource locator (URL)**, which is the protocol used to identify and locate Web pages on the Internet. It is also known as a Web address.

Today there are billions of pages on the Web. Hundreds of thousands of new Web pages are added every week. Because the World Wide Web does not have a system for locating or categorizing content, companies have developed an assortment of Web directories and search engines to help users find what they are looking for.

Search Engines

Two of the most popular search engines are Google and Yahoo. Each has a database of more than four billion Web pages. Many of the most useful and common Web pages are known to all search engines, but there are also many sites and pages that are identified only by one or two search engines. That means it can be useful to check search sites like Teoma and Vivisimo to find sites eluding Google and Yahoo.

Search engines try to return results that relate well to your search terms. But they are also designed to make money for the company. To do that, search engines will place paid advertisers near or high up in the results listings.

Electronic Mail

E-mail represents another revolutionary change prompted by the development of the Internet. The popularity of e-mail is attributable to its instant delivery and to the fact that the sender and receiver do not have to be available at the same time.

For example, an appliance store employee can e-mail an order for new merchandise to a shipper in a different time zone. The shipper can acknowledge the order when she arrives at work, and the merchandise can be prepared for shipment almost immediately.

Intranets and Extranets

An intranet is a private, secure network, usually within a company or organization, that contains proprietary company data and can be accessed only by internal users. Some businesses have developed networks for their customers, employees, partners, and suppliers. These networks, called extranets, enable customers to access data stored on an internal server. A firewall protects the security of sensitive information. A **firewall** is a hardware and software checkpoint for all requests for or inputs of data, incoming and outgoing. The firewall reviews the message to make sure that the data content is safe and acceptable for others to view.

Protecting Digital Data

Anyone who has used a computer for a while knows that digital data is not always safe. Sometimes hard disks crash, and the data stored on them cannot be retrieved. Sometimes files are corrupted and cannot be read. Sometimes files are accidentally deleted. The longest-lasting media for backup files are CDs and

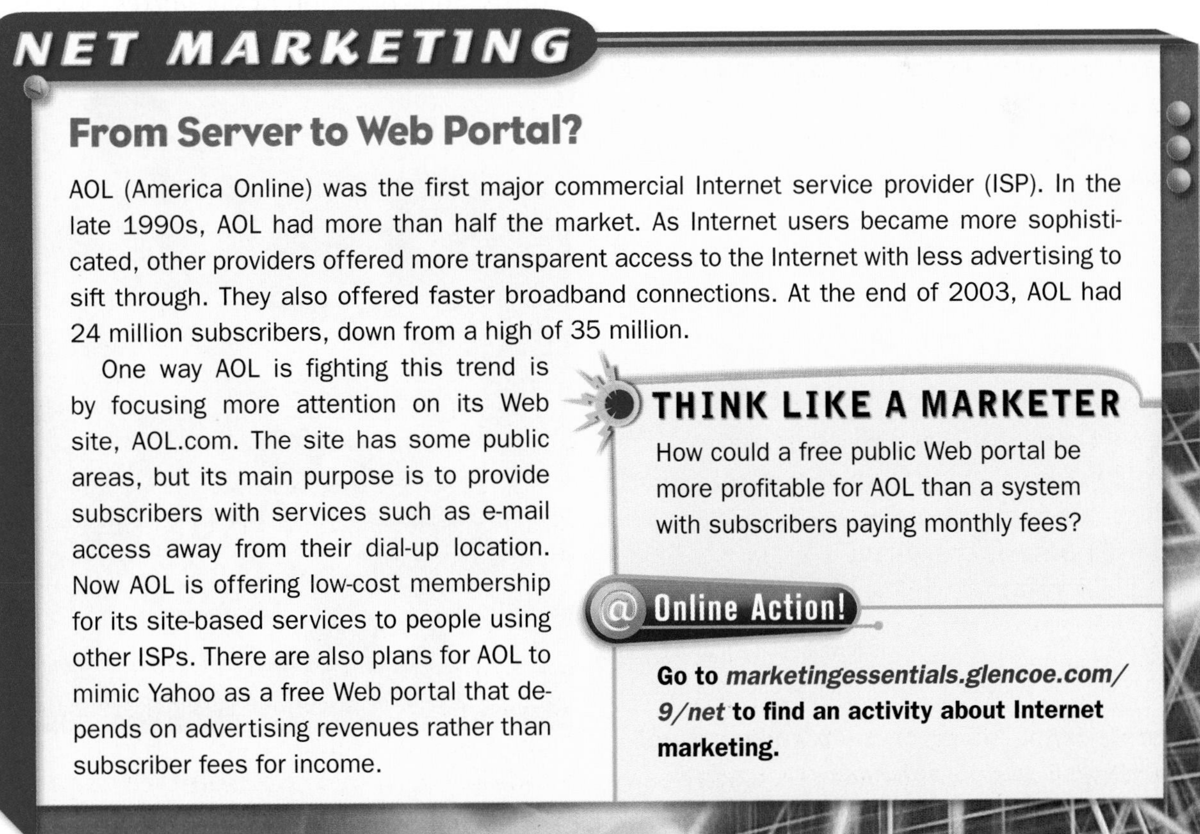

NET MARKETING

From Server to Web Portal?

AOL (America Online) was the first major commercial Internet service provider (ISP). In the late 1990s, AOL had more than half the market. As Internet users became more sophisticated, other providers offered more transparent access to the Internet with less advertising to sift through. They also offered faster broadband connections. At the end of 2003, AOL had 24 million subscribers, down from a high of 35 million.

One way AOL is fighting this trend is by focusing more attention on its Web site, AOL.com. The site has some public areas, but its main purpose is to provide subscribers with services such as e-mail access away from their dial-up location. Now AOL is offering low-cost membership for its site-based services to people using other ISPs. There are also plans for AOL to mimic Yahoo as a free Web portal that depends on advertising revenues rather than subscriber fees for income.

THINK LIKE A MARKETER

How could a free public Web portal be more profitable for AOL than a system with subscribers paying monthly fees?

@ Online Action!

Go to *marketingessentials.glencoe.com/9/net* to find an activity about Internet marketing.

DVDs. Many people use removable, external hard drives because they can be stored off-site, yet are quick and easy to retrieve and access. External drives back up your data with the push of a single button.

Computer files are also vulnerable to viruses, worms, and spyware. Viruses and worms can destroy your data, and spyware can track wherever you go on the Web. It can force you to visit certain sites, and it can collect personal information. Viruses, worms, and spyware can sneak into your system in an attachment to an innocent-looking e-mail message. The best way to protect your data is to use reputable anti-virus and anti-spyware software.

Spam

In 2003, Congress passed the CAN-SPAM law, which bans certain spamming techniques and requires senders to include a valid address. Although the law has made it easier to install filters to block spam, unwanted e-mail is still a problem. The law has merely driven major spammers offshore, beyond the reach of U.S. anti-spam laws.

Web Site Development

A business develops a Web site to inform consumers about the company and its products, enable the business to sell its products, provide related resources, and handle services and inquiries after the sale.

Any Web site's domain name comes from the Internet Corporation for Assigned Names and Numbers (ICANN). The domain name is the part of a URL that identifies a server or service provider. Top-level domains are three-letter extensions, which follow the dot in a Web address. Examples of top-level generic domains include .com and .biz for businesses and .org for nonprofit organizations.

Companies should plan to incur several costs to develop Web sites, including domain name registration, development and maintenance of the Web site, and subscription to a server (if one is not available in-house).

Most business Web sites have similar components that include a branding logo, content, a shopping cart for electronic purchases, a secured payment system for purchases, and general policies related to privacy, shipping, returns, and collection of sales taxes.

•SECURITY **While computers have become indispensable, they are also vulnerable to virus attacks and data theft.**

Name several reasons why the user of a home computer would want to purchase an Internet security software package.

When developing a Web site, the designer creates a site map. A **site map** outlines what can be found on each page within the Web site. This concept in Web site design is known as global navigation. The site map guides a viewer to the desired information and provides links to different parts of the Web site.

A Web site designer prepares a layout grid for every page within a Web site. Layout grids identify all the Web page elements, such as the title of the page, the branding logo, the placement of banner ads, the content, related links, and a navigation bar for movement within the site.

E-Commerce

E-commerce is the process of conducting business transactions on the Internet.

E-commerce sales figures have risen dramatically over the years. In 2000, $28 billion was spent in online shopping in the United States. That translates to less than one percent of the total retail sales figures for the year. In 2003, that had risen to nearly $56 billion, closing in on two percent of all retail sales.

As e-commerce grows, it is redefining the relationship between the seller and the buyer. E-commerce can exist B2B (business to business) or B2C (business to customer). Web markets differ from traditional markets in that they are open for business 24 hours a day, seven days a week. They are also unencumbered by costly middlemen and distribution channels. Additionally, suppliers all over the globe can compete if they can deliver the quality, price, quantity, and service demanded by the customer and are deemed trustworthy financially and ethically.

9.2 AFTER YOU READ

Reviewing Key Terms and Concepts

1. Give four examples of specialized computer systems used for marketing.
2. What are five common uses of the Internet in the workplace?
3. What is the best way to protect digital data?

Integrating Academic Skills

Mathematics

4. For four nations, the following ratios show the numbers of people in millions who have access to the Internet compared to the population in millions. Calculate the percent of the population that has access to the Internet for each country: United States, 185.9/290.34; Australia, 13.05/19.73; Japan, 77.95/127.21; China, 95.8/1,280

Language Arts

5. Do research using consumer magazines and the Internet to learn more about interactive TV. Go to a store to see the features demonstrated. Based on the information you gather, decide if you think the benefits of interactive TV outweigh its potential for invasion of privacy. Use a word processing program to write a paper persuading the reader of your point of view. Use the elements required when writing a paper to persuade.

Check your answers at *marketingessentials.glencoe.com/9/read*

CAREERS IN MARKETING

ERIC MATHIASEN
SENIOR SOFTWARE ANALYST
ORBITZ.COM

What do you do at work?

My first role is that of change or configuration manager. It is my responsibility to make sure changes to the site software have been approved by our software testing team and then are prepared and made active on our Web site in as smooth and problem-free a process as possible. My second function is to work on the installation and deployment of existing site software to new servers or new software to existing servers. My third function is to help track down problems with the Web site when they occur.

What skills are most important to you?

Investigation and tracking. Investigation is important for both finding problems and for finding solutions. Researching problems is a big part of what I do, and to be a good researcher you have to be curious, creative, and persistent. Tracking is important to most professional jobs to make sure you complete all tasks and also to make sure you don't repeat past mistakes.

What is your key to success?

First, be persistent. Don't give up just because things are harder than you expected. Second, stay aware of unexpected opportunities—you never know where a great idea may come from. Third, don't be afraid of failure. Especially when you're starting out, you can learn as much and often more from trying and failing than you can from easy success.

Aptitudes, Abilities, and Skills

Computer and technical skills, organization, strong research and reading skills

Education and Training

A four-year degree in computer science is a good starting point; graduate degrees in related sciences can also be helpful.

Career Path

Entry-level positions might consist largely of routine Web site maintenance and management; these positions can lead to more robust, creative roles.

THINKING CRITICALLY

Why do you think it is harder now for someone to break into a Web-related career without a college degree?

Online Action!

Go to *marketingessentials.glencoe.com/9/careers* for an activity about careers in computer technology.

CHAPTER 9 REVIEW

FOCUS on KEY POINTS

SECTION 9.1

- Computer software applications satisfy business needs for communications, accounting and record keeping, publishing, and graphic design.

SECTION 9.2

- Computer technologies developed especially for marketing fulfill needs in the areas of point-of-sale systems, integrated marketing programs, interactive touch-screen computers, interactive TV, and the Internet.

REVIEW VOCABULARY

Define each of the words below.

1. word processing programs (p. 199)
2. database programs (p. 199)
3. spreadsheet programs (p. 199)
4. desktop publishing programs (p. 200)
5. graphics and design programs (p. 200)
6. presentation software (p. 201)
7. home page (p. 202)
8. hypertext markup language (HTML) (p. 203)
9. communications programs (p. 203)
10. enterprise resource planning (ERP) (p. 206)
11. Internet (p. 208)
12. Internet service providers (ISPs) (p. 208)
13. Wi-Fi (p. 208)
14. World Wide Web (p. 208)
15. hypertext transfer protocol (HTTP) (p. 208)
16. uniform resource locator (URL) (p. 208)
17. firewall (p. 209)
18. site map (p. 211)

REVIEW FACTS and IDEAS

19. How are software applications used in business? (9.1)
20. Give three examples of uses for database programs. (9.1)
21. How can graphics programs be used in marketing? (9.1)
22. Name two examples of interactive technology that are relevant to marketing activities. (9.2)
23. Describe common uses of the Internet in marketing. (9.2)
24. What are the essential components of a Web site? (9.2)

BUILD SKILLS

25. Workplace Skills

The Digital Workplace Work in a group. First, pick a type of business to open together. Then, talk to computer salespeople and use the Internet to find out what computer equipment and software applications are necessary to run that business and how much the technology costs. Make a three- to five-minute presentation of your results to the class.

26. Technology Applications

Wires Do some research on the Internet about the different kinds of connectors (such as wireless transmitters and USB, serial, and Ethernet cables) used to connect computers with monitors, printers, broadband connections, and other computer equipment. Using word processing software, describe four different types of connectors and the equipment they're most often used with.

27. Math Practice

Faster Than Fast A millisecond (ms) is a unit of time used to describe how long it takes a computer to complete an operation. 1 second = 1000 ms. If a computer can execute 25 operations per millisecond, how many operations can it complete in one minute? (Remember, there are 60 seconds in one minute.)

DEVELOP CRITICAL THINKING

28. Technology and Success

Look in the business section of a newspaper and find an article about a large corporation that is losing money and why it is failing. Think about how computers and software applications could help the company. Using a word processing program, write a one-page report outlining your recommendations for technology that can help make the corporation profitable again.

29. Investing in Technology

Imagine you run a business that makes skateboards. You have a budget of $200,000 to invest in increased productivity this year. Improved manufacturing software and the equipment to go with it costs $140,000. A desktop publishing package would cost $55,000. You're also considering design software for $40,000 and more powerful servers that could speed up your office computers and make them more secure for $30,000. You don't have enough employees in your information technology division to take care of any additional software. How do you decide how to spend the productivity budget?

APPLY CONCEPTS

30. Analyzing Computer Use in Marketing Careers

Choose a possible marketing career and use the Internet to research how computers are used in it. Speculate on what new uses computers might have in the future in that career.

Activity Use a word processing program to write a one- to two-page report and present your report orally to the class. Use presentation software, if possible, for supplemental graphics.

31. Data Entry Procedures

Using a spreadsheet program, create a document to track monthly travel expenses for a salesperson. Include columns for miles, parking fees, meals, lodging, airfare, car rentals, and miscellaneous. Enter data in each column. Each entry should be dated. Provide a total for each expense as well as a total for the month.

Activity Save your electronic document on a disk, memory card, or e-mail it to your teacher, so it can be shared and discussed in class.

NET SAVVY

32. The Choice Is Yours

Your boss has asked you to research computer technology that is available for persons with special needs. This is called adaptive or assistive computer technology. Prepare a memo to outlline your findings.

THE DECA CONNECTION

Role Play: Technology Applications

Situation You are to assume the role of cashier at a large supermarket. Your store has recently added a computerized grocery ordering system to the company Web site. This system allows customers to place their grocery orders online, specify a delivery date and time, and select from various payment options. A customer (judge) has complained about the amount of time that it takes to shop for groceries after work.

Activity You are to explain to the customer (judge) the new online shopping service your supermarket is offering.

Evaluation You will be evaluated on how well you meet the following performance indicators:

- Identify ways that technology impacts business
- Analyze technology for use in the sales function
- Describe current business trends
- Use an information system for order fulfillment
- Handle customer inquiries

@ Online Action!

For more information and DECA Prep practice, go to *marketingessentials.glencoe.com/9/DECA*

CHAPTER 10
Interpersonal Skills

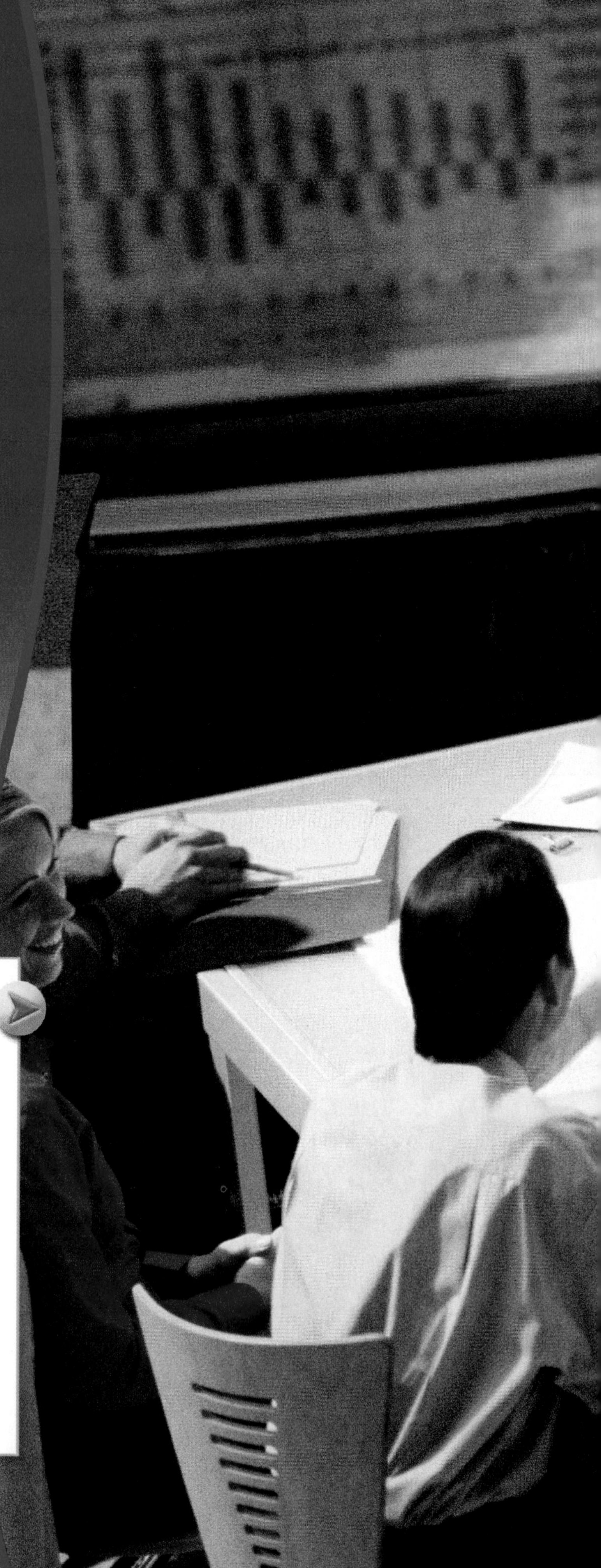

Chapter Objectives

After reading this chapter, you should be able to:

- Recognize the personal traits necessary for ethical action in the workplace
- Identify important interpersonal skills
- Perform effectively in diverse environments
- Manage conflict by using appropriate negotiation skills
- Discuss how to receive and handle customer complaints
- Identify skills needed to be a good team member and provide leadership
- Name six aspects of successful teamwork

GUIDE TO THE PHOTO

Market Talk Good interpersonal skills help employees establish relationships with coworkers and clients. In the diverse marketplace, good interpersonal skills are highly valued. They enable people to work effectively with people of different cultural, religious, and socioeconomic backgrounds.

Quick Think If you were assigned to travel to a foreign country on business, how would you prepare for your interactions with your counterparts there?

THE   CONNECTION

Performance indicators represent key skills and knowledge. Relating them to the concepts explained in this chapter is your key to success in DECA events.

These acronyms represent DECA events that involve knowledge of concepts in this chapter.

AAAL	**FMAL**	**MMS**	**TMDM**
AAML	**FMDM**	**QSRM**	**TSE**
ADC	**FMML**	**RMAL**	**VPM**
BSM	**FSRM**	**RMML**	
EMDM	**HMDM**	**SMDM**	

In all these DECA events you should be able to follow these performance indicators:

- Treat others fairly at work
- Develop cultural sensitivity
- Foster positive working relationships
- Participate as a team member
- Show empathy for others
- Use appropriate assertiveness
- Demonstrate problem-solving skills
- Maintain a positive attitude
- Demonstrate interest and enthusiasm
- Demonstrate responsible behavior and initiative
- Demonstrate honesty and integrity
- Demonstrate ethical work habits
- Demonstrate orderly and systematic behavior
- Demonstrate self-control
- Set personal goals
- Use time-management principles
- Use feedback for personal growth
- Explain the concept of self-esteem

DECA PREP

Check your understanding of DECA performance indicators with the DECA activity in this chapter's review. For more information and DECA Prep practice, go to *marketingessentials .glencoe.com/10/DECA*

Personal Strengths and Interpersonal Skills

OBJECTIVES

- **Recognize the personal traits necessary for ethical action in the workplace**
- **Identify important interpersonal skills**
- **Perform effectively in diverse environments**
- **Manage conflict by using appropriate negotiation skills**

KEY TERMS

- **self-esteem**
- **initiative**
- **time management**
- **assertiveness**
- **flexibility**
- **ethics**
- **equity**
- **negotiation**
- **empathy**

READ and STUDY

BEFORE YOU READ

Connect List five ways your interpersonal skills have helped you form relationships in the past.

THE MAIN IDEA

Self-development and good interpersonal skills are essential in handling a variety of work situations effectively and in working with people of diverse backgrounds.

STUDY ORGANIZER

In a chart like the one below, write down the personality traits and interpersonal skills that are important in good working relationships.

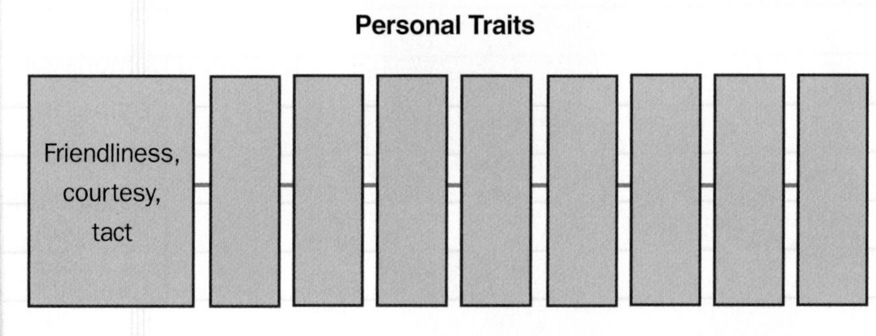

WHILE YOU READ

Evaluate Yourself Make a list of personal traits that you feel you need to improve to be successful in building relationships with people of different backgrounds.

Building Personal Strengths for Good Working Relationships

Successfully interacting with others depends on many factors. A positive self-image, understanding the rules of acceptable behavior, and awareness of the different cultural, religious, and socioeconomic backgrounds of those you are working with are some of these factors.

Self-Esteem and Self-Awareness

Self-awareness is how you perceive yourself. **Self-esteem** is how you perceive your worth or value as a person. It is one of the basic building blocks of successfully interacting with others. Having self-esteem is important because it allows you to believe in yourself and improves your attitude at work.

How do you demonstrate self-esteem in the workplace? When you value yourself and know how you would like to be treated, it allows you to treat others the same way—with respect, friendliness, and patience. Another way you show self-esteem is in your work habits and grooming. Dressing appropriately and behaving in a confident yet courteous way shows that you respect yourself and your work. Arriving at work on time shows that you value yourself as a professional.

Setting goals for your career and personal development is another important aspect of self-awareness and self-esteem. You cannot get anywhere if you do not know where you are headed.

Positive Attitude

Your attitude is your mental outlook, which shapes the way you view people and situations. People with a positive attitude welcome a difficult assignment as a challenge. They look for something positive even when they experience setbacks. They also accept constructive criticism as a way to improve.

Initiative and Responsibility

Initiative means taking action and doing what needs to be done without being asked. If you come up with a new idea, initiative allows you to act on it. Initiative shows that you are enthusiastic about your work.

Accepting responsibility means being willing to be held accountable for your actions. After taking the initiative to begin a job, you must accept responsibility for completing it. Employers and customers value responsible employees because they fulfill their promises.

Self-Control

People who exercise self-control take careful, measured steps and do not act on impulse or emotion. Self-control in the workplace allows you to stop and analyze a situation before reacting to it. This is important when handling conflict. Self-control and orderly behavior inspire confidence in customers and in coworkers. People who cannot control themselves tend to be perceived as overly emotional, irresponsible, inattentive, and uninterested in the customer. They are not likely to be taken seriously.

Creativity

Creativity is the ability to use the imagination to invent. Creativity is used in marketing to think of new products and new ways to present products. It also allows you to find new ways of doing your job. Creativity helps you analyze problems from a new and fresh perspective.

Time Management

Time management means budgeting your time to accomplish tasks on a certain schedule. Time management principles involve establishing goals, setting deadlines, allocating enough time for each task, tackling the most difficult task first, and being realistic. In order to be effective in your work, you must be able to use time wisely. Managing time well is an example of responsible behavior. To manage your time, follow these guidelines:

1. Make a list of the tasks you need to complete.
2. Determine which task is most important considering the time frame you have.
3. Continue to rank the tasks.
4. Create a schedule based on your list.

When you are working on one task, do not let yourself worry about another one. You may, however, be able to work on more than one job at a time. Managing multiple tasks at once is called multitasking.

•CREATIVE SOLUTIONS Creativity enables you to find new ways of doing things. It is a valuable trait to have in many different kinds of work.

What applications does creativity have in marketing?

Stress Management

Stress is a reaction to outside pressure. It can be mental or physical. An example of mental stress might be your reaction if your boss asked you to produce a ten-page research report on competing products by 9:00 A.M. the next day—when you had tickets to a game. Stress can energize, motivate, and excite us. The negative aspects of stress, though, are often harmful. Stress-related anxiety triggers the fight-or-flight mechanism in our bodies. Although this reaction may keep us alive in an emergency, it becomes dangerous when it occurs too often.

New research suggests that a hormone released by bodies under stress suppresses the immune system. Highly stressed people catch colds and flu more often than those who can handle or relieve their stress. Learning to manage stress is a valuable workplace skill.

Stress Relief

Researchers who have studied stress agree that three main elements help prevent stress: regular exercise, a balanced diet, and enough sleep. They also suggest engaging in recreation, making reasonable compromises, and accepting what you cannot change. When you are dealing with stress away from work, try getting a massage or watching a television program or movie. Getting involved in activities you enjoy, such as sports, reading, or listening to music, is a good way to relieve stress. Helping someone in need can help relieve stress by putting things in perspective.

Assertiveness

Assertiveness is standing up for what you believe. People will respect you if you can be assertive without being pushy or aggressive. Show confidence and speak with authority.

For example, suppose you are working with a client who ridicules your opinion. In a very professional and respectful way, you should reassert your contribution. Be sure to point out its strengths in a clear and precise manner. Offer credible support for any claim that you make; valid evidence will put you in a strong position to influence others. Assertiveness is a skill that takes time to learn. Confidence in being assertive comes with experience.

Flexibility

Flexibility allows you to adapt to changing circumstances. A flexible person can learn from others, accept criticism, and grow. To develop flexibility, listen with an open mind. Be willing to try new approaches.

As you will see in the next section, flexibility will help you be a productive team member. Businesses value employees with this trait because flexibility enables a business to move forward and adapt to changing markets.

Ethics in the 21st-Century Workplace

Ethics are the basic values and moral principles that guide the behavior of individuals and groups. In most cultures, ethical behavior includes honesty, integrity, and a sense of fair play. Ethical behavior also means treating all people with respect. People who practice ethical behavior gain the trust of coworkers and clients.

Honesty

Honesty in the workplace is an important part of ethical behavior. It includes telling the truth, maintaining confidentiality, and not spreading gossip. Respect for company property and making an effort to prevent theft are other aspects of workplace honesty. Honesty is the basis for trust, which is essential to a good business relationship.

Respect

The number-one rule when speaking to business clients or customers is to show respect. That applies to interactions with

A MATTER OF ETHICS

Doing the Right Thing

Charlene has been working as a cashier at Johnson Drugs for six months. She loves her job. She gets along well with her supervisor and coworkers, but she has not made friends with any of them yet.

A new employee, Simone, has been very friendly with Charlene. Charlene likes Simone and the fact that she now has a friend at work, but Charlene often hears Simone making fun of a coworker. It seems wrong to Charlene, but she is not sure what to do about it. Simone seems to be doing a good job otherwise.

What's Right?

Charlene does not want to confront Simone and risk losing her friendship. When Charlene considers telling her supervisor, she feels she would be tattling on Simone and perhaps getting her in trouble. Still, just keeping quiet does not feel good, either. Going to work is not very much fun anymore.

THINKING ETHICALLY

What is the right thing for Charlene to do in this situation? How can she deal with the situation in a way that is fair to Simone and her other coworkers? How would you handle a similar situation?

@ Online Action!

Go to *marketingessentials.glencoe.com/10/ethics* to find a project on interpersonal skills in the workplace.

• NEGOTIATING CONFLICTS When negotiating conflict resolution, all parties must be willing to work together to find a fair solution.

What is the key to negotiation?

coworkers as well. You demonstrate respect by listening with an open mind to the other person's point of view, then addressing any differences of opinion with courtesy and tact. This is especially important if there is a disagreement or conflict, for instance, when handling a customer complaint. While it may not always be easy to be courteous and pleasant, you must practice showing respect to others.

Fairness and Equity

People expect to be treated the way others are treated. **Equity** means that everyone has equal rights and opportunities. Never give special privileges to an employee for reasons that are unrelated to his or her work performance.

Sometimes a business establishes standards to maintain fairness. Equality is also protected through both federal and state laws. Such standards and laws can prevent discrimination in procedures such as hiring and firing. For example, employment laws forbid discrimination due to gender, age, religion, or national origin. Federal laws include the Americans with Disabilities Act of 1990, which protects qualified individuals with disabilities from discrimination. If an employee believes that he or she has been the victim of discrimination, the employee can file a complaint with the United States Equal Employment Opportunity Commission (EEOC).

Avoiding Stereotypes

It is important to become aware of prejudices we may have and to eliminate them. Learning about others' interests and experiences helps you understand them better. Interests often reflect values. Experiences shape how we think and view the world. With this understanding, you will find it easier to understand others, and they will be much more likely to understand you. Good workplace relationships and success in marketing are based on mutual understanding.

Managing Conflict

Like stress, conflict in the workplace can be productive or counterproductive. Counterproductive conflict can cause lost time and resources and a decrease in efficiency. Productive conflict can energize a person, group, or organization. Managing conflict requires understanding, skill, knowledge, and experience.

Conflict and Negotiation

Companies can help prevent conflict by creating an atmosphere in which all employees are accepted despite differences in beliefs, values, backgrounds, or experiences. However, no company can completely prevent conflict. When conflicts arise, they must be negotiated.

Negotiation is the process of working with the parties in conflict to find a resolution. Negotiating requires a willingness to work together. The key to successful negotiation is clear communication. As you learned in

Chapter 8, there are four basic skills involved in the communication process: listening, reading, speaking, and writing. Negotiation involves two of these skills: listening and speaking.

Speaking

The first step in negotiation is defining as clearly as possible the problem as each person sees it. Facts and feelings must be presented from each individual's perspective. This usually goes more smoothly when "I statements" are used. For example, avoid the aggressive tone in "You make me mad when you. . . ." Instead, say "I become upset when you. . . ." Instead of saying "Your description of the problem is confusing," say "I am confused about what the problem is." Placing blame should

Case Study

Coming to an Agreement

Herb Cohen is a successful negotiator who has worked for U.S. government agencies, famous sports figures, and large corporations. He has written several best-selling books on negotiation. The most recent is titled *Negotiate This! By Caring, But Not T-H-A-T Much.* It highlights skills Cohen used to help settle an NFL strike and as a consultant during the 1980 Iran hostage crisis. These skills can be applied to issues that arise in everyday life and in the workplace.

Imagine that your mom wants you to wash the dishes. You ask if you can play basketball first, while it is still light outside. That is negotiating! You both win. You play ball and the dishes get washed, too. You probably both feel good about the outcome, an important result of successful negotiation. Negotiating is not about getting your own way, but about coming to agreement.

The Negotiating Process

Cohen emphasizes the importance of caring about your position, but not so much that it prevents you from compromising. Be clear about what you are willing to give up, and what you are not. It is important to make concessions—to give in a little—early in the process. Cohen cautions people not to assume they know what is important to the other person. If you assumed that your mom would be satisfied only if you did the dishes right away, you might not ask if you could play ball first. Thus, you would lose out as a result.

THINK STRATEGICALLY

Suppose you and a friend are planning to spend Saturday afternoon together. Each of you wants to see a movie, but no movies in your neighborhood appeal to both of you. How can you use negotiation skills to decide what to do?

@ Online Action! **Go to *marketingessentials.glencoe.com/10/case* to find a project on negotiations.**

be avoided because it puts people on the defensive. Participants should take some time to plan ahead what they will say. If possible, set a time and place to meet that is convenient for everyone involved. A quiet, neutral place with few distractions is ideal.

Listening

Listening is an active process in which all of your attention is focused on the speaker. Encourage the speaker to share his or her feelings and thoughts. Maintaining eye contact with the speaker shows that you are interested and want to understand what is being said. Planning a response before the speaker's point is made is a distraction that often causes misunderstandings.

Try to empathize, or show empathy, with the person who is speaking. **Empathy** is an understanding of a person's situation or frame of mind. Remember that people of different ages, genders, cultures, and abilities may have had experiences that are unfamiliar to you. Do not make the mistake of assuming that certain viewpoints and behaviors are universal. There are many people in the world with ideas that are very different from yours.

Six simple techniques for negotiating conflict resolution can be helpful:

1. Show respect
2. Recognize and define the problem
3. Seek a variety of solutions
4. Collaborate
5. Be reliable
6. Preserve the relationship

The problem is solved only when both sides reach a common understanding and agreement about what actions are to be taken. Never assume you understand the other person without asking some verification questions. For example, you might ask "Is this what you meant by. . . ?" or "Did I understand correctly when. . . ?"

10.1 AFTER YOU READ

Reviewing Key Terms and Concepts

1. Name five personality traits that help to develop good working relationships.
2. Define ethics and name four ways to apply ethical behavior in the workplace.
3. Explain the two key communication skills necessary to resolve conflict.

Integrating Academic Skills

Math

4. Your company's health insurance plan costs $585 per employee per month. There are 64 employees. Another health insurance company would charge 10 percent less. What would be the total savings per year?

English

5. You were asked to promote a golf tournament for charity. Write a paragraph to explain how you will schedule the steps needed to complete the project.

Check your answers at *marketingessentials.glencoe.com/10/read*

Working Together: Leadership and Teamwork

OBJECTIVES

- **Discuss how to receive and handle customer complaints**
- **Identify skills needed to be a good team member and provide leadership**
- **Name six aspects of successful teamwork**

KEY TERMS

- **teamwork**
- **cross-training**
- **consensus**
- **agreement**

READ and STUDY

BEFORE YOU READ

Predict What do you think are some advantages to working on a team versus working individually?

THE MAIN IDEA

By developing the skills of a good team member, you will help your team achieve its goals.

STUDY ORGANIZER

Draw the chart below. As you read this section, write in six aspects of good teamwork.

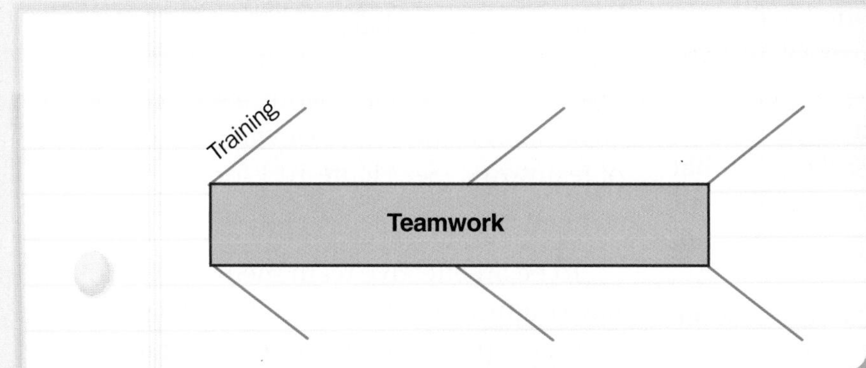

Interpersonal Skills in Marketing

Good working relationships between employees and customers or clients depends on the interpersonal skills of the employees. As an employee, you should be familiar with your company's basic procedures in responding to concerns raised by customers. It is also important to know when you need to refer the customer to someone else. This may happen when an issue needs to be resolved by a manager or when a question involves information that your department does not have.

Connect Focus on each aspect of teamwork and how you can improve your own ability to be a good team member.

Addressing Customers' Concerns

To respond promptly and intelligently to customer concerns, you need to be familiar with company procedures. You should know how to handle the following situations:

- **Requests and questions** You will need to learn the proper procedures for handling customer requests and questions. You will also need to know what you should say to customers if you cannot answer their questions yourself.
- **Directions** You will need to be able to give clear and concise directions to your store or office.
- **Management's role** You will need to know under what circumstances a manager should be called to talk to a customer.
- **Business policies** You will need to be able to explain business policies to customers. These may include return or exchange procedures and the company policy on checks or credit cards.

Addressing Customers' Complaints

Most customers never let the company or store know they have a complaint. Only four to eight percent of customers who have a concern or complaint share their problem with the firm.

If a customer brings you a concern, you have an opportunity to learn something that may improve service. You may also prevent damage to the firm and stop the problem from recurring.

Complaints cover a range of issues. Some are genuine errors on the part of the firm, such as a faulty item or a bad service experience. Others stem from misunderstandings, such as poorly written directions on a product's package. The customer may suggest how the firm can improve its service. Your company should develop a procedure to follow when dealing with customer complaints. If not, follow these guidelines:

- **Listen** First, listen completely and openly to the customer's complaint so that you are sure you understand it.
- **Take the customer aside** If the customer is talking loudly, try to take him or her aside—if possible, into a separate room. A sales counter or desk can seem like a barrier. Standing side by side in a quiet place may ease the tension.
- **Repeat** When appropriate, repeat the facts of the complaint to show that you understand. If you can explain what caused the problem for the customer, state it clearly. Do not place blame on anyone.
- **Get help** If you feel you need assistance from a supervisor, let the customer know this and seek assistance promptly.
- **Establish a plan** Try to reach an agreement with the customer about the next course of action. Suggest only action that is consistent with the company's policy. Then be absolutely certain to follow through on the action agreed upon.

Teamwork

A team is a group of people who work together to achieve a goal. **Teamwork** is work done by a group of people to achieve a common goal.

Teamwork is becoming increasingly important in the business world. According to football coach Vince Lombardi, "Individual commitment to a group effort—that is what makes a team work, a company work, a society work, a civilization work." The following are six aspects of teamwork. (See Figure 10.1 for more detail.)

Training

To be an effective team member, you must have training for all the tasks you will perform. You have probably heard of cross-training in sports. **Cross-training** means preparing to do many different activities.

On the job, people are cross-trained for many tasks on a team. This gives the team flexibility and diverse strengths. Work becomes more enjoyable when you know you will not be doing the same activity every day.

Team Planning

Before you start working on a project, make a plan as a team. Team planning involves setting goals, assigning roles, making agreements, sharing responsibility, and communicating regularly.

Team Goals

Team members must be involved in defining a goal in order to feel committed to it. This results in greater company loyalty and stronger team spirit.

Members should reach a consensus about goals. A **consensus** is a decision to which each member agrees. Therefore, all team members must be allowed to state their opinions. The final agreement may require team members to make a compromise. Being flexible as an individual helps you learn to compromise as a team member.

Assigning Roles

Team projects often work more smoothly if the team appoints a leader who coordinates tasks.

Each person on the team needs to know which part of the process he or she is responsible for each day. Members are usually assigned tasks based on their skills and experience.

Agreements

An **agreement** is a specific commitment that each member makes to the group. When team members make agreements, the team becomes more cohesive and stronger. A team's agreements must be consistent with its goals.

It is important that each team member feel connected to the company's goals as well as to the team's goals. Team loyalty and positive peer pressure help to encourage people to keep their agreements.

Shared Responsibility and Shared Leadership

Shared responsibility and shared leadership mean that each member must feel responsible for the whole team's efforts. Shared leadership also allows all team members to perform some management functions.

Feedback

When giving feedback, make sure you are respectful. If you are overly critical, the feedback

MARKET TECH

Customer Relationship Marketing (CRM)

The more companies know about their customers, the better they can serve them. A wise business develops a database with information about where customers live and what products they purchase. This is part of customer relationship marketing (CRM), which focuses on the customer as key to the success of a business.

Amazon.com Example

When a customer signs in to a personal Amazon.com account and begins browsing the virtual bookshelves, he or she leaves a digital trail. Amazon uses CRM software to collect information about which books the customer looks at and which he or she buys. The company can then direct advertising of similar items to the customer.

A Network of Customer Information

After asking permission, businesses can share information about customers' preferences and buying habits with other businesses. This expands the network of knowledge about the customer. Each piece of information helps to round out the picture, so that the business knows how to sell to each customer better.

THINK LIKE A MARKETER

Besides purchases made, what type of customer information is valuable to marketers?

Online Action!

Go to *marketingessentials.glencoe.com/10/tech* to find a project on customer relationship marketing.

Figure 10.1 Teamwork

- **Succeeding Together** As many businesses move away from a top-down management style toward a team approach, it is important for employees to understand how a team works and what's expected of individual members.

What are some of the interpersonal skills you need to be a valuable team member?

TRAINING

Individual members of a team need to keep up with the team. This means having the necessary skills to do your job and staying current with the best practices in your field.

TEAM PLANNING

Teams are usually assigned projects. Planning how to carry out those projects is the team's responsibility. Teams often include individuals with different strengths; for instance, an advertising team may include an illustrator, a copywriter, a production coordinator, and a marketing specialist.

TEAM GOALS

The team sets goals. For an advertising team, that might mean completing a new ad or an entire advertising campaign by a certain date. Team goals must be aligned with the goals of the company.

DELEGATION/AGREEMENTS

Members of the team are assigned different tasks, depending on their skills. Each team member agrees to complete the assigned task. On an advertising team, the graphic artist lays out graphics on a computer, the copywriter develops slogans and copy, and the production coordinator works with outside vendors.

SHARED RESPONSIBILITY/LEADERSHIP

Everyone on the team shares responsibility for achieving the team's goal. Members of the team usually select a manager, or owner, to keep track of schedules and handle any difficulties that come up.

@ Online Action! **Go to *marketingessentials.glencoe.com/10/figure/1* to find a project on teamwork.**

will not serve its purpose. Instead, it will alienate the team member being evaluated.

Leadership Skills

One definition of leadership is helping members of a group achieve their goals. Leaders need self-confidence and a willingness to take the initiative. They need creativity to solve new or unusual problems. Leaders need problem-solving, social judgment, and communication skills. Problem-solving skills include being able to define the problem, gather information, analyze the problem, and generate plans for a solution. Good leaders understand people and social systems and are able to motivate others to work together. Conflict resolution is also important in helping members of a group work together. Leaders need to communicate their vision to others and be sensitive to their motivations and needs.

Being a Valuable Team Member

What makes a person a good team member? The following list describes valuable attitudes and actions.

- Make the team's goals your top priority.
- In meetings, listen actively and offer suggestions.
- Build positive group dynamics with team members.
- Continue to communicate with team members outside meetings.
- Follow up on what you have been assigned to do.
- Work to resolve conflicts among team members.
- Respect the other members of your team.
- Try to inspire other employees to get involved.

10.2 AFTER YOU READ

Reviewing Key Terms and Concepts

1. Define teamwork and explain how this concept applies to the business world.
2. What personal strengths and interpersonal skills are required of a good leader?
3. What personal traits and interpersonal skills make a person a good team member?

Integrating Academic Skills

Math

4. Your business has decided to start recycling paper products. In exchange, the recycling company will donate 20 boxes of new paper each year to your business. You currently order 150 boxes of paper per year, at $50 per box. If you start recycling with the company, how much money will you save each year?

Economics

5. Research the economic benefits of teamwork in business. Does teamwork increase productivity? How are employees and customers affected?

Check your answers at *marketingessentials.glencoe.com/10/read*

CAREERS IN MARKETING

CARSON LEDFORD
OWNER
TECHNOLOGY PLUS
SALES AND SERVICE

What do you do at work?

I started the company with myself as the only employee and tried to cover all aspects of the business from service provider to bookkeeping. Now with five full-time employees, I focus mainly on sales and customer service. I still maintain a hands-on role, spending about 20 percent of my time in the field providing service to the customer.

What skills are most important to you?

In the beginning when I was the only employee, my technical skills in electronics were the most valuable. The ability to understand the products I serviced and be able to repair them was a must. As my role in the company has changed, I have found my people skills to be more valuable than any other. The most important part of that process is being able to communicate with the customer in a manner that does not confuse them. I believe that good, constant communication with the customer throughout a project is the key to quality solutions.

What is your key to success?

Customer service! Customer service! Customer service! The willingness to provide a quality and affordable service to the customer has been what sets us apart from our competition. We utilize technology, not hide behind it, which allows us to respond quickly to customers' needs. We always return calls promptly to our customers.

Aptitudes, Abilities, and Skills

Technical knowledge, sales ability, strong communication skills

Education and Training

Bachelor's and Master's degrees in computer science and technology are helpful, along with general business degrees to aid in the non-technical side of the business.

Career Path

Many technology professionals begin as freelancers or start their own companies; for others, careers can begin with entry-level IT positions within established companies.

THINKING CRITICALLY

What kind of training might vendors provide to companies such as this, and how would it differ from traditional classroom education?

@ Online Action!

Go to *marketingessentials.glencoe.com/10/careers* to find a research project on technology services.

CHAPTER 10 REVIEW

FOCUS on KEY POINTS

SECTION 10.1

- Good interpersonal skills are necessary for building effective working relationships with coworkers and clients.
- Personality traits such as assertiveness and creativity help people work effectively with others.
- Ethical behavior in today's workplace involves demonstrating respect for people of diverse backgrounds.
- Conflict negotiation requires good communication skills.

SECTION 10.2

- Teamwork means a group of people work together toward a goal.
- Understanding the team goals, the roles assigned to individual team members, and shared responsibilities will help make you a valuable team member.

REVIEW VOCABULARY

Use the following pairs of terms in sentences that show you understand their meanings. Explain how all these words relate to the concept of self-esteem.

1. initiative (p. 219)—time management (p. 219)
2. assertiveness (p. 220)—flexibility (p. 221)
3. consensus (p. 227)—agreement (p. 227)
4. ethics (p. 221)—equity (p. 222)
5. negotiation (p. 222)—empathy (p. 224)
6. teamwork (p. 226)—cross-training (p. 226)

REVIEW FACTS and IDEAS

7. Which personality traits discussed in the text do you feel you need to work on to become a better friend and coworker? (10.1)
8. Explain the importance of initiative to good working relationships. (10.1)
9. How will asking about others' interests and experiences help to prevent bias? (10.1)
10. What is the one thing that a team must do before it can begin its work? (10.2)
11. How can sharing responsibility and leadership be helpful in achieving team goals? (10.2)
12. What are five conventions that can help teams overcome obstacles? (10.2)

BUILD SKILLS

13. Workplace Skills

Interpersonal Communication You are the new manager of a photocopy shop that has three other employees. One of them is an excellent worker, but two who were recently hired often arrive late and tend to make a lot of mistakes. Write a paragraph describing how you will handle the situation and what you will say to your employees.

14. Technology Applications

Researching on the Web Use the Internet to research one of the following topics: (1) Stress management and relaxation techniques; (2) Negotiating conflict resolution; or (3) Gender equity in the workplace. Write a one-page report summarizing your findings.

15. Math Practice

Cross-Training With Math Math is a basic skill that can be helpful to you as a team member. Assume that your boss asks you to determine how much will be discounted from the price of a color printer that has a list price of $1,799 and a discount of 12 percent. What answer would you give her?

DEVELOP CRITICAL THINKING

16. Why Is Cross-Training Important to Teamwork?

Assume that you are employed by a public relations firm as an assistant publicist. Your company is organized into teams. Through regular team meetings and human relations workshops, all the members of your team have some understanding of the roles played by the other team members. The day before a press kit is due to an important client, the senior publicist assigned to produce the press kit calls in sick with the flu. What should you do? Write a one-page essay explaining your answer and why cross-training is valuable in this situation.

17. How Can Business Benefit From Stress Management?

Assume that you work for a shipping company that gets very busy during the holiday season. A month before the company expects its heaviest traffic, your boss calls a meeting and asks for suggestions on how best to handle the increased business. Prepare a short, one-page paper recommending that the human resources department offer a course in stress management. Explain your recommendation.

APPLY CONCEPTS

18. Use Time Management Principles

Imagine that you are an event planner. You have been given the job of planning a marketing career fair to be held at a large convention center. The event is scheduled for the weekend of November 6 and 7, which is six weeks from today.

Activity Use time management principles to create a schedule for planning a marketing career fair to be held six weeks from today. Present the schedule to your class using presentation software.

19. Research Training Opportunities

You have just been hired as the new sales representative for a start-up athletic gear manufacturing company. There is currently no human resources department in the company. Your boss has given you a budget for training and asked you to find appropriate courses in assertiveness and self-esteem, which he considers useful to the job.

Activity Use the Internet to research training in assertiveness and self-esteem. Find out what kinds of classes are available and how they relate to success in business. Pick one and, using a word processing program, prepare the information to present for your boss's approval. Present this information to the class.

NET SAVVY

20. Etiquette

Locate Web sites explaining cultural customs and beliefs that differ from those in the United States. Select one country. Write a 200-word business etiquette guide.

THE 

CONNECTION

Role Play: Motel Front-Desk Clerk

Situation You are to assume the role of front-desk clerk for a family-owned motel in a popular resort area. The main attraction for the motel is that it offers fun family activities like miniature golf tournaments, cookout nights, etc. The staff is a small one, but shares a sense of friendly teamwork. Recently, the housekeepers have complained that they don't hear about upcoming activities planned for guests and feel generally uninformed about activities at the motel.

Activity The motel owner (judge) has asked you for some ideas about ways to make the housekeeping staff feel more a part of the motel's activities.

Evaluation You will be evaluated on how well you meet the following performance indicators:

- Encourage team building
- Explain the nature of staff communication
- Handle employee complaints and grievances
- Assess employee morale
- Address people properly

@ Online Action!

For more information and DECA Prep practice, go to *marketingessentials.glencoe.com/10/DECA*

CHAPTER 11
Management Skills

After reading this chapter, you should be able to:

- Explain how horizontally organized companies differ from vertically organized companies
- Name the three levels of management
- Explain how a self-managing team functions
- Name the three functions of management
- Describe the management techniques used by effective managers
- Explain how to manage employees properly

GUIDE TO THE PHOTO

Market Talk A company usually brings several or more people together, all working in different jobs toward the same goal of business success. How a company organizes its employees determines how well people work together. Managers plan, organize, and control human resources, technology, and materials.

Quick Think List three possible benefits of focusing on teams instead of hierarchy.

THE DECA CONNECTION

Performance indicators represent key skills and knowledge. Relating them to the concepts explained in this chapter is your key to success in DECA events. These acronyms represent DECA events that involve knowledge of concepts in this chapter.

AAAL	**FMAL**	**MMS***	**TMDM***
AAML*	**FMDM***	**QSRM***	**TSE***
ADC*	**FMML***	**RMAL**	**VPM**
BSM	**FSRM***	**RMML***	
EMDM*	**HMDM***	**SMDM***	

In all these DECA events you should be able to follow these performance indicators:

- Explain the concept of management
- Describe the nature of business records
- Describe the nature of budgets
- Describe crucial elements of a quality culture
- Develop project plan
- Explain the nature of overhead/operating costs
- Describe the nature of managerial control (control process, types of control, what is controlled)
- Identify routine activities for maintaining business facilities and equipment
- Orient new employees

All the events with an asterisk (*) also include these performance indicators:

- Describe the role of management in the achievement of quality
- Explain the nature of managerial ethics
- Determine hiring needs
- Establish personnel policies
- Explain the nature of leadership in organizations
- Assess employee performance
- Explain ways to build employee morale

DECA PREP

Check your understanding of DECA performance indicators with the DECA activity in this chapter's review. For more information and DECA Prep practice, go to *marketingessentials .glencoe.com/11/DECA*

SECTION 11.1

OBJECTIVES

- **Explain how horizontally organized companies differ from vertically organized companies**
- **Name the three levels of management**
- **Explain how a self-managing team functions**

KEY TERMS

- **management**
- **vertical organization**
- **top management**
- **middle management**
- **supervisory-level management**
- **horizontal organization**
- **empowerment**

Management Structures

BEFORE YOU READ

Predict What are the benefits of having fewer managers in a business?

THE MAIN IDEA

There are two ways of organizing a business: the traditional or vertical organization with an emphasis on hierarchy, and the horizontal organization with a focus on teams.

STUDY ORGANIZER

In a chart like the one below, take notes on the types of business organization.

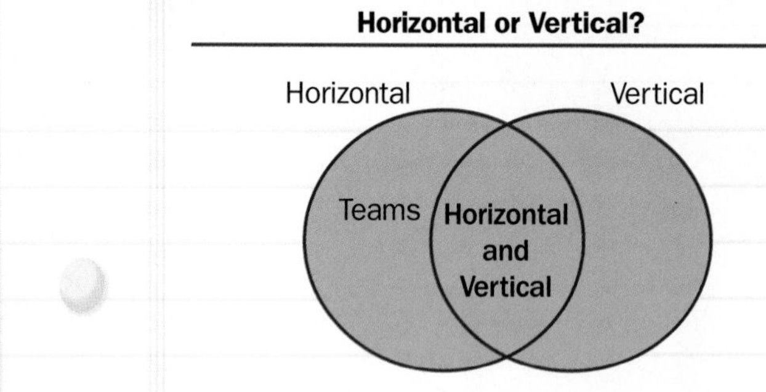

Compare Note differences between vertical and horizontal organization.

Leadership in the 21st Century

Business leaders in the United States and around the world expect many changes in the coming years as a result of globalization. New leaders come from diverse backgrounds. Global competition is creating companies and managers who are united by common goals and ideals.

Types of Management Structure

Management can be defined simply as getting work done through the effort of others. More often, management is considered the process of reaching goals through the use of human resources, technology, and material resources. To facilitate effective management, businesses are generally organized either vertically or horizontally.

Vertical Organization

For a long time, the role of management was to keep an eye on workers. In large, traditional companies, managers reported to higher levels of management. Most managers were responsible for the proper operation of a particular department. The up-and-down structure of this kind of organization is called vertical organization. **Vertical organization** refers to a chain-of-command, hierarchical structure where the tasks and responsibilities of each level of the organization are clearly defined.

Management Levels

In the traditional, vertically organized company, there are three basic levels of management: top management, middle management, and supervisory-level management. Those who make decisions that affect the whole company are **top management**. CEO (chief executive officer), president, COO (chief operating officer), CFO (chief financial officer), and vice president are some top management titles. The functions of top (or senior) management include setting a direction for the company as a whole, identifying resources and methods for meeting goals, and controlling the systems and structures of the company.

GLOBAL MARKET

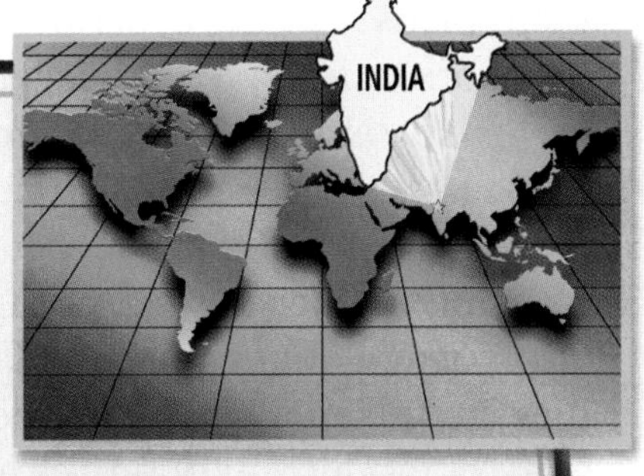

Cultural Adjustments

In 1995, Ranjini Manian founded Global Adjustments, a company that capitalizes on international business both abroad and in India. Global Adjustments offers cross-cultural training for professionals who move to India and for Indian professionals preparing to travel or relocate abroad. The company is based in Chennai (formerly called Madras) in southern India and counts companies such as Ford India, Citibank, Verizon, Morgan Stanley, Siemens, and BMW among its clients.

Management and Etiquette Tutorials The services for foreign professionals arriving in India range from help with finding a place to live or an office to rent, to advice on respecting the Indian custom of blessing new living or working quarters with a religious ceremony. Also available are courses on history and culture, tours of temples and of an Indian home, and even a tutorial Indian lunch to teach foreigners how to eat with their fingers according to Indian custom. Global Adjustments publishes a monthly newsletter with articles about life and culture in India.

Indian professionals can also prepare to travel abroad through Global Adjustments' course on Western management style, dining etiquette, and interview and phone skills.

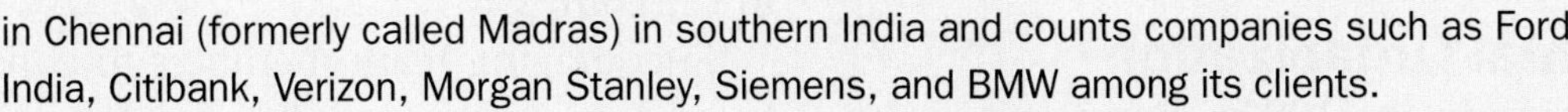

CRITICAL THINKING

What consequences would a lack of knowledge about local culture have on a company?

Online Action!

Go to *marketingessentials.glencoe.com/11/global* to find a research project about globalization and the Internet.

• BRAINSTORMING
Brainstorming is an important activity for self-managing teams.

What else do self-managing teams do?

Middle management implements the decisions of top management. Middle management plans how the departments under them can work to reach top management's goals.

In **supervisory-level management**, managers supervise the activities of employees who carry out the tasks determined by the plans of middle and top management. Supervisors assign duties, monitor day-to-day activities in their department, and evaluate the work of production or service employees.

Horizontal Organization

Beginning in the 1980s, many companies downsized to increase their efficiency and productivity.

These companies needed more than staff cuts to become more efficient. The answer was a new type of management structure—horizontal organization.

In **horizontal organization**, top management shares decision making with self-managing teams of workers who set their own goals and make their own decisions.

Self-Managing Teams

At the heart of horizontal organization is a restructuring of the traditional management hierarchy. Levels of management are eliminated, and the number of supervisors is reduced. This is known as flattening the organization. Instead of reporting up a chain of command, employees are organized into teams that manage themselves.

Self-managing teams in a horizontal organization gather information, analyze it, and take collective action. They are responsible for making decisions, completing tasks, and coordinating their activity with other groups in the company.

Encouraging team members to contribute to and take responsibility for the management process is known as **empowerment**. Empowerment reinforces team spirit and contributes to company loyalty. It can also increase productivity and profits.

Organization by Process

A second characteristic of horizontal companies is organization by process. Self-managing teams are organized around particular processes, such as developing new products or providing customer support. Teams made up of people with different specializations replace functional divisions, like the finance department or engineering department.

•**TEAMWORK** This team is working on the design of a new building.

In a horizontal organization, who would be the manager of this team?

Customer Orientation

The third characteristic of horizontal organization concerns the team's focus. In vertical organizations, workers tend to look to management for direction. In horizontal companies, workers are more likely to focus on the customer.

For example, you can buy Starbucks coffee beans in Starbucks coffee shops, or you can buy them in grocery stores and supermarkets. Different marketing teams within Starbucks focus on each different type of customer. One team is concerned with the wants and needs of the individual who buys beans in the Starbucks store. Another is concerned with the needs of the supermarket chain. By focusing on these different customers instead of on a product or process, managers have direct access to customer feedback. The ideal result is to have satisfied customers, high productivity, large profits, and contented investors.

11.1 AFTER YOU READ

Reviewing Key Terms and Concepts

1. What is the principal difference between the structure of a vertical company and the structure of a horizontal company?
2. What are the three levels of management in a vertical organization?
3. Explain two advantages of horizontal organization.

Integrating Academic Skills

Math

4. Your company produces and markets electronic equipment. Sales last year totaled $2,446,320. The company goal is to increase sales by 12 percent this year. Your division goal is to achieve 25 percent of total sales. What is the dollar value of your division goal?

Social Studies

5. An automobile company is considering locating a new assembly plant in your state. The plant would add about 10,000 jobs and require workers of all different education and training levels. What section of the state would you suggest and why?

Check your answers at *marketingessentials.glencoe.com/11/read*

SECTION 11.2

Management Functions

OBJECTIVES

- Name the three functions of management
- Describe the management techniques used by effective managers
- Explain how to manage employees properly

KEY TERMS

- planning
- organizing
- controlling
- mission statement
- remedial action
- exit interview

READ and STUDY

BEFORE YOU READ

Predict What interpersonal skills should a manager have?

THE MAIN IDEA

As more employees fulfill management positions, understanding basic management functions is essential to your success in the field of marketing.

STUDY ORGANIZER

Draw the chart below. As you read this section, write in management functions and techniques.

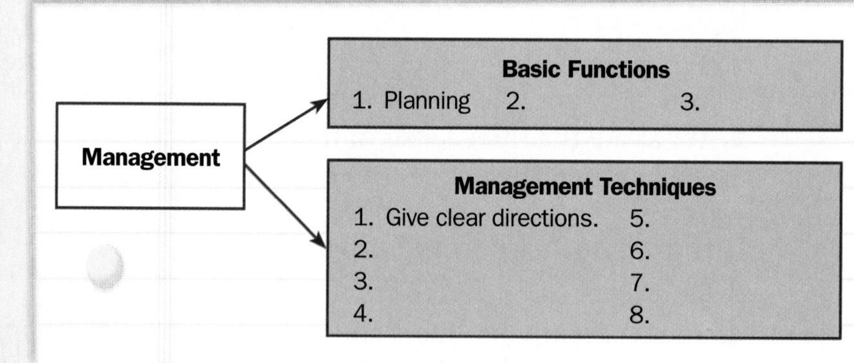

WHILE YOU READ

Practice Consider how you would use each effective management technique that you read about.

What Managers Do

Managers make decisions in addition to supervising and directing the actions of others. Management decisions affect all employees. This means that communicating and motivating people are among the most important of management skills.

Basic Management Functions

All managers perform certain basic functions of planning, organizing, and controlling (see Figure 11.1). **Planning**

Figure 11.1 Management Functions

• **Three Basic Functions** Whether a company is organized vertically or horizontally, the management functions remain the same. Managers plan, organize, and control. Below are the management functions required of the manager, or owner, of a marketing team developing an ad campaign for a new car. In this case, the company structure is horizontal.

What skills are necessary to be a manager?

Planning At the planning stage, the team develops a plan covering the entire life of the ad campaign, from market research to tracking the campaign's effectiveness. The manager, or owner, of the team must be sure that the team's plans and goals are aligned with the company's overall plans.

Organizing Once the plan is set, the manager organizes its execution. With input from other members of the team, the owner delegates responsibilities, determines schedules, makes sure that the efforts of the individual team members are coordinated, and keeps everyone on track to meet team goals.

Controlling When the project is complete, the manager should determine its effectiveness. If it was not successful, the manager must find out what went wrong.

@ Online Action!

Go to *marketingessentials.glencoe.com/11/figure/1* to find a project on management functions.

involves setting goals and determining how to reach them. **Organizing** includes establishing a time frame in which to achieve the goal, assigning employees to the project, and determining a method for approaching the work. **Controlling** refers to setting standards and evaluating performance.

All three of these management functions involve making decisions. Following a formal decision-making process can be helpful when making complicated decisions. This process usually includes the following steps:

1. Define the problem.
2. Identify the options available.
3. Gather information and determine the consequences of each option.
4. Choose the best option.
5. Take action.
6. Evaluate the results.

Planning

Good management planning at any level is realistic, comprehensive, and flexible. It includes plans for the short- and long-range uses of people, technology, and material resources.

To be effective, a management plan should be a written statement that identifies resources that can be used to meet a given goal. The plan should be clear and direct. When completed, the plan should be distributed to and discussed with everyone who is involved.

Organizing

Organizing is a coordinated effort to reach a company's planning goals. It involves assigning responsibility, establishing working relationships, hiring staff to carry out the work, and directing the work of employees.

Controlling

Controlling is the process of comparing what you planned with actual performance. It involves three basic activities: setting standards, evaluating performance according to those standards, and solving any problems revealed by the evaluation.

Before setting standards, many companies compose a mission statement. A **mission statement** is a brief description of the ultimate goals of a company. A mission statement summarizes why a company exists. It identifies products or services offered and the target market.

After a company establishes goals in a mission statement, it adopts standards that are consistent with the goals. Here are some examples of standards:

- Financial standards—profit, cash flow, sales
- Employee standards—productivity, professional conduct, dress
- Customer satisfaction standards—sales returns, customer complaints, repeat business, referrals
- Quality control standards—production line checks for defects in materials or workmanship, repair requests, recalls

Managers use standards to evaluate both company and individual performance. When performance does not meet established standards, managers must identify and solve the problem.

Effective Management Techniques

Whether you become a supervisor in a traditionally organized vertical company or a member of a self-managing team, you will need to develop management skills. The most effective management techniques are usually a matter of common sense.

Give Clear Directions

Directing others requires good communication skills. Good communication is necessary at every level of management. Even the best employees will not be productive if they do not know what they are expected to do.

A supervisor should give all the direction required for each job and encourage employees to ask questions about instructions.

Be Consistent

If you have decided that a job must be completed in a certain way, make sure that all

Case Study

Always Making It Better

Dell Inc. founder Michael Dell learned about keeping costs low and marketing directly to consumers as a young boy selling stamps to collectors. He began the computer business as a 19-year-old college student, selling out of his Texas condo. In the 20 years before he stepped down as CEO, Dell's company reached $40 billion a year in sales.

Driven to Improve

Dell's management has always focused on continuous improvement. Many technology companies spend a significant fraction of revenues on research and development, looking for the "next big thing." At Dell, the goal has been to do better at what is already being done—sell more, cut costs more, improve quality control. When a project concludes successfully, the person responsible gets a little praise, followed by a long discussion of how it could have been done better. This has worked well for employees who have grown up within the company culture.

Even Management Can Improve

Michael Dell does not exempt himself from the drive to improve. In 2001, he and company president Kevin Rollins discovered that employee perceptions of them were quite negative. Dell and Rollins responded by promising that there would be change, and they invited more input from other managers before they made any decisions. Their honesty and responsiveness had an enormous effect on others in management.

THINK STRATEGICALLY

New employees often have difficulty adapting to Dell's management style, and they soon move on. Do you think a management model that depends on filling positions from within the company can be successful in the long run? Why or why not?

@ Online Action!

Go to *marketingessentials.glencoe.com/11/case* to find a research project on management models.

employees follow this standard. Do not make exceptions unless there is a good reason to do so.

Treat Employees Fairly

Whenever possible, do what is best for your employees. Set reasonable standards of performance and apply those standards to everyone. You do not need to say yes to every employee request. However, you should always consider the employees' point of view when making decisions. Listen to suggestions from your employees, and consider acting on them. Take time to explain your reasoning if you believe an employee is wrong. Employees will be more productive when treated fairly.

Be Firm When Necessary

Each situation requiring disciplinary action is different. A friendly suggestion may be all that is necessary to get most employees on the right track. Others may not respond to the friendly approach, and you may have to be direct and firm. Give whatever directions are appropriate, and be certain the employee understands what you expect.

Sometimes employee problems are caused by the inappropriate behavior of one employee toward another. In this case, have a discussion with the employees to solve the problem. Listen to what both parties have to say and be reasonable but firm.

Set a Good Example

Set a good example in everything you do on the job. Doing this one simple thing will make your supervisory job much easier.

Delegate Responsibility

Some supervisors and middle managers do too much work themselves. If a manager is taking work home almost every night, it usually means resources are not being managed well. The manager is probably not delegating enough tasks to others, even though there are capable employees with lighter workloads who would be willing to do more.

As a supervisor, never try to do everything yourself. Organize your work responsibilities, and then decide which ones you can delegate to others. Decide which employee can best handle each task. Take time to teach employees how to do new tasks. Follow up by monitoring and evaluating the tasks that have been delegated. This will allow you more time to concentrate on the most important tasks.

Foster Teamwork

As mentioned earlier, teamwork is especially important in horizontally organized companies. As a manager or group owner, you can foster teamwork in a number of ways. Encourage team members to step outside their areas of specialization and learn about other aspects of the process for which they are responsible. Try to promote honest discussion before decisions are made. Listen respectfully to the comments and opinions of other team members, and encourage others in the group to do likewise. Respond to the comments and concerns of team members to develop a feeling of trust. Treat all team members equally. A team will not succeed if some members are treated unfairly.

Be Ethical

Ethical behavior involves understanding how your actions affect others and striving to make honest and just decisions. Management is responsible for promoting ethical behavior by example.

Employee Motivation

Motivating employees is a key skill for any manager. The more people feel that they are appreciated, the harder they work. Managers should provide frequent feedback to employees and formally evaluate them each year. Identifying long-term goals and rewarding employees who help meet them are important ways to motivate those you manage.

Rewards

It is important to reward smart work, not busy work. A person who looks busy may not necessarily be getting the work done. To get results, reward results.

Identify those workers who value not only speed but quality. Ask them to suggest ways to improve job performance.

Enthusiastic long-term employees are the key to success in most companies. Reward loyalty by investing in continuing education for employees and promoting from within.

Encourage Creativity

A reasonable amount of conformity is necessary in every company in order to maintain standards, but do not let conformity stifle creativity. Encourage employees to be creative, and remind them that they will not be penalized for mistakes. Sometimes, it is necessary to take risks when avoiding conformity.

Human Resources

Without effective managers, team members, and employees, the best technology and material resources would be of little value.

NET MARKETING

Online B2B Marketing

Beginning in the 1990s, online business-to-business (B2B) exchanges allowed purchasing managers to buy supplies through Web sites that access hundreds of vendors rather than by visiting a showroom or meeting a salesperson. About 1,500 online exchanges opened, but by 2001, most were gone because they did not offer their customers service that was personal enough. Purchasing managers wanted familiar suppliers with whom they felt comfortable. The online exchanges that have survived are the ones that have adapted to industry needs.

Zero to Sixty in the Click of a Mouse

For example, Covisint is the auto industry B2B exchange, connecting 22,000 companies. Automakers have instant access to these suppliers. The speed and low cost of Web-based ordering and invoicing are especially useful in auto manufacturing, where parts are ordered many times a day.

An exchange serving trucking companies uses onboard global positioning software to match truckers with shippers in towns they pass through. This increases the efficiency of moving products around the country.

THINK LIKE A MARKETER

Why do you think exchanges are well adapted to the industrial market?

@ Online Action!

Go to *marketingessentials.glencoe.com/11/net* to find a research activity about purchasing through B2Bs.

Most companies have a human resources (HR) department that handles recruitment, hiring and firing, training, and other personnel matters. Employee personnel records are generally maintained in a file within the human resources office. These include records related to an employee's hiring, participation in training programs, performance evaluations, disciplinary action, and commendations.

Recruiting

Recruiting is the process of locating a pool of applicants and selecting employees from this group. Prospective employees can be recruited from a number of different sources, depending on the type of job opening. Sources include current employees, walk-in applicants, media advertising, state employment services, public and private employment agencies, schools, and the Internet.

Current Employees

Most employees welcome the opportunity for a promotion, and many are happy with a lateral move, or transfer. Notices of job openings should be posted where all employees can see them. The notice should include the job title and duties, qualifications, contact name, and sometimes the salary. Current employees are also a good source for referrals.

Walk-Ins

Some applicants simply walk into the human resources office and ask to be considered for one or more types of jobs. They usually complete an application form and may be given information on any jobs that might soon become available. They may take the company's employment tests.

Media Advertising

Most companies use media advertising, in newspapers and on the Internet, to recruit applicants. Blind advertisements that do not disclose the name of the company are usually not very effective. The nature of the job and required qualifications should be clearly indicated in an advertisement.

State Employment Services

State employment offices provide prescreening and testing of prospective applicants. Both state offices and private employment agencies try to match listings of applicants with job openings. State or public agency services are free, but private agencies charge a fee when an applicant is hired.

Schools

High schools can be a good source for jobs that do not require specialized skills. Vocational and technical schools are sources for applicants who have learned a variety of specialized skills. Colleges are the recruiting field for applicants with higher-level skills.

Discrimination and the Law

Laws that prohibit discrimination govern both employers and recruitment agencies. These laws apply even before an employee is hired, so it is important to avoid discriminatory remarks and actions in all recruiting efforts. Federal law prohibits employers from discriminating on the basis of race, color, religion, gender, national origin, age, sexual orientation, or

•ABILITY, NOT DISABILITY
Unemployment is one of the most profound issues facing the disability community. Only 32 percent of Americans with disabilities aged 18 to 64 are working, but two-thirds of those that are unemployed would rather be working.

Do you think it is legal to avoid hiring a disabled job applicant? Explain.

•**THE INTERVIEW** For the company, the purpose of a job interview is to determine whether an applicant can perform well on the job.

As a manager, how would you prepare to interview several applicants for the same job?

disability. The U.S. Equal Employment Opportunity Commission enforces and regulates these laws.

Hiring New Employees

For the employer, the purpose of the interview is to determine whether an individual has the skills and abilities to perform well on the job.

It is a good idea to conduct at least two interviews with applicants who seem well-qualified. It is also a good idea to have at least two people interview final applicants. Prepare interview questions in advance. Ask only questions that are job related. If you are interviewing more than one applicant for the same job, ask each of them exactly the same questions in exactly the same order. You will need to allow the applicant to ask questions, too. It is the interviewer's responsibility to explain such things as wages and benefits.

When the time comes for managers to interview job applicants, they should check to make sure that they will be following all the laws that govern the hiring process. They should remember which kinds of questions are illegal or unacceptable.

Before hiring an applicant, most employers do some pre-employment testing. This may include some type of aptitude test to predict how well an applicant would be able to perform certain tasks. Some companies give personality tests, and many companies will ask prospective employees to be tested for illegal drug use.

Orientation and Training Programs

Orienting new employees includes more than simply training them for their positions. It is important to make new employees feel valued and welcome and to familiarize them with the working environment.

Orientation may take as little as a couple of hours or as long as a few days. It commonly includes the following:

- Tour of the company and introduction to coworkers
- Discussion of the company's history, mission, and values
- Description of what the company does
- Training on equipment, such as cash registers and computers
- Information on where facilities are located
- Information about payroll, benefits, and company policies

All new employees need on-the-job training. As a supervisor, you may train new employees yourself or delegate this task to an experienced employee. Make sure that all job duties are explained and that new employees understand how to complete them.

Scheduling Employees

Employee scheduling is the process of determining which employees should work at what times. Very small companies can handle the scheduling of employees quite simply without any special computer program. Today, though, most companies use some type of computer scheduling.

Handling Complaints and Grievances

Employee complaints or grievances should be taken just as seriously as customer complaints. Most employee complaints fall into one of three categories: complaints about other employees, complaints about the quality of the company's product or service, or complaints about their own work situation. Complaints about other employees should be handled with care and discretion. Conflicts in the workplace can damage morale and productivity.

Some employees do, indeed, care enough about the quality of the company's products or services to bring problems to the attention of management. The complaining employee should be kept informed at every step. If the complaint proves justified, the employee should be rewarded.

Complaints involving the employee's work situation are usually fairly easy to resolve when the issue is salary. Every company should have a pay range for each job and a way to deviate from this range for truly outstanding work. For other work situation complaints, gather the facts, report the findings to the complaining employee, make your decision, and clearly explain to the employee the reasons and nature of your decision.

Assessing Employee Performance

Assessment enables a manager to develop better workers and a more efficient and profitable company.

In many companies, newly hired employees are placed on probation for a period of three to six months. Near the end of the probationary period, the employee is evaluated. If performance is satisfactory, the employee's status is changed to permanent. Usually, all employees are evaluated yearly. In many companies, the employee completes a self-evaluation form, and the supervisor completes the same form on the employee. Then a meeting is scheduled so that the supervisor and the employee can compare and discuss any differences in their completed forms.

Remedial Action

Whenever a supervisor notices that an employee's performance or behavior is substandard, it is the supervisor's responsibility to discuss the matter with the employee. Sometimes, remedial action is necessary. **Remedial action** is a means of encouraging appropriate workplace behavior in order to improve employee performance. Two approaches to remedial action are preventive discipline and corrective discipline.

Preventive Discipline

Preventive discipline focuses on managing employees in a way that prevents behavior that might require directly disciplining an employee. Its intent is to encourage employees to follow the rules. Preventive techniques might include involving employees in setting standards, encouraging employees to meet standards, and communicating standards clearly. Providing training programs for self-discipline and having a method for controlling absences are also helpful.

Corrective Discipline

In some cases, corrective discipline is necessary. Corrective counseling is sometimes effective. This involves a discussion between the employee and a human resources counselor about the problem and what must be done to correct it. When this fails, more severe forms of remedial action are required. This usually begins with an oral warning and an explanation of what will be required. Next is a written warning to the employee with a copy for the employee's personnel file. If the problem is not resolved, the third action is suspension from work without pay. The suspension usually lasts from one to five days and comes with a warning that if the problem is not corrected, the employee may be fired.

Dismissing Employees

Sooner or later, all companies have to face the task of firing an employee for poor performance or bad behavior. Before this decision is made, certain procedures must be followed. In most cases, a supervisor or manager must give the employee verbal and written warnings that her performance or behavior is not acceptable. These warnings should be included on the employee's performance assessment form in the personnel file. The employee may be placed on probation and given time to change.

When a decision is made to dismiss a worker, a letter of dismissal should be written, along with separate checks for final salary and severance pay.

The Exit Interview

When an employee leaves the company, the human resources department will typically arrange an **exit interview**. An exit interview provides the opportunity for both the employee and manager to obtain valuable feedback. Exit interviews are often conducted with human resources personnel rather than the employee's supervisor. An employee always has the right not to participate in an exit interview.

An employee leaving voluntarily may have feedback on overall work conditions that will help the company retain workers in the future.

If the employee is being dismissed, the reason should be discussed in the exit interview. Usually, an employee will be entitled to advance notice of termination. As a manager, you must decide whether to have the employee continue working or leave immediately.

11.2 AFTER YOU READ

Reviewing Key Terms and Concepts

1. What are the basic functions of management?
2. What does it mean to delegate responsibility?
3. What is the purpose of assessing employee performance?

Integrating Academic Skills

Math

4. Retail store clerks are negotiating with their company management for a 7.5 percent increase in their hourly wage. Assume that the average hourly wage of a clerk is $13.75 and that the company has 45 clerks who each work a 40-hour week, for 50 weeks per year. The clerks receive an additional two-week paid vacation each year. What would such a pay raise cost the company per year?

Language Arts

5. Choose a clothing store whose products you purchase or like. Do research to learn what ethical policies the company follows in terms of working conditions for those who produce the clothing. Write a one-page report on what you learn.

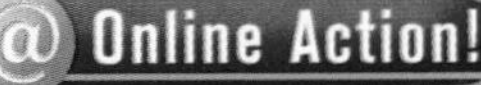

Check your answers at *marketingessentials.glencoe.com/11/read*

CAREERS IN MARKETING

DAN REED
MUSIC DIRECTOR/ OPERATIONS MANAGER WXPN-FM

What do you do at work?
I am the music director and operations manager of WXPN in Philadelphia, a non-commercial radio station. I'm also the talent coordinator of the "World Café," a daily syndicated music show. I'm responsible for all of the contact with the music industry, including new music acquisition, relationships with management and labels, booking artists, and special events coordination. Everything I do is geared toward marketing because if there isn't an audience, there isn't a radio station or show. The biggest creative part of my job is understanding the audience and making sure that they know what we're doing—that's marketing in its purest form.

What skills are most important to you?
I was fortunate enough to attend a high school that had a radio station, so my early, mistake-ridden, trial-and-error training came in 10th, 11th, and 12th grades. I also worked at my college radio station. Besides about 16 years in the radio business, I also worked for five years in the concert business, which has become invaluable experience. Contacts are important—the art of the schmooze should be considered. Get real world experience—a degree is fine, but hardcore work experience is paramount.

What is your key to success?
I work hard, and I let my opinions be heard. Any media or marketing organization runs on ideas, so always be thinking. I've tried to make people believe in me and my work ethic, and I've never backed off tough decisions. Having a sense of humor is very important—I think that laughter has allowed me to disarm many a detractor.

Aptitudes, Abilities, and Skills

Strong interpersonal skills, an outgoing personality, tenacity, and a tough work ethic

Education and Training

A bachelor's degree can be helpful, but real-world experience is often more important.

Career Path

Positions such as this one can begin virtually anywhere within an organization; Reed suggests that individuals seek out new ways to make themselves valuable to the company.

THINKING CRITICALLY

Why do you think "the art of the schmooze" is important in a marketing career?

Online Action!

Go to *marketingessentials.glencoe.com/11/careers* for a career-related activity.

CHAPTER 11 REVIEW

FOCUS on KEY POINTS

SECTION 11.1

- The global marketplace will influence the kind of leadership companies will need in the future.
- Businesses are organized in one of two ways: vertically or horizontally.
- Traditional, vertically organized companies have three levels of management: top management, middle management, and supervisory-level management.
- Horizontal companies have top and middle management. Horizontally organized companies have self-managed teams that set their own goals and make their own decisions.

SECTION 11.2

- Basic management functions are planning, organizing, and controlling.
- Effective management techniques involve properly training employees, letting them know what is expected of them, and treating them fairly.
- In the case of poor performance or unacceptable behavior, the employee should receive warnings. These warnings should be included in the employee's personnel file. A letter of dismissal should be given to the employee at dismissal time, along with the final salary amount due.

REVIEW VOCABULARY

Define each of the following terms in a short sentence.

1. management (p. 237)
2. vertical organization (p. 237)
3. top management (p. 237)
4. middle management (p. 238)
5. supervisory-level management (p. 238)
6. horizontal organization (p. 238)
7. empowerment (p. 238)
8. planning (p. 240)
9. organizing (p. 242)
10. controlling (p. 242)
11. mission statement (p. 242)
12. remedial action (p. 248)
13. exit interview (p. 249)

REVIEW FACTS and IDEAS

14. How do horizontally organized companies differ from traditionally organized companies? (11.1)
15. What are the three levels of management? (11.1)
16. How does a self-managing team function? (11.1)
17. What are the three functions of management? (11.2)
18. What management techniques are used by effective managers? (11.2)
19. What methods can be used to motivate employees? (11.2)

BUILD SKILLS

20. Workplace Skills

Working in Teams Angela is a member of a six-person team. One of the team members, Lou, often arrives at work late. The other team members seem not to notice. Angela feels the quality of Lou's work is being affected by his late arrival. What should she do?

21. Technology Applications

Internet Job Ads Use the Internet to find recruiting sites. Locate an ad for a management opportunity in marketing. Use a word processing program to write a summary of your findings, including the qualifications necessary to apply for the job. Also include the Web address of the site.

22. Math Practice

Plan Office Space Calculate the square feet of space required to organize an office area to accommodate six employees. Each cubicle will be 16 square feet. Plan for three cubicles on each side (for a total of six cubicles) and a 3-foot wide hallway down the middle.

DEVELOP CRITICAL THINKING

23. Organizational Plans

Business organizational structures can mimic existing social structures. For example, a U.S. company doing business with a company in a hierarchical society might use a straightforward, vertically organized management structure to enhance communication with its target market and vendors.

Why might globalization encourage companies to use a mix of both vertical and horizontal organization?

24. Rewarding Job Performance

A material reward for a job well done might include a raise, bonus, or promotion. Do you think nonmaterial rewards such as praise and public recognition motivate and encourage employees as much as financial compensation? Explain your answer. What other types of reward might an employer use to motivate and encourage employees? List a few examples and explain why you think they would be applicable to work situations.

APPLY CONCEPTS

25. Plan an Event

Assume that your school is going to organize a talent show fund-raiser. You will need to form a committee to solicit prizes, advertise, sell tickets, hold a drawing, distribute prizes, and determine expenses and profit.

Activity Create a vertical or horizontal organization plan for your committee. Use visual aids and/or a word-processing program to explain your choice of organization and show how your organization will accomplish the goals of your committee.

26. Develop a Mission Statement

Assume that you are the manager of a new independent retail music store with seven employees.

Activity Use a word processing program to create a mission statement explaining the goals of your business.

NET SAVVY

27. Does the Company Benefit?

You and several coworkers would prefer to work at home and avoid the commute to the office. Browse the Web to research the advantages and disadvantages for the company of having employees work from their homes.

Use a word processing program to write a one-page report that could serve as a basis for a discussion with company management.

THE DECA CONNECTION

An Association of Marketing Students

Role Play: Management Trainee

Situation You are to assume the role of management trainee for a chain of CD and video stores. Your chain of stores is a dynamic and growing one. As a result of this growth, the company is constantly seeking individuals for management positions. The manager of the store where you are assigned (judge) will be making a presentation to some potential management trainees.

Activity You are to prepare information about your company and some of the traits upper management seeks in the individuals it hires for management positions. You are to review your ideas with your store manager (judge).

Evaluation You will be evaluated on how well you meet the following performance indicators:

- Explain the concept of management
- Identify desirable personality traits important to business
- Analyze employer expectations in the business environment
- Explain the nature of managerial ethics
- Make oral presentations

@ Online Action!

For more information and DECA Prep practice, go to *marketingessentials.glencoe .com/11/DECA*

MARKETING INTERNSHIP

A SIMULATED DECA PRODUCT AND SERVICE MANAGEMENT EVENT

Design a Program for Savvy Business Travelers

BASIC BACKGROUND

Cameo Creations recently began expanding its operations internationally and has found that its staff is ill-prepared for the rigors of travel and the expertise needed to conduct business abroad. Although there are many outside consultants and seminars available, the company prefers to keep its training in-house. It wants your firm to propose an interactive training program in a technology that can be used whenever a new employee is hired.

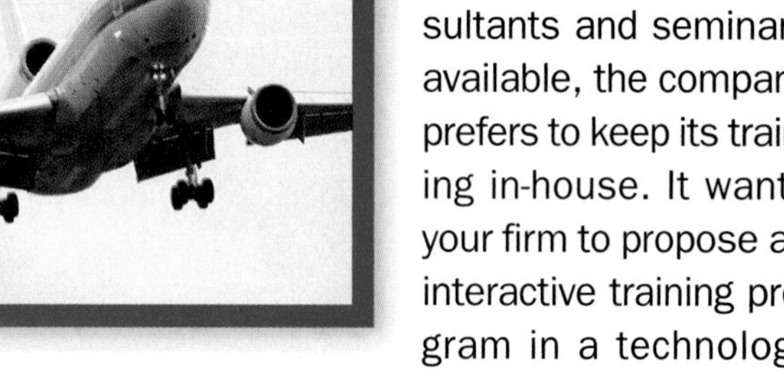

Working Abroad Some topics that were discussed during the initial interview with Cameo Creations executives include: cross-cultural differences in management, communication and interpersonal relations; safety when traveling abroad; foreign currency conversion; jet lag; and technology needed to conduct business in foreign countries, e.g., the right type of cell phone or bringing a power adapter for laptop computers.

YOUR OBJECTIVE

Your objective is to design a reusable training program for Cameo Creations' employees that travel abroad and to convince company executives that your proposal meets their needs. You will need to include the most current information available on technology and the tools that can make international business easier.

ASSIGNMENT AND STRATEGY

- **Conduct research** Research the topics the client wants included in its training program. Research consulting companies that provide cross-cultural workshops to see what topics they generally cover. Interview global business travelers and review business magazines, such as *BusinessWeek, Sales and Marketing Management,* and *Forbes,* and the magazines' Web sites to learn about the practical issues a person needs to know.
- **Design a training program** Select one foreign country or region of the world to use as the basis of your proposal. Outline the topics covered in this program and explain why

you would include them. Describe the interactive activities for participants. Decide on a length and schedule for the program, and how you could evaluate participants. Include a list of the computer equipment and software that the client will need for this training program.

- **What your project should include** To make your project complete, prepare a sample scenario that can be used for role playing exercises to train participants in interpersonal skills when doing business abroad. Include a sample test that can be used to evaluate a participant at the end of the training program. Prepare a flyer that would be distributed to participants to outline the program's major topics.

YOUR REPORT

Use a word processing program and presentation software to prepare a double-spaced report and an oral presentation for your supervisors. See a suggested outline and key evaluation points at *marketingessentials.glencoe.com/internship*

BUILD YOUR PORTFOLIO

Option 1 Internship Report Once you have completed your Marketing Internship project and presentation, include your written outline and a few printouts of key slides from your oral presentation in your Marketing Portfolio.

Option 2 Design Business Seminars Typical business seminars include selling techniques, management skills, customer service, communications skills, and computer training. Create a new kind of seminar and explain why it could succeed. Decide where it will be offered and what the fee will be. Describe the presenters and draw up an outline. Come up with a plan to promote it. Prepare a written report and an oral presentation using word processing and presentation software. See a suggested outline and key evaluation points at *marketingessentials.glencoe.com/portfolio*

@ Online Action!

Go to *marketingessentials.glencoe.com/Unit/4/DECA* to review employee training concepts that relate to DECA events.

UNIT 5 Selling

In this unit you will find

- Chapter 12 Preparing for the Sale
- Chapter 13 Initiating the Sale
- Chapter 14 Presenting the Product
- Chapter 15 Closing the Sale
- Chapter 16 Using Math in Sales

ANALYZE THE AD

The makers of V8 vegetable juice saw an opportunity to gain customers when low-carbohydrate diets became popular. What tone does this ad have?

Market Talk V8 is a "shelf-stable bottled juice," while consumers head to the refrigerator or freezer cases to buy orange juice. Why do you think V8 feels it can compete directly with orange juice?

Think and Write Imagine you work at a health-food store and a customer asks you which is the best choice, V8 or a sports drink. What would you need to know about these two products and about your customer to give a helpful answer?

Go to ***marketingessentials.glencoe.com/u5/ad*** for an extended activity.

Marketing Plan

1 ANALYSIS
- SWOT
- Economic
- Socio-Cultural
- Technological
- Competitive

2 STRATEGY
- Promotion
- Place
- Price
- Product

3 IMPLEMENTATION
- Organization
- Management
- Staffing

4 BUDGET
- Cost of Sales
- Cost of Promotion
- Incomes and Expenses

5 CONTROL
- Evaluation
- Performance Measures
- Performance Analysis

In this unit

Foundations of Marketing
- Communication, Interpersonal Skills

Functions of Marketing
- Selling

CHAPTER 12

Preparing for the Sale

Chapter Objectives

After reading this chapter, you should be able to:

- Define selling and different types of selling situations
- Explain the purpose and goals of selling
- Define consultative selling
- Differentiate between rational and emotional buying motives
- List three levels of customer decision making
- Name sources of product information
- Explain the main focus of preparation in business-to-business selling and in retail selling

GUIDE TO THE PHOTO

Market Talk Product knowledge is what sales skills rest on. In the food industry, salespeople need to know what the products are, their shelf life, and how they are prepared. An apparel salesperson needs to know how garments were manufactured, their style, and specific benefits such as warmth or ease of care.

Quick Think If you worked in the produce section of a grocery store, what questions would customers ask?

Performance indicators represent key skills and knowledge. Relating them to the concepts explained in this chapter is your key to success in DECA events. These acronyms represent DECA events that involve knowledge of concepts in this chapter.

AAAL*	**FMAL***	**MMS**	**TMDM**
AAML*	**FMDM**	**QSRM**	**TSE**
ADC	**FMML***	**RMAL***	**VPM***
BSM	**FSRM**	**RMML***	
EMDM*	**HMDM**	**SMDM**	

In all these DECA events you should be able to follow these performance indicators:

- Explain the nature and scope of the selling function
- Explain company selling policies
- Prepare for the sales presentation
- Acquire product knowledge for use in selling
- Identify product features and benefits
- Identify a customer's buying motives for use in selling
- Differentiate between consumer and organizational buying behavior
- Prospect for customers
- Write sales letters

All the events with an asterisk (*) also include this performance indicator:

- Explain the use of brand names in selling

Some events include additional performance indicators. These are:

BSM Describe customer buying process for services

SMDM Describe customer buying process for services

DECA PREP

Check your understanding of DECA performance indicators with the DECA activity in this chapter's review. For more information and DECA Prep practice, go to *marketingessentials.glencoe.com/12/DECA*

SECTION 12.1

What Is Selling?

OBJECTIVES

- Define selling and different types of selling situations
- Explain the purpose and goals of selling
- Define consultative selling
- Differentiate between rational and emotional buying motives
- List three levels of customer decision making

KEY TERMS

- personal selling
- business-to-business selling
- telemarketing
- consultative selling
- feature-benefit selling
- product features
- customer benefits
- rational motive
- emotional motive
- extensive decision making
- limited decision making
- routine decision making

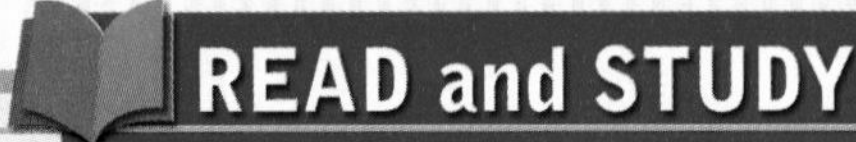

BEFORE YOU READ

Connect When was the last time you purchased something with the help of a salesperson? What was the item and how did the salesperson help you?

THE MAIN IDEA

Selling is a function of marketing that involves one-on-one contact with customers. To be effective in sales, a salesperson must possess product knowledge, as well as an understanding of customers' motives for buying and of the decision-making process.

STUDY ORGANIZER

Create a chart like the one below to record important information about selling situations and customers' decision making.

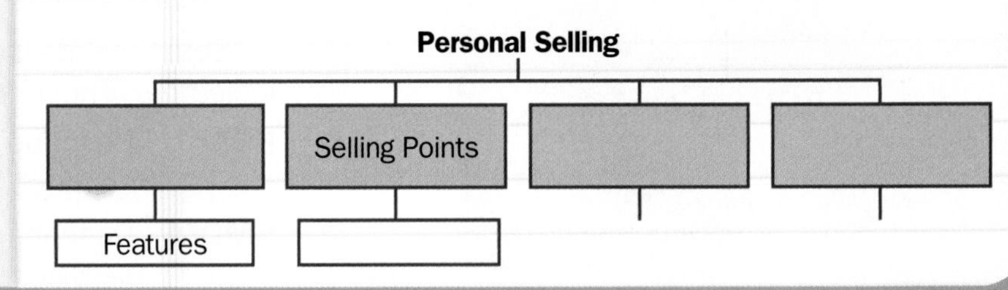

WHILE YOU READ

Connect Think about the last time you shopped. What motives did you have for your purchase, and what product information was important to you?

Selling

Personal selling is any form of direct contact between a salesperson and a customer. The key factor that sets it apart from other forms of promotion is this two-way communication between the seller and the buyer. This communication can take place in a retail setting, in a business-to-business setting, and in telemarketing (over the phone). Salespeople need to research their products and their customers. The more a salesperson knows about both, the better prepared and the more effective she or he will be at offering customers solutions to their problems and meeting their needs. Certain aspects of a salesperson's job will vary depending on where the selling takes place.

Retail Selling

Retail selling is unique because customers come to the store. The salesperson should be available to answer any questions about the product or its features.

Business-to-Business Selling

Business-to-business selling may take place in a manufacturer's or wholesaler's showroom (inside sales) or a customer's place of business (outside sales). In the latter case, it is up to the salesperson to make contact with the customer. Sales representatives, in most cases, will call to make an appointment prior to their visit. In other cases, a sales representative may make a cold call, which means he or she will appear without an appointment.

Telemarketing

The last type of personal selling situation is **telemarketing**, which is the process of selling over the telephone.

In 2003, Congress passed legislation making it more difficult for telemarketers to operate. The new law prohibits telemarketers from calling any phone number that has been registered with the National Do Not Call Registry, established by the Federal Communications Commission. This new law has significantly reduced the number of people telemarketers may contact.

Goals of Selling

The purpose and goals of selling are the same regardless of the sales situations. They are to help customers make satisfying buying decisions, which create ongoing, profitable relationships between buyer and seller. This is important because repeat business is crucial to the success of any company. It is easier and less expensive to keep current customers happy than it is to generate new customers. If a business is successful at keeping customers happy, the customers are likely to pass along positive recommendations to other business associates, friends, and family.

Consultative Selling

Salespeople accomplish these goals by engaging in a process called consultative selling. **Consultative selling** is providing solutions to customers' problems by finding products that meet their needs. A customer may say that she is having a problem with her feet because she stands all day in her new job. Possessing the relevant product knowledge allows an alert salesperson to suggest shoes designed for comfort and support.

Consultative selling goes even further in business-to-business selling. To comply with OSHA standards, an ice cream manufacturer must provide insulated clothing to protect employees who work in freezers that are 20 degrees below zero. In this situation, the sales representative for the insulated clothing company would recommend the garments that had the capacity to keep workers warm in such a cold work environment. Analysis of customer needs combined with product knowledge is the essence of consultative selling. To be effective in consultative selling, you need to be trained in feature-benefit selling.

Feature-Benefit Selling

Matching the characteristics of a product to a customer's needs and wants is a concept called **feature-benefit selling**. Many people believe that customers do not buy products; rather, they buy what the products will do for them. Leather shoes are purchased for their appearance, easy care, comfort, and longevity (see Figure 12.1).

Product Features

A salesperson needs to learn how a product's features will benefit the customer. **Product features** may be basic, physical, or extended attributes of the product or purchase. The most basic feature of a product is its intended use. A person buys an automobile for transportation and a watch to tell time.

Figure 12.1 Feature-Benefit Chart

• **Warm and Dry** **A feature-benefit chart combines product features with corresponding benefits, creating selling points. This chart shows the features and benefits for Columbia Sportswear's Canyon Meadows Jacket.**

What other important product feature is needed to complete this chart?

Product Feature	Customer Benefit
100% nylon Hydro Rip-Stop Fabric	Durable, water/wind resistant, washable
100% nylon Hydro Plus shell	Durable, water/wind resistant, washable
65% polyester & 35% cotton jersey lining	Comfortable, washable
Designed to fold into zippered pouch that is part of the jacket	Packable, great for hiking and trail trips
Radial sleeve and articulated elbow	Free range of motion, comfortable
Colors: abalone, wink, Columbia navy, tilt blue	Unisex colors, offers variety
Sizes: 7/8, 10/12, 14/16, 18/20, 4/5, 6/6x, 2T, 3T, 4T	Children's sizes, covers full age range
Limited warranty	Covers defects in materials and workmanship in outerwear manufactured by Columbia Sportswear Company.

Online Action!

Go to *marketingessentials.glencoe.com/12/figure/1* to find a project on feature-benefit charts.

The physical features of a product differentiate competing brands and models. In buying a vehicle, a consumer might consider the car's engine, gas consumption, appearance, stereo system, and tires, and whether the car has an automatic transmission, air bag, power steering, and antilock brakes.

Additional features add more value to a product and provide the reasons for price differences among product models. An iron that turns itself off after sitting unused will cost more than a basic model without this feature. Extended product features for a vehicle might include the warranty, service policy, and available financing. Customers might consider the reputation of a company to be an extended feature because there is reduced risk in doing business with a secure and well-established company. Customers are faithful to a reputable company that stands behind its products.

Customer Benefits

When the features of a product are developed into customer benefits, they become selling points. **Customer benefits** are the advantages or personal satisfaction a customer will get from a good or service. It is a salesperson's job to analyze the product features from the customer's point of view to determine the benefits. A salesperson will need to answer two questions about each product feature:

1. **How does the feature help the product's performance?** The answer to this question represents the first step in developing a customer benefit. For example, air pockets in the heel of a running shoe cushion the impact on pavement.
2. **How does the performance information give the customer a personal reason to buy the product?** What value is the product to the customer? In the case of the running shoe, the air pockets give the wearer more comfort when running or walking and help to protect the foot from injury.

After identifying the features of a product and their benefits, you should put together a feature-benefit chart. This is a chart in which each product feature is listed with its corresponding customer benefits. In preparing such a chart, remember that the more useful a feature, the more valuable the product is to the customer. Figure 12.1 on page 262 shows a feature-benefit chart for a jacket.

Customer Buying Motives

Salespeople must know what motivates customers to buy and what decisions customers make before the final purchase.

Customers may have rational or emotional motives for making purchases. A **rational motive** is a conscious, logical reason for a purchase. Rational motives include product dependability, time or monetary savings, health or safety considerations, service, and quality. An **emotional motive** is a feeling experienced by a customer through association with a product. Emotional motives are feelings such as social approval, recognition, power, love, or prestige. Many buying decisions involve a combination of both buying motives.

Successful salespeople determine customers' rational and emotional motives in a potential buying situation. Then they suggest the features and benefits of the product that best matches those motives.

Customer Decision Making

Some customers need no help from salespeople, and others require significant time and effort. This difference has its roots in three distinct types of decision making—extensive,

• **MAKING an EXPENSIVE DECISION** Cars are costly and they come in a wide variety. This ad highlights the many features of a minivan.

Suppose a couple with two young children needs a new car. They have never owned a minivan before. Would this require extensive or limited decision making?

limited, and routine. How a person makes a decision is affected by the following factors:

- Previous experience with the product and company
- How often the product is purchased
- The amount of information necessary to make a wise buying decision
- The importance of the purchase to the customer
- The perceived risk involved in the purchase (for example, uncertainty about how the product will function)
- The time available to make the decision

Extensive Decision Making

Extensive decision making is used when there has been little or no previous experience with an item. This category includes those goods and services that have a high degree of perceived risk, are very expensive, or have high value to the customer. A consumer who is buying a first home will use extensive decision making.

Limited Decision Making

Limited decision making is used when a person buys goods and services that he or she has purchased before but not regularly. There is a moderate degree of perceived risk involved, and the person often needs some information before buying the product.

Consumer goods and services in this category might include a second car, certain types of clothing, furniture, a vacation, and household appliances.

Routine Decision Making

Routine decision making is used when a person needs little information about a product. The perceived risk may be low because the item is inexpensive, the product is bought frequently, or satisfaction with the product is high. Some consumer goods and services in this category are grocery items, newspapers, and dry cleaning services. Customers who have developed brand loyalty for a product will use routine decision making.

12.1 AFTER YOU READ

Reviewing Key Terms and Concepts

1. What sets personal selling apart from other forms of promotion?
2. Identify a basic, a physical, and an extended product feature for a camera.
3. What factors influence the level of customer decision making?

Integrating Academic Skills

Math

4. When buying advertising time on television or in magazines, advertisers calculate the cost per thousand (CPM) people reached by the ad. If the cost of advertising was $100,000 and the reach or circulation was 10,000,000 people, what would be the CPM? (Note: M is the Roman numeral for 1,000.)

Civics and Government

5. Research the provisions of the Do Not Call Registry and note its impact on sellers and telemarketers. Prepare a one-page written report on your findings.

@ Online Action! Check your answers at *marketingessentials.glencoe.com/12/read*

SECTION 12.2

Getting Ready to Sell

OBJECTIVES

- **Name sources of product information**
- **Explain the main focus of preparation in business-to-business selling and in retail selling**

KEY TERMS

- **pre-approach**
- **prospect**
- **referrals**
- **endless chain method**
- **cold canvassing**
- **sales quotas**

READ and STUDY

BEFORE YOU READ

Predict Suppose you are starting tomorrow as a tire salesperson. Where would you find information about car tires?

THE MAIN IDEA

As a salesperson, you will need to prepare for the sale by learning about the industry and the products you will be selling. In specific sales situations, you may also need to find customers. The tools and techniques for accomplishing these tasks are covered in this section. You will also review company policies and ethical and legal issues in sales.

STUDY ORGANIZER

Use a chart similar to the one below to take notes about sources of product and industry information and methods of prospecting.

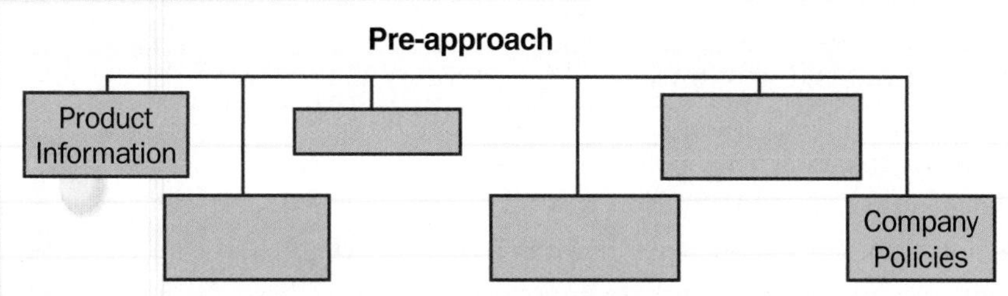

The Pre-Approach

The **pre-approach** is the preparation for the face-to-face encounter with potential customers. In preparing to assist customers, salespeople study their products, keep abreast of industry trends and competitors, research potential customers, and develop familiarity with their company's policies and procedures. They also review ethical and legal issues involved in their selling situation.

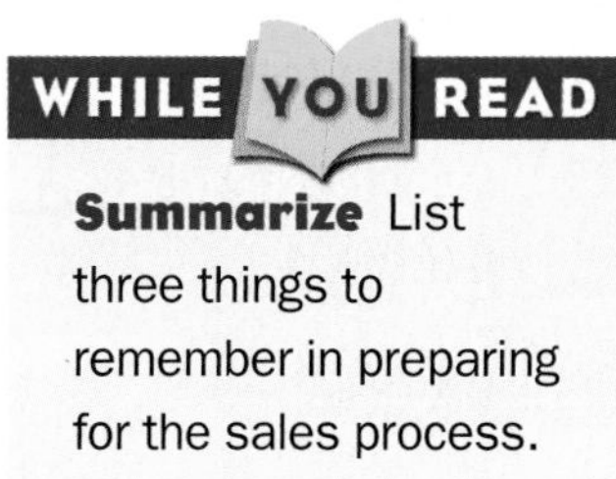

Summarize List three things to remember in preparing for the sales process.

Product Information

Developing product knowledge is easy if you know where to look for the information. Salespeople can generally find all the product information they need through four main sources: direct experience, written publications, other people, and formal training.

Some businesses offer discounts to their salespeople to encourage employees to buy and use the company's merchandise. You can also get direct experience with a product by studying display models or visiting the manufacturing facility to see how the product is made.

Printed materials include user manuals, manufacturer warranties and guarantees, catalogs, and promotional materials. Labels provide important information for clothing items or prepackaged goods. Manufacturers, retailers, and wholesalers often have Web sites where products may be explained and purchased.

Formal training may be the best way to educate salespeople on certain products. Most industrial sales representatives receive much

Case Study

Marketing Pharmaceuticals

When the biotech company Genta was on the brink of selling its first drug, it took two years to recruit a sales force. For most drug companies, the sales division is the heart of the business. The smallest can still employ more than 1,000 salespeople. The largest sales division may reach 3,000, selling everything from hypertension medicines to antibiotics. Genta does not fall into either category.

An Expert Salesforce

Genta recruited 18 experienced salespeople, mostly from other pharmaceutical companies. They all began their careers in primary care—the typical trajectory—before switching to a specialty in oncology—the treatment of cancer. Genta would not release salary figures. Sales reps with no experience can earn a base salary of $80,000, according to Salary.com, a Web site that tracks wages. Bonuses, commissions, and, of course, experience can push that much higher, according to industry executives.

The team is composed of salespeople who won awards for their selling performance, Williams said. They spend their downtime in medical libraries and hospitals, picking up information to share with physicians. They are considered experts in oncology and mingle with physicians, spend time with cancer advocacy groups, and forfeit weekends in an ongoing effort to sell.

THINK STRATEGICALLY

Why do these salespeople have to be experts in oncology?

@ Online Action!

Go to *marketingessentials.glencoe.com/12/case* to find an activity about sales training.

Figure 12.2 How to Develop Employer Leads

• **Finding a Buyer** Many firms generate leads for their sales staff. Leads help salespeople locate potential customers.

How do companies find leads?

1 EMPLOYERS ATTEND TRADE SHOWS

Employers can get leads by attending trade shows. Retailers and other interested business-to-business buyers attend trade shows to learn about new products they may want to buy to resell or to use in their businesses. Attendees are usually good leads for the shows' vendors. Trade shows are often sponsored by trade associations. For instance, the Super Show is sponsored by the Sporting Goods Manufacturers Association (SGMA), the members of which are producers of athletic clothing, footwear, and sports equipment.

2 EMPLOYERS GIVE LEADS

Employers give leads to the sales representatives responsible for the territories in which the prospects are located. Special forms may be used to communicate this information and to track the follow-up action taken by the sales representatives.

3 SALESPEOPLE ACT ON LEADS

Salespeople call to learn more about the prospects. Salespeople make appointments with qualified leads. They then report back to their employer. That way the employer knows that the leads have been followed.

@ Online Action!

Go to *marketingessentials.glencoe.com/12/figure/2* to find a project on employer leads.

MARKET TECH

FOSE—A High-Tech Trade Show

FOSE stands for Federal Office Systems Expo. This exposition has high-tech companies exhibiting their wares for government officials and procurement officers. In 2004 it was held at the Washington (D.C.) Convention Center. Some 500 vendors selling everything from printers, scanners, and software to GPS-equipped digital cameras and high-tech motion-detector systems showcased their products there. Close to 19,000 people attended FOSE in 2004.

Bringing Home Leads

According to Tom Temin, Editor-in-Chief of *Government Computer News* and *Washington Technology* and Senior Vice President for Editorial at *PostNewsweek Tech Media*, "the show was more of a breeding ground for networking and mining sales leads than a place for vendors to close deals. There are deal shows, and this one is not one of those." Large and small companies used gimmicks to get prospects to stop at their booths. One company had a cartoonist, two others had slot machines promising gifts and awards for prizes, while another scanned badges for a raffle.

THINK LIKE A MARKETER

If you had a small company that specialized in software to track agricultural goods, would you pay to exhibit at this show? Why or why not?

@ Online Action!

Go to *marketingessentials.glencoe.com/12/tech* to find an activity about technology and sales.

of their product knowledge through formal training sessions. Information might be funneled informally to the sales staff as new merchandise is received or selected for promotion. Some of this information and even training may be provided by the vendors/manufacturer of the product(s).

Industry Trends

Sales representatives read periodicals related to their trade to gain insight into the industry. As a sales representative for an apparel manufacturer, you might read *Women's Wear Daily*. At the retail level of selling, a sales representative may read consumer fashion magazines, such as *Vogue*, to stay current with up-to-date colors and trends.

Prospecting

Looking for new customers is called prospecting. A **prospect**, or a lead, is a potential customer. Many types of businesses require salespeople to find prospects, while others do not.

Prospecting is especially important in business-to-business selling situations. Salespeople are evaluated on how many new accounts they open through prospecting efforts.

Employer Leads

Some firms employ entire telemarketing teams to generate leads for their sales staffs. They also attend trade shows, where they display their products for review by buyers in the industry.

Interested buyers provide information for follow-up. Other firms rely entirely on their salespeople to find new customers. Many employers do what they can to help locate potential customers for their salespeople.

Directories

The Yellow Pages list businesses that may be potential customers for certain industrial goods and services. Business-to-business sales representatives can use trade and professional directories to locate potential customers. One well-known directory frequently used by sales representatives is the *Thomas Register of American Manufacturers.*

Newspapers

Newspapers provide good leads for some salespeople. For example, engagement announcements provide bridal shops, caterers, florists, and printers with prospects.

Commercial Lists

Salespeople may buy lists of potential customers from companies that specialize in categorizing people by such criteria as education, age, income, credit card purchases, and location. Lists of businesses categorized according to net sales, profits, products, and geographic locations are also available.

Customer Referrals

Satisfied customers often give salespeople **referrals**—the names of other people who might buy the product. Referrals open the market to potential customers whom you might not have reached without a recommendation. When salespeople ask previous customers for names of potential customers, they are said to be using the **endless chain method**. Some companies offer discounts or gifts to customers who give referrals.

Cold Canvassing

In **cold canvassing**, potential customers are selected at random, such as by going door-to-door or selecting names from a telephone directory. This is also sometimes called blind prospecting.

Preparing for the Sale in Business-to-Business Selling

In business-to-business (B-to-B or B2B) sales, pre-approach activities vary depending on whether the sales call is with a previous customer or a new prospect. When dealing with previous customers, salespeople analyze past sales records and review their notes about the buyer's personality, family, interests, and hobbies.

A MATTER OF ETHICS

Sealing a Deal

A software firm in a medium-sized city has been growing, in part thanks to its popular sports-based video games. The company has decided to sell stock and become a publicly traded company. It can use the money it raises to fund new research and development, but it will also have to meet a lot of new accounting requirements. The people who own the company stock will want complete information about the company's financial performance.

Pitching and Wooing

Accounting firms in the city are desperately trying to get the contract with the software company. They treat executives and software designers to expensive dinners and tickets to NBA games. One company is so determined to win the contract that it makes a secret offer to one of the senior executives. It promises to hire the executive's daughter, who recently graduated from college, but has been having trouble getting a job.

THINKING ETHICALLY

How far can a company go to win over a potential customer?

Online Action!

Go to *marketingessentials.glencoe.com/12/ethics* to find an activity about ethics and sales.

When dealing with a new customer, the salesperson must do some homework before jumping into the selling process. Questions that the salesperson should research include the following:

- Does the prospect need this product or service?
- Does the prospect have the financial resources to pay?
- Does the prospect have the authority to buy?

To find answers to these questions, you can make inquiries by calling other sales representatives who sell noncompeting lines. You can read the company's annual reports or subscribe to the database listings of a company like Dun & Bradstreet, which monitors businesses' financial situations. All these things are part of qualifying a prospect. Qualified prospects are prospective customers that meet the necessary requirements established by your firm to conduct business.

Some of the concerns above can be addressed during your telephone conversation with the prospect. By asking tactful questions such as what competing products the prospect carries, you can determine satisfaction with the present supplier. You may find that your product could better satisfy your prospect's needs. Other questions might help to determine how your product could help improve the prospect's business. That will help you in your consultative selling because you will be in a position to offer solutions to current needs and problems.

•SALES TRAINING Formal training may be used to disseminate product information to new and seasoned sales staff. Role playing is often used.

What other information might be important to cover in the formal training of a new sales employee?

Preparing for the Sale in Retail Selling

Since the customer comes to you in retail selling situations, the preparation centers around the merchandise and work area. Retail sales associates are often responsible for merchandising, stock keeping, and housekeeping. Those activities include:

- Straightening, rearranging, and replenishing the stock
- Adjusting price tickets before and after special sales
- Learning where stock is located and how much is available
- Arranging displays
- Vacuuming the floor, dusting the shelves, and keeping the selling area neat and clean

Company Policies and Training

Sales management establishes the guidelines and policies under which salespeople function. Some of their specific duties involve scheduling sales staff, overseeing and evaluating their performance, and training them.

Training

A four-step process is often used by sales managers who are ultimately responsible for training new sales personnel. The four steps are explanation, demonstration, trial, and critique. A sales technique is first explained and then is demonstrated by the person conducting the training. In the next step, the new sales associate performs the newly learned task or demonstrates product knowledge in a role-playing format. The final step involves constructive criticism by the trainer. This plan for sales training works well at all levels of selling. It also helps to reinforce the concept of consultative selling with new and seasoned sales associates when new products are being introduced.

Compensation and Sales Quotas

Salespeople are compensated by straight commission, straight salary, or salary plus commission.

Commission salespeople get paid only when they sell something. Salaried salespeople get paid a set amount regardless of how much they sell. Salary plus commission salespeople generally have a set salary, and their commission rate is lower than those who are paid only commission.

Regardless of the methods of compensation, sales managers often establish sales quotas. **Sales quotas** are dollar or unit sales goals set for the sales staff to achieve in a specified period of time. A plan for meeting a yearly sales quota may be to establish sales quotas for a week, month, or quarter.

Legal and Ethical Issues

Commission sales and sales quotas can create pressure on the sales staff to produce sales. If not schooled properly in selling ethics and legal issues, sales associates may engage in hard-sell tactics or may lie to a prospective customer. For example, if a salesperson knows that it will take four weeks for delivery of an order and promises two-week delivery just to make the sale, that is both illegal and ethically wrong.

It is important to remember that a sales order or purchase order is a legal agreement, a contract between the buyer and seller and signed by both parties. It contains all the elements of a legal contract: an offer, an acceptance, consideration (price and terms), competent parties (buyer and seller), legal form, and legal subject matter.

Another aspect of a sales contract is full disclosure of the facts. In a contract providing services, all services and materials that will be used should be clearly identified.

12.2 AFTER YOU READ

Reviewing Key Terms and Concepts

1. In all selling situations, what can salespeople do to prepare for the sale?
2. What is prospecting?
3. Which of the three sales compensation methods would you prefer? Why?

Integrating Academic Skills

Math

4. Mark has a choice as to how he will be compensated in his new sales position. He may elect to be paid a straight commission of eight percent of sales or a salary of $55,000 plus a two percent commission on sales. Which is a better deal for Mark if sales are projected to be $1,000,000 in his territory? Which method of compensation would you recommend? Why?

Writing

5. To prepare for a sales demonstration with a product of your choice, write a letter to the product's manufacturer. Introduce yourself and tell the reason for writing the letter. Explain why you selected that company's product for your research. Identify the specific information you are requesting. Request the information in a way that makes it easy for the reader to comply.

Check your answers at ***marketingessentials.glencoe.com/12/read***

CAREERS IN MARKETING

NANCY NORTHERN
UNDERWRITING SALES
PUBLIC RADIO PARTNERSHIP

What do you do at work?
I find prospects that will benefit the most from on-air exposure on one of Public Radio Partnership's three radio stations. It is then my responsibility to "court" them. I will send an introduction letter, detailing who I am and a very brief description of how my product can help their business. After sending a few mailers, I follow up with a phone call and attempt to set up an in-person meeting. At this meeting we discuss the prospect's marketing challenges, strengths, weaknesses, and goals for the future.

What skills are most important to you?
Communication is a skill that is necessary in a sales position. You must be able to communicate with your prospects, your clients, and your audience. Another essential skill is writing. Every proposal that I present to a client must be easy to understand while expressing the specific desires of my client. In addition, on-air time restrictions require me to express a large amount of information in a very short period of time.

What is your key to success?
I read books on the market, advertising, marketing, and specific client categories that I am targeting as often as possible. I also attend sales seminars and networking events. Hard work and thick skin are key. Sales can be a very difficult job. There are a lot of highs and lows and a ton of nos. I do not take nos personally; a good sales person can't. I have perseverance and dedication and I am really bad at giving up.

Aptitudes, Abilities, and Skills

Outgoing personality, writing and communication skills, persistence, and self-motivation

Education and Training

Degrees in general business and marketing can be helpful.

Career Path

Sales positions are easy to find, and since many are commission-only, they can be easy to land. Excellent performance within a sales position leads to quick advancement, as a company's sales force is its life blood.

THINKING CRITICALLY

What do you think would be the toughest aspect of a career in sales?

Go to *marketingessentials.glencoe.com/12/careers* to find a career-related activity.

CHAPTER 12 REVIEW

FOCUS on KEY POINTS

SECTION 12.1

- Three types of selling situations are retail, business-to-business, and telemarketing.
- Matching the characteristics of a product to a customer's needs and wants is feature-benefit selling. Customers may have both rational and emotional motives for making a purchase. Three forms of customer decision making are extensive, limited, and routine.

SECTION 12.2

- To prepare for a sale, salespeople study their products, industry trends, competitors, and customers, as well as company policies and legal and ethical selling issues.
- A prospect or lead is a potential customer.
- To prepare for business-to-business selling, research the customer and make appointments with qualified prospects. For retail selling, learn about products, merchandising, stockkeeping, and housekeeping.

REVIEW VOCABULARY

Define each of the key terms below.

1. personal selling (p. 260)
2. business-to-business selling (p. 261)
3. telemarketing (p. 261)
4. consultative selling (p. 261)
5. feature-benefit selling (p. 261)
6. product features (p. 261)
7. customer benefits (p. 263)
8. rational motive (p. 263)
9. emotional motive (p. 263)
10. extensive decision making (p. 264)
11. limited decision making (p. 264)
12. routine decision making (p. 264)
13. pre-approach (p. 265)
14. prospect (p. 268)
15. referrals (p. 269)
16. endless chain method (p. 269)
17. cold canvassing (p. 269)
18. sales quotas (p. 271)

REVIEW FACTS and IDEAS

19. Define personal selling and name three settings where it may occur. (12.1)
20. What are the purpose and goals of selling? (12.1)
21. Explain the concept of feature-benefit selling and how it is related to consultative selling. (12.1)
22. Name five sources that can be used in prospecting. (12.2)
23. What is the difference between the endless chain and cold canvassing methods of prospecting? (12.2)
24. What is the focus of the pre-approach in business-to-business and in retail sales? (12.2)

BUILD SKILLS

25. Workplace Skills

Human Relations As the senior salesperson for a mobile phone company, you are responsible for training a new sales associate in consultative selling and selling ethics. Conduct a role play to demonstrate how you would cover those two topics with a classmate who will play the role of a new sales associate.

26. Technology Applications

Prepare a Script Write the telephone script for a company that wants to qualify the leads it received before passing them along to the sales staff. Assume you work for a local commercial bakery that services independent restaurants, as well as those found in hotels and country clubs, in three adjacent states.

27. Math Skills

Calculating Discounts A store is having a sale: Buy one shirt (priced at $40), get the second one at half price and the third one at one-third of the price.

How much does the second shirt cost? The third shirt? Add an 8.25 percent sales tax. What is the total cost to a customer buying three shirts?

DEVELOP CRITICAL THINKING

28. Job Skills

Scan the newspaper's want ads and ads on monster.com and list the various qualities and skills required for sales positions. Organize your list into three categories:

- General and specific qualities for retail
- General and specific qualities for business-to-business
- General and specific qualities for telemarketing sales positions

What conclusions do you draw from your research?

29. Buying Motives

Suppose you are working as a salesperson in the camera department of a large retailer during the holiday season. What buying motives do you think you will observe among your customers?

APPLY CONCEPTS

30. Writing a Sales Letter

One way to generate leads is to write sales letters to prospective customers. Your prospective customers are DECA chapter advisors and members. Your company is an art gallery that runs auctions for fund-raising projects.

Activity Use your knowledge of buying motives and consultative selling to write a convincing sales letter to generate an interest in this form of fund-raising. Include a means of contacting your company for follow-up by one of your sales representatives.

31. Learning Company Policies and Selling Ethics

Select a company that is of interest to you and to which you have access. Interview the person responsible for orienting new sales associates. Ask questions about company policies, as well as unethical selling practices and sales regulations with which a new employee should be familiar. Also ask about the type of training that is provided.

Activity Prepare a background report on this company. Describe what it sells and how it sells its products. Include the types of sales personnel it employs.

NET SAVVY

32. Finding the Unique Features

Select a product of interest to you that is also fairly new. Use the Internet to research and create a list of all the unique features of your product.

THE 

CONNECTION

Role Play: Preparing for the Sale

Situation Assume the role of part-time employee of a camera store. You want to do a good job, so you spend all the time you can reading about the different cameras your store sells. Your manager (judge) has noticed you studying the camera information and customers asking for you by name. The manager (judge) has also noticed that your sales figures are growing steadily.

Activity The manager (judge) has asked you to explain your selling method so the manager (judge) can encourage the other employees to do the same.

Evaluation You will be evaluated on how well you meet the following performance indicators:

- Acquire product information for use in selling
- Analyze product information to identify product features and benefits
- Prepare for the sales presentation
- Explain key factors in building a clientele
- Explain the selling process

@ Online Action!

For more information and DECA Prep practice, go to *marketingessentials.glencoe.com/12/DECA*

CHAPTER 13
Initiating the Sale

Chapter Objectives

After reading this chapter, you should be able to:

- List the seven steps of a sale
- Explain the importance and purposes of the approach in the sales process
- Demonstrate how business-to-business sales representatives conduct the initial approach
- Name three methods for making the initial approach in retail sales
- Explain why determining needs is an essential step in the sales process
- List three methods for determining needs

GUIDE TO THE PHOTO

Market Talk The approach to the customer is the critical first step in the sales process. It gives the salesperson the opportunity to establish a relationship with the customer, to initiate a conversation, and to focus the customer's attention on the product. The approach can make or break a sale, so it is important to make a good first impression.

Quick Think What might you say to open a conversation with a customer?

THE   CONNECTION

Performance indicators represent key skills and knowledge. Relating them to the concepts explained in this chapter is your key to success in DECA events. These acronyms represent DECA events that involve knowledge of concepts in this chapter.

AAAL*	**FMAL**	**MMS**	**TMDM**
AAML*	**FMDM**	**QSRM**	**TSE**
ADC	**FMML**	**RMAL**	**VPM**
BSM	**FSRM**	**RMML**	
EMDM	**HMDM**	**SMDM**	

In all these DECA events you should be able to follow these performance indicators:

- Explain the selling process
- Establish relationships with clients/customers
- Address the needs of individual personalities
- Determine customer/client needs
- Assess customer/client needs

All the events with an asterisk (*) also include these performance indicators:

- Determine the size and fit of children's apparel
- Determine the size and fit of women's apparel
- Determine the size and fit of men's apparel
- Determine the size and fit of shoes

Some events include additional performance indicators. These are:

VPM	Interpret test results to customers
FMDM	Explain the process of selling stocks
SMDM	Identify risks perceived by customers in purchasing services
TMDM	Determine client's travel preferences/needs

DECA PREP

Check your understanding of DECA performance indicators with the DECA activity in this chapter's review. For more information and DECA Prep practice, go to *marketingessentials.glencoe.com/13/DECA*

The Sales Process

OBJECTIVES

- List the seven steps of a sale
- Explain the importance and purposes of the approach in the sales process
- Demonstrate how business-to-business sales representatives conduct the initial approach
- Name three methods for making the initial approach in retail sales

KEY TERMS

- service approach
- greeting approach
- merchandise approach

READ and STUDY

BEFORE YOU READ

Connect Reflect on ways salespeople have approached you. How effective were their methods?

THE MAIN IDEA

There are seven main steps to the sales process. There are also different styles and methods for approaching customers. What type of approach is appropriate depends on the sales situation. These elements are the foundation of sales skills.

STUDY ORGANIZER

Prepare a chart similar to the one below to identify the steps of a sale.

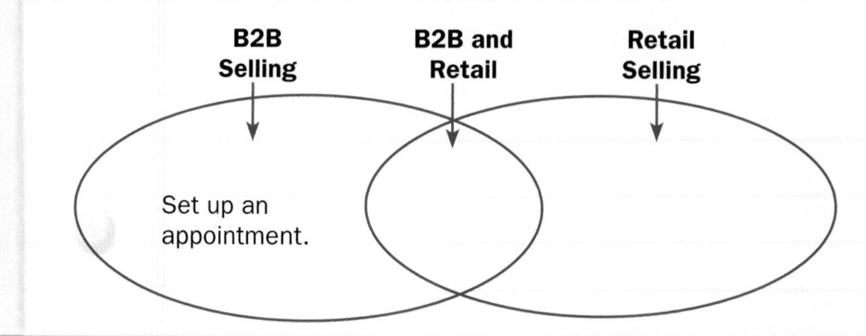

WHILE YOU READ

Connect Think about selling situations where all seven steps of a sale were involved. Recall how the salesperson incorporated each step into the selling process.

The Selling Process

Selling is the process of matching customer needs and wants to the features and benefits of a product or service. The salesperson plays a vital role in this process by gathering information about the customer, then advising the customer about which products would best suit his or her needs and lead to a decision to buy.

There are seven steps to the selling process:

1. **Approaching the customer** greeting the customer face-to-face
2. **Determining needs** learning what the customer is looking for in order to decide what products to show and which product features to present first in the next step of the sale
3. **Presenting the product** educating the customer about the product's features and benefits
4. **Overcoming objections** learning why the customer is reluctant to buy, providing information to remove that uncertainty, and helping the customer to make a satisfying buying decision
5. **Closing the sale** getting the customer's positive agreement to buy
6. **Suggestion selling** suggesting additional merchandise or services that will save your customer money or help your customer enjoy the original purchase
7. **Relationship building** creating a means of maintaining contact with the customer after the sale is completed

In this chapter, we will concentrate on the first two steps in the sales process: (1) the approach and (2) determining the customer's needs. The other five steps will be examined in later chapters.

Approaching the Customer

Salespeople can make or break a sale during their first few minutes with a customer; therefore, the initial approach is critical. Customers who are turned off by the approach will be difficult to win over later on.

The approach sets the mood or atmosphere for the other steps of the sale. It has three purposes: to begin conversation, to establish a relationship with the customer, and to focus on the product.

To begin conversation, you need to be alert to customers' interests. This may be easier in business-to-business selling because you can conduct research prior to the initial meeting. In retail selling, you must observe the customer from the moment he or she enters the store.

To establish a relationship, treat the customer as an individual. You should not stereotype a person because of age, sex, race, religion, appearance, or any other characteristic.

You must be perceptive about the customer's buying style. Some customers like to do business quickly. Others prefer a more methodical, slower pace. In any case, a customer likes to feel important.

To put a customer at ease and establish a positive atmosphere you should be enthusiastic, courteous, and respectful. Show sincere interest by maintaining good eye contact and showing genuine friendliness. Always ask business-to-business customers if it is a good time to see them. This courtesy is appreciated by busy businesspeople.

The Approach in Business-to-Business Selling

In business-to-business selling, the salesperson sets up an appointment in the pre-approach stage of the sale. Arriving early for the appointment will show your customer that you are interested and give you time to organize your thoughts. Introduce your-self and your company with a firm handshake and a smile. Use the customer's name. Some salespeople may give a business card to the customer.

The initial approach depends on your prior dealings with the customer or the work you did in the pre-approach. When meeting with customers you visit frequently, you can be more personal. Comments on recent happenings in the customer's industry or personal recollections about the customer's family, interests, or hobbies can create a smooth initial meeting. Learning what is appropriate to say regarding personal matters is critical. When personal conversation is not appropriate, you can still engage in small talk to establish a relationship with the customer.

Prior research on the prospect conducted in the pre-approach may suggest other possible opening comments. You can also discuss current topics in the industry.

Case Study

Beware of Bias

Wanting to take a pro-active approach with his team, Harry Bradford, a regional sales VP with GlaxoSmithKline turned to Orlando-Ward Associates, a San Diego-based workplace training organization that specializes in live-action drama to address diversity and other interpersonal workplace issues.

Here is an example of a vignette used in such training: You are making your first sales call to Dr. Lee's office in the Chinatown section of San Francisco. Approaching a young Asian woman behind the desk, you say who you are and ask to speak with Dr. Lee for a moment. After a brief pause the woman looks up from her paperwork and deadpans: "You're speaking with Dr. Lee right now." Whoops! After you apologize profusely, Dr. Lee responds that she would be happy to meet with you—about a year from now.

Role Play as Training

After each vignette was presented during the half-day program, the producing director led a discussion with the reps to identify the mistakes made and to brainstorm about more thoughtful approaches. Next, reps were invited to participate in replays, in which the scene is re-enacted but this time with a program participant playing the role of the sales rep. The rep's task is to handle the situation more effectively, without making errors based on cultural or gender stereotypes.

THINK STRATEGICALLY

Why are live-action drama and role playing good sales training methods?

@ Online Action!

Go to *marketingessentials.glencoe.com/13/case* to find a research project on avoiding stereotyping.

The Approach in Retail Selling

When customers are in an obvious hurry, you should approach them quickly. When customers seem undecided, encourage them to look around and ask questions.

The Three Methods of Approach in Retail Selling

There are three methods you can use in the initial approach to retail customers: the service approach, the greeting approach, and the merchandise approach. You must evaluate the selling situation and the type of customer to determine which method is best.

Service Approach

With the **service approach**, the salesperson asks the customer if he or she needs assistance. One way to use this method is to ask, "How may I help you?" An open-ended question such as this one offers the customer a greater opportunity to respond with more than "yes" or "no." It is acceptable when the customer is obviously in a hurry or if you are an order-taker for routine purchases. In most other sales situations, this type of question is ineffective because it usually elicits a negative response, such as "No, I'm just looking." In this case, you lose control of the sales situation. If such a situation occurs, take a moment to remind the customer to ask any questions that he or she may have later on.

Greeting Approach

With the **greeting approach**, the salesperson simply welcomes the customer to the store. This lets the customer know that the salesperson is available for any questions or assistance. The greeting can be a simple one, such as "Good morning."

When you greet the customer, it is important to use a rising tone in your voice. A falling tone sounds unfriendly and would start the sales process off on the wrong note. It is extremely important that the salesperson smile and be friendly.

• THE MERCHANDISE APPROACH The merchandise approach can be used only when a customer demonstrates interest in a product.

What might you say to this customer to demonstrate the merchandise approach?

NET MARKETING

Business E-Mail

Once considered merely a nuisance, spam and other unwanted e-mail have become a costly burden for enterprises. E-mail can spread destructive computer viruses to millions of users in a matter of hours.

An Expensive Problem

Ferris Research estimates that in 2003, the total cost of spam to U.S. businesses in lost productivity was $10 billion. The MX Logic Threat Center reported that 74.4 percent of all e-mail traffic filtered by the company was spam. By 2006, industry analysts expect the economic impact of computer viruses to approach $60 billion worldwide.

THINK LIKE A MARKETER

Assume you work for a company that sells software and services to block spam and provide antivirus protection. Write an attention-getting statement that you could use in conjunction with your greeting and initial approach in a business-to-business selling situation.

@ Online Action!

Go to *marketingessentials.glencoe.com/13/net* to find a project on e-mail security.

If the customers need help, they will tell you how you can assist them. If they are just looking, they will let you know. The greeting approach establishes a positive atmosphere and opens the lines of communication.

Merchandise Approach Method

With the **merchandise approach**, the salesperson makes a comment or asks questions about a product in which the customer shows interest. This method can be used only if a customer stops to look at a specific item. You may open with a statement about the product's features and benefits.

Using Conversation Skills

In the merchandise approach, the salesperson walks up to the customer and starts talking about the merchandise without asking whether the customer wants assistance. The opening comment used in the merchandise approach should be appropriate to the situation. Ideally, it should give the customer some information that is not immediately apparent to the eye.

Notice what interests the customer and make that the focus of your conversation. If a customer is looking at a label, you might say, "That shirt is made of a cotton and polyester blend, so it's machine washable." If a customer is simply looking at an item and you have no indication of the exact interest, you can talk about the item's popularity, its unusual features, or its special values. You can also ask a question about the item, such as "Is that the size you need?" or "Were you looking for a comfortable children's jacket?"

The merchandise approach is usually the most effective initial approach in retail sales because it immediately focuses attention on the product. It also gives you an opportunity to tell the customer something about the features and benefits of the merchandise.

Customers may not see the desired style, size, or color on the selling floor. The merchandise approach can easily clear up any confusion, let the customer know what is available, and open a dialogue with the customer.

13.1 AFTER YOU READ

Reviewing Key Terms and Concepts

1. Do you think all seven steps of a sale are followed in every sale? Why or why not?
2. Why is the initial approach in business-to-business selling different from a retail approach?
3. What are the advantages of the merchandise approach?

Integrating Academic Skills

Math

4. Assuming there is no sales tax on clothing, how much would you charge a customer who needs only two pairs of socks when the sign indicates six pairs are $15.99?

Language Arts

5. Write two merchandise approaches for a product of your choice. Include specific examples of what a salesperson might say or do.

Check your answers at *marketingessentials.glencoe.com/13/read*

Determining Needs in Sales

OBJECTIVES

- **Explain why determining needs is an essential step in the sales process**
- **List three methods for determining needs**

KEY TERMS

- **nonverbal communication**
- **open-ended questions**

READ and STUDY

BEFORE YOU READ

Predict Name three ways you might determine a customer's needs.

THE MAIN IDEA

Determining needs is an early step in the sales process because it frames the rest of the sales presentation. It is also the one step that continues throughout the sales process as you try to match a customer's needs with solutions found in your product line.

STUDY ORGANIZER

Prepare a chart like the one below to review when and how to determine needs in the sales process.

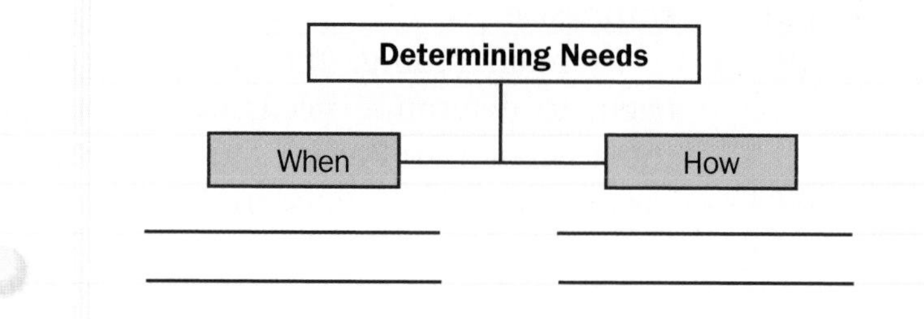

Determining Needs

In this step of the sale, your job is to uncover the customer's problems or reasons for wanting to buy. In some instances, their motives or needs may be quite obvious, but that is not always the case. It is your job to determine those needs so you can offer one or more solutions. Discovering your customer's motivation for buying will help you in the next step of the sale when you are helping the customer select the right product.

WHILE YOU READ

Connect Has a salesperson ever helped you make a choice? What questions were asked?

GLOBAL MARKET

Skateboarding in Brazil

Skateboarding might seem like an all-American sport, but it is also very popular and competitive around the world. Brazil has a thriving skateboarding market. Brazilian skaters started out by making their own skateboards with roller skate trucks and wheels, inspired by American products they often could not afford. However, what started as tinkering has now become a national industry.

Homegrown Success Brazil's government is protective of small firms and trademarks and offers incentives to promote internal commerce. Skateboard products are sold mostly through specialty stores. With imports heavily taxed, domestic brands sell far better than U.S. competitors. Government policies and taxation were determining factors in the creation of domestic skateboard brands and in the growth of the Brazilian skateboard market. Skateboarding shoes, accessories, and clothing are now also manufactured in Brazil for Brazilian brands. The largest board brands are Son, Formigao, Perfect Line, and Stage. Truck brands are Crail, Tracker, and Crazy. The largest wheel manufacturer is Moska. Some of these companies have now expanded into exporting their goods throughout South America and to the United States.

How does knowledge regarding a customer's motivation and value system help in determining needs?

Online Action!

Go to *marketingessentials.glencoe.com/13/global* to find a research project on customer motivation.

When to Determine Needs

The salesperson's focus should be to determine the customer's needs as early in the sales process as possible. Here is an example of what can happen when a salesperson does not determine needs early on.

Salesperson: "This is one of our most popular tennis rackets. It's perfect for you—the grip is the correct size and the large sweet spot can improve your game."

Customer: "That's very interesting; but, I'm not buying the racket for myself. It's actually a gift for my nine-year-old daughter."

After the initial approach, the salesperson could have asked, "Are you interested in a racket for yourself?"

The answer to that simple question could have guided the salesperson into additional questions about the person for whom the racket was being purchased. It also could have helped the salesperson decide which racket to show the customer and which features to emphasize.

In retail selling, the salesperson should begin to determine needs immediately after the approach. In business-to-business selling, needs can be determined in the pre-approach. In both situations, the salesperson should continue determining needs throughout the sales process.

How to Determine Needs

There are three methods used to determine customer needs: observing, listening, and questioning. (See Figure 13.1.)

Observing

When you observe a customer, you look for buying motives that are communicated nonverbally. **Nonverbal communication** is expressing yourself without the use of words. Facial expressions, hand motions, eye movement, and other forms of nonverbal communication can give you clues about a customer's mood and interest in a product.

Observing how long a customer in a retail store looks at a product can give you an initial idea about the level of interest.

In a business-to-business selling situation, you can generally get ideas about a buyer's interests by looking around his or her office.

Listening

Listening helps you pick up clues to the customer's needs. You can use this information for the product presentation. Here's an example.

Customer: "I want a copier for my home business that is simple to use and reliable. My last copier broke down often, which was a problem. I usually make one or two copies at a time. However, occasionally I may make up to 50 copies at once."

From these statements, you have learned that the customer is not looking for a top-of-the-line copier. Since the copier is for a home business, size is a factor.

Questioning and Engaging the Customer

When you begin determining needs, first ask general questions about the intended use of the product and any previous experience with it. Build your questions around words like *who, what, when, where, why,* and *how*. You might ask the following questions of someone who wants to purchase a copier:

- Who will be using the copier?
- What type of copier is the person presently using?

• DETERMINING CUSTOMER NEEDS The sales step of determining customer needs helps a salesperson match those needs with products or services.

What does this ad say about the company's policy of listening to customers' needs?

Figure 13.1 Ways to Determine Customer Needs

• **Observe, Listen, Question** Selling is based on matching a customer's needs or wants with the features and benefits of a product. In the step of the sales process known as determining needs, the salesperson gathers information in order to match the customer's needs and wants with a product. There are three ways to do that.

Is there one best way to determine customer needs?

Observing Customers provide many nonverbal cues about their product interests. By carefully observing a customer, a salesperson can learn a lot about the customer's interests. The salesperson can then use that information to guide the customer to products that might result in a decision to buy.

Listening When a customer is ready to talk, the salesperson should give the customer his or her undivided attention and maintain eye contact. Other guidelines that help to make the salesperson a good listener are not interrupting until the customer has finished, providing feedback, and listening with an open mind.

Questioning Questions can encourage a customer to talk. When asking questions, salespeople should begin with general questions, such as those beginning with *who, what, when, where, why,* and *how.* For instance, this salesperson might ask what color of shoe the woman is shopping for. Salespeople must be careful not to ask a question that is too personal or unintentionally offends the customer. That might quickly put an end to the sale.

@ Online Action! **Go to *marketingessentials.glencoe.com/13/figure/1* to find a project on determining customer needs.**

- How much experience has the person had with copiers?
- How many copies will the person be making every week or month?

How to Refine Your Questioning

Once you have an idea of the customer's general needs, then you can ask more specific questions relating to the product. In the case of the copier, questions could be asked about the need to enlarge or reduce the size of the copy, as well as the need to collate and staple copies.

Open-ended questions are those that require more than a yes or no answer, such as "What do you dislike about the copier you're presently using?" The answer to such a question will provide valuable information about a customer's needs. Always bear in mind that some customers will be protective of their privacy; they may resent even general, nonpersonal questions.

Here are some other dos and don'ts guidelines for questioning:

1. Do ask open-ended questions that encourage customers to do the talking.
2. Do ask clarifying questions to make sure you understand customers' needs. To do this, use opening lines such as "Let me see if I understand you" or "Am I correct in assuming you're looking for a product that can . . .?"
3. Don't ask too many questions in a row. This will make customers feel as if they are being cross-examined.
4. Don't ask questions that might embarrass customers or put them on the defensive. Never ask, "How much do you want to spend?" Instead, ask about the intended use of the product and any past experience. That should give you enough information to determine the correct price range on your own.

13.2 AFTER YOU READ

Reviewing Key Terms and Concepts

1. Why is determining needs an essential step in the sales process?
2. How can you use open-ended questions to encourage customers to do the talking?
3. You are a salesperson in a rug store that carries inexpensive area rugs, medium-priced area rugs, and very expensive handmade area rugs. How would you determine your customer's price range?

Integrating Academic Skills

Math

4. Based on your analysis of the customer's needs, a premium of $1,500 per year is required for long-term health care insurance for your client. Since your client cannot handle this yearly payment, you want to offer a quarterly payment schedule. There is a surcharge of $25 per quarter for this service. What are the quarterly payments for this client?

Language Arts

5. Use the product you used at the end of the last section to write five to ten questions that could be used to determine a customer's needs in the sale of that product.

Check your answers at *marketingessentials.glencoe.com/13/read*

CAREERS IN MARKETING

MELISSA MCINTOSH, MJE
FOUNDER
1214 ENTERPRISES, INC.

What do you do at work?

For my corporate clients in law, real estate, medicine, engineering, architecture, and construction, I can provide a full spectrum of design and print-brokering services so that they have one contact for all their marketing collateral needs. A big part of my job is focused on service: handholding a brochure all the way through the print process with an outside commercial printer, making 900 tweaks to a corporate logo to get it "just right," and making sure I pay attention to the small details.

What skills are most important to you?

The ability to be flexible. Being able to keep from getting frustrated and to move between being a marketing consultant, tech support guru, and graphic artist. Having a background where I've worked with computers since the mid-80s and have learned a lot in the trial and error department has really helped.

What is your key to success?

Very simple: hard, hard work. In any of the jobs I've had, either in education or business, and in owning my own company now, I have never bragged that I'm the smartest, most creative, most cutting edge, or whatever. But how I have always had an edge over the competition is that I'm willing to out-work them. If the "what does it take" requires evenings and weekends to get the job done just a bit better than the other guy, fine.

Aptitudes, Abilities, and Skills

Computer skills, sales and communication skills, versatility, an eagerness to learn and gain new experiences

Education and Training

Degrees in marketing, communication, language, and computer science are helpful.

Career Path

Before starting their own companies, many entrepreneurs work for companies that do the work they want to do. That is their training. To eventually run a marketing consulting firm, the best career track is to work in marketing, sales, and communications departments.

THINKING CRITICALLY

Other than college, what kind of training and classes might be worth pursuing?

Online Action!

Go to *marketingessentials.glencoe.com/13/careers* to find a career-related activity.

CHAPTER 13 REVIEW

FOCUS on KEY POINTS

SECTION 13.1

- Seven steps in the sales process are approach, determining needs, product presentation, overcoming objections, closing the sale, suggestion selling, and relationship building.
- Relationship building is important to create loyal customers.
- The approach step of the sale can make or break the sale.
- The three purposes of the approach are to begin a conversation, build a relationship, and focus on the product.
- The approach in business-to-business selling is different from that in retail selling.
- The three retail sales approaches are service, greeting, and merchandise.

SECTION 13.2

- Determining needs is a step in the sales process that should begin as soon as possible and continue throughout the process.
- Three methods that help in determining needs are observing, listening, and asking questions.

REVIEW VOCABULARY

Work in groups to develop a story about two salespeople using the following terms:

1. service approach (p. 280)
2. greeting approach (p. 281)
3. merchandise approach (p. 282)
4. nonverbal communication (p. 284)
5. open-ended questions (p. 287)

REVIEW FACTS and IDEAS

6. What are the seven steps of a sale? (13.1)
7. What are the main purposes of the approach step in the sales process? (13.1)
8. Write the dialogue and describe the actions that might be taken during an initial business-to-business sales approach by a sales representative from the XYZ Copier Company meeting a new prospect for the first time. (13.1)
9. Why is determining needs an essential step in the sales process? (13.2)
10. List three methods used for determining needs. (13.2)
11. What types of questions should be asked first when determining customer needs? (13.2)
12. When should a salesperson determine needs? (13.2)

BUILD SKILLS

13. Workplace Skills

Human Relations Use the Internet to research different ways of greeting people. Conduct a role play with classmates to demonstrate the proper way to greet customers who are from Japan, Germany, Brazil, and Singapore in a business-to-business setting. Assume you are employed by the XYZ Corporation.

14. Technology Applications

Research During Pre-approach Imagine that you are a sales representative for a tool distributor such as Grainger and you have a meeting with a car dealer who repairs cars on the lot. Using the Internet, research the car dealerships and repair shops to determine the needs that might be met by items in your product line. Prepare a short, one-page report on your findings.

15. Math Practice

Budgeting Your Time You are stuck in traffic, and you are going to be late for your first meeting with a potential customer. You are traveling at ten miles an hour and have five miles to go. If it is 8:00 A.M., at what time can you expect to arrive if you keep traveling at that speed? What should you do? How could you prevent this situation from happening again?

DEVELOP CRITICAL THINKING

16. Why Does the Approach Used in Business-to-Business Selling Differ From the Retail Approach?

Imagine that you are a salesperson selling seeds to garden supply stores. Think of how you would approach the sale using a *retail sales approach*. Do you think that would be an effective approach? Why or why not?

17. Good Observations Lead to Sales

Salespeople must be good communicators in order to initiate conversations with potential customers and gather information about customers' wants and needs. But customers are not always willing to talk. Assume you are a men's clothing salesperson in a large department store and you have a customer who seems reluctant to talk. How might you determine his interests? What skills, besides communication, would you need to do this?

APPLY CONCEPTS

18. Approaching and Determining Needs

Role play the approach and determining needs steps of a sale with a classmate by using a personal product, such as a jacket, calculator, or purse. Assume you work for a retailer.

Activity Make a list of guidelines for listening, observing, and asking questions. At the conclusion of the role play, provide the salesperson with constructive criticism. Change the product and switch roles with your partner to repeat the assignment.

19. Research Selling Etiquette in Foreign Countries

Accepted business etiquette differs from country to country, including manner of greeting, preferred time of day to conduct business, and follow-up. Select one foreign country and conduct research on the Internet and with other sources regarding business etiquette and cultural difference when selling in foreign countries.

Activity What are some of the dos and don'ts? Using a word processing program, write a two-page report of your findings. Cite your sources.

NET SAVVY

20. Selling on the Internet

Select a company that sells its products on the Internet, such as Dell or Gateway computers. Assume the role of a customer and research the questions you should ask in order to decide on the best buy for your needs.

THE DECA CONNECTION

Role Play: Initiating the Sale

Situation You are to assume the role of an experienced employee for a toy store. The holiday season is a few months away, and many new employees have been hired who have had little or no sales training. The store manager (judge) knows that you are studying marketing and has asked you to offer some ideas for basic sales training on the steps of a sale.

Activity You are to present your ideas about training in the steps of a sale to the store manager (judge).

Evaluation You will be evaluated on how well you meet the following performance indicators:

- Explain the selling process
- Prepare for the sales presentation
- Determine customer/client needs
- Demonstrate suggestion selling
- Close the sale

@ Online Action!

For more information and DECA Prep practice, go to *marketingessentials.glencoe.com/13/DECA*

CHAPTER 14
Presenting the Product

Chapter Objectives

After reading this chapter, you should be able to:

- Describe the goal of product presentation
- List four techniques that create a lively and effective product presentation
- Distinguish objections from excuses
- Explain the five buying decisions on which common objections are based
- Demonstrate the general four-step method for handling customer objections
- List seven specific methods of handling objections and note when each should be used

GUIDE TO THE PHOTO

Market Talk Selling an expensive product such as a car relies on both product features and on emotional aspects of decision making. A car salesperson, for example, must be able to relate to the customer on all these levels in order to close the sale.

Quick Think How can the previous sales step, determining needs, help a salesperson do a better job at selling a car?

THE DECA CONNECTION

Performance indicators represent key skills and knowledge. Relating them to the concepts explained in this chapter is your key to success in DECA events. These acronyms represent DECA events that involve knowledge of concepts in this chapter.

AAAL	**FMAL**	**MMS**	**TMDM**
AAML	**FMDM**	**QSRM***	**TSE**
ADC	**FMML***	**RMAL**	**VPM**
BSM	**FSRM**	**RMML**	
EMDM	**HMDM***	**SMDM**	

In all these DECA events you should be able to follow these performance indicators:

- Recommend a specific product
- Demonstrate a product
- Create a presentation software package to support a sales presentation
- Analyze technology for use in the sales function
- Prescribe a solution to customer needs
- Convert customer/client objections into selling points

All the events with an asterisk (*) also include this performance indicator:

- Take a customer's food order

Some events include additional performance indicators. These are:

AAAL Use style characteristics to sell men's and women's apparel

AAML Use style characteristics to sell men's and women's apparel

VPM Suggest needed parts/service as determined by testing

FMAL Recommend quantities and cuts of meat to customers

DECA PREP

Check your understanding of DECA performance indicators with the DECA activity in this chapter's review. For more information and DECA Prep practice, go to *marketingessentials.glencoe.com/14/DECA*

SECTION 14.1

OBJECTIVES

- **Describe the goal of product presentation**
- **List four techniques that create a lively and effective product presentation**

KEY TERMS

- **layman's terms**

Product Presentation

READ and STUDY

BEFORE YOU READ

Predict Do you think selling has a system or method? What might it be?

THE MAIN IDEA

The product presentation step of the sales process is where you get to share your product knowledge with customers. To be effective, you need to first determine customers' needs in order to match those needs with product features and benefits. There are a few techniques that will create an exciting and interesting presentation for your customers.

STUDY ORGANIZER

Copy the chart below. Use the chart to take notes about how to create an effective product presentation.

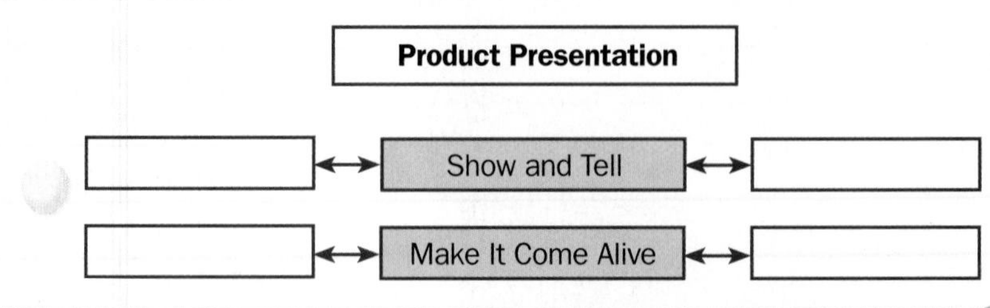

WHILE YOU READ

Connect How can you use what you already know about product knowledge and communication skills to create an effective sales presentation?

Organizing the Product Presentation

Selling is, in many ways, like putting together a jigsaw puzzle. When you do a puzzle, you analyze the various parts by shape and size. You select the straight-edged pieces to use for the frame. When you sell, you analyze your customer's needs and buying motives. Then you use that information to begin framing your product presentation.

Show and Tell

Your first decision in the product presentation step of the sale is what product or products to show your customer. Then you must think about what you are going to say and how you are going to say it. This is the step of the sale where you have the opportunity to share your expertise with the customer. The preparation that you have put into learning about the product or products you sell and how to communicate their selling points will assist you now. In this step, you have the opportunity to match the product features to the customer's needs in consultative selling.

Which Products Do You Show?

After you have learned the customer's intended use of a product, you should be able to select a few samples that match those needs. (See Figure 14.1.) For example, you may select a technically advanced camera for a customer who wants a camera for professional use. Novice customers might want a fully automatic camera.

What Price Range Should You Offer?

When you do not know the customer's price range and your knowledge of the intended use is insufficient to determine a price range, begin by showing a medium-priced product. You can move up or down in price once you begin to get the customer's feedback.

It is not a good idea to introduce price early on in the product presentation unless it is a major selling point because you need time to show your clients/customers how valuable your product is to them. You know yourself that if it is something you really need and want, price becomes less of a factor in a purchase decision.

How Many Products Should You Show?

To avoid overwhelming your customer, show no more than three products at a time. It is difficult for most people to remember all the features of more than three items during a presentation. When a customer wants to see more than three, put away the displayed products in which the customer shows no interest.

MARKET TECH

Worth the Higher Price?

It wasn't long after the invention of the movie camera that people started making home movies, chronicling everything from birthdays to weddings, vacations to baseball games. Over time, the cameras have gotten much smaller and much less expensive. And now, like so many other products, camcorders are digital. Panasonic, Hitachi, and Sony all make DVD camcorders that let you record directly onto a mini DVD-R disc compatible with DVD players. All three companies' models offer useful features, such as a screen of thumbnail images that lets you easily find the video you want to play and a mechanism that prevents you from accidentally recording over your saved videos.

More Features

Sony charges $790 for its camcorder, approximately $130 more than its competitors. Why? Sony's model lets you know exactly how much time is left on your battery. It focuses faster and lets you record in near to total darkness. It also has a sharper, brighter screen and an AC adapter that powers the camera even while the battery is still in place. The company is betting that consumers will be willing to shell out extra money for these extra features.

THINK LIKE A MARKETER

What statements might a customer make that would give you reason to show the new DVD camcorder in the product presentation step of the sale? How would you handle the price objection for the Sony model?

@ Online Action!

Go to *marketingessentials.glencoe.com/14/tech* to find a project on selling technology.

Figure 14.1 Tips for Effective Product Presentation

• Matchmaking The goal of a sales presentation is to match customer needs to the features and benefits of a product. Once you've learned something about your customer's interests and have selected products you believe will interest that customer, you're ready for the presentation. While no advice can guarantee success, the following tips will help to ensure that the process goes smoothly.

What are some other suggestions for product presentation?

DISPLAY AND HANDLE THE PRODUCT

Thinking of how the product will appear to a customer is important. For instance, if you are selling jewelry, an attractive display case will add to the product's appeal. Pick up the jewelry, perhaps showing how it appears in different lighting. Show the customer any special features of the product. When you handle a product, always demonstrate respect for what you are selling.

DEMONSTRATE

Show the customer how the product works. If it is a necklace, demonstrate how the clasp works. If you are selling a product with complicated parts or instructions, using sales aids, such as audiovisual presentations or brochures, helps.

INVOLVE THE CUSTOMER

If possible, let the customer try the product. In makeup sales, salespeople often give away free samples. In car sales, salespeople let the potential buyer drive the car. This allows the customer to experience the product and base the purchasing decision on that experience.

Online Action! **Go to *marketingessentials.glencoe.com/14/figure/1* to find a project on product presentation.**

• PRODUCT FEATURES and BENEFITS A detailed knowledge of product features can help you find the right product for a customer's need.

Which features of this jacket might make it appropriate for snow sports?

What Do You Say?

In this step of the sales process, talk about the product's features and benefits. Tell your customer the product features that match his or her buying motives and needs. Use highly descriptive adjectives and active verbs when describing product features. Avoid unclear words, such as *nice, pretty,* and *fine.*

Avoid slang and double meanings. For example, when selling an expensive suit to a corporate executive, you might not say, "You look cool in that suit."

When selling industrial products, you might use the appropriate jargon to communicate with industrial buyers at their level of expertise. When selling products to retail customers, you should use layman's terms. **Layman's terms** are words the average customer can understand.

Make the Presentation Come Alive

Planning is necessary for an effective product presentation. Consider how you will display and handle the merchandise. What will you do to demonstrate the product's selling points? What sales aids will add to your presentation? Finally, how will you involve the customer?

Displaying and Handling the Product

Creatively displaying the product is the first step in an eye-catching presentation. Some products, of course, lend themselves more naturally to visual display. Others will challenge your creativity. Diamond rings, for example, look great on a black velvet display pad. An attractive display of vacuum cleaners, on the other hand, takes more creative planning.

The way you physically handle a product presents an image of its quality. Handle it with respect and use hand gestures to show the significance of certain features.

Demonstrating the Product

Demonstrating the product in use helps to build customer confidence. This is especially true if you are showing an item that requires manipulation or operation, such as a television, camera, or a computer. To demonstrate the features of a copier, you may show how it can enlarge or reduce a document, as well as organize and staple multiple copies.

To prove selling points or claims made by the manufacturer, you may need to demonstrate a product in a more dramatic way. To prove that a paper towel absorbs water, you can use it to clean up spills. At Saturn car dealerships, salespeople jump up and down on a car door that has been removed to show high durability and dent-proof construction.

Using Sales Aids

When it is impractical to demonstrate the actual product or when you want to emphasize certain selling points, you can use

• PRODUCT DEMONSTRATION Whenever possible, salespeople demonstrate a product's features and benefits. This helps to eliminate any doubts about a product's claims and makes for an effective presentation.

What difficulties or challenges might demonstrating a product present to a salesperson?

• USING TECHNOLOGY The SanDisk Cruzer Mini is just one of many forms of technology that can be used to enhance a product presentation.

Name another technological sales aid.

sales aids in your presentations. Sales aids include samples, reprints of magazine and newspaper articles, audiovisual aids, models, photographs, drawings, graphs, charts, specification sheets, customer testimonials, and warranty information. Computers play an increasingly important role in product presentations as many business-to-business sales representatives make use of computer presentation software.

With a riding lawnmower, you could show the customer complimentary letters or testimonials from satisfied customers as a sales aid, or whatever warranty the manufacturer offers. These tactics help consumers build confidence in the company because it shows that the company stands behind its products. If you were selling this product to retailers for resale purposes, you may even want to use samples of the lawnmower's blade to demonstrate its effectiveness and durability or a video to demonstrate its important features and high-quality construction.

Be creative when determining which sales aids will help you in your particular product presentation. A manufacturer of industrial ovens might show a videotape of how quickly and efficiently the oven performs. An insurance salesperson might use graphs and charts to show how dividends will accumulate or to compare the benefits of one policy with another. He or she might even use a computer to personalize the presentation of that information for each customer and show different policy plans for that person.

Involving the Customer

It is best to get the customer physically involved with the product as soon as possible in the sales presentation. You could have your customers hold and swing golf clubs, try on and walk around in a pair of shoes, use a computer keyboard or mouse, test-drive an automobile, or taste and smell food products. Some cosmetic companies offer free makeovers so customers can see how the products look on their faces.

For a jacket, have the customer try it on and move her arms around to feel the free range of motion the jacket permits. You can also involve your customer verbally during the sales presentation by confirming selling points. You might say, "This jacket is wind and water resistant. Don't you think that feature will come in handy on an outdoor trip?" Pause for the customer's answer. You should only ask a question that is guaranteed to produce a positive response. Getting the customer's agreement on several selling points helps to ensure that you are on the right track with the selected product.

Holding the Customer's Attention

When you involve a customer in the sale, you help the person make intelligent buying decisions. You also help yourself because a customer is generally more attentive when doing more than just listening to what you say.

If you are losing your customer's attention, ask a simple question. You might say, "Now that you've seen the features of this product, what do you think about it?" Regaining your customer's attention is essential if you are to continue with the sales presentation. The key is keeping the customer involved.

14.1 AFTER YOU READ

Reviewing Key Terms and Concepts

1. When you cannot determine a customer's intended price range, what price level of product should you show? Why?
2. For security purposes and to make your sales presentation effective, what would you do if a customer asks to see six pairs of expensive earrings?
3. How could you involve a customer in the product presentation when selling a copying machine for a business? Replacement windows for a home?

Integrating Academic Skills

Math

4. Your customer wants to buy 7 feet of fabric, and the price per yard is $12.50. How much would you charge?

Language Arts

5. Write a detailed plan that covers the product presentation for a product you have researched. For at least two product features, include what you will say, how you will demonstrate that feature, what sales aids you will use, how you will use them, and how you will involve your customer with each feature. When appropriate, incorporate sample dialogue. Prepare this plan using a word processing program.

Check your answers at *marketingessentials.glencoe.com/14/read*

SECTION 14.2

Objections

OBJECTIVES

- Distinguish objections from excuses
- Explain the five buying decisions on which common objections are based
- Demonstrate the general four-step method for handling customer objections
- List seven specific methods of handling objections and note when each should be used

KEY TERMS

- objections
- excuses
- objection analysis sheet
- paraphrase
- substitution method
- boomerang method
- superior-point method
- third-party method

READ and STUDY

BEFORE YOU READ

Predict Why might objections be a useful sales tool?

THE MAIN IDEA

Learning how to handle objections during the sales process will make you a more effective salesperson. You will quickly see that objections are helpful in the sales process by providing an opportunity to further determine customers' needs and problems. Objections are easily managed once you know the basis for them, as well as the general and specific methods that work in various selling situations.

STUDY ORGANIZER

Copy the chart below. Use the chart to take notes about ways to handle objections.

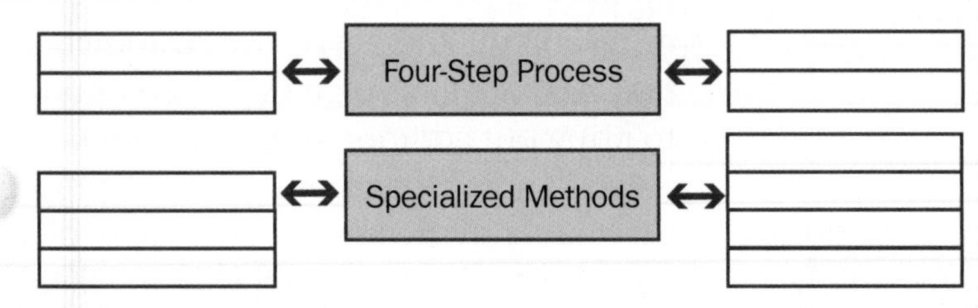

Understanding Objections

Objections are concerns, hesitations, doubts, or other honest reasons a customer has for not making a purchase. Objections should be viewed as positive because they give you an opportunity to present more information to the customer.

Anticipating and planning potential answers to objections will help you feel more confident in your responses to customers. Selecting the most appropriate method for handling those objections will make you a superior salesperson.

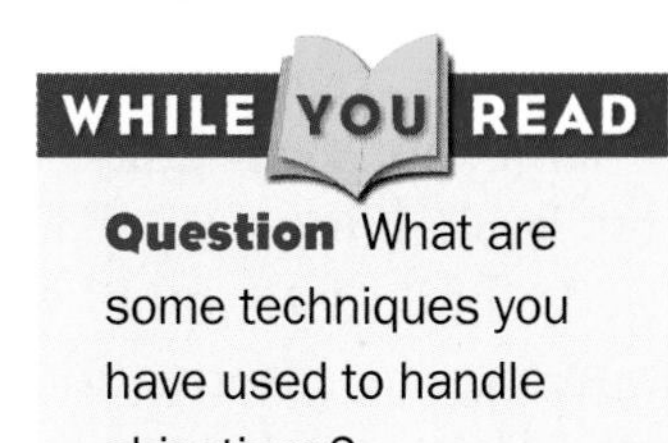

WHILE YOU READ

Question What are some techniques you have used to handle objections?

Objections can be presented as either questions/inquiries or statements. An example of a question or inquiry would be, "Do you carry any other brands?" and a statement would be, "These shoes don't fit me properly." For direct inquiries, you simply answer the question posed. Objections which are statements may require more selling expertise.

Excuses are reasons for not buying or not seeing the salesperson. Customers often use excuses when they are not in the mood to buy or when concealing other objections.

It is often difficult to distinguish between objections and excuses. A statement or question that seems to be an objection may really just be an excuse. When you are faced with this in a retail selling situation, be polite and courteous. Encourage the customer to look around and ask you any questions he or she may have.

In a business-to-business selling situation, the procedure is different. Leave a business card if a potential customer refuses to see you when you make a call and ask if it is possible to see the person at a more convenient time.

There are cases when excuses are actually attempts to hide real objections. "I didn't plan to buy today" may really mean, "I don't like the styles you have available." When you suspect that may be the case, ask additional questions to get to the real reason for the disinterest in your product or products.

•OVERCOMING OBJECTIONS If a customer objects to the price of an eye shadow, you could apply the product to the customer's skin to show its effectiveness and explain that the price per use is low.

How can you find out what a customer objects to about a product?

Plan for Objections

Objections can occur at any time during the sales process and should be answered promptly. A customer who must wait to hear responses to questions or concerns tends to become preoccupied with the objection. When that happens, you may lose the customer's attention and confidence.

Objections can guide you in the sales process by helping you redefine the customer's needs and determine when the customer wants more information. A customer may say, "This item is very expensive." What the person may really mean is, "Tell me why this product costs so much." This objection not only lets you know why the customer is reluctant to buy but also gives you an opportunity to bring out additional selling points.

You should therefore welcome objections; they are not necessarily the sign of a lost sale. Research shows a positive relationship between customer objections and a successful sales outcome.

You can prepare yourself for most objections that might occur in a sales situation by completing an **objection analysis sheet**, a document that lists common objections and possible responses to them. Although the actual objections may be slightly different from those you anticipated, thinking of responses ahead of time gives you an idea of how to handle other objections.

You can incorporate anticipated objections into your product presentation so they do not become objections. You must be cautious about this, however. You do not want to include so many objections in your product presentation that you introduce doubt, especially if none existed before. Saying, "I guess you're worried about the safety of this snowmobile," may introduce a fear that was not a previous concern.

A better way to handle the same situation would be to emphasize the safety features of the vehicle. You might say, "The suspension on this snowmobile is especially designed to keep it stable. It's very safe to operate."

Common Objections

When you list general customer objections you will see that they fall into certain categories. Most objections are based on key decisions the customer must make before buying—decisions about need, product, source, price, and time. This is true for both retail and business-to-business sales situations. The actual objections will vary because of the difference in purchase motivation.

The following are examples of customer objections in a retail situation. They provide a starting point for the creation of an objection analysis sheet.

Need

Objections related to need usually occur when the customer does not have an immediate need for the item or wants the item but does not truly need it. A comment such as, "I really want to get these sandals, but I really don't need another pair," is an objection based on a conflict between a need and a want.

Product

Objections based on the product itself are more common. They include concerns about things such as construction, ease of use, quality, color, size, or style. "I don't buy 100 percent cotton shirts because you have to iron them" is such an objection.

Source

Objections based on source often occur because of negative past experiences with the firm or brand. A business-to-business customer might say, "The last time I placed an order with your company, I received it two weeks after the promised date."

Price

Objections based on price are more common with expensive merchandise. You might

•PROVIDING PROOF In telemarketing, overcoming objections becomes even more challenging than in face-to-face sales situations.

If a customer calls the toll-free number in this ad and questions you about the mattress's construction, what would you say to eliminate any doubt about it?

A MATTER OF ETHICS

Getting Attention

Richard has recently started a small public relations business out of his home in a suburb of Chicago. He has just three employees. They are competing with some of the biggest names in the business, and Richard is having trouble getting the attention of the most desirable clients in town.

It occurs to Richard that if he signs up himself and his employees to volunteer at big charity events, such as a fund-raiser for cancer research or making repairs at homeless shelters, his firm would get some favorable mention as a sponsor. Richard figures he would not even have to tell his employees he had signed them up, because he could call just before the event and say everyone had suddenly "come down with a bad cold." Richard figures no one would be hurt if they did not show up to help... plus, his firm would get some great exposure.

THINKING ETHICALLY

Is it ethical for Richard to volunteer his firm for the charity events, then pull out? Why or why not? What would be a more ethical way for Richard to get attention for his public relations firm?

Online Action!

Go to *marketingessentials.glencoe.com/14/ethics* to find a project on the ethics of getting publicity.

hear statements like, "That's more than I wanted to spend."

Time

Objections based on time reveal a hesitation to buy immediately. These objections are sometimes excuses. Customers usually have a real reason for not wanting to make a purchase on the spot. A customer might say, "I think I'll wait until July when you have your summer sale to buy those sandals."

You will probably hear many different kinds of objections once you begin selling. You should note them for future reference.

Four-Step Process for Handling Objections

Successful salespeople have learned to use a very basic strategy when answering all objections. It consists of four basic steps for handling objections: listen, acknowledge, restate, and answer.

Listen Carefully

Remember to be attentive, maintain eye contact, and let the customer talk.

Acknowledge the Objections

Acknowledging objections demonstrates that you understand and care about the customer's concerns. Some common statements used to acknowledge objections are, "I can see your point," or, "Other customers have asked us the same question."

These acknowledgments make a customer feel that his or her objections are understandable, valid, and worthy of further discussion. It does not mean that you agree with the customer, but it acknowledges the objection. Disagreeing with the customer, or saying, "You're wrong," will put the customer on the defensive, and you might lose the sale.

Restate the Objections

To be sure you understand the customer, you can restate his or her objections in a number of ways:

> "I can understand your concerns. You feel that. . . . Am I correct?"
>
> "In other words, you feel that. . . ."
>
> "Let me see if I understand. You want to know more about. . . ."

Do not repeat the customer's concerns word for word. Instead, paraphrase the

objections. To **paraphrase** is to restate something in a different way. A customer might say, "The style is nice, but I don't like the color." You could paraphrase the objection by asking, "Would you be interested in the jacket if we could find your size in another color?"

Answer the Objections

Answer each objection tactfully. Never answer with an air of superiority or suggest that the person's concern is unimportant.

Think of yourself as a consultant, using the objections to further define or redefine the customer's needs. When price is the objection, go back to determining the customer's needs. Offer a higher-priced item to a customer if it is warranted. Explain the features and benefits of the more expensive model and why that item is better suited to the customer.

Specialized Methods of Handling Objections

There are seven specialized methods for handling objections: substitution, boomerang, question, superior point, denial, demonstration, and third party.

Substitution

Sometimes a customer is looking for a specific brand or model of a product that you do not carry. Or maybe the product you show the customer is not to his or her liking. In any of those cases, you may want to use something called the **substitution method**, which involves recommending a different product that would satisfy the customer's needs. Assume a customer says, "I don't like the way this dress looks on me." In this case you may want to suggest a totally different design that is more becoming on your customer. "Here, why don't you try this dress. It has a completely different look. I think it will fit your style better than the one you just had on."

Boomerang

An objection can be returned to the customer in the same way that a boomerang returns to the thrower. The **boomerang method** brings the objection back to the customer as a selling point. Here is an example:

Customer: "These ski gloves are so lightweight. They can't possibly keep me warm."
Salesperson: "The gloves are so light because of an insulation material called Thinsulate. The manufacturer guarantees that Thinsulate will keep you warmer than fiberfill insulation, without the bulk and extra weight."

When using the boomerang method, you must be careful not to sound as if you are trying to outwit the customer. Use a friendly, helpful tone to explain how the objection is really a selling point.

Question

The question method is a technique in which you question the customer to learn more about the objections. While answering your inquiries, the shopper may even come to realize that an objection may not be valid. Here is an example:

Customer: "I don't see the point of having two sinks in the bathroom, as featured in your suggested layout."
Salesperson: "Do you and another member of your family ever need to get ready to go out at the same time?"
Customer: "Yes."
Salesperson: "Does either one of you have to wait for the other to finish using the sink on those occasions?"
Customer: "Yes. I see your point."

Never ask questions in an abrupt manner; this may seem rude and create a defensive atmosphere.

Superior Point

The **superior-point method** is a technique that permits the salesperson to acknowledge objections as valid yet still offset them with other features and benefits. The superior-point method allows you to admit disadvantages in certain products but then present superior points to offset or compensate for them. This technique puts the

Case Study

Overcoming the Price Objection

When handling the price objection in a business-to-business situation, sell value, not price. You can also conduct a comparison between your product and your competitors' lower-priced products. Take Kellogg Company, which works to educate its customers and potential customers about the benefits of doing business with them.

To maximize perceived value and respond to price objections, Kellogg uses facts about the company. It asks customers to consider the research and development that goes into products, the ongoing support the company will provide, the certainty of on-time delivery, the company's history and reputation, and its market knowledge. Taken together, those factors are worth a lot.

Selling Value as More Than Price

If you want to take this concept a step further, you may use a competitive comparison. This method of handling objections begins with a comparison of product features and return on investment. Then it adds all the value-added aspects of doing business with your company to show how price is not the only factor that should be considered. This competitive comparison method of handling objections can be difficult. It requires a cool head and thorough preparation. Showing customers this comparison of the total package helps a customer see that doing business with a company that has higher-priced products may suit its needs and address its overall situation better than the one with lower-priced products.

THINK STRATEGICALLY

Which of the two methods (perceived value and competitive comparison) would you use to handle a price objection if you were a Kellogg sales representative? Why?

Online Action!

Go to *marketingessentials.glencoe.com/14/case* to find a research project on price objection.

customer in a position to decide between the different features and thus see additional reasons for buying. Here is an example:

Customer: "Your prices are higher than the prices of your competitors."
Salesperson: "That's true. Our prices are slightly higher, but with good reason. We use better quality wool in our garments that will last five to ten years longer than our competitors' garments. Plus, we guarantee the quality for life. You can return the product if you ever have a problem with it and we'll repair it free of charge."

Denial

The denial method is when the customer's objection is based on misinformation. It is best to provide proof and accurate information in answer to objections. This method is also used when the objection is in the form of a question or inquiry. When using the denial method, you

must back up the negative reply with proof and accurate facts. Consider an example:

Customer: "Will this shirt shrink?"
Salesperson: "No, it won't shrink because the fabric is made of 50 percent cotton and 50 percent polyester. The polyester will prevent shrinkage."

Demonstration

The demonstration exemplifies the adage "Seeing is believing." Here is an example:

Customer: "I can't believe that jacket can fold up into itself to become a zippered pouch."
Salesperson: "I'm glad you brought that up. Let me demonstrate how easy it is to stuff this jacket into the pocket pouch here and then zipper it up."

The demonstration method can be quite convincing and should be used when appropriate. Conduct only demonstrations you have tested, and make sure they work before using them on a customer in a sales situation.

Third Party

The **third-party method** involves using a previous customer or another neutral person who can give a testimonial about the product.

Customer: "I can't see how this machine can save me $1,000 in operating costs the first year."
Salesperson: "Frank Smith, one of my customers, questioned the same point when he bought his machine a year ago. He now praises its efficiency and says that his costs have gone down by $1,200. Here's a letter I recently received from him."

In any given sales situation, it is unlikely that you will use all seven methods of handling objections. You will create effective combinations over time that will work best for you.

14.2 AFTER YOU READ

Reviewing Key Terms and Concepts

1. Why should objections be answered promptly?
2. How can you prepare for objections?
3. Which specialized method of handling objections allows you to offset an objection with other features and benefits?

Integrating Academic Skills

Math

4. To overcome a price objection, demonstrate the savings a business-to-business customer will enjoy from purchasing 50 $150 jackets that will last for five years when compared to 50 $80 jackets that will be functional for only a maximum of two years.

Writing

5. Prepare an objection analysis sheet for a silk-and-wool designer blazer. List at least five objections, then write responses to depict methods for handling the objections. Use a word processing program to prepare your written document.

Check your answers at *marketingessentials.glencoe.com/14/read*

CAREERS IN MARKETING

DAVID MODICA
COMMERCIAL PHOTOGRAPHER

What do you do at work?
I specialize in making photographic images for business usage in advertising, documentation, historical preservation, and for competition. Clients come directly and through design and advertising agencies. I'm classified as a commercial photographer rather than a portrait/wedding photographer.

What skills are most important to you?
Photographic skills are obvious necessities, and today those skills are centered around the digital imaging business. Commercial photographers have to know digital cameras and scanning and their applications to paper and Web production. This process starts with capture and runs through color correction and preproduction.

What is your key to success?
Defining my business in great detail and finding a way to survive long enough to develop that business. That means taking jobs you don't necessarily want in the long run to pay bills and doing what is necessary to meet the people you want to work for. Network key industries, spend advertising money wisely, and get involved in your key geographic area.

Aptitudes, Abilities, and Skills

Camera skills, a visually oriented mind-set, knowledge of both the Web and print industries

Education and Training

Specialized courses in photography can be helpful, but hands-on experience, working with established photographers, is essential.

Career Path

Virtually all companies utilize the services of a photographer at some point—whether for a brochure, a newspaper ad, or a Web site. Ad agencies and design houses establish relationships with photographers for their projects.

THINKING CRITICALLY

What are some of the ways businesses use photography to market their products and services?

@ Online Action!

Go to *marketingessentials.glencoe.com/14/careers* to find a research project on photography and marketing.

CHAPTER 14 REVIEW

FOCUS on KEY POINTS

SECTION 14.1

- The goal of the product presentation is to match a customer's needs and wants to a product's features and benefits.
- When selecting products to show your customer during the product presentation, consider needs and price range, and limit your selection to three items at a time.
- To make your product presentation lively and effective, handle the product with respect, demonstrate product features, involve the customer, and use sales aids.

SECTION 14.2

- Objections are reasons for not buying or doubts that occur during a sales presentation.
- You should welcome objections in the sales process because they help clarify a customer's needs and provide an opportunity to introduce additional selling points.
- Common objections are based on five buying decisions: need, product, source, price, and time.
- The four-step method for handling customer objections is: listen, acknowledge, restate, and answer.
- There are seven specific methods of handling objections, each of which can be used in different selling situations: substitution, boomerang, question, superior-point, denial, demonstration, and third-party.

REVIEW VOCABULARY

Define each of the following words in a short sentence.

1. layman's terms (p. 297)
2. objections (p. 301)
3. excuses (p. 302)
4. objection analysis sheet (p. 302)
5. paraphrase (p. 305)
6. substitution method (p. 305)
7. boomerang method (p. 305)
8. superior-point method (p. 305)
9. third-party method (p. 307)

REVIEW FACTS and IDEAS

10. What is the goal of the product presentation? (14.1)
11. Describe some guidelines for what to say during the product presentation. (14.1)
12. What are four techniques that will make the product presentation lively and effective? (14.1)
13. Why are objections important to the sales process? (14.2)
14. List the five buying decisions on which common objections are based. (14.2)
15. Explain the process for handling customer objections. (14.2)
16. Name seven specific methods of handling objections. (14.2)

BUILD SKILLS

17. Workplace Skills

Handling Objections Write a response for each of the following objections and note the specialized method you used.

a. "This is the smallest TV I've ever seen. How will I be able to see the picture?"
b. "Does this blouse need to be dry-cleaned?"
c. "These no-iron cotton dress shirts are awfully expensive."
d. "I like these pants, but I already have two pairs of black pants."
e. "This cell phone is too sophisticated for me; it has too many fancy features I don't need."

18. Technology Applications

Make a Chart Assume you work as a sales associate for an electronics retailer. Select two competing products to compare, focusing on their features and prices. Use spreadsheet, presentation, or word processing software to make a chart that shows this comparison for use in the product presentation step of the sales process. Share your chart with classmates and be prepared to answer their questions and handle objections from them.

19. Math Practice

Determine the Price Your customer wants to buy $6\frac{3}{4}$ square yards of wood flooring for one room of a house and 4 square yards for another room. The price per square foot is $12.50. How much would you charge the customer?

DEVELOP CRITICAL THINKING

20. Selling Points

Tell what is wrong with the following two selling statements and what you would say instead during a product presentation:

a. "This suit is great."
b. "This fabric is made of 420 denier nylon."

21. Communication Skills

Can you use the methods for handling objections in sales to handle objections in other aspects of life? Give three examples of situations when the methods could be useful. Explain which method or methods you would use in each situation, and what the results might be.

APPLY CONCEPTS

22. Present the Product

Select a product, such as cosmetics, life insurance, athletic shoes, skis, and physical fitness equipment. Research the product's features. Be sure to address how the features and benefits satisfy customers' needs.

Activity Use presentation software to support a sales presentation. You may want to include one anticipated objection and an effective response as part of the product presentation.

23. Use Sales Aids

Conduct research on business-to-business products and services, such as integrated computer software, accounting, marketing, advertising, publicity, legal help, and financial consultation to see which selling points lend themselves to display and/or demonstration during the product presentation step of the sale.

Activity Prepare a written report using word processing software. Include graphic illustrations of your ideas, as well, and present them in an oral presentation that uses presentation software.

NET SAVVY

24. Evaluating Web Sites

Visit the Web site of a company of your choice. Evaluate the Web site in terms of ease of navigation, effectiveness of product presentation, and how well it handles customer inquiries and objections. List three positive features of the site.

THE  CONNECTION

Role Play: Teaching Product Presentation

Situation You are to assume the role of assistant manager of a gourmet cooking store. Your store carries high-quality tools, gadgets, and appliances for the home cook. The store often features demonstrations of new products. The store also encourages customers to try new tools and gadgets for themselves by having an area near the store's entrance set up for that purpose. As you are orienting a new employee (judge) to the store, the employee asks why the store has so many product demonstrations.

Activity You are to explain the purpose of the product demonstrations to the new employee (judge).

Evaluation You will be evaluated on how well you meet the following performance indicators:

- Demonstrate product
- Facilitate customer's buying decisions
- Recommend specific product
- Demonstrate suggestion selling
- Sell good/service/idea to individuals

@ Online Action!

For more information and DECA Prep practice, go to *marketingessentials.glencoe.com/14/DECA*

CHAPTER 15
Closing the Sale

Chapter Objectives

After reading this chapter, you should be able to:

- Identify customer buying signals
- List a few rules for closing a sale
- Select appropriate specialized methods for closing a sale
- Explain the importance of suggestion selling
- List the rules for effective suggestion selling
- Demonstrate appropriate specialized suggestion selling methods
- Discuss strategies for maintaining and building a clientele
- Explain the importance of customer service and follow-up
- Explain the concept of customer relationship management

GUIDE TO THE PHOTO

Market Talk Closing the sale means that the customer has made a commitment to buy. A good salesperson knows when a customer is ready to make a buying decision. An effective salesperson also masters techniques and skills to ensure that the customer will be satisfied with the purchase.

Quick Think Why is closing the sale such an important step in the sales process, and why is it not considered the last step?

THE DECA CONNECTION

Performance indicators represent key skills and knowledge. Relating them to the concepts explained in this chapter is your key to success in DECA events. Keep this in mind as you read this chapter and write some notes each time you encounter material that helps you master a key concept. These acronyms represent DECA events that involve knowledge of concepts in this chapter.

AAAL*	**FMAL**	**MMS**	**TMDM***
AASL*	**FMDM***	**QSRM***	**TSE***
ADC	**FMSL**	**RMAL***	**VPM**
BSM*	**FSRM***	**RMML***	
EMDM	**HMDM***	**SMDM***	

In all these DECA events you should be able to follow these performance indicators:

- Close the sale
- Demonstrate suggestion selling
- Sell good/service/idea to individuals
- Sell good/service/idea to groups
- Plan follow-up strategies for use in selling

All the events with an asterisk (*) also include these performance indicators:

- Process special orders
- Process telephone orders

Some events include additional performance indicators. These are:

AAAL/AAML Show customers fashionable ways to accessorize garments
Pack and wrap purchases

QSRM/FSRM Take customer's food order
Recommend additional menu items

FMAL/FMML Pack and wrap purchases

DECA PREP

Check your understanding of DECA performance indicators with the DECA activity in this chapter's review. For more information and DECA Prep practice, go to *marketingessentials.glencoe.com/15/DECA*

How to Close a Sale

OBJECTIVES

- Identify customer buying signals
- List a few rules for closing a sale
- Select appropriate specialized methods for closing a sale

KEY TERMS

- closing the sale
- buying signals
- trial close
- which close
- standing-room-only close
- direct close
- service close

READ and STUDY

BEFORE YOU READ

Predict How can you tell if a customer is ready to buy?

THE MAIN IDEA

At a certain point in the sales process, your customer will be ready to make a purchase. Sometimes, the decision to buy is quick and easy. At other times, it is more difficult. In this section, you will learn how to close a sale.

STUDY ORGANIZER

Prepare a chart like the one below to identify information you need to know in order to close a sale.

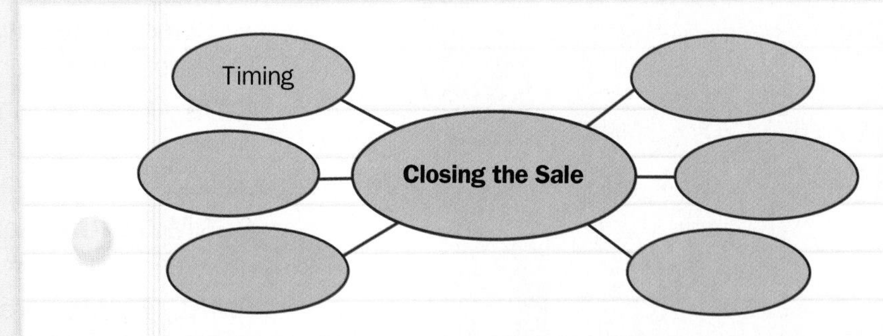

WHILE YOU READ

Question Why do some salespeople find closing the sale difficult, and what can they do to be more effective?

Closing Concepts and Techniques

Closing the sale is obtaining an agreement to buy from the customer. All efforts up to this step of the sale (pre-approach, approach, product presentation, and handling objections) have involved helping your customer make buying decisions.

To close a sale effectively, salespeople need to recognize when a customer is ready to buy. Sales personnel can use general rules and specialized methods to make this phase of the sales process occur seamlessly.

Timing the Close

Some customers are ready to buy sooner than others; therefore, you must be flexible. You may show a customer a product and almost immediately detect an opportunity to close the sale. Other times, you may spend an hour with a customer and still find that he or she is having difficulty making a decision.

Buying Signals

When attempting to close a sale, look for **buying signals**, the things customers do or say to indicate a readiness to buy. Buying signals include facial expressions, body language, and comments.

Trial Close

You may attempt a trial close to test the readiness of a customer and your interpretation of a positive buying signal. A **trial close** is an initial effort to close a sale.

Even if the close does not work, you will learn from the attempt. The customer will most likely tell you why he or she is not ready to buy. If the trial close does work, you will reach your goal of closing the sale. In both cases, you are in an excellent position to continue with the sales process.

General Rules for Closing the Sale

Professional salespeople recognize closing opportunities, help customers make a decision, and create an ownership mentality for the customer. You also want to avoid saying or doing a few things when closing a sale.

Recognize Closing Opportunities

Having a major obstacle removed usually makes a customer receptive to buying the product or service. You can also use effective product presentations to close the sale. Dramatic product presentations often prove important selling points and get a customer excited about owning the product. Take advantage of high customer interest at these times and attempt to close.

Help Customers Make a Decision

When a customer is having difficulty making a buying decision, stop showing additional merchandise. You should also narrow the selection of items by removing those things that are no longer of interest to the customer. You can do this by asking, "Which of these items do you like the least?" Once you get the selection

• IS the CUSTOMER READY to BUY?
A customer might like a product but be hesitant to buy it.

How would you assess if this customer is ready to make a purchase?

down to two, you can help a customer decide by summarizing the major features and benefits of each product. You can also explain any advantages or disadvantages of the item being considered. Both methods help you to focus the decision making on important considerations.

Create an Ownership Mentality

Use words that indicate ownership, such as *you* and *your*. When presenting selling points, say things such as, "When your children are hiking with you and the weather changes, you'll be happy that they have waterproof shoes like these." Look for minor agreements from the customer on selling points that lead up to the close.

Do Not Talk Too Much and Do Not Rush

If you think the customer is ready to make a buying decision, stop talking about the product.

On the other hand, don't rush a customer into making a buying decision. Be patient, courteous, polite, and helpful. Always

Case Study

The Electronic Close

Somewhere in the list of things mobile phones were one day supposed to become was the idea that they would replace credit cards.

Sour Chhor wants to make it happen, and he is closer than you might expect. He is the general manager of a group at Philips Electronics that is focused on developing a technology called near field communications (NFC). This technology is based on radio frequency identification (RFID) and could start turning common mobile phones into the spendthrift's best friend.

New Phone Functions

Consider using the phone to buy concert tickets. Not only will the phone handle payment but it will also become the ticket. Wave it in front of the turnstile at the concert venue, and the phone gets you in the door, where it can also be used to buy a T-shirt.

A Glimpse at the Future

NFC is potentially the next force that will push forward the concept of contactless payments. Credit card companies such as Visa, MasterCard, and American Express, as well as issuing banks like Citicorp's Citibank, J.P. Morgan Chase, and MBNA are testing this technology. ExxonMobil issues its SpeedPass RFID keychain to customers who use them to pay for gas and snacks at gas stations.

THINK STRATEGICALLY

How do you see the future of NFC and RFID technology in relation to the entire sales process? Will it be a positive or negative force?

Online Action!

Go to *marketingessentials.glencoe.com/15/case* to find a research project on sales closes that do not involve human beings.

GLOBAL MARKET

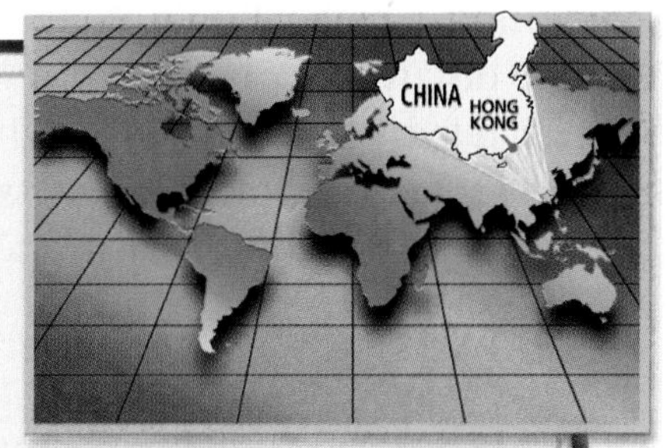

Hong Kong Octopus Is a Hit

The Octopus card, an electronic money card, has become a widely accepted electronic currency in Hong Kong. The card can be used to buy a newspaper at 7-Eleven, a meal at a fast-food restaurant, and even coffee at Starbucks. In all, more than 12,000 locations across Hong Kong accept the card.

A Hard-Working Card Octopus is a stored-value card and works like a debit card. Money is automatically subtracted from the card's monetary value when the card is held over a reading device. This device is a low-range radio transmitter that can be incorporated into doors, turnstiles, and countertops. Because reading devices can detect a card through leather and plastic, many people never remove their card but rather wave their purse or wallet over the reader. There is even a $35 Octopus wristwatch with the card technology built in.

Funds can be added to the cards at machines in subway stations, convenience stores, and via an automatic draw from a bank account.

CRITICAL THINKING

In which specialized closing method would the Hong Kong Octopus card be helpful?

@ Online Action!

Go to *marketingessentials.glencoe.com/15/global* to find a research project about proprietary debit cards.

remember that your primary interest is customer satisfaction.

Specialized Methods for Closing the Sale

Attempt to close the sale as soon as you recognize a buying signal. How you go about this depends on the selling situation. Certain selling situations warrant the use of specialized methods, including the which, standing-room-only, direct, and service closes.

Which Close

The **which close** encourages a customer to make a decision between two items. Follow the general rules for closing a sale and remove unwanted items to bring the selection down to two. Review the benefits of each item and then ask the customer, "Which one do you prefer?"

Standing-Room-Only Close

The **standing-room-only close** is used when a product is in short supply or when the price will be going up in the near future. This close should be used only when the situation honestly calls for it because it may be perceived as a high-pressure tactic. In many situations, a sales person can honestly say, "I'm sorry, but I can't promise that I'll be able to make you this same offer later." This approach is often used in selling high-demand real estate. Customers must often be prompted to act on a hot property that will be off the market quickly.

Direct Close

The **direct close** is a method in which you ask for the sale. You would use the direct close method when the buying signal is very strong. Here are a few direct close approaches: "Can I assume that we're ready to talk about the details of your order?" "It appears you like everything I have shown you. Now we just need to discuss the quantity you will need."

In a retail situation, you might ask about payment: For example, "How would you like to pay for this purchase—cash, check, or credit card?"

Service Close

Sometimes you may run into obstacles or instances that require special services to close the sale. The **service close** is a closing method in which you explain services that overcome obstacles or problems. Such services include gift wrapping, a return policy, special sales arrangements, warranties and guarantees, and bonuses or premiums. You might want to explain the store's return policy when a customer hesitates but seems to be willing to make the purchase anyway. This is an especially good idea when a customer is purchasing the item as a gift for someone else.

Special sales arrangements are used to close the sale when the customer needs help in paying for the item or order.

The Service Close in Business-to-Business Situations

In an industrial selling situation, the sales representative would talk about the terms of the sale, discussing points such as when payment is expected. For example, payment could be due 30 or 60 days after the date of the invoice.

A customer may also need information about credit terms to help him or her decide to buy. In other cases, the customer may need a sample to try out before purchasing large quantities. Sometimes, offering a sampling program is beneficial if it is a new purchase or the buyer is changing vendors and needs proof that your product is a better substitute for the one currently being used.

The Service Close in Retail

In a retail selling situation, the use of credit and checks, as well as special buying plans such as layaway, can be suggested. When a customer questions the quality of the merchandise, perhaps you can explain that a warranty or guarantee is offered on the product. When your business offers the same quality merchandise at the same price as your competitors, your service may be the only factor that affects the buying decision.

Failure to Close the Sale

Do not assume that every sales presentation should result in a sale. Even the best salespeople can sell to only a fraction of the prospects they call on. Research suggests that perseverance is the way to succeed.

In a retail setting, invite the customer to shop in your store again. In a business-to-business selling situation, ask if you may call again. In business-to-business selling, the sale is rarely closed on the first call. Business-to-business salespeople may negotiate with large accounts for over a year before closing the sale. Also remember that every sales contact has the potential to become a successful sale in the future.

Get Feedback

Experienced salespeople capitalize on defeat and come away from an unsuccessful selling experience with something to show for it. It is important to keep in mind that even a customer who does not make a purchase is still a prospect for future business. Be alert to what purchases today's non-buyer might make in the future.

If you have established an excellent rapport with the buyer, you may be able to ask him or her what factors led to the decision to buy from another source. A request for constructive criticism may work for you if you have earned the buyer's respect.

Maintain a Positive Attitude

The attitude of the salesperson who has not made the sale should be no different than that of the successful salesperson. It is very important for the salesperson to smile and be friendly after failing to make a sale. In business-to-business selling situations, it is not uncommon for a buyer to be convinced by a sales presentation but not yet ready to buy.

In such a situation, it is extremely important that the salesperson leave an opening for a return sales call. Return calls can increase sales costs, so consider the situation carefully before bowing out.

Preparing for Future Sales Calls

If you clearly sense an impending turndown, it is better to make a graceful exit, leaving the door open for a future sales call.

Some businesses send questionnaires or call customers to check on how well they were treated by the sales and service staff. The results of these surveys are passed on to salespeople so they can improve their sales techniques.

Success in Sales

One popular misconception about selling is that salespeople are born, not made. It is true that effective salespeople possess certain behavioral characteristics, including confidence, problem-solving ability, honesty, and a sincere desire to be helpful.

However, success in selling is the result of training, apprenticeship, and experience. Learning one's products and how to handle various situations comes with experience and hard work.

15.1 AFTER YOU READ

Reviewing Key Terms and Concepts

1. Why are trial closes beneficial?
2. Why should a salesperson stop talking about a product once a customer gives strong buying signals?
3. A customer seems to be frustrated because she likes three of the items you have shown her. What specialized closing method would you use to make her buying decision easier?

Integrating Academic Skills

Math

4. To close the sale, you offer layaway as an option, which requires a 20 percent deposit. What would the required deposit be on a $350 coat?

Language Arts

5. Write two paragraphs explaining how and when to close a sale. Also write examples of three different specialized methods of closing using a product of interest to you.

Check your answers at *marketingessentials.glencoe.com/15/read*

SECTION 15.2

Customer Satisfaction and Retention

OBJECTIVES

- Explain the importance of suggestion selling
- List the rules for effective suggestion selling
- Demonstrate appropriate specialized suggestion selling methods
- Discuss strategies for maintaining and building a clientele
- Explain the importance of customer service and follow-up
- Explain the concept of customer relationship management

KEY TERMS

- suggestion selling
- customer relationship management

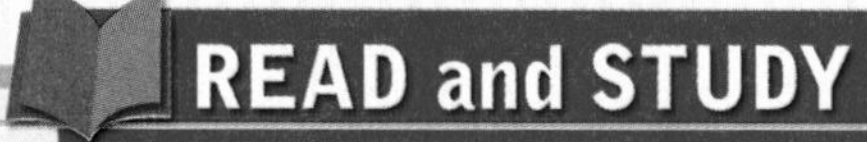

BEFORE YOU READ

Predict What are some ways to maintain customer loyalty?

THE MAIN IDEA

The goal of selling is to help customers make satisfying buying decisions so that they buy from you again. In this section, you will learn how to create a relationship with your customers so that they will continue to do business with you in the future.

STUDY ORGANIZER

Prepare charts similar to the one below to summarize the key points to remember for suggestion selling and maintaining and building a clientele.

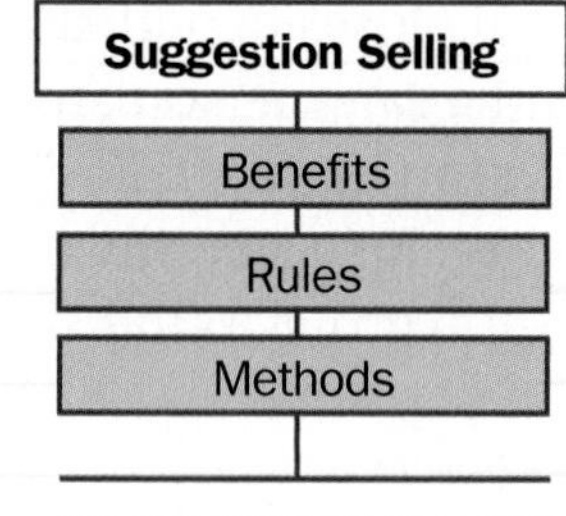

Connect Have you ever experienced suggestion selling? Give examples.

Effective Selling

Maintaining and building a clientele is crucial for future sales. The actual sale is just the beginning of a relationship with a customer. To keep customers, it is important to make a good impression, get to know your customers, and provide excellent customer service.

Suggestion Selling

Suggestion selling is selling additional goods or services to the customer. It involves selling customers other items that will ultimately save time and money or make the original purchase more enjoyable.

Consider the customer who buys an electronic toy for a child, takes it home, and only then realizes that he or she has no batteries for it. The salesperson would have had a sure sale with a suggestion to buy batteries.

Benefits of Suggestion Selling

Suggestion selling benefits the salesperson, the customer, and the company. You benefit because customers will want to do business with you again, and as a result of your efforts, your sales will increase. Since salespeople are often evaluated on their sales figures, you will be viewed as an effective salesperson. Your customer benefits because he or she is more pleased with the original purchase. The firm benefits because the time and cost involved in suggestion selling is less than the cost of making the original sale.

Consider the two purchases in the following chart. The second includes an extra item, a suggestion from the salesperson. Note that the extra time spent on suggestion selling significantly increased the firm's net profits. Expenses rose, but not in proportion to the sales volume. There are two reasons for this. First, less time and effort are needed for suggestion selling compared with the initial sale. Second, certain business expenses (such as utilities and rent) remain the same despite the extra sales activity.

Purchase 1		Purchase 2	
Pants	$75	Pants	$ 75
		Shirt	$ 35
Total	$75	Total	$110
Cost of goods	−$37	Cost of goods	−$55
Gross Profit	$38	Gross Profit	$55
Expenses	−$12	Expenses	−$15
Net profit	$26	Net profit	$40

Rules for Suggestion Selling

Here are five basic rules for suggestion selling:

1. **Use suggestion selling after the customer has made a commitment to buy but before payment is made or the order written.** Introducing additional merchandise before the sale has been closed can create pressure for the customer. The only exception to this rule involves products whose accessories are a major benefit. Let's say you are showing a retailer a new type of video game system. To clinch the sale, you may need to tell the retailer about the exciting new video games that will be sold in conjunction with that new system.
2. **Make your recommendation from the customer's point of view and give at least one reason for your suggestion.** You might say, "For your child to enjoy this toy immediately, you'll need two AAA batteries."
3. **Make the suggestion definite.** Don't ask, "Will that be all?" Instead say, "This oil is recommended by the manufacturer for this engine." In most cases, general questions invite a negative response.
4. **Show the item you are suggesting.** Merely talking about it is not enough. In many cases, the item will sell itself if you let the customer see and handle it. You may put a matching purse next to the shoes a customer has just decided to buy, particularly with some commentary. You might say, "This purse matches your shoes perfectly, doesn't it?"
5. **Make the suggestion positive.** You could say, "Let me show you the matching top to that skirt. It will complete the outfit beautifully."

Suggestion Selling Methods

Three methods are used in suggestion selling: offering related merchandise, recommending larger quantities, and calling attention to special sales opportunities. Figure 15.1 shows an example of using suggestion selling.

Figure 15.1 Suggestion Selling

• **Suggestion Selling in Business-to-Business Sales** Once customers decide to buy, it is a good practice to suggest something specific to help them enjoy their purchase. This practice is known as suggestion selling. Three methods are commonly used in suggestion selling. Let's examine how they might be used by a sales representative for a clothing manufacturer in a business-to-business sale.

What are some examples of suggestion selling?

UP-SELLING

A sales representative may suggest buying larger quantities of goods so a customer qualifies for special discounts, payment terms, or delivery charges. Retailers may also receive free merchandise.

CROSS-SELLING

The sales representative may suggest related merchandise to the retail store buyer. The rationale is that customers may need accessories and related items.

SPECIAL SALES OPPORTUNITIES

When a manufacturer runs a special promotion on products or wants to introduce a new product, it is up to the sales representative to share that information with the retailer.

@ Online Action! **Go to *marketingessentials.glencoe.com/15/figure/1* for a project on suggestion selling.**

Offering Related Merchandise

In some businesses, this method is called cross-selling. You use the opportunity at the end of a sale to introduce another product of possible interest to the customer. Introducing related merchandise is probably the easiest and most effective suggestion selling method.

Recommending Larger Quantities

Suggesting a larger quantity is often referred to as up-selling. This method works in retail settings when selling inexpensive items or when savings in money or time and convenience are involved.

In business-to-business sales situations, the salesperson may suggest a larger quantity so that the customer can take advantage of lower prices or special considerations.

Calling Attention to Special Sales Opportunities

Salespeople are obligated to communicate special sales opportunities to their customers.

In retail sales, routinely inform your customer of the arrival of new merchandise. Regular customers appreciate this special service because they like having the opportunity to see new merchandise before others do.

In business-to-business sales situations, sales representatives often show new items to their customers after they have completed the sale of merchandise requested. Thus, the salesperson establishes a rapport with the customer before introducing new merchandise.

Maintaining and Building a Clientele

Making a sale is the first step in maintaining and building a clientele. After-sale activities by the sales and customer service staff, as well as customer relationship management strategies employed by the company, are two key factors in building a clientele.

After-Sales Activities

After-sale activities include order processing, departure, order fulfillment, follow-up, and customer service. All these activities need to be handled in such a way that it generates repeat business.

Order Processing

In retail selling, bag the merchandise with care. Products such as glassware may require individual wrapping before bagging. Work quickly to bag your customer's merchandise and complete the payment process. In business-to-business sales, complete the paperwork quickly and leave a business card.

Departure

Before the customer departs or before you leave your client's office, reassure the person of his or her wise buying choices. If an item needs special care or specific instructions, take the time to educate your customer about it. You may want to remind the customer, for example, that to get the best results from a Teflon-coated frying pan, it should be preheated. Helpful comments like this will make your customer feel you are interested and concerned.

Always thank your customers. Even when a customer does not buy, express your gratitude for the time and attention given to you. Invite him or her back to the store, or ask for permission to call again in the near future.

Order Fulfillment

In a retail store, fulfillment is a simple process of the customer paying for merchandise and carrying it away. In e-commerce, mail order, or telemarketing sales, order fulfillment gets more complicated. It includes taking the order, financial processing (such as credit card information), picking the right product, packing it well, and shipping it according to the customer's preference. In some companies, fulfillment also includes customer service, technical support, managing inventory, and handling returns and refunds. The goal, of course, is to make the customer happy.

In the new e-commerce economy, success often depends as much on appropriate fulfillment strategies as it does on having the right product at the right price. Some of the most successful online retailers have established

NET MARKETING

Partnership Selling

Digitizing traditional media such as music, photography, or art enables it to be marketed and purchased entirely over the Web. In 2002, IBM announced that the National Geographic Society (NGS) was digitizing and making commercially available 10,000 of its renowned images. NGS planned to add at least 3,000 images a year out of its database of more than 10 million images. IBM provided the computer technology and expertise, and National Geographic provided the images to make this partnership happen.

Better Customer Service

Customers such as advertising agencies, publishers, and others could view, analyze, sort, and purchase NGS images of culture and nature on demand. "IBM's solution is helping NGS serve our customers worldwide more effectively by making our images available in the digital marketplace," said Maura Mulvihill, the National Geographic's image collection vice president.

THINK LIKE A MARKETER

How does IBM demonstrate the concept of partnership selling in the digital marketplace?

Online Action!

Go to *marketingessentials.glencoe.com/15/net* to find a research activity about digitizing media.

their own fulfillment centers to ensure prompt delivery. Amazon.com, BarnesandNoble.com, and Dell Computer all have their own fulfillment centers. Another approach is to outsource fulfillment to a third party. This allows a company to concentrate their resources on marketing the products.

Follow-Up

The follow-up includes making arrangements to follow through on all promises made during the sales process. It also includes checking on your customer's satisfaction with his or her purchase. Here are a few follow-up ideas:

- Call the shipping department to confirm a special delivery date.
- Check to make sure that delivery occurs as promised.
- Call the customer and explain any delay.
- Phone the customer a week or two after the purchase to see if he or she is happy with the selection.
- Send a thank-you note with your business card attached.

Customer Service

Some firms have customer service departments to handle customer inquires and complaints. For example, in some auto dealerships, specific customer service representatives are assigned to each customer to handle appointments and questions with auto problems and regular servicing. In business-to-business sales, customer complaints should be provided to the sales representatives responsible for those customers.

• KEEP TRACK OF CUSTOMERS Most companies maintain a computerized customer database. Such databases must be updated on a regular basis to remain useful.

What should salespeople do to keep a customer database up-to-date?

How these complaints are handled is crucial to maintaining clientele. Customers expect immediate action when they file a complaint. Positive customer-client relations require compassionate and understanding personnel and sales associates who are problem solvers. The main goal is customer satisfaction.

Keeping a Client File

You can use the time immediately after the sale to plan for your next encounter with the customer. Take notes on your conversation with the customer. Keep this in a file for future reference. In retail sales, note a customer's preference in color, style, and size, as well as the person's address and telephone number. In business-to-business selling, record personal information on the buyer's marital status, children, and hobbies to assist with future sales visits. Record changes in buying patterns that may lead to future sales. You also want to note any future service dates for appliances or cars so that you can send a reminder when the time comes. Also be sure to inform your company of any changes you uncover, such as changes in personnel responsible for buying, as well as address or telephone changes so that company files can be kept up to date.

Evaluate Your Sales Efforts

Even if your company has a formal method of reviewing your efforts, you should conduct your own evaluation. In your evaluation, consider the following:

- What were the strong points of your sales presentation?
- What did you do wrong?
- How could you have improved your performance?
- What would you do differently next time?
- What can you do now to solidify your relationship with your customer if you made the sale?

Objective self-evaluation is a helpful tool in any career. Asking yourself these questions can help you improve your selling skills as well as your business skills in general. They will enable you to look forward to your next sales opportunity. That kind of attitude will help you become more effective with each sales contact. It will also help you become more successful in building a strong relationship with your customers.

Customer Relationship Management (CRM)

A popular trend among companies today is **customer relationship management** (CRM), which involves finding customers and keeping them satisfied. CRM provides companies with the means to develop and nurture customer relationships, including lead generation, sales support, customer service, and other after-sales activities.

Technology and CRM

Technology can play a role in this endeavor. Some companies purchase software that can be customized for their business. Others may subscribe to the services of Web-based companies for similar CRM services. For example, Siebel CRM OnDemand and salesforce.com host customer relationship management services. According to a case study at Siebel's Web site, General Orthodontic selected Siebel CRM OnDemand when General Orthodontic realized it needed to manage an overwhelming number of new sales leads. Since it was a start-up company, it also had to keep costs down and still provide a high level of customer service if it wanted to be successful.

The value of a good relationship is not a new idea. Marketers have long recognized that identifying the needs of customers and satisfying them can be profitable. However, only recently have firms made a dedicated effort to use customer relationship management.

By examining successful partnerships in business and elsewhere, marketers have discovered that enduring relationships are built on trust and commitment and require a lot of time and effort to maintain.

Maintaining Contact

To maintain sales accounts, it is important to offer solutions to problems and to stay in contact, acting as a partner or consultant for your customers. For example, a manufacturer of artificial knees or hips may actually be present in the operating room during such a procedure in case there is a question or problem.

You may have seen commercials for IBM and American Express, where they stress their commitment to their customers in providing solutions to their problems, thus demonstrating consultative selling. That commitment signifies their role in relationship building. For example, IBM helped the National Geographic Society with its own photography e-commerce site.

Maintain Relationships

Relationship marketing is alive and well in both traditional and e-commerce marketing. Consider the example set by Harley-Davidson, the motorcycle manufacturer. The company established a club for its members, and it markets services such as motorcycle insurance and travel assistance to those members.

An e-commerce example of relationship marketing is Amazon.com's practice of collecting information about customers' book purchases and then e-mailing personalized information about promotions and merchandise within the customer's established range of interest.

Develop Customer Loyalty

Customer loyalty cannot be taken for granted, especially with the high level of competition in today's market. A company can stay close to its customers and keep them happy by having the sale be the first step in developing a relationship, not the final one.

Think of after-sale activities as part of an ongoing dialog with customers in preparation for future sales. This is simplified with the use of e-mail, which can be used to keep customers informed about sales, new products, and important company news.

Customer Loyalty and Reward Programs

Some companies also reward their regular customers through loyalty programs such as frequent flier programs. E-mailed questionnaires with prize entries or advance notice of special sales are other practices marketers have developed to create and reinforce loyalty. You can also send that information in the mail or have a customer service representative communicate with your customers by phone.

15.2 AFTER YOU READ

Reviewing Key Terms and Concepts

1. Explain how suggestion selling can increase a firm's net profit.
2. List three related items that could be used for suggestion selling after a customer's decision to buy a bicycle.
3. How can a salesperson use the time immediately after the sale to plan for his or her next encounter with that customer?

Integrating Academic Skills

Math

4. You sold a $715 item via the Internet to a European customer, a Japanese customer, and a New Zealand customer. Use the chart below to calculate the total amount due for the product and applicable duties and customs for each of the three customers.

	Europe	Japan	New Zealand
Duties & Customs	20%	9%	50%

Language Arts

5. Write about suggestion selling and measures that can be taken to build and maintain clientele in the sale of a product of your choice. Provide examples of related merchandise that can be suggested in the sale of that product, and specific measures that can be taken in after-sale activities and customer relationship management.

Check your answers at *marketingessentials.glencoe.com/15/read*

CAREERS IN MARKETING

EMILY EBERS-GERMER
SALES REPRESENTATIVE
EBERS & ASSOCIATES
BUSINESS PRINTING

What do you do at work?

My job consists mainly of talking to my customers, setting goals, making cold calls, developing leads, and talking to people and letting them know what I do. Customer service involves keeping the customers I already have. Every one of them is important! I am pretty much available to all my customers by phone, fax, e-mail, cell phone, and through my Web site.

What skills are most important to you?

If I were to hire someone, they would have to have sales experience. You can teach them about printing, but if someone does not have "it," it won't happen. "It" is personality, attitude, the ability to talk to anyone and put a smile on your face whether you mean it or not. You have to open your mouth and ask questions, and find out what people need and what you can do for them.

What is your key to success?

I think my success has been mainly due to my customer service. No customer is too small for me to give them my undivided attention. My base of customers is small businesses. They usually stay with you; they are loyal.

Aptitudes, Abilities, and Skills

Organization and time management, strong people skills, an outgoing personality

Education and Training

Degrees in marketing and general business are helpful, as are industry-specific sales courses.

Career Path

Since most sales representative positions are commission-only, they can be relatively easy to land. Proving yourself in an entry-level sales position can quickly lead to virtually unlimited opportunities.

THINKING CRITICALLY

Why can sales reps find success by focusing on smaller prospects, rather than working to land larger accounts?

Online Action!

Go to *marketingessentials.glencoe.com/15/careers* to find a research project on customer service.

CHAPTER 15 REVIEW

FOCUS on KEY POINTS

SECTION 15.1

- Customer buying signals help a salesperson determine a customer's readiness to buy, which is important in trial closes.
- Close the sale as soon as the customer is ready to buy.
- Use success in answering objections or presenting a product as an opportunity to close.
- Help customers make a decision and create an ownership mentality.
- Four specialized methods for closing a sale include the direct close, the which close, the standing-room-only close, and the service close.

SECTION 15.2

- Suggestion selling is important because it helps generate more sales revenue for a company and helps to create more satisfied customers.
- Three specialized suggestion selling methods are (a) offering related merchandise, also referred to as cross-selling; (b) selling larger quantities, also referred to as up-selling; and (c) calling attention to special sales opportunities.
- After-sales activities and customer relationship management (CRM) are important for maintaining and building a clientele. They include order processing, departure, order fulfillment, follow-up, customer service, and keeping a client file, as well as evaluating your sales efforts.

REVIEW VOCABULARY

Define each of the terms below in a short sentence.

1. closing the sale (p. 314)
2. buying signals (p. 315)
3. trial close (p. 315)
4. which close (p. 317)
5. standing-room-only close (p. 317)
6. direct close (p. 317)
7. service close (p. 318)
8. suggestion selling (p. 321)
9. customer relationship management (CRM) (p. 326)

REVIEW FACTS and IDEAS

10. What are customer buying signals? (15.1)
11. List two rules for closing a sale. (15.1)
12. Why is suggestion selling an important step in the sales process? (15.2)
13. What are two rules for suggestion selling? (15.2)
14. Explain the concept of customer relationship management. (15.2)

BUILD SKILLS

15. Workplace Skills

Making a Sale With another student playing the role of a customer, perform a role-play in which you demonstrate how you would sell an item of clothing to an individual customer. Be sure to complete the sales transaction, too.

If possible, use cash as the method of payment to demonstrate your ability to count back change and use a garment to demonstrate the proper way to fold, wrap, and bag merchandise after the sale.

In order to complete this sales role play, remember to end the sales transaction by thanking the customer and inviting him or her to return again.

16. Technology Applications

Prepare a Sales Presentation Suppose you have some ideas on how to help your company's customer service representatives to cross-sell when they finish answering customer inquiries or solving problems customers have with their phone service. Management likes your ideas and wants you to sell your ideas to the entire group of customer service representatives at the next meeting. Use presentation software to present your ideas.

17. Math Practice

Managing Time Mia is a sales associate for a public relations service firm. She attends an average of 30 client meetings a month. Her manager has recently asked sales associates to increase the number of client meetings they have each month by 25 percent. How many meetings will Mia then have?

DEVELOP CRITICAL THINKING

18. The Service Close

What are some situations that require a service close? List at least three examples and explain why a service close would be needed each time.

19. Explaining and Evaluating Selling Policies

Explain the selling policies of three comparable retailers and evaluate their effectiveness. You may want to consider studying the initial approaches used by sales associates, merchandise return policies, and payment options, as well as any other related selling policy that differentiates one store from the other. Use a word processing program to report your findings.

APPLY CONCEPTS

20. Closing the Sale

Different sales situations call for different closing techniques. If one technique does not work, you may want to try another one.

Activity Respond to the following comments in a role play with a classmate by selecting the most appropriate closing method. After the role play, ask your partner to evaluate your response in terms of the method selected and how effective it was.

a. "I like your product, but I don't have enough money in my store's budget at the current time to buy it right now."

b. "I have tried so many different brands of golf clubs that I can't make up my mind."

c. "My sister is very particular about perfume. What if she doesn't like this fragrance?"

d. "I like these shoes, but I am going to wait until they go on sale before buying them."

21. Maintaining Clientele

Select a business of your choice and note the purpose of the business and its clientele.

Activity Prepare an oral and visual presentation of the skills and strategies that sales personnel should use to build and maintain the firm's clientele. Use presentation software to help organize and deliver your ideas in an effective manner.

NET SAVVY

22. Employing Suggestion Selling

Visit a clothing retailer Web site to find products that can be used for suggestion selling in conjunction with the sale of an outdoor sports jacket. List three ways you would use suggestion selling for a product of your choice.

THE 

CONNECTION

Role Play: Suggestion Selling

Situation You are to assume the role of assistant manager of a women's clothing store. The store has good traffic, and the number of sales per day is good. However, the dollar amount of each sale is decreasing. Your store manager (judge) has decided this is because the sales associates are not making effective use of suggestion selling.

Activity The store manager (judge) has asked you to make a presentation about the use of suggestion selling during the next staff meeting.

Evaluation You will be evaluated on how well you meet the following performance indicators:

- Demonstrate suggestion selling
- Assess customer/client needs
- Sell good/service/idea to individuals
- Close the sale
- Conduct staff meetings

@ Online Action!

For more information and DECA Prep practice, go to *marketingessentials.glencoe.com/15/DECA*

CHAPTER 16
Using Math in Sales

Chapter Objectives

After reading this chapter, you should be able to:

- List all types of retail sales transactions
- Process purchases, returns, and exchanges
- Generate and process sales documentation
- Calculate sales tax, discounts, and shipping charges
- Name the functions of cash registers and point-of-sale (POS) terminals
- Explain the uses for Universal Product Codes (UPCs)
- Make change
- Prepare purchase orders and invoices
- Explain delivery terms

GUIDE TO THE PHOTO

Market Talk An electronic cash register can function as a point-of-sale (POS) terminal if it is connected to a network that keeps track of sales, inventory, and even ordering new merchandise. This new generation of cash registers functions as a sales and a marketing tool.

Quick Think Name a store where you often shop. Is it equipped with conventional cash registers or POS stations? Why do you think this store uses that type of register?

THE  CONNECTION

Performance indicators represent key skills and knowledge. Relating them to the concepts explained in this chapter is your key to success in DECA events. These acronyms represent DECA events that involve knowledge of concepts in this chapter.

AAAL*	**FMAL***	**MMS**	**TMDM***
AAML*	**FMDM***	**QSRM***	**TSE***
ADC	**FMML***	**RMAL***	**VPM***
BSM	**FSRM***	**RMML***	
EMDM	**HMDM***	**SMDM***	

In all these DECA events you should be able to follow these performance indicators:

- Calculate miscellaneous charges
- Process sales documentation
- Analyze technology for use in the sales function
- Prepare invoices
- Use information systems for order fulfillment

The events with an asterisk (*) also include:

- Process cash sales
- Process charge (credit) sales
- Accept checks from customers
- Operate register/terminal
- Prepare cash drawers/banks
- Open/close register/terminal
- Process special orders

Some events include additional indicators:

BSM	Make change
FMDM	Assist with currency exchange
TMDM	Maintain petty-cash fund
HMDM	Perform bucket (room rack) check and resolve discrepancies
RMAL/RMML	Process returns and exchanges
AAAL/AAML	Process returns and exchanges

DECA PREP

Check your understanding of DECA performance indicators with the DECA activity in this chapter's review. For more information and DECA Prep practice, go to *marketingessentials .glencoe.com/16/DECA*

SECTION 16.1

Sales Transactions

OBJECTIVES

- List all types of retail sales transactions
- Process purchases, returns, and exchanges
- Generate and process sales documentation
- Calculate sales tax, discounts, and shipping charges

KEY TERMS

- sales check
- layaway
- on-approval sale
- cash-on-delivery (COD) sale
- sales tax
- allowance

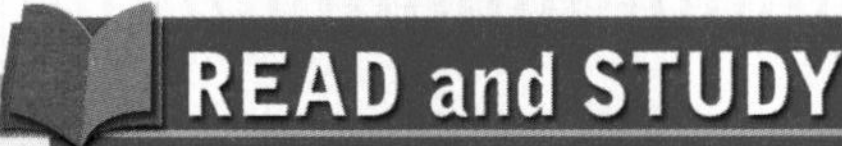

BEFORE YOU READ

Connect Imagine you have just finished shopping at your favorite store and are at the checkout counter. List and describe all the steps that take place before you leave the store.

THE MAIN IDEA

Today, there are many different ways of completing a purchase transaction, but one thing remains true: You still need basic math skills.

STUDY ORGANIZER

Draw the chart below. As you read this section, list six types of retail sales transactions.

Types of Retail Sales Transactions		
1. Cash or check	2.	3.
4.	5.	6.

Summarize List the differences in handling various methods of payment.

Types of Retail Sales Transactions

As a salesperson or cashier, you will handle several types of sales transactions. Most will be cash and debit or credit card sales, but you might also deal with layaway (or will-call) sales, on-approval sales, and cash-on-delivery (COD) sales. You will also handle returns, exchanges, allowances, sales tax, and shipping charges.

Cash or Check Sales

A cash sale is a transaction in which the customer pays for the purchase with cash or a check. The simplest sale occurs when the customer pays in cash. The cashier records the transaction on the register, gives the customer change and a receipt, and wraps the purchase.

When a customer writes a check, you may need to verify his or her identity by requesting a driver's license and another form of identification. Every business has rules about accepting checks. You will have to learn the policy of your company or store.

Sales Checks

A **sales check** is a written record of a sales transaction that includes such information as the date of the transaction, the items purchased, the purchase prices, sales tax, and the total amount due. It is valuable to a customer as an itemized receipt.

In its most complete form, a sales check can contain customer information (name, address, and phone number) and details such as the time of the sale and the identity of the salesperson. While handwritten sales checks are becoming less common than printed ones, some small firms still use them. The salesperson records the transaction by hand in a sales check book that contains at least two copies of each form. One copy is given to the customer and one is retained by the business as a record of the sale.

Math Skills for Handwritten Sales Checks

Some math is necessary when preparing handwritten sales checks. The five steps of this process are shown in Figure 16.1. Occasionally, you will not be given a unit price, and you will need to calculate it on your own. This occurs when items are sold in multiple quantities, such as three reams of paper for $15. To find the selling price of one item in an instance like this, you divide the total price by the number of items: One ream of paper in this example would be $5 ($15 ÷ 3).

When the result of the division is uneven, any fraction of a cent is rounded up and charged to the customer. The price of one ream of paper when three reams are $13.99 is calculated as follows: $13.99 ÷ 3 = $4.6633 or $4.67.

Debit Card Sales

Businesses that have an encrypted, or coded, personal identification number (PIN) pad can ask customers whether they would like to pay with debit or credit. Customers who choose "debit" key in their private PIN. The terminal then dials out and checks to see whether there are enough funds in the customer's account to pay for the sale. If so, the funds are transferred to the merchant's account. The customer does not need to sign a sales draft.

Advantages of Debit Card Payments

The bank that issues the debit card charges the merchant only a flat rate, for example $.59 per sale, regardless of the amount of the sale. They are a convenience to many customers who cannot get approval for a credit card, who prefer not to use a credit card, or who do not carry either a checkbook or large amounts of cash. Most merchants prefer payment by debit card to payment by check because they have access to the money much sooner, there is no risk of insufficient funds, and the cost to the merchant is less than when the customer pays with a credit card.

Credit Card Sales

Statistics show that by accepting credit cards, businesses can increase sales by as much as 40 percent. Primarily because of this potential for increased sales, most businesses today accept one or more of the major credit cards, such as Visa, MasterCard, and American Express.

Credit Card Payment on the Internet

Credit cards are also the most frequently used method of payment for Internet purchases. Many Internet sites also allow the consumer to make purchases with a gift certificate that has a security code the customer must key in. For safety reasons, the payment data (card number, expiration date, security code,

Figure 16.1 Sales Check—Multiple Purchases

• **Adding Complexity** **The basic sales check becomes more complicated when the customer buys several items, or several units of one item.**

How can you be sure that the final sales check is accurate?

Step 1—Multiply unit price times quantity for each item and extend the amounts to the last column. Remember that the last two digits on the right are cents. Place a decimal point to their left, or enter them to the right of the vertical line dividing the last column into two unequal parts.

Step 2—Add item amounts to arrive at a merchandise subtotal. Enter this figure on the appropriate line.

Step 3—Calculate sales tax or look it up in a tax table. Sales tax must be paid by the buyer on all retail sales. It is calculated as a percentage of the merchandise subtotal. In most states, food and prescription medicine are exempt from sales tax, as are shipping charges.

Step 4—Calculate shipping charges. You need to decide if you will use U.S. mail or a specific express mail carrier.

Step 5—Add subtotal, tax, and shipping to get the purchase total. This is the amount the customer will pay.

ODEL'S CAMERA, INC.

1329 Walnut Street • Santa Barbara, CA 93101

NEW CUSTOMER ☐ YES ☐ NO

DATE 6/17/--

NAME Joe Bundy

COMPANY The Daily Times

ADDRESS

CITY & STATE

PHONE (RESIDENCE) PHONE (OTHER)

SOLD BY

TYPE OF SALE: CASH | CHECK ✓ | C.O.D. | CARD TYPE | ACCOUNT | PURCHASE ORDER NO.

CODE	QTY	DESCRIPTION	PRICE	AMOUNT	
6T	1	Olympus digital camera	399.00	399	00
4B	10	Fuji 100 color film	2.80	28	00
	8	Fuji 100 b/w film	3.00	24	00

SPECIAL INSTRUCTIONS

HANDLING	—	—
SUB TOTAL	451	00
TAX	31	57
SHIPPING	—	—
TOTAL AMOUNT	482	57
PAID	500	00
BALANCE	17	43

SHIP VIA:

PAID ON # ____ TC # ____

CC #

7932

@ Online Action! **Go to *marketingessentials.glencoe.com/16/figure/1* to find a project on sales checks.**

cardholder's identity) sent via the Internet are encrypted. This makes it more difficult for unauthorized individuals to gain access to a customer's card numbers.

Credit Card Payment Costs to the Merchant

If your company accepts credit cards, it pays a fee to the bank or agency that handles the billing and record keeping for each card transaction processed. This fee is a percentage of credit sales based on a sliding scale, which means that it varies according to the size of the store account and how the charges are processed.

Suppose your store had Visa sales of $100,000 in one month and that another store had Visa sales of only $2,000 in that same month. Your company would pay a smaller percentage for handling.

Overall, the cost of accepting credit cards typically varies from a low of 1.79 percent for MasterCard and Visa to 3.25 percent for American Express.

How Are Credit Card Payments Processed?

For many businesses, the amount of each credit card sale is electronically deposited in the business's bank account as the sale is made. A credit card sales check, or receipt, is issued by the cash register. With this procedure, the credit card company deducts its service charges from the store's bank account immediately, and the store normally has access to the customers' payment funds the next day. This process is much faster than physically delivering credit card sales checks to a bank.

If manually prepared credit card sales checks are used for these charges, they may be deposited when you deposit checks in your company account. A special deposit slip must be prepared for the bank so that your account is credited quickly.

Getting Credit Authorization

While credit cards are a convenient alternative to more traditional forms of payment, some fraud is always possible. Many retail businesses set a floor limit, a maximum amount a customer is allowed to charge to a credit card, to protect themselves against losses due to the use of stolen or fake credit cards. Illicit charges are disputed by the true cardholder and the credit card company, and the store is liable for only the amount of the floor limit.

Most modern cash registers include an integrated credit authorizer. An electronic credit authorizer can also be a device that reads data encoded on credit cards. The sales clerk inputs the amount of the sale into the device. The data are then transmitted to a computer,

Practice 1: Credit Card Fees

Calculate the impact credit card fees would have on the business described below.

1. At Carol's Pearls and Stones, Visa sales are usually between $13,000 and $15,000 per month. The Visa handling charge is a sliding scale. For $10,000–$14,999, it charges 3 percent of sales; for $15,000–$19,999, 2.5 percent; and for $20,000–$29,999, 2 percent.

   That means that for a purchase of $22,000, Visa collects a 3 percent fee on the first $14,999, a 2.5 percent fee on the next $5,000, and a 2 percent fee on the remaining $2,001. The total Visa collects is $614.99.

   a. Carol had $15,500 in Visa sales one month. How much more did she net than if sales had been $14,300?

   b. How much would Carol have netted in that month if her shop had done $21,000 in Visa sales?

2. Carol has decided to accept the Diners Club card in her shop. The handling charges are 1 percent higher than those for Visa at each sales level. If Carol had $19,000 in Diners Club sales, how much more would she pay in handling fees than she would have for the same amount in Visa sales?

3. Carol had $13,600 in cash sales, $14,800 in Diners Club sales, and $15,200 in Visa sales one month. What were her net sales after handling charges?

Note: Answers to all practice sets at *marketingessentials.glencoe.com*

Case Study

Safety in Internet Sales

How can a small business sell products over the Internet and be certain it will be paid? How can a buyer be certain a Web merchant will not misuse credit card information? In the early days of Web marketing, credit card fraud frightened away many buyers and sellers.

eBay and PayPal

PayPal is a system developed in 1998 to provide safe transactions over the Internet. Originally, most of PayPal's customers were individuals involved in auctions on eBay—the huge Internet auction site. More recently, small online businesses, especially those run by individuals, have been signing up with PayPal. To buy a product from a PayPal client, a purchaser fills out a PayPal registration form, entering credit card and sometimes bank account information. PayPal verifies the information and opens an account for the purchaser.

When someone makes a purchase using PayPal, his or her credit card information is not shared with the merchant. In fact, it is not transmitted over the Web at all, where others might see it. The buyer feels safer making the purchase, and the seller is assured of being paid. PayPal has fraud protection that protects both seller and buyer, making it a more and more popular way to transact business.

THINK STRATEGICALLY

If PayPal charges one percent more to process each transaction than do credit card companies, why would it make sense for a small Web marketer to use the service?

@ Online Action!

Go to *marketingessentials.glencoe.com/16/case* to find a research project on Internet sales.

which returns an approval or a disapproval in less than a minute.

Recording Credit or Debit Card Sales

As a salesperson in retail business, you will probably process many credit card sales. Electronic recording of credit card sales is now common and has replaced manually prepared credit card sales checks. There are usually three copies of each manually prepared sales check—one for the customer, one for the seller, and one for the bank or credit card agency. You might use a mechanical imprinter to transfer the customer's name and account number to the sales slip, or you might write the information on the sales check by hand.

Layaway Sales

Removing merchandise from stock and keeping it in a separate storage area until the customer pays for it is called **layaway**, or will-call. Layaway appeals to many shoppers and increases sales. The customer makes a deposit on the merchandise and agrees to pay for the purchase within a certain time period. The customer receives the merchandise when it is fully paid. If it is not paid for within the agreed-upon time, the goods are returned to stock. The deposit and any money paid need not be returned to the customer.

On-Approval Sales

An **on-approval sale** is an agreement permitting a customer to take merchandise (usually clothing) home for further consideration. Some department and specialty stores extend this special privilege to their regular customers. If the goods are not returned within an agreed-upon time, the sale is final. The customer must then send a check or return to the store to pay for the merchandise. Credit card information may be taken from the customer so that the sale can be processed if the customer keeps the item. This practice is a safe way for retailers to handle on-approval sales because there is much less risk involved.

Cash-on-Delivery Sales

A **cash-on-delivery (COD) sale** is a transaction that occurs when a customer pays for merchandise at the time of delivery. Because the customer must be on hand when the merchandise is delivered, however, COD sales are not as efficient as other types of sales transactions.

A MATTER OF ETHICS

Should You Tell Your Boss?

Mark works at Richard's Flowers, driving the delivery van. One day he notices that Richard has been charging his customers sales tax on the delivery charges. None of the customers has noticed this. Mark knows that in his state there is no tax on labor costs. He feels uncomfortable with the situation, but he likes his boss and doesn't want to lose his job. Mark tells Richard about the overcharging and discovers it has been done by mistake. Richard decides to write a note to all his customers, telling them about the mistake and offering a discount on their next orders.

THINKING ETHICALLY

Did Mark do the right thing by telling Richard that he had noticed the tax on delivery charges? What if Mark had been too afraid of losing his job to talk about it with Richard? If a customer had discovered the tax, how would that have affected Richard's business?

@ Online Action!

Go to *marketingessentials.glencoe.com/16/ethics* to find a project on overcharging.

Sales Tax

A **sales tax** is a percentage fee placed by the government on the sale of goods and services. Rates differ from state to state. State taxes are sometimes combined with local charges.

Who Pays a Sales Tax?

Sales tax is paid only by the final user, or the individual customer who, in most cases, is also the consumer. It does not apply to goods bought for resale. Consumers pay the cost of sales taxes. A sales tax is a regressive tax. It is assessed at a flat rate that applies to persons of all income levels. Thus, although a low-income person and a person with a higher income pay the same sales tax on the same item, the lower-income person is paying a higher percentage of his or her income in making the purchase. For this reason, some states exempt certain items, such as food, clothing, or medication from sales tax.

Sales Tax on the Internet

In the past several years, Internet sales have soared, and some states feel that they should have an easier time collecting tax on all state-to-state sales, including online sales. Legislation is being considered that would set up an Internet sales tax collection system.

The government does not want to put unreasonable burdens on small businesses selling through the Internet. Most of these mom-and-pop businesses do not have sophisticated computer software that could apply every state's unique tax policies to every transaction. But states complain that they cannot expect residents to keep perfect records of all their Internet transactions and to send the states the taxes that are due voluntarily.

Returns, Exchanges, and Allowances

A return is merchandise brought back for a cash refund or credit. Most businesses are happy to make exchanges because they want their customers to be satisfied. (See Figure 16.2.)

An **allowance** is a partial return of the sale price for merchandise that the customer has kept. These are usually given when there is a defect in the merchandise, such as a missing button.

Each of these situations requires a different type of sales transaction. Some businesses adopt a policy of no returns; however, most feel that accepting returns is an important part of good customer relations. Some businesses accept returns but only offer store credit that can be used to pay for other merchandise from the same business instead of a cash refund.

A transaction that involves returning an item for a replacement with the same price is an even exchange.

How to Handle Sales Tax in Return or Exchange Transactions

Suppose Duane decides he needs a laptop computer to help him keep up with his studies, but he wants a less expensive one than the one he was given for his birthday. The original computer was priced at $1,149 (excluding sales tax), and Duane wants to exchange it for

Figure 16.2 Refund Slip

• Refund Policy Most businesses give customers refunds or exchanges under certain circumstances.

Why do stores often insist that the customer have a sales receipt before giving a refund?

Nicky's Dress Shop — **REFUND SLIP**

STORE NO.	DATE	ITEM RETURNED	AMOUNT	
	8/17/--	SKIRT	45	00
NAME	Stacy McClintock			
ADDRESS	777 Seaview Lane			
CITY & STATE	Marblehead, MA 01945			
TELEPHONE NO.	781-882-0252	TAX	3	15
CUSTOMER'S SIGNATURE	*Stacy McClintock*	TOTAL AMOUNT	48	15
EMPLOYEE NO. 6P	AUTHORIZED BY *G. Smith*	REASON FOR RETURN Wrong color		
		No refunds after 30 days; No refunds without receipt.		

@ Online Action! **Go to *marketingessentials.glencoe.com/16/figure/2* to find a project on refunds.**

one priced at $895. To handle this transaction, you refund the difference, $254, plus the sales tax on $254. This procedure is reversed for a customer who wants to exchange an item for one that is more expensive. The customer pays the extra cost of the exchanged item and the extra sales tax on that amount.

Consider how a sales check is prepared. Each item is not taxed individually in multiple purchases; instead, the subtotal is used to calculate the sales tax. When looking at the sales check, simply find the item being returned, calculate the difference between that item and the item the customer is taking in exchange for the item returned, and determine the difference in tax on the two amounts. The customer has already paid tax on the original item, so tax is due only on the difference between the two items.

Shipping Charges

Not all purchases can be bought and carried home: Some items may be too bulky, and others are purchased via the phone or the Internet. Shipping is necessary and adds separate charges. Because delivery charges are generally exempt from sales tax, they are added after the sales tax has been calculated. The cost of shipping merchandise depends on the service used, the weight of the shipment, and the distance it is being sent.

PRACTICE 2

How much will be returned to or paid by the customer in each of the following cases? Assume a sales tax rate of 7 percent.

1. Mr. Williams returned a $330 lamp that did not put out enough light. He chose another style priced at $225. How much will you return to him?
2. Mrs. Crawford returned a $159 printer because it was apparently defective. She chose another model priced at $229. How much more will you charge her?

16.1 AFTER YOU READ

Reviewing Key Terms and Concepts

1. What is a sales check? What important information should it include?
2. How do the fees a merchant must pay for accepting credit card purchases compare with the fees for debit card purchases? What is the main reason merchants are willing to accept credit cards?
3. How are a return, an exchange, and an allowance different from each other?

Integrating Academic Skills

Math

4. A local department store had a 20 percent off everything sale. If you purchased items at $24.95, $5.95, and $34.99, what would be your total bill, assuming the sales tax rate is 5 percent?

Language Arts

5. Write an e-mail message to your boss explaining why your company should (or should not) accept credit card purchases over the Internet.

Check your answers at *marketingessentials.glencoe.com/16/read*

SECTION 16.2

Cash Registers

OBJECTIVES

- **Name the functions of cash registers and point-of-sale (POS) terminals**
- **Explain the uses for Universal Product Codes (UPCs)**
- **Make change**

KEY TERMS

- **Universal Product Code (UPC)**
- **point-of-sale system**
- **till**
- **opening cash fund**

READ and STUDY

BEFORE YOU READ

Predict What do you think are some of the functions performed by cash registers and point-of-sale terminals?

THE MAIN IDEA

The cash register or the point-of-sale station (POS) is the cashier's most important tool in completing a sales transaction. In some instances, it even assumes the cashier's role.

STUDY ORGANIZER

Draw the chart below. As you read this section, write in three methods of entering information in an electronic cash register and three safeguards against theft.

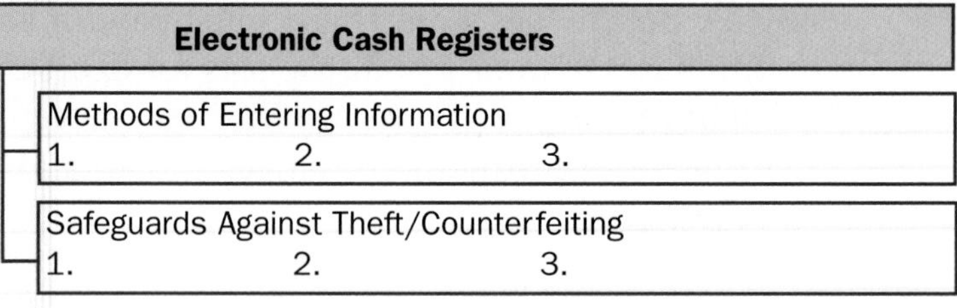

WHILE YOU READ

Compare Create a list of key differences among the methods of recording sales.

Cash Registers and Their Main Functions

After the sale of a product or service is finalized, we say the sale is closed. For accounting and tax purposes, a closed sale must be recorded. In most businesses, cash registers perform this function.

All cash registers, from the simplest to the most complex, perform three basic sales transaction functions:

1. **Recording sales** Cash registers provide a convenient way to enter information about a sale. This usually includes the department, the type of transaction, the salesperson, the amount of the sale, and the form of payment (cash, credit card, gift certificate, etc.). The salesperson also enters the amount of money given by the customer, and the cash register computes the amount of change the customer receives.
2. **Storing cash and sales documents** Cash registers provide a convenient, organized way to keep cash, personal checks, credit sales checks, and refund slips. Coupons and other sales-related documents may also be kept in the cash register drawer.
3. **Providing receipts** Cash registers automatically provide a receipt for the customer. This is the customer's record of the sale and proof of payment.

The Electronic Cash Register

Many businesses today utilize sophisticated electronic cash registers that perform multiple functions in addition to the three basic functions. These may include (1) figuring sales tax, (2) calculating discounts, (3) subtracting and crediting returns, (4) determining the amount due back to the customer, (5) tracking inventory, and, in some instances, even (6) automatically reordering stock.

Entering Data Into an Electronic Cash Register

Sales transaction data are entered into an electronic cash register in several ways:

- **Optical scanning** Supermarkets and other retailers, such as home improvement centers and discount chains, have improved their efficiency in recording sales transactions by installing optical scanners at checkout counters. Salesclerks drag items across the scanner so it can read the bar codes on the product packaging. If the scanner cannot read the code, the salesclerk must key the information manually.
- **Electronic wand entry** Many retailers (especially department and clothing stores) use electronic wands to enter sales transactions. The salesperson moves the point of the wand across the data printed on a tag attached to the article sold.
- **Manual key entry** Even with electronic cash registers, some businesses have their salespeople enter sales transactions manually, often by keying in a Universal Product Code (UPC) using the register keys. All registers provide a numeric keyboard for entry in case other input devices do not function properly.

Universal Product Codes

A **Universal Product Code (UPC)** is a combination bar code and number used to identify a product and manufacturer.

Every item a manufacturer sells must have a different item number. For example, different sizes of the same garment and different size containers of the same product must have distinct UPC codes.

UPCs have two parts: the machine-readable bar code and the human-readable UPC number. Bar codes, consisting of a series of vertical bars, are symbols printed on tags or on product packaging. The UPC number is the series of digits above or below the bar code.

The last number of the code is a check digit based on all the other digits: Every time a scanner reads an item, it uses a formula to calculate the check digit. If the check digit it calculates does not match the check digit it reads, the scanner signals that the item needs to be rescanned. After the coded information is scanned and entered into a register, it can be transferred to a computer for further processing.

Many electronic cash registers are linked to computers as part of a POS (point-of-sale) system. Using the data, the computer can update inventory records with each sale and automatically reorder items in short supply. It can store customer information and make it available for marketing or credit-check purposes. It can also print out financial statements, sales trends, and sales personnel productivity reports.

POS systems have screens that show the names of items scanned and their prices. These displays are usually elevated and angled so customers can easily see the information. After all of the items have been scanned and totaled and tax has been added, the display will show the total amount of the sale. When the customer tenders payment, the amount tendered and the change due the customer are displayed.

Current Trends

Several new trends have emerged and are changing the way business sales transactions are conducted and recorded. Several retailing chains have begun to offer their customers the option of using a self-service checkout. In a self-service lane at a typical grocery store, customers scan their own merchandise and weigh their own produce. They then enter payment in a self-service cash register, which allows them to pay with cash or via credit or debit card.

Integration of Point-of-Sale Information

A **point-of-sale system** combines a cash register with a computer, making it possible to capture information about the transaction at the time of the sale, then apply it to different functions. POS information is now used to trigger replenishment of stock and manufacturing of replacement merchandise.

For example, suppose that on a Saturday afternoon at a store in Atlanta, Georgia, a teenage shopper purchases a plaid skirt, size 8. The clerk processes the transaction at a POS terminal. On the following Monday afternoon, in Hong Kong, a computer technician downloads the information about the sale. On Wednesday, a factory worker in Hong Kong, pulls the same size skirt off the assembly line and boxes it to be shipped to Atlanta. All this happens automatically without anyone at the Atlanta store having to order a replacement.

Radio Frequency Identification

A new technology for sales transactions is radio frequency identification (RFID). With RFID, radio frequencies are used to read labels on products. An RFID tag is placed on cases and pallets by the manufacturer, who then labels each item with an Electronic Product Code (EPC). The tags are read by a radio signal reading machine as a customer passes his or her cart through checkout. This brand new technology makes it possible to read all the items in a cart simultaneously while they are still in the cart.

The Cash Drawer

Currency and checks collected in sales transactions are deposited in the till. The **till** is the cash drawer of a cash register.

Cash Drawer Arrangement

Usually, the till has ten compartments—five in the back and five in the front. Although some companies vary the arrangement, bills are usually kept in the back of the drawer and coins in the front.

In the section for bills, the first compartment on the left often remains empty. It is reserved for checks or other special items. The second compartment contains $20 bills, the third $10 bills, and the fourth $5 bills. The last compartment on the right is used for $1 bills. If a customer uses a larger bill, such as a $50 or a $100, many companies require that it be checked with a head cashier or a manager prior to being placed under the tray, where it is more secure.

In the section for coins, the first compartment on the left is used for silver dollars and half-dollars. The next compartment is for quarters, the following one for dimes, and the one after that for nickels. The last compartment on the right is for pennies.

This arrangement facilitates making change because the bill and coin compartments are related and in descending order of value. Each pair has at least one digit in common. The $20 bills are behind the quarters ($.25). The $10 bills are behind the dimes ($.10). The $5 bills are behind the nickels ($.05), and the $1 bills are behind the pennies ($.01).

Opening Cash Fund

At the beginning of each business day, the manager or other designated person provides a limited amount of money for the cash register, which is called the **opening cash fund**. This fund consists of the coins and currency, or bills, designated for the register for a given day's business. To verify the fund, the assigned person first counts the coins and places them, one denomination at a time, in the correct compartment; then he or she does the same with the currency.

As the coins and currency are counted, the amount is written down and then checked against the amount planned for the register. The change fund is even when the two amounts match exactly. When there is more than planned, the fund is over. If there is less than planned, the fund is short. An opening cash fund that is short or over should be reported immediately to the person who supplied the money so that it can be corrected or accounted for prior to the start of business transactions for that day.

Making Change

A salesperson who handles a large number of cash transactions may run short of certain denominations during the business day. Check your cash drawer during any downtime you have to see if you need any bills or coins, and request the change then. This procedure can prevent delays when customers are waiting for service.

Method 1: Making Change With a POS System

A POS system with a customer display makes it easy to count the correct change due the customer. You simply need to count out the change shown on the display. Begin with the largest denomination when using this type of machine. When the register displays $3.35 due the customer for a $16.65 purchase, select the change from the cash

MARKET TECH

Beyond Bar Codes

Radio frequency identification (RFID) may someday replace the bar codes used on products today. RFID uses miniature circuitry in a durable wireless transmitter called a tag. Some tags are so small that they can be embedded into almost anything—shipping pallets, clothing, credit cards, a tube of lipstick.

How Does It Work?

A tag can contain information about a product, the place of manufacture, its shipping history, and the date and time it was sold to the customer. Electronic readers take the information and feed it into a computer database. A computer can then perform a variety of operations. It can tell the retailer the last time a person purchased toothpaste or how often, and what type of books a customer bought.

RFID on the Road

RFID is already used by ten million motorists in the U.S. in the form of a tiny E-Zpass tag attached to their windshield. The E-Zpass tag allows them to drive through tollbooths and pay electronically.

THINK LIKE A MARKETER

How would RFID affect efficiency in delivering materials from suppliers to manufacturers? How might RFID affect marketing research, advertising, and selling?

Online Action!

Go to *marketingessentials.glencoe.com/16/tech* to find a project on radio frequency identification.

Practice 3: Make Change

How would you make or arrange for change in the following situations using the smallest number of bills and coins possible?

1. A customer gives you a $50 bill and a coupon worth $1 off one item to pay for a $23.19 purchase. What change would you give her?
2. A customer is buying two CDs that total $25.09, including tax. The smallest bills he has are two $20 bills, and he does not want too much change back. What is your response?
3. A customer gives you $30.25 for a $21.25 purchase. How would you count back the change?
4. You are a cashier at Caldwell Drugstore, and a customer gives you $10.75 to pay for a purchase of $3.55. Count the customer's change back to him. Why did he give you the change along with the $10 bill?

drawer by taking out three $1 bills, a quarter, and a dime. The customer knows from the display what change is due; so all you need to do is say aloud "$3.35" as you hand it to the customer.

Method 2: Making Change Without a Customer Display Screen

If your cash register does not have a customer display showing the change due, begin by announcing the total amount of the sale and then count up to the amount tendered. In doing this, be thorough and accurate, and follow these five steps:

1. Once the transaction has been entered in the cash register, announce to the customer the total amount of the sale. You might say, "That will be $16.65."
2. Announce the amount tendered when the customer offers payment in cash, saying, for example, "Out of a $20 bill."
3. Place the $20 on the cash drawer ledge and leave it there until you have given change to the customer. This eliminates most disputes over amount tendered.
4. Count silently while removing change from the cash drawer. The most common method is to count up from the purchase price, taking out smaller denominations of coins and currency first. Use as few coins as possible in making change.
5. Count aloud when handing the change to the customer. Say, "That's $16.65 out of $20. $16.75 (giving the customer a dime), $17 (giving a quarter), $18, $19, and $20 (giving three $1 bills, one at a time)."

Many customers avoid accumulating small change by tendering an odd amount of change to pay for their purchases. A customer might give you $20.39 for a sales total of $18.39. You would use the $.39 to cancel the "odd cents" of the sale and give change for the $20 bill. The same customer might also tender $20.50, in which case you would count the odd cents first, starting at $18.39.

Sales Tally

Salespeople and cashiers who use a cash register must account for the day's sales and money at closing. This process goes by a number of names, including *balancing the cash* and *balancing the till.*

Most cash registers automatically keep a sales tally, or summary of the day's sales. This makes the job of balancing the cash much simpler. The person responsible for each register counts the money and fills out a brief closing balance report. Then he or she removes the tape from the cash register and sends the money, report, and tape to management.

Safeguards Against Theft and Counterfeiting

Every employee who uses a cash register should be familiar with some safeguards against the theft of money. The first rule is to always close the cash drawer between transactions. While you are counting change to a customer, always partially close the drawer. Remove the money tendered by the customer from the register ledge after giving change. You should always lock the register if you leave it.

A customer may interrupt you while you are counting change. It is best to ignore the interruption. Don't allow yourself to get distracted, because this may cause you to make incorrect change. You can respond politely once the transaction has been completed.

Counterfeit bills show up in almost every city at some time, and it is important that cashiers routinely check all currency, particularly larger denominations, such as $20, $50, and $100 bills.

The best way to guard against counterfeit money is to become very familiar with U.S. currency. Every company should have printed information on how to identify counterfeit money. Genuine currency has tiny red and blue fibers embedded throughout. The portrait on a genuine bill appears lifelike and stands out distinctly from the background. Counterfeit portraits are usually lifeless and flat, with details merged into the background. Also, the fine-line printing on the border of a genuine bill is clear and unbroken. On a counterfeit, the lines on the border scrollwork may be blurred and indistinct.

New Currency Design

From time to time, changes are made to the design of U.S. currency to prevent counterfeiting. To make the currency more difficult to reproduce, in the late 1990s the U.S. Department of the Treasury redesigned most denominations with new security features. The redesigned bills include a polymer thread embedded vertically in the bill, concentric fine-line printing, a watermark, color-shifting ink, and an enlarged, off-center portrait. Beginning in 2003, subtle green, peach, and blue colors were featured in the background of $20 bills. The $5, $10, $50, and $100 bills were similarly redesigned. All the older bills will retain their value as long as they are in circulation.

16.2 AFTER YOU READ

Reviewing Key Terms and Concepts

1. What are three functions that all cash registers and POS terminals perform?
2. A customer gives you a $50 bill for a purchase of $34.29. Describe two ways you could count change back to her.
3. What is the Universal Product Code and how is it used?

Integrating Academic Skills

Math

4. The Big 12 Sports Mart sold 20 baseballs and 10 bats to a Little League team. The price for baseballs is $4.25 each and for bats is $17 each. Tax on sales is 7 percent. What is the total cost for the team?

History

5. Research the development of digital scanning technology and write a brief report.

Check your answers at *marketingessentials.glencoe.com/16/read*

SECTION 16.3

Purchase Orders, Invoices, and Shipping

OBJECTIVES

- Prepare purchase orders and invoices
- Explain delivery terms

KEY TERMS

- purchase order (PO)
- invoice
- terms for delivery
- free-on-board (FOB)

READ and STUDY

BEFORE YOU READ

Predict What do you already know about purchase orders and invoices?

THE MAIN IDEA

Writing a purchase order, creating an invoice, and figuring shipping may be part of the sales process, particularly when dealing with business-to-business sales.

STUDY ORGANIZER

Draw the chart below. As you read this section, write in the six types of information needed to complete a purchase order or an invoice.

Information Needed

Purchase Order	Invoice
1. Item number	

WHILE YOU READ

Compare Make a list of similarities and differences between purchase orders and invoices.

Purchase Orders

When a buyer for a business purchases supplies or merchandise from another business (business-to-business sale), the first step in the process is to prepare a purchase order. For vendors—those who sell to other businesses—the equivalent form is the invoice. The calculations for both forms are very similar to those performed by retail salespeople on sales checks.

A **purchase order (PO)** is a legal contract between the buyer and the supplier. This document lists the quantity, price, and description of the products ordered, along with the terms of payment and delivery. In Figure 16.3, notice the information routinely included in a purchase order:

- **Item number** The vendor's catalog designation for the merchandise ordered
- **Quantity** The number of units ordered
- **Description** What is being ordered
- **Unit** How the item is packaged and priced (individually, by the dozen, by the ream, etc.)
- **Unit cost** The price per unit
- **Total** The extension, or the result of multiplying the number of units by the cost per unit

Note that if you order several items on the same PO, the total of all extensions is entered at

Figure 16.3 Purchase Order

•A Legal Document A purchase order is a legal contract between a buyer and a seller.

How would you determine the extension cost of an item from the unit cost?

Mountain-Air

PURCHASE ORDER NUMBER: 1004

Invoice and ship to: Mountain-Air Bicycle Shop
123 State Street
Van Nuys, CA 91423

DATE: Oct. 15, 20 - -

Vendor: Sure-Tread Tire Company
782 Via Camino
Mission Viejo, CA 91626

ITEM NO.	QUANTITY	DESCRIPTION	UNIT	UNIT COST	TOTAL
T781	8	10-inch. wheels	ea.	$ 19.99	$ 159.92
K04	2	14-inch wheels	ea.	21.99	43.98
T77	4	20-inch wheels	ea.	24.99	99.96

TOTAL AMOUNT: $ 303.86
TAX 0.00
TOTAL DUE: $ 303.86

Go to *marketingessentials.glencoe.com/16/figure/3* to find a project on purchase orders.

the bottom of the total column. This amount is used to compute sales tax, if any.

Invoices

When filling an order based on a PO, a vendor will include an invoice with the delivered merchandise. An **invoice** is an itemized list of goods that includes prices, terms of sales, total, taxes and fees, and amount due. The invoice item numbers, quantities, unit costs, and extensions are correct when they match the PO.

Dating Terms

Dating terms state when a bill must be paid and the discount granted for paying early. Ordinary dating occurs when the dating terms are based on the invoice date. Consider, for example, ordinary dating of 2/10, net 30. This means that there will be a two percent discount if the buyer pays within ten days and that the invoice total must be paid within 30 days.

Shipping

As in retail sales transactions, shipping charges are not subject to tax. Therefore, you should add them after the tax is calculated. Shipping services vary greatly, from international companies that specialize in importing or exporting large quantities of goods to the U.S. Postal Service's regular mail service. Private package delivery companies and the post office's Express Mail service compete vigorously with each other in the extremely competitive overnight delivery market. They include Federal Express, UPS (United Parcel Service), and DHL Express.

Parcel Post

Parcel post is one type of standard surface package delivery that is offered by the U.S. Postal Service. Parcel post is a good option if there is time to take packages to the post office and if the customer is willing to wait for delivery.

• **FAST DELIVERY** Businesses can choose from a variety of shipping services offering next-day delivery.

How do you think this drop-off box influenced this person's decision to use Express Mail?

Cash on Delivery (COD)

With COD (cash on delivery) shipping, the postal carrier will collect the amount due from the customer and forward it to the company. The company must prepay the shipping charges. The amount due from the customer may include the total for both the merchandise and the shipping costs. The customer must pay a fee for the COD service, which varies depending on the amount collected.

Up to $500 may be collected on delivery by a postal carrier. Many businesses prefer using UPS for COD shipments. This is because UPS does not limit the amount that can be collected at delivery to $500 and the shipping charges do not have to be prepaid.

Delivery

Part of the selling arrangement negotiated between a buyer and seller involves delivery. This is an important negotiation point in business-to-business transactions. The issues are who will pay for delivery and when change of title (ownership) will take place. The final delivery arrangement between the buyer and seller, called **terms for delivery**, is part of every agreement in business-to-business sales.

Free on Board (FOB)

There are several possibilities for terms for delivery. All are variations of **FOB (free on board)**. FOB destination leaves title and ownership of the goods with the seller until the goods reach their destination. The seller pays for transportation. FOB shipping point makes the buyer responsible for shipping and for any damages during transit. With FOB factory freight prepaid, the seller pays for shipping but the buyer owns the goods in transit. With FOB destination charges reversed, the merchandise becomes the buyer's when goods are received. The buyer pays for shipping, but any damages are covered by the seller.

16.3 AFTER YOU READ

Reviewing Key Terms and Concepts

1. In business-to-business sales, who issues a purchase order (PO)? An invoice?
2. Define extension and explain how an extension is calculated on a purchase order or invoice.
3. You receive an invoice with the dating terms 2/10, net 30. What does that mean?

Integrating Academic Skills

Math

4. Calculate the extensions for these purchases:
   50 reams of printer paper at $5.95 each, 36 pens at $2.20 each, and 24 printer cartridges at $32 each.

Arts

5. You are the buyer for a company that sells computer games. Your boss has asked you to prepare a rough drawing of a new logo to appear on company purchase orders. Prepare a sketch in keeping with the products your company sells.

Check your answers at *marketingessentials.glencoe.com/16/read*

CAREERS IN MARKETING

KEVIN SHARPLES
CUSTOMER SERVICE MANAGER
STAGEPASS.COM INC.

What do you do at work?

We communicate with customers, mostly by e-mail, which has its own unique challenges. The most important is how we address the customer's concerns while being extremely conscious of the tone of our e-mails. Customers generally want to hear that they are, first, understood and second, that there is someone there to help. Taking time to fully understand the problem from the customer's point of view is critical.

What skills are most important to you?

Advertising may bring in business but customer service is what keeps them coming back and affects how they will speak to others regarding your company. The satisfaction comes in finding the resolution to their problem or answer to their question. It is then that you get the reward of a grateful customer, which usually builds loyalty. People remember how they are treated by a company, so the value of this department can never be overrated.

What is your key to success?

It takes a person who doesn't take things personally and welcomes a chance to make a wrong a right. The reward is a very grateful, happy customer. If you've done your job, they usually are appreciative and leave you with a smile and personal satisfaction. The key is you have to care.

Aptitudes, Abilities, and Skills

Writing and communication skills, patience, and problem-solving strengths are all valuable.

Education and Training

General business degrees can be helpful, although many companies prefer to train their customer service and POS staff in-house.

Career Path

Many customer service and POS jobs are entry level and can lead to a variety of different positions within the company.

THINKING CRITICALLY

Why is careful communication so important in a field where most contact takes place via e-mail?

Online Action!

Go to *marketingessentials.glencoe.com/16/careers* to find a research project on customer service.

CHAPTER 16 REVIEW

FOCUS on KEY POINTS

SECTION 16.1

- You may be called upon to handle several types of sales transactions. They may include cash sales, debit card or credit card sales, layaway sales, on-approval sales, and COD sales. You may also handle returns, exchanges, and allowances. Sales tax and shipping charges are normally added to the total price of products sold.

SECTION 16.2

- Most retail businesses today use electronic cash registers to record sales transactions. Many of these registers are linked to computers as part of a point-of-sale (POS) system. Electronic cash registers display the amount of change to be returned to the customer. Some businesses continue to use cash registers that do not display the amount of change to be returned to the customer. Therefore, knowing the two ways to count change as it is given to the customer is important. Some small businesses use handwritten sales checks to record sales.

SECTION 16.3

- To place an order, most companies prepare a purchase order. A purchase order includes the item number, quantity, description, unit, unit cost, and total (or extension) for each item ordered. When filling an order, a vendor prepares an invoice with the delivered merchandise. The invoice includes all of the information on a purchase order plus tax and shipping charges.

REVIEW VOCABULARY

Study each pair of terms and then, in your own words, tell how they are related to each other.

1. sales check (p. 335)—sales tax (p. 339)
2. layaway (p. 338)—on-approval sale (p. 339)
3. Universal Product Code (UPC) (p. 343)—point-of-sale system (p. 344)
4. till (p. 344)—opening cash fund (p. 345)
5. purchase order (PO) (p. 348)—invoice (p. 350)
6. terms for delivery (p. 351)—FOB (free on board) (p. 351)
7. cash-on-delivery sale (COD) (p. 339)—allowance (p. 340)

REVIEW FACTS and IDEAS

8. What are the various types of retail sales transactions? (16.1)
9. Name and explain the general content of sales checks and the basic ways of generating them. (16.1)
10. What is the arrangement of currency and coins in a cash register drawer? (16.2)
11. What are two methods of making change? (16.2)
12. What are two rules for safeguarding money at the cash register? (16.2)
13. Define Universal Product Code (UPC) and explain its uses. (16.2)
14. What are terms for delivery? Give three examples. (16.3)

BUILD SKILLS

15. **Workplace Skills**

Interpersonal Communication You work as a cashier, and today has been exceptionally busy. You give change to a woman for a $10 bill. She claims she gave you a $20 bill. Unfortunately, you neglected to leave the bill out while making change.

How would you handle this situation?

16. **Technology Applications**

Internet Search You work as a cashier in a children's clothing store where an older cash register requires entering the amount of each sale by hand. The owner of the store has asked you to research what POS systems would be appropriate for the store and how much these systems cost.

Use the Internet to do this research. Then use a word processing program to prepare a report.

17. **Math Practice**

Calculate a Sales Total You prepare a purchase order for the following: 144 shirts at $17.85 each, 72 shirts at $16.99 each, 72 shirts at $20.80 each, and 36 shirts at $22.60 each.

What is the total cost of the merchandise ordered?

DEVELOP CRITICAL THINKING

18. **Evaluate the Benefits of Technology**

The Universal Product Code (UPC) system was first used by grocery stores to speed checkout and help them keep track of their inventory.

Why do you think other retailers were so willing to adopt the system? What benefits does it provide them?

19. **Protect Your Business**

The loss to businesses from accepting counterfeit money is a serious problem, as counterfeiters use the latest technology to create ever-better reproductions.

If you were the head of a retail operation how would you protect yourself from this loss?

APPLY CONCEPTS

20. Comparing Purchase Order and Invoice Forms

Ask several local businesses for copies of their purchase orders and invoice forms. Explain to the business owners that you are requesting this information in order to complete a class project. You might also ask about any available information regarding the use of these forms.

Activity Use a spreadsheet program to compare the formats based on ease of use.

21. Comparing Sales Tax Rates

Choose five different states and research the sales tax rates that are applied there.

Activity Create a chart using a spreadsheet program comparing these rates.

NET SAVVY

22. Evaluating Effective Internet Selling

Research how easy it is to purchase items on the Internet. Also research the privacy protection for Internet purchases. Choose three e-tailers that interest you and focus your research on their sites.

Write a brief report detailing your findings, focusing on the strategies you thought were most successful.

THE 

CONNECTION

Role Play: Sales Associate

Situation You are to assume the role of an experienced sales associate for a gift shop located at the historic home of a well-known nineteenth-century author. The gift shop sells copies of the author's books, postcards, and other souvenir items. You are to help orient a new employee (judge) to the overall duties of a sales associate. The new employee (judge) has asked why math is necessary in selling since all the merchandise has price tickets and the register indicates the amount of change to give for cash transactions.

Activity You are to explain to the employee (judge) the importance of math for selling and how those skills will be useful.

Evaluation You will be evaluated on how well you meet the following performance indicators:

- Process cash and charge sales
- Process returns/exchanges
- Prepare cash drawers/banks
- Open/close register/terminal

@ Online Action!

For more information and DECA Prep practice, go to *marketingessentials.glencoe.com/16/DECA*

MARKETING INTERNSHIP

A SIMULATED DECA TECHNICAL SALES EVENT

Selling: LidRock Sales

BASIC BACKGROUND

LidRock sells soft-drink lids that hold mini CDs and DVDs. The current target markets include movie theaters, fast-food chains, and convenience stores—anywhere fountain soft drinks are sold. The content may include songs by popular artists, movie clips, video games, and computer screen savers, as well as special offers by advertisers, such as Internet service providers and other companies that target the demographic that purchases the soft drinks.

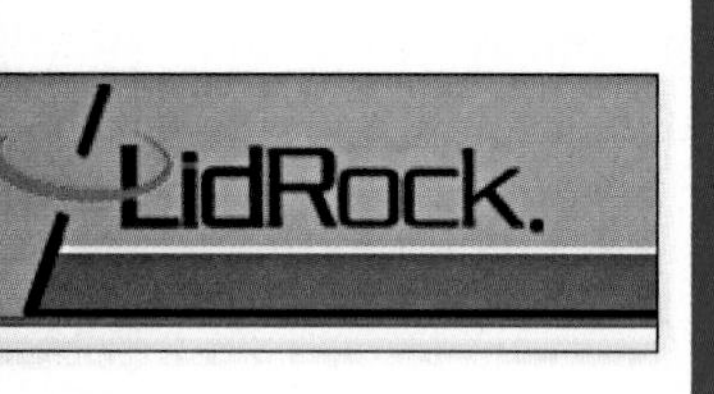

Extra Costs LidRock charges about 70 cents for each lid. The pizza and pasta chain Sbarro has been selling soft drinks with CD lids since 2003. It charges up to $1.50 extra, depending on the drink size and what's on the CD. Regal Cinemas haven't raised the price for drinks with CDs and DVDs.

YOUR OBJECTIVE

Your job is to design a Web-based presentation to sell these lid-tops with CDs and DVDs to businesses you believe would be interested in this new promotional medium. Since travel is expensive, the Web-based presentation must include all the steps of the sale, as well as tips for selling them at the retail level and recommendations for CD and DVD content based on the individual prospects you identified.

ASSIGNMENT AND STRATEGY

- **Get the background** Conduct research on LidRock and other companies that sell CDs and DVDs as promotional products. Investigate prospective customers—what businesses could use lid-top CDs and DVDs as part of their promotional mix? What are the major selling points and anticipated objections for this new medium? Review companies that offer Web conferencing software to see how you can set up an interactive sales presentation.
- **Develop the presentation** Identify three prospective customers and the CDs or DVDs that you would suggest for each one. Begin the written script for LidRock's Web-based sales presentation with an appropriate and attention-getting approach. Explain how the product should be depicted. Anticipate objections and prepare suggested responses. In your

script, provide a few examples of methods for closing the sale. Offer ideas that might convince customers, such as establishing an on-going partnership or creating a related promotion. Be sure to include ideas for training the retail counterpersons who will be selling the fountain drinks. Explain what will be done as a follow-up to ensure success for the customers.

- **What your project should include** Design the Web-based presentation using computer presentation software. It should be interactive and visually interesting, and use the sales techniques you've learned.

YOUR REPORT

Use a word processing program to prepare a written script to accompany the Web-based computer presentation that could be shown to LidRock. Use presentation software for the Web-based presentation and your oral presentation to our client. See a suggested outline and key evaluation points at *marketingessentials.glencoe.com/internship*

BUILD YOUR PORTFOLIO

Option 1 Internship Report Once you have completed your Marketing Internship project and presentation, include your written report and a few printouts of key slides from your oral presentation in your Marketing Portfolio.

Option 2 Preparing a Sales Training Manual Research a product of a company you like and its target market. Use what you learn to prepare a written sales training manual for that product. Prepare your written report using a word processing program. Use presentation software to prepare a program to train new employees in how to sell the product. See a suggested outline and key evaluation points at *marketingessentials.glencoe .com/portfolio*

Online Action!

Go to *marketingessentials.glencoe .com/Unit/5/DECA* to review sales concepts that relate to DECA events.

UNIT 6 Promotion

In this unit you will find

- Chapter 17 Promotional Concepts and Strategies
- Chapter 18 Visual Merchandising and Display
- Chapter 19 Advertising
- Chapter 20 Print Advertisements

Marketing Plan

ANALYZE THE AD

Kellogg's did not stray far from its traditional Corn Flakes logo when it introduced a new variation of its cereal. What impression does this ad make?

Market Talk Ready-to-eat (RTE) cereals came onto the market in the late 1800s. Early on, there were only a few varieties, including Shredded Wheat and Corn Flakes. By 1989, cereal makers were introducing more than 100 new kinds of cereal each year.

Think and Write Visit the cereal aisle of your local grocery store. What brands get prime position, in front of your eyes? Which ones are on the top shelves or down by your feet? Choose a cereal you think could have a better display. List three things you would do to change the product's design and display and to promote it.

Online Action! Go to ***marketingessentials.glencoe.com/u6/ad*** for an extended activity.

1 ANALYSIS
- SWOT
- Economic
- Socio-Cultural
- Technological
- Competitive

2 STRATEGY
- **Promotion**
- Place
- Price
- Product

3 IMPLEMENTATION
- Organization
- Management
- Staffing

4 BUDGET
- Cost of Sales
- **Cost of Promotion**
- Incomes and Expenses

5 CONTROL
- Evaluation
- Performance Measures
- Performance Analysis

In this unit

Foundations of Marketing
- Communication, Interpersonal Skills

Functions of Marketing
- Promotion

CHAPTER 17

Promotional Concepts and Strategies

Chapter Objectives

After reading this chapter, you should be able to:

- Explain the role of promotion in business and marketing
- Identify the various types of promotion
- Distinguish between public relations and publicity
- Write a news release
- Describe the concept of the promotional mix
- Define sales promotion
- Explain the use of promotional tie-ins, trade sales promotions, and loyalty marketing programs

GUIDE TO THE PHOTO

Market Talk Businesses must continually promote their organizations, products, services, and policies to gain customer loyalty and attract new customers. Promotion is an umbrella term that includes many activities. Consumers are well aware of advertising through large billboards. Promotion also includes public relations, publicity, and many forms of direct marketing.

Quick Think What promotional activity have you witnessed in the past week?

THE  CONNECTION

Performance indicators represent key skills and knowledge. Relating them to the concepts explained in this chapter is your key to success in DECA events. These acronyms represent DECA events that involve knowledge of concepts in this chapter.

AAAL	**FMAL**	**MMS***	**TMDM***
AAML*	**FMDM***	**QSRM***	**TSE***
ADC*	**FMML***	**RMAL**	**VPM**
BSM	**FSRM***	**RMML***	
EMDM*	**HMDM***	**SMDM***	

In all these DECA events you should be able to follow these performance indicators:

- Explain the communication process used in promotion
- Explain the role of promotion as a marketing function
- Explain the types of promotion
- Identify the elements of the promotional mix
- Explain the nature of a promotional plan
- Coordinate activities in the promotional mix
- Write a news release

All the events with an asterisk (*) also include these performance indicators:

- Obtain publicity
- Develop a public relations plan
- Analyze use of specialty promotions
- Design a frequency marketing program

Some events include additional performance indicators. These are:

FMDM Promote sales through community service activities

SMDM Select strategies for maintaining fan support

DECA PREP

Check your understanding of DECA performance indicators with the DECA activity in this chapter's review. For more information and DECA Prep practice, go to *marketingessentials .glencoe.com/17/DECA*

Promotion and Promotional Mix

OBJECTIVES

- **Explain the role of promotion in business and marketing**
- **Identify the various types of promotion**
- **Distinguish between public relations and publicity**
- **Write a news release**
- **Describe the concept of the promotional mix**

KEY TERMS

- **promotion**
- **product promotion**
- **institutional promotion**
- **advertising**
- **direct marketing**
- **sales promotion**
- **public relations**
- **news release**
- **publicity**
- **promotional mix**
- **push policy**
- **pull policy**

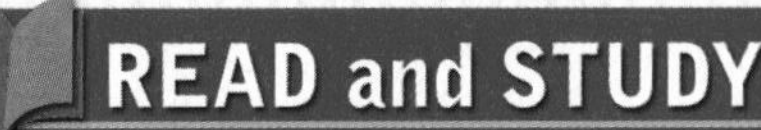

BEFORE YOU READ

Predict What would happen if businesses could not promote their products or services?

THE MAIN IDEA

The combination of advertising, selling, sales promotion, direct marketing, and public relations makes up the promotional mix.

STUDY ORGANIZER

In a chart like the one below, take notes about the five elements of the promotional mix and give examples for each.

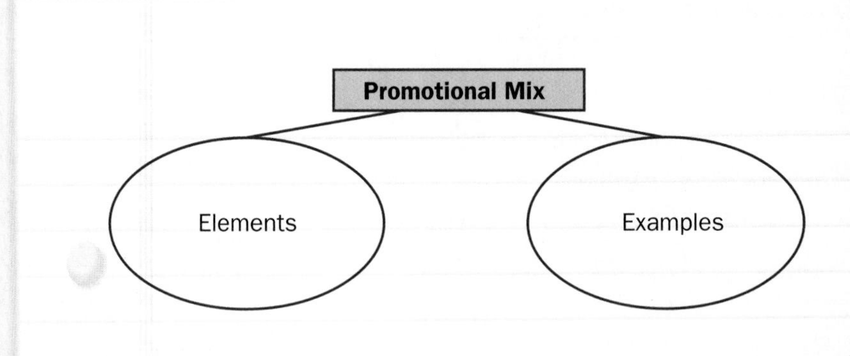

Describe How would you describe the various types of promotion?

The Concept of Promotion

Promotion is persuasive communication. Companies rely on promotion to inform people about their products and services. Companies also use promotional techniques to enhance their public image and reputation and persuade people that their products are valuable. Organizations such as nonprofits rely on promotional activities to educate the public about an issue or trend or to advocate for change in a law or policy. The goals of promotional activities are summarized by the phrase *AIDA*—first attract Attention, then build Interest and Desire, and finally ask for Action.

A business uses **product promotion** to convince prospects to select its products or services instead of a competitor's brands. Promotional activities explain the major features and benefits of the product or service, identify where it is sold, advertise sales, answer customer questions, and introduce new offerings. Product promotion also helps companies foster good relations with existing customers, thereby enhancing their loyalty.

Institutional promotion is used to create a favorable image for a business, help it advocate for change, or take a stand on trade or community issues. As part of its institutional promotional efforts, for example, businesses maintain Web sites to provide news, product and general information, and to answer questions. Although institutional promotions do not directly sell a product or service, these activities do foster a favorable image for the company, which in turn may help sales efforts.

Types of Promotion in the Promotional Mix

The combination of advertising, selling, sales promotion, direct marketing, and public relations makes up the promotional mix. There are five basic categories in the promotion mix and each plays a vital role in promoting businesses and their products. (See Figure 17.1.)

1. Personal selling
2. Advertising
3. Direct marketing
4. Sales promotion
5. Public relations

Through advertising, direct marketing, public relations, and sales promotion, companies communicate with customers in ways other than direct contact. Personal selling, on the other hand, requires direct personal contact with the customer.

Personal Selling

Personal selling requires that a company employ sales representatives who generate and maintain direct contact with prospects and customers. It is one of the costliest forms of promotion. Direct contact can take the form of personal meetings, telemarketing, e-mail contact, and correspondence. Typically, personal selling takes place after—or as a result of—other promotional activities.

Advertising

Advertising is a form of nonpersonal promotion. Companies pay to promote ideas, goods, or services in a variety of media outlets. Advertising can be found everywhere, from magazines, newspapers, television, and Web sites to gymnasiums and city buses. With advertising, a company engages in a one-way communication to the prospect or customer.

Direct Marketing

Direct marketing is a type of advertising directed to a targeted group of prospects and customers rather than to a mass audience. The two forms of direct marketing are printed direct mail, which is sent via regular mail to a home or business, and electronic direct mail.

The goals of direct marketing are to generate sales or leads for sales representatives to pursue. Generally, direct marketing generates a response from the targeted customer by making a special offer, such as a coupon, discount, or special merchandise and delivery terms. Direct marketing gives recipients an incentive to respond by visiting a store or Web site, calling a toll-free number, returning a form, or sending an e-mail.

Both print and electronic direct marketing allows a business to engage in one-way communication with its customers about product announcements, special promotions, bulletins, customer inquiries, and order confirmations. However, as a result of consumer complaints about unwanted electronic direct mailings, Congress passed the CAN-SPAM Act of 2003. This act requires senders of unsolicited

Figure 17.1 Elements of a Promotional Mix

• **Several Strategies, Same Goal** The promotional activities chosen to promote a particular product are known as its promotional mix.

How do the elements in a promotional mix work together?

Advertising Advertising is a one-way communication about a product with a potential customer. Advertising can be done through radio, television, billboards, newspapers, and the Internet.

Direct marketing Direct marketing sends a promotional message to a specific group of customers. It takes the form of printed mail or e-mail.

Sales promotions Sales promotions are activities directed at business or retail customers to boost sales. Sales promotions include coupons, product samples, and point-of-purchase displays.

Public relations Public relations are designed to influence opinion and to create a favorable public image of a person or a product. A campaign to encourage businesses to donate computers to schools is an example.

Personal selling Personal selling requires sales representatives to generate and maintain contact with customers through meetings, by phone, or by e-mail.

Online Action! Go to *marketingessentials.glencoe.com/17/figure/1* to find a project on the promotional mix.

commercial e-mail to give recipients a way to opt out of e-mails, prohibits the use of deceptive subject lines and headers, and requires businesses to provide valid return addresses on their e-mails.

Sales Promotion

According to the American Marketing Association (AMA), **sales promotion** represents all marketing activities—other than personal selling, advertising, and public relations—that are used to stimulate purchasing and sales. The objectives of sales promotions are to increase sales, inform potential customers about new products, and create a positive business or corporate image.

Public Relations and Publicity

Public relations (PR) activities enable an organization to influence a target audience. Often, public relations campaigns try to create a favorable image for a company, its products, or its policies. However, companies can rely upon public relations strategies and techniques for many reasons. One of the goals of a public relations program is to cultivate media relations with reporters who cover a specific industry.

Writing News Releases

Although there are many media tools, one of the most important ones is the **news release**. A news release is an announcement that is sent to the appropriate media outlets.

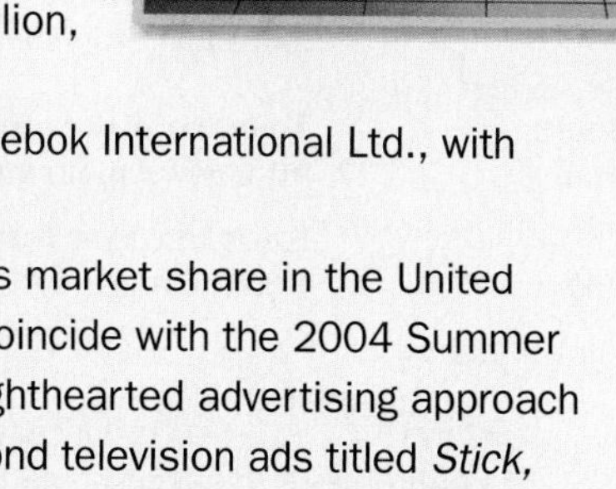

Puma's Advertising Approach

Puma AG is a German company that has an international reputation as an athletic footwear supplier for soccer, track, and baseball.

In 2003, the company had worldwide sales of $1.65 billion, but only 0.25 percent of the U.S. market share for athletic footwear. Puma trailed Nike, which had 45 percent, and Reebok International Ltd., with 9 percent of the U.S. market.

Using the Olympics as a Promotion Theme To increase its market share in the United States, Puma launched an advertising campaign timed to coincide with the 2004 Summer Olympics in Athens, Greece. The company bet that a fun, lighthearted advertising approach would bolster U.S. sales. The company ran 15- and 30-second television ads titled *Stick, Stick, Stick* and featuring Olympic athletes from Jamaica. As the athletes pass in front of different venues, such as markets or parks, viewers hear a loud "boing!" as the baton is passed off. Puma athletic shoes magically appear on the runner's feet.

Compare Puma's ad to most other athletic shoes ads. How is it different?

@ Online Action!

Go to *marketingessentials.glencoe.com/17/global* to find an activity about international marketing.

Figure 17.2 News Releases

• **Step-by-Step Directions** News releases sent via regular mail to media outlets should be double-spaced and printed on letterhead stationery. Margins should be about one-and-a-half inches to allow the editor to make notes. Always type copy so that it is clean, legible, and free of spelling errors. News releases distributed electronically or posted on the company's Web site are limited by the capability of the e-mail program or the Web site design.

What kind of news goes in a news release?

1 The first paragraph should answer the Who, What, When, Where, and Why questions.

MOTORCYCLE RIDING ACCESSORIES HIT THE WEB AT FULL SPEED

Dateline: July 15, 2004 ... Miami Beach, FL
Contact Name: Felix Mosqueda
Contact Phone: 1-888-309-5819
Web Address: http://www.moto-xtreme.com/

MIAMI BEACH, FL - July 15, 2004 - Motorcycle accessories are now just a click away at Moto-Xtreme.com. No more driving to the nearest city to find all of the name brand apparel, riding gear, helmets, boots, exhaust systems, tires and other sought-after accessories.

Enthusiasts of motorcycles, snowmobiles, scooters, personal watercraft and ATV's can search hundreds of products throughout the breathtaking selection at Moto-Xtreme.com, and have accessories delivered directly to their home.

With eighteen years' experience in the motorcycle business, and three years as an online Web source for accessories, the owners of Moto-Xtreme.com are very concerned about safety as well as style and quality. Bringing motorcycle riders the best possible products for safety and luxury is the number one goal at Moto-Xtreme.com.

"I'm X-tremely pleased with your pricing, selection and your speed of service!" states customer Andrew W. Bertsch.

Motorcycle riders will enjoy browsing the best buys, closeouts, discounts and new products sections at the site.

Also, the customer service group is knowledgeable, helpful, and available from 10 A.M. until 9 P.M., providing the best possible service to each individual. Shipping is available at only "a penny" on many major brands.

To learn more about Moto-Xtreme.com, please visit the Web site at:
http://www.moto-xtreme.com/

For an interview or further information, please contact Steve Sharts at 1-888-309-5819.

2 The story with important facts should be developed within the next few paragraphs.

3 When first identifying people in a news release, include the full name and title or position of the person, but avoid using Mr., Ms., Mrs., Dr., etc. After you have used the complete name refer only to the last name in the remaining part of the news release.

4 More information that is slightly less important can follow.

5 The entire news release should be brief—usually one or two pages is enough. If the news release runs more than one page, write "more" at the bottom of each page except the final one. Identify and number each succeeding page at the top. On the last page, put "---30---" or "###" at the bottom to signify the end of the news release.

6 The news release should always include the name, address, and phone number of the contact person sending out the release. All pages should be numbered except for the first page.

@ Online Action! Go to *marketingessentials.glencoe.com/17/figure/2* to find a project on news releases.

The release announces newsworthy developments about the company's products or services, distribution channels, facilities and operations, partners, revenues and earnings, employees, and events. (See Figure 17.2.)

Publicity is one tactic that public relations professionals use. Publicity involves bringing news or newsworthy information about an organization to the public's attention. This process is known as placement.

Although a publicity campaign can be launched to achieve various goals, the main function of publicity is to develop a positive perception or awareness of the organization in the marketplace. The right kind of publicity can create and maintain a company's positive image; negative publicity can devastate it. People like to do business with respectable companies, so companies engage in such image-building activities as sponsoring cultural events, awarding scholarships, and donating land or equipment for public use.

Unlike advertising, the placement of publicity is free. For example, a one-minute story on the evening news about a company costs nothing; fifteen seconds of advertising time on the same broadcast, however, can cost thousands of dollars.

Cost is not the only advantage of publicity. Newspapers, television and radio news programs, and reporters are usually viewed as more objective than advertisers. People are more likely to pay attention to and believe news stories than advertisements. Publicity often appears as a media story or is incorporated into a larger story or report, which makes the information appear more credible to many people.

The disadvantage of publicity is that its content, unlike paid advertising, is not easily controlled by the business that issues it. The media select the context and story angle and decide when and how to present the content. Negative stories, such as one reporting on an accident or an unsafe product, are as likely to get publicized as positive ones about company successes or community contributions. Whenever possible, businesses work to generate positive publicity and avoid negative publicity.

The Concept of Promotional Mix

To reach its promotional goals, an organization develops an effective **promotional mix**—a combination of strategies and a cost-effective allocation of resources. Most businesses use more than one type of promotion to achieve their promotional goals. How do companies decide which mix will be most effective? A business establishes a promotional mix by following a series of steps that range from identifying the target market to measuring the results.

The strategies in the mix are designed to complement one another. Advertising and direct marketing create awareness of a business's product, while public relations helps cultivate a favorable image and brand recognition. Sales promotional activities stimulate sales, reinforce advertising, and support selling efforts. Finally, personal selling builds on all of these previous efforts by completing the sale.

Elements of the promotional mix must be coordinated. For example, national advertising should be reinforced by local promotional efforts. Many consumer product manufacturers give or sell retailers decorations or in-store displays to reinforce a national campaign. At the local retail level, the national and local efforts need to be communicated to the store personnel. Sales personnel should be made aware of coupons, rebates, contests, and any other featured promotional items so that they can encourage customer participation. When promoted products are not available as advertised or when the sales staff is uninformed about a promotion, sales are lost and customers are dissatisfied.

Promotional Budget

In large companies, the marketing department has many roles. It determines the promotional mix, establishes the budget, allocates resources, coordinates the campaign, supervises any outside resources, and measures the results.

It is important to consider all aspects of the promotional mix when developing the promotional budget. Determining the ideal amount for the promotional budget can be difficult. There is no precise way to measure the exact results of spending promotional dollars. Often, a promotional budget is a percentage of sales. Sometimes, the budget is dictated by revenue and includes operational costs.

The Push-Pull Concept

Manufacturers often develop a promotional mix for each segment of the distribution channel. To promote a product to large retailers that sell its products, a manufacturer might want to use a mix of personal selling, advertising, and buying discounts. This type of promotion, known as the **push policy**, is used only with the next partner in the distribution channel. The manufacturer pushes the product to the retailer. The main purpose of the promotion is to convince a retailer to stock the products being promoted. A push strategy relies heavily on personal selling and sales promotion, especially at trade shows. It is a helpful strategy for manufacturers whose products do not have strong brand identity.

The same manufacturer might use a different promotional mix of local and national advertising, in-store displays, sales promotion, and public relations to reach consumers. The **pull policy** directs promotion towards consumers. This pull policy of promotion is designed to create consumer interest and demand. Consumer demand can pull or encourage retailers to carry the product being promoted. This strategy relies heavily on advertising geared to consumers, in addition to premiums, samples, and demonstrations.

17.1 AFTER YOU READ

Reviewing Key Terms and Concepts

1. What is promotion?
2. What is the difference between product and institutional promotion?
3. Describe the concept of promotional mix.

Integrating Academic Skills

Math

4. Your school store management team has established a promotional budget of $750 to be spent in the following manner: $300 for a print advertisement in the school yearbook; $125 for "two-for-one specials" on selected advertised items; $75 for premiums (pencils imprinted with the store name); $250 for a DECA scholarship to build public relations. What percentage of the budget is spent on each promotional category?

Social Studies

5. Watch the evening news on television. Write a 200-word report about a segment you think might be the result of corporate publicity.

Check your answers at *marketingessentials.glencoe.com/17/read*

Types of Promotion

OBJECTIVES

- Define sales promotion
- Explain the use of promotional tie-ins, trade sales promotions, and loyalty marketing programs

KEY TERMS

- sales promotions
- trade promotions
- consumer promotions
- coupons
- premiums
- incentives
- promotional tie-ins

READ and STUDY

BEFORE YOU READ

Predict How do you think a sales force can benefit from promotions?

THE MAIN IDEA

A business must continually promote its products. Sales promotion includes different techniques to increase sales and inform customers about a company's products or services.

STUDY ORGANIZER

Draw a two-column chart like the one below to list examples for each type of sales promotion.

Sales Promotions	
Trade Promotions	Consumer Promotions

Connect List three examples of how you have responded to sales promotions in the past.

Sales Promotion

Sales promotions are incentives that encourage customers to buy products or services. Sales promotions can be used to encourage customers to try a new product, build awareness, increase purchases by current customers, or reward loyalty. Sales promotions are usually supported by advertising activities. They may be either business-to-business (B2B) or business-to-consumer (B2C) oriented.

Trade Promotions

Trade promotions are sales promotion activities designed to get support for a product from manufacturers, wholesalers, and retailers. More money is actually spent on promoting to businesses than to consumers. Major trade promotions include promotional allowances, cooperative advertising, slotting allowances, sales force promotions, and trade shows and conventions. Good business ethics require that trade promotional payments and awards be offered in a uniform manner, that terms be clearly spelled out, and that no one be penalized for not achieving the goals, among other requirements.

Promotional Allowances

Promotional allowances represent cash payments or discounts given by manufacturers to wholesalers or retailers for performing activities to encourage sales. For example, promotional allowances are sometimes used to encourage wholesalers or retailers to stock a large quantity of a product. The cash payment or price discount gives wholesalers and retailers an incentive to sell, so they are more likely to promote the product to customers.

Cooperative Advertising

A manufacturer supports the retailer by helping to pay for the cost of advertising its product locally. This practice is known as cooperative advertising.

Slotting Allowances

A slotting allowance is a cash premium paid by a manufacturer to a retailer to help the retailer cover the costs of placing the manufacturer's product on the shelves. Slotting allowances can range from a few thousand dollars to several million dollars per product. In addition to buying space in the store, slotting allowances also pay for a retailer's discount specials on a product, charges for store shelves, penalties for poor sales, store advertising, and display costs.

Sales Force Promotions

Sales force promotions are awards given to dealers and employees who successfully meet or exceed a sales quota. Such quotas can apply to a specific period of time, such as a month, one day, or a year, or for a particular product or line of products.

Sales force promotions vary from business to business, but they may include cash bonuses or prizes such as merchandise or travel awards.

Trade Shows and Conventions

Trade shows and conventions showcase a particular line of products. One of the largest trade shows is the annual Consumer Electronics Show in Las Vegas, which attracts more than 190,000 manufacturers, retailers, product engineers, and developers. Many participating companies invest millions of dollars in their display booths. Trade shows provide businesses with opportunities to introduce new products, encourage increased sales of existing products, meet customers and partners in the distribution chain, and gain continued company and product support.

Consumer Promotions

Consumer promotions are sales strategies that encourage customers and prospects to buy a product or service. Consumer promotions support advertising, personal selling, and public relations efforts. Major consumer sales promotion devices include coupons, premium deals, incentives, product samples, sponsorships, promotional tie-ins, product placement, loyalty marketing programs, and point-of-purchase displays.

Coupons

Coupons are certificates that entitle customers to cash discounts on goods or services. Manufacturers use coupons to introduce new products, to enhance the sales of existing products, and to encourage retailers to stock and display both.

Coupons are placed on or inside product packages, or printed in newspapers and magazines. Increasingly, companies are

•ENTICE WITH REBATES Coupons are used for a variety of reasons: making a new product more visible, reducing stock, or attracting customers in hopes they will also purchase other merchandise.

What is this rebate offer promoting?

using strategies to drive consumers online to download and print electronic coupons or to redeem printed coupons by purchasing merchandise sold online.

Stores that accept coupons send them to the manufacturers' headquarters or to a clearinghouse to be sorted and passed along to redemption centers. The centers, in turn, reimburse the stores for the face value of each coupon plus a handling charge of about eight cents per coupon. They then bill the manufacturers.

Premiums

Premiums are low-cost items given to consumers at a discount or for free. They are designed to increase sales by building product loyalty, and attracting new customers. They also can persuade nonusers to switch brands.

The fundamental concept behind premium marketing is that people will be more motivated to buy a product when they are offered an added-value gift in exchange. Three types of popular consumer premiums are factory packs, traffic builders, and coupon plans.

Factory packs, or in-packs, are free gifts placed in product packages, or as a container premium. This form of premium is especially popular with cereal manufacturers.

Traffic builders are low-cost premiums, such as pens, key chains, pocket calendars, and coffee mugs, that are given away to consumers for visiting a new store or for attending a special event.

•PREMIUMS Giveaways such as this one encourage customers to visit the store or service provider.

Which two goals does this premium offer seek to accomplish?

Coupon plans are ongoing programs offering a variety of premiums in exchange for labels or coupons obtained from a product or label. A customer might send a manufacturer three soup-can labels in exchange for a recipe book.

Deals

Deals or price packs offer short-term price reductions that are marked directly on the label or package. The deal might feature two similar products bound together for the price of one or two related products, such as Bausch & Lomb's Renu contact lens cleaner and its multipurpose wetting solution.

Incentives

Businesses use **incentives** to promote many products because they create customer excitement and increase sales. Incentives generally are higher-priced products earned and given away through contests, sweepstakes, and rebates.

Contests are games or activities that require the participant to demonstrate a skill. Contest winners win such prizes as scholarships, vacations, and money.

Sweepstakes are games of chance. (By law in most states, no purchase is necessary in order to enter a contest or sweepstakes.)

Rebates are discounts offered by manufacturers to customers who purchase an item during a given time period. Auto and household appliance manufacturers frequently use rebates to encourage customers to buy their products.

Product Samples

Another form of consumer sales promotion is the product sample. A product sample is a free trial size of a product sent through the mail, distributed door-to-door, or given away at retail stores and trade shows. Detergents, toothpastes, shampoos, deodorants, and colognes are frequently promoted this way. Samples are especially important in promoting new products. Drug manufacturers frequently give samples to doctors and dentists so they can let their patients try new products.

Sponsorship

Sponsorship has become an integral part of promotion. The sponsoring company pays a fee for the right to promote itself and its products or services at or on a set location. The location can be a physical site (such as a stadium), an event (such as a concert), a group (such as a car racing team), or a person (such as a golfer or tennis player).

Sponsors often negotiate the right to use logos and names on retail products. A title sponsor is an organization that pays to have its name incorporated into the name of the sponsored location, such as the Mattel Children's Hospital at the University of California in Los Angeles.

Sponsorship is a high-profile promotional medium. Therefore, deals must be able to withstand public and media scrutiny. The effectiveness of the sponsorship is measured among those who actually view the title or logo.

Promotional Tie-Ins, Cross-Promotion, Cross-Selling

Promotional tie-ins are also known as cross-promotion and cross-selling campaigns. These activities involve sales promotional arrangements between one or more retailers or manufacturers. They produce mutually beneficially results.

Partners combine their resources (advertising and sales promotional activities) to conduct a promotion that will create additional sales for each partner. Promotional tie-ins as well as cross-promotional and cross-selling campaigns can be complex and involve several companies. This practice is becoming increasingly popular on the Internet; for example, a traditional marketer will offer an incentive for consumers to go online to make a purchase or receive a discount from an online marketer.

Product Placement

Product placement is a consumer promotion that involves using a brand-name product in a movie, television show, sporting event, or even in a commercial for another product. For example, in the *Survivor* television series, winning teams were given Doritos and Mountain Dew as treats. Strategic product placement helps an organization develop recognition for its products and gain increased exposure. One of the best-known examples for product placement took place in the Warner Brothers movie *You've Got Mail,* which featured America Online (AOL). The onscreen exposure in this movie is said to have cost AOL between $3 and $6 million. As a result, Warner Brothers was able to offset

NET MARKETING

Supermarket Shopping Online

Although online groceries represent only 5 percent of a $400 billion supermarket business, online sales are projected to grow in the future. Many customers prefer the ease of shopping online and filling their virtual shopping carts at home. Items ordered online are delivered the next day for about $10 per order. For some shoppers, the convenience is worth the cost.

Expansion Strategy

While several online grocers have failed in the past because of costly high-tech warehouses and rapid expansions, stores like Albertson's, Publix Super Markets, Inc., and Safeway are limiting their expenses by using individual stores rather than costly warehouses to fill orders. Their e-business segments are also expanding slowly, often one city or neighborhood at a time.

THINK LIKE A MARKETER

Suggest how online grocers can promote online shopping and avoid high promotional costs.

@ Online Action!

Go to *marketingessentials.glencoe.com/17/net* to find an activity about Internet promotion and shopping.

Case Study

Plastic That Pays Back

Credit card companies know that consumers are more loyal to brands than they are to their cards. They understand that consumers will respond to the card with the best (lowest) rate. Consumers will easily switch credit cards. It is not surprising, therefore, that credit card issuers align themselves with consumer brands.

Co-Branding

Many financial institutions offer credit cards branded with the names of consumer companies. This type of arrangement is known as co-branding.

The specifics of co-branded cards vary quite a bit, but generally, for each dollar you charge, you receive a point. Points can be redeemed at affiliated companies—for lattes with your Starbucks-branded card, for chinos with your Gap-branded card, or for flights with your Delta-branded card. The number of accounts offering rewards jumped from 35 million to 56 million in 2003 according to the industry-tracking Nielson Report. According to Synovate, a market-research firm, U.S. households received 263 million pitches for co-branded credit cards in the last quarter of 2003, up 35 percent from the same period the year before.

THINK STRATEGICALLY

Why are loyalty programs involving co-branded credit cards growing in popularity?

Online Action!

Go to *marketingessentials.glencoe.com/17/case* to find an activity about financial marketing.

its production costs and create a realistic film, while AOL received international film exposure for its product and services. Another popular example is the movie character James Bond, who is known as much for his Rolex watch and Aston-Martin as he is for his prowess.

Loyalty Marketing Programs

Loyalty marketing programs, also called frequent buyer programs, reward customers for patronizing a company.

The airline industry instituted one of the first such promotions, the frequent flier program. These programs reward customers with free air travel once they have accumulated a designated amount of travel miles.

The hotel industry has adopted similar programs in which consumers can earn free lodging by spending a designated number of nights or dollar amount on lodging.

Customer loyalty means that customers are so satisfied with a brand or retailer that they continue to buy that brand or patronize that retailer even when they have others from which to choose. Loyalty marketing offers consumers incentives to continue to buy.

Both small and large businesses in many industries have adopted loyalty marketing programs. T.G.I Friday's, a restaurant chain, has a Gold Points card program; customers can earn points and trade them for dining certificates and catalog merchandise.

Online Loyalty Marketing

Online versions of loyalty marketing programs have also become popular. The Internet search engine Yahoo! awards points to Web surfers who buy from certain retailers or visit certain Web sites. Yahoo! has negotiated with the airline industry to allow consumers to convert their points into frequent flier miles.

Point-of-Purchase Displays

Point-of-purchase displays are displays designed primarily by manufacturers to hold and display their products. They are usually placed in high-traffic areas and promote impulse purchases.

By exposing potential customers firsthand to a company's products, point-of-purchase displays stimulate sales and serve as in-store advertising. A complete discussion of visual merchandising and display can be found in Chapter 18.

17.2 AFTER YOU READ

Reviewing Key Terms and Concepts

1. Why do businesses use sales promotions?
2. Explain the difference between trade and consumer promotions.
3. What are the purposes of promotional tie-ins?

Integrating Academic Skills

Math

4. Promotional discounts are given to stores by manufacturers to place products in preferred locations or to pay for ads, displays, or in-store demonstrations. Calculate the store's cost to stock the following items and the percentage of the discount given.

Item	Purchase Amount	Discount Amount	Net Cost to Store	Percent Discount
Snowboards	$5,650	$847.50	_____	_____
CD Players	$535	$42.80	_____	_____

Language Arts

5. Perform an Internet search or visit a library to identify some of the advantages and disadvantages that manufacturers face when they issue product coupons. Identify and label them in a two-column table.

Check your answers at *marketingessentials.glencoe.com/17/read*

CAREERS IN MARKETING

OLGA GARCIA
MANAGER, CORPORATE RELATIONS COORS BREWING COMPANY

What do you do at work?
My position is Manager, Corporate Relations, Coors Brewing Company. My emphasis is on the Latino community, developing relevant corporate initiatives and sales opportunities that enhance the company's image and build brand awareness.

What skills are most important to you?
The ability to communicate effectively both written and verbally, in both Spanish and English, to a variety of audiences: the Latino public, the general market and Latino press, community leaders, internal departments, our distributors, agencies and senior management. A formal education (bachelor and masters degrees) in communications, journalism, government affairs and business administration is very important, as well as formal education in the Spanish language. Continuing education as a professional is critical to success, especially in leadership development.

What is your key to success?
Ongoing evaluation of your career goals with a mentor. A good mentor can help you identify areas of improvement to realize your maximum potential and a game plan to help you achieve your career goals. The work-family life plan should be included in goals to set realistic expectations that can be achieved throughout your life cycle. And don't be afraid to move out of your comfort zone!

Aptitudes, Abilities, and Skills

Communication and interpersonal skills are crucial in this career.

Education and Training

Degrees in communication, business administration, and marketing are all helpful; Masters-level degrees can be especially beneficial.

Career Path

Careers such as this one often begin with entry-level positions within a company's marketing or public relations department, and evolve over time as the employee becomes familiar with the company's products and services, and how best to present them to the public.

THINKING CRITICALLY

How can a mentor help with your career development? How should you go about choosing a mentor?

Go to *marketingessentials.glencoe.com/17/careers* to find a career-related activity.

CHAPTER 17 REVIEW

FOCUS on KEY POINTS

SECTION 17.1

- Promotion is any form of communication a business uses to inform, persuade, or remind people about its products and its image. Promotion includes personal selling, advertising, direct marketing, sales promotion, and public relations.
- Public relations fosters a favorable image about a business, its products, or its policies. Publicity tries to place positive information in the media.

SECTION 17.2

- Sales promotion is a short-term incentive given to encourage consumers to buy a product or service. Sales promotions can be classified as either trade promotions or consumer sales promotions.

REVIEW VOCABULARY

Write a sentence for each of the following terms.

1. promotion (p. 362)
2. product promotion (p. 363)
3. institutional promotion (p. 363)
4. advertising (p. 363)
5. direct marketing (p. 363)
6. sales promotion (p. 365)
7. public relations (p. 365)
8. news release (p. 365)
9. publicity (p. 367)
10. promotional mix (p. 367)
11. push policy (p. 368)
12. pull policy (p. 368)
13. sales promotions (p. 369)
14. trade promotions (p. 370)
15. consumer promotions (p. 370)
16. coupons (p. 370)
17. premiums (p. 371)
18. incentives (p. 372)
19. promotional tie-ins (p. 373)

REVIEW FACTS and IDEAS

20. List the five basic types of promotion. (17.1)
21. What is the purpose of public relations? (17.1)
22. Explain the differences between trade promotions and consumer sales promotions. (17.2)
23. Explain the difference between contests, sweepstakes, and rebates. (17.2)
24. Explain the concept of product placement. (17.2)

BUILD SKILLS

25. Workplace Skills

Human Relations Each month at your company, a certain amount is automatically deducted from managers' paychecks and donated to established charities. Your boss has asked you to participate. You are reluctant because you already donate to your own charities, and you prefer to decide where your money goes. How would you explain your position?

26. Technology Applications

E-Coupons Perform an Internet search to find examples of electronic coupons and use a word processing program to prepare a brief report on the advantages of electronic coupons as promotional devices. Explain how e-coupons are used.

27. Math Practice

Figure Out Promotional Expenditures A large amount of money is spent annually on promotional activities in the United States. The average budget spent on any one campaign breaks down as follows: 53 percent for advertising, 27 percent for sales promotion, and 20 percent for trade promotion.

Use these percentages to calculate the amount a company will spend on each type of promotional expenditure to promote a product in the United States if its overall budget is $1.2 million.

DEVELOP CRITICAL THINKING

28. Understanding Promotional Devices

Research the advantages and disadvantages of coupons as promotional devices. Gather coupons from a local newspaper, magazines, or the Internet. Use these coupons to give specific examples of pros and cons.

29. Researching Publicity

Identify an event that resulted in negative publicity for a business or person. You can find examples by reading through national newspapers (in the business pages) and magazines, or by performing an Internet search. Even simple key words such as *negative publicity* will yield some examples. Summarize the situation for your chosen examples. Explore how the outcome could have been avoided or how negative publicity could have been minimized.

APPLY CONCEPTS

30. Planning Promotions

Plan a promotion for a product of your choice. Describe your target market, as well as the public image you would like for your product. Choose a product name and explain why it will appeal to your audience. Describe where you will sell your product (catalog, retail store, discount store, or industry). Discuss any premiums you might offer to promote your product.

Activity Use a word processing program to write a report about your plan.

31. Analyzing Promotions

Choose a product that is heavily promoted in the marketplace. Answer the following questions in your analysis: What market is being targeted? What type of image is the company trying to project? What types of promotion are used? Are the promotions effective? Why or why not?

Activity Prepare an oral analysis of the product using presentation software.

NET SAVVY

32. Internet Promotions

Perform an Internet search to identify three different retail apparel companies that are of interest to you. Summarize at least one Web-based promotional effort used by each company this year. Include in your summaries what you think the goals of the promotions were.

THE DECA CONNECTION

An Association of Marketing Students

Role Play: Promotional Concepts and Strategies

Situation You are to assume the role of employee of a service station that also has an attached convenience store. The station owner (judge) is an enthusiastic fan of the local professional football team. The station owner (judge) has decided to celebrate the team's victories by offering free coffee on Monday's following a victory by the football team.

Activity The station owner (judge) has asked you to prepare a report with an outline for a promotional plan for the free coffee promotion.

Evaluation You will be evaluated on how well you meet the following performance indicators:

- Develop a sales promotion plan
- Analyze the use of specialty promotions
- Explain the types of promotion
- Identify the elements of the promotional mix
- Prepare simple written reports

@ Online Action!

For more information and DECA Prep practice, go to *marketingessentials.glencoe.com/17/DECA*

CHAPTER 18
Visual Merchandising and Display

Chapter Objectives

After reading this chapter, you should be able to:

- Explain the concept and purpose of visual merchandising
- Identify the elements of visual merchandising
- Describe types of display arrangements
- Understand the role of visual merchandisers on the marketing team
- List the five steps in creating a display
- Explain how artistic elements function in display design
- Describe the importance of display maintenance

GUIDE TO THE PHOTO

Market Talk Window display is often the first contact the customer has with merchandise. This type of display is used especially in fashion retail. Displays can set the tone for the store (high-end, professional, or young and trendy). Window displays can even become a tradition, such as Chicago's Marshall Field's displays.

Quick Think Besides fashion retail, which other business categories rely heavily on displays?

THE  CONNECTION

Performance indicators represent key skills and knowledge. Relating them to the concepts explained in this chapter is your key to success in DECA events. These acronyms represent DECA events that involve knowledge of concepts in this chapter.

AAAL*	**FMDM**	**HMDM**	**RMML***
AAML*	**FMML***	**QSRM***	**TMDM**
FMAL*	**FSRM***	**RMAL***	**VPM***

In all these DECA events you should be able to follow these performance indicators:

- Prepare store/department for special event
- Dismantle/Store displays/display fixtures/forms
- Create promotional signs

All the events with an asterisk (*) also include these performance indicators:

- Explain the use of visual merchandising in retailing
- Describe types of display arrangements
- Maintain displays
- Select and use display fixtures/forms
- Create displays

Some events include additional performance indicators. These are:

AAAL/AAML	Arrange trunk showing (apparel)
FMAL/FMML	Build food marketing displays
FSRM/QSRM	Explain display considerations in food service
RMAL	Plan/Schedule displays/themes with management
RMML	Inspect/Approve displays
VPM	Set up point-of-sale displays and handouts

DECA PREP

Check your understanding of DECA performance indicators with the DECA activity in this chapter's review. For more information and DECA Prep practice, go to *marketingessentials .glencoe.com/18/DECA*

Display Features

OBJECTIVES

- Explain the concept and purpose of visual merchandising
- Identify the elements of visual merchandising
- Describe types of display arrangements
- Understand the role of visual merchandisers on the marketing team

KEY TERMS

- visual merchandising
- display
- storefront
- marquee
- store layout
- fixtures
- point-of-purchase displays (POPs)
- kiosk

BEFORE YOU READ

Predict Why are displays an important part of promotion?

THE MAIN IDEA

Visual merchandising and displays are important promotional strategies to sell products and services, attract potential customers, and create a desired business image.

STUDY ORGANIZER

Use a chart like the one below to take notes on the basics of merchandising and display.

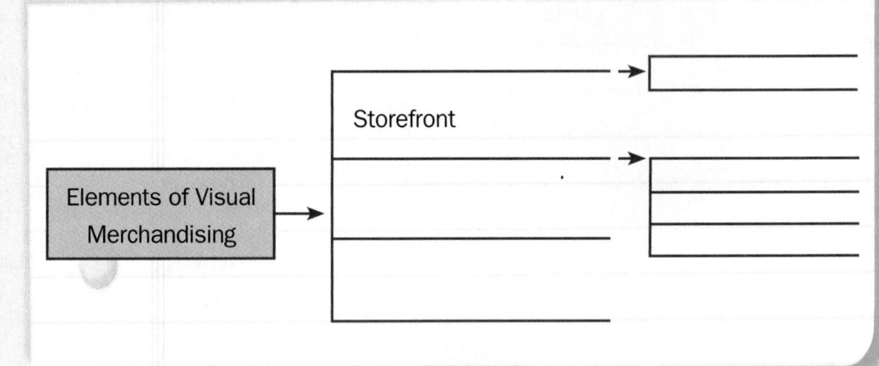

WHILE YOU READ

Connect Think about one of your favorite stores. As you read this section, visualize and list examples of visual merchandising in that store.

Visual Merchandising and Display

Visual merchandising encompasses all of the physical elements that merchandisers use to project an image to customers. Visual merchandising promotes interest in merchandise or services, encourages purchasing, and reinforces customer satisfaction.

The term *visual merchandising* is sometimes used interchangeably with the term *display,* but they are not the same. Display is a much narrower concept and makes up only one element of visual merchandising. **Display** refers to the visual and artistic aspects of presenting a product to a target group of customers. Visual merchandising, by contrast, encompasses the visual and artistic aspects of the entire business environment.

The Role of the Visual Merchandiser

Visual merchandisers are responsible for the total merchandise or service presentation, the overall business/brand image, and even the building and placement of design elements. They are active members of the marketing team that promotes a business and its products or services.

Elements of Visual Merchandising

One goal of visual merchandising is to create a positive shopping experience that will compel customers to return. Merchandisers consider four elements key to achieving this goal: storefront, store layout, store interior, and interior displays.

Storefront

The exterior of a business is known as the storefront. The **storefront** encompasses a store's sign or logo, marquee, banners, awnings, windows, and the exterior design, ambiance, and landscaping. Consider Target stores, which are typically large buildings with bold graphics, a logo, bright red colors, a convenient location near a main highway, and a large, well-lit parking lot to attract customers, provide safety, and assist with security. Storefronts project brand identity and help the company distinguish itself from its competitors and surrounding stores.

Signs

Signs are designed primarily to attract attention, advertise a business, and project brand identity. The design of the sign should be original and easily recognizable. The name, letters, logo, materials, and colors that are used help create the desired store's image. An upscale department store might use an elegant script, while a toy merchandiser would use bright primary colors to reinforce a youthful and playful image.

Marquee

A **marquee** is an architectural canopy that extends over a store's entrance. Marquees can be found over most theater entrances, where names of the latest plays or movies are

A MATTER OF ETHICS

Advertising Food to Children

According to government statistics, about 20 to 30 percent of children in the United States are either overweight or at risk of becoming overweight. The Kaiser Family Foundation reviewed more than 40 studies on the role of the media in childhood obesity.

Television and Fast Food

It found that kids today see an estimated 40,000 television ads a year, compared with about 20,000 a year in the 1970s. Many of today's ads are for candy, cereal, and fast food.

Although the report did not endorse one specific solution to the problem, it recommended that parents limit television viewing time for their children. In addition, the report recommended that food advertisements to children be reduced or regulated.

THINKING ETHICALLY

Do you think that it is ethical to target food ads to children? Why or why not? Should the government develop regulations? Why or why not?

@ Online Action!

Go to *marketingessentials.glencoe.com/18/ethics* to find an activity on ethics and promotion.

• **STORE DISPLAYS** Pet stores organize their displays for each type of pet. Cat food is usually close to accessories displays with cat litter, toys, and water bowls.

How does a display of related items help customers find exactly what they want?

highlighted. Marquees also can display the store's name and its key products as well as hours of operation and a phone number or URL address. A marquee is highly visible, and a company can exploit the space for advertising.

Entrances

Entrances are usually designed with customer convenience and store security in mind. Smaller stores normally have only one entrance, while larger ones have several. The average midsize business needs at least two entrances—one leading in from the street for pedestrians and another adjacent to the parking lot for patrons who drive.

Window Displays

Display windows are especially useful for visual merchandising. Window displays initiate the selling process, create excitement, and attract prospects.

Store Layout

Store layout refers to ways that stores use floor space to facilitate and promote sales and serve customers. A typical store layout divides a store into four distinct spaces:

- **Selling space** is used for interior displays, wall and floor merchandise, product demonstrations, sales transactions, and aisles for customer traffic flow.
- **Storage space** is for items that are kept in inventory or stockrooms.
- **Personnel space** is allocated to store employees for office space, lockers, lunch breaks, and restrooms.
- **Customer space** is designed for the comfort and convenience of the customer and may include sandwich, soda, and coffee shops, in-store restaurants, seating, lounges, and recreation areas for children.

Decisions are made about how much selling space to allocate and the type of interior and window displays to use for various products and related items. Store layout planners and visual merchandisers design traffic patterns to encourage browsing and impulse shopping.

Store Interior

Once the general placement of merchandise has been determined, store personnel can develop the visual merchandising approaches for the building's interior. Mannequins, decorations, comfortable seating, and innovative props are all valuable tools for creating a memorable shopping experience. The selection of floor and wall coverings, lighting, colors, store fixtures, interior signage, and graphics powerfully impact the customers' shopping experience and their image of the store.

Color, Lighting, Graphics, and Paint

Bright colors and light pastels (or plain white) appeal to different types of customers. Stores catering to teens might favor bright colors and lighting. Stores catering to adults often choose pastels and soft, subtle lighting effects. Superstores choose fluorescent or high-intensity discharge lighting, while prestige retailers might install expensive chandeliers.

Interior graphics and signage can be used to promote a particular product brand or a specific line of products, provide directions to various departments, or assist with a special promotional campaign, such as a demonstration, special sale, or a holiday promotion.

Walls are interior features that can be covered to reinforce store image. Walls are also used to display merchandise. Clothing can be hung high up on the walls. This technique has the advantage of both saving space and attracting customers with higher-than-eye-level displays.

Fixtures

The principal installations in a store are the **fixtures**. Fixtures are permanent or movable store furnishings that hold and display merchandise. Basic types of fixtures include display cases, tables, counters, floor and wall shelving units, racks, bins, and stands.

A business cultivating an upscale image might enhance its fixtures by painting them or covering them with textured materials (carpeting, fabric, cork, or reed, for example). A business catering to discount buyers would most likely use basic, unadorned shelf fixtures.

The width of a store's aisles is related to its fixtures. The width of aisles and positioning of the fixtures and displays influence traffic patterns and buying behavior.

Interior Displays

If interior displays are done exceptionally well, they enable customers to make a selection without the assistance of a sales clerk. So it is not surprising that these displays have an important place in the selling environment of today's self-service stores.

Five types of interior displays are closed displays, open displays, architectural displays, point-of-purchase displays, and store decorations. Figure 18.1 illustrates the five types of interior displays.

• **KIDS and BOOKS** Selling children's books requires specific store setup and displays.

List three components of a good book display and store setup for children's books.

Figure 18.1 Types of Interior Displays

• **The Functions of Displays** Retailers use interior displays to show merchandise, provide customers with product information, get customers to shop at the store, reinforce advertising messages, and promote the store's image.

Why are interior displays so effective?

ARCHITECTURAL DISPLAYS

Architectural displays consist of model rooms that allow customers to see how merchandise might look in their homes.

STORE DECORATIONS

Store decorations are displays that often coincide with seasons or holidays. Banners, signs, props, and similar items are used to create the appropriate atmosphere.

OPEN DISPLAYS

Open displays allow customers to handle and examine merchandise without the help of a salesperson. Tables and shelves for groceries or countertop and shelf displays for cosmetics are examples.

CLOSED DISPLAYS

Closed displays allow customers to see but not handle merchandise. They are typical displays in places like jewelry stores, where security or breakage is a concern.

POINT-OF-PURCHASE DISPLAYS

Point-of-purchase displays are designed to promote impulse purchases. They are usually more effective at supporting new products than established ones.

@ Online Action! **Go to *marketingessentials.glencoe.com/18/figure/1* to find a project on interior displays.**

As you can see in Figure 18.1, different sales situations call for different types of displays. Items such as clothing are difficult to showcase in a closed display. The cosmetic department is an example of a typical store area that combines many different displays. Items such as brushes and accessories may be part of an open display; other items could be contained in a closed display to prevent customers from sampling them inappropriately. Finally, a point-of-purchase display may feature a computerized touch screen terminal that can evaluate the best cosmetics for each customer's preferences, coloring, and skin type. These displays complement one another and create a positive, interactive buying experience.

Point-of-Purchase Displays

As explained in Chapter 17, **point-of-purchase displays (POPs)** are a consumer sales promotion device. Most POPs are manufactured units with bold graphics and signage that hold, display, or dispense products. Vending machines and automatic teller machines (ATMs) are examples of point-of-purchase units.

Interactive Kiosks

In recent years, interactive point-of-purchase or retail **kiosks** are playing a growing role in point-of-sale merchandising. Kiosks are typically four feet high, have pedestal-mounted, high-tech screens, and take up less than two square feet of store space. Immediate product availability, more reliable technology, and information services have led to their increased popularity. Photo-finishing stands for processing prints from digital cameras are among the most popular kiosks.

Props

Props, also called properties, are special display elements. Props are generally classified as decorative or functional. Decorative props include background scenery such as rakes, dried leaves, and a wheelbarrow used to project an autumn theme. Functional props include items that hold merchandise, such as mannequins and shirt forms.

18.1 AFTER YOU READ

Reviewing Key Terms and Concepts

1. Why is display considered part of visual merchandising?
2. How does visual merchandising differ from display?
3. What are the four elements of visual merchandising?

Integrating Academic Skills

Math

4. Space productivity is measured by sales per square foot of selling space. What are the sales per square foot for a merchandise category that generated $259,645 in sales for a selling space of 1,602 square feet?

Art

5. Research the Internet and look at storefronts and advertising in magazines to find information and ideas about various display styles. Next, select a product category that interests you. Use a posterboard to draw a display for these products. You may use paint, collage, or any other medium you wish. Be creative.

Check your answers at *marketingessentials.glencoe.com/18/read*

SECTION 18.2

Artistic Design

OBJECTIVES

- List the five steps in creating a display
- Explain how artistic elements function in display design
- Describe the importance of display maintenance

KEY TERMS

- color wheel
- complementary colors
- adjacent colors
- triadic colors
- focal point
- proportion
- formal balance
- informal balance

READ and STUDY

BEFORE YOU READ

Predict What skills and talents would you need to design a store display?

THE MAIN IDEA

Visual merchandisers must know the rules of artistic design in order to create displays that help enhance sales, attract customers, and sustain customer loyalty.

STUDY ORGANIZER

As you read this section, identify the key steps of creating a display in a flow chart like the one below.

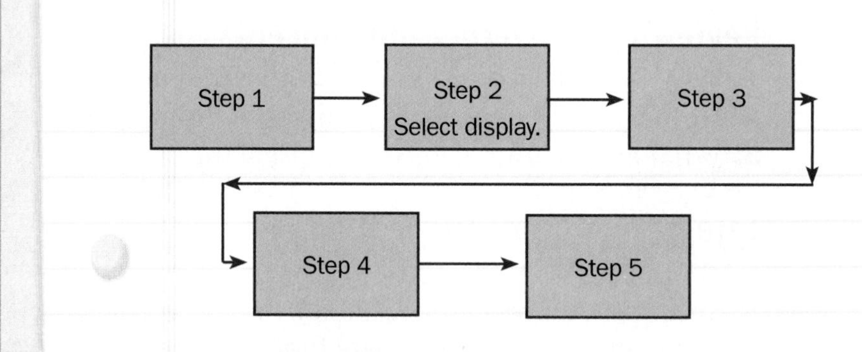

WHILE YOU READ

Connect Think about a display that attracted your attention in the past. List three things that attracted you to it.

Display Design and Preparation

In the retail environment, a display has about four to six seconds to attract a customer's attention, create a desire, and sell a product. This limited time frame means that a business must target its displays carefully to appeal to its customers.

When planning and preparing displays, retailers and merchandisers must carefully consider differences in cultural and ethnic perceptions among their target markets.

Many will employ specialists in cross-cultural and ethnic design and marketing to adapt displays to the target market. All display design and selection involves the following five steps.

Step 1: Selecting Merchandise for Display

The merchandise selected will determine the theme and all other supporting elements of the display. Display merchandise must also be visually appealing and contemporary to attract customers. It must be appropriate for the season and for the store's geographic location.

Step 2: Selecting the Display

The merchandise selected largely determines the type of display that is used. There are four basic kinds of displays: those that feature just one item; similar products; related products, such as camping equipment; and a cross-mix of items, such as a display of a picnic scene, with tables, grills, grilling tools, and aprons.

Step 3: Choosing a Setting

Displays can be presented in a number of different settings. The setting a business selects will depend largely on the image it wants to project.

A realistic setting depicts a room, area, or recognizable locale. The scene could be a restaurant, a park, or a party. Props, such as tables, chairs, plants, risers, books, dishes, and mannequins provide the details.

A semirealistic setting suggests a room or locale but leaves the details to the viewer's imagination. A cardboard sun, a beach towel, a surfing poster, and a sprinkling of sand would be enough to invoke the rest of the beach scene in the viewer's mind.

An abstract setting does not imitate, or even try to imitate, reality. It focuses on form and color rather than reproducing actual objects. Wide bands of torn colored paper used as an accent behind or around merchandise can create an attractive visual image that has little or nothing to do with reality.

Step 4: Manipulating Artistic Elements

The artistic elements of a display include line, color, shape, direction, texture, proportion, motion, and lighting. These elements subtly influence your perception of a display.

Line

Lines within displays are created to direct the viewer's attention. Various types of lines create different impressions. Straight lines suggest stiffness and control, while curving lines suggest freedom and movement. Diagonal lines give the impression of action; vertical lines offer height and dignity; and horizontal lines convey confidence.

Color

Color selection is a critical step in developing displays. The colors selected for a display should contrast with those used on the walls, floors, and fixtures around them. For example, a store decorated in pastels should feature displays that use darker, stronger colors.

The standard **color wheel** shown in Figure 18.2 illustrates the relationships among colors. **Complementary colors** are found opposite each other on the color wheel and are used to create high contrast. Red and green, blue and orange, and yellow and purple are examples of complementary colors.

Adjacent colors, also called analogous colors, are located next to each other in the color wheel and share the same undertones. Successive adjacent colors (such as yellow-orange, yellow, and yellow-green) form families, or groups of colors, that blend well with each other. **Triadic colors** involve three colors equally spaced on the color wheel, such as red, yellow, and blue. Triadic color harmony, as shown by the triangle on the color wheel, creates vivid and contrasting colors. Triadic color schemes can be achieved by rotating the triangle within the color wheel.

Figure 18.2 The Color Wheel

•Color Matters The color wheel is structured to show both similarities and differences in colors. Effective displays use colors that draw customers' attention but don't compete with the product.

How would you use this wheel to create triadic color harmony?

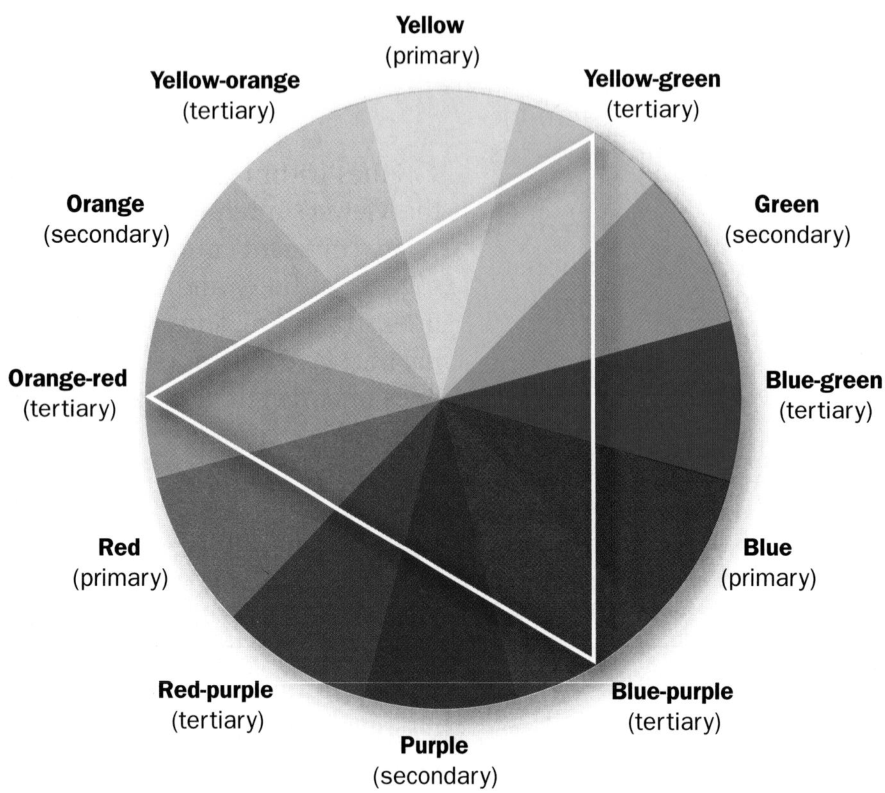

Online Action! Go to ***marketingessentials.glencoe.com/18/figure/2*** to find a project on the use of color in merchandising.

Effective displays use color groupings to create visual calm or excitement. Colors from the warm side of the color wheel, such as red and yellow, convey a festive mood that works well with lower-priced merchandise. Colors from the cool side of the color wheel, such as blue and green, represent calm and refinement. They are often associated with higher-priced merchandise.

Shape

Shape refers to the physical appearance, or outline, of a display. Shape is determined by the props, fixtures, and merchandise used in the display. Squares, cubes, circles, and triangles are some of the shapes that display units may resemble. Displays that have little or no distinct shape—called mass displays—are also possible. Mass displays are often used by dollar stores, discounters, and supermarkets to display large quantities and indicate a low price.

Direction

A good display directs the viewer's eye to the merchandise, moving a viewer's attention

Case Study

The Shopping Buddy

There is a revolution afoot in the world of food shopping: a technology-powered Shopping Buddy. The Shopping Buddy is a cart-based, wireless shopping aid. Several Stop & Shop stores in Massachusetts have started using this new technology. The Shopping Buddy talks the customer through the shopping experience.

Faster, Easier Shopping

The buddy reads the shopper's loyalty card, linking the card and the shopper's history to an 8-inch by 11-inch electronic tablet that is positioned on the cart handle. The wireless browser, combined with sensors embedded in the ceiling, enables the tablet to send and receive data to speed and simplify the shopping experience.

A Virtual Grocery List

The system alerts the shopper to items based on the shopper's preferences and history. It can even place the shopper's deli order and alert her or him when it is ready. It uses sophisticated technology to combine visual merchandising and loyalty marketing.

THINK STRATEGICALLY

How will the Shopping Buddy help increase sales at Stop & Shop stores?

Online Action!

Go to *marketingessentials.glencoe.com/18/case* to find an activity on technology and promotion.

seamlessly from one part of the display to another. This smooth visual flow is called direction. Effective displays create direction by using techniques such as color, repetition, and lighting patterns.

Effective displays should also have a **focal point**, an area in the display that attracts attention first, above all else. A good method of creating an effective focal point is to build the display elements in a triangular shape. The focal point is created by placing the strongest shape at the top, or apex, of the imaginary triangle in the display. A viewer's eyes will naturally travel to the strongest shape within a display. This arrangement helps keep the eyes moving up and over the merchandise. Displays that lack a focal point are said to be unfocused. Typically, an unfocused display contains too many items, too many shapes, or too many props outside the imaginary triangle.

MARKET TECH

Payments by Fingerprint

The Piggly Wiggly grocery store chain has introduced a finger-scanning payment system at more than 100 stores in South Carolina and Georgia. The chain will begin offering a high-tech payment feature allowing customers to pay using their fingerprints. With a touch of the finger to a light-sensitive pad, patrons will be able to pay for their groceries, provided that they have an account in the store's system that can be debited.

Who Is Watching You?

According to Pay By Touch, the San Francisco-based firm whose technology is being used, the system takes 10 seconds to approve a payment by fingerprint. Pay By Touch claims customers' personal information is stored in a secure database and cannot be accessed by unauthorized parties. The company says other stores that have utilized the technology find that three-fourths of their customers sign up to use the fingerprint system. Many privacy advocates, however, oppose fingerprint payment technology. Some consumers are opposed to any technology that can be used to track shoppers.

THINK LIKE A MARKETER

What are the benefits for stores that use fingerprint technology? Can you think of some of the reasons why some consumer organizations do not like this new technology?

@ Online Action!

Go to *marketingessentials.glencoe.com/18/tech* to find an activity on technology and promotion.

Texture

A texture (smooth or rough) is the look of the surfaces in a display. The contrast between the textures used in a display creates visual interest. Products that are smooth, such as flatware, should be placed against backgrounds or props that are rough.

Proportion

Proportion refers to the relationship between and among objects in a display. The merchandise should always be the primary focus of a display. Props, graphics, and signs should be in proportion to the merchandise; they should not dominate the display.

Balance

Display designers also pay attention to balance when creating displays. They place large items with large items and small items with small items to create **formal balance** in a display. When a large item is placed on one side of a display, an equally large item should be placed on the other side for balance. To create **informal balance**, they will place several small items with one large one. An example of an informal display would be one in which an adult mannequin is placed next to several shallow baskets of flowers that are elevated on a prop to the mannequin's height.

Motion

Motion is playing an increasingly important role in display design. Animation can be achieved through the use of motorized fixtures, mannequins, and props. Motion should be used sparingly to accentuate merchandise, not overpower it.

Lighting

Proper lighting is critical to attractive displays. Lighting can help make merchandise appear more attractive. It is recommended that display lighting be two to five times stronger than a store's general lighting. Colored lighting can be used in displays to create

dramatic effects. Lighting used with reflective items such as crystal needs careful attention. Although the lighting in the dressing rooms is technically not part of a display, it should be considered as well. Dressing room lighting that is glaring and unflattering will negatively affect a consumer's buying decisions, no matter how well the merchandise is lit in a display.

Step 5: Evaluating Completed Displays

Do displays enhance the store's image, appeal to customers, and promote the product in the best possible way? Was a theme creatively applied? Were the color and signage appropriate? Was the result pleasing? These are just some of the factors that visual merchandisers consider when evaluating the effectiveness of displays.

Display Maintenance

Once a display has been constructed, it needs to be maintained and eventually dismantled. Individual businesses have different policies regarding the duration of displays. Most businesses check displays daily for damage, displacements, or missing items caused by customers handling the merchandise. Clothing items that are folded and stacked in a display should be organized and restocked frequently. Proper display maintenance can keep the merchandise fresh and attractive to customers.

Poor maintenance can create a negative image not only of the merchandise, but of the store as well. Display fixtures and props should be cleaned and merchandise dusted on a regular basis. Customers are not likely to be enthusiastic about purchasing items that are displayed on dusty or dirty fixtures.

18.2 AFTER YOU READ

Reviewing Key Terms and Concepts

1. Why is the first step in display preparation so important?
2. Name the four basic types of displays.
3. Why is a focal point so necessary in display preparation?

Integrating Academic Skills

Math

4. The *2002 Buyers Report* by Point of Purchase Advertising International estimated POP spending at over $17 billion. If $240 billion is spent on advertising in the United States annually, what percentage of the overall expenditures is the estimated spending on POP advertising?

Art

5. Visit a local supermarket or discount store to observe point-of-purchase (POP) displays. Ask permission to sketch the display on a poster board. Ask the store owner why and how product display choices were made. Annotate your sketch with these comments and answers.

Check your answers at *marketingessentials.glencoe.com/18/read*

CAREERS IN MARKETING

NINA J. MONASTERO, AIA
MONASTERO & ASSOCIATES, INC. ARCHITECTURE AND INTERIOR DESIGN

What do you do at work?
I am an architect and an interior designer who specializes in retail design. We strive to design all aspects of a customer's experience: the way the store environment is shaped, the colors and finishes used in the space, the retail fixtures used, the ways in which merchandise is displayed, the sounds, and the smells, so that all of a customer's senses are affected, and to some extent, controlled, to reinforce the store's message and entice purchases.

What skills are most important to you?
It is imperative to have good listening skills. By that, I mean that I engage in active listening, whereby I make and maintain direct eye contact, don't interrupt, take notes where needed and reflect back on what I think I heard. When meeting with clients, I tend to listen much, much more than speak. Next, an innate design sense, or sense of style is important and should be supplemented by proper training in design, be it through architecture, interior design, graphic design, or industrial design coursework at the college level.

What is your key to success?
Over the course of my career, I have always put my clients, their companies and their needs first, my ego second. My firm and I are not known for having a "style." Rather, we are known for designing the best solutions for our clients. I always try to put myself in their shoes and understand where their issues and ideas may be coming from.

Aptitudes, Abilities, and Skills

Strong interpersonal skills, an eye for design, and a strong sense of creativity

Education and Training

Courses in architecture and interior design can lay the groundwork, fine arts will add depth to the understanding of how space works.

Career Path

Designers usually begin their careers working for an established agency with a reputation. Once individuals have built portfolios of projects, they can think about moving to better opportunities within their companies, with another firm, or on their own as freelancers.

THINKING CRITICALLY

Why would fine arts courses be helpful to someone working in retail space design?

Online Action!

Go to *marketingessentials.glencoe.com/18/careers* to find a career-related activity.

CHAPTER 18 REVIEW

FOCUS on KEY POINTS

SECTION 18.1

- Visual merchandising is an important part of a business's total promotional mix. Visual merchandising and display must be coordinated with advertising, direct marketing, personal selling, and sales promotion efforts.

SECTION 18.2

- Visual merchandising and in-store displays help to sell products and build store and brand image. Businesses create effective displays by using prescribed steps and rules for artistic design to attract customers and to keep them coming back.

REVIEW VOCABULARY

Study each pair of terms and, in your own words, tell how they are related to each other.

1. visual merchandising (p. 382)—display (p. 383)
2. storefront (p. 383)—marquee (p. 383)
3. store layout (p. 384)—fixtures (p. 385)
4. point-of-purchase displays (p. 387)—kiosks (p. 387)
5. color wheel (p. 389)—complementary colors (p. 389)
6. adjacent colors (p. 389)—triadic colors (p. 389)
7. focal point (p. 391)—proportion (p. 392)
8. formal balance (p. 392)—informal balance (p. 392)

REVIEW FACTS and IDEAS

9. What is the purpose of visual merchandising? (18.1)
10. What are the key elements of visual merchandising? (18.1)
11. Why are interior displays important? (18.1)
12. Which type of interior display is most effective for new product introductions? (18.1)
13. What role do visual merchandisers play on the marketing team? (18.1)
14. What are the five steps involved in creating a display? (18.2)
15. What artistic elements function in display design? (18.2)
16. Locate complementary and adjacent colors on the color wheel. How do the colors contrast with each other? (18.2)
17. How are formal and informal balance achieved in a display? (18.2)

BUILD SKILLS

18. Workplace Skills

Human Relations Assume that you are the visual merchandising coordinator for a large department store. You have been asked to update the required skills for display specialists. You must provide a rationale and explain your decisions at a meeting with upper management. How would you prepare for the meeting?

19. Technology Applications

Comparing Display Techniques Visit a department store to observe and evaluate its visual merchandising effectiveness. Review its storefront, store layout, and store interior.

Use a spreadsheet program to create a chart, evaluating the quality of each component.

20. Math Practice

Display Budget Cheryl owns a small fashion retail store in a suburban mall in Georgia. Last year she spent one percent of her profits ($65,489) on props for windows and store displays. This year, she forecasts her display costs at $1,000. How much did she spend last year? What percent increase is she considering this year?

DEVELOP CRITICAL THINKING

21. Technology and Displays

Visit a local supermarket, then a megastore. Briefly describe the technology, if any, that is used in displays, noting its purpose and benefits to both the store and the consumer. Then, make a list and compare and contrast how the technology you observed is used in both types of stores. Does one store use technology more effectively? Explain your evaluation.

22. Evaluating Displays

Visit a shopping mall to observe and evaluate three different window or interior displays. Using a scoring rubric for each display, evaluate and rate each display in terms of the artistic elements from this chapter.

APPLY CONCEPTS

23. Explaining Display Objectives

Conduct an Internet search on the award-winning point-of-purchase (POP) displays recognized by Point of Purchase Advertising International (POPAI). Select one temporary, semipermanent, or permanent POP display to download, then review its objectives.

Activity Use a word processing program to prepare a brief report on your findings.

24. Preparing a Display

Interview a local business owner or manager regarding visual merchandising needs. Ask the business owner whether he or she would participate in a classroom project. Explain that this project involves preparing a display that fits the needs of the business.

Activity As a member of a display team, prepare a display at the local business with selected merchandise and specifications as determined by the business owner.

NET SAVVY

25. Research Display Fixtures

Perform an Internet search to find five suppliers of store fixtures. Write a summary of the products and services provided by each supplier, where the company is located, and its Web site address. Make sure to provide details such as prices and styles of fixtures.

THE DECA CONNECTION

Role Play: Virtual Merchandising and Display

Situation You are to assume the role of assistant manager of an upscale women's designer boutique. The store is currently undergoing a complete renovation and image update. The store's designer (judge) has asked you for some ideas for the new bags and packaging, including shopping bags, hanging garment bags, and mailing packaging. You may include any other sizes of bags you think are necessary.

Activity You are to present your ideas for the new bags and packaging to the store's designer (judge).

Evaluation You will be evaluated on how well you meet the following performance indicators:

- Demonstrate appropriate creativity
- Demonstrate interest and enthusiasm
- Develop a project plan
- Recommend specific products
- Follow directions

@ Online Action!

For more information and DECA Prep practice, go to *marketingessentials.glencoe.com/18/DECA*

CHAPTER 19
Advertising

Chapter Objectives

After reading this chapter, you should be able to:

- Explain the concept and purpose of advertising in the promotional mix
- Identify the different types of advertising media
- Discuss the planning and selection of media
- Identify media measurement techniques
- Explain techniques used to evaluate media
- Summarize how media costs are determined
- Explain promotional budget methods

GUIDE TO THE PHOTO

Market Talk There are many forms of advertising to fit all kinds of budgets. A large company such as Procter & Gamble typically spends 25 to 30 percent of its revenues on advertising, while a small firm might consider spending two percent. Types of ads vary greatly, from carefully crafted television national ad campaigns, to print ads in newspapers and magazines, to a much simpler and cheaper approach, such as leaflet distribution.

Quick Think When planning an advertising budget and strategy, do you think it is important to study how and where the competition is advertising?

THE DECA CONNECTION

Performance indicators represent key skills and knowledge. Relating them to the concepts explained in this chapter is your key to success in DECA events. These acronyms represent DECA events that involve knowledge of concepts in this chapter.

AAAL	**FMAL**	**MMS***	**TMDM***
AAML*	**FMDM***	**QSRM***	**TSE***
ADC*	**FMML***	**RMAL**	**VPM**
BSM	**FSRM***	**RMML***	
EMDM*	**HMDM***	**SMDM***	

In all these DECA events you should be able to follow these performance indicators:

- Explain the types of advertising media
- Explain the nature of direct advertising strategies
- Describe considerations in using databases in advertising
- Calculate media costs

All the events with an asterisk (*) also include these performance indicators:

- Select advertising media
- Buy advertisements
- Develop an advertising campaign
- Use past advertisements to aid in promotional planning
- Prepare promotional budget
- Manage promotional allowances

Some events include additional performance indicators. These are:

ADC Select placement of advertisements
TMDM Select placement of advertisements
FMDM Select placement of advertisements

DECA PREP

Check your understanding of DECA performance indicators with the DECA activity in this chapter's review. For more information and DECA Prep practice, go to *marketingessentials .glencoe.com/19/DECA*

Advertising Media

OBJECTIVES

- Explain the concept and purpose of advertising in the promotional mix
- Identify the different types of advertising media
- Discuss the planning and selection of media

KEY TERMS

- promotional advertising
- institutional advertising
- media
- print media
- transit advertising
- broadcast media
- online advertising
- specialty media
- media planning

READ and STUDY

BEFORE YOU READ

Predict If a business did not advertise, how would potential customers learn about its products?

THE MAIN IDEA

Advertising is an important element of promotion. Businesses use different types of advertising media to promote their images, products, and services.

STUDY ORGANIZER

In a chart like the one below, organize your notes about the types of media used in advertising.

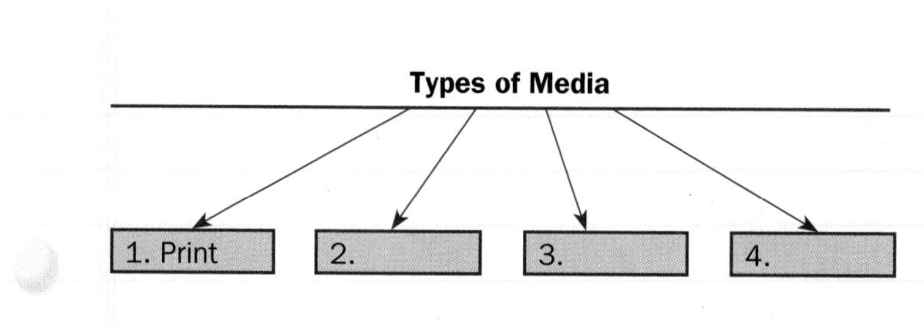

WHILE YOU READ

Connect Think about the many types of advertisements you have seen. How would you classify the different types?

Advertising and Its Purpose

Advertising is everywhere—television, radio, magazines, newspapers, stores, the World Wide Web, billboards, theaters, sports arenas, and even on highway road signs. The average person is exposed to more than 2,000 advertisements every week.

In advertising, advertisers control the message, where it will be seen or heard, and how often it will be repeated.

Promotional and Institutional Advertising

There are two main types of advertising: promotional and institutional. **Promotional advertising** is when the goal is to increase sales. The targets of promotional advertising are consumers or business-to-business customers. Promotional advertising can introduce a new business, change a company image, promote a new product, advertise an existing one, or encourage the use of a particular service. Sometimes, the goal of promotional advertising is to encourage potential customers to ask for information, call for an appointment, go online, or enter a store. This is called generating leads or developing prospects.

Promotional advertising is an effective way to support direct selling efforts, sales promotion activities, visual merchandising, and display efforts.

Institutional advertising tries to create a favorable image for a company and foster goodwill in the marketplace. There are many institutional advertising techniques in use today. Connecting its name to a worthy cause helps a company make a favorable impression on its customers.

Mass Advertising Versus Targeted Advertising

Mass advertising enables companies to reach large numbers of people with their messages. Certain media, such as television and radio, lend themselves to mass advertising. Thanks to today's sophisticated technology, advertisers can also carefully target their messages to select audiences. This is known as targeted advertising. Advertising demonstrates the features and benefits of a product or service. As a result, business customers and general consumers are encouraged to buy the product or service.

Types of Media

Media are the agencies, means, or instruments used to convey advertising messages

•**A SPECIAL PLACE** A state tourism office has placed this ad to advertise Wyoming as a good place to vacation.

List three characteristics of this ad.

to the public. The four general categories of advertising media are print, broadcast, online, and specialty. Figure 19.1 illustrates examples of the different types of advertising media.

Print Media

Print media includes advertising in newspapers, magazines, direct mail, signs, and billboards. This is one of the oldest and most effective types of advertising.

Newspaper Advertising

Newspapers continue to be an important advertising outlet for many consumer-oriented products and services. In 2004, there were 1,456 daily newspapers in the United States. These local papers provide a timely way for companies to reach their target audiences. Many retailers and local companies rely on daily newspapers to advertise their products and services. These papers also offer a variety of options for the size, location, and frequency of insertion of ads. This flexibility enables companies to select the options that best suit their budgets and advertising goals.

Another type of local paper is called a shopper. Shoppers contain little editorial content, but they are delivered free to residents who live in specific areas.

National newspapers, such as *USA Today* and the *Wall Street Journal,* are distributed throughout the country. Advertisers can purchase ad space in the newspaper to reach the entire circulation or buy less expensive space targeted only to specific regions or cities.

Local and national papers often have online editions and sell advertising space for both formats. What are the advantages of newspaper advertising? It is estimated that 55 percent of adults in the United States read a newspaper every day. Advertisers want their ads to be seen, and this high number of readers is very important. Since a newspaper's reach is known, advertisers can target their advertising to people living in certain areas or with certain interests. A newspaper may even offer different neighborhood sections within the same city.

Responses to newspaper ads and coupon sales can be dated and easily tracked. The cost of newspaper advertising is another advantage. It remains relatively low because the paper and print quality is lower and the expense of printing is less than for magazines and direct mail.

Newspaper advertising does have limitations, however. Some newspapers are distributed to subscribers outside the business's target market. Also, newspapers have a limited shelf life because they are read and then thrown away each day. Many newspapers are still printed with black ink or with just a limited number of color pages. Ads are less visually appealing than those found in colorful magazines and direct mail.

Magazine Advertising

Magazines are distributed locally, regionally, or nationally. They can be published as weeklies, monthlies, and quarterlies. *U.S. News & World Report, Time,* and *Newsweek* are examples of national weekly magazines. Regional magazines are often developed to serve the needs of a metropolitan area or region. *Southern Living* is an example of a regional magazine. Some national magazines have regional, state, and city editions.

Magazines can also be classified as consumer or business-to-business. More than 3,000 consumer magazines such as *Reader's Digest, TV Guide, Seventeen, Forbes,* and *Sports Illustrated* are read for personal pleasure or interest. Advertisers can target their audiences through the characteristics of a magazine's subscribers.

Business-to-business magazines, also known as trade publications, interest professionals in specific fields. Examples include *Mass Market Retailers, Advertising Age,* and *Women's Wear Daily.* These publications are cost effective for advertisers who want to reach a target audience with little wasted circulation.

Both consumer and business-to-business magazines have a longer life span than newspapers. People tend to keep magazines for a more extended period of time. This increases the chance that they, and the ads in

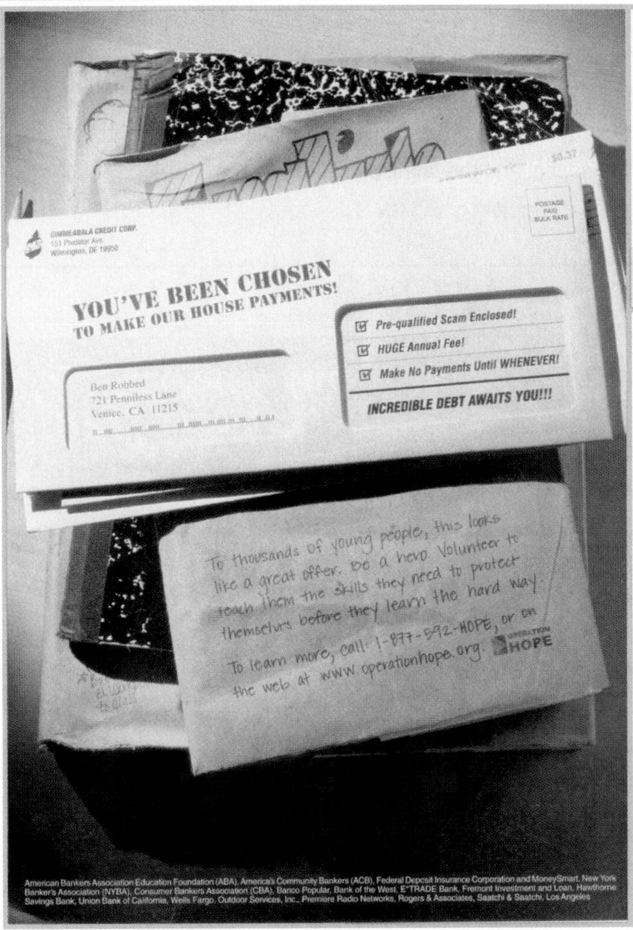

•DIRECT MAIL and ETHICS The Direct Marketing Association (DMA) encourages its members to follow ethical guidelines for the practice of direct mail advertising. In this ad, several banks and banking associations are promoting awareness of direct-mail scams.

Why does this group advertise Operation Hope?

them, will be reread or passed along to others. People also read magazines more slowly and thoroughly than newspapers. Magazines are generally printed in color and have better print quality than newspapers. Magazines also offer a variety of presentation formats, including full-page ads, two-page spreads, gatefolds (a page folded into itself), return cards, and heavy stock inserts.

There are drawbacks to magazine advertising. The cost of advertising in magazines is higher than newspaper advertising. In addition, magazines are often printed a month or two in advance of publication. The deadline for submitting ads is several weeks or months before actual publication, and this requires careful planning.

Direct Mail

Direct marketing is a highly focused form of advertising. The two types of direct marketing are printed direct mail sent to a home or business and electronic direct mail delivered to an e-mail address. Such direct marketing is a good way to keep current customers aware of new products, services, and upcoming sales. It is also a cost effective way to generate leads and qualify prospective customers.

Printed direct-mail advertising takes many forms, including newsletters, catalogs, coupons, samplers, price lists, circulars, invitations to special sales or events, letters, and more. Large retailers and manufacturers send direct-mail catalogs and price lists to current and prospective customers.

The success of direct-mail advertising depends on carefully selecting its target. Direct mail is most effective with existing customers. However, in order to grow, a company must find new customers. Direct-mail advertisers seek new customers first by analyzing their existing customers to build a customer profile. Then, they acquire the names of people or organizations that fit the same profile. Direct

Figure 19.1 Advertising Media

• Promoting Images and Products Media are the agencies, means, or instruments used to convey advertising messages to the public. Below are some examples of advertising media. The advertising media should be determined much in the same way as the advertising message: by the appeal and the target audience.

What are some other advertising media?

MAGAZINES AND NEWSPAPERS

Magazines offer a high level of reader involvement and messages that can be seen repeatedly. Online magazines represent a new advertising opportunity for marketers. Newspapers are a convenient way for a local advertiser to present a message in selected geographic areas.

DIRECT MAIL

Direct-mail advertising sends a message directly to your home or computer. It encourages customers to try new products and usually offers them an incentive for doing so.

TRANSIT ADVERTISING

Transit advertising uses public transportation facilities and vehicles to bring messages to people.

@ Online Action! Go to ***marketingessentials.glencoe.com/19/figure/1*** to find a project on advertising media.

marketing specialty firms sell lists of people's mailing addresses, phone numbers, and e-mail addresses. Names can be sorted according to many different demographic criteria to match the profile of existing customers.

Direct-mail advertising enables advertisers to be highly selective about who will receive the mailing and when the person receives it.

Direct-mail advertisers have a wide choice of printed advertisement formats, such as letters, catalogs, and postcards—limited only by postal regulations. Direct mail also includes electronic advertising campaigns. This flexibility enables direct mailers to test various creative approaches providing valuable input for perfecting future campaigns.

There are disadvantages to direct mail. It can yield a low level of response in relation to the number of items sent. A return of 10 percent for printed direct mail is usually considered excellent. Poorly planned and executed direct mail campaigns usually yield less than a one-half percent response.

Direct mail also has an image problem. Many people think of printed or electronic direct-mail advertising as junk mail.

The cost of printed direct mailing can be high because it includes producing and printing each piece of the mailing, collating it, buying mailing lists, and paying for postage to send it.

Directory Advertising

The best example of a directory that accepts advertising is the telephone directory. In the White Pages, businesses and residents receive a free alphabetical listing of their phone numbers and addresses. In the Yellow Pages, businesses pay for an alphabetical listing and, if desired, a display ad. The listings and ads appear under general category headings.

Directory advertising has some unique advantages. It is relatively inexpensive and can be used to target all demographic groups. For example, telephone directories are found in 98 percent of American households. Directories are usually kept for at least a year or until another is provided. This advantage, however, can also be a disadvantage. Advertisers cannot adjust their information, offers, or message until a new directory is distributed.

Outdoor Advertising

Both local, regional, and national businesses use outdoor signs for advertising. There are two types of outdoor signs: nonstandardized and standardized. Nonstandardized outdoor signs are used by companies at their places of business or in other locations throughout the community. An example is a sign displaying the company's logo at the entrance to its office building.

Standardized outdoor signs are purchased from advertising companies and are provided only in standard sizes. Examples are advertisements to be placed on billboards.

Other types of standardized outdoor signs are posters, painted bulletins, and spectaculars. Posters are pre-printed sheets put up like wallpaper on a wall or billboard. They are changed three to four times each year. Painted bulletins are painted signs that are changed every six months to a year. Spectaculars are outdoor signs purchased or rented from an advertising company. They use lights or moving parts to attract attention. They are common in densely populated metropolitan areas.

Outdoor advertising is highly visible and relatively inexpensive. It provides a 24-hours-a-day, 7-days-a-week message, and can be located to reach specific target markets. Drawbacks of outdoor advertising include limited viewing time, inability to target a specific audience, and increasing government regulations. Outdoor advertising is often restricted to roadways and areas zoned for commercial and industrial uses.

Transit Advertising

Transit advertising can be found on public transportation. It includes printed posters inside trains, taxis, and buses; ads on public benches, bus stop shelters, kiosks, newsstands, and trash cans; and station advertising located near or in subways and in railroad, bus, and airline terminals.

Transit advertising reaches a wide, and sometimes captive, audience. It is economical and has a defined market, usually in urban areas.

Broadcast Media

Broadcast media encompass radio and television. Over a lifetime of 70 years, the average person will spend nearly ten years watching television and almost six years listening to the radio. You can see why advertising through broadcast media is popular. Most of the 1,200 commercial television stations are affiliated with one of the major networks—ABC, CBS, NBC, or Fox. There are about 11,600 local cable systems. More than 66 percent of the estimated 98 million households with a television set are cable television subscribers.

Television Advertising

Television is the ultimate advertising medium for many businesses because it can combine all the creative elements necessary—sight, sound, action, and color—to produce a compelling advertising message. As a result, television is a very effective medium for demonstrating a product's features and benefits.

Television advertising allows companies to direct their advertising messages to audiences with a specific interest such as news, movies, or sports.

Most television advertisements are 30- or 60-second spots. An exception is the infomercial, which is a 30- or 60-minute advertisement. Infomercials promote products such as cookware, exercise equipment, and appliances, using a talk-show type setting. Viewers can order the advertised merchandise by calling a phone number, visiting a Web site, or writing to an address.

There are disadvantages to television advertising. Television has the highest production costs of any type of media and a high dollar cost for the TV time purchased. Prime-time and special event costs can be prohibitive. For example, a 30-second network TV ad for Super Bowl XXXVIII cost $2.25 million, while ABC charged $1.5 million for a 30-second ad during the 2004 Academy Awards.

Smaller companies cannot usually afford the production and placement costs of network television advertising, or they may be forced to buy time in less desirable time slots or rely on smaller and less expensive local or cable TV markets.

Radio Advertising

More than 10,000 AM and FM radio stations reach 96 percent of all people age 12 and over in a given week. This ability to reach a wide audience makes radio an extremely efficient and cost-effective advertising medium.

Radio is a mobile medium that can be heard just about anywhere. It is also a timely medium—radio advertisers can update their messages, ads, and offers daily, even hourly. Radio has the immediacy of newspapers without the high production costs of television.

Radio advertisers can carefully target their audience when they select the station on which to broadcast their ads. Most radio station programming targets a specific segment of the radio listening market.

Radio advertisements are presented in 10-, 20-, 30-, or 60-second time periods. These messages are effective in encouraging people to buy because the announcer or actors—along with background music, jingles, slogans, and sound effects—add excitement, drama, or humor.

However, products and services can only be described, not seen. Advertisers cannot rely on visual involvement to hold a listener's attention. That is why a catchy jingle is important. Radio advertisements also have a short life span.

Online Advertising

Online advertising is a form of advertising that uses either e-mail or the World Wide Web. It is still a small part of overall advertising spending, but it is growing steadily. Online advertising sales totaled $6.5 billion in 2003, generating 1.09 trillion impressions. An impression is a single appearance of an ad on a computer user's screen.

Electronic direct-mail advertising is sent via e-mail. Today, much advertising of this

NET MARKETING

Rich Media Comes to PC Ads

Rich media ads—ones that combine animation, video, and sound with interactive features—are growing in popularity. Jupiter Research predicts that by 2008, advertisers will spend about 39 percent of their online advertising budgets on rich media. Rich media captured only 11 percent of online ad spending in 2003.

What Rich Media Can Do

Rich media ads provide instant, detailed feedback about how long PC users spend viewing an ad and what ad the user viewed next. The ads entice users to make an online purchase or submit demographic data in real time. DoubleClick, a company that distributes online ads, found that rich media ads generate better brand recognition and higher sales activity than static online ads.

AOL and Yahoo work with the Interactive Advertising Bureau to set standards for file size and load time to protect Web surfers with slower Internet connections.

THINK LIKE A MARKETER

How do rich media ads differ from print and broadcast ads in addressing a target market?

Online Action!

Go to *marketingessentials.glencoe.com/19/net* to find an activity on Internet advertising.

type is sent to pre-qualified groups of people. This is known as opt-in e-mail because recipients requested it or authorized it. Many of these e-mails enable the recipient to click through to a company's Web site. This enables companies to track exactly how many people visited their site by clicking on a link in the e-mail. It is also cost-effective, and it is easy to update and personalize the message for each recipient.

Banner and Pop-Up Ads

Most online advertising appears as banner ads. A banner ad comes in various shapes and sizes, but it is usually a rectangle seen at the top, bottom, or side of a Web page.

Similar to banner ads but smaller in size, button ads are placed in a strategic position on a Web page. Some advertisers use pop-up interstitial ads, which are TV-like spots that pop up between Web pages and are inserted in audio or video streams, either live or on-demand. A viewer must click on the ad to get to the advertiser's Web site or close the ad window to resume surfing.

Online advertisers have found that bold colors, top-of-page placement, animation, calls to action, and limited frequency of exposures help increase that number of click-throughs. Even using these techniques, online advertisers report response rates as low as one percent. In other words, for every 100 banner ads, only one in 100 users clicks on the ad to visit the Web site.

Specialty Media

Specialty media, which are sometimes called giveaways or advertising specialties, are relatively inexpensive, useful items featuring an advertiser's name or logo.

To be successful as advertising tools, specialty items must be practical, used frequently, and placed in locations with high visibility. Common items that fit this description include hats, calendars, pens and pencils. Specialty items carry the identity of the business sponsoring them and an advertising message.

The distribution of the items is usually limited. In addition, the items might be given to people who would never consider buying the product or patronizing the business.

Other Advertising Media

Businesses are constantly creating innovative means of transmitting their messages to potential customers. Examples include sports arena billboards, ads in movie theaters and home video rentals. Some advertisers, such as pharmaceutical manufacturers, use DVDs and CD-ROMs.

In-Store Advertising

Increasingly, in-store advertising techniques, such as electronic shelf ads, supermarket cart displays, instant coupon machines, floor mats, and sound systems are being used to advertise products within stores.

Media Planning and Selection

Media planning is the process of selecting the advertising media and deciding the time or space in which the ads should appear to accomplish a marketing objective. To select and compare different types of media, companies rely upon media planning software as well as media cost data and audience information.

To establish the media plan and select the right medium to use, advertisers address three basic questions:

1. Can the medium present the product and the appropriate business image?
2. Can the desired customers be targeted with the medium?
3. Will the medium get the desired response rate?

The media plan provides the opportunity to present a compelling message and project the desired business image to the target market.

19.1 AFTER YOU READ

Reviewing Key Terms and Concepts

1. Describe the two main types of advertising.
2. List the six different kinds of print media.
3. What is media planning?

Integrating Academic Skills

Math

4. In 2003, total advertising expenditures for TV (network, local, and cable) were $48.9 billion. What percentage was spent in each category if network TV totaled $20.4 billion, local TV $16.2 billion, and cable TV 12.3 billion?

History

5. Use the Internet or your local school or community library to research the history of print advertising over time. Prepare a two-page written report.

Check your answers at *marketingessentials.glencoe.com/19/read*

SECTION 19.2

Media Measurement and Rates

OBJECTIVES

- Identify media measurement techniques
- Explain techniques used to evaluate media
- Summarize how media costs are determined
- Explain promotional budget methods

KEY TERMS

- audience
- impression
- frequency
- cost per thousand (CPM)

READ and STUDY

BEFORE YOU READ

Predict Suppose your company ran a four-color ad in *Newsweek* three months ago. How would you measure the response to that ad?

MAIN IDEA

Businesses need to reach as many targeted customers as possible within limited budgets. It is important to calculate costs and measure media effectiveness to best reach a potential audience.

STUDY ORGANIZER

Use a chart like the one below to take notes about media rates.

Media	How Rates Are Determined
Newspaper	

Media Measurement

Media planners must concern themselves with the correct medium to use and its costs as well as how to measure overall advertising effectiveness.

To understand media measurement, you need to become familiar with several key terms. First, the number of homes or people exposed to an ad is called the **audience**. A single exposure to an advertising message is called an **impression**. **Frequency** is the number of times an audience sees or hears an

WHILE YOU READ

Predict If you were charged with selecting advertising media, what kinds of information would you need?

advertisement. **Cost per thousand (CPM)** is the media cost of exposing 1,000 readers or viewers to an advertising impression. Cost per thousand is the comparison tool used to determine the effectiveness of different types of media.

The audience for print media is the total number of readers per issue. Readership in print media is measured by surveys or estimated by circulation. The audience figure is normally higher than its circulation because more than one person can read a single issue of a printed newspaper or magazine. From an advertiser's viewpoint, the audience figure better reflects the actual number of people exposed to an ad.

Television audience measurement is based upon diaries and meter data collected by Nielsen Media Research for a sample of TV viewers in more than 200 TV markets. The measurement of viewing behavior occurs during what are known as sweeps months—February, May, July, and November. The Arbitron Company measures radio audiences in more than 260 markets by collecting diaries of listening behavior. Online audiences are measured through surveys and computer software tracking systems to calculate the number of people who viewed a particular ad.

Knowing the potential audience, how frequently your advertisement will be seen, and its CPM can tell you whether the rates charged by various media are right for your advertising budget.

Media Rates

To reach customers, advertising uses a set format that is defined in terms of time (a 30-second television commercial) or space (a half-page newspaper ad). Media costs vary greatly, not just with type of media but also with geographical location and audience. For example, a quarter-page newspaper ad in a large city daily newspaper could cost four to eight times more than the same-sized ad in a small-town weekly. It is virtually impossible to quote exact rates for each type of media advertising.

Businesses can look up rates in the publications of Standard Rate and Data Service. This company publishes rate cards for most major media according to general categories, such as print media or broadcast media.

Another service important to both advertisers and print media is the Audit Bureau of Circulations (ABC). Print media publishers subscribe to the ABC to verify their circulation figures. A circulation audit is critical to publishers because it enables them to verify circulation numbers to advertisers. Circulation figures are important selling points when publications try to attract and maintain their advertisers.

Newspaper Rates

Newspaper advertising rates are divided into two categories depending on whether the ad is a classified ad or a display ad.

Classified ads are grouped, or classified, into specific categories, such as help wanted, real estate, personals, or auto sales. They are effective for selling everything from services to houses to job openings. People or businesses that buy classified ads usually pay by the word or line of type.

Display ads enable the advertiser to depict the product or service being advertised. Advertisers use a mix of art or photographs, headlines, copy, and a signature or logo of the product or business. Display ads are generally larger than classified ads. Their cost is based upon the amount of space used and the ad's position in the newspaper.

Newspapers quote display advertising rates by the column inch. A column inch is an area that is one column wide by one inch deep. If a newspaper quotes a column inch rate, you simply multiply the number of inches by the number of columns to determine the total number of column inches. Then, multiply the total column inches by the rate. For example, if the rate for a column inch is \$17, then a single ad (called an insertion) that measures four inches long by three columns will cost \$204.

$$\$17 \times 4 \text{ inches} \times 3 \text{ columns} = \$204$$

Factors That Affect Rates

Advertising rates can vary depending on when an advertisement will appear in a paper.

A newspaper may charge a Monday through Thursday rate of $29 per column inch, a Friday rate of $30, a Saturday rate of $32, and a Sunday rate of $35 per column inch.

Where an ad appears is another factor. Display ads are usually sold at run-of-paper rates. Run-of-paper allows the newspaper to choose where to run an ad in the paper or magazine. However, for a higher rate, advertisers can run ads in guaranteed or preferred locations, such as the back cover. The use of color also affects the advertising rate. Color ads are sold at a higher price than black-and-white ads. The frequency of advertising affects the amount charged. The open rate, often referred to as the noncontract rate, is used for infrequent advertisers. It is the highest rate charged for a display ad.

Businesses that advertise in the newspaper frequently may contract with a newspaper to guarantee that they will use a certain amount of space for a specified time period. They are granted contract rates, which are discounted from the open rate. Contracts can be written in a number of ways. A yearly frequency contract guarantees that an advertiser will use a minimum number of column inches each week for 52 weeks. A bulk space contract guarantees that a minimum number of inches will be used when the advertiser chooses, within a 12-month period.

Comparing Rates

The cost per thousand (CPM) measurement is useful in comparing the cost of advertising to reach 1,000 readers in one newspaper with

GLOBAL MARKET

Green Pastures

Almarai is the largest dairy foods company in the Middle East. The company was founded in 1976. Its headquarters are in Riyadh, Saudi Arabia. Almarai, whose name means *green pastures* in Arabic, has developed from a simple dairy farm into a large international business under the guidance of the governing royal family. Today, Almarai exports its dairy products all across the Middle East.

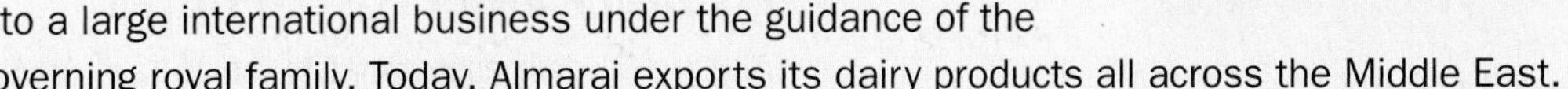

A Focus on Local Tastes Similar companies in developing countries often achieve notable success only to lose the competition for markets once multinational competitors decide to enter the race for customers. A multinational company with well-funded and experienced marketing and advertising departments is hard to beat. But Almarai won such a challenge against giant Nestle by tailoring its marketing and advertising to Middle Eastern preferences. The company's success rests on its focus on local taste for fresh, full-fat milk (sold in plastic bottles that look like old-fashioned glass milk bottles), regional products such as *labneh* (a soft cheese made from yogurt), and yogurt with no artificial color or flavor.

CRITICAL THINKING

Why might multinational companies find it difficult to market their products in a foreign market?

Online Action!

Go to *marketingessentials.glencoe.com/19/global* to find an activity on international advertising.

the cost of advertising to reach 1,000 readers in another newspaper. The comparison is made by using the following formula:

Cost of the ad × 1,000/Circulation = CPM

Suppose the cost of an ad in the *Times* is $500, and the paper has a circulation of 500,000. Its CPM would be calculated as follows:

$500 × 1,000/500,000 = $500,000/500,000
= $1 per 1,000 readers

Suppose the cost of an ad in the *Tribune,* a competing paper, is $600, and the paper has a circulation of 300,000. Its CPM would be calculated as follows:

$600 × 1,000/300,000 = $600,000/300,000
= $2 per 1,000 readers

All other things being equal, an advertiser would probably choose the *Times* over the *Tribune* because it would cost less per 1,000 readers. Of course, all other things might not be equal. The *Tribune's* circulation could include more of the advertiser's target market, or the paper could offer a special ad placement. CPM is a convenient measure that enables advertisers to compare costs.

Magazine Rates

Magazine rates are based on circulation, the type of readership, and production techniques. To calculate the actual cost of magazine advertising, you need to become familiar with terms found on magazine advertising rate cards, including bleed, black-and-white rates, color rates, premium position, and discounts.

Bleed means that half- or full-page ads are printed to the very edge of the page, leaving no white border. Magazines generally charge between 15 to 20 percent extra for bleeds.

The lowest rates that magazines offer for display ads are black-and-white rates for black-and-white advertisements. Color rates are offered for color ads. Each time the magazine adds color to the ad, the rates increase.

Magazine Rate Card

General Rates

RATE BASE: Rates based on a yearly average of 1,100,000 net paid A B C
A member of the Audit Bureau of Circulation

SPACE UNITS	BLACK & WHITE	BLACK & ONE COLOR	FOUR COLOR
1 page	$16,000	$19,630	$23,300
2 columns	11,620	14,560	18,170
½ page	10,130	13,550	17,200
1 column	5,920	9,530	12,180
½ column	3,020		
Covers			
Second Cover			$25,520
Third Cover			23,300
Fourth Cover			27,020

BLEED CHARGE: 15%
AGENCY COMMISSION: 15%
CASH DISCOUNT: 2% 10 days, net 30 days

Bleed accepted in color, black & white, and on covers, at an additional charge of 15%. No charge for gutter bleed in double-page spread.

Premium Positions: A 10% premium applies to advertising units positioned on pages 1, 2, and 3. A surcharge of 5% applies to bleed units in premium positions.

Rate Change Announcements will be made at least two months in advance of the black & white closing date for the issue affected. Orders for issues thereafter at rates then prevailing.

ISSUANCE AND CLOSING DATES

A. On sale date approximately the 15th of month preceding date of issue.

B. Black & white, black & one color, and four-color closing date, 20th of the 3rd month preceding date of issue. Example: Forms for August issue close May 20th.

C. **Orders for cover pages noncancellable. Orders for all inside advertising units are noncancellable 15 days prior to their respective closing dates.** Supplied inserts are noncancellable the 1st of the 4th month preceding month of issue. Options on cover positions must be exercised at least 30 days prior to four-color closing date. If order is not received by such date, cover option automatically lapses.

•AD RATES Ad rates are based on color.

Based on this magazine rate card, what is the cost of a half-page, four-color ad paid in ten days from the issuance of the invoice?

Premium position refers to ad placement. Ads placed in premium positions, such as on the back cover or the inside of the first page, are more expensive to buy.

Rate Discounts

Frequency discounts are offered to advertisers who run the same ad several times during the year. The magazine may publish an entire schedule of rates for the number of times during the year an advertiser contracts to advertise. The rate per issue decreases as the frequency increases.

Another discount is a commission—a percentage of sales given by the magazine to the advertising agency for placing the ad for the advertiser. A typical commission is 15 percent.

Take a look at the rate card. You would calculate the cost of a full-page, four-color advertisement with bleed as follows:

$23,300	1 page, four-color rate
× .15	bleed
$ 3,495	extra for bleed

Case Study

Generating New Revenue

Magazines are trying to boost advertising revenues with new crossover and promotional tie-in deals. Some of the ideas include partnering with successful television channels and making distribution arrangements with mass merchandisers.

For example, the music video cable channel MTV crossed over from television to print by launching an MTV magazine. Major advertisers in the first edition included Nike, Pepsi, the NBA, and Procter & Gamble. The model for this crossover was ESPN. The sports station began *ESPN The Magazine* in 1998, and it has a circulation of 1.7 million.

Trying Something New

Time Inc., a large magazine publisher, is considering a new kind of distribution tie-in deal, including a new women's magazine. This new magazine would be sold only through mass retailers. To attract scarce ad dollars, magazine publishers are also partnering with the makers and sellers of consumer products. However, experience shows that only four out of ten new magazines survive.

Talk Show Crossovers

The publisher of the magazine *Rosie* hoped to profit from the popularity of talk show host Rosie O'Donnell. It shut down after a year and a half. In contrast, talk show host Oprah Winfrey's magazine *O* has been a success.

THINK STRATEGICALLY

Considering the survival rate for new magazines, why do media companies view crossovers to be a smart way to create new revenues?

@ Online Action!

Go to *marketingessentials.glencoe.com/19/case* to find an activity on media advertising.

$23,300	1 page, four-color rate
+ 3,495	bleed
$26,795	for 1 page, four-color, with bleed

An ad agency placed the ad and it took the commission and the cash discount. The total cost of the above ad to the agency would be:

$ 26,795	1 page, four-color, with bleed
× .15	ad agency's commission
$ 4,019.25	

$ 26,795.00	1 page, four-color, with bleed
− 4,019.25	agency's commission
$ 22,775.75	net cost of ad to agency after commission
× .02	cash discount percentage if paid within 10 days of invoice
$ 455.52	cash discount
$ 22,775.75	net cost of ad to agency after commission
− 455.52	cash discount
$ 22,320.23	net cost to advertising agency for one full-page, four-color ad with bleed after cash discount and agency commission

As with newspapers, the CPM can be used to compare the cost of advertising in several magazines. If a magazine has a circulation of two million and charges $35,000 for a full-page, black-and-white ad, the CPM for such an ad would be $17.50.

$$\$35{,}000 \times 1{,}000/2{,}000{,}000 = \$17.50$$

Online Rates

Online advertising rates are based upon the type of format the customer desires. Banner ads, rich-media enhanced banner ads, button ads, and interstitial ads are some of the options. Online advertising rates are set on a CPM rate of page views. Rates vary based on the volume of monthly page views.

Radio Rates

When purchasing radio time, a business needs to decide what kind of radio advertising to use. There are three options: network radio advertising, national spot radio advertising, and local radio advertising. It is important to know the difference between spot radio and spot commercials. Spot radio refers to the geographical area an advertiser wants to reach with its advertising. Spot commercials are advertising messages of one minute or less that can be carried on network or spot radio.

Businesses with a national customer base usually choose network radio advertising or national spot radio advertising. Network radio advertising is a broadcast from a network studio to all affiliated radio stations throughout the country.

The following radio times are listed from most expensive to least expensive:

Class AA:	Morning drive time: 6 A.M. to 10 A.M.
Class A:	Evening drive time: 4 P.M. to 7 P.M.
Class B:	Home worker time: 10 A.M. to 4 P.M.
Class C:	Evening time: 7 P.M. to midnight
Class D:	Nighttime: midnight to 6 A.M.

Weekend rates may differ from weekday rates.

Rates are higher during early morning and late afternoon listening times, also called drive times. Radio stations also offer less costly, run-of-schedule (ROS) airtimes. ROS airtime allows a radio station to decide when to run the ad.

Television Rates

Advertising rates for television also vary with time of day. It is more expensive, for example, to advertise during the prime time hours of 7 P.M. to 10 P.M. than during other hours. The rates charged for other time slots, such as day (9 A.M. to 4 P.M.), late fringe (10:35 P.M. to 1:00 A.M.), or overnight (1 A.M. to 5 A.M.) are lower due to smaller numbers of viewers. Advertisers try to play their messages during the time slots that enable them to reach the most customers.

Promotional Budget

The promotional budget considers not only the cost for developing and placing or airing advertising but also the cost of staffing the department or campaign. The advertiser must consider short- and long-term benefits of the effort or campaign. Four common promotional budgeting methods are percentage of sales, all you can afford, following the competition, and objective and task.

1. In the percentage of sales method, the budget is decided based on a percentage of past or anticipated sales. For example, the current budget for advertising might be five percent of last year's sales or five percent of projected sales for the coming season. In either case, the advertising budget is tied to figures that could be too high or too low for current market condition.
2. If a company follows the all you can afford method, it first pays all expenses, then applies the remainder of funds available to promotional activities. This method is often used for only a short period of time. It is popular in small businesses, especially Internet and other start-up companies. The objective is to build sales and reputation quickly in the beginning.
3. When employing a following the competition method, an advertiser matches its competitor's promotional expenditures or prepares a budget based on the competitor's market share. This method is generally considered to be weak because it is based on the competitor's objectives.
4. With the objective and task method, the company determines goals, considers the necessary steps to meet goals, and determines the cost for promotional activities to meet the goals. This method considers a company's current situation and where it wants to be. This is the most effective of the four methods because it focuses on the company's goals and how it will reach them.

19.2 AFTER YOU READ

Reviewing Key Terms and Concepts

1. What is the cost per thousand (CPM) measurement?
2. What determines the rates television and radio stations charge for advertising?
3. Name the four methods used to create a promotional budget.

Integrating Academic Skills

Math

4. Calculate the CPM for an ad in a magazine that has a circulation of 1.7 million and charges $35,000 for a full-page, black-and-white advertisement.

Civics/Government

5. Perform an Internet or library search on how the government tries to prevent deceptive advertising. Find at least three laws, rules, or regulations established to assist the consumer with advertised products or services.

@ Online Action!

Check your answers at *marketingessentials.glencoe.com/19/read*

CAREERS IN MARKETING

JUAN GUILLERMO TORNOÉ
PARTNER
HISPANIC DIVISION
WIZARD OF ADS, INC.

What do you do at work?

I work in a marketing and advertising consulting firm, Wizard of Ads, Inc. I handle all the media research and negotiation for our mainstream clients, currently 40+ of them located in 38 cities across the United States and Canada. I personally research and negotiate each one of the individual markets where our clients are located, maximizing their advertising budgets' performance. From a couple thousand dollars to several million dollars per market, depending on the client's size, we get the most efficient and effective media buys for the dollar in each of those markets.

What skills are most important to you?

Not diminishing formal education, which most certainly created an extremely strong foundation as well as an invaluable skills tool box, it has been through real-world work experiences that I have obtained the best training to do my job. I was blessed with the opportunity to work on and learn about message development, strategy, media negotiation, human persuasion, and "why people do the things they do" with the president of my company.

What is your key to success?

I have realized that success is a journey, not a destination. I have had to learn to rejoice on each individual milestone accomplished, and then keep on moving toward the next one. The keys to reaching those milestones have been awareness of opportunities, the willingness to take risks, hard work, and perseverance.

Aptitudes, Abilities, and Skills

Creativity, writing and communication skills, and an analytical mind

Education and Training

Degrees in marketing, psychology, communication, and general business are helpful.

Career Path

Many careers at marketing and advertising agencies are launched through unpaid internships or entry-level assistant positions. Successful employees usually become responsible for large client accounts and entire ad campaigns.

THINKING CRITICALLY

Why would a marketing professional benefit from a study of art, sociology, and religion?

Online Action!

Go to *marketingessentials.glencoe.com/19/careers* to find a career-related activity.

CHAPTER 19 REVIEW

FOCUS on KEY POINTS

SECTION 19.1

- The main purpose of advertising is to present a message that encourages the customer to buy the product or service or to accept an idea. Businesses must choose the most appropriate advertising media for their target market; for example, Web sites, newspapers, radio, or television. A business then prepares a media plan.

SECTION 19.2

- Choosing the correct medium to use from all the available types of media is a very complex effort. Media planners must concern themselves not only with the correct medium to use and its costs, but also with how to measure overall advertising effectiveness. Once a company decides on its promotional methods and goals, it must create a promotional budget.

REVIEW VOCABULARY

Organize the class into two teams for a game of "Marketing Tic-Tac-Toe." Team members will give the definition for the terms and will place an "X" or "O" on the board for each correct definition.

1. promotional advertising (p. 401)
2. institutional advertising (p. 401)
3. media (p. 401)
4. print media (p. 402)
5. transit advertising (p. 405)
6. broadcast media (p. 406)
7. online advertising (p. 406)
8. specialty media (p. 407)
9. media planning (p. 408)
10. audience (p. 409)
11. impression (p. 409)
12. frequency (p. 409)
13. cost per thousand (CPM) (p. 410)

REVIEW FACTS and IDEAS

14. What is advertising? (19.1)
15. List the four main categories of advertising media. (19.1)
16. What three basic questions are used to develop a media plan? (19.1)
17. What are the two forms of broadcast advertising? (19.1)
18. What is online advertising? (19.1)
19. What factors affect newspaper ad rates? (19.2)
20. What is the most effective way to create a promotional budget? (19.2)

BUILD SKILLS

21. Workplace Skills

Communication A coworker believes that advertising is a waste of money and suggests that products would be cheaper without it. Develop a ten-minute oral presentation on the benefits of advertising.

22. Technology Applications

Ads in Schools and Gyms Research the Internet to find information about the advantages and disadvantages of advertising in school buildings and athletic facilities. What restrictions, if any, would you recommend for such advertising? Use a word processing program to develop a one-page paper on the topic.

23. Math Practice

CPM Calculations Calculate the CPM for a $35,000 ad in the following magazines based upon circulation figures from the first six months of 2003.

Magazine	Total Paid	CPM
Reader's Digest	11,090,349	
People	3,628,982	
Cosmopolitan	2,860,024	
Ebony	1,798,844	

DEVELOP CRITICAL THINKING

24. Analyzing Printed Direct Mail

Analyze the printed direct mail that either you or your family receives in a two-week period, such as reply cards, incentive discounts, product samples, credit card offers, inserts with utility bills, or letters. Attach your analysis and the direct mail samples to a poster board for display.

25. Advertising a Start-Up

Suppose you and your best friend have created a new formula for a shampoo. You decide you want to manufacture several hundred bottles of this shampoo. Part of your business plan involves developing a promotion strategy. What type of advertising would you choose? Why?

APPLY CONCEPTS

26. Analyzing Radio Listening

Listen to your favorite radio station for one hour. List the products advertised, characterize the advertising approach taken, and identify the sponsor as either national or local.

Activity Use a spreadsheet computer program to prepare an advertising log for one hour of your radio listening.

27. Creating a Media Plan

Develop a media plan for a product of your choice using billboards, radio ads, magazines, television commercials, and/or newspapers for a one-month period. Assume that you have $125,000 to reach a target audience of 10,000 people. The CPM for an ad in each medium is as follows:

Medium	CPM
Billboard	$2.05
Radio ad, drive time	$8.61
Magazine, one-page color ad	$9.35
TV commercial, 30 seconds in prime time	$17.78
Newspaper, one-third page, black-and-white	$22.95

Activity Use a word processing program to develop a plan that identifies how you will use the above media.

NET SAVVY

28. Finding Resources

Perform an Internet search for *B to B: The Magazine for Marketing Strategists.* Select one of the business Web sites named on B2B's Top 100 list. Browse the Web site and prepare a summary about the resources that are available on the site.

THE 

CONNECTION

Role Play: Develop an Advertising Plan

Situation You are to assume the role of manager of the cosmetics department of a small, locally owned department store. You are to develop an advertising plan and coordinate an in-store promotional plan to announce the new lipstick colors for the upcoming spring season. The new colors are inspired by flowers and include shades of lilac, rose, hyacinth, violet, and hibiscus red.

Activity You are to select appropriate advertising media and make suggestions for an in-store promotion that will coordinate with one another. You are to present your ideas to the department store manager (judge).

Evaluation You will be evaluated on how well you meet the following performance indicators:

- Explain the types of advertising media
- Select advertising media
- Analyze use of specialty promotions
- Develop a sales promotion plan
- Demonstrate appropriate creativity

@ Online Action!

For more information and DECA Prep practice, go to *marketingessentials.glencoe.com/19/DECA*

CHAPTER 20

Print Advertisements

Chapter Objectives

After reading this chapter, you should be able to:

- Discuss how advertising campaigns are developed
- Explain the role of an advertising agency
- Identify the main components of print advertisements
- Explain the principles of preparing an ad layout
- List advantages and disadvantages of using color in advertising
- Describe how typefaces and sizes add variety and emphasis to print advertisements

GUIDE TO THE PHOTO

Market Talk There are many different types of print ads. Magazines, newspapers, and direct mail are the most common venues for these ads. Preparing a print ad requires a high degree of expertise, since the writing style and graphics can vary greatly depending on the product and where the ad will run.

Quick Think Take a quick look at a daily newspaper and at a monthly magazine. Compare the types of ads you see.

THE DECA CONNECTION

An Association of Marketing Students

Performance indicators represent key skills and knowledge. Relating them to the concepts explained in this chapter is your key to success in DECA events. These acronyms represent DECA events that involve knowledge of concepts in this chapter.

AAAL	**FMAL**	**MMS***	**TMDM***
AAML*	**FMDM***	**QSRM***	**TSE***
ADC*	**FMML***	**RMAL**	**VPM**
BSM	**FSRM***	**RMML***	
EMDM*	**HMDM***	**SMDM***	

In all these DECA events you should be able to follow these performance indicators:

- Explain components of advertisements
- Write promotional messages that appeal to targeted markets
- Create a Web site

All the events with an asterisk (*) also include this performance indicator:

- Evaluate the effectiveness of advertising

Some events include additional performance indicators. These are:

EMDM Explain the use of advertising agencies
Write content for use on the Internet

FMDM Write direct-mail letters
Explain the use of advertising agencies

HMDM Explain the use of advertising agencies

SMDM Explain the use of advertising agencies
Write direct mail letters

TMDM Explain the use of advertising agencies
Design a company's catalogs
Design a company's brochures

DECA PREP

Check your understanding of DECA performance indicators with the DECA activity in this chapter's review. For more information and DECA Prep practice, go to *marketingessentials .glencoe.com/20/DECA*

SECTION 20.1

Essential Elements of Advertising

OBJECTIVES

- Discuss how advertising campaigns are developed
- Explain the role of an advertising agency
- Identify the main components of print advertisements

KEY TERMS

- advertising campaign
- advertising agencies
- headline
- copy
- illustration
- clip art
- signature
- slogan

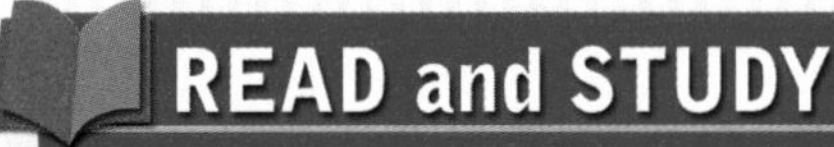

BEFORE YOU READ

Predict Think of print ads you have seen recently. What key elements do they have in common?

THE MAIN IDEA

Successful advertising campaigns help to sell products and services. Marketers must know what the essential elements are and how they are used to develop effective advertisements.

STUDY ORGANIZER

Use a chart like the one below to take notes about the components of a print ad.

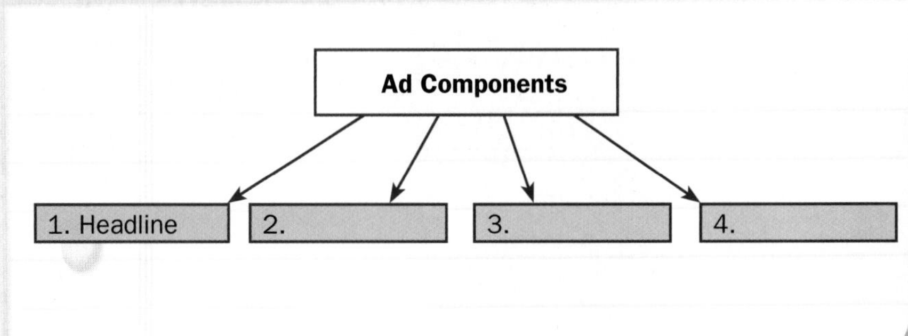

Connect Think of a product you like. How would you advertise it?

The Advertising Campaign

To advertise a product or service, a company must plan an advertising campaign. An **advertising campaign** is a group of advertisements, commercials, and related promotional materials and activities that are designed as part of a coordinated advertising plan to meet the specific goals of a company. An integrated advertising campaign involves the creation and coordination of a series of advertisements around a particular theme.

Planning an integrated advertising campaign involves a series of steps:

1. **Identify the target audience** Advertisers must analyze the potential market and decide who should receive their messages.
2. **Determine objectives** They identify their goals, such as increasing brand awareness, or increasing knowledge about the product.
3. **Establish the budget** Advertisers decide what to spend over a specific period of time.
4. **Develop the message** They develop the theme and messages based on the product's features, benefits, and uses.
5. **Select the media** They choose which media, such as TV, radio, Internet, or print, will be most effective.
6. **Evaluate the campaign** Advertisers use market research to see if the campaign met its objectives.

Advertising Agencies

Advertising agencies are independent businesses that specialize in developing ad campaigns and crafting the ads for clients. Full-service agencies plan the entire advertising campaign by setting objectives, developing advertising messages and strategies, completing media plans, selecting media, and coordinating related activities, including sales promotion and public relations. Larger advertising agencies employ specialists, such as copywriters, graphic artists, media experts, marketing researchers, and legal advisers, to help with the development and execution of campaigns.

Limited-service agencies specialize in one aspect of the campaign, such as creative services, media planning, or media buying. Larger companies are increasingly selecting specialists, such as those who concentrate only on Internet advertising, to develop different aspects of the advertising campaign. Global consumer brands also make use of specialty agencies to develop or tailor campaigns to specific countries, ethnic groups, or other target markets.

Technology and e-commerce opportunities have led many businesses to employ in-house staff for some advertising functions, such as Web site development and maintenance. Some companies supplement in-house resources with the work of freelance professionals or limited-service agencies.

New Models for Advertising Agencies

New models for advertising agencies include business formats such as creative boutiques, project team agencies, and virtual agencies.

A creative boutique is a specialized service agency that helps businesses with creative production. In a creative boutique, the advertiser develops the message and copy but outsources the design and production of the advertisement to the boutique. This type of organization enables the advertiser to create ads much faster than a traditional agency could.

Agencies organized around a project team provide copywriting, creative execution, and media placement without the overhead of a larger agency. Teams can come together to do one project, then move on to the next when the ad campaign is complete.

In a virtual agency, one individual coordinates the work of a network of experienced freelancers. A freelancer is a self-employed person who sells work or services by the hour, day, or job, rather than working on a regular salary basis for one employer. One of the benefits of this type of agency is that it has lower overhead, which means lower costs for the client.

Developing Print Advertisements

Although they are only one part of an advertising campaign, print advertisements are very important to most campaigns. As Figure 20.1 shows, print advertisements have four key elements: headline, copy, illustrations, and signature. Some advertisements also include the company's slogan. Each of the four key elements enhances the overall theme. The four fundamental elements of a print advertisement are applicable for ads in other media, too. As you read this section,

Figure 20.1 Parts of a Print Advertisement

- **The Components of Advertising Success** Print advertisements usually contain four elements: headline, copy, illustrations, and signature. Some advertisements also include the company's slogan, which is often presented with or near the signature.

How do the elements of an ad work together?

IT'S A BIT OF
A CONTROL FREAK.
FORD EXPLORER

WITH ITS INNOVATIVE INDEPENDENT REAR SUSPENSION AND AVAILABLE ADVANCETRAC™ STABILITY CONTROL SYSTEM, FORD EXPLORER IS READILY EQUIPPED TO DELIVER PRECISE HANDLING ON ANY ROAD YOU TRAVEL. NO WONDER FORD EXPLORER HAS BEEN AMERICA'S MOST TRUSTED SUV 11 YEARS RUNNING.

Ford
IF YOU HAVEN'T LOOKED AT FORD LATELY...
LOOK AGAIN.

1 **Headlines** attract readers, arouse interest, and get them to look at the illustration and copy.

2 **Copy** represents the selling message in the ad.

3 **Illustrations** help expand on the copy by showing how the product works or how it is used.

4 **The signature**, or logotype (logo), is the identification symbol for a business.

5 **A slogan** is a catch phrase or small group of words that are combined in a special way to identify a product or company.

Online Action! Go to *marketingessentials.glencoe.com/20/figure/1* to find a project on print advertisements.

think of ways these concepts would apply to preparing television and radio commercials, as well as online advertising.

Headline

The **headline** is the phrase or sentence that attracts the readers' attention to a particular product or service. Headlines must grab attention fast and hold it. They must convince the reader that it is in his or her best interest to read the ad. A headline should also lead readers into the ad's illustration and make them want to read the copy to learn more about the product's or service's benefits. Research shows that headlines that use words such as *you, your, how,* and *new* attract the most attention.

Writing Effective Headlines

Before writing a headline, a copywriter must know the needs of the target market. These needs might relate to price, delivery, performance, reliability, service, or quality. The headline must identify a benefit of the product or service, such as how it meets a consumer need. Effective headlines stress these benefits by making a promise, asking a question, posing a challenge, or using a testimonial.

Most headlines are brief. Research has shown people cannot process more than seven words at one time.

In a recent study, creative directors from major advertising agencies analyzed award-winning print ads to determine what their headlines had in common. They discovered that 32 percent of the headlines used familiar sayings with a twist. For example, "When it rains, it pours" (Morton Salt) or "I think, therefore IBM" (International Business Machines). About 23 percent of the headlines made use of opposites such as "up/down" and "lie/truth." For example, "Does she, or doesn't she?" (Clairol hair coloring) or "Hand-built by robots" (Fiat Strada).

A MATTER OF ETHICS

Do You Want My Opinion?

A proposed Federal Communications Commission (FCC) rule would allow national cable television companies, like Comcast, to own local newspapers as well. According to some critics, ownership of two or more main sources of local information would stifle competition and limit expression of differing viewpoints.

News Sources

According to Nielsen Media Research, Inc., about 35 percent of consumers rely on local broadcast television as their primary source of local news, 30 percent rely on newspapers, 25 percent on radio, and the remainder rely on the Internet. If this FCC rule were passed, a large media giant could control the coverage of political races, business, and other issues.

THINKING ETHICALLY

Do you think that it is ethical for one media company to own both the television station and the newspaper in a community? Why or why not?

@ Online Action!

Go to *marketingessentials.glencoe.com/20/ethics* to find an activity on ethics and advertising.

Copy

The **copy** is the selling message of a written advertisement. It details how the product or service meets the customer needs identified in the headline. As with headlines, copy should be developed only after the market is thoroughly researched. It should be based on the business objectives for the advertising campaign. For example, is your advertising designed to introduce a new product, build an image, attract new customers, answer inquiries, or generate sales to existing customers?

• MOTIVATING a CUSTOMER Every headline should have a single focus or main idea. Headlines should motivate the reader to try a product or service.

What is the main idea of this ad?

Here are some tips to create compelling, effective copy:

1. Your copy should be viewed as a conversation and written in a very personal, friendly manner.
2. Good copy, like a good headline, is simple and direct. Copy can vary from a few words to several paragraphs. Copy does not need to be extensive to get a message across. Copy can be viewed as an educational tool, a testimonial to the benefits of using the product, or a description of how an institution can help you.
3. Copy should appeal to the senses. Through the words, the customer should be able to see, hear, touch, taste, or even smell a product. This can be done through using descriptive adjectives and action words.
4. Your copy should tell the who, what, when, where, why, and how of your product. Remember that facts about your product are more powerful than claims. Use case histories, statistics, performance figures, dates, and quotes from experts whenever possible.
5. Add desire and urgency to the copy. Use key words such as *new, improved, introducing, save,* and *easy* to establish immediate contact with the reader. They arouse interest, encourage awareness, and create desire and urgency.
6. Advertising copy should provide a personal call to action now or in the near future. It should always be in the second person and in the active rather than the passive voice. Including a phrase to encourage acting immediately, such as *last chance, limited supply, ends in two weeks,* or *special bonus offer*, helps create a sense of urgency and need for action.

Other techniques for keeping your copy personal include using contractions and short sentences. For example, "we are" would be written as "we're" and "you are" would be changed to "you're." Write in short sentences and avoid the use of commas. Too many commas and long sentences will distract the reader.

Illustration

The **illustration** is the photograph, drawing, or other graphic elements used in an advertisement. Its primary functions are to attract and hold attention and to encourage action. It should also integrate the headline and copy. The illustration, together with the headline, should motivate the prospect to read at least the first sentence of the copy.

The illustration and graphic elements should transmit a message that would be hard to communicate with words alone. For example, illustrations can show the product, how the product works, and safety features. Illustrations should also project the desired image or benefit—for example, convenience, entertainment, leisure, or status.

Photographs should be used in advertisements when a sense of reality is necessary. Drawings are often used to show a part of a product that the reader would not normally see. Cut-away drawings and illustrations of constructed or manufactured products and equipment can help show important features not visible in a photograph. They can also help the reader understand how a product works.

Sources for Illustrations

Businesses often use clip art in their print advertisements. **Clip art** takes the form of images, stock drawings, and photographs. Suppliers, manufacturers, or trade associations often provide clip art for print advertisements. Clip art can also be found in published books, on CD-ROMs, and on the Web. Because clip art is ready for reproduction and printing, it is inexpensive, quick, and easy to use. When

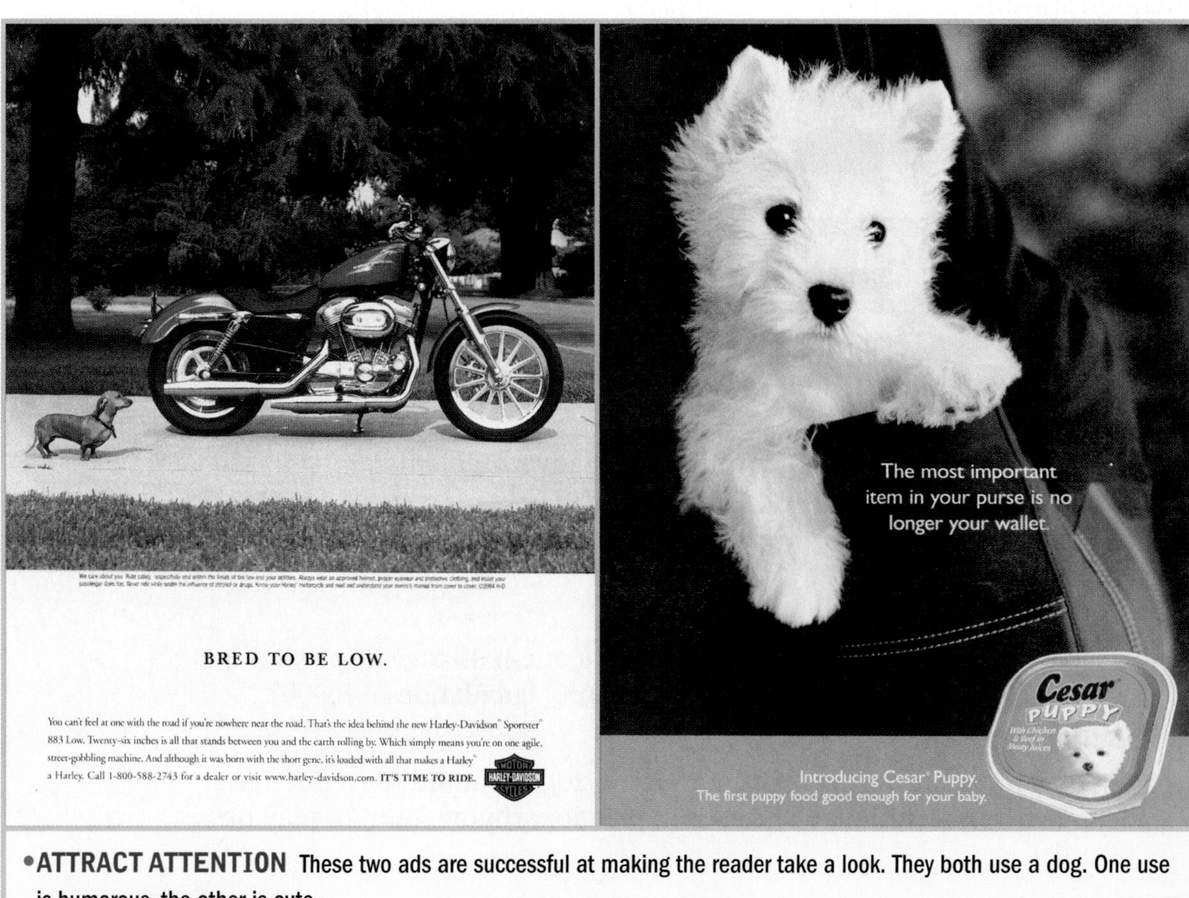

•ATTRACT ATTENTION These two ads are successful at making the reader take a look. They both use a dog. One use is humorous, the other is cute.

Besides animals, name two other visual components that are commonly used in advertising.

stock artwork is not sufficient, professionals may be hired to photograph or illustrate situations or products.

Signature

The **signature**, or logotype (logo), is the distinctive identification symbol for a business. A well-designed signature gets instant recognition for a business. No advertisement is complete without it.

In national ads, the signature is the name of the firm. It may also include the corporate symbol and slogan. The signature in local advertisements usually includes the business's name, address, telephone number, business hours, or slogan. Many advertisers also include their Web site address in the signature.

Slogan

A **slogan** is a catchy phrase or words that identify a product or company. Each of these advertising slogans had the power to attract attention and arouse interest for the company or its product. To support a firm's signature, many businesses create and use slogans that help customers identify the firm and its image.

Here are techniques copywriters use when developing slogans for advertising campaigns:

- Alliteration uses repeating initial consonant sounds—"Welcome to the World Wide Wow" (AOL).
- A paradox is a seeming contradiction that could be true—"The taste you love to hate" (Listerine mouthwash).
- Rhyme uses rhyming words or phrases—"Give a hoot, don't pollute" (United States Forest Service).
- A pun is a humorous use of a word that suggests two or more of its meanings or the meaning of another word similar in sound—"Time to Re-Tire" (Fisk Tires).
- A play on words cleverly uses words to mean something else—"Let your fingers do the walking" (Yellow Pages).

20.1 AFTER YOU READ

Reviewing Key Terms and Concepts

1. What steps should be followed when developing an advertising campaign?
2. Why are headlines so important in print advertisements?
3. What is the main purpose of advertising copy?

Integrating Academic Skills

Math

4. What is the cost per thousand (CPM) of a one-half-page display ad that costs $75 in a newspaper with a community circulation of 8,000?

Reading or Language Arts

5. Make up slogans for five products. Each slogan should use a different copywriting technique (alliteration, paradox, rhyme, pun, or play on words).

Check your answers at *marketingessentials.glencoe.com/20/read*

SECTION 20.2

Advertising Layout

READ and STUDY

BEFORE YOU READ

Predict How do you think color affects the viewer's reaction to an ad?

MAIN IDEA

Advertisements have only a few seconds to attract a targeted audience. Advertisers need to understand effective design principles when developing ad layouts to attract the attention of the desired audience quickly.

STUDY ORGANIZER

Use a chart like the one below to take notes on the principles of ad design.

Tips for Developing Effective Ad Layouts

1. Leave white (unused) space.
2. ____________
3. ____________
4. ____________

OBJECTIVES

- Explain the principles of preparing an ad layout
- List advantages and disadvantages of using color in advertising
- Describe how typefaces and sizes add variety and emphasis to print advertisements

KEY TERMS

- ad layout
- advertising proof

Developing Print Advertising Layouts

An **ad layout** is a sketch that shows the general arrangement and appearance of a finished ad. It clearly indicates the position of the headline, illustration, copy, and signature.

Components of Effective Ad Layouts

Ad layouts should be prepared in exactly the same size as the final advertisement. The illustrations should be large

WHILE YOU READ

Evaluation Think of a product you are interested in. How would you design an ad for it?

MARKET TECH

In-Store Advertising Increases

In-store television advertising is gaining in popularity. Since more people are watching cable and satellite television channels, it has become difficult for national advertisers to reach a mass audience via regular network television. But a large and diverse number of people still shop on a regular basis at supermarket and discount chains. Tesco PLC, Britain's largest supermarket chain, is installing television sets in 300 of its stores. In between news clips, recipe tips, and beauty advice, the screens will show ads for products in the aisles. In the United States, Wal-Mart stores also have television sets that carry advertising messages.

How to Get Shoppers' Attention

To be effective, in-store ads must be very attention-getting, since customers are at the store to shop and not to watch television. In-store ads can be very creative and often use the actual store as a setting for the ad. For example, Unilever created an ad for its Axe deodorant that featured an attractive male using the product. The ad showed women in the store running after him because they were attracted to the scent.

THINK LIKE A MARKETER

What are some reasons why in-store TV advertising is becoming more popular with mass-market retailers?

Online Action!

Go to *marketingessentials.glencoe.com/20/tech* to find an activity on technology and advertising.

enough to show the product in use and grab attention through size, humor, or dramatic content. Ads that feature large visuals (60 to 70 percent of the total ad) are the best attention-getters. The image projected in the layout should be appropriate for the target audience.

The best ads contain a focal point and lines of force that guide the reader to the copy through photographs and illustrations. One technique is to create a Z layout. Place the most dominant item (typically the headline or illustration) on the top of the Z. Since a reader's eye will normally follow the path of the Z, place copy on the line going down and your signature and "call to action" at the bottom of the Z.

Using Color in Print Advertisements

A color ad is usually more realistic and visually appealing and commands the reader's attention more than a black-and-white advertisement does. In fact, research proves that color newspaper ads can increase the readership of ad copy by as much as 80 percent over black-and-white ads. Studies have also shown that full-color ads are usually more cost effective than two-color ads (usually black and another color) because of their increased response rates.

Adding another color can increase costs by as much as 35 percent. Therefore, when businesses use color in advertisements, the added cost must be continually measured against the desired results.

Select the appropriate colors for your product and target market. For example, red is used for passion, excitement, and power. It is often used in automobile and food advertising. Also, when developing ads for global markets or ethnic groups within the United States, an advertiser must be sensitive to the different meanings that color conveys to people of other cultures and countries.

• **LETTERING** This ad is a good example of the use of fonts and type sizes to attract attention and impart information.

What is your reaction to the size of the words Break Out?

Selecting Typefaces and Type Sizes for Print Advertisements

Many typefaces and type sizes are effective for use in print ads. Advertisers make sure to select styles and type sizes that are distinctive, yet appropriate for the business and target audience.

The look and appearance (design) of the type is called the typeface. A complete set of letters in a specific size and typeface is called a font. The appearance of the typeface affects the entire character of an advertisement.

Type size is measured in points. There are 12 points to one pica, and 6 picas to 1 inch. So a point is about 1/72 of an inch. Your word processing program allows you to choose the size of type you want, usually within a range of 8 to 72 points.

One way to classify typefaces is to consider whether they are serif or sans serif. A serif typeface has short crosslines at the upper and lower ends of the letters. Times Roman and Palatino are two commonly used serif fonts. Here are examples of these fonts in 10-point and 24-point type. Can you see the crosslines at the top and bottom of the letters T and P?

Times Roman, 10-point

Times Roman, 24-point

Palatino, 10-point

Palatino, 24-point

A sans serif font is one that is *sans* (French for "without") any crosslines. These fonts are popular because their simple design makes them very easy to read. Some common sans serif fonts are Arial, Helvetica, and Futura. Here are some examples:

Case Study

Advertising to Reach Young Males

Video games reach 18- to 34-year old males more effectively than perhaps any other medium. A recent Nielsen Media Research study found that young men were watching seven percent less prime-time television than a year earlier.

Activision, a Santa Monica, California, video game publisher, and Nielsen Entertainment are planning to help advertisers evaluate the effectiveness of video game ads. They are proposing an evaluation method that is similar to Nielsen Media Research's famous method of rating television shows.

Watching Gamers

The new system will track how many gamers see the ads in video game content, how often they see them, and how well they recall them. This system works with console-based games, by far the industry's largest sector, with real-time measurement data relayed through an Internet connection. It is estimated that video game product placement costs between $20,000 and $100,000, a fraction of the cost of a network TV ad. The new service, which is still in development, is likely to employ a small gadget to measure game-playing behavior, much as Nielsen's TV-rating service uses set-top devices to monitor TV-viewing habits. Gamers' ability to recall ads is likely to be measured using telephone surveys and other follow-up methods.

THINK STRATEGICALLY

What products would you advertise in video games?

Go to *marketingessentials.glencoe.com/20/case* to find an activity on targeted advertising.

Arial, 10-point

Helvetica, 16-point

Futura, 24-point

The preferences and characteristics of the target market will dictate the choice of typeface. A study done by the Newspaper Advertising Bureau found that nearly one-third of readers over 65 were not reading ads because the type was too small. This means that a 14-point font would be a better choice than 10-point for ads designed to reach readers over 65. Type that is too small or difficult to read will lower the readership of an ad. Many companies use serif typefaces and 12-point font sizes in most ad copy.

Large, bold type is usually chosen when the words contained in a headline are to be shouted. Smaller, lighter type is usually chosen when the words in a headline are to be whispered. In general, print advertisers should use one typeface for headlines and prices and another typeface for copy. You can add variety and emphasis by using different sizes of typefaces, italics, boldface, and combinations of capital and lowercase letters. The message may remain the same, however, capitalizing different words may change the effect.

Checking Advertising Proofs

When advertisements are first created, an **advertising proof** is developed. The advertising proof shows exactly how an ad will appear in print. Many proofs are now delivered in a digital format. This practice helps to cut production costs and speed up production.

The advertising proof is sent to the advertiser for review and approval. Before giving final approval of a written advertisement, the advertiser makes an evaluation based on the following criteria:

- The ad should be bold enough to stand out on a page, even if it is placed next to other ads.
- The overall layout should look clean and uncluttered and should guide the reader through the copy.
- The typefaces and type sizes should be easy to read and help to emphasize the message.
- The signature should be apparent and distinctive.
- The intended message and image projected must be appropriate for the target audience.

In addition, it is important to make sure that all prices are accurate and all brand names and company names are correctly spelled. Any errors found in the proof must be marked and returned for correction before the ad is published.

20.2 AFTER YOU READ

Reviewing Key Terms and Concepts

1. How can you create a focal point and eye movement in a print ad?
2. What size typeface would you use to attract attention in an ad? Why?
3. What is shown on an advertising proof?

Integrating Academic Skills

Math

4. If a Web banner ad has a click-through rate of one percent and was sent to 15,000 people, how many people visited the banner Web site?

Reading/Language Arts

5. Investigate the Better Business Bureau's (BBB) Code of Advertising. Select one of the BBB's basic advertising principles (comparative prices, claims of free, cents-off sales, etc.) to research and develop a short oral report on the standards for the specific advertising practice.

Check your answers at *marketingessentials.glencoe.com/20/read*

CAREERS IN MARKETING

RANDALL RENSCH
FREELANCE ADVERTISING COPYWRITER

What do you do at work?

Writing is usually done in stages: concept, approval, headlines and basic copy, approval, then finished draft and polish. Sometimes we have to do it overnight. And, once in a great while, we have to do it over. I used to view my services as simply copywriting. Over time, it became apparent that for many clients I was as much a creative consultant. So if I have a concern about an existing concept, I will voice it and offer alternatives. So that's about half of what I do. The other half consists of running my business: billing, filing, computer repair, and writing self-promotional material.

What skills are most important to you?

Obviously, the ability to write is the real core. But advertising copywriting isn't just writing. It's also business writing and salesmanship, all imperceptibly rolled into one task. People skills are also very important. Some ability to concentrate, self-motivate, and run a small business are also important.

What is your key to success?

Niche specialization. Write copy about industrial products, or fashion, or Web sites, whatever. The key to my success is my flexibility. A client knows that I see problems and solutions from a broad perspective, that I bring new angles and ideas from related fields, and that whatever they need in a pinch, I'm able to deliver.

Aptitudes, Abilities, and Skills

Writing and communication skills, time management, research ability, and self-motivation

Education and Training

Degrees in communication, language arts, marketing, or general business are helpful.

Career Path

Copywriting positions within companies like ad agencies and marketing firms offer a point of entry to this career, which has abundant room for growth both within a company and as a freelancer.

THINKING CRITICALLY

Why is it important for a writer to focus on one or more areas of specialty?

Online Action!

Go to *marketingessentials.glencoe.com/20/careers* to find a career-related activity.

CHAPTER 20 REVIEW

FOCUS on KEY POINTS

SECTION 20.1

- Print advertisements usually contain four key elements: headline, copy, illustrations, and signature. Some advertisements also include the company's slogan, which is often presented with or near the signature. Each of the four key elements enhances the overall theme of a product promotion. The four fundamental elements of a print advertisement are applicable to ads in other media.
- An advertising campaign coordinates a series of ads around a theme. Ad agencies specialize in developing ad campaigns and crafting ads for clients.

SECTION 20.2

- Businesses need to follow ad layout principles when developing print advertisements. Companies can turn to a variety of sources for helping in developing their ad layouts, including newspaper advertising salespeople, magazine representatives, and advertising agency personnel (such as art directors, copywriters, or account executives).

REVIEW VOCABULARY

1. advertising campaign (p. 422)
2. advertising agencies (p. 423)
3. headline (p. 425)
4. copy (p. 425)
5. illustration (p. 427)
6. clip art (p. 427)
7. signature (p. 428)
8. slogan (p. 428)
9. ad layout (p. 429)
10. advertising proof (p. 433)

REVIEW FACTS and IDEAS

11. How are advertising campaigns developed? (20.1)
12. What is the role of an advertising agency? (20.1)
13. What are the four essential elements of a print ad? (20.1)
14. What should illustrations show about a product? (20.1)
15. List five principles that should be followed in developing print advertising. (20.2)
16. Why is color important in print advertisements? (20.2)
17. How can variety be provided when selecting typefaces? (20.2)

BUILD SKILLS

18. Workplace Skills

Human Relations A customer wishes to purchase an item that was advertised improperly in a print advertisement. The item actually costs more than the advertised price. When told about the higher price, the customer is upset and angry, but she still wants the product. What procedures would you use to calm the customer and still complete the sale?

19. Technology Applications

Design an Ad Layout Using a desktop publishing program, select a product that you would advertise for a target audience of your choice. Develop an advertising proof and then write a paragraph describing why your layout would attract and appeal to your target audience.

20. Math Practice

Figure Out Advertising Credit Your hardware store has a cooperative arrangement with a manufacturer of garden tools. The store receives a 3.5 percent advertising credit on total yearly sales. What is your advertising credit on sales totaling $42,000?

DEVELOP CRITICAL THINKING

21. Investigating Advertising Agencies

Perform an Internet search for Advertiser and Agency Red Books. Select one of the top 25 advertising agencies by billings. Summarize the types of services it provides to clients. Would you select this company for your ad campaign? Why or why not?

22. Circulation and Ads

Why are media circulation numbers key to the business of print ads? What do they determine? To give examples that illustrate your answer, you should research advertising rates for one or two publications of your choice. As you work to find out this information, also note whether the publication you have selected is distributed nationwide or regionally. How does this type of information influence promotion decisions?

APPLY CONCEPTS

23. Creating an Advertising Campaign

Design an advertising campaign of any length for a service, product, or company of your choice. Imagine that you will present the campaign to a prospective client. Research the appropriate budget and media.

Activity Prepare a summary of your campaign to present in class. Explain and justify your choices. Bring visuals such as a poster-sized sketch of your main ad or a graphic representation of all the campaign components and how they work together.

24. Creating an Advertising Layout

Select a product that interests you and develop an ad layout, including a sketch of the design, a headline, copy, illustration, and signature.

Activity Create an 8 1/2" by 11" print advertising layout sketch. Prepare a summary explaining the parts of the ad and why you think they are effective.

NET SAVVY

25. Ad Research

Select a product or service that interests you and conduct an Internet search to find an ad for it. You might select either an ad, a banner, or a button. Analyze how this ad works and list three reasons you think it is effective.

THE  CONNECTION

Role Play: Ad Designer

Situation You are to assume the role of part-time employee of a locally owned jewelry store located in a small town. You are a high school student and a member of the school's field hockey team that has just won the state championship. The store's owner (judge) is thrilled and has decided to run an ad in the local newspaper to congratulate the team.

Activity The jewelry store owner (judge) has asked you to create a draft outline of the ad. The ad should contain the name of the store, the high school team name, and mention you as an employee. You are to present your draft of the ad to the jewelry store owner (judge).

Evaluation You will be evaluated on how well you meet the following performance indicators:

- Explain components of advertisements
- Analyze costs/benefits of company participation in community activities
- Explain the nature of positive customer/client relations
- Demonstrate appropriate creativity
- Prepare simple written reports

@ Online Action!

For more information and DECA Prep practice, go to *marketingessentials.glencoe.com/20/DECA*

MARKETING INTERNSHIP

A SIMULATED DECA ADVERTISING CAMPAIGN EVENT

Pitch a New Client

BASIC BACKGROUND

POGO is trying to get off the ground. The start-up air taxi service is looking for investors to put its business plan into action. It intends to offer short flights on six-seat mini-jets to and from small airports of the customer's choosing and on the customer's own schedule. Its plan calls for each of its mini-jets to fly 1,500 hours a year, or about 750 two-hour trips.

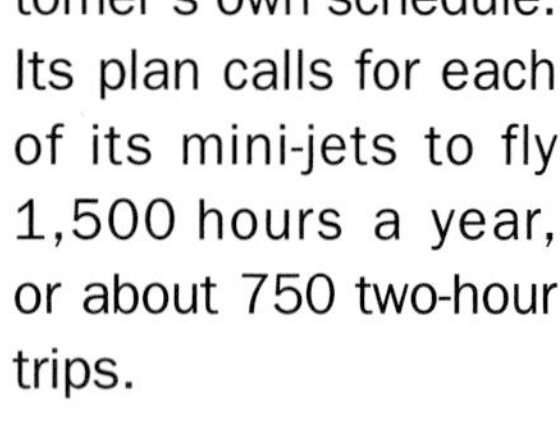

Expensive . . . and Economical Like a taxicab, the cost per mile is set, regardless of the number of passengers. It's pricey for someone flying alone, but if a company has four executives going to the same destination, POGO's price is pretty close to the cost of four first-class seats on a regular airline. The main selling point is convenience: There are no long waits at the airport and no fear of losing one's luggage. The target market is a mid-level executive who earns at least $150,000 a year and flies once every five or six weeks.

YOUR OBJECTIVE

Your firm would like to sign POGO as a client. The plan is to sell the company on your firm's ability to promote the business to its target market. Your objective is to prepare an effective marketing proposal to present to POGO.

ASSIGNMENT AND STRATEGY

- **Get the background** To get started you will need to conduct the opportunities and threats portion of a SWOT analysis for POGO and a competitive assessment. For example, look at the cost of first-class tickets on commercial airlines, as well as the cost to charter a small jet for routes that POGO might want to fly.

  Research attitudes about air travel. Learn what annoys most airline travelers, especially business travelers, and how POGO's service could remove or reduce those annoyances.

  Decide which media are best suited to reach POGO's target market.

- **Write the proposal** Begin your proposal by identifying POGO's main problem in one sentence. Then write a statement of purpose—what your firm intends to do to help POGO achieve its goals. Tell what you did to prepare for this

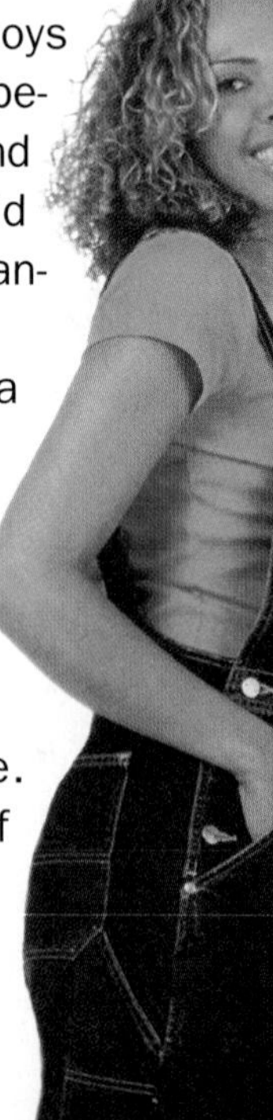

presentation. Include a time line or work plan that outlines how to proceed.

Consider all the elements of a promotional mix: selling, advertising, sales promotion, and public relations. Provide rationale for your recommendations.

- **What your project should include** Be sure to tell how POGO will differentiate itself from its competitors. To make your project complete, create a sample of one or more of your promotional ideas.

YOUR REPORT

Use a word processing program and presentation software to prepare a double-spaced report and an oral presentation for POGO. See a suggested outline and key evaluation points at *marketingessentials.glencoe.com/internship*

BUILD YOUR PORTFOLIO

Option 1 Internship Report
Once you have completed your Marketing Internship project and presentation, include your written report and a few printouts of key slides from your oral presentation in your Marketing Portfolio.

Option 2 Creating a Promotional Plan
A client (choose an existing company) wants a new, trendy promotional plan. Start with a SWOT analysis, a competitive assessment, and identify a target market. Then design a cutting-edge proposal that addresses your client's needs. Provide sample promotional materials. Prepare your written proposal using a word processing program and use presentation software for your oral presentation. See a suggested outline and key evaluation points at *marketingessentials.glencoe.com/portfolio*

@ Online Action!

Go to *marketingessentials.glencoe.com/Unit/6/DECA* to review promotion concepts that relate to DECA events.

UNIT 7 Distribution

In this unit you will find

- **Chapter 21** Channels of Distribution
- **Chapter 22** Physical Distribution
- **Chapter 23** Purchasing
- **Chapter 24** Stock Handling and Inventory Control

Marketing Plan

1 **ANALYSIS**
SWOT
Economic
Socio-Cultural
Technological
Competitive

2 **STRATEGY**
Promotion
Place
Price
Product

3 **IMPLEMENTATION**
Organization
Management
Staffing

4 **BUDGET**
Cost of Sales
Cost of Promotion
Incomes and Expenses

5 **CONTROL**
Evaluation
Performance Measures
Performance Analysis

ANALYZE THE AD

This Florida's Natural ad suggests that the company's juice is fresher than its competitors' products. How does the ad communicate this message?

Market Talk Refrigerated orange juice easily outsells frozen, concentrated juice. Distribution of refrigerated juice has to happen quickly because the juice will spoil if it does not make it into the stores fast enough.

Think and Write Flip through a newspaper and find advertisements for three food items and two other consumer products. Research how these products are distributed from the grower or manufacturer to the consumer. Is fast distribution part of how the products are marketed? What are some reasons to distribute nonfood items quickly? Write a paragraph describing your findings.

@ Online Action! **Go to *marketingessentials.glencoe.com/u7/ad* for an extended activity.**

In this unit

Foundations of Marketing

Business, Management, Entrepreneurship

Functions of Marketing

Distribution

CHAPTER 21
Channels of Distribution

Chapter Objectives

After reading this chapter, you should be able to:

- Explain the concept of a channel of distribution
- Identify channel members
- Compare channels of distribution for consumer and industrial products
- Explain distribution planning
- Name and describe the three levels of distribution intensity
- Explain the effect of the Internet on distribution planning
- Describe the challenges of distribution planning for international markets

GUIDE TO THE PHOTO

Market Talk Products may pass through many hands before reaching the consumer or industrial user. Use of channels of distribution depends on many factors, including the product, the target audience, supply and demand, and costs associated with each channel.

Quick Think For most products, there are several channels that can be used to move products from the producer to the end user. How would you decide which is the best?

THE DECA CONNECTION

Performance indicators represent key skills and knowledge. Relating them to the concepts explained in this chapter is your key to success in DECA events. Keep this in mind as you read this chapter and write some notes each time you encounter material that helps you master a key concept. These acronyms represent DECA events that involve knowledge of concepts in this chapter.

AAAL	**FMAL**	**MMS***	**TMDM***
AAML*	**FMDM***	**QSRM***	**TSE***
ADC*	**FMML***	**RMAL**	**VPM**
BSM	**FSRM***	**RMML***	
EMDM*	**HMDM***	**SMDM***	

In all these DECA events you should be able to follow these performance indicators:

- Explain the nature and scope of distribution
- Explain the nature of channels of distribution
- Coordinate distribution with other marketing activities
- Explain the nature of channel-member relationships

All the events with an asterisk (*) also include these performance indicators:

- Explain the nature of channel strategies
- Select channels of distribution
- Evaluate channel members

Some events include additional performance indicators. These are:

BSM Discuss the nature of service intermediaries

EMDM Explain distribution issues and trends in e-commerce

DECA PREP

Check your understanding of DECA performance indicators with the DECA activity in this chapter's review. For more information and DECA Prep practice, go to *marketingessentials .glencoe.com/21/DECA*

SECTION 21.1

Distribution

OBJECTIVES

- **Explain the concept of a channel of distribution**
- **Identify channel members**
- **Compare channels of distribution for consumer and industrial products**

KEY TERMS

- **channel of distribution**
- **intermediaries**
- **wholesalers**
- **rack jobbers**
- **drop shippers**
- **retailers**
- **brick-and-mortar retailers**
- **e-tailing**
- **agents**
- **direct distribution**
- **indirect distribution**

READ and STUDY

BEFORE YOU READ

Predict What do you already know about distribution?

THE MAIN IDEA

As you know, the marketing mix includes decisions about product, place, price, and promotion. In this chapter, you will explore the place decision—where and how the product will be distributed and sold in the marketplace. Making the correct place decision has an impact on the entire operation of a business.

STUDY ORGANIZER

Draw the chart below. As you read this section, write in the routes taken to distribute products to consumers (A–E) and to industrial users (A–D).

Consumer Products	Industrial Products
A.	A.
B.	B.
C.	C.
D.	D.
E.	

WHILE YOU READ

Compare List the different channels and how they are used to distribute products to consumers and to industrial users.

Distribution: How It Works

How do you get somebody to buy your product? By marketing it! Now the question is how does that product get to your customers? This is the place decision, one of the four Ps of the marketing mix.

To make a place decision, marketers must decide on their channel of distribution. The **channel of distribution** is the path a product takes from its producer or manufacturer to the final user. When the product is purchased for use in a business, the final user is classified as an industrial user. When the product is purchased for personal use, the final user is classified as a consumer.

Using shampoo as an example, you can see how the same product may be classified as both a consumer and an industrial product. Manufacturers of shampoo sell their product to the customer through retail operations but

THANKS TO MISSISSIPPI, VEHICLES THAT ARE AHEAD OF THEIR TIME ARE EVEN FURTHER AHEAD OF THEIR TIME.

Speed is nothing new to Nissan. So when they decided to build a state-of-the-art plant in Canton, Mississippi, they wanted it done, well, really, really fast. That's when Mississippi put the pedal to the metal. Preparation and site work for the 2.5 million square-foot plant was completed in just five months (more than a year faster than average). A water and wastewater system was finished in 12 months. A new freeway interchange in 14 months. In fact, Mississippi helped Nissan go from groundbreaking ceremonies to groundbreaking vehicles, like the all-new Nissan Quest minivan, in just 25 months. Proving what Nissan had known from the start: when it comes to business, Mississippi is built for speed. To learn more, visit us at mississippiandnissan.com.

U.S.-assembled Nissans consist of domestic and globally sourced parts. Nissan and Nissan model names are Nissan trademarks. Always wear your seat belt, and please don't drink and drive. © 2003 Nissan North America, Inc.

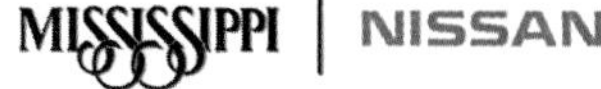

• **FASTER DELIVERY** Nissan, a Japanese auto manufacturer, has built a plant in Mississippi, so many Nissans sold in the U.S. are also built in the U.S.

What consequences do you think having a North American plant has in terms of distribution?

NET MARKETING

How Will They Find You?

You have started an online auto parts business. You have great sources for parts, good relationships with your suppliers, and an attractive Web site. All you need is for customers to find your site among thousands of similar ones. Someone might search for "discount auto parts" on a search engine such as Google or Yahoo. What determines which merchants come up on top? Learning how search engines determine which sites are listed first is key to a successful Web business.

What Is a Good Web Page Design?

Your site's title should include words that will attract searchers—something like "Discount VW Vintage Auto Parts," where each word points to something a searcher might target. Each page of your site needs a different title. A meta-tag, a short but complete description of what is on the site, is also essential.

THINK LIKE A MARKETER

What can happen if you include words in your title that do not reflect the content of your Web page?

Online Action!

Go to *marketingessentials.glencoe.com/21/net* to find an activity on the Internet and distribution.

also may sell it to hair salons and hotel chains as an industrial product for use in a business.

Channel Members

Businesses involved in sales transactions that move products from the manufacturer to the final user are called **intermediaries** or middlemen. Intermediaries reduce the number of contacts required to reach the final user of the product. Suppose four customers wanted to buy a digital camera made by Nikon. If Nikon sells directly to consumers, it would have to make four separate sales transactions. By using an intermediary, such as CompUSA, the number of contacts Nikon must make is reduced to one.

Intermediaries are classified on the basis of whether they take ownership (title) of goods and services. Merchant intermediaries take title; agent intermediaries do not. Agent intermediaries, usually called agents, are paid a commission to help buyers and sellers get together. The two major types of merchant intermediaries are wholesalers and retailers.

Wholesalers

Businesses that buy large quantities of goods from manufacturers, store the goods, and then resell them to other businesses are called **wholesalers**. Their customers are retailers. Wholesalers may be called distributors when their customers are professional or commercial users, manufacturers, governments, institutions, or other wholesalers. In either case, they take title to the goods they buy for resale.

Two specialized wholesalers are rack jobbers and drop shippers. **Rack jobbers** are wholesalers that manage inventory and merchandising for retailers by counting stock, filling it in when needed, and maintaining store displays. As the name implies, they provide the racks for display of the product in a retail store. They bill the retailer only for the goods

sold, not for all the items on display. Products that are handled by rack jobbers include CDs, hosiery, health products, and cosmetics.

Drop shippers own the goods they sell but do not physically handle the actual products. They deal in large quantities of items in bulk, such as coal, lumber, and chemicals that require special handling. Drop shippers sell the goods to other businesses and have the producer ship the merchandise directly to the buyers.

Retailers

Retailers sell goods to the final consumer for personal use. Traditional retailers, called **brick-and-mortar retailers**, sell goods to the customer from their own physical stores. These retail stores buy their products from manufacturers or wholesalers. They serve as the final link between the manufacturer and consumer. To build good customer relationships, they often have special services, such as offering credit or providing delivery.

A number of non-store retailing operations serve the customer. They include automatic retailing (vending machines), direct mail and catalog retailing, TV home shopping, and online retailing (or e-tailing).

Vending service companies buy manufacturers' products, such as drinks, snacks, and travelers items, and sell them through vending machines that dispense goods to consumers. These companies often place their vending machines in stores, office buildings, hospitals, airports, schools, and other institutions for free.

•GETTING the GOODS to CUSTOMERS Barnes & Noble stores in New York City provide an extra service to their customers: same-day delivery.

How does this illustrate the importance of thinking about distribution?

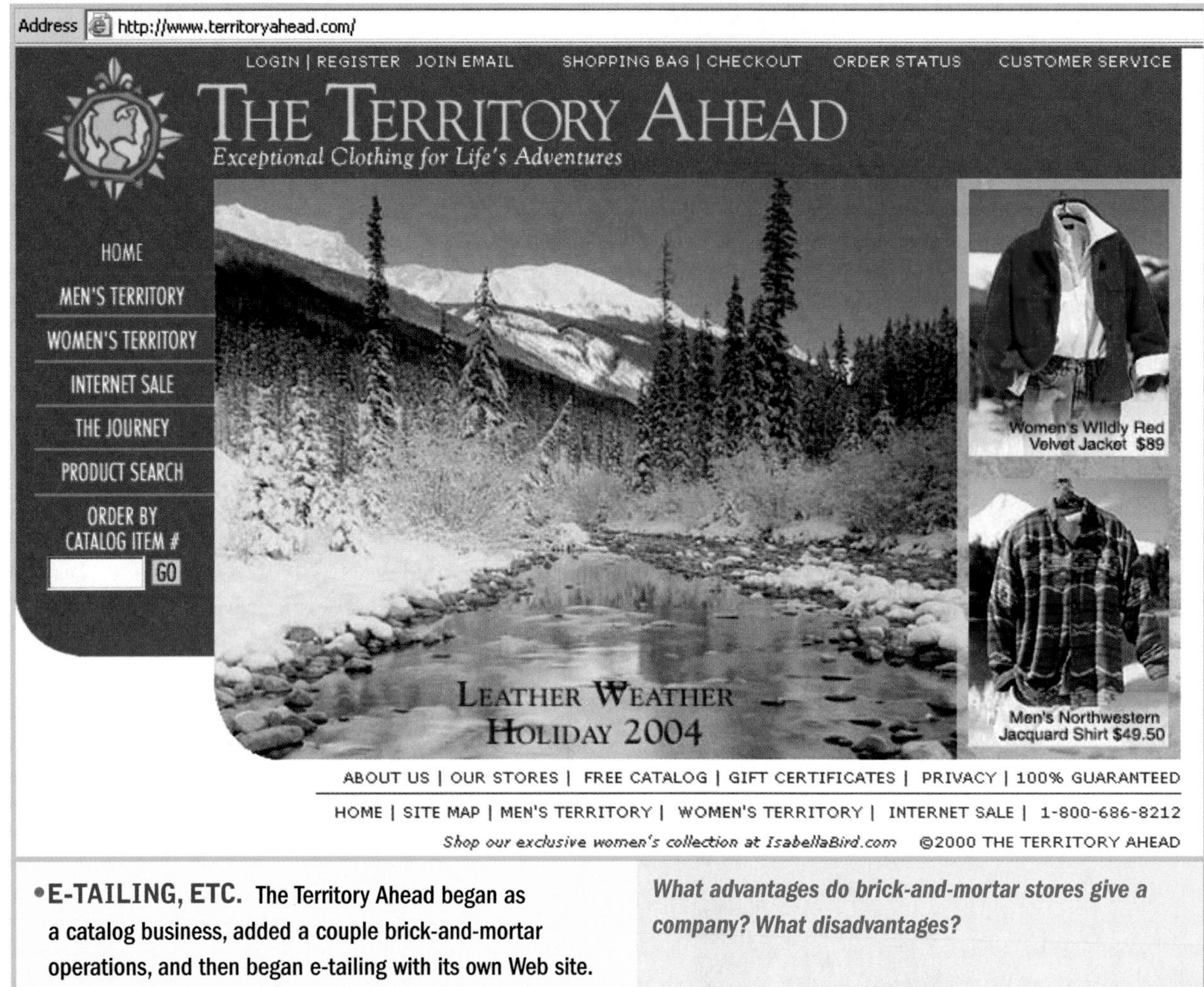

• E-TAILING, ETC. The Territory Ahead began as a catalog business, added a couple brick-and-mortar operations, and then began e-tailing with its own Web site.

What advantages do brick-and-mortar stores give a company? What disadvantages?

Direct mail and catalogs also reach the final consumer. Many large brick-and-mortar retailers produce their own catalogs to reach consumers who prefer shopping at home. There are also catalog houses that buy goods from different manufacturers and display them in a catalog for sale to the customer.

Television home shopping networks are TV stations that sell products to consumers. These companies buy the products in set quantities and sell them via television programs. Consumers phone in their orders while watching shows. One example of this is the Home Shopping Network (HSN).

Online retailing, or **e-tailing**, involves retailers selling products over the Internet to the customer. Some of the big e-tailing companies are found only on the Internet, such as amazon.com or overstock.com.

Not to be left out of the Internet revolution, many brick-and-mortar retailers, such as Target and Williams-Sonoma, have created Web sites. Some of the top e-tailing sectors are air travel, books, and hardware.

Agents

Unlike wholesalers and retailers, agents do not own the goods they sell. **Agents** act as intermediaries by bringing buyers and sellers together. There are two different types of agents: manufacturers' representatives and brokers.

Independent Manufacturers' Representatives

Independent manufacturers' representatives work with several related (but noncompeting) manufacturers in a specific industry. They are not on any manufacturer's payroll. Instead, they are paid commissions based on what they sell.

An independent manufacturers' agent might carry a line of fishing rods from one manufacturer, lures from another, insulated clothing for hunters from a different manufacturer, and outdoor shirts from still another manufacturer.

Brokers

A broker's principal function is to bring buyers and sellers together in order for a sale to take place. Brokers usually do not have a continued relationship with either party. They negotiate the sale, are paid a commission, and then look for other customers. Food brokers, however, are an exception to this rule. Food brokers represent several manufacturers of products sold in supermarkets, convenience stores, and other specialty food stores.

Direct and Indirect Channels

Channels of distribution are classified as direct or indirect (see Figures 21.1 and 21.2). **Direct distribution** occurs when the producer sells goods or services directly

Case Study

Changing Channels

Gateway Computers was founded with a $10,000 loan by Theodore Waitt on his parents' Iowa farm in 1985. It grew to become a major computer producer, selling directly to consumers over the phone and on the Web. After acquiring eMachines, a low-end PC company, early in 2004, Gateway was the number three PC producer in the United States.

In 1996, Gateway became the first "bricks-and-clicks" computer seller (with both online sales and its own stores). There were over 300 Gateway stores where customers could order computers for delivery.

The Wrong Channel?

Company stores were never profitable, and in April 2004 Gateway closed all its stores, returning to phone and Web-based sales. eMachines had been available at other retail outlets, including Best Buy, and Gateway expanded into that channel for its own branded computers and consumer electronics.

Part of being a direct distributor is developing an especially close relationship with customers. Selling Gateway products in third party retail outlets will affect the control the company has over that relationship, but there is a trade-off in terms of a wider market for Gateway.

THINK STRATEGICALLY

What reasons can a direct distributor have to open brick-and-mortar or bricks-and-clicks operations?

Go to *marketingessentials.glencoe.com/21/case* to find an activity on channels of distribution.

Figure 21.1 Distribution Channels—Consumer Products

• **Getting the Goods in Consumers' Hands** Products are distributed to consumers through five channels. Historically, most consumer goods were not distributed using direct distribution (channel A) because consumers became accustomed to shopping in retail stores. E-commerce is changing that for some products.

Which channel is used most often for items that go out of date quickly or need servicing?

CHANNEL A

Manufacturer/Producer Directly to Consumer

There are five ways in which direct distribution is used for consumer goods.

1. Selling products at the production site.
2. Having a sales force call on consumers.
3. Using catalogs or ads to generate sales.
4. Using telemarketing.
5. Using the Internet to make online sales.

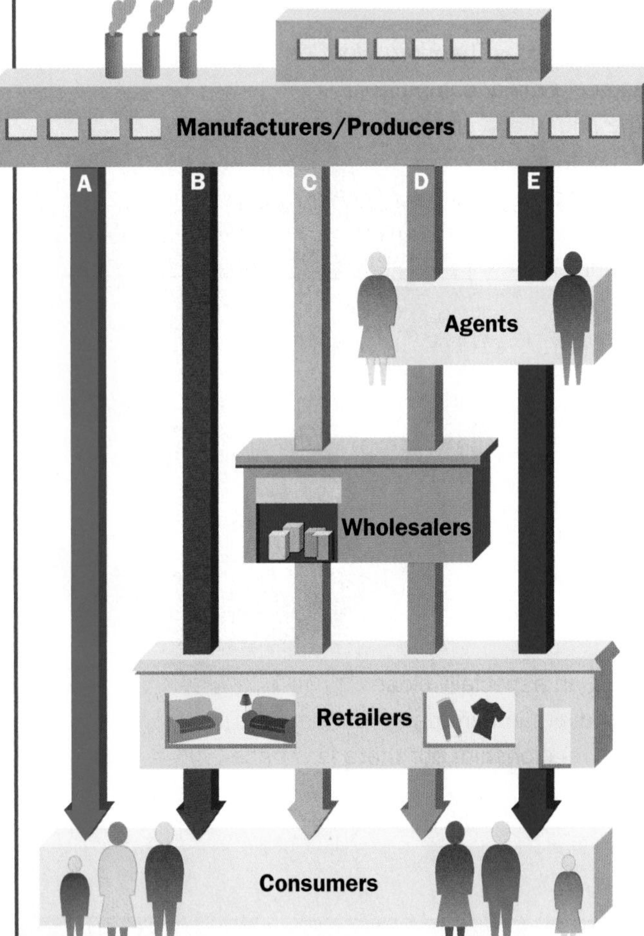

CHANNEL B

Manufacturer/Producer to Retailer to Consumer

This is the most commonly used channel for merchandise that dates quickly or needs servicing.

CHANNEL C

Manufacturer/Producer to Wholesaler to Retailer to Consumer

This is the most common distribution method for staple goods, which are items that are always carried in stock and whose styles do not change frequently.

CHANNEL D

Manufacturer/Producer to Agents to Wholesaler to Retailer to Consumer

This is the channel for manufacturers who wish to concentrate on production and leave sales and distribution to others.

CHANNEL E

Manufacturer/Producer to Agents to Retailer to Consumer

This is the channel chosen by manufacturers who do not want to handle their own sales to retailers. The agent simply brings the buyer and seller together.

Online Action!

Go to *marketingessentials.glencoe.com/21/figure/1* to find a project on distribution channels for consumer products.

Figure 21.2 Distribution Channels—Industrial Products

• **Getting the Goods to Businesses** Industrial buyers have different needs than retail buyers, so they use different channels of distribution. The least common channel in the consumer market—direct distribution (channel A)—is the most common in the industrial market. Industrial products and services are distributed through four channels.

Which channel is most often used to distribute major equipment used in manufacturing?

CHANNEL A

Manufacturer/Producer Directly to Industrial Users

This is the most common method of distribution for major equipment used in manufacturing and other businesses. The manufacturer's sales force calls on the industrial user to sell goods or services. Note: All methods of direct distribution listed for the consumer market are used in the industrial market as well.

CHANNEL B

Manufacturer/Producer to Industrial Distributors to Industrial Users

This channel is used most often for small standardized parts and operational supplies needed to run a business. Industrial wholesalers (distributors) take ownership of the products, stock them, and sell them as needed to industrial users.

CHANNEL C

Manufacturer/Producer to Agents to Industrial Distributors to Industrial Users

Small manufacturers who do not have the time or money to invest in a direct sales force may prefer this channel. The agent sells the goods to the industrial wholesaler who stores, resells, and ships them to the industrial user.

CHANNEL D

Manufacturer/Producer to Agents to Industrial Users

This is another channel used when a manufacturer does not want to hire its own sales force. The agent represents the manufacturer for sale of the goods but does not take possession or title. The merchandise is shipped directly from the manufacturer to the industrial user.

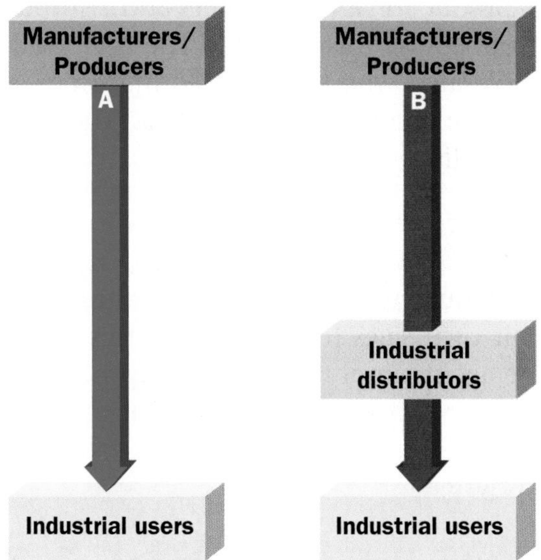

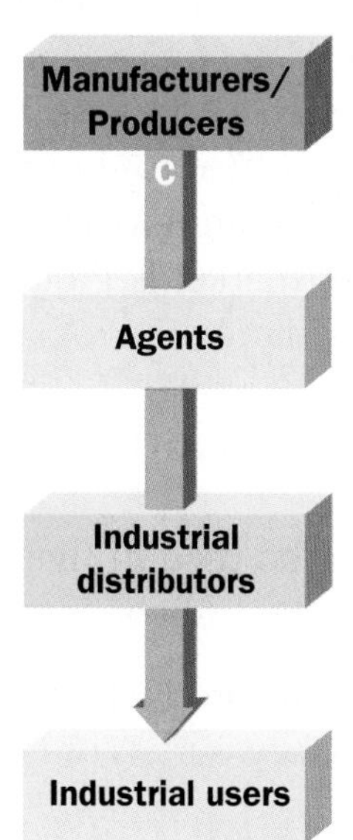

Online Action!

Go to *marketingessentials.glencoe.com/21/figure/2* to find a project on distribution channels for industrial products.

to the customer, with no intermediaries. **Indirect distribution** involves one or more intermediaries. Both consumer markets and industrial markets use direct and indirect channels of distribution.

Examples of Channels of Distribution

Different channels of distribution are generally used to reach the customer in the consumer and industrial markets.

When selling to the industrial market, a manufacturer would sell paper napkins to industrial distributors who, in turn, would sell the napkins to restaurants.

When selling to the consumer market, the company would sell napkins to a wholesaler or use food brokers to sell to retailers such as grocery stores or party supply shops. Not every option works best for every kind of product or company.

Despite the potential for success that any product may seem to have, it can fail if the wrong channels of distribution are used.

Distribution Channels for Consumer Products and Services

Few consumer products are marketed using direct distribution (channel A) because consumers have become accustomed to shopping in retail stores. The most common indirect channel in the consumer market is Producer to Retailer to Consumer (channel B).

Manufacturer/Producer Directly to Consumer (Channel A)

Direct distribution can be used in five different ways to deliver products to consumers:

1. Selling products at the production site. Examples include factory outlets or farmers' roadside stands.
2. Having a sales force call on consumers at home. Examples include Avon and Tupperware.
3. Using catalogs or ads to generate sales.
4. Having sales representatives call consumers on the telephone (telemarketing). The National Do Not Call registry has greatly limited this method.
5. Using the Internet to make online sales.

Manufacturer/Producer to Retailer to Consumer (Channel B)

This channel is used most often for products that become out of date quickly or need regular servicing. Clothing and automobiles are sold this way. Chain stores and online retailers use this channel.

Manufacturer/Producer to Wholesaler to Retailer to Consumer (Channel C)

This method of distribution is most often used for staple goods, which are items that are always carried in stock and whose styles do not change frequently. The manufacturer sells to the wholesaler, who then handles the sales, warehousing, and distribution of the goods to retailers. Consumer goods sold this way include supermarket items, flowers, candy, and stationery supplies.

Manufacturer/Producer to Agents to Wholesaler to Retailer to Consumer (Channel D)

Manufacturers who prefer to concentrate on production and leave sales and distribution to others use this channel. The agent sells to wholesalers who are involved in storage, sale, and transportation to retailers. The retailer then sells to consumers.

Manufacturer/Producer to Agents to Retailer to Consumer (Channel E)

Manufacturers who do not want to handle their own sales to retailers use this channel. The agent simply brings the buyer and seller together. Expensive cookware, meat, cosmetics, and many supermarket items are sold this way.

Distribution Channels for Industrial Products and Services

Industrial users shop differently and have different needs from consumers, so they use different channels of distribution. The least used channel in the consumer market—direct distribution (channel A)—is the most used channel in the industrial market.

Manufacturer/Producer Directly to Industrial Users (Channel A)

This method of distribution is most often used for major equipment used in manufacturing and other businesses. The manufacturer's sales force calls on the industrial user to sell goods or services. For example, a Xerox sales representative sells copiers directly to manufacturers and commercial businesses.

Manufacturer/Producer to Industrial Distributors to Industrial Users (Channel B)

This channel is used most often for small standardized parts and operational supplies needed to run a business. Industrial wholesalers (distributors) take ownership of the products, stock them, and sell them as needed to industrial users. For example, a restaurant supply wholesaler buys pots, pans, utensils, serving pieces, and paper products from various manufacturers to sell to restaurant owners.

Manufacturer/Producer to Agents to Industrial Distributors to Industrial Users (Channel C)

Small manufacturers who do not have time or money to invest in a direct sales force may prefer to use the services of an agent. The agent represents the manufacturer for sale of the goods but does not take possession or title. The agent sells the goods to the industrial wholesaler who stores, resells, and ships them to the industrial user.

Manufacturer/Producer to Agents to Industrial Users (Channel D)

This is another channel used when a manufacturer does not want to hire its own sales force. The merchandise is shipped directly from the manufacturer to the industrial user. Construction equipment, farm products, and dry goods are often marketed this way.

21.1 AFTER YOU READ

Reviewing Key Terms and Concepts

1. What term describes the path a product takes from producer to final user?
2. What is the function of intermediaries?
3. Name the two main types of distribution channels.

Integrating Academic Skills

Math

4. Assume a manufacturer makes an item that costs $2.50 to produce. The markup when sold to the distributor is 35 percent. What is the cost to the distributor? When the distributor sells this item to the retailer, the markup is 40 percent. How much will the retailer pay for the item?

Language Arts

5. Using standard outline form, organize the following information into a Distribution Channel Members Outline: stores, wholesalers, retailers, merchant intermediaries, rack jobbers, agent intermediaries, drop shippers, intermediaries, direct mail operations, and independent manufacturers' representatives.

Check your answers at *marketingessentials.glencoe.com/21/read*

SECTION 21.2

Distribution Planning

OBJECTIVES

- **Explain distribution planning**
- **Name and describe the three levels of distribution intensity**
- **Explain the effect of the Internet on distribution planning**
- **Describe the challenges of distribution planning for international markets**

KEY TERMS

- **exclusive distribution**
- **integrated distribution**
- **selective distribution**
- **intensive distribution**
- **e-marketplace**

BEFORE YOU READ

Predict What do you already know about distribution planning?

THE MAIN IDEA

Distribution decisions affect the entire company, so it is important for you to know how these decisions are made. It is also helpful to know how these decisions are carried out in different markets, including international markets and e-marketplaces.

STUDY ORGANIZER

In a chart like the one below, note the main components of distribution planning.

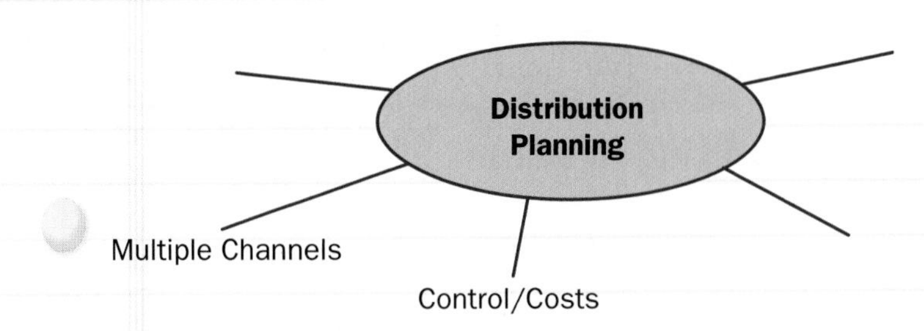

Analyze Determine ways the Internet might facilitate the use of channels of distribution.

Understanding Distribution Planning

Distribution planning involves decisions about a product's physical movement and transfer of ownership from producer to consumer. In this chapter, we address only transfer of ownership concerns. Distribution decisions affect a firm's marketing program. Some of the major considerations are the use of multiple channels, control versus costs, intensity of distribution desired, and involvement in e-commerce.

Multiple Channels

A producer uses multiple channels when its product fits the needs of both industrial and consumer markets. J & J Snack Foods sells its pretzels, drinks, and cookies to supermarkets, movie theaters, stadiums, and other sports arenas. It also sells to schools, colleges, and hospitals. The producer must identify the best channel for each market.

Control Versus Costs

All manufacturers and producers must weigh the control they want to keep over the distribution of their products against costs and profitability.

Who Does the Selling?

A manufacturer must decide how much control it wants over its sales function. It can use its own sales force or hire agents to do the selling.

A direct sales force is costly. In-house sales representatives are on the company payroll, receive employee benefits, and are reimbursed for expenses. The manufacturer, though, has complete control over them. It can establish sales quotas and easily monitor each sales representative's performance.

With an agent, a manufacturer loses some of its control over how sales are made. This is because agents work independently, running their own businesses. However, the relative cost of using agents can be lower than hiring an in-house sales staff. No employee benefits or expenses must be paid because agents are independent businesspeople. Another benefit is that agents are paid a set percentage of sales, assuring that the cost of sales is always the same in relation to the sales generated.

Distribution Intensity

Distribution intensity has to do with how widely a product will be distributed. There are three levels of distribution intensity: exclusive, selective, and intensive.

Exclusive Distribution

Exclusive distribution involves protected territories for distribution of a product in a given geographic area. Dealers are assured that they are the only ones within a certain geographic radius that have the right to sell the manufacturer's or wholesaler's products. Prestige, image, channel control, and a high profit margin for both the manufacturer and intermediaries are characteristic of this distribution strategy. Franchised operations are examples of exclusive distribution planning.

Wholesalers may also sponsor voluntary groups in which a retailer agrees to buy and maintain a minimum inventory of the wholesaler's products. One example of a voluntary group sponsored by a wholesaler is the National Auto Parts Association (NAPA). Retailers affiliated with NAPA buy most of their stock from NAPA and participate in its promotions.

Some manufacturers own and run their own retail operations. This variation on exclusive distribution is **integrated distribution**. The manufacturer acts as wholesaler and retailer for its own products. The Gap sells its clothing in company-owned retail stores.

Selective Distribution

Selective distribution means that a limited number of outlets in a given geographic area are used to sell the product. The goal is to select channel members that can maintain the image of the product and are good credit risks, aggressive marketers, and good inventory planners.

Intermediaries are selected for their ability to cater to the final users that the manufacturer wants to attract. Dana Buchman sells its clothing only through top department stores that appeal to the affluent customers who buy its merchandise. It does not sell its goods in a chain megastore or a variety store with a very different target market.

Intensive Distribution

Intensive distribution involves the use of all suitable outlets to sell a product. The objective is complete market coverage, and the ultimate goal is to sell to as many customers as possible, wherever they choose to shop. Motor oil is marketed in quick-lube shops, farm stores, auto parts retailers, supermarkets, drugstores, hardware stores, warehouse clubs, and other mass merchandisers to reach the maximum number of customers.

E-Commerce

E-commerce is the means by which products are sold to customers and industrial buyers through the Internet. You already learned that e-tailing is retail selling over the Internet. This online shopping location is called the **e-marketplace**.

In 2004, Internet travel bookings were estimated at $54 billion, which was 23 percent of the travel industry's revenues. Consumers have also become accustomed to buying books, toys, and other goods online.

E-marketplaces for B2B operations provide one-stop shopping and substantial savings for industrial buyers. Online catalogs of products supplied by different companies make it easier for corporate buyers to compare prices and get the best deal. E-marketplaces provide smaller businesses with the exposure that they could not get elsewhere.

In each of the past five years, a greater proportion of B2B trade has taken place via the Internet. This trend is expected to continue for some time.

Legal and Ethical Considerations in Distribution

In most cases, businesses may use whatever channel arrangement they desire. Laws affecting channels generally prevent exclusionary tactics that might keep other companies from using a desired channel. The Clayton Antitrust Act of 1914 prevents exclusive arrangements that substantially lessen competition,

GLOBAL MARKET

Marketing Multiculturalism

Convention and visitors' bureaus in many American cities provide guides, maps, and other information about ethnic history and culture they hope will appeal to African Americans, Hispanics, or Asians. They act as marketing agents for their areas, indirectly bringing potential consumers to local businesses.

Destination Marketing Convention bureaus have always marketed their cities in different ways to different business or professional groups. Destination marketers recognize that focusing on ethnic history, food, and cultural events and activities can attract tourists and business travelers—and dollars—from different ethnic groups. In addition to convention bureaus, groups representing minority businesses, such as the African American Chamber of Commerce, publish brochures promoting black-owned businesses to African American visitors to their city. Such groups, along with many city governments, help support festivals and celebrations of ethnic holidays such as Chinese New Year, Cinco de Mayo, or Kwanzaa.

CRITICAL THINKING

How could businesses promote a city's Cinco de Mayo celebration to visitors?

@ Online Action!

Go to *marketingessentials.glencoe.com/21/global* to find an activity on distribution and multicultural marketing.

create a monopoly, or in which one party did not commit to the agreement voluntarily.

Some distribution practices meet legal requirements but may be ethically questionable. The American Marketing Association (AMA) Code of Ethics lists the following responsibilities in the area of distribution:

- Not manipulating the availability of a product for purpose of exploitation
- Not using coercion in the marketing channel
- Not exerting undue influence over the reseller's decision whether to handle the product.

Distribution Planning for Foreign Markets

Foreign market environments require that businesses adjust their distribution systems. They also give businesses a chance to experiment with different distribution strategies. For example, in the United States, General Motors distributes automobiles through franchised retail car dealerships. However, in Taiwan, GM owns its own retail dealerships and sells cars directly to consumers. In Taiwan, GM is free from franchise dealer constraints and has been able to test systems for selling cars to consumers directly over the Internet.

Cultural considerations should also be weighed when planning distribution in foreign markets. For example, when Reebok wanted to sell its athletic shoes in Europe, it studied European culture and found that Europeans visit sporting goods stores far less often than Americans. The company decided to distribute Reebok's shoes through hundreds of traditional retail shoe outlets. Within one year of adopting this distribution strategy, Reebok's sales in France doubled.

21.2 AFTER YOU READ

Reviewing Key Terms and Concepts

1. Why might a company decide to use multiple distribution channels?
2. What are the factors a company must consider when choosing between a direct sales force and independent sales agents?
3. What are two advantages that e-commerce provides in B2B sales?

Integrating Academic Skills

Math

4. Assume manufacturer A had sales of $3,500,000 and sales expenses of 8 percent for outside sales agents. Manufacturer B, a rival company, had sales of $5,750,000 for the same period. Its sales expenses were $402,500. Which company had the lowest rate of sales expenses?

Language Arts

5. Look up the definitions for each of the following words in the American Marketing Association's Code of Ethics: *manipulate, availability, exploit, coercion, exert,* and *undue*. Then, rewrite each of the statements from the code in your own words.

Check your answers at *marketingessentials.glencoe.com/21/read*

CAREERS IN MARKETING

JUSTIN STERLING MOODY
OWNER
FUSIONIST.COM

What do you do at work?

I own and operate a network of online stores, focused on high-quality products from the hip-hop and underground youth cultures.

We build everything, from the store section to the entire Web site. My resume includes bobmarley.com, fatburger.com, mearone.com, saberone.com, shopbelton.com, awolone .com and fusionist.com.

I also manage the inventory and distribution of products sold through Fusionist, and I provide consultation concerning print media projects.

What skills are most important to you?

My most important skill is customer service. Learning how to use a computer is absolutely essential, too. Although you don't need a degree to start your own business, everyone needs to experience college or some type of skill training school.

What is your key to success?

My key to success is to never quit. If you try and try again, you are bound to get it right.

Aptitudes, Abilities, and Skills

Strong interpersonal skills, technical knowledge, and ability to maintain the IT back-end of a Web site

Education and Training

Many Web entrepreneurs are entirely self-taught, although courses do exist focusing on e-commerce and Web marketing.

Career Path

For many Web retailers, careers begin as a hobby, selling and shipping products that are of personal interest. Larger operations can often develop over time if demand is great enough, and if the logistics of the operation can keep up with this demand.

THINKING CRITICALLY

Why is customer service often considered the most valuable skill an entrepreneur can possess?

@ Online Action!

Go to *marketingessentials.glencoe.com/21/careers* to find a career-related activity.

CHAPTER 21 REVIEW

FOCUS on KEY POINTS

SECTION 21.1

- Manufacturers or producers may choose one or more paths (channels) to distribute products to the final user.
- The channels used to distribute consumer products usually differ from those used to distribute to the industrial market.

SECTION 21.2

- Manufacturers or producers may use multiple channels of distribution to reach different markets. Product distribution in foreign markets often requires special planning.
- Distribution intensity may be exclusive, selective, or intensive.

REVIEW VOCABULARY

Working in a group, choose a company and explain how it sells products to consumers and industrial buyers. Include the following terms:

1. channel of distribution (p. 444)
2. intermediaries (p. 446)
3. wholesalers (p. 446)
4. rack jobbers (p. 446)
5. drop shippers (p. 447)
6. retailers (p. 447)
7. brick-and-mortar retailers (p. 447)
8. e-tailing (p. 448)
9. agents (p. 448)
10. direct distribution (p. 449)
11. indirect distribution (p. 452)
12. exclusive distribution (p. 455)
13. selective distribution (p. 455)
14. intensive distribution (p. 455)
15. integrated distribution (p. 455)
16. e-marketplace (p. 456)

REVIEW FACTS and IDEAS

17. A marketer makes a place decision by selecting channels of distribution. What does this mean? (21.1)
18. What is another name for intermediaries? Name two types of intermediaries. (21.1)
19. Name five non-store retailing methods. (21.1)
20. What is the most common method of distribution for consumer products and services? For industrial products and services? (21.1)
21. What are the key questions a firm must consider in establishing a distribution plan? (21.2)
22. Explain why manufacturers sometimes use exclusive distribution. (21.2)
23. How do the costs of having a direct sales force differ from the costs of using independent sales agents? How do the controls differ? (21.2)
24. Name the three levels of distribution intensity and give one advantage of each. (21.2)

BUILD SKILLS

25. Workplace Skills

Writing Your sporting goods manufacturing company wants to sell its exercise equipment products to fitness centers, schools, and individual consumers. As the assistant marketing manager, you have been asked to give your opinion on distribution channels. Write a memo (or an e-mail message) to your marketing manager identifying the channels that you think would best serve each market.

26. Technology Applications

Compare Shipping Costs Your company uses 24-inch mailing tubes to ship its products. Log onto the Internet and locate three distributors for this item. Using a word processing program, create a table comparing the information from each source such as quantities in which the tubes are sold and the stated per item cost. Also compare shipping and handling charges.

27. Math Practice

Calculate Savings The price of a best-selling paperback is $9.00 at a local bookstore. You can purchase the same book through an e-tailer for $6.20 plus 20 percent for shipping charges. How much will you save by purchasing the book through the e-tailer?

DEVELOP CRITICAL THINKING

28. Researching Key Concepts

Interview a marketing manager of a local manufacturer to learn what distribution channels the company uses to sell its products. Or, interview the buyer of a local retail business to learn which channels it uses to purchase its goods. Ask the person you are interviewing to explain how these decisions were made.

29. Select a Level of Distribution

Which level of distribution (intensive, selective, or exclusive) would you choose for the following products:

- Personal computers
- Cashmere sweaters
- A new brand of shampoo
- A new hybrid car

APPLY CONCEPTS

30. Determining Distribution Intensity

Design a product for a manufacturing company to produce. Define the market for your product. Then select the level of intensity that you think would be best for the distribution of your product.

Activity Use a word processing program to describe your product, your intended market, and your preferred distribution intensity. Provide your rationale for the level of intensity that you chose.

31. Compare E-Commerce to Brick-and-Mortar Shopping

Select a destination for a weekend trip. Log onto a travel site on the Internet. Using the Web site, determine what it will cost you to fly to your destination. Then investigate hotel expenses for a two-night stay. Record your information. Next, ask a local travel agent to help you plan the same trip.

Activity Write a brief report comparing the results of your two shopping experiences. Describe the pros and cons of each method.

NET SAVVY

32. Internet Searches and Marketing

Select a product you would like to purchase. Use a search engine to find e-tailers selling the product or log on to the Web sites of companies that you know would sell the product you wish to purchase.

THE DECA CONNECTION

An Association of Marketing Students

Role Play: Channels of Distribution

Situation You are to assume the role of assistant manager of a lighting and lamp store. Your store manager is considering adding a line of lamps from a new vendor. The vendor will ship lamps purchased from the line directly to the customer. The direct shipping means a delay of one day longer than your store delivery. This also means the store can sell the lamps at somewhat lower prices since the store does not have to store the lamps at the warehouse or deliver them to customers.

Activity You are to explain to a customer (judge) why waiting the extra day for delivery means lower prices for these lamps.

Evaluation You will be evaluated on how well you meet the following performance indicators:

- Explain the relationship between customer service and distribution
- Explain storing considerations
- Handle customer inquiries
- Explain channel-member relationships

@ Online Action!

For more information and DECA Prep practice, go to *marketingessentials.glencoe.com/21/DECA*

CHAPTER 22
Physical Distribution

Chapter Objectives

After reading this chapter, you should be able to:

- Describe the nature and scope of physical distribution
- Identify transportation systems and services that move products from manufacturers to consumers
- Name the different kinds of transportation service companies
- Explain the concept and function of inventory storage
- Identify the types of warehouses
- Discuss distribution planning for international markets

GUIDE TO THE PHOTO

Market Talk Marine transportation is one of the oldest methods of moving goods. Many major cities developed next to bodies of water because the ability to transport goods facilitated the growth of commerce.

Quick Think Barges and container ships are used to transport goods on bodies of water. What are some other forms of transportation?

THE  CONNECTION

Performance indicators represent key skills and knowledge. Relating them to the concepts explained in this chapter is your key to success in DECA events. Keep this in mind as you read this chapter and take notes each time you encounter material that helps you master a key concept. These acronyms represent DECA events that involve knowledge of concepts in this chapter.

AAAL*	**FMAL***	**MMS**	**TMDM**
AAML*	**FMDM**	**QSRM**	**TSE**
ADC	**FMML***	**RMAL***	**VPM***
BSM	**FSRM**	**RMML***	
EMDM*	**HMDM**	**SMDM**	

In all these DECA events you should be able to follow these performance indicators:

- Explain the nature and scope of distribution
- Explain the nature of warehousing
- Explain shipping processes
- Use an information system for order fulfillment

All the events with an asterisk (*) also include these performance indicators:

- Complete documents used in shipping goods
- Trace lost shipments
- Select best shipping method
- Analyze shipping needs

Some events include additional performance indicators. These are:

EMDM Fulfill orders

Analyze capabilities of electronic business systems to facilitate order fulfillment

Assess order fulfillment processes

DECA PREP

Check your understanding of DECA performance indicators with the DECA activity in this chapter's review. For more information and DECA Prep practice, go to *marketingessentials.glencoe.com/22/DECA*

SECTION 22.1

Transportation Systems and Services

OBJECTIVES

- Describe the nature and scope of physical distribution
- Identify transportation systems and services that move products from manufacturers to consumers
- Name the different kinds of transportation service companies

KEY TERMS

- physical distribution
- transportation
- common carriers
- contract carriers
- private carriers
- exempt carriers
- ton-mile
- carload
- freight forwarders

BEFORE YOU READ

Predict Why is distribution so important to the marketing concept of place?

THE MAIN IDEA

To succeed in today's business environment, a company must deliver its products to customers around the country and throughout the world in the most efficient and effective way.

STUDY ORGANIZER

Use a figure like the one below to list the advantages and disadvantages of each type of transportation system.

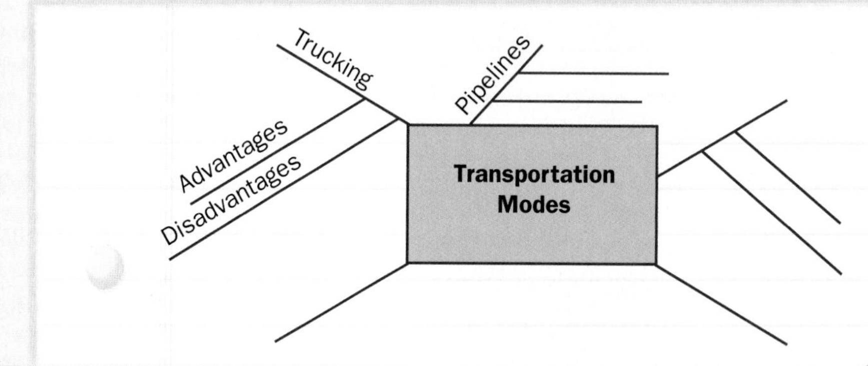

WHILE YOU READ

Read for Details
Keep a list of government agencies that regulate the physical distribution of goods.

The Nature and Scope of Physical Distribution

After a company decides on its channels of distribution, it must plan for actually moving its products through those channels. Physical distribution is the key link between a business and its customers. **Physical distribution** comprises all the activities that help to ensure that the right amount of product is delivered to the right place at the right time.

Physical distribution is also known as logistics. It involves order processing, transporting, storing, stock handling, and inventory control of materials and products. Figure 22.1 presents an overview of these functions. Physical distribution is the third-largest expense for most businesses. It is surpassed only by the costs of material and labor.

Businesses need to make the physical distribution system as efficient and cost effective as possible. At the same time, physical distribution needs to be coordinated with other business functions, such as purchasing, finance, production, packaging, and promotion. Suppose a business has planned to launch promotional ads for a new product available on a certain date. If the distribution system is unreliable, the product may not arrive at stores in time. This error will cost the business customers and cause the business to lose credibility.

Types of Transportation Systems

Transportation is the marketing function of moving a product from the place where it is made to the place where it is sold. Transportation costs are a significant part of each sale; therefore, manufacturers, wholesalers, and retailers look for the most cost-effective delivery methods.

There are five major transportation systems, or modes, which move products, including trucks, railroads, waterways, pipelines, and air carriers. Figure 22.2 shows the percentage of freight carried by each transportation mode.

Trucking

On certain U.S. highways, such as the Ohio Turnpike, about 30 percent of the miles driven are driven by commercial vehicles. Trucks, or motor carriers, are the most frequently used transportation mode. They carry higher-valued products that are expensive for a business to keep in inventory. They also carry products such as produce that have very limited shelf life. Lightweight shipments transported over moderate distances are generally handled by trucks—nearly 80 percent of those shipments weigh less than 1,000 pounds each. Businesses use trucks for virtually all intracity (within a city) shipping and for 26 percent of the intercity (between cities) freight traffic in the United States.

State and federal transportation agencies regulate motor carriers used for interstate (between states) commerce. For example, they regulate the number of hours motor carrier operators can drive without stopping and the length of their rest periods. State transportation agencies regulate fuel taxes, safety issues, and rates charged for intrastate (within a state) trucking.

Types of Carriers

Businesses that use trucks to move their products have several different options. They can use for-hire carriers, private carriers, or a combination of both. For-hire carriers include common carriers and contract carriers.

Common carriers provide transportation services to any business in their operating area for a fee. Carriers can change their rates or geographical areas, as long as they do not charge rates that are different from their published rates. More than one-third of all motor freight is handled by common carriers. Less-than-truckload carriers provide shipments in which freight from multiple shippers are consolidated into a single truckload.

Contract carriers are for-hire carriers that provide equipment and drivers for specific routes, according to agreements between the carrier and the shipper. A contract carrier can provide services on a one-time basis or on a continuing basis.

Contract carriers usually transport goods for more than one business, and they can charge different rates to each business. However, they must file their contracts with the appropriate state or federal regulatory agency.

A major advantage of using for-hire carriers is that the business does not need to invest in transportation equipment. However, for-hire carriers offer less flexibility for special pick-ups or handling, rush deliveries, and direct shipments.

Figure 22.1 Physical Distribution

- **Moving and Counting** Physical distribution involves the functions of order processing, transportation, storage, stock handling, and inventory control.

How does physical distribution work?

TRANSPORTATION

Transportation involves the actual physical movement of products. It is estimated that up to eight percent of a company's sales revenue is spent on the transportation function.

ORDER PROCESSING

The purchase of a product initiates the movement of products through a physical distribution system.

STORAGE

The storage function facilitates the movement of products through the distribution channel as products are sold.

STOCK HANDLING

Receiving, checking, and marking items for sale are important steps in the physical distribution system.

INVENTORY CONTROL

Proper inventory control ensures that products are kept in sufficient quantities and available when requested by customers.

Online Action! Go to *marketingessentials.glencoe.com/22/figure/1* to find a project on physical distribution.

Figure 22.2 Transportation Systems

• **The Importance of Single-Mode Transportation Systems** This pie chart shows the percentage of freight in ton-miles shipped by each mode of transportation.

Why do you think the percentage carried by trucks is so large?

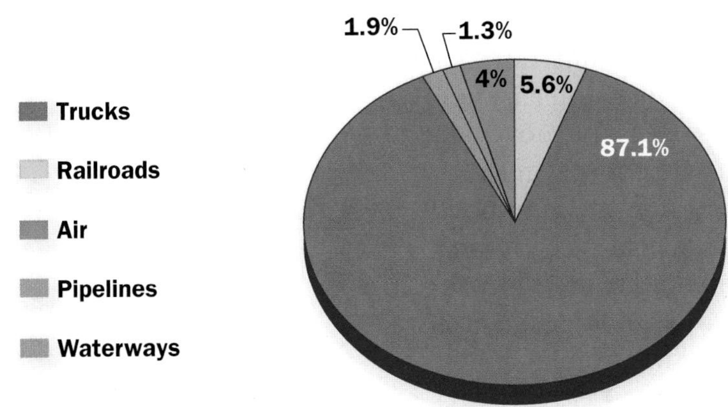

Source: Bureau of Census, 1997

Online Action! Go to *marketingessentials.glencoe.com/22/figure/2* to find a project on modes of transportation.

Private Carriers

Private carriers transport goods for an individual business. The transportation equipment can be owned or leased to meet the specific transportation needs of the business. Significant capital investment is required, however, if a business decides to own and maintain its own private fleet.

Cost is a major factor in selecting transportation. Starting a private carrier operation requires a large investment in equipment and facilities. However, private carriers let a business maintain total control over equipment, maintenance, availability, routes, delivery times, and handling procedures. This also allows a business to rapidly change schedules, routes, and delivery times to meet customers' needs.

Many businesses use a combination of private and for-hire carriers. They may use their own trucks for local deliveries and common or contract carriers for shipments beyond their local service areas.

Exempt carriers are free from direct regulation of rates and operating procedures. In most cases, they carry agricultural products. Their rates are lower than those charged by common carriers because of their exempt status. Local transportation firms may also receive exempt status if they make short-distance deliveries within specified trading areas in cities.

Some disadvantages of trucks are that they cost more than rail and water carriers, and they are susceptible to delays due to traffic jams and road conditions. Trucks are also subject to size and weight restrictions, which can vary state-to-state.

Intermodal Transportation

Intermodal transportation combines two or more transportation modes to maximize the advantages of each. Piggyback service is carrying loaded truck trailers over land on railroad flatcars. Trucks will then take the trailers to their destinations. Fishyback service is shipping loaded truck trailers over water on ships and barges. Piggyback and fishyback services combine advantages of truck transportation with the lower costs of rail and marine transportation.

Railroads

Railroads are another major form of transportation in the United States. Trains transport nearly six percent of the total intercity ton-miles of freight. A **ton-mile** is the movement of one ton (2,000 lbs) of freight one mile.

Trains are important for moving heavy and bulky freight, such as coal, steel, lumber, chemicals, grain, farm equipment, and automobiles over long distances. Refrigerated cars keep perishable products such as milk or fresh vegetables from spoiling over long distances. Other specially designed freight cars haul combustible or hazardous materials, such as chemicals.

•TWO IS BETTER THAN ONE Often, intermodal transportation is used to get goods to the customer.

Why might a company use both rail and road shipping methods?

Pricing and Delivery Services

Shippers pay lower rail transportation rates if they fill an entire boxcar. A **carload** is the minimum number of pounds of freight needed to fill a boxcar. Carload weights are established for different classifications of goods. Once a shipment reaches the minimum weight, the shipper pays the lower rate, regardless of the physical size of the shipment. Rates charged for less-than-carload shipments are more expensive because partial carloads have to be unloaded at each destination.

Advantages and Disadvantages of Railroad Transportation

Railroads are one of the lowest cost transportation modes because trains carry large quantities at relatively low per unit costs. Trains need 50 to 70 percent less energy than a motor carrier to transport freight, and they are seldom slowed or stopped by bad weather. This makes trains one of the safest modes of transportation.

The biggest disadvantage of rail transport is the lack of flexibility. Trains can pick up and deliver goods only at stations along designated rail lines.

Marine Shipping

Barges and container ships transport merchandise within the United States and around the world. Container ships carry their loads in either 20- or 40-foot-long standardized truck-size containers. The United States Maritime Commission regulates U.S. marine shipping.

Waterways

Inland shipping is shipping from one port to another on connecting rivers and lakes. The St. Lawrence Seaway, which is a combination of rivers, canals, and lakes, and the Mississippi and Ohio Rivers are all internal shipping routes that give ocean-going vessels access to the heartland of America.

Intracoastal shipping is the shipping of goods on inland and coastal waterways between ports along the same coast. For example, shipments can be sent from Virginia to North Carolina through the Great Dismal Swamp Canal.

International waterways are the oceans and rivers that connect continents and countries. Almost all overseas nonperishable freight is transported by container ships and barges because of the low cost. Products commonly shipped by international waterways include heavy equipment, steel, ore, forest products, grain, and petroleum.

Advantages and Disadvantages of Marine Shipping

The biggest advantage of marine transportation is the low cost: container ships and barges are the cheapest form of freight transportation. However, they are also the slowest form of transportation.

Marine shipping has other disadvantages. Buyers that are located far from the port city must have products off-loaded from container ships onto railroad cars or motor carriers to reach their destination. This added cost of distribution reduces some of the cost advantages of marine shipping.

Marine shipping is affected by bad weather and seasonal conditions. Great Lakes shipping, for example, is closed for two to three months in the winter.

Pipelines

Pipelines are usually owned by the company using them, and in these instances, they are considered private carriers. There are more than 200,000 miles of pipelines in the United States.

Pipelines are most frequently used to transport oil and natural gas. They move crude oil from oil fields to refineries, where it is processed. The refined products, such as gasoline, are then trucked to retail outlets such as your local gasoline station.

Advantages and Disadvantages of Pipelines

The construction of pipelines requires a high initial investment, but operational costs are relatively small. Pipeline transportation has the best safety record among all major transportation systems. Products carried through pipelines move slowly but continuously,

MARKET TECH

Scan and Bag as You Shop

National grocery chain, Albertsons, Inc., has introduced a Shop 'n' Scan system for shoppers who can scan and bag their groceries while they shop. Here are Albertsons' steps to using the system:

1. Take a Preferred Card to the Shop 'n' Scan display, scan the card, and wait for a handheld scanner to light up.
2. Use the scanner, store grocery bags, and a shopping cart while shopping.
3. Scan each item and place it in a bag.
4. If you return an item, scan it, and press the minus key.
5. If you can't remember whether you picked up something, scroll your list with the up and down keys.
6. Press the "i" key to see offers available only to Shop 'n' Scan customers.
7. At checkout, point the scanner at the "end of trip" bar code at the register and pull the trigger. That transfers your grocery list and prints a receipt. Pay as you would otherwise. There's no need to take your groceries out of the bags.
8. Place the scanner in a return rack.

THINK LIKE A MARKETER

What are some store and customer advantages and disadvantages for self-scanning devices?

Online Action!

Go to *marketingessentials.glencoe.com/22/tech* to find a project on scanning devices.

•IT WILL BE THERE TOMORROW Air transportation is a growing segment of the transportation industry.

What items are generally sent by air?

suffer minimal product damage or theft, and are not subject to delivery delays due to bad weather. The risk of a pipeline leak is low, but when a leak does occur, the damage to the environment can be extensive.

Air Cargo Services

Currently, air cargo services are less than one percent of the total ton-miles of freight shipped. High-value, low-weight, time-critical items such as overnight mail are often shipped by air. Certain high-value products, such as emergency parts, instruments, and medicines may also be shipped by air. Air cargo has space restraints, so products transported in smaller containers are well suited to this form of shipment.

The Federal Aviation Administration (FAA) regulates air transportation, but airlines and air transport companies set their own rates. Air cargo service carriers offer such things as wide-bodied jets that can ship more goods and specialized packaging designed to help prevent damage.

Advantages and Disadvantages of Air Transportation

The greatest advantage for air transportation is its speed. This fast delivery time allows businesses to satisfy customers who need something quickly. It also reduces inventory expenses and storage costs.

The greatest disadvantage of air transportation is its cost. It is by far the most expensive form of distribution. Air cargo rates are at least twice as costly as truck rates. Other disadvantages of air cargo services include mechanical breakdowns and delays in delivery caused by bad weather.

Transportation Service Companies

Transportation service companies handle small- and medium-size packages. Some examples of these companies are the U.S. Postal Service, express delivery services, bus package carriers, and freight forwarders.

U.S. Postal Service

The U.S. Postal Service ships small packages by parcel post or first-class mail. For an extra fee, parcel post can be insured against loss or damage. Parcel post can also be express-mailed at higher rates to guarantee next-day delivery.

Express Delivery Services

Express delivery services specialize in delivering small, lightweight packages and high-priority mail usually weighing less than 150 pounds. Express delivery companies, such as Federal Express, DHL, and United Parcel Service, can deliver nationally or internationally by airplane, truck, bus, or train. Rates are based on speed of delivery, size and weight of package, distance to be sent, and type of service used. Regular service usually takes from two to three days; more expensive, next-day service is also available.

Over the last 35 years, express carriers have become a more important part of physical distribution. Federal Express, which began operations in 1971, transports an average of 3.1 million shipments daily. It has a worldwide fleet of 643 aircraft, 136,000 employees, and more than 1,000 service centers serving 215 countries.

DHL, a pioneering express delivery carrier, started shipping from San Francisco to Honolulu in 1969. It was the first carrier to introduce express international shipping via airplane to Eastern Europe in 1983 and to China in 1986. Today, DHL is the largest company that specializes in international express shipping. It can send packages to approximately 635,000 destinations in more than 233 countries and territories.

Bus Package Carriers

Bus package carriers provide transportation services for packages weighing less than 100 pounds. Bus package carriers, such as Greyhound, can provide same-day or next-day service to cities and towns along their scheduled routes. As with other forms of shipping, the cost of bus package transportation depends on the weight of the package and the distance it will travel.

Freight Forwarders

Freight forwarders are private companies that combine less-than-carload or less-than-truckload shipments from several different businesses and deliver them to their destinations. They gather small shipments into larger lots and then hire a carrier to move them, usually at reduced rates. By combining shipments, freight forwarders can often obtain truckload or carload rates and lower transportation costs for shippers. Freight forwarders also provide logistical services that help businesses select the best transportation methods and routes.

22.1 AFTER YOU READ

Reviewing Key Terms and Concepts

1. What is physical distribution?
2. Why is transportation important in marketing a product?
3. Which mode of transportation would you use to ship fresh flowers from Hawaii to New York? Why?

Integrating Academic Skills

Math

4. The *George A. Stinson* is the second largest freighter on the Great Lakes. Normally, it carries 57,000 tons of taconite ore each voyage between Superior, Wisconsin, and Detroit, Michigan. Now, due to lower lake levels, it can only carry 55,000 tons per trip. At an average cost of $5 per ton, how much revenue is lost per trip?

Civics and Government

5. The Transportation Security Administration (TSA) was established to protect the nation's transportation systems. Research and write a 200-word paper about security measures used to balance safety and security with ensuring freedom of movement for people and commerce.

Check your answers at *marketingessentials.glencoe.com/22/read*

SECTION 22.2

Inventory Storage

OBJECTIVES

- Explain the concept and function of inventory storage
- Identify the types of warehouses
- Discuss distribution planning for international markets

KEY TERMS

- storage
- private warehouse
- public warehouse
- distribution center
- bonded warehouse

READ and STUDY

BEFORE YOU READ

Predict How do you think inventory storage relates to a product's price?

MAIN IDEA

Inventory storage allows a business to keep its products for a certain period of time in a safe location until they are needed or ready to be sold.

STUDY ORGANIZER

In a chart like the one below, take notes about various types of warehouses.

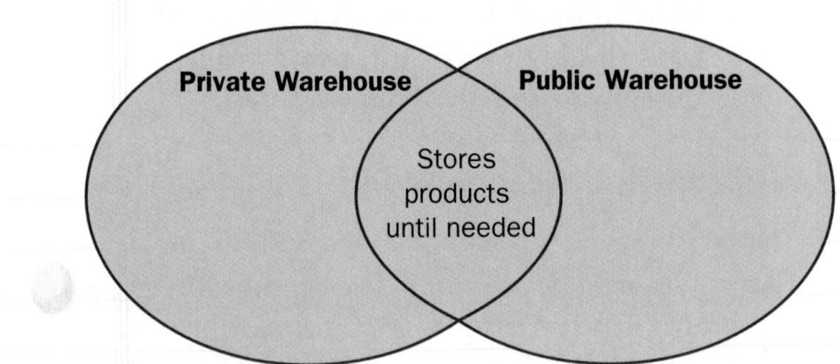

WHILE YOU READ

Analyze Think about products that need to be stored and others that do not. What are the differences between these types of goods?

The Storage of Goods

Some products, such as books, need to be manufactured in large quantities in order to be cost effective, and those products need to be kept safe and clean until they are sold. **Storage** is a marketing function and refers to the holding of goods until they are sold. The amount of goods stored is called an inventory. We will talk more about inventories in Chapter 24.

There are many reasons why storing goods is an essential activity for most businesses. First of all, products are stored until orders are received from customers. Products might also need to be stored because production has exceeded consumption or demand decreases. Sometimes, agricultural commodities such as corn, wheat, and soybeans may only be available during certain seasons. Commodity storage makes these products available year-round and ensures that their price remains relatively stable. Some purchasers buy in quantity to get discounts on their purchases and then store the items until they are needed. Finally, products may be stored at convenient locations to provide faster delivery to customers.

The costs involved in storing products include space, equipment, and personnel. Storage also means spending money (or capital) on inventory rather than investing it in another activity that could provide a larger return.

Most products are stored in warehouses, or facilities in which goods are received, identified, sorted, stored, and dispatched for shipment.

Private Warehouses

A **private warehouse** is a facility designed to meet the specific needs of its owner. A private warehouse is valuable for companies that move a large volume of products. Specialized conditions, such as a temperature-controlled environment, may be built into the facility. Private warehouses often house other parts of the business operation, such as offices.

A disadvantage is that private warehouses are costly to build and maintain. In a recent survey, large retailers reported spending 51 percent of their total physical distribution costs on warehouse expenses; transportation costs accounted for the remaining 49 percent. Private warehouses should be considered only when a significant amount of merchandise needs to be stored, thus making the total operating costs lower than those of public warehouses.

Public Warehouses

A **public warehouse** offers storage and handling facilities to any individual or company that will pay for its use. Public warehouses not only rent space but also provide additional services to businesses. These services include shipment consolidation, receiving, unloading, inspecting, reshipping, order filling, and truck terminal operation services. Public warehouses are helpful to businesses that have low- to medium-volume storage needs or seasonal production.

A MATTER OF ETHICS

Big Stores, Big Controversy

A major discount retailer with operations in multiple countries is trying to do more expanding at home. But it has seen fierce opposition. Some cities and counties have even enacted legislation banning stores that fit the retailer's description: 200,000-square-foot stores that use more than 10 percent of the space for food.

Ask the Voters

In 2004, following months of controversy about building a store near a major city, the retailer went directly to the voters. If approved, the retailer could have built a store without going through normal environmental reviews, traffic studies, and public hearings. Even though the retailer spent nearly $1 million to persuade voters to approve the construction, voters rejected the proposal.

THINKING ETHICALLY

Do you think that it is ethical for a city government to write ordinances banning a type of business? Why or why not?

Online Action!

Go to *marketingessentials.glencoe.com/22/ethics* to find a project on local government regulation of business development.

Case Study

Trucking and Wireless Technology

When Schneider National signed a deal in 1988 to equip its fleet with a satellite tracking and communication system from Qualcomm, the trucking giant was taking a big gamble on new and unproven technology.

The gamble paid off. The lines of drivers who once waited to use pay phones to call the home office, wasting precious on-duty hours, disappeared. Instead, drivers use text messaging to communicate with the home office via an in-cab or handheld wireless device.

Hot Spots and Wireless Modems

Instead of phone banks, truck stops are installing hot spots enabled with Wi-Fi technology. Drivers can log on to the Internet with laptops and PDAs equipped with wireless modems just by entering one of the hot spots and registering.

Schneider National now also writes its own software programs to integrate vehicle-location data and driver communications into its dispatch process and fleet management. In addition to new uses for existing data, Schneider National is also looking to add a tracking system that will locate trailers when doing intermodal transport.

How do you think Schneider National's customers benefit from this technology?

Online Action! **Go to *marketingessentials.glencoe.com/22/case* to find a research project on software and logistics.**

Distribution Centers

A **distribution center** is a warehouse designed to speed delivery of goods and to minimize storage costs. The main focus in a distribution center is on sorting and moving products, not on storing them. Distribution centers are planned around markets rather than transportation requirements. They can cut costs by reducing the number of warehouses and eliminating excessive inventory.

Some businesses such as paint companies Sherwin-Williams and Benjamin Moore use their distribution centers to physically change the product for the final customer. Their distribution centers perform additional functions such as mixing ingredients, labeling, and repackaging for shipments to retailers.

Distribution centers also consolidate large orders from many sources and redistribute them as separate orders for individual accounts or stores within a chain. Merchandise normally stays only a very short time in a distribution center.

Bonded Warehouses

Bonded warehouses, either public or private, store products that require the payment of a federal tax. Imported or domestic products cannot be removed until the required tax is paid. Although they are charged storage fees, businesses can save on taxes by taking goods out of storage, and hence paying the tax, only when they are needed.

Distribution Planning for International Markets

Selling to customers in the international marketplace requires more planning than selling to domestic customers. Businesses that sell internationally must follow United States export laws as well as the import laws of the countries to which they are selling. Some countries also have legal restrictions about how products may be transported. Businesses frequently have to handle bureaucratic regulations, language barriers, and negotiations.

To deliver their goods successfully, businesses must understand other countries' physical transportation systems. In some less developed nations, the postal system may not be reliable enough to assure delivery of packages by mail. Other countries may not have well-developed roads and highway systems to support dependable truck deliveries. In China, for example, many goods are transported by bicycle or carts pushed by hand.

It is important to understand how retail institutions in other countries differ from American retail institutions. In some parts of the world, retailers have little or no capacity for refrigeration. American-style supermarkets are rare in developing countries due to the lack of refrigeration and storage facilities. In Japan, the term *supermarket* refers to a type of retail outfit that sells food as well as clothing, furniture, and appliances.

22.2 AFTER YOU READ

Reviewing Key Terms and Concepts

1. Give four reasons why merchandise is stored.
2. How does a distribution center differ from a warehouse?
3. What is a bonded warehouse?

Integrating Academic Skills

Math

4. One measure of warehouse productivity is the cost per order. Cost per Order = Total Warehouse Cost/Total Orders Shipped. What is the Cost per order for a company that has a total warehouse cost of $531,000 and shipped a total of 900 orders in a one-year period?

Language Arts

5. Use the Web sites for the American Trucking Association (ATA), the Association of American Railroads (AAR), the National Transportation Library, and other business news sources to research the latest issues impacting the transportation industry. Summarize these issues in a one-page report.

@ Online Action!

Check your answers at *marketingessentials.glencoe.com/22/read*

CAREERS IN MARKETING

STEVE ROBERTS
OWNER/OPERATOR
ZNRCDS.COM
MUSIC MAIL ORDER

What do you do at work?

My duties include logistics, inventory management, and Web site inventory maintenance. Logistics includes everything from the physical tasks of pulling orders, stocking new product, and maintaining the warehouse, to making sure that the processes are in place and evaluated on a regular schedule for their effectiveness. Inventory management includes ordering product, re-ordering and re-stocking product as needed, and processing returns for defective or overstock products. Web site inventory maintenance means making sure that the site will allow the customer to order only those products currently in stock so as to minimize the occurrence of out-of-stock and back-ordered items.

What skills are most important to you?

A background in inventory management and loss prevention is essential. Without these skills it would be impossible to manage a process during which you have no actual contact with the customer, such as an interactive e-commerce Web site. If customers have no confidence that their order will be filled not only in a timely manner but also completely, they will likely find somewhere else to shop.

What is your key to success?

First, put in place systems and processes that remove obstacles to customer service. Second, evaluate the effectiveness of the systems and processes on a regular schedule and make changes or adjustments as needed. Third, ask your customers what obstacles still exist, then, based on their input, revisit steps one and two.

Aptitudes, Abilities, and Skills

Inventory management, time management, strong computer skills, and organizational ability

Education and Training

High-level courses and degrees are offered in the areas of logistics and workflow, although many warehousing and inventory managers are entirely self-taught.

Career Path

Many on-the-floor warehouse jobs are entry level, while higher-level positions involve managing the overall process. Often, employees starting on the floor are promoted to managing positions as they stay with the company and develop new skills.

THINKING CRITICALLY

Why would skills in loss prevention, typically associated with running a retail store, be helpful to someone operating an e-commerce Web site?

Online Action!

Go to *marketingessentials.glencoe.com/22/careers* to find a career-related activity.

CHAPTER 22 REVIEW

FOCUS on KEY POINTS

SECTION 22.1

- Physical distribution links a business and its customers. Physical distribution comprises all the activities that help to ensure that the right amount of product is delivered to the right place at the right time. Physical distribution is also known as logistics. It involves transporting, storing, order processing, stock handling, and inventory control of materials and products. The different kinds of transportation include marine, air, pipeline, and land transportation, which includes both trucking and railroads.

SECTION 22.2

- Storage is the marketing function of holding goods until they are sold. Storing goods is an essential activity for most businesses. Products are stored in warehouses or distribution centers until orders are received from customers. Globalization is increasing the importance of international distribution.

REVIEW VOCABULARY

Define each of the below terms in a short sentence.

1. physical distribution (p. 464)
2. transportation (p. 465)
3. common carriers (p. 465)
4. contract carriers (p. 465)
5. private carriers (p. 467)
6. exempt carriers (p. 467)
7. ton-mile (p. 468)
8. carload (p. 468)
9. freight forwarders (p. 471)
10. storage (p. 472)
11. private warehouse (p. 473)
12. public warehouse (p. 473)
13. distribution center (p. 474)
14. bonded warehouses (p. 475)

REVIEW FACTS and IDEAS

15. Explain the components of physical distribution. (22.1)
16. Name transportation systems and services that are used to move goods from one place to another. (22.1)
17. What are the different kinds of transportation service companies? (22.1)
18. What is inventory storage? Explain how it is used. (22.2)
19. What are the different kinds of warehouses? (22.2)
20. Name at least three reasons why planning is important for distribution in international markets. (22.2)

BUILD SKILLS

21. Workplace Skills

Human Relations You are a clerk in a warehouse. A carton of snack items has been damaged during a shipment. As you are filling out a report for the damaged merchandise, a coworker suggests you have some of the snacks because the warehouse will never miss them.

What would you say to your coworker? How do you believe management would view your coworker's suggestion?

22. Technology Applications

Prepare an Oral Presentation Select one of the vocabulary terms dealing with physical distribution. Use presentation software to develop a 10- to 15-minute presentation on different aspects associated with the term selected.

23. Math Practice

Calculate Price A large manufacturer can save 29 percent by using piggyback service. The cost of shipping the manufacturer's products without the piggyback service will total $75,255. How much money will the manufacturer save by using the service?

DEVELOP CRITICAL THINKING

24. The Rise of International Distribution

Why is knowledge of international physical distribution increasingly important? How has the Internet influenced the importance of international distribution? List three reasons why these developments are limited to free enterprise and the global economy.

25. Shipping and Receiving

Imagine you are a shipping and receiving supervisor for a large furniture manufacturer located in the midwestern part of the United States. Your distribution manager has asked you to evaluate the current distribution system used at your company. The company is deciding between a common carrier, its own private fleet, or a combination of both to transport its products.

Identify the pros and cons of each transportation alternative and write a memo to your manager detailing your analysis. Make sure to include supporting details.

APPLY CONCEPTS

26. Investigating Intelligent Transportation Systems (ITS)

Perform an Internet search on the ITS program initiative of the U.S. Department of Transportation to add information technology to commercial vehicle operation.

Activity Write a one-page report detailing how technology is being used to improve safety, transportation time, and fuel costs.

27. Interviewing a Small-Business Owner

Interview a local businessperson about how product shipments are received within the business. Then select one specific transportation mode (such as trucking, air cargo carriers, etc.).

Activity Summarize in a one- to two-page report which products are received, how often, and what payment arrangements are involved.

NET SAVVY

28. Express Carriers

Using an Internet search engine, investigate a small-package express carrier (e.g. FedEx, DHL, UPS) or the U.S. Postal Service and prepare a report on its online services and technologies currently available to shippers. What are the goals of these online services? How can shippers use online technology and Web sites to market their own products and services?

THE DECA CONNECTION

An Association of Marketing Students

Role Play: Physical Distribution

Situation You are to assume the role of an experienced employee at the warehouse of a grocery supplier. You are familiar with the operation of the business and with filling orders from the individual grocery stores that your warehouse supplies. The warehouse manager has asked you to explain the warehouse operation to a new employee (judge).

Activity You are to explain to a new employee (judge) how the merchandise gets to your warehouse and how orders from the individual grocery stores you supply are filled and delivered.

Evaluation You will be evaluated on how well you meet the following performance indicators:

- Explain the nature of warehousing
- Explain the shipping process
- Explain storing considerations
- Explain the nature of channels of distribution
- Explain the nature of channel-member relationships

Online Action!

For more information and DECA Prep practice, go to *marketingessentials.glencoe.com/22/DECA*

CHAPTER 23
Purchasing

Chapter Objectives

After reading this chapter, you should be able to:

- Define the terms used to describe organizational buyers
- Explain how planning purchases differs between an industrial market and a resellers' market
- Describe the six-month merchandise plan and explain its calculations
- Explain the concept of chain store buying
- List the three types of purchase situations
- Explain the criteria for selecting suppliers
- Name the factors involved in negotiating terms of a sale
- Describe the various Internet purchasing methods

GUIDE TO THE PHOTO

Market Talk Buyers in the apparel industry view designs before purchasing new collections. New designs are presented at private business meetings or at trade shows.

Quick Think What are some other sources of information about suppliers of products, materials, and services?

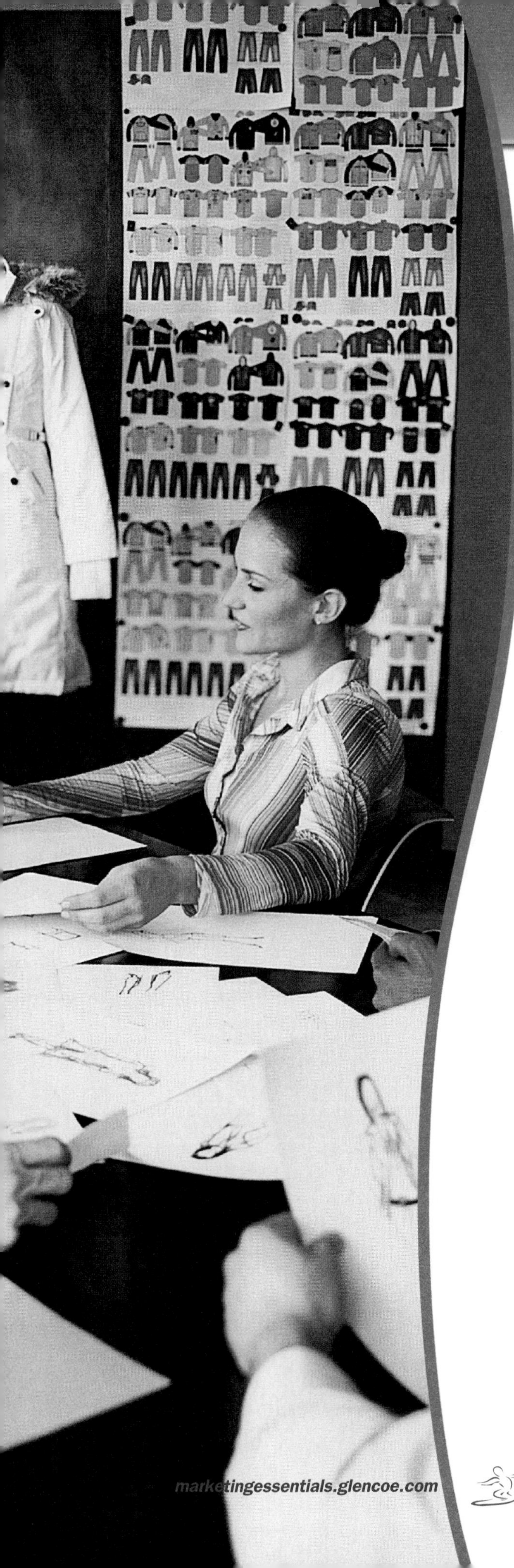

THE   CONNECTION

Performance indicators represent key skills and knowledge. Relating them to the concepts explained in this chapter is your key to success in DECA events. These acronyms represent DECA events that involve knowledge of concepts in this chapter.

AAAL	**FMAL**	**MMS***	**TMDM***
AAML*	**FMDM***	**QSRM***	**TSE***
ADC*	**FMML***	**RMAL**	**VPM**
BSM*	**FSRM***	**RMML***	
EMDM*	**HMDM***	**SMDM***	

In all these DECA events you should be able to follow these performance indicators:

- Explain the nature and scope of purchasing
- Explain company buying/purchasing policies
- Explain the nature of the buying process
- Explain the nature of buyer reputation/vendor relationships
- Conduct vendor search

All the events with an asterisk (*) also include these performance indicators:

- Negotiate contracts with vendors
- Review performance of vendors

Some events include additional performance indicators. These are:

EMDM	Explain the impact of the Internet on purchasing
HMDM **FSRM** **QSRM**	Prepare food specifications (specs) for purchasing food items Plan quantities of food items to order

DECA PREP

Check your understanding of DECA performance indicators with the DECA activity in this chapter's review. For more information and DECA Prep practice, go to *marketingessentials.glencoe.com/23/DECA*

SECTION 23.1

OBJECTIVES

- **Define the terms used to describe organizational buyers**
- **Explain how planning purchases differs between an industrial market and a resellers' market**
- **Describe the six-month merchandise plan and explain its calculations**
- **Explain the concept of chain store buying**

KEY TERMS

- **organizational buyers**
- **wholesale and retail buyers**
- **six-month merchandise plan**
- **open-to-buy (OTB)**
- **centralized buying**
- **decentralized buying**

The Role of the Buyer

BEFORE YOU READ

Predict What do you already know about the role of the buyer?

THE MAIN IDEA

The purchasing function in any business is important because the costs associated with running a business are often a direct result of the competence of the person responsible for buying the goods and services required to run the business.

STUDY ORGANIZER

Use a chart like the one below to write two or three sentences describing each of the following: industrial market, resellers market, government market, and institutional market.

Market	Notes
Industrial	
Resellers	
Government	
Institutional	

Compare List the similarities and differences of the four markets listed above.

Planning Purchases

Organizational buyers purchase goods for business purposes, usually in much greater quantities than the average consumer. Much of what they buy requires technical knowledge and knowledge of the operations of the firm, especially in manufacturing and service operations. Having a handle on the business trends that affect their industry is also important, especially when buying for resale purposes.

Industrial Markets

In manufacturing and service businesses, the people responsible for purchasing may be called purchasing managers, industrial buyers, or procurement managers. Although the job titles may differ, the key function is to buy goods and services for use in the business.

In manufacturing businesses, planning purchases often requires industrial buyers to be directly involved with production planning. To get an idea of the responsibilities involved, consider the case of a purchasing manager for an outerwear apparel manufacturer.

The purchasing manager would review the company's master production schedule for details of production needed to meet sales requirements. Let's say that the marketing department predicts the company will sell 500 Style No. 1900 jackets in the coming season. The purchasing manager must know how much fabric, insulation, and thread and how many zippers it takes to produce one Style

• BUY to SELL Purchasing and inventory control go hand in hand. Buyers need to know what sells and what does not. Companies need to figure out their projected sales to order the correct quantities of merchandise.

What can happen if a store's shelves run out of a popular item?

No. 1900 jacket. This is called a bill of materials. The total of all the materials necessary to make one jacket can be multiplied by 500 to determine exactly what needs to be purchased to meet the sales goal.

To determine when to buy those items, the purchasing manager would be responsible for materials requirement planning (MRP). MRP includes an analysis of when to make the purchases so they are available when needed according to the production schedule. The purchasing manager must therefore know the capacity of the manufacturing facility. He or she must be sure the company has room for the supplies, raw materials, and inventory of finished goods.

Time lines and delivery of all supplies must be followed and checked on a regular basis to maintain the master production schedule. This ensures that everything is as it should be for manufacturing to progress at an appropriate rate.

Case Study

Maximizing Purchasing Power

Trader Joe's, a specialty grocer based in California, has 210 U.S. stores. It had estimated sales in 2003 of $2.5 billion, up 13 percent over 2002. The company operates differently from most grocers, selling only about 2,500 different items rather than the 40,000 a large chain supermarket carries. Buyers search for bargains around the world. When they find high-quality items at especially low prices, they buy large quantities, lowering the price further with volume discounts. Trader Joe's buys only from producers, not from wholesalers. Of its products, 20 percent to 25 percent are imported, and it has developed its own brands for about 80 percent of its products.

Joe Coulombe began the business in 1958 as a chain of neighborhood convenience stores. He later expanded store space and began selling gourmet cheeses and wines at much lower prices than other food retailers. In 1979, the company was bought by Theo Albrecht, co-owner of the German Aldi food store chain, whose purchasing and marketing strategy is similar, focusing on a few items (700 in Aldi stores) and emphasizing store brands. Aldi sells to the low end of the market, focusing on budget items. Trader Joe's targets sophisticated buyers who still want to save money.

THINK STRATEGICALLY

From a purchasing standpoint, how can it benefit Trader Joe's to be owned by a German company? With a 13 percent increase in sales from 2002 to 2003, how much of an increase in purchases would you advise in a merchandise plan for Trader Joe's?

@ Online Action!

Go to *marketingessentials.glencoe.com/23/case* to find an activity about purchasing and the grocery business.

NET MARKETING

How to Choose a B2B?

Internet B2B suppliers have greatly increased in number as e-commerce has become mainstream. How can a purchaser wisely choose a vendor from the many thousands available? There are hundreds of directories listing B2Bs that simply provide links to their Web sites with no commentary. Services that provide directories, list the kinds of transactions vendors provide, and rate them on their performance are more helpful—and they do exist.

Online Information

Purchasinga2z is a Web site providing news reports about purchasing issues, research and ratings of B2B businesses and links to other sources of information. VerticalZOOM is another such service. It also features customer feedback on specific vendors, giving buyers an extra piece of the puzzle. The Internet may make purchasing easier, but it takes research to identify the right supplier when there are so many possibilities.

THINK LIKE A MARKETER

As the buyer for a new hip-hop fashion boutique, how will you find sources or know if a quoted price is reasonable?

Go to *marketingessentials.glencoe.com/23/net* to find activities about purchasing and the Internet.

Resellers' Markets

The resellers' market is found in wholesaling and retailing operations, where the person responsible for purchasing is simply called a buyer. **Wholesale and retail buyers** purchase goods for resale; they forecast customers' needs and buy the necessary products. Buyers must plan far in advance of the selling season to know how much of each item to purchase.

Six-Month Merchandise Plan

Buyers plan their purchases by preparing a **six-month merchandise plan**, the budget that estimates planned purchases for a six-month period.

The first figure calculated on a merchandise plan is the planned sales figure. In most cases, this is determined by using the previous year's monthly sales figures and adjusting them to reflect the firm's current-year sales goal.

Suppose sales for a particular month last year were $100,000, and this year's goal is to increase sales by 10 percent. This year's planned sales for the month would be calculated as follows:

Desired increase: $\$100{,}000 \times .10 = \$10{,}000$
Planned sales: $\$100{,}000 + \$10{,}000 = \$110{,}000$

You could also reach the same result in a single step:

$$\$100{,}000 \times 1.10 = \$110{,}000$$

The company goal for the current year is derived from a study of last year's sales, current market and economic conditions, and an analysis of the competition. Projection of accurate planned sales figures is important because all other figures on the merchandise plan are computed on the basis of this figure.

Buyers must ensure that there is enough stock to accommodate the sales volume planned. This is also known as beginning-of-the-month (BOM) inventory. To project this figure, a buyer checks the previous year's records for how much stock was needed in relation to monthly sales. Sales were $40,000 in a given month and the BOM stock for that month was $120,000; therefore, the stock-to-sales ratio is 3 to 1. The buyer can apply that same ratio to the planned figure for another month if economic and market conditions are similar.

Here is how the BOM figure on the merchandise plan would be calculated. Suppose the stock-to-sales ratio is 2:1 (usually reported as 2). This means that to accommodate a given sales volume, it is necessary to keep twice that amount of stock on hand. BOM inventory should be twice the amount of anticipated sales; if sales are $5,000, then the BOM would be $10,000.

The end-of-the-month (EOM) stock figure is closely related to the BOM stock figure. The BOM stock figure for any given month is the EOM stock figure for the previous month.

Planned retail reductions take into account reductions in the selling price, shortages of merchandise caused by clerical mistakes, employee pilferage, and customer shoplifting. Such reductions in earnings and merchandise shortages ultimately affect the amount of money that must be planned for purchases.

Planned retail reductions can be calculated in two different ways. One is to calculate reductions as a percentage of planned sales. Suppose planned reductions have historically been 10 percent of planned sales. If planned sales for the month are $25,000, planned reductions for that month would be calculated as follows:

$$\$25{,}000 \times .10 = \$2{,}500$$

Some companies set goals of reducing planned reductions from the previous year. Assume that a firm's goal is to reduce this year's planned reductions by 5 percent from last year's figure. Last year's reductions were $700; therefore this year's planned reductions would be figured this way:

Desired decrease: $\$700 \times .05 = \$35$
Planned reductions: $\$700 - \$35 = \$665$

This result could also be reached in a single step: $\$700 \times .95 = \$665$

The planned purchase entry shows the retail-dollar purchase figures a firm needs to achieve its sales and inventory projections for

• PURCHASING as a SALES TOOL Athleta, a catalog and e-tail business that targets women who play sports, sends advance notice of merchandise that has just been purchased.

How can the purchasing power and savvy of a company become a sales tool?

Figure 23.1 Six-Month Merchandise Plan

• **Making Merchandise Plans** This nearly completed model merchandise plan is based on the following assumptions: sales are expected to increase by 10 percent over last year; last year's stock-to-sales ratios should be used to compute this year's BOM stock figures; this year's planned reductions should be 5 percent lower than last year's; and the planned BOM for August is $264,000.

What are the planned purchase figures for May through July?

Spring Season 20___ Department Toys

No. 6124

		February	March	April	May	June	July	Total
Sales	Last year	82,000	96,000	90,000	100,000	94,000	80,000	
	Plan	90,200	105,600	99,000	110,000	103,400	88,000	
	Actual							
Retail Stock BOM	Last year	328,000	336,000	297,000	360,000	291,400	224,000	
	Plan	360,800	369,600	326,700	396,000	320,540	246,400	
	Actual							
Retail Reductions	Last year	12,300	14,400	13,500	15,000	14,100	12,000	
	Plan	11,685	13,680	12,825	14,250	13,395	11,400	
	Actual							
Purchases	Last year	N/A	N/A	N/A	N/A	N/A	N/A	
	Plan	110,685	76,380	181,125				
	Actual							

@ Online Action! Go to ***marketingessentials.glencoe.com/23/figure/1*** to find a project on merchandise plans.

each month. All the figures discussed previously—planned sales, BOM stock, and reductions—are needed to determine planned purchases (P). That includes planned sales (PS), planned EOM/BOM stock, and planned reductions (R). The formula for planned purchases is

(PS + EOM stock + R) − BOM stock = P

Assume that planned sales are $10,000, planned EOM stock is $25,000, planned reductions are $500, and BOM stock is $20,000. Using the formula, planned purchases would be arrived at this way:

($10,000 + $25,000 + $500) − $20,000 = $35,500 − $20,000 = $15,500

Figure 23.1 shows a nearly completed merchandise plan.

Open-to-Buy

During the buying season, a buyer may want to know the **open-to-buy (OTB)**. This is the amount of money left for buying goods after all purchases received and on order have been considered. It is calculated this way:

$$P - (\text{goods received} + \text{goods ordered}) = \text{OTB}$$

Assume that merchandise received against the planned purchase figure computed above is \$6,500 thus far and merchandise on order against it is \$2,000. The present OTB would be as follows:

$$\$15{,}500 - (\$6{,}500 + \$2{,}000) = \text{OTB}$$
$$\$15{,}500 - \$8{,}500 = \$7{,}000$$

This \$7,000 figure represents the retail value of the goods that the buyer may purchase at the time. However, the problem is not solved here.

There is a way to determine the actual money the buyer has to spend. You must calculate the markup percentage used by the buyer and deduct that figure from the retail value. Assume that the markup percentage is 45 percent based on the retail value of the merchandise. The formula for determining the OTB at cost is shown below:

$$100\% - \text{markup}\ \% = \text{\% attributed to cost of the item}$$
$$\text{\% attributed to cost} \times \text{retail value} = \text{OTB at cost}$$
$$100\% - 45\%\ \text{markup} = 55\%\ (\text{cost})$$
$$55\%\ (\text{cost}) \times \$7{,}000\ (\text{retail}) = \$3{,}850\ \text{OTB at cost}$$

Therefore, in the end, the buyer has \$3,850 to spend with all other costs considered. You can see how this extra step makes a big difference in the final amount.

Planning Purchases for a Chain Store Operation

Buying for all branches in a chain store operation is usually done in a central location (company headquarters) and is called **centralized buying**. Buyers involved in centralized buying generally buy all the items for a department or part of a department. There may be three buyers for women's shoes—one in charge of casual shoes, another of traditional shoes, and still another of better shoes. To coordinate the efforts of those three buyers, there would be a merchandise or division manager. This person would oversee all shoe buyers, which may include those for men's, children's, and women's shoes.

Chain stores use centralized buying to create a unified image for the chain. Another benefit of centralized buying is the quantity discounts that stores can negotiate with vendors because of the large volume of goods that they purchase at one time.

Decentralized Buying

Sometimes, chain stores want to have special goods in their stores that are not available elsewhere in the chain. In these cases, local store managers or their designated buyers are authorized to make special purchases for their

PRACTICE

On a separate sheet of paper, practice the following calculations that are necessary for creating a six-month merchandise plan:

1. Last March a shop had sales of \$7,300. The owner's goal is to increase sales by 8 percent for this year. What would be the planned sales for this March?
2. Last year's BOM for March was \$10,950. Calculate the stock-to-sales ratio.
3. What should be the BOM stock figure for this March?
4. Planned reductions have historically been 10 percent of sales. Using this figure, what would be the planned reductions for this March? The owner would like to cut planned reductions by 5 percent this year. Last year's reductions for the month was \$750, therefore what would be this year's target figure?
5. Using the figures given or calculated in numbers 1, 3, and 4, determine the planned purchases for the shop if the EOM stock figure for March is \$12,000.
6. Assuming merchandise received and ordered amounted to \$1,850, what would be the open-to-buy position at retail?
7. The customary markup for an item is 60 percent. What is OTB at cost?

Note: Answers to this practice set are available at *marketingessentials.glencoe.com*

individual stores. This is **decentralized buying**. Decentralization is when authority for retail decisions is made at lower levels in the organization.

Retailers constantly make trade-offs between the efficiency gained through centralized buying and the greater sales potential obtained through decentralized buying decisions that tailor merchandise to local markets.

Government Markets

Just as there are special markets, such as industrial or resellers', there are also buyers for government markets. Government units are the federal, state, and local agencies responsible for purchasing goods and services for their specific markets. There are approximately 85,000 government units in the United States. These would include the Federal Aviation Administration (FAA), departments of sanitation, public libraries, and local school boards.

Government markets make up one of the largest single markets for retail goods and services in the world. In the United States, the federal government is a huge consumer of goods, ranging from food for school lunches to equipment for the military. A large portion of the federal government's buying is centralized. However, no one federal agency is responsible for all government buying.

Institutions

One final segment of the market cannot be overlooked when discussing buying power. This market includes institutions and nonprofit organizations that do not compete in the business world in the same way retailers and wholesalers do. These institutions include hospitals, schools, colleges, churches, civic clubs, and foundations that do not work solely for profit. Institutions and nonprofit organizations may have unique buying requirements.

23.1 AFTER YOU READ

Reviewing Key Terms and Concepts

1. What are three job titles that can be used to describe people responsible for purchasing in manufacturing and service businesses?
2. How is a bill of materials used in planning purchases?
3. What are two benefits of centralized buying?

Integrating Academic Skills

Math

4. You are ordering tourist maps of your area for resale in your store. The cost of 500 maps is $625. The cost of 1,000 maps is $1,125. Calculate the per-item cost for each quantity of maps.

Geography

5. You want to become an industrial purchaser for the automobile manufacturing industry. Go to local car dealerships to research three different makes and models of cars. Obtain a brochure describing each model you research. Learn where each model is manufactured. Use your brochures to create a classroom map showing where each automobile is manufactured.

Online Action!

Check your answers at *marketingessentials.glencoe.com/23/read*

The Purchasing Function

OBJECTIVES

- List the three types of purchase situations
- Explain the criteria for selecting suppliers
- Name the factors involved in negotiating terms of a sale
- Describe the various Internet purchasing methods

KEY TERMS

- want slips
- consignment buying
- memorandum buying
- reverse auction

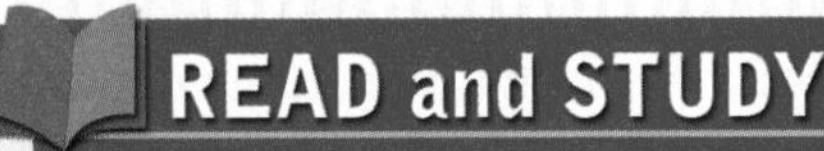

BEFORE YOU READ

Predict What do you already know about the purchasing function?

THE MAIN IDEA

Knowing the details of the purchasing function will give you a better idea of what is involved in the overall job description. It is especially important to recognize the impact of the Internet on the purchasing function. You can expect changes in job descriptions for buyers in the near future due to the significant increase in online purchasing.

STUDY ORGANIZER

In a chart like the one below, write in three types of purchase situations and four criteria for selecting suppliers.

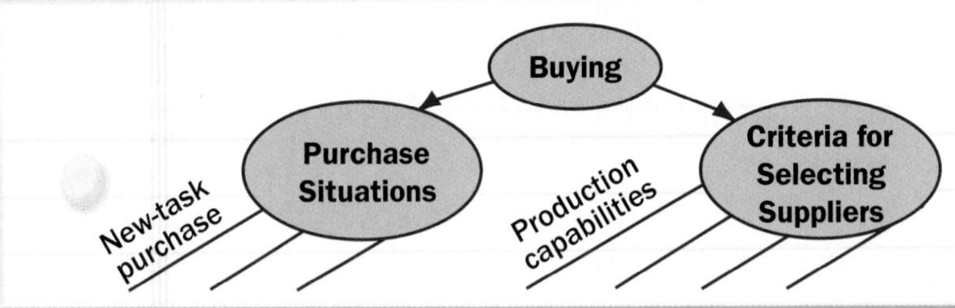

WHILE YOU READ

Compare List the differences among the types of purchase situation.

The Buying Process

There are many types of purchase situations. The ways suppliers are selected, how terms are negotiated, and how the Internet is used are changing the entire process.

Types of Purchase Situations

How difficult is the task of a purchasing manager or a buyer? The answer depends on which type of purchase situation is considered. Let's review the three types of purchase situations: new task purchase, modified rebuy, and straight rebuy.

New-Task Purchase

In a new-task purchase situation, a purchase is made for the first time, possibly triggered by a formerly unrecognized need, a new manufacturing process, or organizational change. This can be the most complicated buying situation, because it involves a first-time purchase. In a retail or wholesale operation, salespeople prepare **want slips**. These are customer requests for items that are not carried in the store. The buyer evaluates want slips to determine if the requests warrant the purchase of new merchandise.

Modified Rebuy

In a modified-rebuy situation, the buyer has had experience buying the good or service, but some aspect of the purchase changes. Perhaps the buyer is purchasing from a new vendor because the previous vendor went out of business or increased prices significantly. Other reasons for investigating new vendors may come from an analysis of the competition (through comparison shopping) or from current trade information (found in trade journals or trade shows).

Finally, retail buyers may hire the services of a resident buying office. Resident buying offices are retailers' representatives in a geographic area where many suppliers of a given product are located. New York City's garment

GLOBAL MARKET

Stocking Challenge

Ikea is one of the largest privately held companies in the world, with over 200 furniture stores in 31 countries, employing over 75,000 people and generating over 12 billion in sales annually. It all started in 1956 in southern Sweden when a local entrepreneur figured out that he could transport furniture more easily by taking it apart and packing it flat. The customer would put it together and the furniture prices could be lowered. Several decades later, the concept still works.

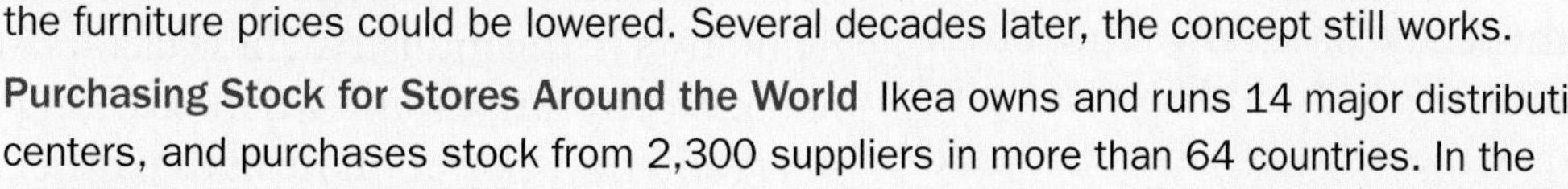

Purchasing Stock for Stores Around the World Ikea owns and runs 14 major distribution centers, and purchases stock from 2,300 suppliers in more than 64 countries. In the past few years, Ikea acquired a number of its own factories, some of which function as training units and set standards for other suppliers for production economy, quality, and environmental awareness.

To secure supplies and help suppliers develop, Ikea is also partnering as joint owners or financiers in a number of countries including Poland, Slovakia, Russia, Romania, and Bulgaria.

CRITICAL THINKING

Why did Ikea decide to purchase its own factories?

@ Online Action!

Go to *marketingessentials.glencoe.com/23/global* to find an activity about purchasing and international business.

• WHERE ARE CLOTHES MADE? Clothes you buy in the U.S. are often manufactured abroad. Hong Kong is a central market for the garment industry.

Look at the tags on a few items of clothing (yours or at a store). List the countries where the clothes were made.

district, for example, is a central market for apparel. Resident buying offices send information to retail buyers on a regular basis. They inform buyers about new merchandise offerings, closeouts, or fashion trends.

Straight Rebuy

In a straight-rebuy situation, the buyer routinely orders the goods and services purchased from the same vendor(s) as in the past. Staple goods such as office supplies fall into the straight-rebuy category for wholesale and retail buyers. The purchase of certain manufacturing supplies may be considered a straight rebuy. (See Figure 23.2 for a recap of types of purchases.)

Selecting Suppliers

The criteria for selecting suppliers fall into a few key categories. They include production capabilities, past experience, product and special buying arrangements, and special services.

Production Capabilities

When dealing with a source for the first time, buyers may request specific information about the source's production capabilities. They may even visit a facility in person to see it in operation. Buyers may solicit business references to determine the source's reputation in the industry. These factors would be extremely important when selecting suppliers and transportation firms as partners in a just-in-time production arrangement.

Production capabilities for some companies go beyond the actual physical plant into ethical and social issues, such as a review of facilities to ensure that they are not sweatshops. Sweatshops are factories characterized by poor working conditions and negligent treatment of employees.

Past Experiences

Many buyers maintain resource files that document past experiences with vendors. All basic information, such as products carried,

Figure 23.2 Types of Purchases

• Stocking Up A purchasing manager may be faced with three buying situations: the new-task purchase, the modified rebuy, and the straight rebuy. The level of difficulty varies depending on the type of purchase.

What circumstances might lead to a modified rebuy type of purchase?

NEW-TASK PURCHASE

A new-task purchase is a first-time buy. This is the most complicated buying situation. It may be triggered by the identification of a previously unrecognized need or the decision to switch vendors. New-task purchases often involve input from a buying committee, as shown here.

MODIFIED REBUY

In a modified rebuy, the buyer has had experience buying the item, but is changing something about the purchase: perhaps the product line, the vendor, or the grower.

STRAIGHT REBUY

With a straight rebuy, the buyer repeats a purchase that was made in the past. This buyer is reordering shoes he already carries in his store in order to replenish stock.

Go to *marketingessentials.glencoe.com/23/figure/2* to find a project on types of purchases.

prices, delivery and dating terms, and the names of sales representatives, is recorded. Also noted are evaluations of products, delivery performance, and customer service. A major factor in selecting a supplier is the quality of goods it offers. Retail buyers keep accurate records of customer returns and the reasons for them. Returns relating to the quality of the goods may cause a vendor to be dropped as a supplier.

Special Buying Arrangements

Suppliers may have special policies regarding merchandise returns and sales arrangements. Two special types of sales and return policies are called consignment buying and memorandum buying.

In **consignment buying**, goods are paid for only after the final customer purchases them. The supplier owns the goods until the wholesaler or retailer sells them. Many suppliers offer consignment buying as an incentive when introducing a new line of goods. However, a problem arises with consignment buying when merchandise is stolen or damaged, raising the question of who is responsible and who must pay.

Memorandum buying occurs when the supplier agrees to take back any unsold goods by a certain pre-established date. The buyer pays for all the goods purchased but is later reimbursed for all the goods returned in accordance with the agreement. This buying arrangement allows for returns.

Special Services

Businesses today demand more services from their suppliers than just the basic return policy. Suppliers must keep up with these services to stay competitive.

One special service that many retailers are requesting or demanding is the placement by manufacturers of universal product codes (UPCs) on goods. Having the codes on all products saves the retailer time because individual items do not have to be marked with a price. It also helps retailers keep track of what they have in stock.

Negotiating Terms

Buyers must negotiate prices, dating terms, delivery arrangements, and discounts. You learned about dating terms and delivery arrangements in Chapter 16. Discounts are any reductions from the quoted price. Such reductions are generally granted for the buyer's performance of certain functions. These will be discussed in Chapter 26.

Dating terms include when a bill must be paid and the discount permitted for paying early. You learned about ordinary dating (2/10, net 30) in Chapter 16, but there are several variations for specific situations. A company may allow the dating terms to take effect later than the invoice date. This type of dating, which is known as advance dating, is sometimes offered to businesses as an incentive to buy before the buying season. An invoice may be dated January 15 and include the following advance dating terms: 2/10, net 30, as of March 1.

In other situations, additional days may be granted for the discount (called extra dating). This special dating may be used to encourage a buyer to purchase new merchandise. In still another situation, the terms begin when the buyer's firm receives the goods, which is called ROG dating (receipt of goods).

Internet Purchasing

Business-to-business (B2B) e-commerce has revolutionized the purchasing function for businesses in the industrial and reseller markets. Organizational buyers account for 80 percent of the total dollar value of all online transactions. Increased use of online buying is expected to continue. This is partly because organizational buyers have come to depend heavily on timely supplier information, and such information can be easily and quickly conveyed via the Internet. Another reason is that businesses have found that online purchasing dramatically reduces marketing costs for many types of products and services.

Most of the B2B e-commerce transactions are routine purchases of products such as office supplies. The Internet makes the process more efficient.

Many companies have their own Web sites from which other companies may make purchases directly. Growing in popularity, however, are electronic exchanges where registered users can buy and sell their goods online. Most of these electronic exchanges are in specific industries, such as the NECX Global Electronics Exchange, an open market for electronic components, computer products, and networking equipment.

Another Internet purchasing trend involves online auction companies. An auction usually involves having a seller set an asking price and buyers try to outbid each other. In other cases, a reverse auction takes place. In a **reverse auction**, companies post what they want to buy and suppliers bid for the contract.

Purchasing online through third parties has both advantages and disadvantages. The biggest advantage is lower prices. However, as with most businesses on the Internet, privacy is a problem. Some companies fear that competitors will know how much was paid for materials and supplies. To combat that problem, some big companies, like Intel and General Electric, have decided to run their own reverse auctions. GE spent just $15,000 to write its own reverse auction software. This has inspired other companies to follow.

GE's trading process network (TPN) enables GE buyers to post requests for quotes, negotiate, and place orders with global suppliers. The TPN has lowered GE's purchasing costs by over 20 percent.

Another problem with the online purchasing process, especially in a reverse auction, is that unknown companies could artificially deflate prices by bidding low prices. Such a practice would benefit buyers but cause bad relationships with suppliers.

23.2 AFTER YOU READ

Reviewing Key Terms and Concepts

1. What are three ways a buyer can acquire information that is helpful in a modified-rebuy situation.
2. How does the buyer's payment for goods differ between consignment and memorandum buying?
3. Name one advantage and one disadvantage of purchasing online.

Integrating Academic Skills

Math

4. Vendor A sells 144 (1 gross) coffee mugs at $496.50 with free shipping. Dating terms are 2/10, net 30. Vendor B's offer is $3.15 per mug for one gross, with shipping charges of $25, and payment is COD. Which vendor is offering the better deal?

Language Arts

5. You received a delivery that does not meet your specifications. Use a word processing program to write a letter to the supplier describing the problem and requesting the action you would like taken.

@ Online Action!

Check your answers at *marketingessentials.glencoe.com/23/read*

CAREERS IN MARKETING

JACOB SCHOENLY
OWNER
SYNTHETIC SPACE
FURNITURE LIGHTING & ACCESSORIES

What do you do at work?

The company is a small operation, and so I wear many hats. I maintain the Web site, select and purchase the vintage items that we resell, respond to customer inquiries, and process and ship orders.

What skills are most important to you?

Perhaps the most important skill as a small business owner is the ability to multitask. Each day brings a variety of tasks that need to be fulfilled, and the person running a business has to ensure that everything is accomplished. This often means that if the owner wants something done, and done right, he has to do it himself. Beyond skills, there are important personality traits, such as honesty and reliability, that can help you make your business a success.

I am a strong believer in education. A solid liberal arts education is all that you need in order to begin a successful career. Such an education serves as a strong foundation for more specific on-the-job training that an employee might need. If someone is looking to start a business in a particular field, then prior work experience in that field can be helpful but is not an absolute requirement.

What is your key to success?

Loving what I do. When you feel that way about your job, it no longer seems like work. I also strive to treat customers the same way that I would like to be treated, offering service that meets or exceeds their demands.

Aptitudes, Abilities, and Skills

Creativity, interpersonal skills and an outgoing personality, the ability to multitask and prioritize goals and demands

Education and Training

A liberal arts degree, coupled with real-world work experience in your chosen field, makes for a solid beginning.

Career Path

Retail store owners might begin their career working for someone else, or they might open up their own shop right away. Often, niche retailers are driven by the owner's personal interests and hobbies.

THINKING CRITICALLY

Why is a love for one's career so valuable?

@ Online Action!

Go to *marketingessentials.glencoe.com/23/careers* to find a career-related activity.

CHAPTER 23 REVIEW

FOCUS on KEY POINTS

SECTION 23.1

- Organizational buyers in industrial and resellers' (wholesale and retail) markets purchase goods in much greater quantities than the average consumer.
- Buyers for government markets make purchases of goods and services for one of the largest single markets in the world.

SECTION 23.2

- The three types of purchase situations are new-task purchase, modified rebuy, and straight rebuy.
- The primary criteria for selecting suppliers are (1) production capabilities, (2) past experience, (3) special buying arrangements (such as consignment buying and memorandum buying), and (4) special services.
- The Internet has revolutionized purchasing in the industrial and resellers markets, and online buying is expected to grow in coming years.

REVIEW VOCABULARY

Write one sentence for each group of vocabulary terms, using each term in context.

1. organizational, wholesale, and retail buyers (pp. 482, 485)
2. six-month merchandise plan and open-to-buy (OTB) (pp. 485, 487)
3. centralized versus decentralized buying (pp. 488, 489)
4. want slips (p. 491)
5. consignment, memorandum buying, and reverse auction (pp. 494, 495)

REVIEW FACTS and IDEAS

6. List three titles for manufacturing or service business buyers. (23.1)
7. Identify the type of planning used to guide purchasing by organizational buyers and that used by buyers for the resale market. (23.1)
8. What is the six-month merchandise plan? What four figures must be calculated in order to complete a six-month merchandise plan? (23.1)
9. What method of buying is used by chain stores? Why? (23.1)
10. List three types of purchase situations that a buyer may encounter. (23.2)
11. What criteria do buyers use to evaluate suppliers? (23.2)
12. What factors are negotiable in determining the terms of a sale? (23.2)

BUILD SKILLS

13. Workplace Skills

Human Relations You are a division manager. Top-level management has instructed you to require your buyers to use online buying for the purchase of standardized products. Some of your longtime buyers are not computer literate and value the relationships they have established with their suppliers. Write an outline of the points you will present to your buyers. Make sure your outline includes:

- Problems you can anticipate
- How you would handle those problems

14. Technology Applications

Writing a Memo You work as a salesclerk in a men's clothing store. Several young customers have inquired about a popular line of clothing that you do not sell. You believe updating the young men's department would increase sales. Using a word processing program, create and complete a want slip for this line of clothing. Then write a memo to accompany your request, explaining to your buyer the merits of your proposal.

15. Math Practice

Discounts Suppose you own a craft supplies store, and you place an order with a fabric manufacturer for several bolts of printed cotton. The manufacturer offers you a 17 percent trade discount. The total list price is $1,016.14. How much do you have to pay?

DEVELOP CRITICAL THINKING

16. Analyzing Institutional Buying

Interview an institutional buyer in your community. Find out what kinds of products they buy and why, and what unique buying requirements they have. Report your findings to your class.

17. Internet Purchasing

Why is online buying popular in industrial markets? Explain your answer using two or three examples.

APPLY CONCEPTS

18. Developing a Six-Month Plan Spreadsheet

Use a spreadsheet program to create a six-month merchandise plan using the data shown in Figure 23.1 of your text. Learn how to write formulas so that your worksheet will automatically calculate the figures for the current year's planned sales, BOM, planned reductions, and planned purchases.

Activity Note these formulas on the bottom of your worksheet. Change the expected sales increase to five percent and the planned reductions to 10 percent. Enter the data and complete the plan.

19. Selecting a Vendor

Do an Internet search on printer cartridge suppliers. Read the details from two of the top-rated suppliers. Using a word processing program, report on the services, prices, and product quality of each of these two suppliers.

Activity Report, as a buyer, which supplier you would use. Explain your rationale.

NET SAVVY

20. Chain Store Buyer

Conduct an Internet search using the phrase *popular chain stores*. Also search through a national online job board. Read through descriptions of store buyer positions and make a list of common qualifications for these positions.

THE DECA CONNECTION

An Association of Marketing Students

Role Play: Fashion Buyer

Situation You are to assume the role of assistant buyer for the women's sportswear department of a large department store chain in the upper Midwest of the United States. Your department sells a large number of cotton turtleneck tops each year. The buyer (judge) has used one vendor for many seasons. The vendor can no longer supply seasonal fashion colors but is able to supply the basic colors. The buyer (judge) has asked you to help find a vendor to supply the fashion color turtlenecks in a comparable quality and price.

Activity You are to explain to the buyer (judge) how you will go about finding a new vendor for the turtlenecks.

Evaluation You will be evaluated on the following performance indicators:

- Conduct vendor search
- Explain the nature of buyer reputation/vendor relationship
- Explain company buying/purchasing policies
- Negotiate contracts with vendors
- Explain the nature of the buying process

@ Online Action!

For more information and DECA Prep practice, go to *marketingessentials.glencoe.com/23/DECA*

CHAPTER 24
Stock Handling and Inventory Control

Chapter Objectives

After reading this chapter, you should be able to:

- Describe the receiving process
- Explain stock handling techniques used in receiving deliveries
- Describe the process for providing effective inventory management
- Explain the types of inventory control systems
- Discuss the relationship between customer service and distribution
- Analyze sales information to determine inventory turnover
- Discuss technology and inventory management

GUIDE TO THE PHOTO

Market Talk The receiving process is an important part of inventory control. Proper procedures for handling of incoming stock allow businesses to move products to market in a smooth and timely manner.

Quick Think How does technology help control inventory?

THE DECA CONNECTION

Performance indicators represent key skills and knowledge. Relating them to the concepts explained in this chapter is your key to success in DECA events.

These acronyms represent DECA events that involve knowledge of concepts in this chapter.

AAAL*	**FMAL***	**MMS**	**TMDM***
AAML*	**FMDM**	**QSRM***	**TSE**
ADC	**FMML***	**RMAL***	**VPM**
BSM	**FSRM***	**RMML***	
EMDM	**HMDM***	**SMDM**	

In all these DECA events you should be able to follow these performance indicators:

- Explain the receiving process
- Describe the use of technology in the distribution process

Events with an asterisk (*) also include:

- Explain stock-handling techniques used in receiving deliveries
- Determine processing priorities
- Check incoming stock
- Reconcile shipping/receiving discrepancies
- File claims for lost/damaged goods
- Process returns to vendors
- Maintain inventory levels
- Complete inventory counts
- Explain the nature of inventory control systems
- Calculate inventory shrinkage

Some events include additional performance indicators. These are:

EMDM	Explain types of unit inventory control systems
AAAL/AAML	Transfer stock to/from branches
RMAL/RMML	Transfer stock to/from branches

DECA PREP

Check your understanding of DECA performance indicators with the DECA activity in this chapter's review. For more information and DECA Prep practice, go to *marketingessentials.glencoe.com/24/DECA*

The Stock Handling Process

OBJECTIVES

- Describe the receiving process
- Explain stock handling techniques used in receiving deliveries

KEY TERMS

- receiving record
- blind check method
- direct check method
- spot check method
- quality check method
- source marking
- preretailing marking method

READ and STUDY

BEFORE YOU READ

Predict What are some ways to prepare merchandise to sell?

THE MAIN IDEA

All businesses must have a stock handling process in place to accept deliveries of materials or products. The receiving process must be done efficiently and correctly to ensure that proper inventory levels are maintained at all times.

STUDY ORGANIZER

Copy the flow chart organizer below. Use the chart to identify key steps in the stock handling process.

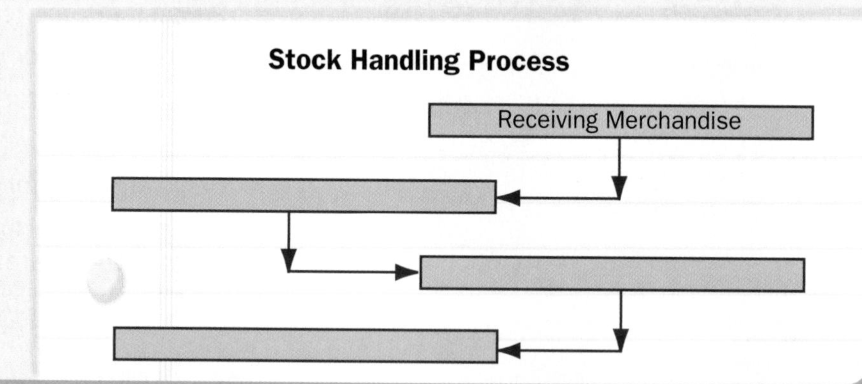

WHILE YOU READ

Question When an order for materials or products is received, what are some problems that might occur at delivery?

Stock Handling

Manufacturing companies depend on suppliers to deliver parts or raw materials used in making finished products accurately and on time. When these parts or materials are delivered to the warehouse, plant, or store, they must be received into stock and information about them must be recorded and tracked. For example, suppose a door handle manufacturer has a contract with an automobile assembly plant to supply door handles for pickup trucks. They deliver door handles almost every day to keep pace with production at the assembly plant.

Whether a business receives raw materials, parts, or merchandise for resale, it needs a process to handle the items. The steps in the stock handling process include receiving goods, checking them, marking the goods with information, if necessary, and delivering them to a place where they will be used, stored, or displayed for sale. The receiving clerk at the truck assembly plant who checks in the door handles must make sure that the correct part has been delivered, that the right number are there, and that they get to the assembly line in time to be installed on the pickup truck doors. The receiving clerk must also make sure that information about the parts is recorded in the system so that inventory levels are correct and the accounts payable department knows to pay the invoice from the door handle manufacturer.

Receiving Stock

Stock ordered by a business is received, checked, and, in retail settings, often marked with a selling price before it is transferred to the sales area.

Facilities

Where stock is placed when it is received depends on the type and size of the business. Smaller businesses may use a backroom or may even place items in store aisles when they are received. Many businesses, however, have enough space to devote an area of a loading dock, or first floor to receiving.

Large businesses and chain stores sometimes have separate warehouses or distribution centers where merchandise is received and stored before it is taken to the department or branch store that needs it. Facilities such as these have large bays with loading docks that open at the height of the bed of a truck for easy unloading.

Receiving Records

Every business records information about the goods it receives either manually or electronically in a **receiving record**. The items on a receiving record depend on the needs of the business. They can include the following:

- A receiving number
- Person who received the shipment
- Shipper of the merchandise
- Place from which the goods were shipped
- Name of the carrier
- Number of the carrier
- Number of items delivered
- Weight of items delivered
- Condition of the goods received
- Shipping charges
- Department or store that ordered the merchandise
- Date the shipment was received

Each set of goods received is assigned a receiving number. Some businesses include this number on a record called an apron. An apron is a form that is attached to the invoice that accompanies the goods received before they move through checking and marking. The apron system helps prevent the payment of duplicate invoices because the invoice is only paid when the proper information is recorded on the apron.

The receiving number may be called an apron number for businesses using this system. In retail businesses, the apron is often prepared by a store's buyers. For example, Lydia buys accessories for a women's clothing shop. She prepares apron forms for a shipment of scarves she ordered when they arrive. These forms will travel through the system with the scarves as they are inspected, priced, prepared for display, and finally placed on the sales floor. The apron lists the steps the scarves take to reach the selling floor and includes the receiving number, the department number, the purchase order number, any terms on the purchase order and on the invoice, routing information, and the date the shipment was checked.

Checking Merchandise

Merchandise is checked to verify quantity and condition; cartons are checked for damage, and the goods are sorted and counted.

A MATTER OF ETHICS

Quality Control

Carlo had recently returned to work after raising a family. He got a job at a furniture manufacturer as a receiving clerk and was soon promoted to department manager. Upon receiving and inspecting a shipment of padding from a supplier, Carlo noticed that the quality of the padding was not according to the buyer's specifications that were listed on the purchase order.

Risk a Large Order or Not?

Carlo suspected that either a mistake had been made or the supplier had shipped the wrong merchandise. But when he reported his findings to the buyer, he was told to ignore the situation. The buyer said that the company needed the padding immediately to complete a large order. He said if the order was not completed by the end of the week, the company would lose the business altogether and that could jeopardize everyone's job.

THINKING ETHICALLY

Do you think that Carlo should report his findings or follow the buyer's request to ignore the situation? Explain.

Online Action!

Go to *marketingessentials.glencoe.com/24/ethics* to find a project on the use of inferior materials.

Some businesses use specially trained employees called receivers to inspect and record newly arrived merchandise.

In the past, checking merchandise was a time- and labor-intensive process. Today, however, electronic data interchange systems minimize the time required for this process. For example, the door handle manufacturer's distribution center can notify the truck assembly plant in advance with information about which cartons of door handles to expect each day and the contents of each carton. Upon receipt at the assembly plant, coded shipping box labels are electronically scanned, the carton's contents are identified, and the information is automatically transferred to an inventory management computer system.

Methods of Checking

There are four methods that are frequently used to check merchandise: the blind check, the direct check, the spot check, and the quality check. Figure 24.1 illustrates the methods of checking merchandise.

The **blind check method** requires the receiver to write the description of the merchandise, count the quantities received, and list them on a blank form or dummy invoice. The list or dummy invoice is then compared to the actual invoice after the blind check is made. The blind check method is considered the most accurate checking method, but it can be time consuming. The blind check method is used when the merchandise needs to be moved quickly to the sales floor and the actual invoice has not yet been received from the seller. Invoices often follow the shipment of goods by two or more days.

With the **direct check method**, the merchandise is checked directly against the actual invoice or purchase order. This procedure is faster than the blind check method, but errors may not be found if the invoice itself is incorrect. Some receivers do not completely check the total number of items once they see the amount listed on the invoice: if the amount looks correct, they may not bother to take an actual count.

The **spot check method** is a random check of one carton in a shipment (such as one out of every twenty). The carton is checked for quantity, and then one product in the carton is inspected for quality. When the contents are as stated on the invoice, the remaining cartons

Figure 24.1 Checking Merchandise

• **Four Methods** When a shipment is received, it must be checked to determine if the merchandise arrived in the right quantities and in good condition. Once a time- and labor-intensive process, it has been greatly simplified by electronic data interchange systems, which transfer information about the order to the receiver. The merchandise must still be checked manually for accuracy and quality assurance. Four methods of checking are commonly used.

What method would likely be used for new-task purchases?

BLIND CHECK

With this method, the receiver counts and records the quantities delivered on a dummy invoice. That information is then compared to the original invoice. This method is considered the most accurate but may be time consuming.

DIRECT CHECK

When using the direct check method, the receiver checks merchandise against the original invoice. This procedure is faster than the blind check. Errors may be introduced, however, if the receiver relies on the amount on the invoice rather than actually counting the merchandise delivered.

SPOT CHECK

A spot check is a random check of one carton in a shipment. The carton is checked for quantity and quality. If it passes inspection, the remaining cartons are assumed to be in the same condition. This method is often used for checking supermarket and drugstore deliveries.

QUALITY CHECK

A quality check is done whenever the workmanship and general characteristics of the merchandise received must be examined. This type of check is usually done for products such as furniture and products with artistic value, such as vases and paintings. Often this check is performed by the buyer, not a receiver.

@ Online Action! Go to *marketingessentials.glencoe.com/24/figure/1* to find a project on checking merchandise.

are assumed to be the same. Spot checking is often used for products such as canned goods, paper products, and pharmaceuticals.

The **quality check method** is done to inspect the workmanship and general characteristics of the received merchandise. Although a receiver can do a quality check, a buyer often performs this check. The merchandise is checked to determine whether the quality of the goods received matches the quality of the products, which were ordered. If the goods are damaged, a damage report is prepared. Damaged goods should not be discarded without the authorization of the supplier.

Returning Merchandise

Careful checking practices can save a business large amounts of money. All incorrect items, damaged merchandise, and items ordered but not received are identified and reported according to the policies of the business. When this is done, the business can get proper credit or adjustments from the carrier or the seller.

Upon return of the merchandise, the seller issues a credit memorandum. A credit memorandum is notification that the buyer's account has been credited for the value of the returned merchandise.

Marking Merchandise

After it has been received and checked, merchandise must be marked with the selling price and other information. Different methods may be used for various kinds of merchandise. The most common method of marking price is with a UPC, however a hand-operated pricing machine or pricing tickets can be used as well.

Universal Product Codes (UPCs) are widely used in business today for tracking merchandise (see Chapter 16). UPCs originate with the Uniform Code Council (UCC). A manufacturer pays an annual fee to the UCC for permission to use the UPC system. Many businesses receive goods that are preticketed with prices and UPCs.

UPCs are often used for **source marking**. With this method, the seller or manufacturer marks the price before delivering the merchandise to the retailer. Merchandise can be moved directly from the receiving area to the sales floor. The UPCs are scanned at the checkout area, and the price stored in the computer for that code is entered for the sale.

Some businesses use a **preretailing marking method** of marking merchandise. With the preretailing marking method, pricing information is marked in advance on the purchase order. This information is entered in the buyer's computer system, and prices are available for marking merchandise as soon as it is received. Preretailing marking is normally used for staple items that are unlikely to have price changes between the time of the order and receipt of the merchandise. It saves time because merchandise can be price marked immediately.

Finally, merchandise can be marked with the familiar price tickets. In large stores, price tickets are prepared by hand or by machine in a marking room or in a stock room. Gum labels are used on merchandise with a flat, hard surface such as books. Pin tickets are used on merchandise that will not be damaged by the pinholes, such as socks or scarves. String or plastic tags are used for larger articles, such as dresses, shirts, and suits. The pricing ticket also helps when a customer needs to return an item to a store as it is difficult to return an item that has no tags.

Price Ticket Information

The price ticket identifies the price of the merchandise. Other important information may also be included on the price ticket. Many businesses include information such as store numbers, model or style numbers, color, sizes, fabrics, manufacturer's number, and lot numbers. This information is useful for tracking merchandise. It helps a business determine which items, sizes, and colors are popular with customers.

Transferring Merchandise

In a retail environment, once merchandise is received, checked, and marked, it is ready to be moved to the sales area. But if it remains on the shelf too long without being sold, it is often transferred to other departments or areas within the store. Older stock is generally transferred from a department or store to a warehouse at the beginning of each selling season. Old merchandise must be removed from the department sales areas to make room for new merchandise. The old merchandise is put on sale for a short time, and the merchandise that does not sell is transferred to a warehouse or distribution center.

Transferred merchandise is accompanied by a form describing the items, style numbers, colors, sizes, cost, and retail prices. Duplicate copies of the transfer forms are retained as a record of merchandise on hand.

Stock transfers between departments can occur when merchandise is carried by more than one department or when the demand for merchandise in one department creates a need for additional merchandise. Stock transfers can also occur when the merchandise is used for sales promotions, such as displays, advertising illustrations, or fashion shows or when the merchandise is used for installation or repairs in various departments.

Stock transfers between stores can occur to meet unexpected demand or to fill requests by customers. A customer may find the perfect pair of pants, but find that the branch of the store is sold out. Some stores will call another local store to have it send over the right size. Finally, stock transfers from store to distribution outlet can occur when off-season and nonsalable merchandise is moved to surplus or discount stores. A store may choose to transfer all of its winter clothing to an outlet store if the stock doesn't clear out during after-season sales.

24.1 AFTER YOU READ

Reviewing Key Terms and Concepts

1. List the four main steps in the stock handling process.
2. What are the four methods used for checking merchandise?
3. How do UPC codes assist with the stock handling process?

Integrating Academic Skills

Math

4. A stationery store calculated the cost of price marking its merchandise to be $54,000 a year in employee time. The store estimates that it can save 33 percent of this cost by switching to source marking for most of its merchandise. What is the amount of the savings?

Social Studies

5. Research the history and development of the Universal Product Code (UPC). Use a word processing program to write a one-page paper on the beginning of UPC in the supermarket industry and its use on most manufactured products today.

@ Online Action!

Check your answers at *marketingessentials.glencoe.com/24/read*

SECTION 24.2

Inventory Control

OBJECTIVES

- Describe the process for providing effective inventory management
- Explain the types of inventory control systems
- Discuss the relationship between customer service and distribution
- Analyze sales information to determine inventory turnover
- Discuss technology and inventory management

KEY TERMS

- inventory
- inventory management
- just-in-time (JIT) inventory system
- perpetual inventory system
- physical inventory system
- cycle counts
- stockkeeping unit (SKU)
- dollar control
- unit control
- inventory turnover
- basic stock list
- model stock list
- never-out list
- real-time inventory systems

READ and STUDY

BEFORE YOU READ

Predict What would happen if stores and businesses did not maintain correct inventories?

MAIN IDEA

The inventory a business owns represents money tied up in products until the inventory is sold. A well-managed and controlled inventory increases the profits of a business.

STUDY ORGANIZER

Copy the concept map below. Use the map to record aspects of perpetual and physical inventory systems.

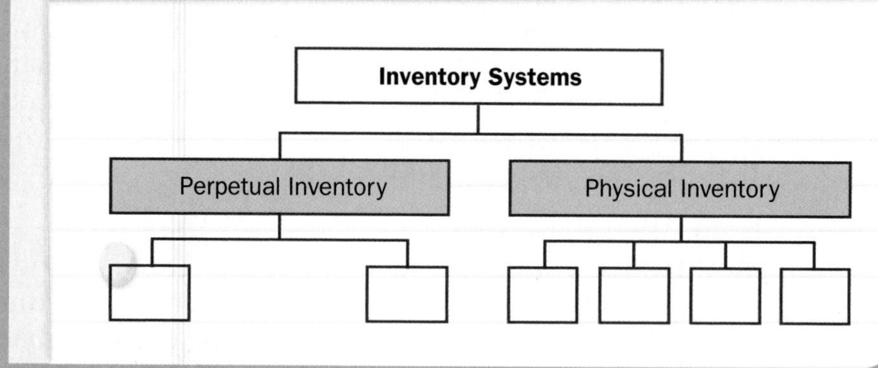

WHILE YOU READ

Question How would shopping be different if there were no plan for inventory management?

Inventory Management

Inventory refers to all the goods stored by a business before they are sold. Inventory includes raw materials, components purchased from suppliers, manufactured sub-assemblies, work in process, packaging materials, and finished goods. In a retail store, inventory includes all goods available for resale.

Inventory management is the process of buying and storing these materials and products while controlling costs for ordering, shipping, handling, and storage. This is usually the responsibility

•COUNTING the MERCHANDISE Inventory accuracy is important to any business.

What are three ways to monitor inventory?

of the supply chain manager whose job it is to maintain just the right level of inventory to meet the supply and demand needs of a business. Having the wrong merchandise in stock, holding too many slow-selling items, or storing too few fast-selling ones are problems the supply chain manager faces every day.

Unnecessarily high inventories can create many problems for a business. In addition to using up valuable storage space, they may increase personnel costs for security and warehouse staff, may cause higher inventory insurance premiums, and may lead to increased interest expenses for a business. Businesses lose money and reduce profits when they manage their inventories poorly.

Distribution, Inventory Management, and Customer Service

The most important goal of any department within a business is to meet the needs of its customers. Every department in today's business environment must be customer oriented if the overall business is to be successful.

Just-in-Time Inventory

A **just-in-time (JIT) inventory system** controls the flow of parts and material into assembly and manufacturing plants. A JIT inventory system coordinates demand and supply such that suppliers deliver parts and raw materials just before they are needed for use. Plants keep only small stocks on hand to avoid tying up money and inventory space.

Computer link-ups tell suppliers and transportation companies which items are needed and when to deliver them to meet production needs. Parts are delivered on a schedule—just in time for use in the production process. A late shipment can bring an entire manufacturing operation to a standstill.

Inventory management is complex because a business has to correctly anticipate demand for its products while trying to keep overall inventory investment as low as possible. Retail businesses are expected to:

- Maintain the right quantities of merchandise without running out of stock
- Keep a wide product assortment (with low inventory investment) without compromising on customer needs and wants
- Purchase merchandise at large volumes to gain the lowest prices while not buying more than it will sell
- Keep a current inventory on hand

Good inventory management balances the costs of inventory with the benefits of maintaining a large inventory. The costs of inventory include not only the cost of the items in stock, but also storage, insurance, and taxes. Inventory ties up a business's working capital—money that could be used for other purposes. It is not effective for a company to maintain large inventory holdings if that money could be spent more effectively somewhere else or invested. Effective inventory management helps increase working capital and allows a business to use its savings to pay for other business expenses.

Inventory Systems

Two methods of tracking inventory are the perpetual inventory system and the physical inventory system.

Perpetual Inventory System

A **perpetual inventory system** tracks the number of items in inventory on a constant basis. The system tracks all new items purchased and returned, as well as sales of current stock. An up-to-date count of inventory is maintained for purchases and returns of merchandise, sales and sales returns, sales allowances, and transfers to other stores and departments. With a perpetual inventory system, a business keeps track of sales as they occur.

Manual Systems

In a manual system, employees gather paper records of sales and enter that information into the inventory system. These records can include receiving department records, sales checks, price tickets, cash register receipts, stock transfer requests, and other documents used for coding and tabulation.

Merchandise tags are used to record information about the vendor, date of receipt, department, product classification, color, size, and style. The merchandise tags from items sold are sent in batches to a company-owned tabulating facility or to an independent computer service organization where the coded information is analyzed through the use of computer software.

Computer-Based Systems

Computer-based systems to control inventory are increasingly popular, even among smaller businesses. They are also faster and more accurate than manual systems. A point-of-sale terminal uses hand-held laser guns, stationary lasers, light pens, or slot scanners to feed sales transaction data directly from Universal Product Codes (UPCs), sales checks, or merchandise tags into a computer. Businesses then use computer-generated information printouts at different times for review and action.

Electronic Data Interchange (EDI) involves computer-to-computer information exchanges and relays of sales information directly to a supplier. The supplier then uses the sales transaction data to ship additional items automatically to the business.

Physical Inventory System

Under a **physical inventory system**, information about stock levels is not maintained on an ongoing basis. Rather, every so often, stock is visually inspected or actually counted to determine the quantity on hand. Inventory data can be captured in many ways, from high-tech methods to manual counts. Some of the most popular methods for larger retailers are scanned bar codes and keypad entry onto handheld devices.

Even if a perpetual inventory system is used, physical inventories are still conducted periodically or on a regular annual basis. A physical inventory allows a business to calculate its income tax, determine the correct value of its ending inventory, identify any stock shortages, and plan future purchases. There are several methods used for physical inventory control.

Inventory Counting Methods

To count inventory, businesses often use a combination of methods. Regular employees or outside inventory service companies can be used to count inventories. Larger national retailers tend to use outside companies such as Washington Inventory Services, RGIS, or smaller regional or local companies more than regular company employees. After the counting is finished, the total value of the inventory is determined. This value is reported on the business's financial statements.

Physical Inventory Method

The most popular method of inventory management is the physical inventory. Most businesses physically count inventory at least once a year, some conduct them on a semiannual basis, and fewer on a quarterly or even more frequent basis. Inventory clerks usually work in pairs: one counts merchandise while the other records the count. Physical inventories are usually wall-to-wall store inventories which often require that the business close temporarily to conduct the inventory.

Cycle Count Method

Many businesses use **cycle counts** either in combination with an annual physical inventory or alone to track inventory. In this method, the entire inventory is never counted at one time. A small portion of the inventory is physically counted each day by stockkeeping units so that the entire inventory is accounted for on a regular basis. A **stockkeeping unit (SKU)** is a unit or a group of related items. Manufacturers' representatives do a variation of the cycle count method. The representative

Case Study

Bar Codes Meet New Standards

The Uniform Code Council, an industry group for retailers in the United States and Canada, is requiring that all bar code scanners read a new global Universal Product Code. Beginning in January of 2005 all point-of-sale scanners must be upgraded to read an extra number (up from 12 to 13 digits). Rather than the existing 12-digit bar code used in North America, the 13-digit bar code is widely used in Europe.

Global Codes

The new 13-digit code gives retailers information about the country of origin, the manufacturer, individual product information, and a single check digit to verify accuracy and to control inventory. The first two digits give country information. For example, numbers from 00–13 represent companies in the U.S. and Canada, while higher numbers represent other countries. The next five digits identify manufacturers from throughout the world who have registered their own unique code with regional authorities like the Uniform Code Council.

The next five numbers are assigned to individual products by each manufacturer. The previous 12 numbers are used mathematically to come up with a final number or check digit. The last number verifies that a product has been scanned correctly. Scanning and technical problems will occur for most retailers because the software written for tracking sales, orders, and inventory control will need to be re-designed for the new bar code.

THINK STRATEGICALLY

While many consumer and retailers may experience initial technical difficulties with scanners and software, why are U.S. and Canadian retailers moving to the new 13-digit bar code standard?

Go to *marketingessentials.glencoe.com/24/case* to find a research project on UPCs and inventory.

visits a business on a regular basis, takes the stock count, and writes the order. Unwanted merchandise is removed from stock and returned to the manufacturer through a predetermined, authorized procedure.

Visual Control Method

Visual control is sometimes used to monitor physical inventory levels. Smaller businesses often place stock cards on pegboards with stock numbers and descriptions for each item displayed. The stock cards specify the number of each item to be kept in stock. It can be somewhat inaccurate because it does not account for misplaced merchandise. The amount to reorder is the difference between the number on hand and the specified number to be stocked. The number to stock may be an estimate of sales for a typical period of time.

Trends in Inventory Methods

As business becomes increasingly more competitive, efficient and effective inventory management methods will be implemented. Some predicted future trends related to inventory methods will be the almost universal recording of inventories using SKU and/or UPC codes, greater use of technology in taking inventories, increased use and frequency of cycle counts by SKU, increased use of Internet technologies to link with vendors, and increased vendor participation.

Using Both Systems

A business does not have to choose between a physical inventory system and a perpetual inventory system. Most businesses find it most effective to use both systems. The perpetual system gives an up-to-date inventory record throughout the year. The physical system gives an accurate count that can be compared to the perpetual records to identify any errors or problems. The two systems actually complement each other.

The perpetual inventory records are used to help the business track sales and manage its merchandise. After a physical inventory is taken, the ending inventory amount becomes the beginning inventory for the year that follows. Purchases by the business during the year are added to this amount, while sales are subtracted. Ending inventory is calculated in the example that follows.

Number of Items for 1/1/05 to 6/30/05		
Beginning inventory, 1/1/2005		1,000
Net purchases (purchases less purchases and allowances returned)	+ 300	
Merchandise available for sale		1,300
Less net sales (sales less returns and allowances)	– 1,050	
Ending inventory, 6/30/2005		250

Sometimes, the ending inventory shown in the perpetual inventory system does not match the physical count of inventory. When the physical count shows less merchandise than is supposed to be in inventory, a stock shortage or shrinkage has occurred. Employee and customer theft, receiving errors, incorrect counting, and selling errors can cause shortages for a business.

In the previous example, all records for purchases and sales are ongoing in a business; therefore the data represents a perpetual inventory system. The ending inventory figure of 250 items is the perpetual inventory. However, as you know, it is possible that this is not the most accurate count. If the physical inventory system showed ending inventory of 225, a stock shortage of 25 would have occurred (250 – 225 = 25). It is not until the physical inventory is taken that the company really knows if its ending inventory records are correct. It is still helpful, however, to use the perpetual inventory as a good estimation.

Stock Control

Stock control involves monitoring stock levels and investments in stock so that a business is run efficiently. Planning those stock levels and monitoring them requires the use of several different systems. They include dollar versus unit control methods, inventory turnover calculations, and three stock lists (model, basic, and never-out).

Dollar Versus Unit Control

Inventory management involves both dollar control and unit control of merchandise held in inventory. **Dollar control** represents the planning and monitoring of the total inventory investment that a business makes during a stated period of time. A business's dollar control of inventory involves information about the amount of purchases, sales, dollar value of beginning and ending inventory, and stock shortages. This information helps a business determine the cost of goods sold and the amount of gross profit or loss during a given period of time. By subtracting operating expenses from the gross profit, the business can determine its net profit or loss.

Unit control refers to the quantities of merchandise that a business handles during a stated period of time. Unit control allows the business to keep inventory adjusted to sales and lets the business determine how to spend money available under a planned budget. In a unit control inventory system, merchandise is tracked by stockkeeping unit. Tracking the SKUs gives valuable sales information on those items that are successful and those that are not selling. A business can use this information to make better merchandising decisions. Sales promotions can be run to sell slow-moving items or to spotlight popular ones.

Unit control records also allow purchasing personnel to see what brands, sizes, colors, and price ranges are popular. By keeping track of this information, buyers can understand customer preferences and order accordingly. Finally, unit control records specify when items need to be ordered. When a minimum stock amount is reached, an order is placed for more stock. This system ensures that adequate assortments are available and helps avoid out-of-stock situations.

Inventory Turnover

The most effective way to measure how well inventory is being managed is to look at inventory turnover. **Inventory turnover** is the number of times the average inventory has been sold and replaced in a given period of time. The higher the inventory turnover rate, the more times the goods were sold and replaced. In retailing and wholesaling operations, the key is moving inventory so there is cash available to buy more fast-selling merchandise. High turnover rates mean that merchandise is selling quickly. That means higher profit for the business because its money is not tied up in inventory. Inventory turnover is also a good measure of success for businesses to use in evaluating vendors and products from year to year. Businesses use inventory turnover rates to compare a particular store's entire operation with the operations of similar stores.

Inventory turnover rates for selected retailers are available from trade associations and commercial publishers. One such publisher is Dun & Bradstreet, which publishes *Industry Norms and Key Business Ratios*. Inventory turnover rates can be calculated in dollars (retail or cost) or in units.

Stores that keep records of the retail value of stock compute their inventory turnover rates as follows:

$$\frac{\text{Net sales (in retail dollars)}}{\text{Average inventory on hand (in retail dollars)}}$$

When net sales during a period are $49,500 and average inventory is $8,250, the inventory turnover is 6:

$$\frac{\$49{,}500}{\$8{,}250} = 6$$

To determine the average inventory, use inventory amounts for each of the months included in the time period being considered. Total these, as shown in the second column below, and then calculate the average.

Month	Inventory	Net Sales
January	$ 50,000	$ 10,000
February	55,000	15,000
March	68,000	20,000
April	64,000	19,000
May	63,000	21,000
June	60,000	20,000
Totals	$360,000	$105,000

MARKET TECH

Picking Up the Speed

Picking orders in distribution centers can represent 30 to 40 percent of the total labor cost. So, increasing the speed it takes for order picking and selection can save time and money. Radio frequency (RF) terminals can speed up order selection by showing a worker the best sequence to pick up requested orders. Speed is increased, because the order selector does not have to read the entire pick ticket to look for the items, arrange the pick sequence, and find the item location.

Initial Costs

However, warehouse management system (WMS) software must be purchased to use radio frequency picking. The computer program is needed to arrange the orders in the best possible picking sequence. The order selector, using a RF handheld terminal, sees only one item at a time shown on the terminal. Besides the software, handheld RF terminals costing about $4,000 each need to be purchased, and an RF network including installation, antennas, and access points needs to be erected. Extra RF terminals also need to be purchased for spares and for use by storage and distribution supervisors.

THINK LIKE A MARKETER

How would you justify to upper management a capital investment in distribution technology such as radio frequency terminals?

Online Action!

Go to *marketingessentials.glencoe.com/24/tech* to find a project on warehouse management software.

To get the average inventory for the six-month period, divide by the number of months.

$$\frac{\$360{,}000}{6} = \$60{,}000$$

Finally, to calculate inventory turnover, divide total net sales (see the third column above) by average inventory.

$$\frac{\$105{,}000}{\$60{,}000} = 1.75$$

This figure means that the average inventory was sold and replaced 1.75 times during the six-month period.

When only cost information about inventory is available, inventory turnover can be calculated with this formula:

$$\frac{\text{Cost of goods sold}}{\text{Average inventory on hand (at cost)}}$$

When a store wants to look at the number of items carried in relation to the number of items sold, it calculates its stock turnover rates in units with this formula:

$$\frac{\text{Number of SKUs sold}}{\text{Average SKUs on hand}}$$

Stock Lists

There are three plans used to monitor different types of goods—staple items, fashionable items, and very popular items. They are the basic stock list, model stock list, and never-out list.

A **basic stock list** is used for those staple items that should always be in stock. This list specifies products that a store should always carry based upon the type of business. A basic stock list in a men's clothing store would include items such as T-shirts, underwear, and dress socks. The basic stock list at a card store would include birthday cards, blank cards, thank you cards, and cards for special occasions, such as weddings and anniversaries.

Based on expected sales for a given period, a basic stock list specifies the minimum amount of merchandise that should be on hand for particular products. It shows the quantity of items that should be reordered, as well as the colors, styles, and sizes that should be carried. Retailers assign each product a code for ease in recording when the products are purchased and sold.

A **model stock list** is used for fashionable merchandise. Fashion items change relatively rapidly; therefore, these lists are less specific than basic stock lists. The information contained in model stock lists identifies goods by general classes (blouses, skirts, dresses, slacks) and style categories (short sleeve, long sleeve), sizes, materials, colors, and price lines. Style numbers are not included because each manufacturer's style numbers change each year. Although model stock lists identify how many of each type of item should be purchased, the buyer must actually select specific models at the market. A **never-out list** is used for best-selling products that make up a large percentage of sales volume. Items are added to or taken off the list as their popularity increases or declines.

The Future of Inventory Management

Because most customers who buy online expect their orders to be filled immediately, the ability to process and ship orders without delay has become essential to the success of e-businesses. This has brought about **real-time inventory systems**. Real-time inventory management is an Internet technology that connects applications, data, and users in real time. This technology lets a company constantly track every product it sells from when it is manufactured, or when it arrives in the warehouse, to when the customer orders it online, and to when it arrives at the buyer's door.

24.2 AFTER YOU READ

Reviewing Key Terms and Concepts

1. Explain the difference between a perpetual and a physical inventory system.
2. Name the three different inventory counting methods.
3. What is the difference between dollar control and unit control as they relate to inventory management?

Integrating Academic Skills

Math

4. What is the inventory turnover rate (at cost) for a school store if the cost of goods sold equals $15,000 and the average inventory on hand (at cost) equals $3,000? What does your answer represent?

Science

5. Investigate smart cards or radio frequency identification (RFID) tags and develop a one-page report on the scientific principles involved with this technology.

Check your answers at *marketingessentials.glencoe.com/24/read*

CAREERS IN MARKETING

ANGIE VITTITOW
BUSINESS SYSTEMS ANALYST
UPS SUPPLY CHAIN SOLUTIONS

What do you do at work?

I provide support for multiple clients in a third-party logistics environment. This includes supporting warehouse management order and inventory management systems. I train new employees, author documentation, and spec out modifications to improve the visibility of current inventory or to improve the quality of cycle counts and annual physical inventories. I work with the warehouse operations management to improve processes. I also work on new client implementations. Included in this are system design, warehouse layout, process design, and testing.

What skills are most important to you?

Without a doubt, written and verbal communication skills are at the top of the list. I work with all levels of employees. I must be able to understand the operator's vision and translate that to specifications for software developers. When training, I must find a way to make sure the light bulb goes on for everyone, regardless of different learning styles. There is frequent interaction with our third-party clients. Presenting the company's best image to the client is very important.

What is your key to success?

The ability to keep an open mind and good communication skills. Hard skills are important but soft skills will take you where you want to go.

Aptitudes, Abilities, and Skills

Excellent communication skills, organization, and time management

Education and Training

Technology-related degrees as well as degrees in general business are useful.

Career Path

Entry-level positions in logistics and operations can lead to a number of careers centered around the inner workings of a company.

THINKING CRITICALLY

Why is keeping up with technology so crucial?

Online Action!

Go to *marketingessentials.glencoe.com/24/careers* to find a career-related activity.

CHAPTER 24 REVIEW

FOCUS on KEY POINTS

SECTION 24.1

- Successful stock management procedures help control costs and ensure the continuation of business operations. The steps in the stock handling process include receiving goods, checking them, marking the goods with information, if necessary, and delivering them to their selling or storing location. Methods of checking merchandise include the blind check method, the direct check method, the spot check method, and the quality check method.

SECTION 24.2

- Inventory is one of the most costly parts of operations for many businesses. Inventory management is the process of buying and storing products for sale while controlling costs for ordering, shipping, handling, and storage. Inventory systems include perpetual inventory systems and physical inventory systems. Technology is changing the way inventory is controlled. Retail businesses have implemented standards such as UPCs, EDI, and SCM to take advantage of computerized systems. Real-time inventory systems let businesses track all stages of a product, from manufacture to delivery.

REVIEW VOCABULARY

Define each of the following key terms in a short sentence.

1. receiving record (p. 503)
2. blind check method (p. 504)
3. direct check method (p. 504)
4. spot check method (p. 504)
5. quality check method (p. 506)
6. source marking (p. 506)
7. inventory (p. 508)
8. inventory management (p. 508)
9. just-in-time (JIT) inventory system (p. 509)
10. perpetual inventory system (p. 510)
11. physical inventory system (p. 510)
12. cycle counts (p. 511)
13. stockkeeping unit (SKU) (p. 511)
14. dollar control (p. 513)
15. unit control (p. 513)
16. inventory turnover (p. 513)
17. basic stock list (p. 514)
18. model stock list (p. 515)
19. never-out list (p. 515)
20. real-time inventory system (p. 515)

REVIEW FACTS and IDEAS

21. Why is a receiving record important? (24.1)
22. What are stock handling techniques? (24.1)
23. What is the inventory management process? (24.2)
24. What are some methods used to monitor inventory under a physical inventory system? (24.2)
25. How do you calculate stock turnover rates? (24.2)
26. Give three examples of technological developments in the retail industry related to inventory management. (24.2)

BUILD SKILLS

27. Workplace Skills

Presenting Information Use the resources at a public library to research the inventory turnover rates of two competing companies.

28. Technology Applications

Presenting Information Find an article about potential privacy issues related to radio frequency identification at the library or on the Internet. Use a word processing program to prepare a summary focusing on the article's main points. Identify the name of the article, the author, source, and date of publication.

29. Math Practice

Calculating Inventory Turnover Calculate the inventory turnover rate (at retail) for the six-month period, given the following information.

Month	Average Inventory	Net Sales
July	$45,000	$15,000
August	$53,000	$20,000
September	$48,000	$21,000
October	$42,000	$32,000
November	$44,000	$35,000
December	$44,000	$38,000

DEVELOP CRITICAL THINKING

30. Checking Merchandise

Why must merchandise be checked after it has been received? Explain the consequences of not checking received merchandise properly.

31. Real-Time Service

Review the definition of real-time inventory system and research this inventory method on the Internet. After you read a few articles about it, answer the following questions: How can a real-time inventory system improve customer service? Why would a global business be particularly interested in real-time inventory systems?

APPLY CONCEPTS

32. Researching Storage

Perform an Internet search on the potential hazards caused by the storage of goods and materials in warehouses, retail stores, or restaurants.

Activity Use a word processing program to compose a one-page report detailing some of the risks investigated and steps to minimize the risks. Organize your report by types of business.

33. Improving Inventory Management

Research business magazines to find an example of a company that has improved its inventory management system.

Activity Use presentation software to create an oral presentation describing the situation and how the solution increased profits.

34. Investigating Inventory Technologies

Use the Internet, your school media center, or local library to investigate how technologies such as RFID, Warehouse Management Systems, UPC codes, ECR computer systems, or Electronic Data Interchange are impacting inventory management.

Activity Use a word processing program to compose a one-page report with the source and date of your information cited.

NET SAVVY

35. Develop a Prospectus

Using an Internet search engine, identify a software company that specializes in inventory management systems. Use a word processing program to write a one-page prospectus on the company. Include its Web site address and some of the services the company offers.

THE 

CONNECTION

Role Play: Stock Handling and Inventory Control

Situation You are to assume the role of assistant grocery manager for a large grocery store. A customer has just returned a package of frozen broccoli that was purchased earlier today. The frozen broccoli is covered with ice crystals, appears to have freezer burn, and generally has an old appearance. The customer service clerk (judge) has refunded the customer's money and asks you how this situation could have occurred.

Activity You are to explain to the customer service clerk (judge) about stock handling and proper handling and rotation of frozen foods.

Evaluation You will be evaluated on how well you meet the following performance indicators:

- Explain storing considerations
- Store food products to prevent contamination and spoilage
- Explain stock-handling techniques used in receiving deliveries
- Process returned/damaged products
- Inspect food deliveries

@ Online Action!

For more information and DECA Prep practice, go to *marketingessentials.glencoe.com/24/DECA*

MARKETING INTERNSHIP

A SIMULATED DECA PRODUCT AND SERVICE MANAGEMENT EVENT

Sell GPS Technology to Consumers

BASIC BACKGROUND

Your firm's newest client, Street-Smarts, specializes in Global Positioning System (GPS) products. GPS uses satellites to provide navigational information. The police, the military, and aviation used the technology for years before it became available on the consumer market. Other companies marketing GPS products include Timex, Garmin Inc., and Thales Navigation.

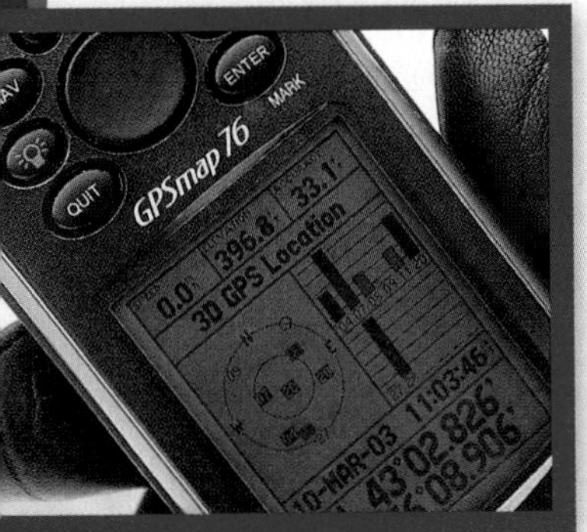

Pinpointing Locations Some automobiles are equipped with GPS to help direct drivers to their destinations. Handheld GPS devices are currently on the market for runners, hikers, cyclists, and outdoor sports enthusiasts. Geocaching and other games that make use of GPS are on the rise. Tourist attractions and museums are using the devices as tour guides.

Street-Smarts has asked for your firm's help in defining consumer markets, choosing products, and suggesting channels of distribution for its products.

YOUR OBJECTIVE

Your objective is to suggest the products Street-Smarts should market to consumers for personal use, who should be the target market(s), and the channel(s) of distribution that should be used to get the products into their hands.

ASSIGNMENT AND STRATEGY

- **Conduct research** To get started, analyze Street-Smarts' competitors and the market for GPS products. Learn about GPS technology, especially devices that are currently marketed to consumers for personal use. Research the emerging trends and markets for GPS. Examine the marketing of GPS products, including target markets, pricing, and distribution.
- **Develop the plan** Begin your proposal with an overview of the current consumer market for GPS technology, including emerging trends. Include a history of the growth of this market.

  Cover the four Ps of the marketing mix (product, place, price, and promotion). Then devise an effective distribution plan. Recommend products you think Street-Smarts should market, identify target markets, and suggest prices for the products.

Discuss the distribution channels you would include, the costs involved, and the volume of products you suggest distributing. Provide reasons for your recommendations.

- **What your project should include** To make your project complete, suggest how Street-Smarts should set up its sales and marketing departments for the consumer market. If you suggest working with resellers, include promotional materials that might be used to persuade resellers to carry this line of consumer GPS products. If you suggest a Web site, provide a sample site map and home page design.

YOUR REPORT

Use a word processing program and presentation software to prepare a double-spaced report and an oral presentation for Street-Smarts. See a suggested outline and key evaluation points at *marketingessentials.glencoe.com/internship*

BUILD YOUR PORTFOLIO

Option 1 Internship Report
Once you have completed your Marketing Internship project and presentation, include your written report and a few printouts of key slides from your oral presentation in your Marketing Portfolio.

Option 2 E-Commerce Plan
From books to groceries, electronics to entertainment, more and more e-commerce companies are succeeding. Create your own e-commerce business. Conduct a situation analysis to support the selection of the business. Develop ideas for purchasing, inventory control, warehousing, and shipping, as well as your Web site design. Prepare a written report and an oral presentation using word processing and presentation software. See a suggested outline and key evaluation points at *marketingessentials.glencoe.com/portfolio*

Online Action!

Go to *marketingessentials.glencoe.com/Unit/7/DECA* to review distribution concepts that relate to DECA events.

UNIT 8 Pricing

In this unit you will find

- **Chapter 25** Price Planning
- **Chapter 26** Pricing Strategies
- **Chapter 27** Pricing Math

ANALYZE THE AD

Orbitz, an online company, provides travel services on its Web site. What does this ad say to you? How is Orbitz competing for Linda's business?

Market Talk Travel companies such as Expedia.com, Hotel.com, or Travelocity attract customers with competitive rates, powerful visuals, and fast, 24-hours-a-day service. Which of these three elements do you see in this Orbitz ad?

Think and Write Read the travel section of your local newspaper, browse the Internet to research competing travel Web sites. Make a list of companies in this market. Select two companies from your list and pick a travel destination. Find out about airfares, hotel and rental car rates from these two sites. Write a paragraph to explain which company you would select for your trip and why.

Online Action! **Go to *marketingessentials.glencoe. com/ u8/ad* for an extended activity.**

Marketing Plan

1 **ANALYSIS**
SWOT
Economic
Socio-Cultural
Technological
Competitive

2 **STRATEGY**
Promotion
Place
Price
Product

3 **IMPLEMENTATION**
Organization
Management
Staffing

4 **BUDGET**
Cost of Sales
Cost of Promotion
Incomes and Expenses

5 **CONTROL**
Evaluation
Performance Measures
Performance Analysis

In this unit

Foundations of Marketing
- Economics
- Business, Management, Entrepreneurship

Functions of Marketing
- Pricing

CHAPTER 25
Price Planning

Chapter Objectives

After reading this chapter, you should be able to:

- Recognize the different forms of pricing
- Discuss the importance of pricing
- Explain the goals of pricing
- Differentiate between market share and market position
- List the four market factors that affect price planning
- Analyze demand elasticity and supply and demand theory
- Explain how government regulations affect price planning

GUIDE TO THE PHOTO

Market Talk Cell phone companies advertise in various ways to target very specific markets. Family plans that allow parents and children to stay connected during the day are very popular; so are plans geared toward college students.

Quick Think The first cell phone cost about $600. Now you can get a phone for free or for a modest sum when signing up for a plan. Think of three reasons why the price of cell phones has changed so much in recent years.

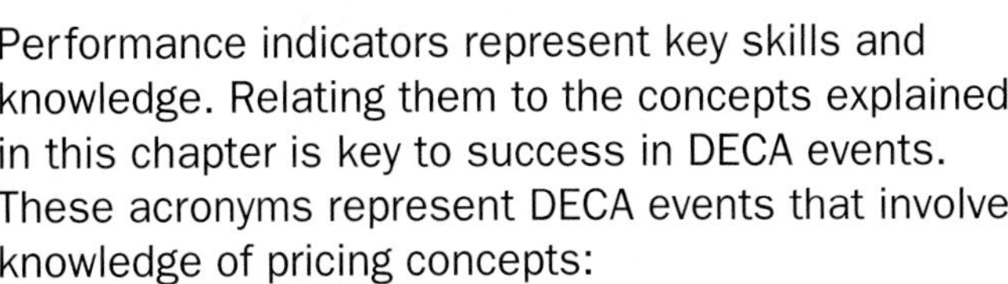

Performance indicators represent key skills and knowledge. Relating them to the concepts explained in this chapter is key to success in DECA events. These acronyms represent DECA events that involve knowledge of pricing concepts:

AAAL	**FMAL**	**MMS**	**TMDM**
AASL	**FMDM**	**QSRM**	**TSE**
ADC	**FMSL**	**RMAL**	**VPM**
BSM	**FSRM**	**RMML**	
EMDM	**HMDM**	**SMDM**	

In all these DECA events, you should be able to follow these performance indicators:

- Explain the nature and scope of the pricing function
- Describe the role of business ethics in pricing
- Explain the use of technology considerations for pricing

Some events include additional performance indicators. These are:

BSM Explain the concept of price in services marketing

ADC Explain the concept of price in the advertising industry

EMDM Describe Internet pricing models

FMDM Explain the concept of price in the financial services industry

HMDM Explain the concept of price in the hospitality industry

SMDM Explain the concept of price in sports and entertainment marketing

TMDM Explain the concept of price in the travel and tourism industry

DECA PREP

Check your understanding of DECA performance indicators with the DECA activity in this chapter's review. For more information and DECA Prep practice, go to *marketingessentials .glencoe.com/25/DECA*

Price Planning Considerations

OBJECTIVES

- Recognize the different forms of pricing
- Discuss the importance of pricing
- Explain the goals of pricing
- Differentiate between market share and market position

KEY TERMS

- price
- return on investment (ROI)
- market share

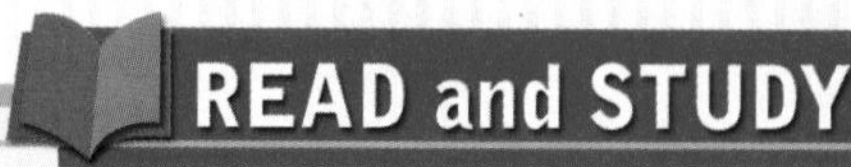

BEFORE YOU READ

Predict What do you already know about pricing?

THE MAIN IDEA

Price—one of the four Ps of the marketing mix—is an essential element in marketing a product to the correct target market. Price comes in a variety of forms. Pricing goals are directly related to a company's goals.

STUDY ORGANIZER

Use a chart like the one below to take notes about the scope and significance of pricing and the major goals of pricing.

Scope and Significance	Goals

Analyze Find three main ideas in this section and jot them down on a piece of paper.

What Is Price?

Price is the value in money (or its equivalent) placed on a good or service. It is usually expressed in monetary terms, such as $40 for a sweater. It may also be expressed in non-monetary terms, such as free goods or services in exchange for the purchase of a product. The oldest form of pricing is the barter system. Bartering involves the exchange of a product or service for another product or service, without the use of money. For example, a business might exchange some of its products for advertising space in a magazine or newspaper. Some companies also will exchange advertising spots on their Web pages as a form of bartering, or an equal trade.

Relationship of Product Value

The value that a customer places on an item or service makes the difference in them spending $25,000 or $80,000 on a new auto or $20 or $150 on a concert ticket. Value is a matter of anticipated satisfaction—if consumers believe they will gain a great deal of satisfaction from a product, they will place a high value on it. They will also be willing to pay a high price.

A seller must be able to gauge where a product will rank in the customer's estimation—whether it will be valued much, valued little, or valued somewhere in between. This information can then be considered in the pricing decision. The seller's objective is to set a price high enough for the firm to make a profit and yet not so high that it exceeds the value potential customers place on the product.

Various Forms of Price

Price is involved in every marketing exchange. The fee you pay a dentist to clean your teeth, the amount you pay for a new pair of shoes, and minor charges such as bridge tolls and bus fares are all prices. Rent is the monthly price of an apartment. Interest is the price of a loan. Dues are the price of membership. Tuition is the price you pay for an education. Wages, salaries, commissions, and bonuses are the various prices that businesses pay workers for their labor. Price comes in many forms and goes by many names.

Importance of Price

Price is an important factor in the success or failure of a business. It helps establish and maintain a firm's image, competitive edge, and profits.

Many customers use price to make judgments about products and the companies that make them. A higher price means better quality from an upscale store or company to some customers; to other customers, a lower price means more for their money.

NET MARKETING

Let Your Fingers Do the Comparison Shopping

PriceGrabber.com is a fast, convenient way to locate and compare products, merchants, and prices online. Since 1999, PriceGrabber's innovative comparison shopping technology has made online shopping informative and effective. Savvy shoppers save time, money, and effort by using PriceGrabber to find the right product from the best merchant at the best price.

Ratings and Costs

Besides product pictures, descriptions, and specifications, PriceGrabber offers merchant and product ratings with narratives that give customers the lowdown on products and merchants.

A site feature called *BottomLinePrice* estimates total delivery costs, including applicable sales tax and shipping charges based on the delivery address.

THINK LIKE A MARKETER

Could a comparison shop site be useful to a marketing manager working for an electronics company? Explain your answer.

Online Action!

Go to *marketingessentials.glencoe.com/25/net* to find a project on pricing sites.

Advertising strategies are closely aligned to a firm's image. Wal-Mart's slogan, "Always Low Prices. Always." is a perfect example of how a company can use price as the main thrust of its advertising strategy. Some retailers stress that they offer the lowest prices in town or promise that they will beat any other store's prices. In such cases, price plays an important role in establishing the edge a firm enjoys over its competition.

Finally, price helps determine profits. Marketers know that sales revenue is equal to price times the quantity sold. In theory, sales revenue can be increased either by selling more items or by increasing the price per item. However, the number of items sold may not increase or even remain stable if prices are raised. Figure 25.1 shows what may happen.

It is also important to remember that an increase in price can increase profits only if costs and expenses can be maintained. You will explore this limitation later in the chapter.

Goals of Pricing

Marketers are concerned with earning a profit, or return on investment, as their primary goal of doing business. There are times, however, when two other pricing goals become important: gaining market share and meeting the competition.

Earning a Profit

Return on investment (ROI) is a calculation that is used to determine the relative profitability of a product. The formula for calculating rate of return on investment is as follows:

Rate of Return = Profit/Investment

Profit is another word for return, which explains the expression *return on investment.*

Assume your company sells watches to retailers for $9 each. Your cost to make and market the watches is $7.50 per unit. Remember that profit is money earned by a

Figure 25.1 ***Projected Effects of Different Prices on Sales***

- **Increased Price or Increased Sales?** An increase in the price of an item may not produce an increase in sales revenue.

Explain why an increase in price does not always mean an increase in revenue.

Price per Item ×	Quantity Sold =	Sales Revenue
$50	200	$10,000
$45	250	$11,250
$40	280	$11,200
$35	325	$11,375
$30	400	$12,000
$25	500	$12,500

Online Action! **Go to *marketingessentials.glencoe.com/25/figure/1* to find a project on pricing and sales.**

•THE 99-CENT HAMBURGER Wendy's and other fast-food chains all compete for customers. They offer similar menus and similar prices.

Could a fast-food chain set its prices much lower or higher than its competitors? Why or why not?

business minus costs and expenses, so that your profit on each watch is $1.50:

$$\$9 - \$7.50 = \$1.50$$

and your rate of return is 20 percent:

$$\$1.50/\$7.50 = .20$$

Your rate of return on investment is 20 percent.

A company may price its products to achieve a certain return on investment. Let's say that your watch company wants to achieve a return on investment of at least 25 percent on a new model. To determine the price at which the new watch would have to sell, you would work backward. Start with a target price, the price at which you want to sell the new watch. Then, determine how your company can get costs down so that that price will generate your target return. When you take into consideration the suggested retail price you think consumers are willing to pay for the watch, target pricing takes on another dimension. You will learn more about target pricing for the final consumer in Chapter 26.

Gaining Market Share

A business may forgo immediate profits for long-term gains in some other area. One goal, for example, might be to take business away from competitors. The business is trying to increase its market share in this case. For example, Nintendo's GameCube systems sold for $80 less than other similar systems, which helped to increase its market share from 19 percent to 37 percent in 2003. **Market share** is a firm's percentage of the total sales volume generated by all competitors in a given market. Businesses constantly study their market share to see how well they are doing with a given product in relation to their competitors.

Visualize the total market as a pie. Each slice of the pie represents each competitor's share of that market. The biggest slice of the pie represents the firm that has the largest percentage of the total sales volume. Marketers are also interested in their market position. Market position is the relative standing a competitor has in a given market in comparison to its competitors.

Improving Market Share and Market Position

To monitor market position, a firm must keep track of the changing size of the market and the growth of its competitors. Competitors are ranked according to their total sales volume. Thus, the company or brand with the highest sales volume would be ranked number 1.

Pricing is one means of improving market share and market position. Other means of accomplishing the same goals may involve increased advertising expenditures, changes in product design, and new distribution outlets.

Meeting the Competition

Some companies simply aim to meet the prices of their competition. They either follow the industry leader or calculate the average price and then position their product close to that figure. Airline pricing appears to follow this pattern. Most airlines charge around the same price for the service provided.

How else do you compete when you don't want to rely on price alone? You compete on the basis of other factors in the marketing mix. These nonprice competing factors might include quality or uniqueness of product, convenience of business location or hours, and level of service. For example, Commerce Bank is open seven days a week and offers hours from 8:30 A.M. until 8:00 P.M. during weekdays. Automobile manufacturers are now competing with warranties and maintenance agreements, some offering coverage for five or ten years, or 50,000 or 100,000 miles, respectively. A computer store may offer free installation of software and training to teach you how to use your new software.

25.1 AFTER YOU READ

Reviewing Key Terms and Concepts

1. Provide an example of how pricing is related to a firm's image and promotion of that image.
2. What means, other than price, do marketers have to accomplish the goal of improving market share or market position?
3. Provide two examples of how businesses compete when they don't want to compete on price.

Integrating Academic Skills

Math

4. A cosmetic company has developed a new line of mascara. Each tube of mascara costs $6.50 to make and market and it is sold for $10. What is the rate of return on investment?

Geography

5. Why may the price of a concert ticket vary depending on where the concert is held within the United States? What if the concert is held in another country?

Check your answers at *marketingessentials.glencoe.com/25/read*

SECTION 25.2

Factors Involved in Price Planning

OBJECTIVES

- List the four market factors that affect price planning
- Analyze demand elasticity and supply and demand theory
- Explain how government regulations affect price planning

KEY TERMS

- break-even point
- demand elasticity
- law of diminishing marginal utility
- price fixing
- price discrimination
- unit pricing
- loss leader

READ and STUDY

BEFORE YOU READ

Predict What are two factors that can influence prices?

THE MAIN IDEA

Pricing a product may seem like an easy task, until you take into consideration all the factors affecting that decision. Skipping even one aspect of this process could cost a business millions of dollars in lost sales or even in fines or lawsuits from not following the laws and ethics governing pricing decisions.

STUDY ORGANIZER

Draw the chart below. As you read this section, note each step of the pricing process and its consequence. Use these notes to review before a test.

Factors That Affect Price	Consequences
Costs and expenses	Determine a company's profits

Market Factors Affecting Prices

How do businesses make pricing decisions? The answer is not an easy one, as you have probably already realized. Constant changes in the marketplace force businesses to review their pricing decisions frequently. Four key market factors that must be considered when reviewing and establishing prices are: costs and expenses, supply and demand, consumer perceptions, and competition. Most price planning begins with an analysis of costs and expenses, many of which are related to current market conditions. The cost of raw materials may increase a manufacturer's costs to make an item.

Connect As you read this section think of what you have just learned about the goals of pricing.

Costs and Expenses

In today's competitive economic environment, businesses constantly monitor, analyze, and project prices and sales in the light of costs and expenses. They do this because sales, costs, and expenses together determine a firm's profit. Many factors have to be considered when raising or lowering prices even if the impulse to increase or decrease is a direct, seemingly logical reaction to events in the marketplace.

Responses to Increasing Costs and Expenses

When oil prices go up, you will often see an increase in rates charged by airlines, shipping companies, and gas stations. How else could businesses maintain their profit margins? Let's look at other options.

Some businesses have found that price is so important in the marketing strategy of a product that they hesitate to make any price changes. They will reduce the size of an item before they will change its price. A candy

Case Study

99¢ Only: Spending in Order to Earn

99¢ Only Stores' low-budget roots helped it increase sales to $863 million in 2003, up 21 percent over previous years. Their strategy? Cutting-edge warehouse and in-store stock-tracking and technology, and a frugal management culture that counts every penny.

Spend to Keep Prices Low

Expensive computer gear and cutting-edge automation are not exactly what you would expect to find behind the scenes at a retailer so price-conscious that it sells everything for $0.99 each. Net profit margins are 8.3 percent, which may not sound spectacular, but consider this: Kroger Co., the supermarket chain, has net margins of only 2.1 percent, while margins at the super-efficient Wal-Mart Stores Inc. come in at just 3.1 percent.

Yet, even with sales of $863 million, IT investments at 99¢ Only Stores are as spare as Robert Adams, Vice President of information services, can make them. 99¢ Only spends less than $5 million a year on IT, not a huge budget for a company this size.

Knowing Who Likes to Save

Where other dollar stores target low- to moderate-income neighborhoods, 99¢ Stores looks for areas with a high-income demographic. "Rich people like to save money too, and they do it in higher volumes," says founder David Gold. Case in point: The 18,000-square-foot 99¢ Only store adjacent to Beverly Hills rakes in the chain's highest annual gross sales, averaging $10 million.

THINK STRATEGICALLY

Why do you think 99¢ Only store management chose to invest in warehouse and in-store technology despite their reputation for containing costs?

Online Action!

Go to *marketingessentials.glencoe.com/25/case* to find a research project on discount stores.

manufacturer might reduce a candy bar from 4 to 3.5 ounces rather than increase its price.

Manufacturers drop features their customers don't value. Some airlines have stopped serving meals and offer only beverages. Eliminating a small portion of its service helps the company to stay competitive.

Some manufacturers respond to higher costs and expenses by adding more features or upgrading the materials in order to justify a higher price. For example, the Ford Motor Company designed more comfortable supercabs on some of its trucks and charged more for those models.

Responses to Lower Costs and Expenses

Prices may occasionally drop because of decreased costs and expenses. Aggressive firms are constantly looking for ways to increase efficiency and decrease costs. Improved technology and less expensive materials may help create better-quality products at lower costs. Personal computers have fallen in price because of the improved technology.

Break-Even Point

Manufacturers are always concerned with making a profit. They are especially concerned, however, in two situations—when marketing a new product and when trying to establish a new price. In these circumstances, manufacturers carefully analyze their costs and expenses in relation to unit and dollar sales. To do this they calculate their break-even point.

The **break-even point** is the point at which sales revenue equals the costs and expenses of making and distributing a product. After this point is reached, businesses begin to make a profit on the product.

Suppose a toy manufacturer plans to make 100,000 dolls that will be sold at $6 each to retailers and wholesalers. The cost of making and marketing the dolls is $4.50 per unit, or $450,000 for the 100,000 dolls. How many dolls must the toy manufacturer sell to cover its costs and expenses? To calculate the break-even point, the manufacturer must divide the total amount of costs and expenses by the selling price:

$$\$450{,}000 \div \$6 = 75{,}000$$

To break even, the firm must sell 75,000 dolls. After 75,000 are sold, the firm will begin to make a profit.

Supply and Demand

In Chapter 3, you learned about supply and demand theory. You might recall that demand tends to go up when price goes down and down when price goes up. This statement is accurate as a general rule. However, demand for some products does not respond readily to changes in price. The degree to which demand for a product is affected by its price is called **demand elasticity**. Products are said to have either elastic demand or inelastic demand.

Elastic Demand

Elastic demand refers to situations in which a change in price creates a change in demand. Changes in the price of steak can serve as an example. If the price of steak were $8 per pound, few people would buy steak; if the price were to drop to $5, $3, and finally $2 per pound, however, demand would increase at each price level.

Law of Diminishing Marginal Utility

These increases would not continue indefinitely, however. At some point, they would be limited by another economic law—the **law of diminishing marginal utility**, which states that consumers will buy only so much of a given product, even though the price is low. Let's say that detergent went on sale, and you bought five bottles of it. Three weeks later a new sale is announced for the same detergent, but you already have enough to last for months; therefore, you don't take advantage of the new sale.

Inelastic Demand

Inelastic demand refers to situations in which a change in price has very little effect on demand for a product. If milk prices were to increase, parents with young children may still pay the higher price. During the holiday season, you may see parents willing to pay a higher price for a popular toy than they would normally pay. Since there is no substitute for that toy, it is an example of inelastic demand.

Factors Influencing Demand Elasticity

There are five factors that determine whether demand is elastic or inelastic. They are: brand loyalty, price relative to income, availability of substitutes, luxury versus necessity, and urgency of purchase. See Figure 25.2 for details.

Consumer Perceptions

Consumer perceptions about the relationship between price and quality or other values also play a role in price planning. Some consumers equate quality with price. They believe a high price reflects high quality. A high price may also suggest status, prestige, and exclusiveness.

Some businesses create the perception that a particular product is worth more than others by limiting the supply of the item in the market. They do this by coming out with a limited edition of a certain model and charging a higher price. Why? The reasoning is that the value of the item will increase as a result of its exclusiveness.

Service and Consumer Perceptions

Personalized service can add to a consumer's perceptions about price. Many consumers

Figure 25.2 Demand Elasticity

• **What Determines Demand Elasticity?** Demand elasticity varies with five factors. Most depend on the consumer's personal situation or attitudes about the purchase.

How does demand elasticity work?

1 *Brand Loyalty*
Some customers will not accept a substitute product, even though there are many competing brands. In such situations, demand becomes inelastic because customers are loyal to one brand.

2 *Price Relative to Income*
If the price increase is significant relative to one's income, demand is likely to be elastic.

3 *Availability of Substitutes*
When substitutes are readily available, demand becomes more elastic.

4 *Luxury Versus Necessity*
When a product is a necessity (such as medicine for a sick person), demand tends to be inelastic. When a product is a luxury, just the opposite is true.

5 *Urgency of Purchase*
If a purchase must be made immediately, demand tends to be inelastic.

@ Online Action!
Go to *marketingessentials.glencoe.com/25/figure/2* to find a research project on demand elasticity.

GLOBAL MARKET

GERMANY

Wal-Mart's Prices Too Low In Germany

In Germany, Wal-Mart was involved in a price war with its two major competitors, the Aldi and Lidl chains. Wal-Mart's response to its competitors' low prices for sugar was to lower its price for sugar to below cost. Wal-Mart also lowered its prices on margarine and milk, but not because of competition. When Wal-Mart experienced a sudden price increase by its suppliers of margarine, it decided not to risk losing market share by passing those increases on to its customers. Wal-Mart dropped milk prices to meet competitors' prices.

Supreme Court Ruling Germany's Superior Court ruled against Wal-Mart because its pricing practices were harmful for small- and medium-sized competitors. The basis of the Supreme Court's ruling questioned whether the pricing practices were "objectively justified" under the circumstances. The Supreme Court ruled that Wal-Mart did not violate the law with the price on margarine because it was only for a short period of time, as Wal-Mart looked for a new supplier. Wal-Mart's below-cost prices for milk were not justified because it was reacting to illegal pricing practices by its competitors, which hurt small businesses. The court maintained that Wal-Mart should have reported its competitors' pricing actions to the German Federal Cartel Office.

CRITICAL THINKING

Do you agree with the German court decision? Why or why not? How could have Wal-Mart avoided this legal tangle?

@ Online Action!

Go to *marketingessentials.glencoe.com/25/global* to find a research project about marketing and economic activity in Europe.

are willing to pay more for items purchased from certain businesses because of the service those businesses might offer.

Marketers can charge slightly higher prices because consumers are willing to pay for the added service. Five-star restaurants offer fancy place settings and an attentive wait staff to make your dining experience elegant.

Competition

Price must be evaluated in relation to the target market and is one of the four Ps of the marketing mix. A company can use a lower price when its target market is price conscious. When its target market is not price conscious, a company can resort to various forms of non-price competition.

Nonprice competition minimizes price as a reason for purchase; instead, it creates a distinctive product through product availability and customer service. The more unusual a product is perceived to be by consumers, the greater the marketer's freedom to set prices above those of competitors.

Marketers change prices to reflect consumer demand, cost, or competition. When products are very similar, price often becomes the sole basis on which customers make their purchase decisions. Shoppers are more likely to buy the less expensive brand if they see no difference between products. Because of this, competitors must watch each other closely. When one company changes its prices, others usually react.

When competitors engage in a fierce battle to attract customers by lowering prices, a price war is the result. The problem with price wars is that firms reduce their profits while trying to undercut their competitors' prices and attract new customers. This may result in excessive financial losses and, in some cases, actual business failure. According to *PC World,* it took two years for the home scanner market to stabilize after a two-year price war. The battle put many vendors out of business.

Legal and Ethical Considerations for Pricing

Federal and state governments have enacted laws controlling prices. Marketers must be aware of their rights and responsibilities regarding price fixing, price discrimination, resale price maintenance, minimum pricing, unit pricing, and price advertising. Some pricing practices, while legal, may not be ethical. Thus, ethical pricing considerations are also important.

Price Fixing

Price fixing occurs when competitors agree on certain price ranges within which they set their own prices. Price fixing can be proved only when there is evidence of collusion. This means that there was communication among the competing firms to establish a price range. Price fixing is illegal because it eliminates competition. The federal law against price fixing is the Sherman Antitrust Act of 1890, which outlawed monopolies.

Price Discrimination

Price discrimination occurs when a firm charges different prices to similar customers in similar situations. The Clayton Antitrust Act of 1914 defines price discrimination as creating unfair competition. The Robinson-Patman Act was passed in 1936 to strengthen the provisions of the Clayton Act. The Robinson-Patman Act prohibits sellers from offering one customer one price and another customer a different price if both customers are buying the same product in similar situations.

The Robinson-Patman Act was intended to help smaller retailers compete with the large chain stores.

Unit Pricing

A number of states have passed laws to make it easier for consumers to compare similar goods that are packaged in different sizes or come in different forms (such as frozen and canned foods). **Unit pricing** allows consumers to compare prices in relation to a standard unit or measure, such as an ounce or a pound. Food stores have been most affected by these laws and have responded with shelf labels and computer records of unit prices.

Resale Price Maintenance

Manufacturers' resale price maintenance policies have come under scrutiny by legal authorities. Historically, manufacturers would set a retail price for an item and force retailers to sell it at that price. The manufacturer would punish retailers that sold the item for a lower price by withholding deliveries or refusing promised discounts or allowances. This practice of punishing retailers was outlawed in 1975 in the Consumer Goods Pricing Act.

A manufacturer may suggest resale prices in its advertising, price tags, and price lists. There can even be an agreement to fix the maximum retail price as long as the price agreement is not an "unreasonable restraint of trade" or considered "anti-competitive." A business cannot coerce current customers into adhering to such prices. It can tell customers in advance that they will not be permitted to sell its products if they break the established pricing policy. The difference between "coercing customers" and "telling them in advance" is the fine line manufacturers with such policies must walk.

Unfair Trade Practices Law

Unfair Trade Practices Law, also known as Minimum Price Law, prevents large companies with market power from selling products at very low prices to drive out their competition. In general the federal law prohibits pricing that has a predatory intent or that harms competition or consumers. Many states have enacted "sales below cost" or "unfair sales" statutes that may prohibit certain below-cost pricing, even though they would be permitted under federal law. The state laws were enacted to prevent retailers from selling goods below cost plus a percentage for expenses and profit. Some states have passed such laws that cover all products, while others have included only specific products, such as gasoline, milk, or insurance.

In states where minimum price laws are not in effect, an item priced at or below cost to draw customers into a store is called a **loss leader**. This means the business takes a loss on the item to lead customers into the store. Retailers select highly popular, well-advertised products to use as loss leaders.

Price Advertising

The Federal Trade Commission (FTC) has developed guidelines for advertising prices. The FTC's price advertising guidelines forbid a company from advertising a price reduction unless the original price was offered to the public on a regular basis for a reasonable and recent period of time. Another rule says that a company may not say its prices are lower than its competitors' prices without proof based on a large number of items.

Also, a premarked or list price cannot be used as the reference point for a new sale price unless the item has actually been sold at that price.

Bait-and-switch advertising, in which a firm advertises a low price for an item it has no intention of selling, is illegal. For example, when a customer comes in and asks for the advertised item, salespeople switch the customer to a higher-priced item by saying that the advertised product is out of stock or of poor quality.

Pricing Ethics

Most ethical pricing considerations arise when interpreting pricing laws. Some businesses like computer chip makers and pharmaceutical companies spend a lot of money for research and development of new products. Once a product is created, its manufacturing cost may be small. When you compare its selling price to its manufacturing cost, the price may seem unusually high, but if you include the costs of development, the price may seem warranted. However, if you set a price higher than normal for a product in high demand, you are price gouging. Gouging is unethical and against the law in some states during national and state emergencies due to natural disasters or strikes.

25.2 AFTER YOU READ

Reviewing Key Terms and Concepts

1. In response to increased costs and expenses, what four pricing options might a business consider?
2. What five factors affect demand elasticity?
3. What U.S. government agency regulates price advertising?

Integrating Academic Skills

Math

4. Calculate the break-even point for a music CD that cost $12 to make and market and that will be sold for $15. The total quantity that will be sold at that price is 200,000.

Civics and Government

5. On the Internet or at your library, research the Robinson-Patman Act and list three forms of discrimination this legislation prevents.

Check your answers at *marketingessentials.glencoe.com/25/read*

CAREERS IN MARKETING

John L Daly
Pricing Consultant
Executive Education, Inc.

What do you do at work
I develop customized Microsoft Excel computer models for companies to price their products. My clients are usually manufacturing companies who are in highly competitive environments with thin profit margins. Most companies price their products using average accounting costs without an understanding of the real economics behind their pricing decisions. As a result, it is common for companies to overprice easy, high volume sales opportunities (what operating people would call gravy) and underprice difficult low-volume opportunities (what operations people would call dogs).

What skills are most important to you?
In general, the discipline of marketing, which includes a knowledge of the customer and how much the customer is willing to pay, sets the upper limits of price. The lower limits must be set by a knowledge of the real economics of the selling situation. Pricing is a discipline that requires a strong knowledge of both marketing and cost accounting.

What is your key to success?
I have a deep intuitive understanding of three disciplines: marketing, activity-based costing and information systems. Without any one of these three, I would not be able to do an effective job as a pricing professional. Pricing professionals should have an in-depth knowledge of the more quantitative aspects of marketing.

Aptitudes, Abilities, and Skills

Discipline and organizational skills, reading and research ability, strong mathematical and analytical skill

Education and Training

Advanced degrees in marketing, general business and accounting are very useful in this career.

Career Path

Careers in pricing may begin with entry-level research positions within established pricing firms.

THINKING CRITICALLY

Why is it common for companies to set prices incorrectly on products or services that are an easy sell?

Online Action!

Go to *marketingessentials.glencoe.com/25/careers* to find a research project on careers in marketing.

CHAPTER 25 REVIEW

FOCUS on KEY POINTS

SECTION 25.1

- Price is the money value placed on a good or a service. There are many forms of price: fees, fares, tuition, rent, wages, commissions, etc.
- Pricing is a key factor in the success or failure of a product or service, and therefore of a business. It establishes an image, a competitive edge, and determines profits. Revenue = price × quantity sold.
- The goals of pricing are: earning a profit, gaining market share, and meeting the competition. Market share is a company's percentage of the total sales volume generated by all companies in a given market. Market position is the standing a company has in its market compared to its competitors.

SECTION 25.2

- Four factors affect pricing: costs and expenses, supply and demand, consumer perceptions, and competition.
- The law of supply and demand means that, in general, demand goes up when price goes down and demand goes down when price goes up. Demand elasticity is the degree to which price affects demand. If a change in price creates a change in demand, demand is said to be elastic. If change in price has little effect on demand, demand is inelastic.
- Legal and ethical issues play a key role in pricing. Government regulations control price fixing, price discrimination, resale price maintenance, minimum price, unit pricing, and price advertising.

REVIEW VOCABULARY

Define the key terms below.

1. price (p. 526)
2. return on investment (ROI) (p. 528)
3. market share (p. 529)
4. break-even point (p. 533)
5. demand elasticity (p. 533)
6. law of diminishing marginal utility (p. 533)
7. price fixing (p. 536)
8. price discrimination (p. 536)
9. unit pricing (p. 536)
10. loss leader (p. 537)

REVIEW FACTS and IDEAS

11. What are the different forms of pricing? (25.1)
12. Why is pricing important? (25.1)
13. What are the main goals of pricing? (25.1)
14. What is the difference between market share and market position? (25.1)
15. Name and explain the four market factors that affect price planning. (25.2)
16. What is demand elasticity and how does it alter supply and demand theory? (25.2)
17. What role do government regulations play in the pricing process? Give one example. (25.2)

BUILD SKILLS

18. Workplace Skills

Interpersonal Communication Prepare a memo addressed to your staff of marketing consultants regarding the need for accurate accounting for the time they spend on their clients' projects. Explain the role they play in the ethical pricing practices of your firm. Include an explanation of the firm's rules regarding padding the bill and doing work for a client beyond the original contract.

19. Technology Applications

Spreadsheet Use a spreadsheet program to prepare a pie chart depicting market share enjoyed by competitors in a hypothetical $900 million market for specialty frozen pizza. Use these fictional figures to represent each brand's sales.

Brand	Sales (× 1,000)
Salerno	225,000
Ciccone	180,000
Marie's	135,000
Infantino	126,000
Aurora's	108,000
Angelo's	90,000
Other	36,000

20. Math Practice

Return on Investment Determine the return on investment for the following two toys:

	Ringo Wrango	Pingo Pango
Manufacturing costs	$ 5.00	$ 7.50
Marketing expenses	$ 2.50	$ 4.00
Selling price	$ 17.00	$ 14.75

Based on return on investment, which toy is more profitable for the company?

DEVELOP CRITICAL THINKING

21. Study the Competition

Select a product that interests you and note its price. Research other brands of that product and their prices. Which brands compete on price and which ones use nonprice competition to win customers? Summarize your findings in a 150-word paragraph.

22. Consumer Perceptions

Select a product and explain why and how consumer perceptions might have influenced its pricing. Write a short list of reasons and be prepared to discuss them in class.

APPLY CONCEPTS

23. Identify Price

You must determine the price you will charge retailers for a box of disposable cleansing cloths, which is a new product. Competing brands retail for between $5.99 and $6.99. Assume your cost of manufacturing and marketing this new product is $2.75 per box. Remember to include a profit margin in the price you will charge retailers. To be competitive, you need to consider the suggested retail price that retailers will charge the final consumer. In this example, assume retailers will double the price they pay for the item when calculating the price they charge their customers. You expect to make 200,000 boxes of these disposable cloths at the price you will be charging retailers.

Activity What will be your break-even point? Use a word processing program to prepare a written report.

24. Research and Debate Price Gouging

Use the Internet to research the topic of price gouging from a legal and ethical standpoint. Find out if your state has a gouging law. Note specific instances and court decisions regarding price gouging. Include issues concerning prescription drugs in your research. Look at issues from a free market perspective and from a consumer's point of view.

Activity Use a word processing program to write a 200-word report of your findings and participate in a debate with classmates about price gouging.

NET SAVVY

25. A Fair Price?

Browse travel Web sites Travelocity, Orbitz, Expedia, and Priceline. Determine and list three differences in pricing factors between these dot-coms and brick-and-mortar travel agencies or major airlines.

THE DECA CONNECTION

Role Play: Management Trainee

Situation You are to assume the role of management trainee for a unisex clothing store that specializes in jeans and trendy clothing. The store's buyer (judge) wants your opinion about whether or not to carry a new brand of jeans that would sell for $10 more than your most expensive brand. Even at the $80 retail price, you think they will sell.

Activity In ten minutes, you will be meeting with the store buyer to share your thoughts and opinions. What will you say?

Evaluation You will be evaluated on how well you meet the following performance indicators:

- Explain the nature and scope of the pricing function
- Explain factors affecting pricing decisions
- Identify strategies for pricing new products
- Explain the nature of sales forecasts
- Persuade others

@ Online Action!

For more information and DECA Prep practice, go to *marketingessentials.glencoe.com/25/DECA*

CHAPTER 26
Pricing Strategies

Chapter Objectives

After reading this chapter, you should be able to:

- Name three pricing policies used to establish a base price
- Explain the two polar pricing policies for introducing a new product
- Explain the relationship between pricing and the product life cycle
- Describe pricing strategies that adjust the base price
- List the steps involved in determining a price
- Explain the use of technology in the pricing function

GUIDE TO THE PHOTO

Market Talk Product prices change all the time. Sometimes a new product or new technology becomes more common, so prices drop. At other times, retailers and service providers have sales and promotion events.

Quick Think Name a product you like whose price has changed in the past few years. Why did the price change?

THE  CONNECTION

Performance indicators represent key skills and knowledge. Relating them to the concepts explained in this chapter is your key to success in DECA events. These acronyms represent DECA events that involve knowledge of concepts in this chapter.

AAAL	**FMAL**	**MMS***	**TMDM***
AAML*	**FMDM***	**QSRM***	**TSE***
ADC*	**FMML***	**RMAL**	**VPM**
BSM	**FSRM***	**RMML***	
EMDM*	**HMDM***	**SMDM***	

In all these DECA events you should be able to follow this performance indicator:

- Explain factors affecting pricing decisions

All the events with an asterisk (*) also include these performance indicators:

- Select approach for setting a base price
- Identify strategies for pricing new products
- Select product-mix pricing strategies
- Use psychological pricing to adjust base prices
- Select promotional pricing strategies used to adjust base prices
- Determine geographic pricing strategies to adjust base prices
- Identify segmented pricing strategies
- Set prices
- Adjust prices to maximize profitability

Some events include additional performance indicators. These are:

FMDM Describe factors affecting the prices of financial services/products

ADC Describe factors affecting the prices of advertising services

SMDM Set event prices

TMDM Set price of group tour

DECA PREP

Check your understanding of DECA performance indicators with the DECA activity in this chapter's review. For more information and DECA Prep practice, go to *marketingessentials.glencoe.com/26/DECA*

Basic Pricing Policies

OBJECTIVES

- Name three pricing policies used to establish a base price
- Explain the two polar pricing policies for introducing a new product
- Explain the relationship between pricing and the product life cycle

KEY TERMS

- markup pricing
- cost-plus pricing
- one-price policy
- flexible-price policy
- skimming pricing
- penetration pricing

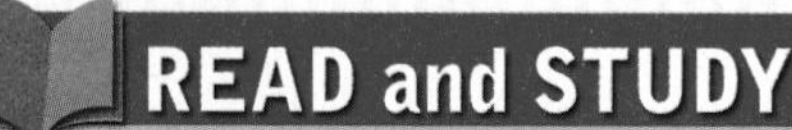

BEFORE YOU READ

Predict Name four reasons why prices vary.

THE MAIN IDEA

You already know the factors that influence pricing decisions. This will help you understand key pricing concepts. Establishing a base price from which price adjustments may be made is the focus of this section. This includes the various situations and company policies that can affect the pricing of a product.

STUDY ORGANIZER

Use a chart like the one below to take notes about the pricing policies that can affect the base price for a product.

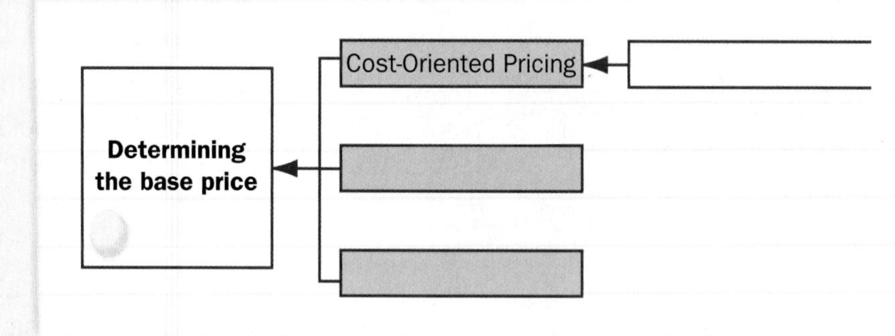

Analyze Identify policies and situations that marketers use to establish the base price for new and old products.

Basic Pricing Concepts

A major factor in determining the profitability of any product is establishing a base price. Cost, demand, and competition influence pricing policies and are important in establishing a base price for a product. Each factor is the basis for a different method of setting the base price of any given product: cost-oriented pricing, demand-oriented pricing, and competition-oriented pricing.

Cost-Oriented Pricing

In cost-oriented pricing, marketers first calculate the costs of acquiring or making a product and their expenses of doing business; then they add their projected profit margin to these figures to arrive at a price. Markup pricing and cost-plus pricing are two of the most common methods of cost-oriented pricing.

Markup Pricing

In **markup pricing**, resellers add a dollar amount (markup) to their cost to arrive at a price. For example, if an item cost $10 and the percentage of markup on cost is 40 percent, the retail price would be $14 ($10 × .40 = $4.00; $10 + $4 = $14). Thus, a markup, generally expressed as a percentage, is the difference between the price of an item and its cost. Markup pricing is used primarily by wholesalers and retailers, who are involved in acquiring goods for resale. The markup on products must be high enough to cover the expenses of running the business and must include the intended profit.

Cost-Plus Pricing

In **cost-plus pricing**, all costs and expenses are calculated, and then the desired profit is added to arrive at a price. Cost-plus pricing is used primarily by manufacturers and service companies. The method is more sophisticated than markup pricing because all fixed and variable expenses are calculated separately. Fixed expenses are those expenses that do not change based on production. Fixed expenses include things such as rent, interest on loans, executives' salaries, advertising, and insurance. Variable expenses are associated with the production of the good or service and include costs related to labor and supplies. When a manufacturer is running at full capacity, the percentage of fixed expenses allocated to each product becomes smaller. This permits the manufacturer to charge a lower unit price

•PRICING WIRELESS SERVICE The demand for cell phone service has increased tremendously in the past years.

How has demand affected prices in this case?

for goods. Figure 26.1 illustrates how cost-plus pricing can be used to calculate price for a manufacturer.

Demand-Oriented Pricing

Marketers who use demand-oriented pricing attempt to determine what consumers are willing to pay for given goods and services. The key to this method of pricing is the consumer's perceived value of the item. The price set must be in line with this perception or the item will be priced too high or too low for the target market. Inappropriate pricing could cause the product to fail.

Demand-oriented pricing relies on the basic premises of supply-and-demand theory and on demand elasticity factors. The higher the demand, the more a business can charge for a given good or service, even though the good or service and its cost do not change.

Competition-Oriented Pricing

Marketers may elect to take one of three actions after learning their competitors' prices: price above the competition, price below the competition, or price in line with the competition (going-rate pricing). There is no relationship between cost and price or between demand and price in this pricing method.

Competitive-bid pricing, one type of competition-oriented pricing strategy, determines the price for a product based on bids submitted by competitors to a company or government agency. In such cases, some companies will try to enter the lowest bid in order to obtain the contract.

Establishing the Base Price

To establish the base price or price range for a good or service, all three pricing approaches can be used.

Figure 26.1 Cost-Plus Pricing for a Manufacturer

• **Variable Costs** The example below is for a plain pair of pants.

How would the addition of details, such as four pockets, affect the price to the business customer and ultimately to you, the final consumer?

PLENTY OF PANTS CLOTHING MANUFACTURER: UNIT PRICE FOR A PAIR OF PANTS	
Materials (fabric, thread, zipper, buttons)	$7.50
Labor (piecework)	$1.50
Fixed expenses (overhead)	$.25
Intended profit	$2.25
Final price to business customer	$11.50

Online Action! **Go to *marketingessentials.glencoe.com/26/figure/1* to find a project on cost-plus pricing for manufacturers.**

Case Study

Voice Over Internet Protocol

Once upon a time, there was only one telephone company in the United States. After the government broke up the monopoly in 1982, consumers had many more choices. The invention of mobile phones expanded the number of service providers, and the invention of telephoning through the Web (Voice over Internet Protocol) in the mid-1990s expanded that number again. With all those companies vying for customers, the competition is fierce.

Price Wars

Dozens of companies in the United States offer phone service through high-speed Internet connections. Some compete by adding features such as voice mail or call waiting, but most compete with price.

Verizon and AT&T charged $29.95 to $34.95 per month for unlimited calling in the U.S. in 2004. Some competitors charged $20 to $25 per month. Even cheaper plans limit the number of minutes. Skype uses a different business model, charging about 2.3 cents per minute for calls in the United States.

But some industry insiders warned there was no way to stay in business without charging $35 per month per customer, especially if the government decides VoIP providers need to collect the same taxes that traditional phone service providers collect.

What additional changes in this service do you predict for the future and how will those changes affect the pricing plans now offered by providers?

@ Online Action! **Go to *marketingessentials.glencoe.com/26/case* to find an activity on new cost-saving technology.**

Cost-oriented pricing helps marketers determine the price floor for a product, or the lowest price for which it can be offered and still make a profit. Demand-oriented pricing determines a price range for the product that is defined by the price floor and the ceiling price (the highest amount consumers would pay). Competition-oriented pricing may be used to ensure that the final price is in line with the company's pricing policies such as always offering prices lower than competitors. Combining pricing considerations offers a good range within which a company can establish its base price. If a company decides to go with the competition-oriented pricing strategy, it still knows how much it can lower its prices if necessary, based on the cost-oriented pricing figures.

Reseller Considerations

Manufacturers may also consider the prices they will charge resellers (wholesalers and retailers) for their products in order to establish a base price. This can be done in one of

Figure 26.2 Pricing Backward From the Retail Price

• Determining the wholesale price One way for a manufacturer to arrive at a wholesale price is to subtract all the markups for channel members from the suggested retail price.

What problem would this manufacturer have if its costs and expenses totaled $37?

Manufacturer's suggested retail price (MSRP)	**$75**
Retailer's markup *(40% of retail price)*	**−$30**
Wholesaler's price to retailer *(Subtract retailer's markup from MSRP)*	**$45**
Wholesaler's markup *(20% of wholesale price)*	**−$9**
Manufacturer's price to wholesaler *(Subtract wholesaler's markup from the price paid by wholesalers)*	**$36**

• Remember this amount must cover costs, expenses, and profit for the manufacturer.

@ Online Action!

Go to *marketingessentials.glencoe.com/26/figure/2* to find a project on pricing backward.

Figure 26.3 Pricing Forward From the Manufacturer's Cost

• Marking up cost In this pricing method, the starting point is the manufacturer's cost. At each step, a reseller adds a markup to arrive at a new price. The reseller then charges its customers the new price. The final price is the price to the consumer.

What do you see as the basic difference in markup percentage between calculating pricing forward and pricing backward?

Cost of producing the item	**$30.00**
Manufacturer's expenses and intended profit *(20% of cost)*	**+6.00**
Manufacturer's price to wholesaler *(Cost plus expenses plus intended profit)*	**36.00**
Wholesaler's markup *(25% of price wholesaler paid for item)*	**+9.00**
Wholesaler's price to retailer *(Manufacturer's price to wholesaler + markup)*	**45.00**
Retailer's markup *(66.67% based on price paid to wholesaler)*	**+30.00**
Retailer's base price to consumer	**$75.00**

@ Online Action!

Go to *marketingessentials.glencoe.com/26/figure/3* to find a project on pricing forward.

two ways. You can work backward from the final retail price to find the price for the wholesalers. You can also do this in reverse, working forward from costs and expenses to the final retail price. Figures 26.2 and 26.3 illustrate these two methods.

In Figure 26.2, which describes the steps in working backward, the suggested retail price is set first, on the basis of consumer demand and competition. Next, the markups desired by the wholesalers and retailers are deducted sequentially from the suggested retail price. Finally, the base price that the manufacturer will charge the wholesaler is determined. Note that the price to the wholesaler must be high enough to cover the manufacturer's costs, any expenses, and the intended profit.

Figure 26.3 illustrates the steps for working forward from the manufacturer's cost. Expenses and intended profit must be considered, and then the wholesaler's and retailer's markups are added to the manufacturer's price to arrive at the base selling price. Competition and consumer demand may be left out of the pricing decision if the price is set at this point.

Pricing Policies and Product Life Cycle

A basic pricing decision every business must make is to choose between a one-price policy and a flexible-price policy. A business also needs to consider how a new product will be introduced into the marketplace. That choice will determine the pricing decisions that follow as the product moves through its life cycle.

One-Price Versus Flexible-Price Policy

A **one-price policy** is one in which all customers are charged the same prices. Prices are quoted to customers by means of signs and price tags, and no deviations are permitted. Most retail stores employ this policy. A one-price policy offers consistency and reliability. It also allows retailers to estimate sales and profit because they know the set price.

A **flexible-price policy** is one in which customers pay different prices for the same type or amount of merchandise. This kind of policy permits customers to bargain for merchandise. Most retail stores avoid using flexible pricing because it can cause legal problems and it may keep some customers away. A flexible-price strategy is common for goods such as used cars, artwork, antiques, furniture, and selected jewelry. One disadvantage of a flexible-price policy is that it does not offer consistent profits. It can be difficult to estimate sales revenue because of the fluctuations in price. However, with computer technology and huge databases, this may be changing.

Product Life Cycle

Products move through four stages: introduction, growth, maturity, and decline. Pricing plays an important role in this sequence of events.

New Product Introduction

A business may elect to price a new product above, in line with, or below its competitors depending on the philosophy of the business and market conditions. When a going-rate strategy is not used to introduce a new product, two methods may be used: skimming pricing or penetration pricing.

Method 1 **Skimming pricing** is a pricing policy that sets a very high price for a new

• PRICING ELECTRONICS Computers and other electronic appliances quickly go out of date as new technology emerges and becomes more common.

How does this fast product life cycle affect pricing?

MARKET TECH

Pricing and Promotion Software

Chances are you have seen circulars in the mail or in the Sunday newspaper promoting special markdowns or "everyday low prices" at local stores. Stores used to rely on laborious calculations and even guesswork to set prices and decide what products to put on sale. Today, computer software can handle that job.

No More Guesswork

Retail chains including Radio Shack, Albertsons, and Longs Drugs use what is known as retail revenue management software or customer demand software to make pricing decisions.

The computer programs use information collected by point-of-sale terminals, such as sales volume and price. The software combines these data with other factors, including sales and volume goals, price sensitivity, and the prices that the chains pay for their goods.

After crunching the numbers, the software recommends prices and suggests products to put on sale or otherwise promote.

THINK LIKE A MARKETER

Why is the information collected at point-of-sale (POS) terminals not enough for this software to accomplish a complete price analysis?

Online Action!

Go to *marketingessentials.glencoe.com/26/tech* to find an activity on pricing and technology.

product. This kind of policy can be used any time demand is greater than supply. Such a policy is designed to capitalize on the high demand for a product during its introductory period.

Businesses that use this method recognize that the price will have to be lowered once the market for the product changes to more price-conscious customers. While the product is hot, the business will enjoy a high profit margin. Another advantage of skimming pricing is that the price may be lowered without insulting the target market.

One disadvantage of skimming pricing is that the high initial price generally attracts competition. In addition, if the initial price is far above what consumers are willing to pay, sales will be lost and profits diminished.

Method 2 **Penetration pricing** is the opposite of skimming pricing; the price for a new product is set very low. The purpose of penetration pricing is to encourage as many people as possible to buy the product and thus penetrate the market. This type of pricing is most effective in the sale of price-sensitive products (items with elastic demand). Sony used a penetration pricing strategy when it introduced its first PlayStation game console.

To penetrate the market quickly with penetration pricing, mass production, distribution, and promotion must be incorporated into the marketing strategy. The product should take hold in a short period of time. This allows the marketer to save on fixed expenses (through mass production) and to increase the profit margin (through volume sales).

The biggest advantage of penetration pricing is its ability to capture a large number of customers in a relatively short period of time. This blocks competition from other companies.

If the product is not in high demand, however, the lower price will cause the marketer to suffer a bigger loss than it would have if a higher initial price had been set.

Other Product Stages

Pricing during subsequent periods in a product's life cycle is determined by which pricing method was originally used, skimming or penetration. Sales increase rapidly during the penetration stage, and total costs per unit decrease because volume absorbs fixed costs. The main goal of marketers is to keep products in this stage as long as possible.

Sales of products introduced with skimming pricing should be monitored. Once sales begin to level off, the price should be lowered to appeal to the price-conscious target market.

Very little price change will be made in the growth stage for products introduced with penetration pricing. When demand decreases and sales begin to level off, competition is generally very keen. Marketers look for new market segments to hold the prices for their products. A baking soda marketer may stress noncooking uses for baking soda, such as deodorizing refrigerators.

The marketer's principal goal during the maturity stage is to stretch the life of a product. Some companies reduce their prices. Others choose to revitalize products in this stage by adding new features or improvements, or by looking for new target markets. Another option is to seek new markets in other nations in the global marketplace. Products that have been made obsolete in the United States by technological advances may be in the introductory or growth stage in other places. By using techniques like these, marketers can significantly extend a product's life cycle. When such efforts are not successful, however, a product moves into its decline.

Sales decrease and profit margins are reduced in the decline stage. Companies are forced to reduce the price to generate sales. To maintain profitability, marketers try to reduce manufacturing costs or cut back on advertising and other promotional activities. Once a product is no longer profitable, it is phased out.

26.1 AFTER YOU READ

Reviewing Key Terms and Concepts

1. Name and explain the two most common methods of cost-oriented pricing.
2. What is the key to demand-oriented pricing?
3. What three actions may marketers elect to follow in competition-oriented pricing?

Integrating Academic Skills

Math

4. Use the "pricing backward from retail price" approach to calculate the manufacturer's price to a wholesaler for a product that has a suggested retail price of $200. Assume that the retailer's markup on the retail price is 40 percent and the wholesaler's markup is 20 percent.

Civics and Government

5. What is competitive-bid pricing, and why must marketers understand this policy if they want to sell goods and service to the government?

Check your answers at *marketingessentials.glencoe.com/26/read*

Strategies in the Pricing Process

OBJECTIVES

- Describe pricing strategies that adjust the base price
- List the steps involved in determining a price
- Explain the use of technology in the pricing function

KEY TERMS

- product mix pricing strategies
- price lining
- bundle pricing
- geographical pricing
- segmented pricing strategy
- psychological pricing
- prestige pricing
- everyday low prices (EDLP)
- promotional pricing

BEFORE YOU READ

Predict How and why do you think prices change?

THE MAIN IDEA

Now that you know how to establish a base price, you need to learn how and why price adjustments are made. Price adjustments are a marketer's way of being creative with pricing. These strategies help businesses stay competitive. Using the right pricing strategy can help increase sales and profitability for a company, as you will see in the examples provided.

STUDY ORGANIZER

Create an outline of this section to identify the strategies for adjusting prices and the steps in setting prices.

Price Adjustment Strategies

1. Product mix strategies
   a. Price lining
   b.
   c.
   d.
   e.
2.

Connect Note pricing strategy examples from your own experience.

Adjusting the Base Price

Marketers can use specific pricing strategies to fit different economic and market conditions. To adjust base prices, marketers may employ any one or more of the following pricing strategies: product mix, geographical, international, segmented, psychological, and promotional pricing, as well as discounts and allowances. Using these strategies in the appropriate situations helps businesses remain competitive.

Product Mix Strategies

Product mix pricing strategies involve adjusting prices to maximize the profitability for a group of products rather than on just one item. With this method, one product may have a small profit margin while another may be high to balance the effect of the lower priced one. They include price lining, optional product pricing, captive product pricing, by-product pricing, and bundle pricing.

Price Lining

Price lining is a special pricing technique that sets a limited number of prices for specific groups or lines of merchandise. A store might price all its blouses at $25, $35, and $50. When deciding on the price lines, marketers must be careful to make the price differences great enough to represent low, middle, and high quality items. Price lines of $25, $26, $27, and $28, for example, would confuse customers because they would have difficulty discerning their basis.

An advantage of price lining is that the target market is fully aware of the price range of products in a given store. In addition, price lining makes merchandising and selling easier for salespeople, who can readily draw comparisons between floor and ceiling prices.

Optional Product

Optional product pricing involves setting prices for accessories or options sold with the main product. One example is options for cars. All options need to be priced so that a final price for the main product can be established.

Captive Product

Captive product pricing sets the price for one product low but compensates for that low price by pricing the supplies needed to operate that product high. Ink-jet printers are low in price, but the ink cartridges required to operate the printers have high prices.

By-Product

By-product pricing helps business get rid of excess materials used in making a product by using low prices. Wood chips that are residual by-products from making furniture may be sold at a very low price to other manufacturing companies that use that material in making their products.

Bundle Pricing

With **bundle pricing**, a company offers several complementary products in a package that is sold at a single price. The one price for all the complementary products and the main item is lower than if a customer purchased each item separately. Computer companies use bundle pricing when they include software in the sale price of a computer. Bundling helps businesses sell items (parts of the package) that they may not have sold otherwise, which increases their sales and revenue.

Geographical Pricing

Geographical pricing refers to price adjustments required because of the location of the customer for delivery of products. The delivered price includes the cost of the item and delivery charges. In this pricing strategy, the manufacturer assumes responsibility for the cost and management of product delivery.

International Pricing

When doing business internationally, marketers need to set prices that take into consideration costs, consumers, economic conditions, and the monetary exchange rate. Costs may include shipping, tariffs, or other charges. Consumers' income levels and lifestyles will require adjustments to the price.

Segmented Pricing Strategies

A **segmented pricing strategy** uses two or more different prices for a product, even though there is no difference in the item's cost. Used correctly, this strategy helps businesses optimize profits and compete more effectively. Four factors can help marketers use segmented pricing strategies: buyer identification, product design, purchase location, and time of purchase.

Buyer Identification

Recognizing a buyer's sensitivity to price (demand elasticity) is one way to identify a customer segment. For example, to attract customers on fixed incomes, some businesses offer senior citizen and student discounts. Airlines offer different classes of travel—first class and coach. First-class travelers pay a significantly higher price to get to the same destination.

Product Design

Manufacturers may also create different prices for different product styles that do not reflect the cost of making the item but, rather, the demand for a given style.

Purchase Location

Purchase location involves pricing according to where a product is sold and/or the location of the good or service. Tickets for Broadway shows in New York City will be priced higher than those for the same show when it goes on the road.

Time of Purchase

Some types of businesses experience highs and lows in sales activity. During peak times, they are able to charge more because of increased demand. Telephone companies often charge more for long-distance calls made during business hours, a peak time.

Psychological Pricing Strategies

Psychological pricing strategies are pricing techniques that help create an illusion for customers. They are often based on a buyer's motivation for making a purchase and purchasing habits. Among common psychological pricing techniques are odd-even pricing, prestige pricing, multiple-unit pricing, and everyday low prices (EDLPs).

Odd-Even Pricing

A technique that involves setting prices that all end in either odd or even numbers is known as odd-even pricing. This strategy is based on the psychological principle that odd numbers ($.79, $9.95, $699) convey a bargain image. Even numbers ($10, $50, $100) convey a quality image. Whether or not this is true, you will find that many marketers follow the odd-even technique in an effort to project a certain image.

Prestige Pricing

Prestige pricing sets higher-than-average prices to suggest status and high quality to the consumer. Many customers assume that higher prices mean better quality. Rolls-Royce automobiles, Waterford crystal, and Rolex watches are all prestige priced.

Multiple-Unit Pricing

Some businesses have found that pricing items in multiples, such as three for $1.00, is better than selling the same items at $.34 each. Multiple-unit pricing suggests a bargain and helps to increase sales volume.

Everyday Low Price

Everyday low prices (EDLP) are low prices set on a consistent basis with no intention of raising them or offering discounts in the future. Everyday low prices are not as deeply discounted as promotional prices might be, which creates sales stability. Other benefits include reduced promotional expenses and reduced losses due to discounting.

Promotional Pricing

Promotional pricing is generally used in conjunction with sales promotions where prices are reduced for a short period of time. Common types of promotional pricing are loss leader pricing (discussed in Chapter 25), special-event pricing, and rebates and coupons.

Loss Leader Pricing

Loss leader pricing is used to increase store traffic by offering very popular items of merchandise for sale at below-cost prices. The theory behind this practice is that customers will be attracted by the low price. Once in the store, they will buy regularly priced merchandise in addition to the loss leader item.

Special-Event

In special-event pricing, items are reduced in price for a short period of time, based on a specific happening, such as back-to-school,

Presidents' Day, or anniversary sales. Manufacturers offer special promotions to wholesalers and retailers willing to advertise or promote a manufacturer's products.

Rebates and Coupons

Rebates are partial refunds provided by the manufacturer to consumers. To receive the rebate, a customer buys the product and then sends in a rebate form along with the product proof of purchase and a store receipt. Manufacturers offer rebates to wholesalers and retailers too, for purchasing certain quantities of goods prior to running promotions that will generate business for those resellers. Coupons allow customers to take reductions at the time of purchase. Coupons may be found in newspapers, advertisements, product packages, and even on sales receipts printed by retailers, such as supermarkets.

Discounts and Allowances

Discount pricing involves the seller offering reductions from the usual price. Such reductions are generally granted in exchange for the buyer's performance of certain functions. These include cash discounts, quantity discounts, trade discounts, seasonal discounts, and special allowances.

Cash Discounts

Cash discounts are offered to buyers to encourage them to pay their bills quickly. Terms are generally written on the invoice, for example, 2/10, net 30 means that a 2 percent discount is granted if the bill is paid in ten days.

Quantity Discounts

Quantity discounts are offered to buyers for placing large orders. Sellers benefit from large orders through the lower selling costs involved in one transaction as opposed to several small transactions. Quantity discounts also offer buyers an incentive to purchase more merchandise than they originally intended to purchase.

A MATTER OF ETHICS

Reward or Punishment?

Some supermarkets offer special discounts on selected items to customers who have a frequent shopper card, but not to those without one. Consider two customers at the checkout counter, both purchasing the same loaf of bread. The customer with a card pays $2.00 for a loaf of bread, while the other without a card pays $2.99. Frequent shopper cards are available to all customers who request one.

Opting Out

Some customers simply do not want their purchases traced through participation in a frequent shopper program. They feel it is an invasion of their privacy. However, they also object to paying higher prices than other customers.

THINKING ETHICALLY

Are loyalty-card programs ethical?

@ Online Action!

Go to *marketingessentials.glencoe.com/26/ethics* to find an activity on ethics and pricing.

There are two types of quantity discounts: noncumulative and cumulative. Noncumulative quantity discounts are offered on one order, while cumulative quantity discounts are offered on all orders over a specified period of time. Cumulative discounts may be granted for purchases made over six months, for example, in which case all purchases for that period are used to determine the quantity discount offered. In other cases, buyers may be

required to sign a contract that guarantees a certain level of business. Advertisers who agree to use a specified number of column inches in their newspaper ads might be charged cheaper contract rates. Generally, the more you advertise, the less you pay per column inch.

Trade Discounts

Trade discounts are not really discounts at all but rather the way manufacturers quote prices to wholesalers and retailers. Many manufacturers establish suggested retail prices, or list prices, for their items. They grant discounts from the list price to members of the channel of distribution. A manufacturer might grant wholesalers a 40 percent discount from the list price and retailers a 30 percent discount.

The manufacturer might also quote the discounts in series, such as 25 percent and 10 percent for retailers and wholesalers, respectively. Series, or chain, discounts are calculated in sequence, with discounts taken on the declining balance as shown below. The example is based on a list price of $50.

Retailer's discount
$50 × .25 = $12.50

Cost to retailer
$50 − $12.50 = $37.50

Wholesaler's discount
$37.50 × .10 = $3.75

Cost to wholesaler
$37.50 − $3.75 = $33.75

In series discounts, note that the wholesaler's discount is based on the retailer's discount, not the original list price.

Seasonal Discounts

Seasonal discounts are offered to buyers willing to buy at a time outside the customary buying season. Manufacturers offer discounts to obtain orders for seasonal merchandise early so that production facilities and labor can be used throughout the year.

Other businesses use seasonal discounts to cut anticipated costs. Many retailers, for example, drastically reduce prices on swimsuits after the summer season. Such retailers prefer to sell this merchandise at a lower markup than pay the costs of warehousing it until the following year. A variation on this device is used by vacation resorts. They offer vacationers lower rates to encourage use of resort facilities during the off-season.

Allowances

Trade-in allowances go directly to the buyer. Customers are offered a price reduction if they sell back an old model of the product they are purchasing. Consumers are generally offered trade-in allowances when purchasing new cars or major appliances. Companies are usually granted such allowances when purchasing machinery or equipment.

The Pricing Process and Related Technology

The pricing process is ongoing, as you will see in the steps of determining a price. As one of the four Ps of the marketing mix, pricing is the most flexible because pricing strategies and prices can be changed quickly.

Steps in Determining Prices

There are six basic steps that are used to determine prices (see Figure 26.4):

Step 1: Establish pricing objectives
Step 2: Determine costs
Step 3: Estimate demand
Step 4: Study competition
Step 5: Decide on a pricing strategy
Step 6: Set prices

Step 1: Establish Pricing Objectives

The first step in the process of pricing a product is to determine the pricing objectives. Pricing objectives must conform to the company's overall goals: making profit, improving market share, and meeting the competition. To be effective, pricing objectives should be specific, time sensitive, realistic, and measurable. Increasing sales of a given product is not a good pricing objective. Increasing unit or dollar sales by 20 percent in one year compared

Figure 26.4 Six Steps in Determining Price

• **A Set Procedure** Whether setting a price to launch a new product or adjusting the price of an existing product to increase sales, the process of determining price is the same.

What are some factors affecting this process?

STEP 1: ESTABLISH PRICING OBJECTIVES

The main goals of pricing are to make a profit, increase market share, and stay competitive. Remember that objectives should be time sensitive, realistic, and measurable. The objective for this product might be to increase market share by ten percent in the coming year.

STEP 2: DETERMINE COSTS

Costs are an important consideration in pricing. A company must price its product high enough above costs to make a profit. Costs for a soft drink manufacturer include raw materials, bottling, and labor.

STEP 3: ESTIMATE DEMAND

Through market research, a company must determine the size of the market and how much customers would be willing to pay for their product.

STEP 4: STUDY COMPETITION

Knowing what the competition charges for similar products is key to determining price. If a company prices its product too low, it misses out on potential profit, too high and it risks losing customers to the competition.

STEP 5: DECIDE ON A PRICING STRATEGY

The pricing strategy for a product depends on a variety of factors, including whether the product is being sold to segmented markets, whether there is a seasonal market, and where the product is sold. When a company sells soft drinks at a sporting event, purchase location is an important factor in determining price.

STEP 6: SET PRICES

Based on all the information gathered in the first five steps, a company sets a price for its product. Remember, though, that this price is subject to change.

Online Action!

Go to *marketingessentials.glencoe.com/26/figure/4* to find a project on pricing.

with the previous year would be better. Why? Because the latter objective satisfies the requirements of being time-sensitive (one year) and it is specific and measurable (20 percent increase). At the end of one year, a company can evaluate the pricing objective to see if it was met. If not, the company can review the objective and the pricing strategies used to reach that objective.

Step 2: Determine Costs

For resellers (wholesalers and retailers), costs involved in the purchase of a product from their vendors and freight charges constitute the cost of the item. Businesses that provide services must take into account the cost of supplies used in conjunction with performing the service and the cost of labor help. A hair salon's shampoo, gels, hair spray, dyes, permanent wave solutions, and the like, as well as employee salaries, all need to be considered when determining the cost of providing those services. In manufacturing, the cost of materials and labor used in the manufacture of the product makes up the cost of an item. Costs can vary due to ever-changing economic conditions. A business needs to maintain accurate records and keep abreast of any change in its costs, which may affect its ultimate pricing decision.

Step 3: Estimate Demand

Marketers will study the size of the market to determine the total number of possible customers for a given product. For example, let's say the market is for a new soft drink. Sales of soft drinks for the past few years would be studied to see if sales were on the rise or the decline. Additional research might be conducted with consumers to see how they viewed soft drinks versus other beverages, such as water and juice alternatives. From their basic research, estimates would be made regarding the percentage of potential customers who might buy that new product. Much of this analysis is based on supply-and-demand theory and on the exceptions that occur because of demand elasticity.

Step 4: Study Competition

Studying your competitors is the next step in the process. You need to investigate what prices your competitors are charging for similar goods and services. Businesses subscribe to services that provide competitive information on a daily basis.

Step 5: Decide on a Pricing Strategy

Steps 2 through 4 help to establish a base price. In Step 5, you need to revisit the pricing objectives and decide on a pricing strategy or strategies that will help you accomplish your objectives. Everything you learned in Section 26.2 will help you in this endeavor. However, you must remember that as economic and market conditions change, strategies may require changes too.

Step 6: Set Prices

The final step is to set the price that will be quoted to customers, which is the published price that can be found on price tickets, company Web sites, and price sheets, as well as printed in catalogs and promotional materials. For that reason, it is important that all the above steps are carefully considered. Marketers must decide on how often they want to change their published prices. In addition to the cost of changing printed materials, customers' reactions to price changes must be considered.

Pricing Technology

Technology related to pricing can be seen in data that are now made available to marketers when making pricing decisions, as well as in the vehicles for providing price information to customers.

Smart Pricing

Smart pricing, as it is sometimes called, allows marketers to make intelligent pricing decisions based on an enormous amount of data that Web-based pricing technology crunches into timely, usable information. For example, Northern Group (a Canadian retailer) uses software that combines sales data with inventory data. The result is pricing recommendations that the pricing team can decide to accept or reject. Historical sales data are compared with current sales data from the store's point-of-sale system, as well as with its merchandising system, which includes the inventory levels for specific items. Combining all these data helps to suggest prices for new merchandise, as well as when to take markdowns, if any, on current merchandise in stock. This system gives this company the ability to adjust prices according to changing market conditions.

Communicating Prices to Customers

To complement these advances in pricing decisions, electronic gadgets provide customers with real-time pricing information. Retailers that invest in electronic shelves and digital price labels can change prices quickly and easily. They also can send messages to shoppers while they are in the store alerting them to deals on goods of interest to the customer based on their buying habits.

We have already seen kiosks in retail stores where customers can scan a product to determine its price. In supermarket chains, we have seen self-check-out counters, where customers scan their own merchandise and pay for the products without the assistance of a clerk. With these new technological advances, price-marking techniques, such as printed price tags, are quickly becoming a thing of the past in certain industries.

Upcoming Technology: RFID

Upcoming technology that will revolutionize pricing and inventory control is called radio frequency identification, or RFID. RFID is wireless technology that involves tiny chips imbedded in products. A chip has an antenna, a battery, and a memory chip filled with a description of the item.

26.2 AFTER YOU READ

Reviewing Key Terms and Concepts

1. What is the key factor in deciding price lines?
2. Why does bundling discourage comparison shopping?
3. Name four factors that can help marketers use segmented pricing strategies.

Integrating Academic Skills

Math

4. Determine the price a wholesaler would pay for an item with a list price of $35 if the series trade discounts were 40 percent and 10 percent for retailers and wholesalers, respectively.

Geography

5. What factors would come into play when setting the price for a child's bicycle if you were selling it in Mexico or China?

@ Online Action!

Check your answers at *marketingessentials.glencoe.com/26/read*

CAREERS IN MARKETING

RYAN WILSON
CO-OWNER
VEGAN ESSENTIALS

What do you do at work?

I run a new organic food store. With the hiring of additional employees, my position has become a bit more focused in the past year rather than running almost everything myself. Now, my primary focuses are setting a pricing policy, marketing, product research, customer service, and purchasing.

What skills are most important to you?

General management skills from having to run so many aspects of a business. Internet marketing, customer and vendor relations, and product research are other much needed skills. Setting pricing, researching competition's prices and setting the right pricing policy for products that are not widely marketed is a challenge. In retrospect, the jobs I had to do working for others were far easier because my position was focused in one direction.

What is your key to success?

Dedication. There have been countless 12–15 hour days, slow periods, vendor problems, and numerous other issues we've come across, and the only way to be successful has been to persevere through the rough times and keep looking forward. Never lose sight of what you want to accomplish with your business.

Aptitudes, Abilities, and Skills

Organizational skills, general business management, creativity, and flexibility

Education and Training

Many successful retailers have no higher education whatsoever, but general business, management, and accounting degrees can all be helpful.

Career Path

Retail careers often begin with entry-level positions in established stores. Niche retailers often spring from a personal hobby or interest (as in the case of this vegan-oriented store).

THINKING CRITICALLY

What can a business do to make sure its prices are competitive?

@ Online Action!

Go to *marketingessentials.glencoe.com/26/careers* to find a career-related activity.

CHAPTER 26 REVIEW

FOCUS on KEY POINTS

SECTION 26.1

- Establishing a base price for a product can be accomplished by combining cost-oriented, demand-oriented, and competition-oriented policies, as well as considering resellers' needs.
- Businesses must decide whether to use a one-price policy or a flexible pricing policy.
- The product life cycle needs to be considered in the pricing process. Two polar pricing strategies for the introduction of a product are skimming pricing and penetration pricing.

SECTION 26.2

- Once a base price is established, price adjustments are made with the use of specific pricing strategies. These strategies include product mix pricing, geographical pricing, international pricing, segmented pricing, psychological pricing, and promotional pricing, as well as discounts and allowances.
- There are six steps used to determine prices: establishing pricing objectives, determining costs, estimating demand, studying competition, deciding on a strategy, and setting the actual price.
- Pricing technology has revolutionized the way businesses make pricing decisions and adjustments to prices.

REVIEW VOCABULARY

Review each set of terms below. Note what they have in common.

1. markup pricing and cost-plus pricing (p. 545)
2. one-price policy and flexible-price policy (p. 549)
3. skimming pricing and penetration pricing (pp. 549, 550)
4. product mix pricing strategies, price lining, and bundle pricing (p. 553)
5. geographical pricing and segmented pricing strategy (p. 553)
6. psychological pricing, prestige pricing, everyday low prices (EDLP), and promotional pricing (p. 554)

REVIEW FACTS and IDEAS

7. List three pricing policies that can be used to establish a base price. (26.1)
8. What are two polar pricing methods that may be used when a new product is introduced into the market? (26.1)
9. Explain the relationship between pricing and the product life cycle. (26.1)
10. What are six types of pricing strategies that may be used to adjust the base price? (26.2)
11. List the six steps in the pricing process. (26.2)
12. Provide an example of how technology is used in pricing. (26.2)

BUILD SKILLS

13. Workplace Skills

Human Relations You work for a department store in the women's dress department. A customer approaches you with two dresses that are identical, except that the one from the petite department is not marked down, while the other one is. None of the petite dresses have been marked down because the buyer for that department did not elect to do so.

How will you handle this customer who wants to buy that dress style in the petite size?

14. Technology Applications

Computer Skills Set up a spreadsheet to demonstrate bundle pricing of a computer and needed software. Show the savings to a customer when buying the advertised bundle price as compared with buying each item separately.

15. Math Practice

Incentives Promotional discounts are given to stores by manufacturers to place products in preferred locations or to pay for ads, displays, or in-store demonstrations. Calculate the store's net cost to stock the following items and the percentage of the discount given.

Item	Purchase Amount	Discount Amount	Net Cost to Store	Percent Discount
Snowboards	$5,650	$847.50	________	________
CD Players	$535	$42.80	________	________

DEVELOP CRITICAL THINKING

16. Pick Your Discount

If you were a small business with little storage space, which type of quantity discount would be better for you: cumulative or noncumulative? Why?

17. Life Cycle

Select a product that interests you and research its pricing history and its competition. You can complete these research steps on the Internet, through the company site and through competitors' sites; you can also research companies on their sites at your local library. Make a list of details such as how long a product has been on the market and any product improvements. In which product life cycle stage is it? Why?

APPLY CONCEPTS

18. Cost-Plus Pricing

Using cost-plus pricing, establish a price for a car wash fund-raiser. The local community center will allow you to use its parking lot and water supply for $10.00 per hour from 9:00 A.M. to 5:00 P.M. on a Saturday. To arrive at prices you can advertise, you must purchase all the cleaning supplies and determine how much you will use per auto. Since this is a learning experience, your labor costs will be $2 per hour per worker.

Activity Write a short report that outlines your pricing strategy and calculations and be ready to share it with your classmates.

19. Using the Six-Step Method for Determining Price

Use the six-step method for determining the price of a new hat fad. Competition for this hat will be with similar trucking hats. Your cost to make the hat is $15. Your company expects a gross profit from the sale of the hats to be at least 20 percent.

Activity Prepare a written report to depict the decisions you made in each step. Include all your research and calculations to justify the price you will charge retailers and the suggested retail price for this new hat.

NET SAVVY

20. Comparison Shopping

Browse computer companies' Web sites, such as Dell, IBM, HP, and Gateway, to see pricing strategies in action. Try to find the best price for a laptop computer for your firm. What pricing strategies made comparison shopping difficult?

THE 

CONNECTION

Role Play: Assistant Buyer

Situation Assume the role of assistant buyer for a costume jewelry store. You are ordering a shipment of earrings in five styles from a supplier. The cost of the earrings is $1.50 per pair. You know that if you set too low a selling price the earrings will not sell well. The buyer (judge) has asked you to prepare a pricing strategy for the earrings. Among the decisions you must make is whether to price all the styles at one price point or to price the different styles at separate price points.

Activity Present your pricing strategy to your supervisor (judge).

Evaluation You will be evaluated on how well you meet the following performance indicators:

- Explain factors affecting pricing decisions
- Use psychological pricing to adjust base prices
- Select promotional pricing strategies used to adjust base prices
- Set prices
- Adjust prices to maximize profitability

Online Action!

For more information and DECA Prep practice, go to *marketingessentials.glencoe.com/26/DECA*

CHAPTER 27
Pricing Math

Chapter Objectives

After reading this chapter, you should be able to:

- Explain how a firm's profit is related to markup
- Use the basic formula for calculating a retail price
- Calculate dollar and percentage markup based on cost or retail
- Calculate markdown in dollars
- Calculate maintained markup in dollar and percent
- Utilize a general procedure for figuring discounts
- Calculate discounts in dollars and percentages
- Calculate net amounts

GUIDE TO THE PHOTO

Market Talk Many convenience stores are now offering coffee and other hot beverages, which offer high profit margins and bring in lots of repeat business.

According to *Supermarket News,* hot beverages delivered hefty gross margins in excess of 53 percent in 2002.

Quick Think Why do you think hot beverages bring in high profits?

THE DECA CONNECTION

Performance indicators represent key skills and knowledge. Relating them to the concepts explained in this chapter is your key to success in DECA events. These acronyms represent DECA events that involve knowledge of concepts in this chapter.

AAAL	**FMAL**	**MMS***	**TMDM***
AAML*	**FMDM***	**QSRM***	**TSE***
ADC*	**FMML***	**RMAL**	**VPM**
BSM	**FSRM***	**RMML***	
EMDM*	**HMDM***	**SMDM***	

In all these DECA events you should be able to follow this performance indicator:

- Explain factors affecting pricing decisions

All events with an asterisk (*) also include these performance indicators:

- Determine cost of product
- Determine discounts and allowances that can be used to adjust base prices
- Set prices
- Adjust prices to maximize profitability

Some events have additional performance indicators. These are:

ADC	Set price of advertising services
SMDM	Set event prices
FMDM	Describe factors affecting the price of financial services/products
	Set prices of financial services/products
EMDM	Describe the impact of e-commerce on pricing decisions

DECA PREP

Check your understanding of DECA performance indicators with the DECA activity in this chapter's review. For more information and DECA Prep practice, go to *marketingessentials.glencoe.com/27/DECA*

Calculating Prices

OBJECTIVES

- Explain how a firm's profit is related to markup
- Use the basic formula for calculating a retail price
- Calculate dollar and percentage markup based on cost or retail
- Calculate markdown in dollars
- Calculate maintained markup in dollar and percent

KEY TERMS

- gross profit
- maintained markup

READ and STUDY

BEFORE YOU READ

Predict How do you think prices are calculated?

THE MAIN IDEA

Pricing and profit have a direct relationship to one another. Retailers use different formulas for calculating prices and related markups and markdowns.

STUDY ORGANIZER

Use a chart like the one below. Insert the basic formula for calculating a retail price in the middle circle. Use the other circles to record each formula you encounter in this chapter.

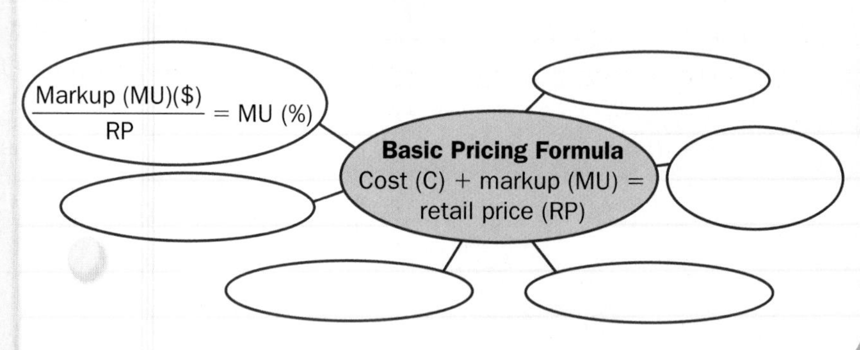

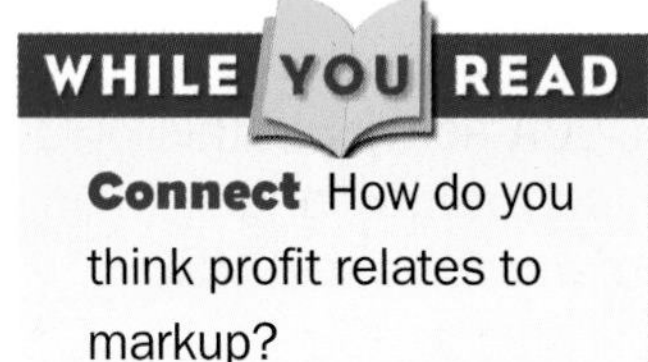

Connect How do you think profit relates to markup?

Profit and Markup

A businessperson says, "We made a profit of $50—buying the radio for $100 and selling it for $150." The businessperson is only partially correct. The difference between the retail price of $150 (which is equal to 100 percent) and the $100 cost (66⅔ percent) is the markup, or margin, of $50 (33⅓ percent), not the profit. Profit is the amount left over from revenue after the costs of the merchandise and expenses have been paid. The markup (margin) on an item, however, is the same as gross profit. **Gross profit** is the difference between sales revenue and the cost of goods sold. Expenses must still be deducted in order to get net (actual) profit. Therefore, a business must have a markup high enough to cover expenses and provide the profit needed to be successful.

Let's compare profit with retail markup by using the above figures and sales of 300 radios. Look at Figure 27.1 for this comparison. On an income statement, sales revenue would be $45,000 (100 percent), less cost of goods sold of $30,000 (66⅔ percent), which would equal gross profit of $15,000 (33⅓ percent). If expenses were $9,000 (20 percent), the gross profit (33⅓ percent) would be enough to cover expenses and earn a net profit of $6,000 or 13⅓ percent ($6,000 divided by $45,000; or 33⅓ percent − 20 percent).

Basic Markup Calculations

Retailers and wholesalers use the same formulas to calculate markup. We will use only retail prices here to make these formulas easier to understand. Note, however, that wholesale prices can be substituted in any of the formulas.

The most basic pricing formula is the one for calculating retail price. It states in mathematical terms a relationship that has been discussed in the last two chapters: retail price is a combination of cost and markup. Knowing these two figures will enable you to calculate retail price. Here's how.

Cost (C) + markup (MU) = retail price (RP)

For example,

$14 + $6 = $20

Two other formulas can be derived from this basic formula—cost and markup.

Retail price (RP) − markup (MU) = cost (C)

$20 − $6 = $14

Retail price (RP) − cost (C) = markup (MU)

$20 − $14 = $6

You will rely on these three formulas throughout this chapter. The formulas and their terms will be cited in abbreviated form (for example, as C + MU = RP).

PRACTICE 1

Use the retail price formula and its variations to do the following problems.

1. A calculator costs $3.50, and the markup is $1.49. What is its retail price?
2. A children's DVD retails for $29.99, and its markup is $10.04. What is its cost?

Note: Answers to all practice sets in this chapter at *marketingessentials.glencoe.com*

Percentage Markup

In the examples shown, markup was expressed as a dollar amount. In most business situations, however, the markup figure is generally expressed as a percentage. We will distinguish between these two forms of markup (dollar and percentage) throughout the rest of the chapter. In calculations, dollar markup will be represented with the abbreviation MU($) and percentage markup with the abbreviation MU(%).

Expressing markup in either dollar or percentage form is not the only choice that wholesalers and retailers have in making markup calculations. They may also elect to compute their markup on either cost or retail price if they choose to use the percentage form.

Most choose to base the markup on retail price for three reasons. First, the markup on the retail price sounds like a smaller amount. This sounds better to customers who know the markup percentage and can make the price seem reasonable.

Second, future markdowns and discounts are calculated on a retail basis. Third, profits are generally calculated on sales revenue. It makes sense to base markup on retail prices when comparing and analyzing data that play a role in a firm's profits.

Here are the steps that are used to calculate the percentage markup on retail. They will be

Figure 27.1 How Profit and Loss Relate to Markup

• **Calculating the Price** Before retailers or wholesalers set the price of an item, they must determine how much margin, or markup, they need on the item to sell it at a profit. That involves writing an income statement. Let's look at how these calculations work together to determine the markup.

How much markup is enough?

Sales revenue equals the price of an item times the quantity sold. This is the total amount of money generated by sales of a particular item. For example, if 300 radios are sold at $150/radio, sales revenue will be 300 × $150 = $45,000.

Cost of goods is the cost to purchase or make the items for sale. In the example of the radio, the cost to the retailer is $100/radio. For 300 radios, then, the cost is 300 × $100 = $30,000.

Income Statement		
Sales revenue (300 items @ $150/item)	$45,000	100%
Cost of goods sold	$30,000	66 2/3%
Gross profit	$15,000	33 1/3%
Less expenses	$ 9,000	20%
Net profit	$ 6,000	13 1/3%

Gross profit is the difference between sales revenue and the cost of goods sold: $45,000 – $30,000 = $15,000.

Expenses are the costs of running the business that sells the item. In the case of the radio sales, these costs are $9,000.

Net profit is the amount left over from revenue after the costs of the merchandise and expenses have been paid: $45,000 – $30,000 – $9,000 = $6,000. The owner of the electronics store decides that this is a sufficient profit and sets the retail price at $150.

The **retail price** is the price of the item to the customer, or the sticker price. The radio in our example will cost a customer $150.

Retail Pricing		
Retail price (unit price)	$150	100%
Unit cost	$100	66 2/3%
Markup (margin)	$ 50	33 1/3%

The **unit cost** is the cost per item to the retailer or wholesaler. In our example, each radio costs the retailer $100.

The **markup**, or **margin**, is the difference between the unit cost and the retail price, or the amount added to the unit cost to cover expenses and provide a profit. In our example, that is $150 – $100 = $50.

Online Action! Go to ***marketingessentials.glencoe.com/27/figure/1*** to find a project on pricing.

easier to follow if we have an example to work with. Assume that you want to calculate the percentage markup on a pair of bookends that Wright's Department Store stocks for $49.50 (cost) and sells for $82.50 (retail price).

STEP 1 Determine the dollar markup.

RP − C = MU($)
$82.50 − $49.50 = $33.00

STEP 2 To change the dollar markup to the percentage markup, divide it by the retail price. The result will be a decimal.

MU($)/RP = MU(%) on retail
$33.00 divided by $82.50 = .4

STEP 3 Change the decimal to a percentage by shifting the decimal point two places to the right. This figure is the percentage markup on retail.

.40 = 40%

Retailers may find the percentage markup on cost to be helpful. The calculation is the same, except for Step 2. Using the same facts from above, you calculate the percentage markup on cost as follows:

STEP 1 Determine the dollar markup.

RP − C = MU($)
$82.50 − $49.50 = $33.00

STEP 2 To change the dollar markup to the percentage markup, divide by cost.

MU($)/C = MU(%) on cost
$33.00 divided by $49.50 = .6667

STEP 3 Change the decimal to a percentage. This figure is the percentage markup on cost.

.6667 = 66.67%

PRACTICE 2

Calculate the percentage markup in each of these situations.

1. The retail price of a music CD is $11.99 and the cost is $7.80. (A) What is the percentage markup based on cost price? (B) Based on retail price? Round your markup percentages to the tenths place.
2. A gas grill costs $220, and its markup is $179.99. (A) Find its percentage markup on cost price. (B) Calculate the retail price, and then (C) calculate its percentage markup on retail price. Round percentages to the tenths place.
3. A gallery sells a framed print for $100, and its markup is $50. (A) What is its percentage markup on cost price? (B) On retail price?

Markup Equivalents Table

You would notice a correlation between the two figures if you calculated enough problems using the formulas for computing percentage markup based on cost and retail. This correlation led marketers to develop a calculation aid called a Markup Equivalents Table, a portion of which is shown in Figure 27.2. The table lists markup percentages based on retail and the equivalent percentages based on cost. To use the table, you locate the percentage markup on retail and read its cost equivalent in the adjacent column or vice versa.

PRACTICE 3

Use the markup equivalents table in Figure 27.2 to answer the following questions:

1. When the markup on retail is 31 percent, what is its equivalent markup on cost?
2. The markup on cost is 22 percent; what is its equivalent markup on retail?

Cost Method of Pricing

Sometimes marketers know only the cost of an item and its markup on cost. In such a situation, they use the cost method of pricing.

Consider a board game that a toy store buys for $8.50 and sells for cost plus a 40 percent markup on cost. To arrive at the retail price, follow these steps:

STEP 1 Determine the dollar markup on cost. Multiply the cost by the percentage markup on cost in decimal form.

$C \times MU(\%) = MU(\$)$
$\$8.50 \times .40 = \$3.40$

STEP 2 Add the dollar markup to the cost to get the retail price.

$C + MU(\$) = RP$
$\$8.50 + \$3.40 = \$11.90$

Often, the situation is not that simple. Suppose you have the cost, but the only markup figure you know is the markup on retail. What will you do? You cannot use the markup percentage on retail to calculate the markup in dollars unless you know the retail price. This is the perfect time to use the Markup Equivalents Table (see Figure 27.2). You can convert the markup on retail to the markup on cost and apply it to the cost of the item to arrive at the markup in dollars.

Here is an example: A marketer knows that the customary markup for a particular cosmetics firm is 33.3 percent based on retail and that the cost of its most popular lipstick is $8.00. To project the lipstick's retail price, follow these steps:

STEP 1 Use the markup equivalents table to get all the information in the same form (cost). Find the cost equivalent of a 33.3 percent markup on retail.

Markup Percent on Retail	Markup Percent on Cost
32.0	47.1
33.3	50.0
34.0	51.5

STEP 2 Apply the cost method to determine the retail price. First calculate the dollar markup on cost.

$C \times MU(\%) = MU(\$)$
$\$8.00 \times .50 = \$4.00$

NET MARKETING

Shopping Auctions

Internet shopping auctions provide a means for buyers and sellers to get the merchandise they want through a bidding system. The seller establishes a price where bidding starts. Buyers respond by placing bids for the goods they want to purchase. One of the largest Internet shopping auctions is eBay. However there are others. Some of them are even specialized, like ones for sports memorabilia.

Setting a Price

Some items are in great supply or there is not a lot of demand for them. Usually the prices on those items are relatively low, such as a cookbook for $3 or a chair for $6. For other items that are more rare, prices can soar; for example, a 1961 Mickey Mantle baseball card for $102.

THINK LIKE A MARKETER

Identify an item you own that you might want to auction off on the Internet. At what price would you start the bidding?

Online Action!

Go to *marketingessentials.glencoe.com/27/net* to find an activity on online pricing.

Figure 27.2 Markup Equivalents

• **Markup Equivalents Table** This sample markup equivalents table allows users to convert markups on retail to markups on cost and vice versa.

A 23.1 percent markup based on retail is equal to what markup percent based on cost?

Markup on Retail	Markup on Cost	Markup on Retail	Markup on Cost
4.8%	5.0%	25.0%	33.3%
5.0	5.3	26.0	35.0
6.0	6.4	27.0	37.0
7.0	7.5	27.3	37.5
8.0	8.7	28.0	39.0
9.0	10.0	28.5	40.0
10.0	11.1	29.0	40.9
10.7	12.0	30.0	42.9
11.0	12.4	31.0	45.0
11.1	12.5	32.0	47.1
12.0	13.6	33.3	50.0
12.5	14.3	34.0	51.5
13.0	15.0	35.0	53.9
14.0	16.3	35.5	55.0
15.0	17.7	36.0	56.3
16.0	19.1	37.0	58.8
16.7	20.0	37.5	60.0
17.0	20.5	38.0	61.3
17.5	21.2	39.0	64.0
18.0	22.0	39.5	65.5
18.5	22.7	40.0	66.7
19.0	23.5	41.0	70.0
20.0	25.0	42.0	72.4
21.0	26.6	42.8	75.0
22.0	28.2	44.4	80.0
22.5	29.0	46.1	85.0
23.0	29.9	47.5	90.0
23.1	30.0	48.7	95.0
24.0	31.6	50.0	100.0

Go to *marketingessentials.glencoe.com/27/figure/2* to find a project on markups.

STEP 3 Then calculate the retail price.

C + MU($) = RP
$8.00 + $4.00 = $12.00

Retail Method of Pricing

Another way to compute the retail price when all you know are cost and the markup on retail is to use the retail method. This method is based on changing the information that you already have into retail figures.

Let's consider an example: The owner of a sporting goods store wants to know what the markup and retail price should be for a sun visor that costs $6.75. His customary markup based on the retail price is 40 percent. The steps that he follows in his calculation are as follows:

Case Study

The Vuitton Money Machine

Luxury Priced Right

Louis Vuitton handbags and rivals Gucci, Prada, Coach, and Hermes price their handbags very high to attract the luxury market. The Vuitton machine is running mighty smoothly right now. With $3.8 billion in annual sales, it is about twice the size of runners-up Prada and Gucci. Vuitton maintained double-digit sales growth and the industry's fattest operating margins as rivals staggered through a global downturn that started early in 2001. That power was underscored in March 2003, when Vuitton reported a record-high 45 percent operating margin. Some Vuitton bags retail for $1,000 or more. And no Vuitton bag is ever marked down.

Manufacturing Differences

According to Andrew Gowen, an analyst who visited the factories of Vuitton and competitor Hermes, they are "worlds apart. Vuitton's factory is still labor-intensive, but there is a balance between mechanization and handmade. At Hermes, it looks like you stepped into the 14th century, just rows and rows of people stitching." Hermes bags cost more, but the company's operating margins are only about 25 percent, which is the industry's average margin.

THINK STRATEGICALLY

What word could you use instead of "margin" if you were speaking about the pricing function? Why do you think Louis Vuitton's margins are so high in comparison to its competitors and the industry in general?

@ Online Action!

Go to *marketingessentials.glencoe.com/27/case* to find an activity on luxury pricing.

GLOBAL MARKET

China's Auto Industry and the WTO

When China joined the World Trade Organization (WTO) in 2001, it lowered tariffs and raised quotas on automobiles. Tariffs on imported cars dropped from a range of 70 percent to 80 percent of the list price to 50 percent to 60 percent. By 2006, duties should have sunk to 25 percent, which is still high by world standards but low enough to put autos within the reach of China's growing upper middle class.

New Designs What is good for buyers is bad news for China's automakers, which will experience intense competition from imported autos. As the state phased out rules dictating which models each manufacturer can assemble, manufacturers were free to design new cars aimed at quality- and cost-conscious buyers. Eventually, lower prices and wider choices should create a thriving auto industry.

By 2004, China's auto production ranked fourth in the world, according to peoplesdaily.com. However, an increase in import quotas and further tariff cuts put pressure on domestic manufacturers' margins according to John Bailey, a director at Standard & Poor's Corporate Ratings and Infrastructure Ratings in Hong Kong.

CRITICAL THINKING

How do changing tariffs and quotas on imported autos sold in China affect Chinese automakers' margins?

Online Action!

Go to *marketingessentials.glencoe.com/27/global* to find an activity on price and international marketing.

STEP 1 Determine what percentage of the retail price is equal to cost. This is a matter of subtracting the known retail markup percent from 100 percent, which represents the retail price.

RP(%) − MU(%) = C(%)
100% − 40% = 60%

STEP 2 To determine the retail price, divide the cost by the decimal equivalent of the percentage calculated in Step 1.

$6.75 divided by .60 = $11.25

STEP 3 Calculate the dollar markup.

RP − C = MU($)
$11.25 − $6.75 = $4.50

STEP 4 Check your work by multiplying the retail price you calculated in Step 2 by the percentage markup on retail given originally. The answer will match the dollar markup you calculated in Step 3, if your retail price is correct.

RP × MU(%) = MU($)
$11.25 × .40 = $4.50

You can use a visual device called the retail box (see Figure 27.3) to help you remember this sequence of calculations. This retail box organizes your information and makes it simple to check your work.

PRACTICE 4

Calculate retail price and markup in these two problems by using the retail method. Then double-check your answer to see if your retail price is correct.

1. (A) Find the retail price and (B) dollar markup for a bag of chips that costs $1.81 and has a 4 percent markup on retail. (C) Double-check your answer.
2. A lamp costs the retailer $20 and has a 60 percent markup on retail. Calculate this lamp's (A) retail price and (B) dollar markup. (C) Double-check your answer.

Calculations for Lowering Prices

When a business lowers its prices, a new sale price must be calculated, as well as a new markup. Let's look at the steps used in calculating markdowns (lowered prices), maintained markups, and the actual sale prices derived from these calculations.

Markdowns

To reduce the quantity of goods in stock, a business will sometimes mark down merchandise by a certain percentage (MD[%]).

This reduction is based on the retail price. Consider as an example a record store that wants to mark down by 25 percent CDs that originally sold for $16. The steps for calculating the sale price (SP) are as follows:

STEP 1 Determine the dollar markdown. Multiply the retail price by the percentage markdown.

RP × MD(%) = MD($)
$16 × .25 = $4

STEP 2 To determine the sale price, subtract the markdown from the retail price.

RP − MD($) = SP
$16 − $4 = $12

Another way to arrive at the same answer is to consider what percentage of the original price will equal the sale price. The procedure is still two steps long, but the percentage calculation is so easy that you can probably do it in your head and save some time. Here are the steps involved.

STEP 1 Determine what percentage of the original price will equal the sale price. This is simply a matter

Figure 27.3 Retail Box

	$	%		$	%
Retail Price	M 11.25	J 100	Retail Price	M	J 100
Markup	N 4.50	K 40	Markup	N	K
Cost	O 6.75	L 60	Cost	O	L

Computation:	L = J − K	L = 100 − 40 = 60%
	M = O ÷ L	M = $6.75 ÷ .60 = $11.25
	N = M − O	N = $11.25 − $6.75 = $4.50
Check:	M × K = N	11.25 × .40 = $4.50

• **The Retail Method** To compute the retail price using the retail method, fill in the boxes following the letter sequence (J-O). Note that the box labeled "J" (RP%) is always 100 percent. The amounts that go in the boxes labeled K (MU%) and O (C$) are usually known.

Why is this retail box an example of the retail method for calculating markup?

Go to *marketingessentials.glencoe.com/27/figure/3* to find a project on retail pricing.

•**SALES as ADVERTISING** Many stores widely publicize their sales as a way of attracting shoppers.

Why would a store that is closing put its merchandise on sale?

of subtracting the markdown percentage from 100 percent.

RP(%) − MD(%) = SP(%)
100% − 25% = 75%

STEP 2 To find the sale price, multiply the retail price by the decimal equivalent of the percentage calculated in Step 1.

RP × SP(%) = SP
$16 × .75 = $12

PRACTICE 5

Calculate the sale price.

1. A suit that sells for $350 is to be marked down by 40 percent. What is its new price?

Maintained Markup

When a marketer marks down goods, the markup and markup percentage change. The difference between an item's final sale price and its cost is called the **maintained markup**.

Maintained Markups and Pricing Strategies

Businesses must plan for markdowns; doing so is part of being profitable and competitive in the marketplace. Reductions in the original retail price include employee discounts, damaged goods allowances, and special sales events. For businesses to enjoy the profit margin they need to be successful, they must take these factors into account.

The concept of maintained markup becomes extremely important in planning the original price of the item and all future markdowns.

Let's consider an example. Assume that a video game that cost Zap Electronics $25 to manufacture and originally sold for $50 is marked down 20 percent. The maintained markup (expressed in both dollars and as a percentage) is calculated as follows:

STEP 1 Calculate the new sale price.

100% – 20% = 80%
$50 × .80 = $40

STEP 2 To determine the maintained markup in dollars (MM$), subtract the cost from the sale price.

SP – C = MM($)
$40 – $25 = $15

STEP 3 To determine the maintained markup percentage, divide the maintained markup in dollars by the sale price. Note: Round percents to the tenths place.

MM($) ÷ SP = MM(%)
$15 ÷ $40 = .3750
.375 = 37.5%

PRACTICE 6

Now try the same type of computation on your own.

1. A digital audio player that costs the retailer $126 to stock sells for $299.99 (retail price). The retailer wants to mark down the player 20 percent. (A) Determine the sale price and (B) maintained markup in dollars, and then (C) calculate the maintained markup percentage. Round the markup percentage to the tenths place.

27.1 AFTER YOU READ

Reviewing Key Terms and Concepts

1. What income statement term is the same as markup?
2. What steps are used to calculate prices according to the cost method?
3. When is the initial markup the same as the maintained markup? Explain.

Integrating Academic Skills

Math

4. Determine the retail price of an item that cost the business $89 and has a markup of $50.

Writing

5. Write a two-page paper on research comparing prescription drug prices in Canada with prices for the same drugs sold in the United States.

Check your answers at *marketingessentials.glencoe.com/27/read*

Calculating Discounts

OBJECTIVES

- **Utilize a general procedure for figuring discounts**
- **Calculate discounts in dollars and percentages**
- **Calculate net amounts**

KEY TERMS

- **employee discounts**

READ and STUDY

BEFORE YOU READ

Connect When did you last purchase a discounted item?

THE MAIN IDEA

Discounts affect the final price a customer will pay. Therefore, it is essential that you learn how to calculate discounts and the net price payable.

STUDY ORGANIZER

In the center of the diagram below record the procedures for calculating discounts and the net amount payable. In the other circles, note examples of discounts.

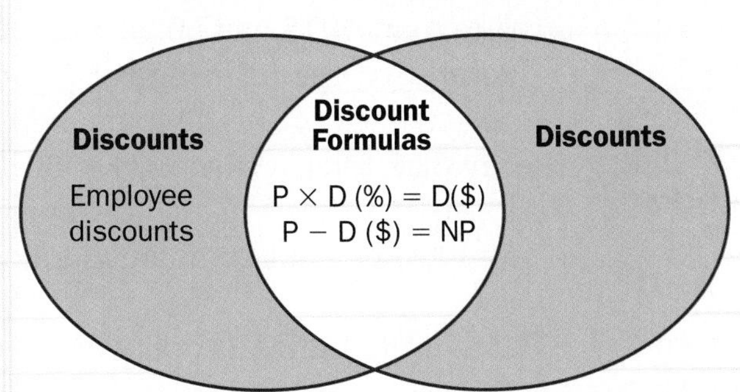

Predict Compare the two methods of calculating discounts and net amounts to decide when each method should be used.

Discounts

Discounts and allowances are price adjustments often taken by employees for purchases and offered by vendors to their customers. Knowing how to calculate discounts and the resulting net amounts is important because they affect the prices customers ultimately pay for the products you are selling or buying.

Recall that a discount is a reduction in the price of goods and services sold to customers. Retailers may offer discounts to their employees as a job benefit or to encourage their employees to purchase their goods. Vendors offer discounts to their customers to encourage prompt payment and stimulate business. There are two different ways you can go about calculating discounts and net amounts.

The first way is to calculate the discount and then subtract the discount from the original price. You would use this method if you wanted to know the dollar amount of the discount and the net amount. Here is an example of this two-step method.

STEP 1 Multiply the price (P) by the discount percentage [D(%)] to get the dollar amount of the discount [D($)].

P × D(%) = D($)

STEP 2 Subtract the discount from the price to get the net price (NP), or the amount that the customer will actually pay.

P − D($) = NP

Here is an example. A business is offering a 35 percent discount on an item that sells for $150.

$150 × .35 = $52.50
$150 − 52.50 = $97.50

When you simply want to know the net amount due, you can also follow a two-step process. Using the above example, those calculations would be as follows:

STEP 1 Subtract the discount percent from 100 percent. This figure represents the net price's percentage equivalent (NPPE).

100% − D(%) = NPPE
100% − 35% = 65%

STEP 2 Then multiply the original price by that net price's equivalent percentage to get the net price.

P × NPPE = NP
$150 × .65 = $97.50

Employee Discounts

Discounts offered by employers to their workers are **employee discounts**. Employee discounts encourage employees to buy and use their company's products. In so doing, businesses hope employees will project confidence in and enthusiasm for those products. This is especially important for the sales staff and customer service representatives, so they can speak about the products from firsthand experience. Employee discounts can range from 10 percent to 30 percent for entry-level employees and as high as 50 percent or more for top-level executives.

Discounts from Vendors

Some common types of discounts offered by manufacturers and distributors are cash, trade, quantity, seasonal, and promotional, all of which were already explained in Chapter 26. The following section explains how each of these types of discounts is calculated.

Cash Discounts

Recall from Chapter 26 that a cash discount is a discount offered to buyers to encourage them to pay their bills quickly. Consider the invoice terms 3/15, net 60.

Recall that the first number (3) represents the percentage of the discount applicable to the invoice total. When that total is $1,000 and the customer takes advantage of the discount, the calculations are as follows:

STEP 1 Determine the dollar discount.

P × D(%) = D($)
$1,000 × .03 = $30

STEP 2 Determine the net price.

P − D($) = NP
$1,000 − $30 = $970

Cash discounts can also be calculated on a unit basis. The net unit price listed on the invoice for 100 items at $10 each is determined as follows:

STEP 1 Determine the dollar discount.

$P \times D(\%) = D(\$)$
$\$10.00 \times .03 = \$.30$

STEP 2 Determine the net price.

$P - D(\$) = NP$
$\$10.00 - \$.30 = \$9.70$

The net amount payable by the customer would still be the same, of course—$970 ($9.70 × 100).

If you wanted to determine the net price simply, you could subtract 3 percent from 100 percent and take 97% of $10 ($10 × .97 = $9.70).

Trade Discounts

Trade discounts are based on manufacturers' list prices. They are not really discounts but are the way manufacturers quote prices to wholesalers and retailers. They are called trade discounts because different prices are offered to different lines of trade (for example, wholesalers versus retailers), in a series, such as 40 percent and 20 percent. The 40 percent discount is offered to the retailer and the series of discounts 40 percent and 20 percent is offered to the wholesaler. To figure 40 percent and 20 percent trade discounts for a wholesaler's invoice totaling $8,450, you would do the following:

STEP 1 Determine the first dollar discount.

$P \times D(\%) = D(\$)$
$\$8{,}450 \times .40 = \$3{,}380$

STEP 2 Determine the declining balance.

$P - D(\$) = DB$
$\$8{,}450 - \$3{,}380 = \$5{,}070$

STEP 3 Take the second discount off the declining balance in Step 2

$DB \times D\ (\%) = D\ (\$)$
$\$5{,}070 \times .20 = \$1{,}014$

STEP 4 Determine the net price

$DB - D(\$) = NP\ (\$)$
$\$5{,}070 - \$1{,}014 = \$4{,}056$

Sometimes, retailers or wholesalers want to calculate the net unit price of individual items listed on an invoice. In those cases, using the result of subtracting the discounts from 100 percent would be faster. Assuming one of the items on that above invoice was $84.50, you would multiply $84.50 × .60 = $50.70; then you would multiply $50.70 × .80 = $40.56 (net unit price).

PRACTICE 7

Determine the amounts payable by the following customers.

1. Alliance Trucking receives an invoice in the amount of $325,000 showing the terms 2/10, net 30. The invoice lists five trucks at $65,000 each. (A) If Alliance takes advantage of the discount, what will be the net amount due on the invoice? (B) The net price per truck?
2. A manufacturer gives retailers a 55 percent trade discount. The invoice received by Oliver's Department Store totals $2,907.40. (A) What is the dollar amount of the store's discount? (B) What is the amount payable to the manufacturer?
3. A manufacturer gives wholesalers discounts of 40 percent and 10 percent. The invoice received by Industrial Wholesaler totals $193,300. What is the net amount payable to the manufacturer?

Quantity Discounts

Quantity discounts are offered to buyers for placing large orders. Sellers benefit from large orders because the selling costs for one transaction are lower than for several small transactions. Quantity discounts are meant to encourage buyers to buy in bulk and purchase more merchandise than they originally intended to purchase. These discounts may be quoted either as a percentage of price or as part of a quantity price list like this:

No. of items	1–24	25–48	49–72
Unit price	$.95	$.90	$.85

Using the above table, if you purchased 50 items, you would pay $.85 each. Your total bill would be $42.50 ($.85 × 50).

•SCHOOL SUPPLIES DISCOUNTS The price of school supplies varies depending on the time of year.

When are school supplies likely to be discounted and why?

Sometimes, businesses offer cumulative quantity discounts, whereby a certain minimum purchase must be made during a specified period of time for the discount to be activated. A firm may offer a 2 percent cumulative quantity discount to any company that purchases $3,000 worth of products in a six-month period. If a firm's purchases total $2,500 during that period, no discount is given; if they total $4,000, however, the discount is allowed.

For example, let's say a manufacturer offers a 5 percent cumulative quantity discount for purchases that total at least $5,000 in a three-month period. Suppose Kathy's Flowers placed the following orders:

January 15: $1,000; February 28: $2,000; March 10: $3,000. The total purchases of $6,000 would meet the dollar requirement within the three-month period. Thus, Kathy's net amount payable would be $5,700 ($1,000 + $2,000 + $3,000 = $6,000 × .95 = $5,700). If Kathy's Flowers had not placed the March 10 order, the total for the three-month period would be only $3,000, so no discounts would be permitted.

Promotional Discounts

Promotional discounts are given to businesses that agree to advertise or in some other way promote a manufacturer's products. When the promotional discount is quoted as a percentage, it is calculated in the same way as a cumulative discount.

Sometimes, marketers are granted a dollar amount as a promotional discount. In such cases, they may want to determine the net purchase price or the percentage of the promotional discount for themselves. Consider an example. The Cycle Shop buys Speedy bicycles for $10,000 and is granted a $250 promotional discount for displaying the bikes in its store window during the month of March. To determine the percentage discount, follow these steps:

STEP 1 Divide the dollar discount by the original price. The answer will be a decimal.

D($) divided by P = D(%)
$250 ÷ $10,000 = .025

STEP 2 Change the decimal to a percentage by shifting the decimal point two places to the right. This figure is the percentage discount. When necessary, round the percentage to the tenths place.

.025 = 2.5%

Seasonal Discounts

Sellers offer seasonal discounts to encourage buyers to purchase goods long before the actual consumer buying season. Purchasing beach towels before January 27 or ski apparel before May 1 might qualify retailers for seasonal discounts.

Seasonal discounts are calculated in the same way as other discounts. PNC, Inc. offers an 8 percent seasonal discount to all buyers who purchase winter coats before August 1. An order placed on July 20 for $1,500 worth of parkas would qualify for the discount. However, if that order was placed on August 1, PNC, Inc. would not grant the 8 percent discount.

PRACTICE 8

Now try these problems involving quantity, promotional, and seasonal discounts.

1. Suppose a firm is required to buy $10,000 worth of goods by September 15 in order to qualify for a 10 percent cumulative quantity discount. (A) Would a firm that purchased $8,000 worth of goods on September 1 get the discount? (B) What about one that purchased $11,500 worth on September 20?
2. A manufacturer offers a retailer $3,775 as a promotional discount for advertising a certain product. What is the percentage discount if the total invoice was $75,500? Round percentage discount to the tenths place.
3. Regal Shoe Company offers retailers a 6 percent discount for placing orders by May 1. A retailer takes advantage of the offer and purchases $117,344 worth of shoes by the cutoff date. What is the net amount payable on the invoice?

27.2 AFTER YOU READ

Reviewing Key Terms and Concepts

1. The dating terms on a $7,000 invoice are 3/10, net 30. If the buyer takes advantage of the cash discount, what will be the net amount due?
2. If a promotional discount involved receiving a free case of items you purchased, how can you calculate the percent of the discount offered?
3. Why do sellers offer seasonal discounts to customers?

Integrating Academic Skills

Math

4. How much would you charge a customer who purchased 40 items, based on the following quantity price list?

Number of items	0–12	13–36	37–49	50–74
Unit price	$4.50	$4.25	$4.00	$3.75

Art

5. Prices for artwork vary immensely. Use the Internet to locate artwork that appeals to you. Price the artwork and write a short report on the variations you found in prices and any discounts offered.

Check your answers at *marketingessentials.glencoe.com/27/read*

CAREERS IN MARKETING

BILL BUCKALEW
PRICING CONSULTANT
DEMAND CURVE, INC.

What do you do at work?
My job is to help companies achieve financial goals through better pricing. A good strategy puts the company in a position to be successful, while a bad strategy assures that the company will fail. As a pricing consultant, it is important to know which pricing strategy will increase the company's chances for success.

What skills are most important to you?
Price analysis requires the ability to access and manipulate large data sets. It is important for a good consultant to be able to pull data from many diverse data sources and transform that data into information that people can use to make decisions. Skills that are important, then, are data query, statistical analysis, and reporting. Some tools that can be used to assist this process are SQL, MS-Access, MS-Excel, and report-generators like Crystal Reports or Business Objects.

What is your key to success?
To consistently increase the value of the products or services the company is supplying. Increasing the value of the product or service forces upward price pressure in the marketplace. When customers realize the benefits of the company's offering they are willing to pay more to purchase... and the pricing consultant gets paid!

Aptitudes, Abilities, and Skills

Analytical skills, strong computer and technical ability, and mathematical aptitude are all critical.

Education and Training

Degrees in economics are essential in this career; other math-intensive courses are also helpful to the pricing analyst.

Career Path

Entry-level positions can begin in the accounting department of any major company; many price analysts also work in a freelance capacity.

THINKING CRITICALLY

Why is a thorough understanding of basic principles of economics so important for this career?

Online Action!

Go to *marketingessentials.glencoe.com/27/careers* to find a career-related activity.

CHAPTER 27 REVIEW

FOCUS on KEY POINTS

SECTION 27.1

- Gross profit on an income statement is the same as gross margin or markup in pricing. The basic formula for markup is Cost + Markup = Retail Price. Markups may be computed on cost or retail prices and in dollars or percentages.
- To calculate a markdown, multiply the markdown percent by the retail price. To arrive at the sale price, subtract the dollar markdown from the original retail price.
- Maintained markup is the difference between sale price and cost.

SECTION 27.2

- The procedure for calculating discounts is to multiply the price by the discount percentage and then to subtract that amount from the original price to arrive at the net price. Another method for calculating the net price is to subtract the discount percent from 100 percent. Multiply the resulting percentage by the original price to arrive at the net price.
- Cash discounts are offered to customers with dating terms such as 2/10, net 30. The "2" represents the discount percentage. Trade discounts are often quoted in series, such as 40 percent and 20 percent. To calculate the net price with a series of discounts, multiply each sequential discount by the declining balance.
- Quantity discounts may be quoted on a quantity price list that provides unit prices for specific quantities purchased. Promotional discounts are often granted in dollar amounts. To determine the percentage of discount offered in a promotion, divide the promotional discount by the original price paid for the merchandise in an order. Seasonal discounts have qualifying purchase date requirements.

REVIEW VOCABULARY

Explain the meanings of the following terms by giving an example of each.

1. gross profit (p. 567)
2. maintained markup (p. 575)
3. employee discounts (p. 578)

REVIEW FACTS and IDEAS

4. Explain how a firm's profit is related to markup. (27.1)
5. What is the most basic formula you need in order to calculate retail price? (27.1)
6. How are the dollar and percentage markups calculated, based on cost and based on retail? (27.1)
7. What is the two-step procedure for calculating a discount and net amount? What is the two-step procedure for calculating just the net price? (27.2)
8. A company is granted a $250 promotional discount for including a product in its flyer. What percentage is this discount of the $5,000 invoice? (27.2)

BUILD SKILLS

9. Workplace Skills

Business Ethics The store where you are working as a cashier is having a huge sale with selected items marked down 30 to 50 percent. The discounts are taken at the register. Your friend asks you to take a 50 percent markdown on an item that is not on sale. What would you do?

10. Technology Applications

Computing Prices Prepare a spreadsheet that shows how retail prices are calculated using the retail method. Use a 40 percent markup on retail and the following items and their costs:

Item	Retail Cost
Model #314	$20
Model #315	$35
Model #316	$42

Record the formulas you used in your spreadsheet calculations.

11. Math

Calculate: Percentage Markup A card store buys boxes of candy for $5.50 and puts a $4.49 markup on each box. (A) What is the percentage markup on cost? (B) The percentage markup on retail?

DEVELOP CRITICAL THINKING

12. What Is the Retail Price?

Suppose a buyer wanted to buy goods that cost $300 and the customary markup on retail was 20 percent.

Demonstrate two methods that could be used to calculate the retail price. Identify each method when showing your calculations. Finally, explain why you chose the two calculation methods.

13. Company Discounts

A vendor offers Company XYZ a cumulative discount of six percent on orders of at least $10,000 placed within a six-month period. Company XYZ purchases $8,000 within three months and $4,000 a month later.

What is the amount payable by Company XYZ? Make sure you show all the steps in your calculations.

APPLY CONCEPTS

14. Trade Discounts and Maintained Markup

Local schools and businesses have inquired about receiving a discount if they purchase bagels for resale. Prepare a discounted price list that shows at least five different price options for different quantities purchased. Assume your cost to make and market one bagel is $.35. At present, you sell one bagel in your retail store for $.60. Be sure your trade discounts still generate gross margins of no less than 27 percent, which is essential to remain profitable.

Activity What trade discounts would you offer these resellers?

15. Understanding Markup and Gross Profit

Trade organizations often publish average markup (margins) for a given product category. Research the retail prices of two competing products from each of the three categories noted below.

Product Category	Average Retail Markup Percent
Small Appliances	30%
Videos	25%
Clothing	50%

Activity Use a spreadsheet to calculate the cost of those items. Analyze the costs and markup in dollars you calculated, as well as the sales volume required to generate $100,000 in gross profit for each of the products you researched.

NET SAVVY

16. Free Goods and Coupons

Find a Web site that offers free goods and coupons. Do manufacturers' coupons affect the retailer's markup percentages?

THE DECA CONNECTION

Role Play: Pricing Math

Situation Assume the role of manager of the children's department of a department store. The buyer (judge) has asked you to select three slow selling merchandise styles for markdowns. The styles you have selected are 10 infant sleepers that currently are selling for $20 each; 6 girls cotton crewneck sweaters selling for $25 each; and 11 boys wool sweaters selling for $30 each. The buyer has asked you to take a 30 percent markdown on each item.

Activity Determine the new selling price for each of the styles receiving a markdown, and send a buyer a report of those new prices.

Evaluation You will be evaluated on how well you meet the following performance indicators:

- Determine discounts and allowances that can be used to adjust base prices
- Explain the nature and scope of the pricing function
- Explain factors affecting pricing decisions
- Demonstrate orderly and systematic behavior

@ Online Action!

For more information and DECA Prep practice, go to *marketingessentials.glencoe.com/27/DECA*

MARKETING INTERNSHIP

A SIMULATED DECA PRODUCT AND SERVICE MANAGEMENT EVENT

Pricing Toys

BASIC BACKGROUND

Tri-Star Toys is introducing two new products influenced by Japanese pop culture. One is a trading card game called Laszot. The other is a line of 12-inch stuffed animals called Mie Dolls. Each doll is supposed to have a unique trait, such as being friendly or mischievous.

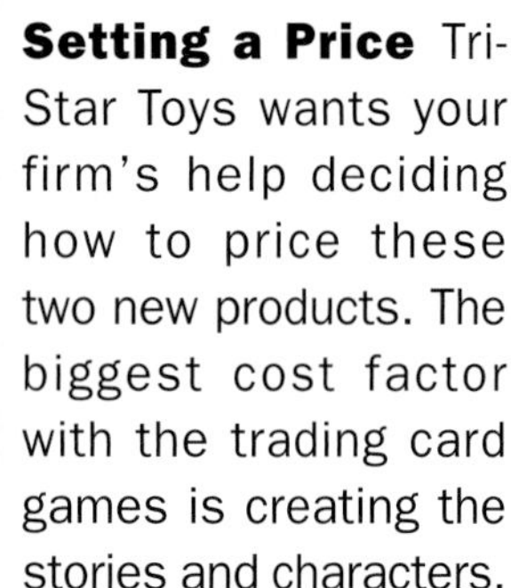

Setting a Price Tri-Star Toys wants your firm's help deciding how to price these two new products. The biggest cost factor with the trading card games is creating the stories and characters. Assume a cost of $.25 per card for the initial production. For the dolls, assume an initial cost of $4.50. Marketing expenses are $0.05 per trading card and $1.00 per doll. Demand for both items depends on conditions in the marketplace, which you will need to determine.

YOUR OBJECTIVE

Your objective is to prepare an effective pricing and retail strategy for Tri-Star's two new products. The company wants to make a 15 percent profit off the products in the first year. You will need to identify a price for sale to wholesalers, retailers, and e-commerce sites, as well as a suggested retail price for those businesses to charge their customers. Base your conclusions on research and analysis of current market conditions.

ASSIGNMENT AND STRATEGY

- **Get the background** To get started you will need to conduct a situation analysis and competitive assessment for these two new products made by the Tri-Star Toy Company. Learn all you can about the markets for trading card games and dolls, some of which may be collectibles.

  You may want to look at the introductions of other trading card games, including Pokemon and Yu-Gi-Oh, and other dolls, such as Ugly Dolls and Beanie Babies.

- **Write the pricing proposal** Begin your proposal by reviewing the reason the client hired your firm.

  Then, provide background information you learned from your situation analysis and competitive assessment.

  Use your research to justify your assumptions as you go through the six steps of pricing a product.

The six steps are: (1) establish pricing objectives; (2) determine costs; (3) estimate demand; (4) study competition; (5) decide on a pricing strategy; and (6) set prices.

- **What your project should include** Show the math you used to arrive at suggested prices for wholesalers, retailers, and e-commerce sites, as well as the suggested prices for retail customers. Also create a table that depicts your competitive price analysis. Create other tables and figures as needed to show relationships among data.

YOUR REPORT

Use a word processing program and presentation software to prepare a double-spaced report and an oral presentation for Tri-Star Toys. See a suggested outline and key evaluation points at *marketingessentials.glencoe.com/internship*

BUILD YOUR PORTFOLIO

Option 1 Internship Report Once you have completed your Marketing Internship project and presentation, include your written report and a few printouts of key slides from your oral presentation in your Marketing Portfolio.

Option 2 Multi-tiered Pricing Strategies A designer of high-priced apparel is thinking of also designing moderate-priced fashions. After doing some research, including a situation analysis, create a pricing plan for this designer. It should include a suggested target market and customer profile, distribution, and pricing strategies. Prepare a written report and an oral presentation using word processing and presentation software. See a suggested outline and key evaluation points at *marketingessentials.glencoe.com/portfolio*

Online Action!

Go to *marketingessentials.glencoe.com/Unit/8/DECA* to review pricing concepts that relate to DECA events.

UNIT 9 Marketing

In this unit you will find

Information Management

Marketing Plan

ANALYZE THE AD

This ad for Mountain High Yoghurt represents a very specific demographic group. Why do you think this group was targeted?

Market Talk Marketing research can analyze results by demographic factors, including income, age, and ethnicity. Companies often make marketing decisions based on the results of their research.

Think and Write Imagine you visit friends in a neighboring state and find out everybody at your friends' high school wears a different brand of jeans than people at your high school wear. List four questions you would ask your friends to discover why a different brand of jeans is popular in their state.

Online Action! Go to *marketingessentials.glencoe.com/u9/ad* for an extended activity.

1 ANALYSIS
SWOT
Economic
Socio-Cultural
Technological
Competitive

2 STRATEGY
Promotion
Place
Price
Product

3 IMPLEMENTATION
Organization
Management
Staffing

4 BUDGET
Cost of Sales
Cost of Promotion
Incomes and Expenses

5 CONTROL
Evaluation
Performance Measures
Performance Analysis

In this unit

Foundations of Marketing
- Business, Management, Entrepreneurship

Functions of Marketing
- Marketing Information Management

CHAPTER 28
Marketing Research

Chapter Objectives

After reading this chapter, you should be able to:

- Describe the purpose of marketing research
- Explain the characteristics and purposes of a marketing information system
- Identify procedures for gathering information using technology
- Identify the methods of conducting marketing research
- Discuss trends and limitations in marketing research

GUIDE TO THE PHOTO

Market Talk Market research is the process of obtaining the information needed to make sound marketing decisions. A well-known market research company is Nielsen Media Research. The company specializes in television audience research. In other words, Nielsen finds out who watches what show, where, and when. The heart of the company's national ratings is the Nielsen People Meter, an electronic device placed on television sets in some 5,100 U.S. households.

Quick Think Name two ways the Nielsen ratings can be used in marketing.

THE DECA CONNECTION

Performance indicators represent key skills and knowledge. Relating them to the concepts explained in this chapter is your key to success in DECA events.

These acronyms represent DECA events that involve knowledge of concepts in this chapter.

AAAL	**FMAL**	**MMS**	**TMDM***
AAML*	**FMDM**	**QSRM***	**TSE**
ADC	**FMML***	**RMAL**	**VPM**
BSM	**FSRM***	**RMML***	
EMDM	**HMDM***	**SMDM**	

In all these DECA events you should be able to follow these performance indicators:

- Describe the need for marketing information
- Explain the nature and scope of the marketing-information management function
- Explain the role of ethics in marketing-information management
- Explain the nature of marketing research in a marketing-information management system
- Explain the use of databases in organizing marketing data
- Design a database for information analysis
- Use a database for information analysis

All the events with an asterisk (*) also include this performance indicator:

- Describe information helpful to retailers in planning

Some events include additional performance indicators. These are:

BSM/SMDM	Identify research methods used to evaluate service quality
EMDM	Explain privacy issues in e-commerce
	Explain the nature of data mining

DECA PREP

Check your understanding of DECA performance indicators with the DECA activity in this chapter's review. For more information and DECA Prep practice, go to *marketingessentials.glencoe.com/28/DECA*

OBJECTIVES

- Describe the purpose of marketing research
- Explain the characteristics and purposes of a marketing information system
- Identify procedures for gathering information using technology

KEY TERMS

- marketing research
- marketing information system
- database marketing
- database

Marketing Information Systems

BEFORE YOU READ

Predict List some reasons why you think that some new businesses have almost immediate success while others fail miserably.

THE MAIN IDEA

Successful companies must be able to understand the needs and wants of customers. Marketing research provides information to help a business plan, solve problems, and make decisions regarding its products and services.

STUDY ORGANIZER

Use a chart like the one below to take notes about the main concepts in this section.

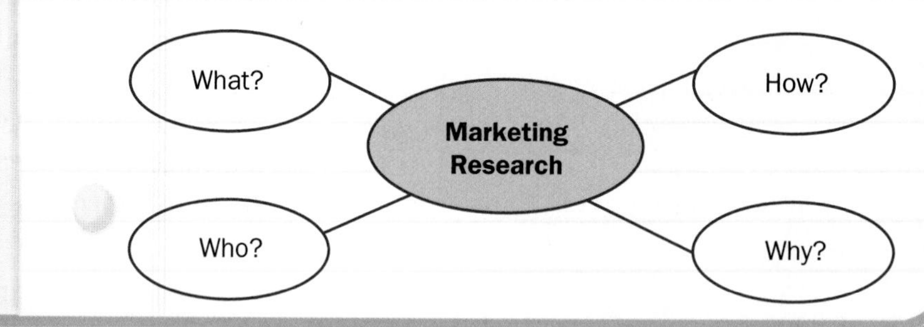

Analysis Compare and contrast the terms *market* and *marketing research.*

Defining Marketing Research

One of the largest American sports shoe manufacturers wants to introduce its new, best-selling shoe in overseas markets. A famous basketball player in the United States wears the shoe and the ad shows him shooting hoops in locations around the world. The commercial is aired in three European countries, translated into each country's official language. However, the sales are disappointingly low. What went wrong?

Even though the ad has a global focus, it does not have global appeal, at least not in Europe. Careful marketing research would have shown that basketball is not as popular in Europe as it is in the United States. Few people purchased the shoe because there were few people who could relate to the sport associated with the product.

According to the Marketing Research Association, **marketing research** involves the process and methods used to gather information, analyze it, and report findings related to marketing goods and services. Information obtained through marketing research is used to identify marketing opportunities, solve marketing problems, implement marketing plans, and monitor marketing performance.

Marketing research is most often used by companies to:

- Determine consumers' attitudes and preferences
- Test product features
- Determine market size and growth potential
- Learn about competitive products
- Determine buying cycles
- Understand how the company is perceived by the public

Before developing a product, marketers can conduct research to determine the type of product customers want. The research can minimize potential losses when introducing the new product. Consumers accept only one out of every ten new products introduced into the marketplace; therefore, gaining information about consumer likes and dislikes is important.

Why Is Marketing Research Important?

Businesses that do not pay attention to what consumers are buying and why are likely to make costly marketing mistakes.

The information obtained from research helps businesses increase sales and profits. Research answers questions about what products to produce, at what price to sell the products, who will buy the products, and how the products will be promoted.

Research also helps businesses solve marketing problems and gauge the potential of new ideas. For example, Stouffer's spent almost 13 years doing marketing research and development before starting its Lean Cuisine product line. Stouffer's studied consumers' interest in health and dieting. They conducted consumer panels to find out what dieters liked and disliked about diet meals. Using the information, the company developed its product, tested its package design, and held pilot sales of the product in several large cities before national distribution. The product was a tremendous success, with over $125 million in sales after the first year of national distribution.

Research also helps a company keep track of what is happening with its current markets. Through research, a company can determine its major competitors, what its competitors are offering, which products consumers prefer, and how satisfied customers are with its product.

Who Uses Marketing Research?

Small businesses usually do not have separate research specialists or departments. There, marketing research is done informally by the owners, managers, or employees, or they hire outside service providers who specialize in market research. Larger companies often have in-house research departments and marketing personnel to plan and conduct marketing research. But even larger companies sometimes contract with outside research companies because of their specialized expertise. It is estimated that $6.2 billion was spent in 2001 on marketing research conducted in the United States by the largest 180 marketing research firms and in-house groups.

Trade associations representing various manufacturers, wholesalers, and retailers conduct marketing research. Industry trade associations, such as the National Retail Federation, collect

A MATTER OF ETHICS

Conducting Research

Fun Foods has hired Manuel's marketing firm to learn what 20- to 30-year-old women want in a nutrition bar. Manuel's bosses have written a 20-minute marketing survey and sent him and his colleague, Jason, to the mall to interview young women. But when Manuel tells shoppers how long the survey will take, they don't want to participate.

Misleading Respondents

Jason has had no trouble finding women to interview. When they take their lunch break, Manuel asks Jason the secret of his success. Jason says, "I say the survey will take only five minutes. When they realize more than ten minutes have gone by and they look uneasy, I tell them we're almost done."

THINKING ETHICALLY

Is Jason's behavior ethical? If Manuel decides to keep telling the truth, what should he do when he and Jason submit their results to their bosses?

Online Action!

Go to *marketingessentials.glencoe.com/28/ethics* to find an activity about ethics and marketing research.

industry data to help their members understand the markets for their products.

Nonprofit organizations, such as hospitals, conduct patient satisfaction surveys to improve on programs and services.

Marketing Information Systems

The data collected in marketing research must be sorted and stored so that the results can be put to good use. Many businesses have sophisticated marketing information systems to organize, collect, and store marketing research data for future decisions. A **marketing information system** is a set of procedures and methods that regularly generates, stores, analyzes, and distributes information for use in making marketing and other business decisions. Most marketing information systems rely heavily on data about current customers, overall product sales reports, and inventory levels. Marketers use marketing information systems in many ways, including designing advertising campaigns, developing promotional plans, and selling directly to customers. Data that should be part of a marketing information system include:

- Customer profile data, such as the results of previous marketing studies regarding buying behavior, shopping patterns, customer demographics, and lifestyles research
- Company records, such as sales results, expenses, supplier data, and production schedules
- Competitors' records, such as their prices, products, and market share
- Government data, such as price trends, new regulations and laws, and future projections for the economy
- Marketing research reports that are produced and sold by research firms

Database Marketing

Information technologies have made the collection and analysis of data for decision making much easier. **Database marketing**, or customer relationship management (CRM), is a process of designing, creating, and managing customer lists. These customer lists contain information about individuals' characteristics and transactions with a business. Customer lists are developed from customer touch points such as face-to-face sales, direct-mail responses, telephone or e-mail purchases, service requests, or Web site visits. Marketing lists can also be obtained through third-party companies that specialize in selling databases of names and addresses to specific markets.

Once a customer list is developed, it can be used for locating, selecting, and targeting customers with special programs and services.

Ways To Collect Data

Many businesses create special programs to assist in data collection by furnishing "valued customer cards," which add the customer's identity to the purchase. Customers complete an application, which entitles them to special rewards. Over time, the store collects data on customer purchases and analyzes it to better understand household demographics, lifestyles, and purchase behavior.

Consumer Databases

Information about consumers and their buying habits are stored in computer databases. A **database** is a collection of related information about a specific topic. For example, REI, an outdoor recreational products retailer, has a database of people to whom it sends its catalogs. American Express maintains a database of its card members and their addresses, plus what they buy, where they buy it, where they eat out, and how much money they spend. The company uses the information to send their card members special offers on products, hotels, restaurants, and travel.

Many companies that collect information about their customers often sell that information to others. Banks that provide mortgage loans often share the names and addresses of the borrowers with insurance companies that then send information about mortgage insurance to the borrower. This exchange of information among businesses has led to complaints of invasion of privacy.

Consumer Privacy

The government has created regulations regarding protecting the privacy of consumers. Banks now offer detailed privacy statements that ensure the protection of clients' personal information. Other businesses offer their clients the option of being added to mailing lists, instead of automatically making their contact information available.

28.1 AFTER YOU READ

Reviewing Key Terms and Concepts

1. Why is marketing research important?
2. Besides individual businesses, who else conducts marketing research?
3. What is a marketing information system?

Integrating Academic Skills

Math

4. According to the European Society for Opinion and Marketing Research, $16 billion was spent on marketing research in 2003. The world's top 25 marketing research companies had total revenues of $10.5 billion. What percentage of the overall research dollars does this represent?

Communication

5. Use the Internet, school media center, or local library to investigate the concept of customer relationship management (CRM). Write a one-page paper on the benefits of business-to-consumer relationships and the specific strategies that can be used to establish them.

@ Online Action!

Check your answers at *marketingessentials.glencoe.com/28/read*

SECTION 28.2

Types, Trends, and Limitations of Marketing Research

OBJECTIVES

- Identify the methods of conducting marketing research
- Discuss trends and limitations in marketing research

KEY TERMS

- quantitative research
- qualitative research
- attitude research
- market intelligence
- media research
- product research

READ and STUDY

BEFORE YOU READ

Predict Many new products are introduced to the marketplace every year. What do you think would happen if marketing research were not used in product development?

THE MAIN IDEA

Using more than one type of research often improves a business's ability to solve problems and successfully market a product.

STUDY ORGANIZER

Use a chart like the one below to note the differences between quantitative and qualitative research.

Predict What kinds of marketing research do successful businesses conduct?

Types of Marketing Research

The type of research businesses conduct depends on the problem that they are trying to solve. **Quantitative research** answers questions that start with "how many" or "how much." This type of research usually gathers information from large numbers of people. Quantitative research relies heavily on surveys or questionnaires to obtain information.

Qualitative research focuses on smaller numbers of people (usually fewer than 100) and tries to answer questions about "why" or "how." This type of research relies heavily on in-depth interviews, rather than surveys that have been constructed ahead of time. Most marketing research efforts combine both quantitative and qualitative methods. (See Figure 28.1 for a breakdown of money typically spent on market research in the United States.)

Research is not limited to products; it is also conducted to answer questions about attitudes and behaviors, market segments, advertising media, brands, prices, employees, and every other aspect of marketing. (See Figure 28.2.)

Attitude Research

Attitude research, also known as opinion research, is designed to obtain information on how people feel about certain products, services, companies, or ideas. Satisfaction studies conducted by mail surveys or telephone interviews are the most common ways to get at individuals' opinions. Customers are usually asked to rate "how satisfied" they are with a product or service they purchased or used.

Opinion polls are another example of attitude research. The Gallup Organization conducts opinion polls on politics, elections, business and the economy, social issues, and public policy. Based on random samples of the population, opinion poll results can be generalized to the entire population. A business considering a major expansion might be interested in the attitude of the general population toward the economy.

Consumer panels, also called focus groups, are groups of people who are questioned to provide information on research issues.

Market Intelligence

Market intelligence is concerned with the size and location of a market, the competition, and the segmentation within the market for a particular product or service. Existing market data and new research are used to assemble a profile of present and potential customers, competitors, and the overall industry. Market intelligence helps define potential

Figure 28.1 U.S. Market Research Spending by Category

• **How Marketing Research Dollars Are Spent** In 2001, syndicated spending represented the largest segment of U.S. marketing research expenditures.

What type of research is represented by the survey segment in this figure?

Segment	Annual Spending ($ million)	Percent of Total	Percent Increase Over Previous Year
Qualitative	1,120	18.2	+5.2
Syndicated	2,573	41.8	+9.2
Survey	2,466	40.0	–1.4

Source: *Marketing News Supplement,* June 11, 2002

Go to *marketingessentials.glencoe.com/28/figure/1* to find a project on marketing research spending.

Figure 28.2 Types of Marketing Research

• **What Do Marketers Need to Know?** Marketing research covers all the activities used to gather, analyze, and report information related to marketing. This broad field can be broken down by types of research and defined by the purpose of the research.

How do you find out the kind of marketing information you need to know?

ATTITUDE AND OPINION RESEARCH

Marketers conduct this type of research to discover how people feel about their products, services, or ideas. Satisfaction surveys, such as those sent after a visit to the hospital, and opinion polls, such as those used by political campaigns, are examples of this type of research.

MARKET INTELLIGENCE

Research is used to gather information about an existing or potential market for market intelligence. It defines the size, location, and makeup of the market. This type of research is often done before a new product launch. It is used to guide the marketing efforts for the new product.

MEDIA RESEARCH

This type of research is used to determine the effectiveness of the various media to advertise a good or service. It can be conducted before or after a media campaign.

PRODUCT RESEARCH

This type of research is used to gather information about a product's design, packaging, and usage. It is used to discover how customers react to a new product design or packaging. It can also be used to gather information about how a competing product is designed and packaged.

Online Action! **Go to *marketingessentials.glencoe.com/28/figure/2* to find a project on types of marketing research.**

target markets for a particular product or service and how to reach potential customers.

A company's existing and projected sales data are part of market intelligence. Sales data help businesses project the potential sales for a product and anticipate problems related to future sales. Sales trends for various products may also be compared to determine whether a product's sales are increasing or declining.

Sales Forecasting

Sales forecasting is an attempt to estimate the future sales of an existing product. A total estimate of a market is calculated, company and competitor sales are analyzed, and then an individual share is estimated for a business.

The share that is assigned to a business is called its market share or sales penetration of

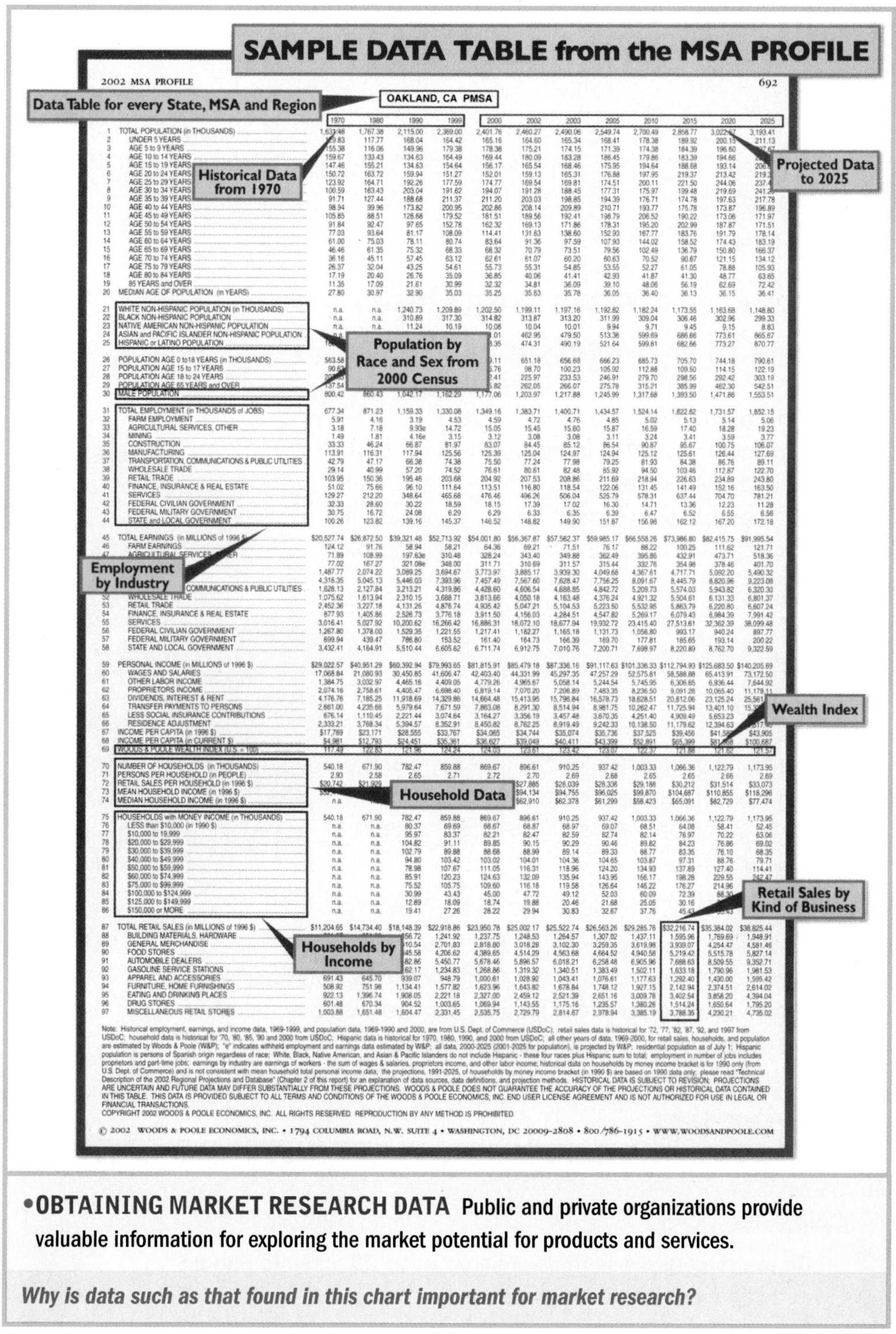

•OBTAINING MARKET RESEARCH DATA Public and private organizations provide valuable information for exploring the market potential for products and services.

Why is data such as that found in this chart important for market research?

the market. Based on its research findings, the business can then try to increase its market share through changes in the product, pricing, promotion, or distribution strategies.

Market share estimation and market segmentation research studies are used for new products and services in both consumer and industrial markets. The goal of market share and segmentation studies is to investigate the potential markets for new products and to define characteristics of the target market.

Specialized software programs can assist with forecasting. These computer programs analyze current market data and use this information to predict future sales.

Economic Forecasting

Economic forecasting is an attempt to predict the future economic conditions of a city, a region, a country, or other part of the world. This research requires extensive knowledge of economic statistics and trend indicators.

Case Study

Ad Agency Launches a Video Game Unit

Young & Rubicam, a large, full-service advertising agency, teamed up with Bounce, an event marketing group, in 2004 to start a video game promotional unit called Bounce Interactive Gaming (BIG).

Ad agencies became more interested in video games in 2003, when Nielsen data showed that men aged 18 to 34—an appealing demographic group for advertisers—were watching less prime-time TV. And Jupiter Research expects that, by 2009, 63 million people in the U.S. will spend at least five hours a week playing video games.

Target Audience

BIG markets products to fans of video games. The company signs deals with video game makers to embed products in the games in the form of a brand of beverage or car, for example. It also hosts video game events sponsored by its products. These events include tournaments for top players or live-satellite feeds to watch tournaments in action.

Captive Audience

Advertising through video games has advantages over advertising on TV. Gamers stay in the room during the course of the game, unlike TV watchers, who sometimes leave the room during commercial breaks. Gamers keep their attention focused on the screen, while TV watchers can lose their concentration. A gamer might also like a product just because it is used by the gamer's onscreen character.

THINK STRATEGICALLY

What are some strategic reasons for a large full-service advertising agency to establish a video game promotional unit?

@ Online Action!

Go to *marketingessentials.glencoe.com/28/case* to find an activity about advertising and market research.

Several federal agencies collect information on key economic indicators, such as new building construction, inflation rates, money supply, and consumer and producer price indexes. Most businesses rely on government data to predict economic conditions, and then they adjust their business activities accordingly.

Businesses use research on general economic conditions to help plan for long-range expansion. This research helps to determine whether to cut costs when unfavorable economic conditions, such as higher interest rates or raw materials costs, are predicted.

Media Research

Media research, also known as advertising research, focuses on issues of media effectiveness, selection, frequency, and ratings. Businesses often conduct research to determine which media are most effective for getting an advertising message to a particular market.

Media research studies brand awareness, advertising recall, brand image, effectiveness of advertising copy, and audience size for a particular type of advertising.

Media Advertising Measures

Important statistics for media measurement include audience, frequency, reach, and ratings. Audience is the number of homes or people exposed to a particular advertising medium. Frequency is the number of times a viewer in the audience sees or hears an ad. Reach is the percentage of the target audience that will see or hear an ad at least once, while ratings are the total number of audience impressions delivered over a set period of time.

To obtain these important media advertising measures, businesses often request information from the print, broadcast, and electronic media of interest to them. In most cases, the information received would include a rate card listing the advertising costs, its circulation or viewership figures, deadline dates, and other requirements for submission of an advertisement. Other information might

MARKET TECH

A New Local Rating System

Nielsen Media Research, Inc. is replacing all of its paper-based viewer diaries with a sample of viewers that use people meters in local television markets.

Local People Meter

People meters automatically track viewing as people change channels. Since 1987, the company has used the method to determine national television ratings. Now, it is establishing a similar system for local television ratings. While the old system provided ratings data only four times a year, the new local ratings will be available on a nightly basis. The new system will allow Nielsen to give demographic data by age, race, and gender on a local television market.

Equal Measurement?

The system is not without controversy. Some politicians and the National Minority Business Council say the new system is flawed because it undercounts minority groups. However, Nielsen says that 21.6 percent of African Americans are being measured under the new rating system, compared to 19 percent with the old system.

THINK LIKE A MARKETER

Why are local television ratings important?

Online Action!

Go to *marketingessentials.glencoe.com/28/tech* to find an activity about technology and market research.

concern the age, income, interests, hobbies, occupations, and attitudes of readers, subscribers, or viewers. Another way to measure advertising research on the various media is to subscribe to *Standard Rate and Data Service* (SRDS), which publishes rates and data for the advertising industry.

Researching Print Advertisements

Marketing researchers can use different techniques to get people's reactions to an advertisement. To determine the ad's effectiveness, readers are asked about the extent to which they noticed the ad, remembered it, and associated it with the advertised brand. The ad is also measured on its ability to change the consumer's beliefs, attitudes, or intended behavior. Using consumer panels is another technique for measuring print advertising effectiveness.

Readership in print media is measured by surveys or estimated by circulation. The Audit Bureau of Circulations provides circulation data on more than 1,500 daily and weekly newspapers and 1,000 periodicals. Mediamark Research and Simmons Market Research Bureau provide audience data. They conduct recent reading studies to see if participants can recall a magazine logotype, have read the magazine, and can remember where they read it during in the past month.

Researching Broadcast Media

Most broadcast ad testing research is done on television commercials. Testing research can use quantitative or qualitative research techniques, such as personal interviews, theater tests, in-home testing, or focus groups, to get reaction to planned TV advertisements.

Nielsen Media Research, Inc. provides audience measurement information for the television industry. Nielsen estimates the audience by measuring the viewing habits of 13,000 people in 5,000 homes. Nielsen's measurement information is recorded by "people meters" on TV sets, VCRs, cable boxes, and satellite dishes that automatically monitor program viewing. Nielsen counts the number of viewers in meter-equipped households to get the number of households using TV, the share of the audience that is tuned to a particular station, and the rating, or percentage of viewers, for a particular television program at a particular time. Broadcast and cable network providers, program developers, distributors, and advertisers use this information to decide on which television programs to advertise.

The Arbitron Ratings Company assembles important data on radio advertising. Arbitron produces radio audience measurements and sells software that analyzes advertising expenditure data. Continuous audience measurement in 267 local markets serving 2,300 radio stations makes it the largest radio audience service in the world. Arbitron contacts more than two million consumers a year and collects more than one million diaries to compile its radio station rating reports. Diaries are records on which people report such viewer data as who is watching or listening to a station and what programs are tuned in.

Using the Internet

The effectiveness of Internet advertising is often measured with tracking studies. Tracking studies can be either Web-centric or user-centric. The Web-centric method logs the total number of people who have visited a Web site and stores the results on the Internet provider's network. The user-centric method involves metering software in a sample household or business that tracks computer usage and Web sites that are visited. The information gained from user-centric tracking can be compiled and analyzed to get an audience profile for a certain Web site.

Product Research

Product research centers on evaluating product design, package design, product usage, and consumer acceptance of new and existing products. Many new products and their packages are designed, tested, changed, and introduced each year. Product research is also conducted to collect information about competitive products. Concept testing is often used in the early stages of product development (see Chapter 30). Concept testing, product positioning, and pricing studies are frequently done with focus groups or in-depth interviews to get initial consumer reaction to a product or service idea.

Trends in Marketing Research

The nature and scope of marketing research is rapidly changing to keep pace with a changing marketplace. The trend toward a global marketplace means increased international competition for U.S. companies, which must improve or change products frequently to hold on to their customers. In this environment, product quality and customer satisfaction are the keys to business success. Research that measures these qualities has become the fastest growing form of marketing research.

Another important trend is the use of both internal and external information in managing a business. Total quality management (TQM) programs place a premium on gathering and using database research in improving business operations.

Limitations of Marketing Research

The amount of information that can be gathered is limited by the amount of money and time a company can afford to spend on the equipment and by the number of personnel needed to conduct the research.

Marketing research information also has its limitations. Customers in a test market situation may say they want a particular product, but there is no guarantee they will actually buy the product when it is sold.

28.2 AFTER YOU READ

Reviewing Key Terms and Concepts

1. What are the two types of marketing research?
2. What are the four major areas within marketing research?
3. List at least two trends facing marketing researchers today.

Integrating Academic Skills

Math

4. Assume that you are planning to purchase an exercise and fitness center targeted to women aged 21 to 49 in your city. By doing market research using results from the Consumer Expenditure Surveys and the U.S. Census Bureau, you learn that 1,550 households in your target market spend $475 a year on fitness and recreation. There is one other fitness center that serves 25 percent of your target market. What would be your annual sales forecast for the center?

Geography

5. Investigate a country of your choice and develop a two-page paper on its location, population demographics, and its culture. As part of your report, indicate recommendations for conducting marketing research in the country.

Check your answers at *marketingessentials.glencoe.com/28/read*

CAREERS IN MARKETING

MICHELLE DAY
SENIOR RESEARCH ANALYST
THE STEVENSON COMPANY

What do you do at work?
Clients and I work together to develop a survey tool to question current or potential customers. We implement this survey and analyze the results to gain a better understanding of customers' opinions of the question at hand. This information is compiled into a format that is presented to clients, who are then able to meet the needs of their customers and make better business decisions based on the results.

What skills are most important to you?
Computer skills and communication skills are critical to this job. Other important skills are analyzing, organizing, and time management. Communication is also very important, both effective oral communication with the client to understand their questions and objectives, and written communication to draft the surveys and present the results to the client in a clear and logical format.

What is your key to success?
Both continuing to learn and receiving constructive criticism have helped me succeed in my job. I have continued to learn by completing an MBA, attending applicable training seminars, and asking questions of those who are more experienced than I am. I welcome constructive criticism from these more experienced professionals, who can help me improve upon the skills I have.

Aptitudes, Abilities, and Skills

Computer skills, communication skills, time management, an analytical mind

Education and Training

Degrees in marketing, communication, or general business are helpful.

Career Path

A successful career path can begin with an assistant position in a marketing department, and continue with responsibilities as market research data analyst.

THINKING CRITICALLY

How are market surveys useful to a business?

Online Action!

Go to *marketingessentials.glencoe.com/28/careers* for a career-related activity.

CHAPTER 28 REVIEW

FOCUS on KEY POINTS

SECTION 28.1

- Marketing research involves the marketing function that links the consumer, customer, and public to the marketer through information. Marketing information is used to identify marketing opportunities, solve marketing problems, implement marketing plans, and monitor marketing performance. A marketing information system is a set of procedures and methods that regularly generates, stores, analyzes, and distributes marketing information for use in making marketing decisions.

SECTION 28.2

- Marketing research is usually divided into two broad types of research: quantitative and qualitative. Marketing research involves the process and methods used to gather information, analyze it, and report findings related to marketing goods and services. The nature and scope of marketing research are rapidly changing to keep pace with a changing marketplace. Marketing research information provides much information but does have limitations.

REVIEW VOCABULARY

Write each of the following vocabulary terms on the front of a 5" × 8" index card with the correct definition on the reverse. Review the terms and definitions by quizzing another marketing student.

1. marketing research (p. 593)
2. marketing information system (p. 594)
3. database marketing (p. 594)
4. database (p. 595)
5. quantitative research (p. 596)
6. qualitative research (p. 597)
7. attitude research (p. 597)
8. market intelligence (p. 597)
9. media research (p. 601)
10. product research (p. 602)

REVIEW FACTS and IDEAS

11. What is marketing research? (28.1)
12. What is the primary function of a marketing information system? (28.1)
13. What is a marketing database? (28.1)
14. How does quantitative research differ from qualitative research? (28.2)
15. What is attitude research? (28.2)
16. What is market intelligence? (28.2)
17. Why do businesses conduct media research? (28.2)
18. Give an example of one research technique used for new product development and one for product usage research. (28.2)
19. Name one trend and one limitation of marketing research. (28.2)

BUILD SKILLS

20. Workplace Skills

Human Relations You have a part-time job in the marketing research department of a large corporation. You and three coworkers are gathering information through mailed surveys. Your supervisor wants each of you to complete at least 30 surveys a day, which can be difficult. One coworker makes changes to incomplete or missing responses on some surveys that have been returned. What should you do?

21. Technology Applications

Analyzing International Trends Use presentation software to present an oral report on the international trends affecting marketing research efforts in the pharmaceuticals market.

22. Math Practice

The Cost of Direct Mail Research Assume that your company plans to send a marketing questionnaire to 30 percent of the names on a mailing list of 5,000 people. The mailing list was purchased from another company for $0.30 per name. Each questionnaire costs $0.10 to print; mailing costs are $0.36 (including the envelope and return envelope) each; and the cost of writing the questionnaire, analyzing the information, and preparing the report is $15,000. What is the total cost?

DEVELOP CRITICAL THINKING

23. Press Review

Review current business publications such as the *Wall Street Journal, Business Week, Forbes, Money, Advertising Age, Brandweek,* and *Sales & Marketing Management.* Find one current research activity and write a one-page report on the nature and scope of the research activity.

24. Marketing Across the Planet

Select a country and an industry or product that interests you. Research this industry or this product in the country of your choice and in the United States, consider how it is marketed, who the target market is, whether there is any import or export exchange. Take notes as you conduct research on the Internet and at the library. Be ready to explain your answer and provide examples. How has the global economy affected marketing research?

APPLY CONCEPTS

25. Identifying Market Factors

Use the Internet to find the U.S. Census Bureau Web site and research your city or state's population, income, education, trading area, and purchasing power. Consult city or state offices for additional market information. For example, you may contact your area's chamber of commerce.

Activity Using presentation software, create an oral report highlighting these marketing factors.

26. Evaluating Research Agencies

Use the Internet to investigate companies that provide customer research, online database searches, and information-brokering services.

Activity Identify four questions that you would ask of a large research agency before you would use its services for media research.

NET SAVVY

27. Researching Market Researchers

Visit the Web site for the American Marketing Association to find Marketing Research Services. Investigate one of the listed companies.

Develop a company profile in 100 to 150 words, describing the company's history, number of employees, and the marketing research that it conducts.

THE DECA CONNECTION

An Association of Marketing Students

Role Play: Marketing Research

Situation You are to assume the role of assistant manager of a small hardware store. The store's sales have been steady, but not growing at the rate they should. The store's owner (judge) is concerned about the lack of sales growth and has asked you for some ideas about how to remedy this situation.

Activity You are to suggest some ways to determine the solution to the lack of sales growth and make your suggestions to the hardware store's owner (judge).

Evaluation You will be evaluated on how well you meet the following performance indicators:

- Describe the need for marketing information
- Assess marketing-information needs
- Identify information monitored for marketing decision making
- Demonstrate interest and enthusiasm
- Address people properly

@ Online Action!

For more information and DECA Prep practice, go to *marketingessentials.glencoe.com/28/DECA*

CHAPTER 29

Conducting Marketing Research

Chapter Objectives

After reading this chapter, you should be able to:

- Explain the steps in designing and conducting marketing research
- Compare primary and secondary data
- Collect and interpret marketing information
- Identify the elements in a marketing research report
- Design a marketing research survey
- Administer a marketing research survey

GUIDE TO THE PHOTO

Market Talk Companies need to find out who their customers are, what they need or want, their opinions, and how much they spend on what. There are many ways of doing market research.

Quick Think Why do you think companies conduct marketing research and testing in different markets?

THE  CONNECTION

Performance indicators represent key skills and knowledge. Relating them to the concepts explained in this chapter is your key to success in DECA events. These acronyms represent DECA events that involve knowledge of concepts in this chapter.

AAAL	**FMAL**	**MMS**	**TMDM***
AAML	**FMDM**	**QSRM**	**TSE**
ADC	**FMML**	**RMAL**	**VPM**
BSM	**FSRM**	**RMML**	
EMDM	**HMDM***	**SMDM**	

In all these DECA events you should be able to follow these performance indicators:

- Identify information monitored for marketing decision making
- Describe sources of secondary data
- Search the Internet for marketing information
- Monitor internal records for marketing information
- Collect marketing information from others
- Conduct an environmental scan to obtain marketing information
- Describe the use of technology in the marketing-information management function
- Describe techniques for processing marketing information
- Interpret descriptive statistics for marketing decision making
- Write marketing reports
- Present report findings and recommendations

Events with an asterisk (*) include this performance indicator: Complete a property analysis. **HMDM** and **FMDM** also include additional performance indicators: Explain the concept of product in the hospitality industry and in the financial services industry respectively.

DECA PREP

Check your understanding of DECA performance indicators with the DECA activity in this chapter's review. For more information and DECA Prep practice, go to *marketingessentials .glencoe.com/29/DECA*

The Marketing Research Process

OBJECTIVES

- Explain the steps in designing and conducting marketing research
- Compare primary and secondary data
- Collect and interpret marketing information
- Identify the elements in a marketing research report

KEY TERMS

- problem definition
- primary data
- secondary data
- survey method
- sample
- observation method
- point-of-sale research
- experimental method
- data analysis

READ and STUDY

BEFORE YOU READ

Predict Why do you think that an organized process is necessary to conduct marketing research?

THE MAIN IDEA

Businesses that want to increase their customer base must have information about the attitudes and behaviors of current and prospective customers. Marketing research can provide insight for strategies that will increase sales and profits.

STUDY ORGANIZER

Construct a flow chart like the one below to record the steps in conducting marketing research.

The Marketing Research Process

Step 1: Define the Problem

WHILE YOU READ

Predict Consider the sequence of steps in marketing research. What would happen if one of the steps were omitted?

The Marketing Research Process

The five steps that a business follows when conducting marketing research are defining the problem, obtaining data, analyzing the data, recommending solutions, and applying the results. Each step is performed sequentially to arrive at solutions to a problem or research issue. Figure 29.1 provides more details about each step in the research process.

Figure 29.1 The Marketing Research Process

• Five Steps Marketing research helps businesses find solutions to problems. There are five steps in the marketing research process, beginning with defining the problem or research issue and ending with applying the results of the research. Following the steps in sequence is important, since each step depends on the steps that preceded it.

What can researchers do after the data are analyzed?

1 DEFINING THE PROBLEM

The problem or research issue is identified and goals are set to solve the problem.

2 OBTAINING DATA

Researchers obtain data from primary and secondary sources.

3 ANALYZING DATA

Researchers compile, analyze, and interpret the data.

4 RECOMMENDING SOLUTIONS

Researchers come up with potential solutions to the problem and present them in a report.

5 APPLYING THE RESULTS

The research results are put into action.

Online Action!

Go to *marketingessentials.glencoe.com/29/figure/1* to find a project on the marketing research process.

Step 1: Defining the Problem

The most difficult step in the marketing research process is defining the problem. **Problem definition** occurs when a business clearly identifies a problem and what is needed to solve it. That is, the business identifies a research question and the information that is necessary to answer it.

Take, for example, a convention and resort center that wants to know if its staff, services, and facilities are meeting the needs of its guests. The business needs this information so that it can continually improve its services as a resort and convention destination.

With the problem defined, the researcher can create objectives for the study that will help answer the research problem. Objectives might include: determine how satisfied different categories of guests are with reservation procedures, accommodations, guest services, and meeting and recreational facilities.

Objectives are used to develop the actual questions that will be included in the research instrument. You will learn more about writing questions later in this chapter. For now you simply need to know that objectives and questions must correlate with one another. Here are two examples:

- **Objective:** Determine guest satisfaction with facilities.
  Question: On a scale of 1 to 5, with 1 being poor and 5 being excellent, how would you rate the following resort facilities? (list of facilities)
- **Objective:** Determine if vacationers and convention-goers differ in levels of satisfaction with the resort and convention center.
  Question: What was the primary purpose of your visit?

This question is necessary so that ratings by guest type can be analyzed separately. If this question was not included in the research instrument, the above objective could not be accomplished.

Because money and time are limited, each business has to determine which problems and issues are the most important to address at a given time.

Step 2: Obtaining Data

The second step in the marketing research process is obtaining data. During this second step, data are collected and examined in terms of the problem or problems being studied.

The word *data* means facts. There are two types of data used in marketing research: primary and secondary. **Primary data** are data obtained for the first time and used specifically for the particular problem or issue under study. **Secondary data** have already been collected for some purpose other than the current study. Secondary data are less expensive to collect than primary data. Therefore, it is most cost effective for a company to decide what secondary data it can use before collecting any primary data.

How Secondary Data Are Obtained

Secondary data are obtained from both internal sources (sources within the company) and external sources (sources outside the company). An excellent source of internal secondary data is the marketing information system of a business. As explained in Chapter 28, a marketing information system is an internal method of getting data used to measure monthly sales, determine the geographic distribution of customers, track customer buying patterns, and identify popular items on the market. Secondary data are most often collected in the following ways:

Internet Sources

The Internet has increased the availability of secondary data from a variety of sources. Since most companies have a Web address, some secondary information is available for free through a company's home page. A company's description of its products, services offered, locations, sales revenue, number of employees, product specifications, and pricing is often available. But since Web site information is used primarily for promotional

NET MARKETING

Paying Your Bills Online

One in four American households now pays bills online each month. Online bill pay makes paying bills quick and convenient. Some services even allow users to establish their own payment schedule.

There are two approaches to Internet bill payment. Each month a person may go to a specific company's Web site and pay a particular bill, such as the water bill. This usually means making stops at the Web sites of several companies.

One-Stop Bill Pay

The other method uses consolidation. Banks, credit card companies, and portals such as Yahoo, MSN, and Quicken let consumers pay multiple bills in one place. Most portals charge a monthly fee. AOL Bill Pay is an exception: America Online subscribers can make Internet bill payments for free.

AOL does not act as a payment intermediary, but it provides links to the Web sites of each company, where transactions take place directly between the consumer and merchant. AOL says its research shows that most people prefer to make payments at a merchant's Web site, because they get faster credit for last-minute payments. Payments handled by an intermediary can take five days or longer to clear.

THINK LIKE A MARKETER

Why is AOL offering a free online bill paying service, rather than charging for the service?

Online Action!

Go to *marketingessentials.glencoe.com/29/net* to find an activity about the Internet and marketing research.

purposes, all information should be verified through other, more objective sources.

Digital dossiers, which provide company profiles on public corporations, income statements, and balance sheets, are also available online. These reports and databases can be purchased for a fee from business clearinghouses, such as Hoover's Online, Factiva, Standard and Poor's NetAdvantage, LexisNexis, and Mergent Online.

U.S. and State Government Sources

State departments of commerce and small business development centers assist with business and economic development activities and can also provide useful information.

Data collected by U.S. government agencies regarding population demographics, specific markets, industries, products, economic news, export information, and legislative trends can be accessed on the Internet for free or for a nominal cost. FedWorld and the Federal Web Locator are two Web directories with links to most government Web sites that provide such data. The Small Business Administration, U.S. Department of Commerce, U.S. Census Bureau, U.S. Securities and Exchange Commission, and the Bureau of Labor Statistics can also be excellent sources for secondary data.

Publications such as the *Census of the Population* and the *Statistical Abstract of the United States* contain hundreds of tables, graphs, and charts that can be useful when analyzing information, such as income, age, and family size, in areas as small in size as zip codes.

Specialized Research Companies

An active and growing number of specialized research companies, or syndicated services, also offer secondary data for business needs.

Specialized companies sell demographic data, five-year forecasts, consumer purchase information, business data, census information, and consumer classification reports to businesses. Syndicated services make this data available in print and electronic formats.

An example is Mediamark Research, Inc. (MRI), which provides comprehensive demographic, lifestyle, product usage, and exposure data to all forms of advertising media. MRI is the nation's leading producer of multimedia audience research for advertisers, agencies, and magazines. The company also provides research in consumer marketing, brand loyalty, promotional opportunities, and trade marketing services, as well as many other types of market research services.

Business Publications and Trade Organizations

Secondary data can also be obtained in business publications such as *Forbes, BusinessWeek,* the *Wall Street Journal,* and *Sales & Marketing Management.* National and statewide trade associations often publish secondary data in articles, reports, and books.

Examples of trade associations for marketing research include the Advertising Research Foundation, American Association for Public Opinion Research, American Marketing Association, Council of American Survey Research Organizations, and the Marketing Research Association. Check the *Small Business Sourcebook* or the *Encyclopedia of Business Information Sources* to identify major books, trade journals, and organizations for specific business categories.

Advantages of Secondary Data

The greatest advantage of secondary data is that they can be obtained easily, because the data are on the Internet; in corporate, public, and college libraries; or available for purchase from syndicated services. The U.S. Census Bureau can provide nationwide data that would cost any firm a great deal of time and money to research on its own.

Disadvantages of Secondary Data

There are two major disadvantages associated with secondary data. First, the existing data may not be suitable for the problem under study.

The other disadvantage is that secondary data may sometimes be inaccurate. Federal census data are collected every ten years. As a result, projections based on the most recent census may not be correct for the current year.

How Primary Data Are Obtained

Primary research data can be obtained through company research projects or specialized research organizations. Large companies frequently have their own marketing research staff to conduct primary research for the company. However, both large and small companies make use of research organizations. National research organizations often contract with businesses and organizations to provide attitude and opinion, market, media, and product research services. AC Nielsen, Arbitron, Synovate, IMS Health, and Westat are some of the leading research organizations in the United States. Primary data may be collected using three methods: the survey method, the observation method, and the experimental method.

The Survey Method

The **survey method** is a research technique in which information is gathered from people through the use of surveys or questionnaires. It is the most frequently used method of collecting primary data.

When designing a survey, marketers must determine the number of people to include in their survey. Researchers can survey the entire target population if it is small. This is called a census. Usually, though, researchers cannot survey the entire target population, because the population is too large, and time and money are limited. Instead, researchers use a sample of the entire target population to get survey results. A **sample** is a part of the target population that represents it accurately. The size of the sample depends on the amount of money the company has to spend and the degree of accuracy that is needed. Generally speaking, the larger the sample, the more accurate the results.

After determining the size of the population to survey, a marketer must decide what type of survey to conduct. Surveys can be conducted in person, by phone (using personal calls and prerecorded messages), by mail (regular and e-mail), or by using the Internet. When the marketer has decided exactly how to conduct the survey, he or she then writes the questions according to the specific needs of that survey type.

Technological Methods

Survey research can now be conducted through online surveys and focus group chat sessions on the Internet. Fax broadcasting allows businesses to send questionnaires to a select group of fax numbers. Automated dialers increase the number of telephone survey responses by placing multiple calls and automatically rejecting those with busy signals and answering machines. Digital surveys allow a prerecorded voice to qualify a respondent and then ask a series of survey questions. Interactive voice response is similar to voicemail as callers are greeted by a recorded voice that leads them through a series of questions. Responses can be given using the telephone keypad.

Interviews

The personal interview involves questioning people face-to-face. Since door-to-door interviews are expensive, researchers often conduct interviews in central locations. Because this type of interview began in shopping malls, it is called a mall intercept interview.

A form of personal interview is the focus group interview. A focus group interview involves eight to twelve people who are brought together to evaluate advertising, a particular product, package design, or a specific marketing strategy under the direction of a skilled moderator.

The moderator must direct the discussion to accomplish the objectives of the study. Focus group facilities usually include conference rooms, observation rooms, and audiotape and videotape equipment.

•MARKET RESEARCH Conversations with consumers are essential to market researchers who need accurate market intelligence on which to base their strategies.

How would research about an existing product differ from research about a brand new one?

A major advantage of personal interviews is that it is often easier to get people to respond to personal interviews than to mail, phone, or Internet surveys. A disadvantage, however, is the cost associated with personal interviews. Personal surveys are easy to administer, but it takes time to get survey responses tabulated for data analysis.

The telephone interview is quick, efficient, and relatively inexpensive. However, this method is now limited by the new Do-Not-Call registry rules.

A mail survey is a relatively inexpensive way to reach a potentially large audience. With a direct-mail survey, a business can use visual presentation techniques. Respondents are generally honest in their responses, and they find mail surveys to be less intrusive.

Unfortunately, even a successful response rate for mail surveys is only ten percent. Average response rates can be improved for questionnaires by offering some type of incentive to complete them.

Internet-based surveys are quick and eliminate data entry, since the responses are automatically tabulated when the survey is completed.

Internet-based research allows for real-time data collection, multiple-choice questions, and open-ended, text-based answers. A drawback is that Internet surveys are limited to individuals who have access to the Web. Also, many people dislike receiving uninvited e-mail surveys.

The Observation Method

The **observation method** is a research technique in which the actions of people are watched and recorded either by cameras or by observers. Properly performed and recorded observations supply better results than those obtained with survey techniques.

Another use of observation called mystery shopping is used to view the interaction between customers and employees. A mystery shopper is a researcher who poses as a customer and goes into a business to observe employees and operations.

One disadvantage of the observation method is that it cannot measure attitudes or motivation. Observation provides information on what the person does, but not why the person does it.

Observation research is faster than personal interviews, and people are unaware that they are being observed, so they are acting as they normally would. This type of research is also cost effective.

Point-of-sale research is a powerful form of research that combines natural observation with personal interviews to get people to explain buying behavior. Point-of-sale researchers observe shoppers to decide which ones to choose as research subjects. After observation, researchers approach the selected shoppers and ask them questions. They can easily remember the reason why they purchased a product because customers have just made the decision to buy.

The Experimental Method

The **experimental method** is a research technique in which a researcher observes the results of changing one or more marketing variables while keeping other variables constant under controlled conditions. The experimental approach is often used to test new package designs, media usage, and new promotions.

The experimental method is infrequently used for marketing research because of the cost of setting up the research situation and the inaccuracy of the responses.

Step 3: Analyzing the Data

The third step in the marketing research process is data analysis. **Data analysis** is the process of compiling, analyzing, and interpreting the results of primary and secondary data collection.

A-P Super Service, Inc., surveyed customers about the quality of the auto mechanics' repair service. The number of customers who returned the survey was 120. Answers to questions were organized so that the percentage of men and women responding to each question could be shown clearly. Data were cross-tabulated to determine such things as how men and women differ in their perceptions of the service. The answers to a question about the quality of service might be presented as shown below. The number of respondents is given in parentheses after the question.

Question: How would you rate the quality of service provided by A-P Super Service, Inc? (N = 120)

Rating	**Men**	**Women**
Excellent	30%	60%
Good	15%	10%
Average	20%	20%
Fair	20%	5%
Poor	15%	5%

As you can see, female customers of A-P Super Service, Inc., have a more favorable impression of the quality of service than the male customers do. This information shows the owner that the shop's image among its male customers needs to be improved.

Data Mining

Data mining is a computer process that uses statistical methods to extract new information from large amounts of data. A database may contain subtle relationships or patterns that only a mathematical search process can identify.

Step 4: Recommending Solutions to the Problem

The conclusions drawn from the research are usually presented in an organized and well-written report. Recommendations must be clear and well supported by the research data. A typical research report includes the following:

- Title page
- Acknowledgments of people who assisted in the research effort
- Table of contents
- List of tables, figures, charts, and graphs
- Introduction (includes the problem under study, its importance, definitions, limitations of the study, and basic assumptions)
- Review of the research information (including the results of any secondary data reviewed for the research effort)
- Procedures used (research technique or techniques used to obtain primary data)
- Findings
- Recommendations
- Summary and conclusions
- Appendixes
- Bibliography

Step 5: Applying the Results

In evaluating the research, managers may find that the research was inconclusive, additional research is needed, or the research suggests specific courses of action. After the research has been completed and changes made, a business should carefully monitor the results. A business needs to know whether the specific actions taken are successful. The research effort has been a success if decisions made as a result lead to increased profits through better sales, increased efficiency, or reduced expenses.

29.1 AFTER YOU READ

Reviewing Key Terms and Concepts

1. Name four sources of information to use in collecting secondary data.
2. What are two advantages and two disadvantages of using secondary data?
3. How does survey research differ from observation research?

Integrating Academic Skills

Math

4. Research indicates that 80 percent of a flower shop's customers live within one mile of the store, another 15 percent live within two miles of the store, and the remaining 5 percent live within five miles of the store. Compute the number of customers who live within the various trading areas if the population of the entire area is 14,240.

Reading and Language Arts

5. Research a company in your community to find out how it collects demographic information about its customers. Write a 250-word report on how customer information (name, address, phone, occupation, age, spending patterns, etc.) is collected and used.

Check your answers at *marketingessentials.glencoe.com/29/read*

SECTION 29.2

The Marketing Survey

OBJECTIVES

- Design a marketing research survey
- Administer a marketing research survey

KEY TERMS

- validity
- reliability
- open-ended questions
- forced-choice questions

READ and STUDY

BEFORE YOU READ

Predict Why is the survey method an important tool for obtaining information?

THE MAIN IDEA

Businesses need valid and reliable data to make good decisions. Marketing researchers need to know how to construct survey instruments that provide the necessary information to assist in the decision-making process.

STUDY ORGANIZER

Complete an outline of Section 29.2 by listing headings, subheadings, and key concepts.

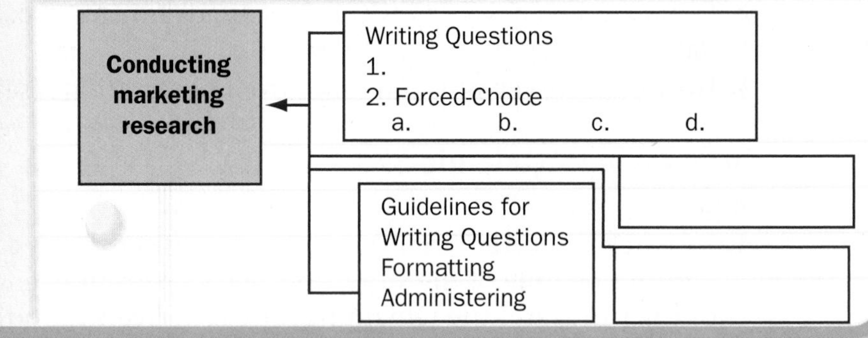

Compare and Contrast How do written survey instruments and scripted interviews differ?

Constructing the Questionnaire

As a major form of quantitative research, questionnaires should provide data that have validity. A questionnaire has **validity** when the questions asked measure what was intended to be measured. A researcher designs a questionnaire to measure a retail store's customer service. Questionnaires that are poorly written or that do not address customer service will not have validity.

Research questionnaires should also have reliability. **Reliability** exists when a research technique produces nearly identical results in repeated trials. Reliability requires that the questions ask for the same type of information from all the respondents. Questions should be clear and easily understood so that all participants understand the question in the same way. Asking a respondent in a restaurant survey, "Was your food hot?" would not yield a reliable answer. "Hot" could be interpreted as either the level of spiciness or the temperature of the food.

To be valid and reliable, a questionnaire must be properly written, formatted, and administered.

Writing Questions

Survey questions can be either open-ended or forced-choice. **Open-ended questions** ask respondents to construct their own response to a question. "What changes or additions to this coat would you recommend?" is an example of an open-ended question. Some surveys have a space for general comments or suggestions on the survey instrument. This is also a type of open-ended question. Open-ended questions generate a wide variety of responses that are sometimes difficult to categorize and tabulate. As a result, most researchers prefer forced-choice questions.

Forced-choice questions ask respondents to choose answers from possibilities given on a questionnaire. Forced-choice questions are the simplest questions to write and the easiest to tabulate. They can be two-choice questions, multiple-choice questions, rating or ranking scales, and level of agreement scales.

Yes/No Questions

Two-choice questions give the respondent only two options, usually yes or no. Yes/no questions should be used only when asking for a response on one issue. You could use a yes/no question to ask "Was our facility clean?" or "Was our facility well maintained?", but not to ask "Was our facility clean and well maintained?" The customer may have different answers for the two issues that the question addresses. Having a question that asks about more than one issue decreases validity and reliability.

Yes/no questions are most often used as filter questions. Filter questions help to guide respondents to answer only those questions that apply.

In cases where there is a range of choices and yes/no questions are not appropriate, you would use multiple-choice questions, rating scale questions, or level of agreement questions.

Multiple-Choice Questions

Multiple-choice questions give the respondent several choices. When constructing multiple-choice questions, it is important to make the options mutually exclusive and comprehensive enough to include every possible response. In order to be sure that all options are covered, many surveys have a space for the option "other." A rental company might ask its customers the following question:

When you have a choice of all the car rental companies listed below, which do you prefer? (check only one)

- ☐ Alamo
- ☐ Avis
- ☐ Budget
- ☐ Dollar
- ☐ Enterprise
- ☐ Hertz
- ☐ National
- ☐ Thrifty
- ☐ Other ________

Offering the choice of "other" increases reliability. If "other" was not an option, respondents who use an unlisted car rental service might not answer at all or might pick an inaccurate answer from the list just to give an answer. This action would cause misleading results.

Rating Scale Questions

Other forced-choice questions may ask respondents to rate a product or service based upon a scale. A variety of scales may be used, such as a rating scale from very satisfied to very dissatisfied, or from excellent to poor.

GLOBAL MARKET

Test Marketing for the Hispanic Market

There are many all-purpose household cleaning products available in the United States, but not many of them have been targeted specifically at Hispanic consumers.

Colgate-Palmolive began marketing its Mexican brand, Fabuloso, in the United States in 1997. Since then, its market share has been growing. It rolled out a fabric softener called Suavitel at the same time. Suavitel's share of the Hispanic market in the United States has already topped 10 percent.

Challengers Procter & Gamble added to the competition by introducing Gain fabric softener, in addition to its Gain and Ariel detergents that were already targeted at Hispanic consumers.

SC Johnson challenged Fabuloso all-purpose cleaner by introducing Glade Cleaner-Limpiador. "Limpiador" means "cleaner" in Spanish. The company test-marketed the product in upstate New York in 2004. Glade Cleaner-Limpiador was priced at $2.35 for 30.4 ounces at one store in Rochester, New York. It comes in red and purple bottles that look similar to Fabuloso's packaging. Companies that are introducing new products for the Hispanic market often use stronger scents than in their other products. Glade considered scents including country meadow and lavender for its all-purpose cleaner.

Which type of primary research data and methods might these manufacturers have used?

Online Action!

Go to *marketingessentials.glencoe.com/29/global* to find an activity about international marketing research.

The following is an example of a rating question that might be used to rate the front desk staff of a resort.

How would you rate your reception by the front desk staff?

Helpfulness
Excellent Good Fair Below Average
Check-In Speed
Excellent Good Fair Below Average
Offering Info About Resort
Excellent Good Fair Below Average
Use of Your Name
Excellent Good Fair Below Average

Level of Agreement Questions

When assessing attitudes or opinions, it is often a good idea to write statements that describe those attitudes or opinions. Then you can ask respondents for their level of agreement with the statements. Commonly used options include *strongly agree* (SA), *agree* (A), *neutral* (N), *disagree* (D), and *strongly disagree* (SD). The following are examples of statements that might be used in a health-related questionnaire.

Indicate your level of agreement with the following statements based on your personal preference:

"I am extremely health conscious."
SA A N D SD
"I do not like vegetables."
SA A N D SD
"Eating low-cholesterol foods is important to me."
SA A N D SD
"The cafeteria should serve heart-healthy foods."
SA A N D SD

As you can see, if someone had to answer yes or no to these questions, the researcher might not get an accurate picture. That is why it is often easier to use descriptive statements for research on attitudes and opinions.

Basic Guidelines for Writing Questions

Each question should be written clearly and as briefly as possible. Use the same ranking or rating scales for all similar questions. It is important not to ask leading questions, which suggest a correct answer. An example of a leading question is: "Do you prefer X or the more reasonably priced Z?" The phrase "more reasonably priced" could cause respondents to answer Z.

You should avoid any bias, which is a systematic error introduced by encouraging one outcome or answer over the others. It is also important to avoid questions that might cause a respondent to guess at the meaning of your question. The following is an example of a question that might cause a respondent to guess:

Case Study

Re-Inventing the Potato

The United States Potato Board wanted to find out why potato sales revenue had not kept up with population growth or the consumer price index.

The Board contracted with the Perishables Group, a specialized research group for growers, shippers, suppliers, commodity boards, and retailers to do the research.

Digging In

The Perishables Group used secondary data: consumer research related to meal trends, food consumption diaries, focus groups, consumer intercepts, lifestyle issues, and census data. To obtain primary data, they interviewed grocery store executives. Category concept testing was done on packaging, cross-merchandising, and secondary locations.

A New Recipe

Research by the Potato Board and the Perishables Group led to the following recommendations: Minor packaging changes were needed, sales could be increased by displaying potatoes in or near meat departments, and better merchandising of bag and bulk varieties was needed. The partners also developed a Retail Marketing Toolkit that provided consumer, trade, and new merchandising concept research, as well as recommendations for assortment, pricing, promotion, and a menu of merchandising options to increase potato sales.

THINK STRATEGICALLY

Why did the United States Potato Board contract with a research group to study sales of potatoes?

@ Online Action!

Go to *marketingessentials.glencoe.com/29/case* to find an activity about marketing research.

How many students in your high school drink coffee on a daily basis?

- ☐ Less than 10
- ☐ 10–49
- ☐ 50–99
- ☐ 100–149
- ☐ 150–199
- ☐ over 200

Without asking every student, the respondent cannot answer the question without guessing.

When a survey questionnaire is finished, it is a good idea to pretest the wording of the questions. This pretest allows for correction of any misleading questions, directions, or problems on the questionnaire.

Formatting

Questionnaires must have excellent visual appearance and design to appeal to respondents. You should use dark ink, preferably black, on light paper and type that is easy to read. The questionnaire should be short enough to be answered quickly. Section headings or numbers should be placed on all individual survey sections. Numbers should be placed on all individual questions. If your questionnaire requires more than one page, place a note at the bottom of each page to continue to the next page.

Content Formatting

Directions for completing the questionnaire must be clear for each section or group of questions.

General demographic questions about gender, age, ethnic background, and education are typically grouped together at the end of

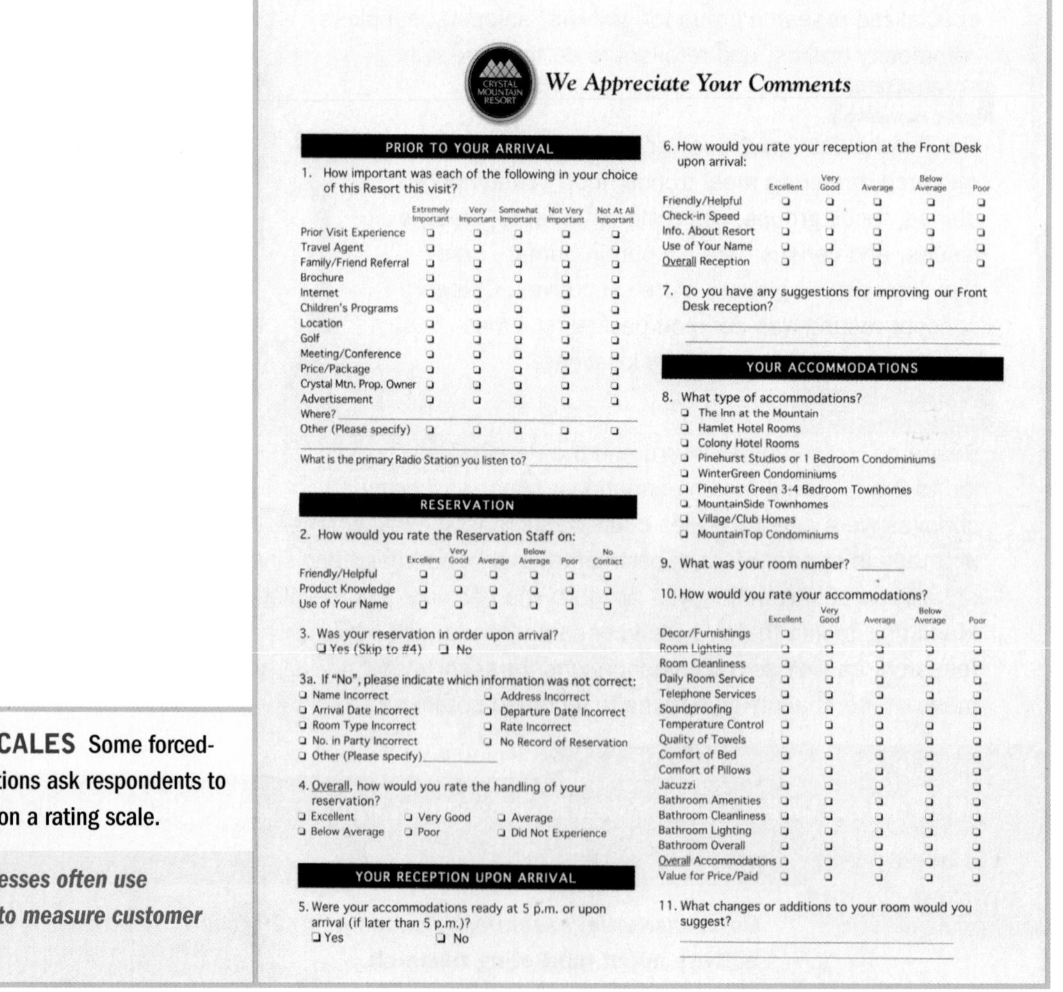

CRYSTAL MOUNTAIN RESORT

We Appreciate Your Comments

PRIOR TO YOUR ARRIVAL

1. How important was each of the following in your choice of this Resort this visit?

	Extremely Important	Very Important	Somewhat Important	Not Very Important	Not At All Important
Prior Visit Experience	❑	❑	❑	❑	❑
Travel Agent	❑	❑	❑	❑	❑
Family/Friend Referral	❑	❑	❑	❑	❑
Brochure	❑	❑	❑	❑	❑
Internet	❑	❑	❑	❑	❑
Children's Programs	❑	❑	❑	❑	❑
Location	❑	❑	❑	❑	❑
Golf	❑	❑	❑	❑	❑
Meeting/Conference	❑	❑	❑	❑	❑
Price/Package	❑	❑	❑	❑	❑
Crystal Mtn. Prop. Owner	❑	❑	❑	❑	❑
Advertisement	❑	❑	❑	❑	❑
Where? ________					
Other (Please specify)	❑	❑	❑	❑	❑

What is the primary Radio Station you listen to? ________

RESERVATION

2. How would you rate the Reservation Staff on:

	Excellent	Very Good	Average	Below Average	Poor	No Contact
Friendly/Helpful	❑	❑	❑	❑	❑	❑
Product Knowledge	❑	❑	❑	❑	❑	❑
Use of Your Name	❑	❑	❑	❑	❑	❑

3. Was your reservation in order upon arrival?
❑ Yes (Skip to #4) ❑ No

3a. If "No", please indicate which information was not correct:
❑ Name Incorrect ❑ Address Incorrect
❑ Arrival Date Incorrect ❑ Departure Date Incorrect
❑ Room Type Incorrect ❑ Rate Incorrect
❑ No. in Party Incorrect ❑ No Record of Reservation
❑ Other (Please specify)________

4. Overall, how would you rate the handling of your reservation?
❑ Excellent ❑ Very Good ❑ Average
❑ Below Average ❑ Poor ❑ Did Not Experience

YOUR RECEPTION UPON ARRIVAL

5. Were your accommodations ready at 5 p.m. or upon arrival (if later than 5 p.m.)?
❑ Yes ❑ No

6. How would you rate your reception at the Front Desk upon arrival:

	Excellent	Very Good	Average	Below Average	Poor
Friendly/Helpful	❑	❑	❑	❑	❑
Check-in Speed	❑	❑	❑	❑	❑
Info. About Resort	❑	❑	❑	❑	❑
Use of Your Name	❑	❑	❑	❑	❑
Overall Reception	❑	❑	❑	❑	❑

7. Do you have any suggestions for improving our Front Desk reception?
____
____

YOUR ACCOMMODATIONS

8. What type of accommodations?
❑ The Inn at the Mountain
❑ Hamlet Hotel Rooms
❑ Colony Hotel Rooms
❑ Pinehurst Studios or 1 Bedroom Condominiums
❑ WinterGreen Condominiums
❑ Pinehurst Green 3-4 Bedroom Townhomes
❑ MountainSide Townhomes
❑ Village/Club Homes
❑ MountainTop Condominiums

9. What was your room number? ________

10. How would you rate your accommodations?

	Excellent	Very Good	Average	Below Average	Poor
Decor/Furnishings	❑	❑	❑	❑	❑
Room Lighting	❑	❑	❑	❑	❑
Room Cleanliness	❑	❑	❑	❑	❑
Daily Room Service	❑	❑	❑	❑	❑
Telephone Services	❑	❑	❑	❑	❑
Soundproofing	❑	❑	❑	❑	❑
Temperature Control	❑	❑	❑	❑	❑
Quality of Towels	❑	❑	❑	❑	❑
Comfort of Bed	❑	❑	❑	❑	❑
Comfort of Pillows	❑	❑	❑	❑	❑
Jacuzzi	❑	❑	❑	❑	❑
Bathroom Amenities	❑	❑	❑	❑	❑
Bathroom Cleanliness	❑	❑	❑	❑	❑
Bathroom Lighting	❑	❑	❑	❑	❑
Bathroom Overall	❑	❑	❑	❑	❑
Overall Accommodations	❑	❑	❑	❑	❑
Value for Price/Paid	❑	❑	❑	❑	❑

11. What changes or additions to your room would you suggest?
____
____

• **RATING SCALES** Some forced-choice questions ask respondents to reply based on a rating scale.

Why do businesses often use rating scales to measure customer satisfaction?

a questionnaire. This is because respondents are more likely to answer personal questions after completing the other questions. The only time such information is placed at the beginning of a questionnaire is to qualify a respondent. For example, if an interviewer wanted to study the views of people in their twenties, he or she might ask, "Are you between the ages of 20 and 30?" If the person answers yes, the interviewer would administer the survey. If the answer is no, then the person would not be included in the study.

Administering the Questionnaire

All surveys should have deadlines for completion. A mailed questionnaire should be sent first-class with a hand-signed cover letter, and it should be personalized if the potential respondent is known. The cover letter should explain the purpose of the survey and the deadline for returning the questionnaire. A postage-paid return envelope should be included with the questionnaire for the respondent's convenience.

In-Person Surveys

Questionnaires that are not mailed should have a brief explanation of the survey's purpose placed on the questionnaire itself. A plan should be established for selecting participants in an unbiased way. In a personal interview, reactions to visual materials such as ads or actual product samples can be collected.

Incentives

Many questionnaires offer incentives to encourage people to participate. For example, a company may enter each respondent's name into a drawing for a cash prize. Or, each participant may receive a coupon for the company's product.

29.2 AFTER YOU READ

Reviewing Key Terms and Concepts

1. When is a survey valid?
2. What guidelines should be followed to ensure that a questionnaire is effective?
3. Name three techniques to make the format of a questionnaire appealing.

Integrating Academic Skills

Math

4. A retailer conducts a traffic study to estimate yearly sales. Use the following data to estimate yearly sales for the retailer: 1,500 people pass the store each day, seven percent enter the store and spend an average of $14, and the store is open 360 days during the year.

Civics and Government

5. Find a newspaper article dealing with an opinion poll on a local, state, or national issue. Write a 100-word summary of when and how the poll was conducted, and what the results indicated.

@ Online Action!

Check your answers at *marketingessentials.glencoe.com/29/read*

CAREERS IN MARKETING

D. CLAY KELLY
DIRECTOR OF MARKETING
STRAND ASSOCIATES, INC.

What do you do at work?
My primary job is to support the efforts of our staff as we seek new work opportunities. Our "product" is professional services, namely engineering design. I make visits to city and county leaders as well as state and federal officials whose jobs are related to construction and capital improvements projects that require engineering services. My goal is to develop a relationship between the decision makers and our firm so that we are completely in tune with the needs of the client.

What skills are most important to you?
People skills are the most important. I fully believe that everyone is a salesperson or a marketer, regardless of their position or chosen career. This applies to almost anyone, whether you're a farmer selling cattle, a businessperson trying to increase market share, or a religious leader creating interest in a specific belief.

What is your key to success?
You have to believe in what you're marketing. In my case, I'm marketing the professional capabilities of my fellow engineers. I am convinced they are among the best in our business and they are dedicated to helping our clients succeed. A reputation is built over a lifetime, but can be destroyed in a moment. Protect your integrity as you would your life and success will be yours in the richest sense of the word.

Aptitudes, Abilities, and Skills

Verbal, written, and interpersonal skills are crucial; public speaking is equally essential.

Education and Training

General business degrees are helpful, along with degrees in marketing and economics, and industry-specific courses.

Career Path

Marketing careers arise within virtually all medium to large companies, often through entry level jobs, marketing or otherwise.

THINKING CRITICALLY

Why is public speaking such a valuable skill?

Online Action!

Go to *marketingessentials.glencoe.com/29/careers* to find a career-related activity.

CHAPTER 29 REVIEW

FOCUS on KEY POINTS

SECTION 29.1

- The five steps that a business follows when conducting marketing research are defining the problem, obtaining data, analyzing the data, recommending solutions, and applying the results. The steps are performed sequentially to arrive at solutions to a problem or research an issue.

SECTION 29.2

- Questionnaires should provide data that are valid and reliable. Marketing surveys may include open-ended and forced-choice questions. Forced-choice questions include yes/no, multiple-choice, rating scale, and level of agreement questions.
- To obtain unbiased data and increase response rates, market researchers must follow guidelines when constructing, formatting, and administering surveys.

REVIEW VOCABULARY

Write one correct sentence on conducting marketing research for each of the following terms.

1. problem definition (p. 612)
2. primary data (p. 612)
3. secondary data (p. 612)
4. survey method (p. 614)
5. sample (p. 614)
6. observation method (p. 616)
7. point-of-sale research (p. 616)
8. experimental method (p. 616)
9. data analysis (p. 616)
10. validity (p. 618)
11. reliability (p. 619)
12. open-ended questions (p. 619)
13. forced-choice questions (p. 619)

REVIEW FACTS and IDEAS

14. Identify in correct order the five steps used in designing and conducting a research study. (29.1)
15. What is the difference between primary and secondary data? Why should researchers consider one type first? (29.1)
16. Identify the three methods used to collect primary data. (29.1)
17. What is the survey method of research? Describe four ways to conduct surveys. (29.1)
18. Identify the elements in a final marketing research report. (29.1)
19. When constructing the options for multiple-choice questions, what is important to remember? (29.2)
20. When do you use level of agreement questions on a questionnaire? (29.2)
21. Name two examples of how bias can be introduced into a questionnaire. (29.2)
22. What can be done when administering a question to encourage people to participate? (29.2)

BUILD SKILLS

23. Workplace Skills

Human Relations You are employed in a shopping mall where a natural observation study is occurring. Your coworker thinks that this research technique is an invasion of privacy and is threatening to tell customers that they are being observed. How should you handle this situation?

24. Technology Applications

Using Secondary Data Sources Locate the U.S. Census Bureau's Web site and the County Business Patterns Economic Profile for your county. Use this profile to identify the number of employees in your county and the annual payroll for your county. Find the total estimated employment by size of business and locate the industry area in your county that employs the most people. Make a graphic representation of the data that you found.

25. Math Practice

Research Costs What would be the per person costs to complete a phone, mail, or Internet survey for 500 people given the following costs:
Phone: $250 for phone; $1250 for interviewers; $1250 for data entry
Mail: $500 for printing/postage; $2,000 to open envelopes and enter data
Internet: $250 create/deliver; $5 to convert data.

DEVELOP CRITICAL THINKING

26. Language Arts

Write a one- to two-page paper addressing the question, "Can business risks be eliminated by conducting marketing research?" Provide a supporting rationale for your answer. Explain what types of risk can be eliminated and why. Try to give specific company examples each time.

27. Conducting a Focus Group

The owner of a cosmetics boutique wants to conduct a focus group to determine whether carrying some organic beauty products would be a good business move. However, this owner does not have a marketing budget and is unwilling to pay several thousand dollars to an outside market research company.

What could the owner do to still have a focus group while keeping costs down?

List at least three ideas and explain why each idea would bring in valuable market research data.

APPLY CONCEPTS

28. Finding a Marketing Research Firm

Locate the Web page of *Quirk's Marketing Research Review*. Search for a firm in your state or city that performs marketing research.

Activity Develop a one-page profile that includes the company name, a company description, research services it provides, and the industries, markets, or audiences served.

29. Constructing a Questionnaire

Construct a 15-item written survey instrument that would assess student satisfaction with a current policy affecting your school community, such as student parking. Use a combination of yes/no, multiple-choice, rating scale, and level of agreement questions.

Activity Share your final document in class. Brainstorm on possible improvements. Form groups of two or three and administer the questionnaire to students on campus during lunch and recess breaks. Share the results and the experience in class.

NET SAVVY

30. Market Research Online

Perform an Internet search for the WorldOpinion Web site. Select "Periodicals" then click on "The Frame." Look in the archives for an article about a recent trend or issue within the field of marketing research. Identify the title of the article, date, and author, and complete a 50-word summary of the trend or issue.

THE DECA CONNECTION

Role Play: Marketing Research

Situation You are to assume the role of researcher at a marketing research company. You have recently been assigned a high school student as a summer intern (judge). The duties are that the intern (judge) assist you with your tasks and in turn, you are to provide the intern (judge) training in the marketing research your company conducts. Today you are going to explain the sources of marketing data, particularly secondary data.

Activity You are to explain to the intern (judge) the importance of secondary data and sources of that data.

Evaluation You will be evaluated on how well you meet the following performance indicators:

- Identify information monitored for marketing decision making
- Describe sources of secondary data
- Search the Internet for marketing information
- Monitor internal records for marketing information
- Collect marketing information from others (e.g., customers, staff, vendors)

@ Online Action!

For more information and DECA Prep practice, go to *marketingessentials.glencoe.com/29/DECA*

MARKETING INTERNSHIP

A SIMULATED DECA MARKETING RESEARCH EVENT

Research Male Grooming Products

BASIC BACKGROUND

The male grooming industry is big—with estimates between $5 billion and $8 billion in annual sales, and it's still growing. Some large companies already active in this market include Unilever, Procter & Gamble, Estee Lauder, and Nivea. Two smaller companies enjoying success are American Crew and Sharps. Sharps' brands include products such as Kid Glove Shave Gel and Guck-in-a-Puck for hair styling.

Branching Out Your firm's client, G&G Cosmetics, is looking to take advantage of the trend of sales growth in male grooming by starting a new line of products for the "modern-day guy." Currently G&G makes cosmetics and personal grooming products for young women of different ethnic backgrounds. Its competitively priced products are sold in department stores. To grow its business, however, it now must expand into other markets.

YOUR OBJECTIVE

Your objective is to conduct a marketing research study of the target market. You need to provide G&G Cosmetics with a customer analysis and recommendations on how to create and market products for this new target market.

ASSIGNMENT AND STRATEGY

- **Get the background** To get started you need to conduct secondary research on the personal grooming industry for men. Find out sales figures, profitability, pricing strategies, and the most popular products. Then, identify questions to ask in a marketing research study.

  You will need to learn what grooming products are used by the target market, what their motivations are, what needs and wants are not being met, where they shop, and what media are part of their daily or weekly routine.

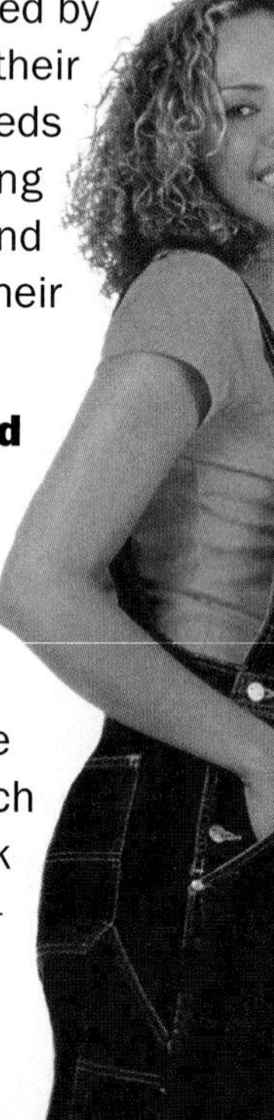

- **Conduct the research and write the report** State G&G Cosmetics' main problem and the objectives of the study.
- **Choose a format** Decide on the marketing research format(s) that will work best to achieve the objectives. Identify the target population and how participants will be selected.

Design the instrument you will use (written questionnaire, focus group questions, etc.).

Conduct the study and take note of any incidents that may create bias or limit your study's conclusions. Highlight the most important findings and include tables and charts to make it easy to see the details of your findings.

Use your data to provide recommendations and a plan to implement those recommendations for the client. Include a section on the limitations of your study.

- **What your project should include** Include samples of all materials used in your marketing research study and examples of any marketing ideas in your recommendations.

YOUR REPORT

Use a word processing program and presentation software to prepare a double-spaced report and an oral presentation for G&G Cosmetics. Use Glencoe's *Marketing Research Project Workbook* as a resource. See a suggested outline and key evaluation points at *marketingessentials.glencoe.com/internship*

BUILD YOUR PORTFOLIO

Option 1 Internship Report Once you have completed your Marketing Internship project and presentation, include your written report and a few printouts of key slides from your oral presentation in your Marketing Portfolio.

Option 2 Conducting a Customer Satisfaction Study Design a customer satisfaction survey for a company of your choice. After conducting the study, explain the methodology, conclusions from your findings, limitations, and recommendations. Prepare your written report using a word processing program and use presentation software for your oral presentation. See a suggested outline and key evaluation points at *marketingessentials.glencoe.com/portfolio* and use Glencoe's *Marketing Research Project Workbook* as an additional resource.

@ Online Action!

Go to *marketingessentials.glencoe.com/Unit/9/DECA* to review information management concepts that relate to DECA events.

UNIT 10

Product and

In this unit you will find

- **Chapter 30** Product Planning
- **Chapter 31** Branding, Packaging, and Labeling
- **Chapter 32** Extended Product Features

Service Management

Marketing Plan

ANALYSIS
1 SWOT
Economic
Socio-Cultural
Technological
Competitive

STRATEGY
2 Promotion
Place
Price
Product

IMPLEMENTATION
3 Organization
Management
Staffing

BUDGET
4 Cost of Sales
Cost of Promotion
Incomes and Expenses

CONTROL
5 Evaluation
Performance Measures
Performance Analysis

ANALYZE THE AD

Friskies is a leading cat food brand sold in the United States and in several foreign countries. How does this ad try to appeal to cat owners?

Market Talk Many cat food brands, including Friskies, 9Lives, and Whiskas, feature pictures of cats on their packaging. Iams and Hill's Science Diet are exceptions. Why would they choose not to feature pictures of cats?

Think and Write Look through a grocery store and find five items with appealing packaging that makes you more inclined to buy the product. For each product, note what makes the packaging effective. Does effective packaging have any similarities, even for different kinds of products? Does it make you willing to pay more for the product?

Online Action! Go to *marketingessentials.glencoe.com/u10/ad* for an extended activity.

In this unit

Foundations of Marketing
Business, Management, Entrepreneurship

Functions of Marketing
Product/Service Management

CHAPTER 30
Product Planning

Chapter Objectives

After reading this chapter, you should be able to:

- Describe the steps in product planning
- Explain how to develop, maintain, and improve a product mix
- Identify the four stages of the product life cycle
- Describe product positioning techniques

GUIDE TO THE PHOTO

Market Talk Businesses plan, position, and manage products and services they create. This process includes determining the product mix and the product mix strategies. For example, a fashion manufacturer must be aware of current trends and anticipate upcoming ones before sending new garment designs to the production line.

Quick Think What do you think it takes for a new product to be successful?

THE  CONNECTION

Performance indicators represent key skills and knowledge. Relating them to the concepts explained in this chapter is your key to success in DECA events. These acronyms represent DECA events that involve knowledge of concepts in this chapter.

AAAL	**FMAL**	**MMS***	**TMDM***
AAML*	**FMDM***	**QSRM***	**TSE***
ADC*	**FMML***	**RMAL**	**VPM**
BSM	**FSRM***	**RMML***	
EMDM*	**HMDM***	**SMDM***	

In all these DECA events you should be able to follow these performance indicators:

- Explain the nature and scope of the product/service management function
- Identify the impact of product life cycles on marketing decisions
- Describe the use of technology in the product/service management function
- Explain business ethics in product/service management
- Explain the concept of product mix
- Describe factors used by marketers to position products/businesses

The events with an asterisk (*) include these indicators:

- Plan product mix
- Determine services to provide customers
- Explain the role of customer service in positioning/image
- Develop strategies to position product/business

HMDM and **FMDM** include additional performance indicators: Explain the concept of product in the hospitality industry and in the financial services industry respectively.

DECA PREP

Check your understanding of DECA performance indicators with the DECA activity in this chapter's review. For more information and DECA Prep practice, go to *marketingessentials .glencoe.com/30/DECA*

SECTION 30.1

OBJECTIVES

- Describe the steps in product planning
- Explain how to develop, maintain, and improve a product mix

Product Planning, Mix, and Development

KEY TERMS

- product planning
- product mix
- product line
- product item
- product width
- product depth
- product modification

READ and STUDY

BEFORE YOU READ

Connect Recall a recent shopping trip. Can you name a new consumer product you discovered?

THE MAIN IDEA

Product planning allows a business to design marketing programs that increase sales by making products that customers want.

STUDY ORGANIZER

With a flow chart like the one below, represent the seven key steps in product development.

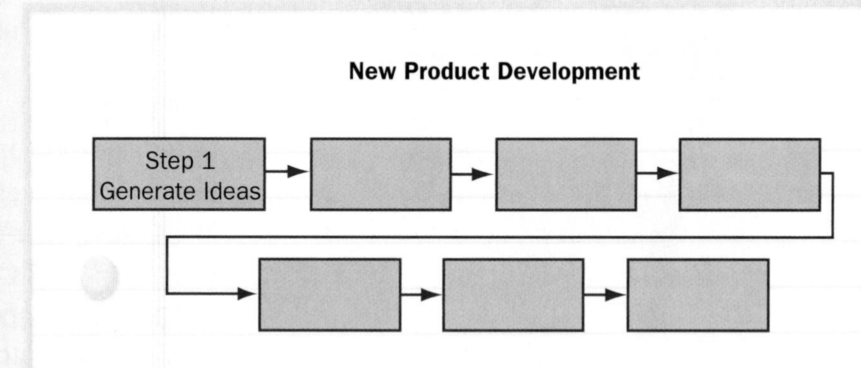

WHILE YOU READ

Analysis What marketing activities must occur prior to launching a new product?

Product Planning

A product is anything a person receives in an exchange. A product can be a tangible item (a notebook PC), a service (auto repair), an idea (a plan for a marketing campaign), some other abstract good (an education), or a combination of all of these concepts. A product, therefore, includes its physical features, the seller's reputation, the seller's services, and the way the product is viewed by people. **Product planning** involves making decisions about what features should be used in selling a business's products, services, or ideas. These decisions relate to product features, such as packaging, labeling, and branding, as well as to services, such as product warranties, that are necessary to support the product. Product planning allows a business to coordinate existing products and features offered to customers, add new products, and delete products that no longer appeal to customers. Product planning requires creativity as well as the ability to interpret current customer needs and forecast new trends.

Product Mix

Product mix includes all the different products that a company makes or sells. A large manufacturer may have a variety of products in different categories. For example, Kraft Foods, the second-largest food and beverage manufacturer in the world, has hundreds of products in five areas: snacks, beverages, cheese, groceries, and convenience meals. Kraft's key brands include Kraft, Kool-Aid, Maxwell House, Nabisco, Oscar Mayer, and Post products.

A retailer's product mix is made up of all of the different products the store sells. Retail stores must plan their product mix carefully because they cannot offer all the products that customers may want.

Variations in Product Mixes

Have you ever heard of *El Caserio* or *Trakinas?* Both are brands that Kraft sells outside the United States. El Caserio is a popular cheese in Spain. Trakinas is a cookie sold in Brazil, Thailand, and China. Kraft has a diverse international market and therefore carries different product mixes for different customer needs across the world.

The type and number of products to be carried must be based on the objectives of the business, the image the business wants to project, and the market it is trying to reach. This makes product mixes unique to each business. Even similar types of businesses can offer different product mixes.

Product Items and Lines

A **product line** is a group of closely related products manufactured or sold by a business. Examples include all the car models produced by the Pontiac division of General Motors or all the cereals produced by Kellogg's. Retailers frequently sell more than one product line.

A **product item** is a specific model, brand, or size of a product within a product line. Typically, retailers carry several product items for each product line they sell. A Harley-Davidson motorcycle dealer might carry several Softail models, such as the Night Train, Deuce, or Heritage Softail Classic.

Product Width and Product Depth

The width and depth of its product offerings define a product mix. **Product width** refers to the number of different product lines a business manufactures or sells. **Product depth** refers to the number of items offered within each product line.

A retailer that sells three brands of jeans—Levi's, Lee, and Guess—has a product width of three. The product depth is the number of sizes, price ranges, colors, fabric type, and styles for each brand.

Product mix strategies vary with the type of business. Red Lobster restaurants, which specialize in seafood dinners, have considerable product depth within a narrow product line (seafood entrées). Other restaurants may offer broader menus that include steak, chicken, pork, and pasta dinners as well as seafood. Their product mix may have greater width but less depth than Red Lobster's.

Both manufacturers and retailers must decide on the width and depth of their product mix. To determine its product mix, a business needs to identify its target market, its competitors, and the image it wants to project. After a target market and an image are identified, a business must determine which product lines and items to manufacture or sell. Businesses must also periodically review whether its existing product lines need to be expanded, modified, decreased, or eliminated.

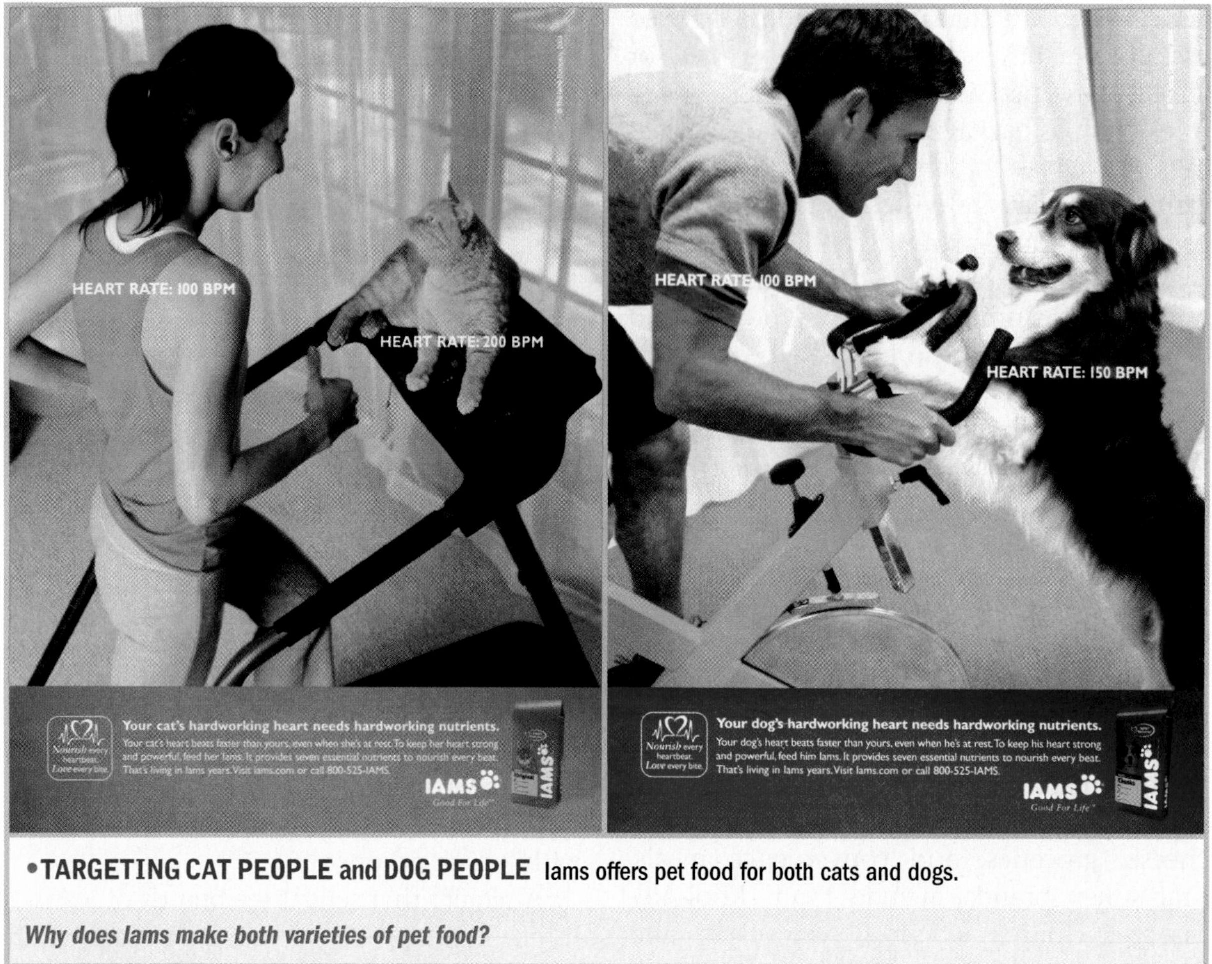

• TARGETING CAT PEOPLE and DOG PEOPLE Iams offers pet food for both cats and dogs.

Why does Iams make both varieties of pet food?

Product Mix Strategies

A product mix strategy is a plan for determining which products a business will make or stock. Businesses can use different product mix strategies depending on their resources and objectives. Some businesses develop completely new products to add to their existing product lines. Others expand or modify their current product lines. Sometimes businesses drop existing products to allow for new product offerings.

To make these decisions, a business must take an objective look at sales as well as other factors such as current trends. A product that has experienced success in the past may not continue to thrive if it fails to respond to changing consumer wants and needs.

Developing New Products

Successful new products can add substantially to a company's overall sales and boost its market share. Often a slight variation of the original or existing product can lead to increased sales.

Procter & Gamble (P&G), the number-one U.S. maker of household products, devotes roughly 15 percent of its research and development budget to developing new products. Innovative P&G products that have created new consumer-goods categories include Febreze odor removers, the Swiffer dry-mop system, and the Dryel home dry-cleaning kit.

According to one study, new products (those less than five years old) account for about 35 percent of total sales for major consumer and industrial goods companies. New products also can help a company's image by building a reputation among customers as an innovator and leader. In addition, a new product may increase markups and profits to sellers because its price tends to be 10 to 15 percent higher than that of older, comparable products.

New product development generally involves seven key steps (see Figure 30.1):

1. Generating ideas
2. Screening ideas
3. Developing a business proposal
4. Developing the product
5. Testing the product with consumers
6. Introducing the product (commercialization)
7. Evaluating customer acceptance

Generating Ideas

New product ideas come from a variety of sources, including customers, competitors, channel members, and company employees. Current and existing customers are frequently involved in focus groups or idea sessions designed to generate new product concepts in as many categories as possible. Creativity is essential for new product development.

Many companies that manufacture consumer packaged goods use a task force approach to new product development. With this approach, employees from different departments, such as marketing, sales, manufacturing, finance, and research and development, take a new concept from the idea stage through the steps of product development. Companies that manufacture and sell industrial products often establish venture teams that are independent of any particular department. Venture teams normally develop new products that are not part of the existing business.

Screening Ideas

During the screening process, ideas for products are evaluated. They are matched against the company's overall strategy, which defines customers, target markets, competitors, and existing competitive strengths.

During the screening process, new ideas are evaluated for potential conflicts with existing products.

A screening might involve concept testing with consumers. Consumers would be asked to identify attributes they liked and disliked about the new concept and to indicate how willing they would be to buy such a product. The purpose of the screening stage is to find the products that deserve further study. A large number of products are rejected in the screening stage, making it an important preliminary step.

Developing a Business Proposal

A product idea that makes it through the screening process is evaluated in terms of its profit potential. A business proposal is developed to evaluate the new product in terms of the size of the market, potential sales, costs, profit potential, technological trends, overall competitive environment, and level of risk. During this stage, production requirements must be considered. How long will it take to create and introduce the new product? Can it be produced efficiently and at a competitive price? The business plans a program to study the feasibility of making and marketing the new product.

Developing the Product

During product development, the new product idea takes on a physical shape, and marketers develop a marketing strategy. The company makes plans relating to production, packaging, labeling, branding, promotion, and distribution.

During this phase of product development, technical evaluations are made to see whether the company can produce the new product and whether it is practical to do so. The Ben & Jerry's ice cream company had difficulties when it first developed Cherry Garcia ice cream. The original idea was to add whole chocolate-coated cherries to the ice cream. But the whole cherries were too large to go through the production machinery, which caused the chocolate to break off the cherries. After numerous tests, the company finally added the cherries and the chocolate separately.

In addition to detecting difficulties with product production, tests are conducted on products to see how they will hold up

Figure 30.1 The Steps in New Product Development

• **Getting an Idea Into a Consumer's Hands** Developing new products involves several key steps.

How does an idea lead to a product?

Steps 1 and 2

GENERATING AND SCREENING IDEAS

Generating ideas involves tracking cultural trends and observing customer behaviors. Screening ideas for new products includes eliminating possibilities until one or two ideas are selected for development and a business proposal is written.

Steps 3, 4, and 5

WRITING A BUSINESS PROPOSAL/ DEVELOPING THE PRODUCT/ TESTING THE PRODUCT

A business proposal evaluates the proposed product in terms of size of market, potential sales, costs, profit potential, technology, the competition, and the level of risk involved. During the development stage, a prototype is made for testing.

Step 6

INTRODUCING THE PRODUCT

If customer response is favorable, the product is introduced into the marketplace.

Step 7

EVALUATING CUSTOMER ACCEPTANCE

After the product has been introduced, marketers track customer acceptance.

@ Online Action! Go to *marketingessentials.glencoe.com/30/figure/1* to find a project on the process of new product development.

during normal and not-so-normal use by the consumer. A new product may be tested for durability in the lab by machines that will reproduce the actions or motions that the product will undergo during use. Technical problems should be detected at this stage so that they can be corrected before full-scale production begins.

The government requires extensive testing in various stages for some products, such as prescription drugs and genetically engineered food products. These tests end with testing on human beings to determine side effects and problems with the product's safety. Getting final approval from the government for use by the general public can take years.

Testing the Product With Consumers

New products frequently are test-marketed in certain geographic areas to see whether consumers will accept them. Larger companies establish research and development departments that work with marketing staff, marketing research staff, and outside research companies to develop and test new products.

Not every new product needs to be test-marketed. A focus group evaluation during development can provide additional input into final product design, uncovering potential problems before production.

In some cases, the costs of test marketing, focus group evaluations, or direct marketing tests to sample households may be too high. Marketers may forgo testing of other products because they do not yet have a product to be evaluated. Sometimes a company delays test marketing because it does not want to give competitors information that might help them get a competing product on the market.

Introducing the Product

This stage is also called commercialization. Introducing a new product can be expensive. For example, to convince adults to use Crest Whitening Expressions toothpaste in cinnamon, citrus, and herbal mint flavors, Procter & Gamble spent $80 million on a marketing campaign.

A MATTER OF ETHICS

Hold the Sugar

Suppose you are developing a new low-sugar doughnut. The new doughnut is designed to attract dieters and diabetics. A regular, glazed doughnut has 10 grams of sugar and 200 calories. More than half of the calories come from 12 grams of fat.

Fast-food makers are introducing lower-calorie products because of changing diet trends. In addition, consumers have filed lawsuits in which they claim that their health has been adversely affected by foods that are high in fat and sugar.

Lawmakers Weigh In

In 2004, the U.S. House of Representatives passed legislation that would ban lawsuits seeking damages because fast food caused weight gain or health problems resulting from obesity. Proponents of the so-called cheeseburger bill argue that such lawsuits are frivolous and ignore personal responsibility for healthy eating. Opponents of the bill argue that the fast-food industry should not be given federal protection from such lawsuits.

THINKING ETHICALLY

Do you think that companies should be immune from lawsuits over their food content?

@ Online Action!

Go to *marketingessentials.glencoe.com/30/ethics* to find an activity about ethics and product development.

New products must be advertised to introduce their benefits to consumers. A new or revised distribution network may be needed. The company may need to develop training programs for its sales force. To pay these costs, the company must get its new products into the market as quickly as possible.

Evaluating Customer Acceptance

The purpose of this step is to evaluate customer acceptance of the product and the marketing strategies used to introduce the product.

One way to obtain customer responses is to study sales information. Scanning equipment and computer systems can be used to compile large amounts of sales and market data on existing and new products. From this information, customized reports can be prepared. These reports help answer key questions such as:

- How often do customers buy the new product?
- When did customers last buy the new product?
- Where are the best customers for our new product?
- What new products are customers buying?

Developing Existing Products

Companies constantly review their product mix to see if they can further expand their product lines or modify existing products. They do this in order to build on an already established image, to appeal to new markets, and to increase sales and profits. Companies that have successful product lines often add products to those lines in order to take advantage of customers' positive attitudes toward the brand name.

One disadvantage of adding new products to a company's product mix is the cost factor. Adding products or product lines increases inventory, promotion, storage, and distribution costs. New products also may take sales away from existing products and may require additional training for sales representatives who sell the products. Finally, when a brand or corporate name is placed on a new product and the product proves to be unpopular, poorly made, or harmful, all products with the corporate name suffer.

Two ways of developing existing products are line extensions and product modifications.

Line Extensions

Companies can expand product offerings by adding new product lines, items, or services, which may or may not be related to current products. To illustrate this strategy, think of all the varieties of Tylenol, such as Tylenol Flu, Tylenol Cold, and Tylenol Allergy Sinus. These products also come in a variety of forms, such as tablets, caplets, and gel caps. Each of these products is a line extension of the original Tylenol product.

A line extension is intended to be a different product that appeals to somewhat different needs of consumers. In essence, the company wants to provide a wider range of choices to increase product depth within a line. Line extensions are easy to market because customers are already familiar with the original product on which the extension is based.

Product Modifications

A **product modification** is an alteration in a company's existing product. Modified products may be offered in new and different varieties, formulations, colors, styles, features, or sizes. Product modifications are a relatively quick and easy way to add new products to a company's product line.

When modifying a product, the old product often is phased out. Packaging may be modified to appeal to consumers and attract them to the new product.

Deleting a Product or Product Line

Sometimes companies decide that they will no longer produce or sell a particular product or, even a whole product line. There can be many reasons for this move.

Obsolescence

Changes in customer interests and technology have caused many products to be dropped. For example, older models of desktop computers have been dropped because newer models are faster and less expensive to produce.

Loss of Appeal

As consumer tastes change, companies drop products that no longer appeal to the old tastes. These products may have some lasting loyalties that generate revenue, but the manufacturers must decide whether these benefits are really worth the expense of keeping the item in their product mixes.

Changes in Company Objectives

Sometimes a product does not match a company's current objectives. In 1993, Sears sold one of its subsidiaries, Coldwell Banker real estate company, for this reason. For several years, Sears had lost market share to other retailers. The company sold some unrelated businesses to focus on its retail objectives.

Replacement With New Products

To encourage retailers to cover costs of putting a new product onto limited shelf space, manufacturers pay slotting fees. Slotting fees for cereal and paper goods often reach $50,000 or more. According to a Federal Trade Commission study in 2003, a nationwide product launch might cost $2 million in slotting fees alone. Slotting fees help the retailer balance the costs associated with accepting a new product. A retailer must mark down eliminated products and pay for software, labor, and materials to change price labels and enter a new product into the inventory.

Lack of Profit

Product developers may drop products when sales reach such a low level that the return on sales does not meet company objectives.

Conflict With Other Products in the Line

Sometimes products take business away from other products in the same product line. Increased sales of one product can cause decreased sales of another product.

30.1 AFTER YOU READ

Reviewing Key Terms and Concepts

1. Why is product planning important to a business?
2. What is the difference between product planning and product mix?
3. What are the three major strategies for developing an effective product mix?

Integrating Academic Skills

Math

4. According to Productscan Online, a new product database, there were 33,677 new product introductions in 2003, compared to 21,986 in 1993. By what percentage did new product introductions increase during that decade?

Reading/Language Arts

5. Perform an Internet search or visit your school or local library to obtain information about slotting fees. Write a one- to two-page paper on the advantages and disadvantages of slotting fees from a manufacturer's and retailer's perspective.

Online Action! Check your answers at *marketingessentials.glencoe.com/30/read*

Sustaining Product Sales

OBJECTIVES

- Identify the four stages of the product life cycle
- Describe product positioning techniques

KEY TERMS

- product life cycle
- product positioning
- category management
- planograms

READ and STUDY

BEFORE YOU READ

Contrast How do you think marketing strategies differ for a new product and for an established one?

THE MAIN IDEA

After products are introduced in the marketplace, they go through different stages of growth and decline. It is important to understand the different marketing strategies used to sustain product sales over time.

STUDY ORGANIZER

Create a chart like the one below to record each stage in the product life cycle. List each stage's sales characteristics and marketing strategies.

Stages in the Product Life Cycle

Stages	Sales Characteristics	Marketing Strategies
Introduction		

Connect Think of why you purchase certain products or services.

The Product Life Cycle

A **product life cycle** represents the stages that a product goes through during its life. There are four stages of the life cycle: introduction, growth, maturity, and decline (see Figure 30.2). As each stage in the product life cycle is reached, marketers must adjust their product mix and their marketing strategies to ensure continued sales.

Managing During the Introduction Stage

When the product is introduced to the market, the company focuses its efforts on promotion and production. The major goal is to draw the customer's attention to the new product. The company works to build its sales by increasing product awareness. Special promotions may get the customer to try the new product. The costs of introducing a product are high. Therefore, this is usually the least profitable stage of the life cycle.

Managing During the Growth Stage

During the growth phase of the product life cycle, the product is enjoying success as shown by increasing sales and profits. Much of the target market knows about and buys the product. Advertising may now focus on consumer satisfaction, rather than on the benefits of new products. By this time, the competition is aware of the success of the product and is likely to offer new products in order to compete. To keep its product sales growing, the company may have to introduce new models or modify the existing product to offer more than the competition.

Managing During the Maturity Stage

A product reaches the maturity stage when its sales level off or slow down. The product may have more competition now, or most of the target market may already own the product.

Figure 30.2 *The Product Life Cycle*

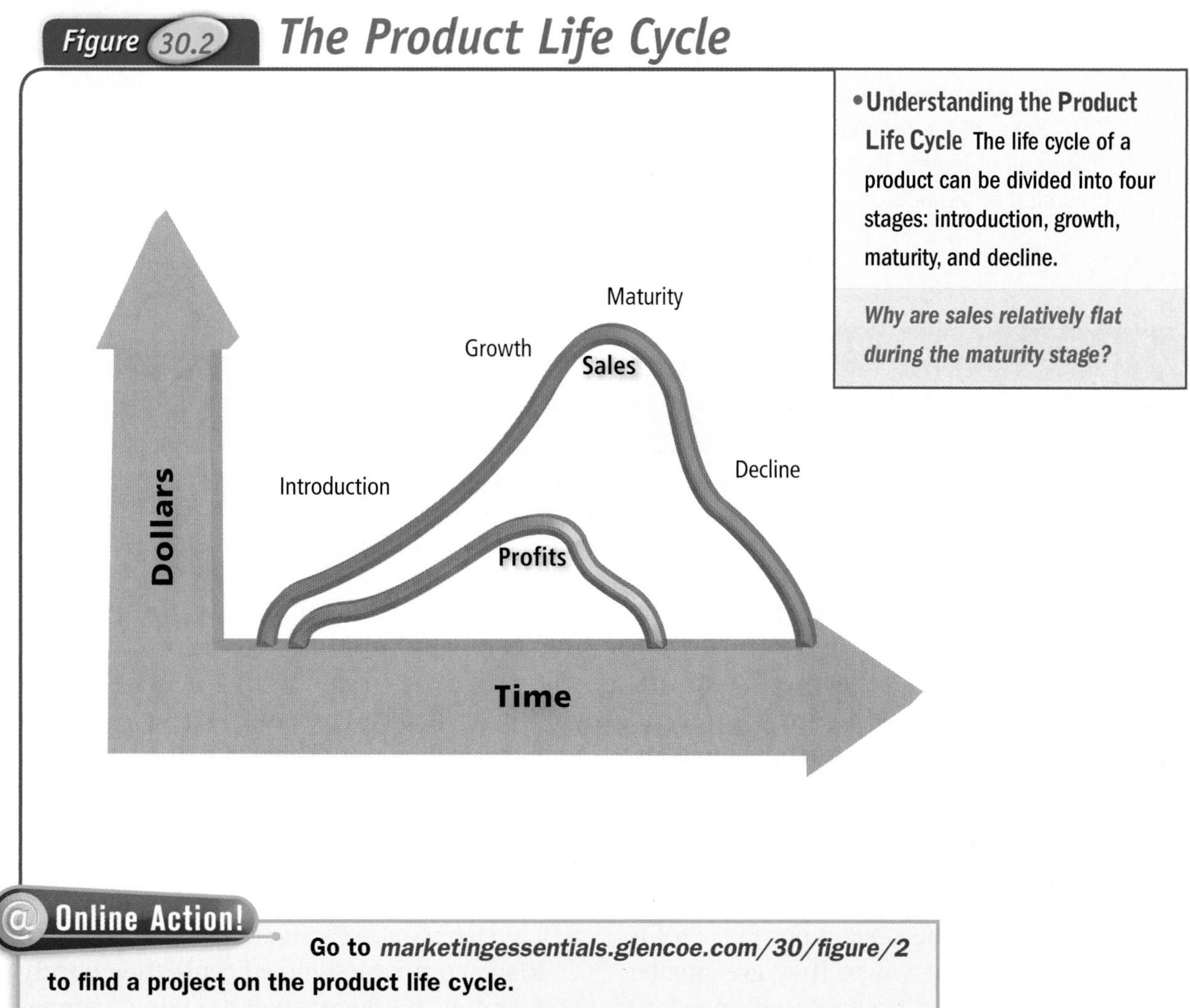

• **Understanding the Product Life Cycle** The life cycle of a product can be divided into four stages: introduction, growth, maturity, and decline.

Why are sales relatively flat during the maturity stage?

@ Online Action! Go to *marketingessentials.glencoe.com/30/figure/2* to find a project on the product life cycle.

Case Study

Snowboarding Without Snow

Winter snowboarding has grown in popularity. From 1997 to 2002, the number of snowboarders doubled to 5.6 million, according to the National Sporting Goods Association. A new product now allows snowboarders to do urban snowboarding after the snow melts. No bindings, boots, or warm clothing is required.

The new boards have a long, hourglass shape, center wheels, and wide-set wheels to simulate a snowboarding ride. The boards are designed to allow riders to slalom down steep streets better than they can with skateboards.

A New Product for an Existing Market

In 1996, Steen Strand designed a prototype of the new board as a project for his master's degree in design at Stanford University. Strand's Freebord X-80 gives the sensation of snowboarding because it has the ability to rotate 360 degrees while on descent. The Freebord X-80 offers two swiveling wheels that sit near the nose and tail of the board. Weight is displaced from the center of the board to the wheels, which spins the board in circles as well as turns it sharply uphill to control speed.

Sales of the Freebord X-80 are expected to double this year. Freebords are so hot in Asia that a Taiwanese company has already developed its own version of the board.

Compare Freebords X-80s to skateboards in the product life cycle. What marketing strategies would you use for the Freebord X-80?

@ Online Action! **Go to *marketingessentials.glencoe.com/30/case* to find an activity about product development.**

During this stage, a company spends more of its marketing dollars fighting off the competition. As advertising expenses climb, the company may have to decide whether it can continue to improve the product to gain additional sales.

Managing During the Decline Stage

During the decline stage, sales fall. Profits may reach the point where they are smaller than the costs. Management will need to decide how long it will continue to support the product. Besides dropping the product, the company can use other product mix strategies to try to gain further sales from a declining or failing product. These strategies include selling or licensing the product, recommitting to the product line, discounting the product, regionalizing the product, and modernizing or altering the product.

Sell or License the Product

Many companies sell or license their poorly performing products to risk-taking companies. Risk-taking companies try to rejuvenate the product by changing the product's image or introducing it to a new market.

Recommit to the Product Line

Some companies decide that a declining product has other possible uses that can help improve sales.

Even with recommitment and advertising of new product uses, there is no guarantee that a product will continue to have enough sales. Eventually, it may need to be discontinued.

Discount the Product

Many declining product lines can be saved from deletion by discounting them to compete with cheaper store or private brands.

Regionalize the Product

Sometimes companies decide to sell declining products only in the geographical areas where there is strong customer loyalty. The Nabisco Food Group markets its My-T-Fine desserts only in northeastern states where it still has a significant customer base. By marketing its product only in that area, the company avoids the cost of national advertising and distribution.

Modernize or Alter the Product Offering

Some products can be altered or modernized to avoid deletion. Products can be completely redesigned, packaged differently, or reformulated. Tide laundry detergent—available in powder form in a box—was redesigned as New Tide. The product was also introduced in liquid form and repackaged in a plastic bottle.

Companies spend large amounts of money to develop and promote consumer and industrial products. As a result, they are reluctant to delete products without trying one of the above strategies. When products must be dropped, a company needs to plan the move carefully to avoid disappointing customers and damaging the company's overall image.

Product Positioning

The focus of **product positioning** is the image that a product projects. The goal of product positioning is to set the product apart from the competition. Product positioning refers to the efforts a business makes to identify, place, and sell its products in the marketplace. To position their products, businesses identify customer needs and determine how their products compare to the competition. A number of strategies are used to position products in the marketplace.

Positioning by Price and Quality

Companies frequently position their products in a product line on the basis of price and quality. A company may offer an economy line, a mid-priced line, and a luxury line. Positioning by price and quality stresses high price as a symbol of quality or low price as an indication of value.

The Ford Motor Company deliberately positions its Focus as an economical compact car while still emphasizing quality. It positions its Mustang as a high-performance car. Promotional efforts are aimed at creating price and quality images for these products. This strategy enables Ford to give each of its products a unique position in the marketplace.

Positioning by Features and Benefits

Products are often associated with a feature, attribute, or customer benefit. OT, a line of personal care products for boys ages 9 to 16, was introduced in 2004. Research had indicated that preteen and teenage boys were dissatisfied with choices available in personal care products. The product line includes shampoo, deodorant, body wash, hair gel, and pomade with rugged names such as Pit Defense and Body Slam. Procter & Gamble, under a licensing agreement with OT Overtime LLC, is promoting the products with bold product names, formulas, and colors to match the intensity of overtime play in sports.

Positioning in Relation to the Competition

Some businesses position their products to compete directly with the products of other companies. Positioning in relation to

MARKET TECH

DVR Benefits at a Low Cost

A digital video recorder, or DVR, is a neat way to watch TV. With a DVR system, you can pause or rewind live TV and can record any program for viewing later without complicated programming and the need to keep blank tapes handy.

But buying a DVR can be costly. What if your budget is limited?

A Cheaper Alternative

If you have a plain old Windows PC, you can turn it into a DVR by using a product from SnapStream Media, a small company from Houston. SnapStream's Beyond TV 3 includes DVR software for Windows and the necessary hardware—an external TV tuner from Hauppauge Computer Works that plugs into the computer with a simple USB cable. This package is sold on the SnapStream.com Web site. No service fee is charged.

Because this bundled product is really two products that are only loosely integrated, there are multiple installation processes—one for the Hauppauge tuner, one for the most recent tuner hardware updates, and a third installation of the Beyond TV 3 software itself.

THINK LIKE A MARKETER

What potential problems can you foresee with bundled products that try to replicate more expensive products at a lower cost? Do you think that this product will be successful?

Online Action!

Go to *marketingessentials.glencoe.com/30/tech* to find an activity about technology and product development.

the competition is a common strategy when a firm is trying to solidify an advantage over another firm.

It is not always a good idea to compete head-to-head with the industry leader. It might be better to compete by showing that you are the underdog. Southwest Airlines does a good job of that by telling potential customers that they are the low-fare alternative to full-service airlines.

Positioning in Relation to Other Products in a Line

Individual products may be positioned in relation to other products in the same line. Starting with the original Palm Pilot fit-in-your-pocket organizer, the company has introduced other handheld products that not only organize information but have added features. For example, the Zire handheld will play MP3s, show photos, and play video clips. The Tungsten handheld allows the user to use e-mail and surf the Web, and the Treo line has all these features plus a phone.

Category Management

Many manufacturers and retailers are adopting a process for marketing and selling their products known as category management. **Category management** is a process that involves managing product categories as individual business units. A category may include a group of product lines with the same target market and distribution channels. The process is designed to put manufacturers and retailers in closer touch with customer needs.

The category manager is responsible for all the brands for one generic product category, such as foods, beverages, or health and beauty products. The category manager is responsible for the profits or losses of the product mix and product lines in the category. The position evolved out of the position of product manager. The difference between the two job titles is that a category manager is responsible for a generic category and has more interaction with other managers from finance, production, and research and development. A product manager handles a particular product and has more direct interaction with the company's sales force.

The manufacturer can customize a product mix within a category according to customer preference on a store-by-store basis. Using scanned data on product sales and other market data, manufacturers assist retailers with their product mix. In examining product mix, a manufacturer determines which of its products a particular retailer does not carry. It also identifies products that would have strong sales potential for both the retailer and the manufacturer. This analysis helps the manufacturer to recommend an optimum product mix by projecting sales volume and profits for a retailer. The manufacturer then suggests adding or deleting certain items to its product mix. If the category manager feels that one product is decreasing sales of other products in the same category, this product may be discontinued.

Another way manufacturers can help retailers is through **planograms**. A planogram is a computer-developed diagram that shows retailers how and where products within a category should be displayed on a shelf at individual stores. This maximizes a product's potential. Placement can also be used to highlight other products that can be used in conjunction with a product. Manufacturers can even customize planograms for specific types of stores. Each store can then stock more of the products that appeal to people in its trading area and fewer products that have limited appeal to its customers.

30.2 AFTER YOU READ

Reviewing Key Terms and Concepts

1. What is the focus and goal of product positioning?
2. List four strategies used to position products in the marketplace.
3. What is category management?

Integrating Academic Skills

Math

4. The Dryers Company has two declining products and is considering deleting one of them from its product line. Product A costs $65 per unit to produce and sells for $110. The storage, distribution, and promotion costs average $4.30 per unit. Last year, 19,500 units were sold. Product B costs $38 to produce and sells for $72. Its storage, distribution, and promotion costs average $7.50 per unit. Last year, 56,000 units were sold. Of the two products, which is the less profitable and should be deleted?

History

5. Perform an Internet search or visit a school or local library to investigate the history of a popular consumer product. Write a one-page report on when and where it was introduced, how it is used, and who manufactures it today.

Check your answers at *marketingessentials.glencoe.com/30/read*

CAREERS IN MARKETING

MACK HANAN
PRINCIPAL
GREENSTREEM.COM LLC

What do you do at work?
I specialize in the creation and take-to-market implementation of fast-growth business models, both for mature businesses of Fortune 500 corporations, and for start-up and early stage companies. I specialize in companies that deal with high-tech or cutting-edge technologies in one way or another.

What skills are most important to you?
It is important to have a strong market sense, as well as an up-to-date understanding of technology. I also have to stay informed on the interplay between social trends and government policy compliance. Strategic creativity is important, as are the ability to lead the adoption of change and people skills as a team leader.

What is your key to success?
I am a zealous advocate of creative strategies, and I work hard to ensure their effective application. It is important to always remain dedicated to my client's objectives. Also, I understand that my compensation is based solely on the performance of my work. In other words, the old adage that the customer is king is still true. So is the rule that good, expert work will be rewarded.

Aptitudes, Abilities, and Skills

Strong understanding of technology as it applies to your chosen industry

Education and Training

High-level business degrees are helpful, with an emphasis on studies in your chosen field of specialty.

Career Path

High-level consultants might begin their careers as employees of a firm, helping apply technology to business and marketing needs. The path of such a career is largely determined by interests, passion, and aptitude.

THINKING CRITICALLY

Why is continuing education crucial in most careers?

Online Action!

Go to *marketingessentials.glencoe.com/30/careers* to find a career-related activity.

CHAPTER 30 REVIEW

FOCUS on KEY POINTS

SECTION 30.1

- Product planning involves deciding what features are needed to sell a business's products, services, or ideas. A product mix strategy is the plan for how the business determines which products it will make or stock. Businesses can use different product mix strategies depending on their resources and their objectives.

SECTION 30.2

- A product life cycle represents the stages that a product goes through during its life (introduction, growth, maturity, and decline). The goal of product positioning is to set the product apart from the competition. Category management is a process that involves managing product categories as individual business units.

REVIEW VOCABULARY

Contrast the following groups of vocabulary terms.

1. product planning (p. 634)/product mix (p. 635)
2. product line (p. 635)/product item (p. 635)
3. product width (p. 635)/product depth (p. 635)
4. product modification (p. 640)/product life cycle (p. 642)
5. product positioning (p. 645)/category management (p. 646)/planograms (p. 647)

REVIEW FACTS and IDEAS

6. What is the difference between a product item and a product line? (30.1)
7. Compare and contrast product depth and product width. (30.1)
8. What types of criteria are used to screen new product ideas? (30.1)
9. Explain how marketers evaluate customer acceptance of a new product. (30.1)
10. What are four reasons for expanding a product line? (30.1)
11. What strategies might a business use during a product's growth stage? (30.2)
12. What strategies might a business use during a product's maturity stage? (30.2)
13. List the strategies that a company can use during a product's decline stage. (30.2)
14. Explain the concept of product positioning. (30.2)

BUILD SKILLS

15. **Workplace Skills**

Human Relations You are the manager of a large grocery store that has recently remodeled. An exasperated customer confronts you because he cannot find a product. He complains that the new organization of products makes no sense. What might you do to pacify the customer and encourage him to continue shopping at the store?

16. **Technology Applications**

Technology and Car Features Investigate how technological improvements have impacted cars in the past five years. Using a word processing program, prepare a written report of 150 to 200 words about one technological development and its effect on the kinds of features offered in today's cars.

17. **Math Practice**

Slotting Fees Retailers sometimes charge manufacturers slotting fees for helping to introduce merchandise. Assume that a small retail chain charges $5,000 per store for a new brand of hot dogs, while a mass market merchandiser charges $20,000 per store for the same product. To how many stores could you sell your brand of hot dogs if your company has a slotting allowance budget of $90,000 and must include at least two mass market stores?

DEVELOP CRITICAL THINKING

18. **Investigating New Product Development**

Perform an Internet search for a sports-related product that is being introduced. Write a one-page report on the product, its intended users, and your rationale for believing that the product will or will not be successful.

19. **Green Products for Green Marketing**

In response to the development of a market for ecologically sound products, manufacturers are designing products that are safe for the environment, or they are adapting current products to fit the green market.

Choose a company that interests you, describe its current product line, and suggest ways one or several products could be modified to be environmentally friendly. Finally, explain how the product modifications you are suggesting would affect the company's marketing strategies.

APPLY CONCEPTS

20. Identifying Product Mix

Explore a Web site for a car manufacturer, such as Ford, General Motors, DaimlerChrysler, Honda, Toyota, or another one of your choice. Identify the product mix offered by the car manufacturer.

Activity Write an outline detailing one product line and the primary market for each product in that product line.

21. Presenting Width and Depth of a Product Line

Investigate a consumer product, such as digital cameras, cellular phones, handheld gaming devices, cosmetics, or sporting equipment, by a specific manufacturer. Identify the width and depth of the selected product line.

Activity Prepare a chart presenting your findings. List each product line as a separate column heading. Then list particular product names in the columns under the appropriate product line.

NET SAVVY

22. Product Line Extensions

Find a food product manufacturer's Web site (Campbell's Soup, J. M. Smucker, Dean Foods, Kellogg's, Hershey Foods, General Mills, H. J. Heinz, Kraft, Del Monte) to obtain five examples of product line extensions. Use presentation software to give an oral report on the name of the original product and the line extensions for the product.

THE DECA CONNECTION

An Association of Marketing Students

Role Play: Product Planning

Situation You are to assume the role of sales associate for a store that sells decorative pillows for the home. The store's owner (judge) has decided to introduce a new line of tapestry pillows imported from England. The store's owner (judge) has asked you for ideas and suggestions to help introduce this new line. The new pillow line will have a retail selling price of $70 to $80 each. This is 10 percent higher than current selling prices.

Activity You are to present your ideas and suggestions for introducing the new pillow line to the store's owner (judge).

Evaluation You will be evaluated on how well you meet the following performance indicators:

- Explain the concept of product mix
- Plan product mix
- Describe factors used by marketers to position products/businesses
- Develop strategies to position products/businesses
- Explain the nature and scope of product/service management function

@ Online Action!

For more information and DECA Prep practice, go to *marketingessentials.glencoe.com/30/DECA*

CHAPTER 31

Branding, Packaging, and Labeling

Chapter Objectives

After reading this chapter, you should be able to:

- Discuss the nature, scope, and importance of branding in product planning
- Identify the various branding elements
- List three different types of brands
- Explain how branding strategies are used to meet sales and company goals
- Explain the functions of product packaging
- Identify the functions of labels

GUIDE TO THE PHOTO

Market Talk Branding, packaging, and labeling are part of the product planning strategy to create perceived product differences or emphasize real differences. Labels have distinctive lettering and design. Nutrition information is another important component of food product labels such as cereals.

Quick Think Is it important for a product to be associated with a specific label and packaging? Why or why not?

THE DECA CONNECTION

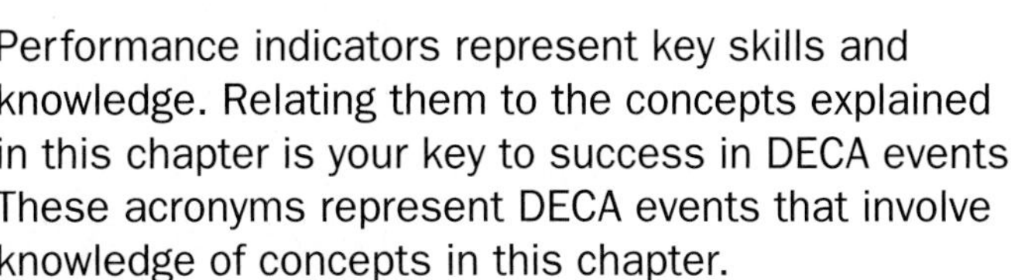

Performance indicators represent key skills and knowledge. Relating them to the concepts explained in this chapter is your key to success in DECA events. These acronyms represent DECA events that involve knowledge of concepts in this chapter.

AAAL*	**FMAL***	**MMS**	**TMDM**
AAML*	**FMDM**	**QSRM**	**TSE**
ADC	**FMML***	**RMAL***	**VPM***
BSM	**FSRM**	**RMML***	
EMDM*	**HMDM**	**SMDM**	

In all these DECA events you should be able to follow these performance indicators:

- Explain the nature of branding
- Describe the uses of grades and standards in marketing

All the events with an asterisk (*) also include this performance indicator:

- Explain the use of brand names in selling

Some events include additional performance indicators. These are:

EMDM	Use the Internet to build brand equity Optimize a business's Web site placement with major search engines and directories
HMDM	Explain the nature of product extensions in the hospitality industry
TMDM	Explain the nature of product extensions in the travel and tourism industry
SMDM	Explain the use of branding in sports and entertainment marketing, Explain logo rights
AAML	Explain fashion-brand images
AAAL	Explain fashion-brand images
FMML	Identify major product categories and classifications of food products in grocery stores

DECA PREP

Check your understanding of DECA performance indicators with the DECA activity in this chapter's review. For more information and DECA Prep practice, go to *marketingessentials .glencoe.com/31/DECA*

SECTION 31.1

OBJECTIVES

- Discuss the nature, scope, and importance of branding in product planning
- Identify the various branding elements
- List three different types of brands
- Explain how branding strategies are used to meet sales and company goals

KEY TERMS

- brand
- brand name
- trade name
- brand mark
- trade character
- trademark
- national brands
- private distributor brands
- generic brands
- brand extension
- brand licensing
- mixed brand
- co-branding

Branding Elements and Strategies

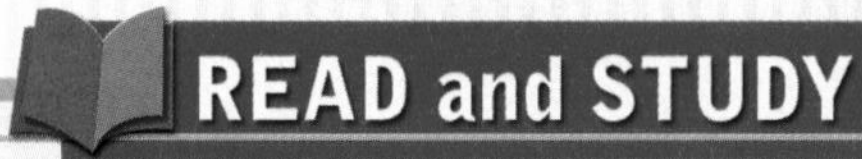

BEFORE YOU READ

Connect Have you or a member of your family recently shopped for or purchased an automobile? How did you know about the benefits and characteristics of the vehicle before you saw it in person?

THE MAIN IDEA

The name of a company and the names of its products or services need to project a positive image. Selecting, promoting, and protecting that image, or brand, is an integral part of the marketing function.

STUDY ORGANIZER

In a chart like the one below, take notes on the branding process.

Analyze Why are brands so important to the success of a business?

Branding

Branding is an important component of the product planning process. A **brand** is a name, term, design, symbol, or combination of these elements that identifies a product or service and distinguishes it from its competitors. A brand can be used to identify one product, a family of related products, or all products of a company. Brands connote any number of benefits,

If product planners do not consider these factors when designing packaging, companies run the risk of losing business as well as eroding their brand images.

Contemporary Packaging Issues

Product packaging offers companies unique opportunities to incorporate the latest technologies and address lifestyle changes as well as environmental, social, and political concerns.

Aseptic Packaging

Aseptic packaging incorporates a technology that keeps foods fresh without refrigeration for extended periods. The process involves separately sterilizing the package and the food product, and filling and sealing the package in a sterile environment. Canning and bottling are aseptic methods of food storage.

Environmental Packaging

Companies are trying to develop packages that respond to consumer demand for environmentally sensitive designs. Recent public opinion surveys show that most Americans support less wasteful packaging. They are even willing to pay more for products that reduce waste. In response to consumer concern, companies are making more packages that are reusable, recyclable, and safer for the environment.

Many companies that manufacture spray products such as hair products, air freshener, and paint have switched from using aerosol cans to pump dispensers, which do not release ozone-destroying chlorofluorocarbons, or CFCs, into the atmosphere.

Cause Packaging

Some companies are also using their packages to promote social and political causes.

GLOBAL MARKET

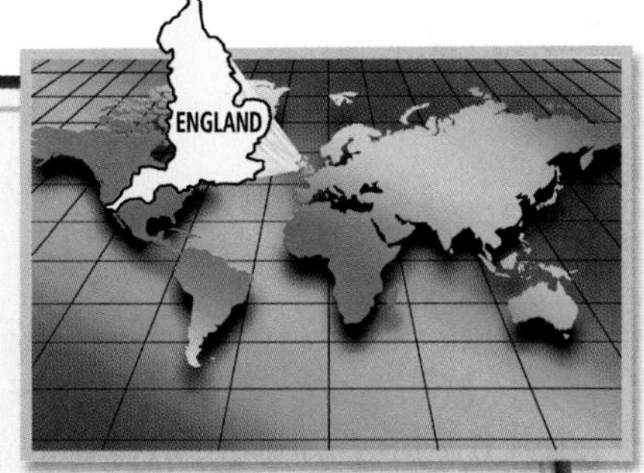

They Got Sole

High fashion can have very humble beginnings. Dr. Martens boots, known as Doc Martens, are the invention of a British orthopedic physician who wanted to create work shoes for people with foot problems. They were an immediate hit among fashion trendsetters, became a British cultural symbol, and are now popular on many continents.

Their popularity is in part due to their broad appeal. In the United States, musicians and rockers of the grunge, alternative, garage band, and ska scenes wore them in the late 1980s and 1990s. But they were also part of the mainstream marketplace.

Regional Differences But not everyone likes the same Docs. Europeans wear Doc Martens in bright colors, such as reds, greens, and blues. In Japan, younger women and some men like classic mid-calf-high boots in colors. Americans prefer black, brown, and tan. Americans are more likely to buy hiking boot styles because of a more casual lifestyle.

Aside from the color differences, all Doc Martens have certain design elements in common. According to the company's marketing director, all Docs have a thick, deeply treaded sole that extends beyond the upper and heavy stitching, often in white, along its seams.

CRITICAL THINKING

How can marketers develop a global brand but still address local needs?

@ Online Action!

Go to *marketingessentials.glencoe.com/31/global* to find a project on global marketing of brands.

• YOGURT on a MISSION The Stonyfield Farm yogurt company prints messages on the lids of its containers. Stonyfield Farm donates ten percent of its profits each year to efforts that help protect or restore the Earth. The company also strives to educate consumers on key health and environmental issues.

What message is the labeling of this product sending?

This practice is known as **cause packaging**. The issues on the packages may be totally unrelated to the products inside. Ben & Jerry's ice cream cartons promote saving the rain forests and express opposition to the use of bovine growth hormone to stimulate milk production in cows.

Printing messages on packages encourages consumers to participate in or think about issues. In many ways, cause packaging is also a company's attempt to differentiate its products from those of its competitors.

Labeling

A **label** is an information tag, wrapper, seal, or imprinted message that is attached to a product or its package. The main function of a label is to inform customers about a product's contents and give directions for use. Labels also protect businesses from legal liability if a consumer is injured during the use of its product. Fear of litigation, consumer pressure, government regulation, and concern for consumer safety are all factors that have compelled manufacturers to place more detailed information on labels.

There are three kinds of labels: brand, descriptive, and grade.

The **brand label** gives the brand name, trademark, or logo. For example, some bananas are stamped with the Chiquita brand label. Although this is an acceptable form of labeling, it does not supply sufficient product information.

A **descriptive label** gives information about the product's use, construction, care, performance, and other features. For example, food labels include product illustrations, weight statements, dating and storage information, ingredients, product guarantees, and the manufacturer's name and address. Product illustrations must represent what is in the package. Weight statements give the net weight of the entire product minus the package or liquid in which it is packed.

Date and storage information is necessary for food items. Date information includes the "packed on" date (date food was packed), the "sell by" date (last date product should be sold), the "best if used by" date (last date for use for top quality), and the expiration date (date after which the product should not be used). Storage information tells how the product should be stored to have the least waste and best quality. Descriptive labels do not necessarily always contain all the information that consumers need when making a buying decision.

Nonfood labels usually provide consumers with instructions for the proper use and

Case Study

Looking for the Cool Factor

The Wrigley company has not spent a lot of time remaking its products over the years. It has been making its Juicy Fruit and Spearmint flavors for more than 100 years, and its Doublemint brand for more than 90 years. But recently the company wanted to expand its sales and extend its brand. So the company turned to Skippies for advice.

Ask the Teens

Skippies, short for School Kids with Income and Purchasing Power, are a target market segment that is getting more attention from market researchers. Teenagers spent $170 billion on products for themselves or their family households in 2003, up from $155 billion in 2000 according to a survey conducted by Teenage Research Unlimited.

Once Wrigley consulted with the Skippies, it introduced a new kind of Juicy Fruit in Strappleberry and Grapermelon flavors. Instead of having the normal long, flat shape with shiny foil around each stick, the new gum is candy-coated individual pieces packaged in blisterpacks. The gum package is flatter and wider than the traditional gum package and it has an inner case that slides out. The company also launched a tongue-twister contest on its Web site, offering free gum to winners. The traditional Juicy Fruit sticks are still on the market.

THINK STRATEGICALLY

Why are companies attempting to make connections with the youth market? Are there any problems with remixing a traditional brand?

Online Action!

Go to *marketingessentials.glencoe.com/31/case* to find a project on marketing to teens.

care of products. They also give manufacturers a convenient place to communicate warranty information and product use warnings. Notices of electrical hazard, flammability, and poisonous ingredients are required on the labels of certain categories of products. Due to increased international business, labels might contain symbols in addition to words. These symbols give graphic instructions on how to wash, cook, or care for the product.

The manufacturer's name and address is provided so consumers can write for more information or to register a complaint. Many packages include the company's Web address, encouraging consumers to visit for more information. Some labels include a customer service phone number that consumers can contact for questions or problems.

A **grade label** states the quality of the product. For example, eggs are grade-labeled AA, A, and B; corn and wheat are grade-labeled 1 and 2; and canned fruit is often grade-labeled A, B, or C.

Labeling Laws

In the past, the public has criticized companies for failing to offer complete and truthful information on product labels. Consumers also complained about the lack of uniformity in labeling. As a result of these complaints and concerns, labeling laws were established. Many package labels must now meet local, state, and federal standards. Federal mandates require that the name and address of the manufacturer, packer, or distributor and the quantity of contents appear on labels. These standards prevent manufacturers from misleading consumers with deceptive or incomplete packaging labels.

The Fair Packaging and Labeling Act (FPLA) of 1966 established mandatory labeling requirements and authorized the U.S. Food and Drug Administration (FDA) and the Federal Trade Commission (FTC) to establish packaging regulations. A 1992 amendment to the FPLA called for packages of selected products to include metric measurements. The amendment, which went into effect in 1994, mandates that product weight be listed in American and metric weights and measures.

In today's global marketplace, companies must also consider the labeling laws of other countries. Some countries require bilingual labels. Others require that every ingredient in a product be listed on the label.

The Federal Food and Drug Administration

The federal Nutrition Labeling and Education Act passed in 1990 and enacted in 1994 protects consumers from deceptive labeling. This act, which is administered by the FDA, requires that labels give nutritional information on how a food fits into an overall daily diet. Labels must clearly state the amount of calories, fat, carbohydrates, sodium, cholesterol, and protein in each serving, as well as the percentage of a daily intake of 2,000 calories. The act also regulates health claims and defines descriptive terms to make them consistent on all products. These terms and phrases include *light* and *lite, free* (as in *fat free, salt free, cholesterol free*), *low, reduced,* and *good source of.*

The FDA also requires that manufacturers of certain products place health warnings on their packages. Beginning in 1989, all alcoholic beverage labels had to carry the following statement: "According to the Surgeon General, women should not drink alcoholic beverages during pregnancy because of the risk of birth defects. Consumption of alcoholic beverages impairs the ability to drive a car or operate machinery and may cause health problems." Similar warnings of health risks are required on cigarette package labels.

The FDA also has proposed new regulations on genetically modified foods. The FDA is developing guidelines for voluntary labeling as to whether food products contain genetically modified organisms.

The Federal Trade Commission

Another federal agency involved with product labeling is the Federal Trade Commission (FTC). The FTC is also responsible for monitoring advertising that is false or misleading.

The Care Labeling Rule, first introduced in 1972, requires that care labels be placed in textile clothing. The care labeling rules ensure that specific information about the care of garments be detailed on labels, including information related to washing, drying, and ironing.

The FTC released guidelines in 1992 for companies to follow when making environmental claims on product labels. Previously, many environmental terms had definitions that were not clear. When using the term *recycled* to describe the content of its products, a company must now show proof that it has retrieved or recovered a designated amount of scraps or materials from the waste stream. The term *recyclable* can be used only if the product or package can be re-used as raw material for a new product or package. The terms *ozone safe* and *ozone friendly* can be used only if the products do not contain any ozone-depleting chemicals. The terms *degradable, biodegradable,* and *photodegradable* can be used only if the product will decompose into elements found in nature within a reasonably short period of time after disposal.

U.S. Department of Agriculture

The rise of specialty markets for organic foods, which totaled $11 billion in sales in 2002, has compelled the U.S. Department of Agriculture (USDA) to issue legal standards and certification requirements for organic labels. The National Organic Rule dictates that companies must reserve the words *100 percent organic* and *organic* for use with foods that are produced without hormones, antibiotics, herbicides, insecticides, chemicals, genetic modification, or germ-killing radiation. The certified organic label requires both products and producers to be certified.

The Country of Origin Labeling (COOL) Act signed in 2002 will take effect in September of 2006. This new law is also administered by the USDA and will require that a country-of-origin label be placed on all fruits, vegetables, peanuts, meats, and fish in the future.

31.2 AFTER YOU READ

Reviewing Key Terms and Concepts

1. Why is a package important to product planning?
2. What are the main functions of product packaging?
3. What three federal agencies regulate labeling laws?

Integrating Academic Skills

Math

4. Robinson & Provost, Inc., a name branding agency, was paid $15,000 by Happy Wanderers Travel Agency for the research and development of the agency's corporate trade name and trademark. Robinson & Provost's graphic designer was paid $6,475 for her creative work on this project. Her salary was what percentage of the entire amount?

Civics and Government

5. Use the Internet or library resources to study one of the federal labeling laws explained in this chapter. Write a one- to two-page report on how the government enforces the law that you investigated.

Check your answers at *marketingessentials.glencoe.com/31/read*

CAREERS IN MARKETING

TRACEY MCFALL
OWNER
KINDHEARTED WOMEN, BABY CARE PRODUCTS

What do you do at work?

I develop and create formulas and recipes for cosmetic and body care products such as lotions, body butters, hair conditioners, baby care products, and the like. I test, package, label, and advertise my products myself. I have a partner who makes baby diapers and diapering supplies. Development of effective formulas requires not only knowledge of raw materials and how they do what they do, but some knowledge of basic chemistry as well.

What skills are most important to you?

The ability to listen to customer feedback. Sometimes I may love a product, but it is not selling. I need to do a little troubleshooting and find out why. Adjustment may be needed in ingredients, marketing, and/or pricing. Sometimes the problem is as simple as a label design flaw or an unappealing bottle or jar—I guess another important skill is the ability to be a bit of a detective.

What is your key to success?

Secure financial backing; research and know your market. Set aside a fair amount for advertising and track what works and what doesn't, be diverse while remembering you can't do it all—you still need a niche. Never sacrifice product quality or your moral values for sales. Most of all, be patient, and remember that most small businesses fail within the first year.

Aptitudes, Abilities, and Skills

Creativity, research skills, product knowledge, customer service and communication skills

Education and Training

Degrees in marketing, communication, and general business are useful.

Career Path

This is an entrepreneurial career, which means it can start anywhere. Product development positions at large corporations are high-level positions, though, and require substantial marketing and product design experience.

THINKING CRITICALLY

How might someone in this entrepreneurial career benefit from a marketing degree?

Online Action!

Go to *marketingessentials.glencoe.com/31/careers* to find a career-related activity.

CHAPTER 31 REVIEW

FOCUS on KEY POINTS

SECTION 31.1

- A brand is a name, term, design, or symbol (or combination of these elements) that identifies a product or service. Brands can include a number of elements, such as a trade name, brand name, brand mark, trade character, and trademark. Branding strategies include brand extensions, brand licensing, mixed branding, and co-branding. Effective use of different brand strategies can increase sales of branded products and maximize company revenues.

SECTION 31.2

- The functions of packaging include promoting and selling the product, defining product identity, providing information, expressing benefits and features to customers, ensuring safe use, and protecting the product. The main function of a label is to inform customers about a product's contents and give directions for use. Labels also protect businesses from legal liability that may occur if a consumer misuses the product.

REVIEW VOCABULARY

Define each of the key terms below.

1. brand (p. 654)
2. brand name (p. 655)
3. trade name (p. 655)
4. brand mark (p. 656)
5. trade character (p. 656)
6. trademark (p. 656)
7. national brands (p. 657)
8. private distributor brands (p. 657)
9. generic brands (p. 658)
10. brand extension (p. 658)
11. brand licensing (p. 658)
12. mixed brand (p. 659)
13. co-branding (p. 659)
14. package (p. 660)
15. mixed bundling (p. 661)
16. price bundling (p. 661)
17. blisterpack (p. 661)
18. aseptic packaging (p. 663)
19. cause packaging (p. 664)
20. label (p. 664)
21. brand label (p. 664)
22. descriptive label (p. 664)
23. grade label (p. 666)

REVIEW FACTS and IDEAS

24. What is the difference between brand extension and brand licensing? (31.1)
25. Why is a mixed-brand strategy used in product planning? (31.1)
26. What is a grade label? (31.2)
27. Name three types of packaging and explain their uses. (31.2)

BUILD SKILLS

28. Workplace Skills

Research Skills Select one line of products that is of interest to you. Identify the various brands sold in that product line. Use the Internet and corporate Web sites to find out specific product information. List the similarities and differences among the products.

29. Technology Applications

The Recycling Process Research the process used to recycle paper, cardboard, glass, plastic, wood, or other packaging materials. Create a chart that illustrates and describes the type of recycling process for the material selected.

30. Math Practice

Brand Valuation Perform an Internet search on the mathematical method used by Interbrand to determine brand valuation. Summarize the procedure in a written one-page report.

DEVELOP CRITICAL THINKING

31. For Kids Only

A few brands of yogurt now package their product in soft plastic tubes that can be squeezed. The concept is that it is yogurt on the go. This idea might have targeted a broad market segment, but instead, those companies have single-mindedly chosen to target primary and middle-school-aged children and their families.

Why do you think manufacturers chose this market segmentation? How does the packaging relate to the target market?

32. Global Brands

Large multinational companies often sell their products all around the globe. For example, Unilever sells a deodorant soap called Rexona in Africa, Australia, and the Middle East, and in most of Europe. In Great-Britain, the same soap is called Sure while in the United States it is called Degree.

What factors do you think companies such as Unilever consider before introducing a product with a specific label and packaging to a specific market?

APPLY CONCEPTS

33. Investigating Brand Licensing

Investigate an existing brand licensing arrangement. Use business publications or online sources such as *Brandweek, Adweek, BusinessWeek, Fortune, Forbes, Marketing News,* or Creative Magazine.com to find applicable information.

Activity In a one-page paper, summarize the companies involved and how the licensing arrangement was established.

34. Understanding Product Packaging

Locate the Web site of a food products manufacturer of your choice, such as Hormel, Hershey's, General Mills, Kellogg's, H.J. Heinz, Del Monte, or Campbell's. Review the site and the company's product lines. Select one product line and identify how the package for the product fulfills one or more of the functions of packaging identified in this chapter.

Activity Use presentation software to create a report based on your research.

NET SAVVY

35. Advergames

Locate an advergame Web site. Some possible choices include the sites of Procter & Gamble, Wrigley, Kellogg's, Kraft, Pepsi, McDonald's, General Mills, or Hershey's. Play one of the sponsored games. Prepare an oral presentation with an accompanying electronic presentation describing the game, how it is played, and what you liked and disliked about the game.

THE DECA CONNECTION

An Association of Marketing Students

Role Play: Branding, Packaging, and Labeling

Situation You are to assume the role of assistant manager of a discount store. Your store carries merchandise with well-known manufacturer brands, merchandise with the store's brand, and some merchandise with generic branding. Many new employees find the different types of brands difficult to understand and explain to customers.

Activity You are to explain the three types of brands to the store's sales staff (judge) during an upcoming staff meeting. Be sure to include examples of each type of brand in your presentation.

Evaluation You will be evaluated on how well you meet the following performance indicators:

- Explain the nature of branding
- Describe factors used by marketers to position products/businesses
- Develop strategies to position products/businesses
- Explain the concept of product mix
- Conduct staff meetings

@ Online Action!

For more information and DECA Prep practice, go to *marketingessentials.glencoe.com/31/DECA*

CHAPTER 32
Extended Product Features

Chapter Objectives

After reading this chapter, you should be able to:

- Identify different types of warranties
- Explore the importance of warranties in product planning
- Identify the major provisions of product safety legislation
- Explain consumer responsibilities and rights related to product performance
- Describe the importance of credit
- Explain various sources of consumer credit
- Identify the types of credit accounts extended to consumers
- Discuss how businesses use trade credit

GUIDE TO THE PHOTO

Market Talk Extended product features such as warranties and the use of credit affect product planning and relate to consumer rights and responsibilities. If a consumer buys a pair of shoes and the soles fall apart on the first day the customer wears the shoes, the product might be defective and might be covered by a manufacturer's warranty.

Quick Think Would a warranty cover the same shoes if they fall apart after a month of wear? Explain your opinion.

Performance indicators represent key skills and knowledge. Relating them to the concepts explained in this chapter is your key to success in DECA events. These acronyms represent DECA events that involve knowledge of concepts in this chapter.

AAAL	**FMAL**	**MMS***	**TMDM**
AAML	**FMDM***	**QSRM**	**TSE**
ADC	**FMML**	**RMAL**	**VPM**
BSM	**FSRM**	**RMML**	
EMDM*	**HMDM**	**SMDM**	

In all these DECA events you should be able to follow these performance indicators:

- Explain warranties and guarantees
- Identify consumer protection provisions of appropriate agencies
- Explain business ethics in product/service management
- Describe legal issues affecting businesses
- Explain the purpose and importance of credit

The events with an asterisk (*) also include:

- Make critical decisions regarding acceptance of credit cards

Some events include additional indicators:

VPM Describe the role of warranties and guarantees used in vehicle and petroleum marketing

AAML/MML Explain factors affecting extension of credit. Determine credit worthiness of customers. Close credit accounts. Establish collection procedures.

FMDM Determine credit worthiness. Place a hold on customer accounts. Analyze credit rating system. Collect receivables.

DECA PREP

Check your understanding of DECA performance indicators with the DECA activity in this chapter's review. For more information and DECA Prep practice, go to *marketingessentials .glencoe.com/32/DECA*

SECTION 32.1

Warranties

OBJECTIVES

- Identify different types of warranties
- Explore the importance of warranties in product planning
- Identify the major provisions of product safety legislation
- Explain consumer responsibilities and rights related to product performance

KEY TERMS

- warranty
- express warranty
- full warranty
- limited warranty
- implied warranty
- warranty of merchantability
- warranty of fitness for a particular purpose
- disclaimer

READ and STUDY

BEFORE YOU READ

Predict Why do you think warranties are a good marketing tactic?

THE MAIN IDEA

Sellers use warranties to encourage customers—wholesalers, retailers, or consumers—to purchase a product or service. Warranties can boost sales, but they can also pose product and customer service problems.

STUDY ORGANIZER

In a chart like the one below, take notes about extended features and warranties.

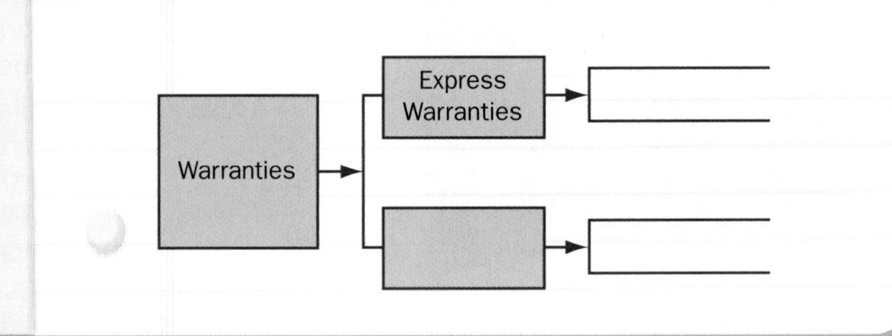

WHILE YOU READ

Analysis Why are warranties and guarantees both essential components of product planning?

Warranties

Extended product features offered after the sale, such as warranties, often determine the likelihood of repeat sales. A **warranty** is a promise or guarantee given to a customer that a product will meet certain standards. Typically, these standards apply to materials, workmanship, and performance.

Guarantee is another term for warranty. The major difference between a guarantee and a warranty is the promotional value of the promise. The term guarantee (or guaranteed) is usually used in conjunction with promotional phrases such as money-back guarantee, results guaranteed, guaranteed for 1,000 hours of use, or satisfaction guaranteed.

A warranty, on the other hand, is usually framed as a series of specific promises. An example is, "Norm's Body Shop will repair any defects in workmanship billed on the repair invoice unless caused by or damaged from unreasonable use, maintenance, or care of the vehicle, excluding paint work if the vehicle's original finish is defective."

Typical warranties set time or use limits for coverage and restrict the seller's liability. The most familiar language is usually found in auto warranties: "Warranty ends at 36 months or 36,000 miles, whichever occurs first."

Role of Warranties in Product Planning

Warranties are an important element of product planning because they help increase sales and profits (see Figure 32.1). Customers often make purchasing decisions based on warranties.

Businesses are not required by law to issue warranties, although most do to assure their customers that their products and services meet quality standards. For some companies, notably automobile manufacturers, warranties play a prominent role in product advertising. Warranties are also significant to businesses because:

- They direct a company to focus on customer satisfaction.
- They require a company to adhere to performance standards.
- They generate customer feedback.
- They encourage quality in product development.
- They boost promotional efforts.

Warranties come in two different forms, express and implied. These forms, in turn, can be divided into specific types.

Express Warranties

An **express warranty** is one that is explicitly stated, in writing or verbally, to encourage a customer to make a purchase. A written warranty can appear in a number of places: on the product packaging, in the product literature, in an advertisement, or as part of a point-of-purchase display. The location of the warranty should be accessible to customers before purchase. The warranty must always be clearly worded so that customers can easily understand its terms. Spoken warranties, however, even if clearly worded, may not be enforceable unless they are also in writing.

Here is an example of how an express warranty works. A broadcast advertisement shows that a portable MP3 player will operate while the user jogs. You purchase the player and discover almost immediately that it shorts out when you jog. You are entitled to whatever relief the warranty specifies. Now imagine that the MP3 product package features a runner using the product in the rain. You find that the product shorts out in the rain. Once again, you are entitled to warranty relief because the illustration constitutes a promise of performance, even though the promise is not a written one. There are two types of written warranties: a full warranty and a limited warranty.

Full Warranty

A **full warranty** guarantees that if a product is found to be defective within the warranty period, it will be repaired or replaced at no cost to the purchaser. A manufacturer who offers a full warranty agrees to repair a defective product "within a reasonable time and without charge."

Limited Warranty

A **limited warranty** may exclude certain parts of the product from coverage or require the customer to bear some of the expense for repairs resulting from defects. It is not uncommon, for example, for a limited warranty to specify that the manufacturer will pay

Figure 32.1 Warranties and Product Planning

• **Appealing to the Customer** Following are some of the ways warranties affect product planning.

Why do companies issue warranties?

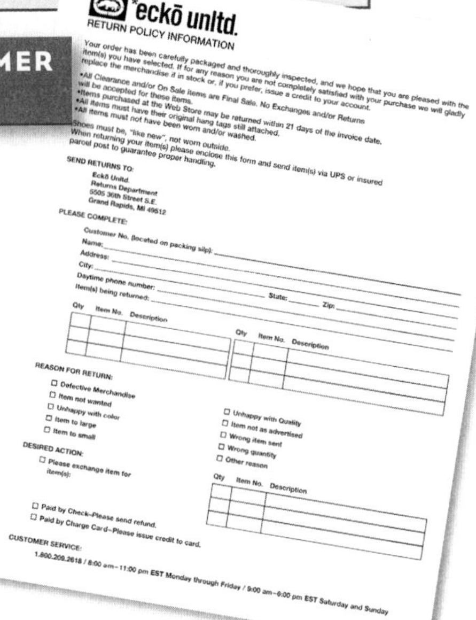

*eckō unltd.
RETURN POLICY INFORMATION

Your order has been carefully packaged and thoroughly inspected, and we hope that you are pleased with the item(s) you have selected. If for any reason you are not completely satisfied with your purchase we will gladly replace the merchandise if in stock or, if you prefer, issue a credit to your account.

•All Clearance and/or On Sale items are Final Sale. No Exchanges and/or Returns will be accepted for these items.
•Items purchased at the Web Store may be returned within 21 days of the invoice date.
•All items must have their original hang tags still attached.
•All items must not have been worn and/or washed.
Shoes must be, "like new", not worn outside.
When returning your item(s) please enclose this form and send item(s) via UPS or insured parcel post to guarantee proper handling.

SEND RETURNS TO:
Eckō Unltd.
Returns Department
5505 36th Street S.E.
Grand Rapids, MI 49512

PLEASE COMPLETE:
Customer No. (located on packing slip):
Name:
Address:
City:
Daytime phone number: State: Zip:
Item(s) being returned:

Qty	Item No.	Description

Qty	Item No.	Description

REASON FOR RETURN:
☐ Defective Merchandise
☐ Item not wanted
☐ Unhappy with color
☐ Item to large
☐ Item to small
☐ Unhappy with Quality
☐ Item not as advertised
☐ Wrong item sent
☐ Wrong quantity
☐ Other reason

DESIRED ACTION:
☐ Please exchange item for item(s):

Qty	Item No.	Description

☐ Paid by Check–Please send refund.
☐ Paid by Charge Card–Please issue credit to card.

CUSTOMER SERVICE:
1.800.209.2618 / 8:00 am–11:00 pm EST Monday through Friday / 9:00 am–6:00 pm EST Saturday and Sunday

FOCUS ON CUSTOMER SATISFACTION

Warranties help to guide expectations for product performance.

SET CLEAR STANDARDS OF PERFORMANCE

Warranties and company policies that set specific standards tell the customer how the product is manufactured or how it will perform.

GENERATE CUSTOMER FEEDBACK

Product or warranty registrations help provide customer feedback about the product.

ENCOURAGE QUALITY CONTROL

Quality manufacturing is necessary since products that are defective or cannot be repaired must be replaced under a warranty program.

BOOST PROMOTIONAL EFFORTS

Long-term warranties speak for the reputation of the company and the confidence it has in its products.

@ Online Action! **Go to *marketingessentials.glencoe.com/32/figure/1* to find a project on the role of warranties.**

for replacement parts but charge the customer for labor or shipping.

Implied Warranties

Most major consumer purchases are covered by written warranties provided by manufacturers. When there are no written warranties, implied warranty laws apply. An **implied warranty** is one that takes effect automatically by state law whenever a purchase is made. There are two types of implied warranties: a warranty of merchantability and a warranty of fitness for a particular purpose.

Warranty of Merchantability

A **warranty of merchantability** is the seller's promise that the product sold is fit for its intended purpose. Some examples are a gasoline-powered lawnmower that will cut the grass or an electric power saw that will cut wood.

Warranty of Fitness

A **warranty of fitness for a particular purpose** is used when the seller advises a customer that a product is suitable for a particular use, and the customer acts on that advice. A customer, for example, might buy a small truck based on a salesperson's recommendation that it will pull a trailer of a certain weight. The dealership must take back the truck and refund the buyer's money if it turns out that the truck cannot tow the anticipated load.

Warranty Disclaimers

Warranties often have disclaimers to protect the businesses issuing them. A **disclaimer** is a statement that contains exceptions to and exclusions from a warranty. Disclaimers are used to limit damages that can be recovered by a customer. A common form of disclaimer limits recovery to a refund of the purchase

• A ROOF WITH COVERAGE A 50-year warranty on a metal roof appeals to consumers who want low-maintenance roofing.

Why might a 50-year warranty help justify a higher price?

A MATTER OF ETHICS

Using Credit Wisely

Credit card issuers make money on credit card interest rates and special fees. Late payment fees can run from $15 on small balances to up to $39 dollars on larger balances. Late payment fees or additional fees are charged to customers who exceed their authorized credit limits, do not pay their minimum charges within the payment grace period, take cash advances, or transfer balances from one card to another. For example, to get a cash advance, a credit card user has to pay a minimum fee of two to three percent of the advanced amount plus a minimum charge of $2 to $10. Late payment and cash advance fees increased at the same time many credit card issuers have introduced introductory rates of zero to three percent to attract new customers. The average U.S. household's credit card debt is nearly $9,000.

THINKING ETHICALLY

Do you think that late payment fees are fair to customers? Why or why not?

@ Online Action!

Go to *marketingessentials.glencoe.com/32/ethics* to find an activity about ethics and credit.

price. It can specifically exclude any other costs that may have been incurred by the owner as a result of product failure. Another common disclaimer waives customers' rights under implied-warranty laws.

Role of Extended Warranties

Extended warranties or service contracts provide repairs or preventive maintenance for a specified length of time beyond a product's normal warranty period. Customers pay extra for such a contract at the time of purchase or shortly afterward. Costs range from a few dollars on a low-cost item to hundreds or even thousands of dollars on a higher-priced item, such as a car. There is often a deductible amount, which the customer pays before work is performed.

Extended warranties are beneficial to both businesses and customers. Businesses benefit by receiving additional money (and more profit, if the product performs as expected) on the original sale of a product. Customers benefit from the assurance of long-term satisfaction with their purchase.

There are also disadvantages to service contracts. *Consumer Reports* magazine estimates that only 12 to 20 percent of people who buy extra repair or service protection ever use it.

Other Extended Product Features

In addition to warranties, product planners create additional extended product features to boost customer satisfaction. These features include delivery, installation, billing, service after the sale, directions for use, technical assistance, and training.

Businesses gain feedback by conducting customer service and satisfaction surveys. After an initial purchase, customers are frequently asked to submit product registration cards to gain customer data and ideas for product and service improvements.

Consumer Laws and Agencies

Business people need a working knowledge of relevant federal, state, and local laws. Manufacturers must be sure that their products meet all legal requirements. They must be safe, adequately labeled, and properly advertised; if they are not, the manufacturer could face fines or product recalls.

Larger companies often employ consumer affairs or legislative specialists to advise management about legal requirements. Smaller companies often join trade associations to stay informed about existing and pending laws that affect their products.

Federal Statutes

Making sure products meet all federal product safety standards is an important function of product planning. Cars and trucks, for example, have their emission standards set by the Environmental Protection Agency (EPA), their price stickers regulated by the Federal Trade Commission, and any potentially dangerous design flaws investigated by the National Highway Traffic Safety Administration.

Magnuson-Moss Consumer Product Warranty Act

Many of the warranty features have their origins in a federal statute called the Magnuson-Moss Consumer Product Warranty Act of 1975. This statute governs written warranties for all consumer products costing $15 or more. It sets minimum standards for such warranties, rules for making them available before a product is sold, and provisions for lawsuits against manufacturers if a warranty is not fulfilled. The Federal Trade Commission enforces this act.

Consumer Product Safety Act

Other federal statutes protect consumers by forcing companies to manufacture and sell safe products. The Consumer Product Safety Act of 1972, for example, established the Consumer Product Safety Commission (CPSC). This agency monitors the safety of more than 15,000 nonfood items, such as toys; household, outdoor, sports, recreation, and specialty products; and appliances. The agency issues standards for the construction, testing, packaging, and performance of these products to protect the public from unreasonable risks of serious injuries or deaths. When the CPSC finds any product defective or dangerous, it can do any of the following:

- Issue a product safety alert.
- Require that warning labels be attached to the product.
- Recall the product and order repairs.
- Withdraw the product or prohibit its sale.

Since its inception, the CPSC has recalled more than 4,000 products. In June of 2004, Payless ShoeSource, Inc., voluntarily recalled 441,000 Smart Fit and Teeny Toes athletic shoes because the eyelet lace holder can detach, posing a choking hazard for children.

To ensure consumer awareness of product recalls, notices for unsafe children's products, appliances, toys, and other items are placed in all U.S. Postal Service offices.

Food, Drug, and Cosmetic Act

The Food, Drug, and Cosmetic Act of 1938 is another federal statute designed to ensure that products will be safe. Safe in this case means pure, wholesome, and effective. It covers features such as informative labels and truthful advertising. The Food and Drug Administration is responsible for the safety of drugs, medical devices, foods, and some food supplements; it also enforces the act. The agency also regulates the advertising and sale of imported and exported foods, drugs, cosmetics, medical devices, animal drugs, animal feed, and products that emit radiation.

State Statutes

Many states have passed their own consumer protection laws. Most are aimed at preventing poorly made or poorly serviced products.

The most common form of state regulation affects service businesses. Most states require certain individuals such as auto mechanics, realtors, and police and fire safety officers to meet training requirements. It is necessary to hold a license or state certification before legally practicing in those professions. The process frequently involves testing and the payment of a substantial fee.

Lemon Laws

Nearly all states have lemon laws to protect customers. Lemon laws are statutes designed to protect consumers from poorly built cars. Under most lemon laws, a car is a lemon if it is out of service at least 30 days during the first year of ownership or if four attempts have been made to fix the same problem. Lemon owners are entitled to a refund or a comparable replacement car.

•CHECKING SAFETY **Underwriters Laboratories (UL) is a multinational corporation that tests products for safety. Products that pass the tests can bear a UL mark.**

Why might a consumer prefer to buy a product with a UL mark?

Many states have incorporated arbitration programs into their lemon laws. In arbitration, an impartial third party, such as a representative of the Better Business Bureau, decides the crucial issues—for example, whether a vehicle is a lemon and how much the refund should be. In most cases, the arbitrator's ruling is not binding on the parties. The owner can sue the carmaker in a court of law if he or she is not satisfied with the outcome. The principal benefit of arbitration is that it saves all parties the long delays and excessive costs often associated with a lawsuit.

Consumer Rights and Responsibilities

Consumers have a right to expect quality products at fair prices. What happens when the extended features fail? Consumers can take several steps when they have not been adequately protected by a warranty.

- The consumer should contact the business that sold the product or provided the service via phone, letter, or the Internet.
- If the problem is still unresolved, the consumer should contact the local, state, or federal offices that can assist with consumer complaints. Contact information can be found on the World Wide Web or in a telephone directory.
- Finally, if the problem is still not resolved, consumers can take legal action.

Consumers can sue manufacturers or retailers on at least three grounds: breach of federal law (written warranty), breach of state law (implied warranty), and negligence. Negligence means failure to take proper or reasonable care.

When a company does not fulfill its warranty or when it shows carelessness, consumers have the right to take a case to court. Courts have held manufacturers and retailers liable for defects in products or when injury is caused by use of the product. Individuals can also bring food suppliers to court if unhealthy practices or bad food cause sickness.

Consumers, cities, and states can file class action suits against manufacturers who make unsafe products. Class action suits are lawsuits filed by more than one party. It is estimated that Bridgestone/Firestone has spent over $1.5 billion in product recalls and legal fees since 2000 on cases related to some of its tires being involved in SUV rollover accidents.

Businesses can take steps to minimize liability suits during product planning. Manufacturers should examine product design and consider what might go wrong. Products should be tested thoroughly. Besides federally mandated tests, there are extensive use tests that manufacturers can do to make suggestions for recommended product use. Manufacturers should give special attention to package design and provide warnings on the package and labels about any potential hazards involved in using the product. When a manufacturer suspects a problem with a product, it is often more cost effective to recall that product than to risk liability and a damaged reputation.

Private distributors can limit their liability by questioning manufacturers before accepting a product for sale. They should obtain the manufacturer's test data and determine the company's ability to stand behind the product before it is put on store shelves.

As a final line of defense against product liability, businesses should encourage their customers to be responsible consumers. They should take every opportunity to remind customers of their duty to be informed. Customers are responsible for reading and following the safety directions provided with products. This is especially important with items for children, such as car seats, cribs, and even toys.

32.1 AFTER YOU READ

Reviewing Key Terms and Concepts

1. List the different types of warranties.
2. What is the role of warranties in product planning?
3. What are the basic provisions of federal product safety laws?

Integrating Academic Skills

Math

4. In 2004, the state of Michigan gave $47.8 million of the $1 billion it received from the 1998 national tobacco award settlement to biomedical research and new business development. What percentage of Michigan's settlement award does this amount represent?

Communication

5. Warranties are written in legal terms and many consumers find them hard to understand. Using a warranty from a household appliance, electronic equipment, or other consumer product you or your family recently purchased, rewrite the warranty in language that is clear and easy to understand.

Check your answers at *marketingessentials.glencoe.com/32/read*

Credit

OBJECTIVES

- Describe the importance of credit
- Explain various sources of consumer credit
- Identify the types of credit accounts extended to consumers
- Discuss how businesses use trade credit

KEY TERMS

- credit
- 30-day accounts
- installment accounts
- revolving accounts
- budget accounts

READ and STUDY

BEFORE YOU READ

Predict Over 185 million U.S. consumers have at least one credit card. Why do you think credit cards are so popular?

THE MAIN IDEA

Extending credit to customers or accepting credit cards for purchases is an important part of product planning. The wise use of credit can be a great benefit to a business and its customers.

STUDY ORGANIZER

In a chart like the one below jot notes about credit's features.

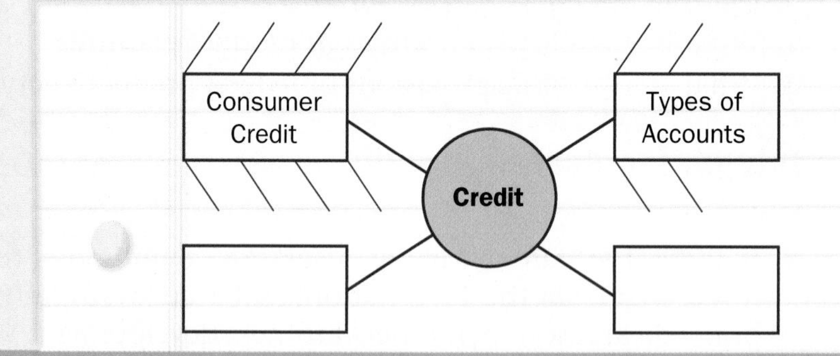

WHILE YOU READ

Connect Based on your prior knowledge about credit, what are the advantages and disadvantages of using credit for purchases?

Credit and Its Importance

Credit enables businesses or individuals to obtain products or money in exchange for a promise to pay later. Credit allows most consumers to make major purchases such as homes, autos, appliances, furniture, and recreational vehicles. Consumers also use credit to make less costly purchases, such as meals, clothing, groceries, and movies.

The use of credit is essential to the U.S. and global economies. According to CardWeb, in 2004 there were over 185 million credit cardholders.

Role of Credit

Businesses and consumers alike use credit to purchase goods and services. Credit is also used between manufacturers, wholesalers, and retailers to buy materials, equipment, supplies, and services for use either within their businesses or to sell to other businesses.

Millions of people and thousands of businesses would not be able to buy necessary goods and services without credit. By extending credit to its customers, a business provides a purchasing incentive and enhances its sales and profits.

Consumer Credit

Companies that offer credit, such as banks, department stores, and oil companies, typically issue credit cards. Customers fill out credit applications to provide information about their sources of income and credit history. If they meet the company's lending criteria, they are issued a credit card and agree to a credit contract that establishes the rules governing the use of the card.

Credit cards are issued with credit limits based on customers' ability to pay and their payment histories. A credit limit is a preapproved dollar amount. Customers can accumulate balances up to that amount. Credit limits can range from as little as $500 for first-time cardholders to tens of thousands of dollars.

Purchases made by credit cards go through a computerized preapproval process prior to the purchase. This assures the company that a customer has not exceeded his or her credit limit.

Bank Credit Cards

Banks or their subsidiaries issue bank credit cards. Visa and MasterCard sponsor bank credit cards, but these companies do not issue them directly. Banks such as BankOne and Citibank that issue credit cards set their own fees and interest rates.

An annual fee is a flat yearly charge similar to a membership fee. Interest rates are tied to other lending rates such as the prime rate or the Treasury bill rate. These are called variable-rate plans. Others are not explicitly tied to changes in other rates and are called fixed-rate plans.

Retailers who belong to a bank credit card system either electronically process credit card sales or mail the credit card forms to the bank for payment. First, the bank deducts a service fee from the sale amount. Then, it remits the balance to the retailer.

Store and Gasoline Cards

Some businesses are large enough to offer their own credit cards, known as proprietary or house cards. Examples of stores and gasoline companies that issue credit cards are Home Depot, Target, and Shell. Usually, proprietary cards do not have an annual fee, but they do have high interest rates. A business also prefers when customers use proprietary cards because it receives income from finance charges. Finance charges on unpaid credit card balances are very expensive. Interest rates of 18 percent or even 21.6 percent are high, but not uncommon.

Travel and Entertainment Cards

Some travel and entertainment companies such as American Express, Diners Club, and Discover issue charge cards with annual fees and service charges; they require that transaction balances be paid in full each month. These types of cards are often accepted for nontravel and entertainment-related goods and services. Travel and entertainment charge card companies also charge retailers higher service fees than credit card companies do for processing the payment. Some businesses are unwilling to pay these fees, so these cards are not universally accepted.

Rebate Cards

Rebate cards offer some type of reward or incentive to consumers who use them. These cards are frequently co-branded and offer rewards in cash, airline miles,

Case Study

Rewards Cards

Rewards cards pay a consumer one point per dollar charged. Since many card issuers no longer charge annual fees to have a card, consumers who pay off their balances each month actually earn money by using rewards cards.

Citibank recently introduced a diamond rewards card that enables cardholders to buy CDs and videos for 1,700 to 2,150 points. Gift certificates are awarded after 500 points are earned. Buy-to-save rewards programs have been launched in the last few years. Upromise is a college savings plan and Nestegg puts a portion of cardholders' spending into retirement accounts.

A Good Deal?

Consumers who do not pay their balance off every month find that the interest charges cost many times more than the free merchandise. For example, if you charge $5,000 to a rewards card, you would receive credits worth about $50. But every month that the balance goes unpaid costs the consumer $41.25 (based on a 9.9 percent annual interest rate).

Only about a quarter of cardholders pay off their balances every month! Rewards programs are targeted to the cardholders who maintain revolving balances. Experts estimate that about 20 to 40 percent of Americans have rewards cards today.

THINK STRATEGICALLY

Why are credit card companies issuing rewards cards?

@ Online Action! **Go to *marketingessentials.glencoe.com/32/case* to find an activity about rewards cards.**

telecommunication service, or special merchandise offers. Individuals who plan to carry balances on a rebate credit card should search for a card with the lowest interest rate. Those who use a credit card for convenience, however, and pay the balance every month may find that rebate cards offer the best deal. Rebate cards have higher interest rates because they are subsidizing membership costs by offering special incentives on future purchases. The Chase PerfectCard Visa, for example, enables you to earn three percent back on your credit purchases for gasoline and one percent on all other purchases. However, the card carries a high annual rate.

Affinity Cards

Affinity cards are credit cards issued by banks to demonstrate a consumer's loyalty to a team, university, charity, business, or other organization. The organization solicits its members or customers to offer them an affinity card to help with brand promotion. The card issuer returns a small percentage (usually less than one percent) of the interest to the organization and reward points or miles to the customer.

Debit Cards

A variation of the credit card is the debit card. When consumers pay for purchases with a debit card, they are authorizing the seller to withdraw funds directly from their bank account at the time of sale to pay for the purchase.

Special Customer Cards

These cards enable customers to receive reduced prices or reward certificates for cash discounts on future purchases. For the business, they provide marketing research information about customers' purchase patterns. Examples include grocery store club cards.

Secured and Unsecured Loans

Loans are also a form of credit. Consumers and businesses can obtain secured loans and unsecured loans for the purchase of goods and services. In secured loans, something of value, such as property, motor vehicles, machinery, or merchandise is pledged as collateral (security). The collateral helps to ensure that a loan will be repaid; if the loan is not repaid, the lender keeps the secured items to cover the debt.

Consumers and businesses can also obtain unsecured loans, which represent a written promise to repay a loan. Unsecured loans do not require collateral but rely on the excellent credit reputation of the borrower who pledges to repay the loan.

In either case, a credit contract is signed to detail payment terms and penalties for not meeting those terms.

Types of Accounts

Four major consumer credit plans are in use today: regular or 30-day accounts, installment accounts, revolving accounts, and budget accounts. The dollar amount a customer pays to use credit is called the finance charge. A finance charge may include interest costs and other charges associated with transactions.

Regular

Regular charge accounts, or **30-day accounts**, enable customers to charge purchases during a month and pay the balance in full within 30 days after they are billed. There is no finance charge for this type of credit plan as long as the bill is paid on time.

Installment Accounts

Installment accounts, or time payment plans, allow for payment over a period of time. Installment accounts are normally used for large purchases, such as a college education, travel, automobiles, appliances, and furniture. Installment accounts offer a certain interest rate over a set period of time. Installment accounts sometimes require a down payment and a separate contract for each purchase.

•CREDIT for MILES Many credit card companies and airlines offer frequent flier programs and credit cards that can accumulate frequent flier miles.

What are the pros and cons of these credit cards?

MARKET TECH

Cash or Charge?

McDonald's customers are now able to pay for their burgers and fries in about 6,000 of the restaurants using credit and debit cards. The world's largest restaurant chain, with 31,000 restaurants in 199 countries, McDonald's has signed agreements with Visa, MasterCard, American Express, and Discover. As of 2004, McDonald's did not plan to launch credit or debit cards with its own logo.

A Happy Meal for Credit Cards

In the past, if McDonald's franchises (80 percent of its restaurants are franchises) wanted to accept credit or debit cards, they had to negotiate individual agreements with credit card companies and banks. The company's agreement with major credit card brands, however, saves its franchises the trouble of negotiating individual agreements. Prior to 2004, only 3,000 McDonald's restaurants accepted cashless payments.

Credit cards, which were once used mostly for big-ticket items, are now being used for the everyday transactions such as paying tolls, buying gasoline and groceries, or reserving movie tickets to build up frequent-flier miles or promotional bonus points.

THINK LIKE A MARKETER

Why have fast-food restaurants like McDonald's been slow to accept payment by credit card?

Online Action!

Go to *marketingessentials.glencoe.com/32/tech* to find an activity about technology and product features.

Revolving Accounts

With **revolving accounts**, the retailer determines the credit limit and payment terms. The minimum payment is usually a certain percentage on the balance owed or a minimum dollar amount, such as $15. The customer can choose to pay more than the minimum payment to reduce the balance owed. An interest charge is added to the unpaid balance for the billing period.

Customers can make purchases up to the credit limit when using a revolving account. Under most credit card arrangements, regular accounts become revolving accounts if the full amount is not paid for the billing period. Most billing cycles are 25-day periods.

Budget Accounts

Budget accounts allow for the payment of a purchased item over a certain time period without a finance charge. The most typical interest-free time period is 90 days, but some businesses have extended the time period to as much as one year. Some retailers who handle expensive products, such as furniture and appliances, offer budget accounts. Budget accounts do not require the customer to pay any interest charges if the amount owed is paid within the interest-free time period. Finance charges are applied if the amount is not paid within the specified time period. Offering budget accounts is one way that a company can stay competitive.

Business Credit

Business credit, or trade credit, is similar to consumer credit in that money is lent for goods and services. Suppliers sell raw materials, equipment, and inventory to businesses that agree to pay for these items with credit. Businesses often use credit for the same reasons that individual consumers do.

Unlike consumer credit, trade credit does not involve the use of a card. Credit memorandums, letters of credit, and credit drafts are used in trade credit arrangements. Money is lent and the parties involved in the transaction agree to payment terms.

Legislation Affecting Credit

Many government regulations protect consumers and their credit standing along with providing information on the proper use of credit.

The Truth in Lending Act of 1968 requires that lenders disclose information about annual percentage rates, the name of the company extending credit, and the amount financed. It also requires lenders to provide the total purchase price minus any down payments and taxes, the actual finance charge in dollars, a payment schedule, and late payment penalties.

The Fair Credit Reporting Act of 1971 requires that a lender report the name and address of the credit bureau that was used when a consumer is denied credit. The act gives consumers the opportunity to check their credit histories for errors that prevent them from obtaining credit.

The Equal Credit Opportunity Acts of 1975 and 1976 set guidelines for the review of applications for credit. These acts also prohibit discrimination based on age, gender, race, religion, or marital status.

The Fair Debt Collection Act of 1980 prevents businesses from harassing or abusing customers to collect debts.

The Fair Credit and Charge Card Disclosure Act of 1988 helps consumers by requiring credit card issuers to provide information about card costs to open credit and charge accounts.

The Fair and Accurate Credit Transactions Act of 2003 requires businesses to verify identities and addresses before opening accounts to fight identity theft. Consumers will also be able to receive free credit reports each year, correct errors more easily in their credit files, and opt out of sharing their information for marketing purposes.

32.2 AFTER YOU READ

Reviewing Key Terms and Concepts

1. Why is credit important as an extended product feature?
2. What are five sources of consumer credit?
3. List the four major consumer credit plans.

Integrating Academic Skills

Math

4. The average American charges $3,000 per year on a credit card. How many years would it take to earn 25,000 miles for a free airline trip, if the rebate was two miles earned per $1 spent with an airline affinity card?

Civics and Government

5. Perform Internet or library research on one of the federal laws regarding consumer credit. Prepare a 150-word paper on the purpose and provisions of the selected legislation.

Check your answers at *marketingessentials.glencoe.com/32/read*

CAREERS IN MARKETING

JEFF KRAUSE
PRODUCT DEVELOPMENT CONSULTANT

What do you do at work?
Industrial design encompasses nearly every discipline needed to take any product from a mere idea to a more or less completely functional physical reality. I create sketches, hand renderings or computer-generated renderings, non-functional or functional physical examples of the concept, as well as 3D computer-generated models of the design. If an industrial designer is properly experienced, he or she can also supply most of the specifications needed for the product to be "tooled" and actually manufactured.

What skills are most important to you?
A modern industrial designer uses a blend of aesthetic skills, mechanical design, and a knowledge of numerous manufacturing processes. This includes the ability to mentally visualize shapes and mechanisms in 3D, and create mock-ups, appearance prototypes, and even working prototypes. Advanced skills include Computer-Aided Design (CAD).

What is your key to success?
Success as an industrial designer means being good at interpreting the concepts of others and maintaining their intent throughout. But they do need to make the originator's vision their own, and along the way they evolve that vision into a product that can be manufactured inexpensively in the real world.

Aptitudes, Abilities, and Skills

An artistic eye, strong computer skills, and a real-world understanding of what products work

Education and Training

Helpful courses include graphic design, arts, mechanical design, and CAD.

Career Path

Most industrial designers begin work within an established firm, but the market is ripe for freelancers with experience under their belt and a portfolio of their work.

THINKING CRITICALLY

Why is it important for an industrial designer to be able to imagine and visualize in 3D?

Online Action!

Go to *marketingessentials.glencoe.com/32/careers* to find a career-related activity.

CHAPTER 32 REVIEW

FOCUS on KEY POINTS

SECTION 32.1

- Warranties are an important element of product planning because they help to increase sales and profits. Customers often base their purchasing decisions on the availability of warranties. A working knowledge of relevant federal, state, and local laws regarding warranties is essential for businesspeople.

SECTION 32.2

- Credit enables businesses or individuals to obtain products or money in exchange for a promise to pay later. The use of credit is essential to our economy. Many government regulations protect consumers and their credit standing along with providing information on the proper use of credit.

REVIEW VOCABULARY

Construct a crossword puzzle using the following vocabulary terms. Below the puzzle, include appropriate clues for the down and across spaces.

1. warranty (p. 674)
2. express warranty (p. 675)
3. full warranty (p. 675)
4. limited warranty (p. 675)
5. implied warranty (p. 677)
6. warranty of merchantability (p. 677)
7. warranty of fitness for a particular purpose (p. 677)
8. disclaimer (p. 677)
9. credit (p. 682)
10. 30-day accounts (p. 685)
11. installment accounts (p. 685)
12. revolving accounts (p. 686)
13. budget accounts (p. 686)

REVIEW FACTS and IDEAS

14. What is a warranty? (32.1)
15. What is the difference between an express warranty and an implied warranty? (32.1)
16. How does a full warranty differ from a limited warranty? (32.1)
17. What is a warranty disclaimer? (32.1)
18. Explain the advantages and disadvantages for extended warranties or service contracts. (32.1)
19. Compare and contrast credit and credit limits. (32.2)
20. What is the difference between a credit card and a debit card? (32.2)
21. How do travel and entertainment charge cards differ from bank, store, and gasoline credit cards? (32.2)
22. What is the difference between consumer and business credit? (32.2)
23. How does the Fair and Accurate Credit Transactions Act of 2003 assist consumers? (32.2)

BUILD SKILLS

24. Workplace Skills

Communication Perform an Internet search on available credit cards from a selected bank, store, gasoline, or travel and entertainment credit card company. Write a one- to two-paragraph description of the card, features, current interest rate, and grace period for payment.

25. Technology Applications

Obtaining a Warranty Quote Use the Internet to find a direct marketer of extended warranties. Obtain a quote for the following items:

- A car
- A recreational vehicle
- A motorcycle
- A boat

26. Math Practice

Consolidating Debt A household has $9,000 in credit card debt and pays three percent per month interest on all credit card payments. The family gets an offer for a new card. It promises no minimum payment for three months on all balance transfers and then a five percent interest rate thereafter.

Assuming that the household pays only the interest each month on a $9,000 balance, under which scenario will the customer spend less money over the course of a year? What other information would you need to know to advise the customer about consolidating credit cards?

DEVELOP CRITICAL THINKING

27. Defective Warranty

What steps should consumers follow if they believe a product's warranty has not adequately protected them?

28. Consumer Credit Regulations

List three reasons why it is necessary to have federal and state legislation regulating consumer credit.

APPLY CONCEPTS

29. Finding the Better Business Bureau

Research a Better Business Bureau located in your state.

Activity Use presentation software to create an oral report that summarizes the various services it provides and where it is located.

30. Comparing Credit Cards

Locate the Web site for the Board of Governors of the Federal Reserve System and find information about comparison shopping for bank credit cards. The board's site provides information on interest rates, grace periods, annual fees, and telephone numbers for the 150 largest banking institutions offering credit cards.

Activity Prepare a spreadsheet using computer software that compares the advantages and disadvantages of three credit cards. Compare annual fees, annual percentage rates, and other pertinent information.

NET SAVVY

31. Learn How to Use Credit

Use the library or the Internet to investigate how to use credit wisely. Research by reading advice in personal finance columns in newspapers and on Web sites. Prepare a one-page report on tips for using credit wisely.

THE DECA CONNECTION

An Association of Marketing Students

Role Play: Extended Product Features

Situation You are to assume the role of sales associate for a costume jewelry store. The store carries earrings, necklaces, bracelets, and watches that are appealing to younger customers. The merchandise price points are at the high end of the range for costume jewelry. All the merchandise carries a lifetime guarantee. If a watch needs to be repaired or items need stones replaced, the item must be sent to the customer service center, not returned to the store.

Activity You are to explain the store's lifetime guarantee to a customer (judge) who is purchasing a watch for $175.

Evaluation You will be evaluated on how well you meet the following performance indicators:

- Explain warranties and guarantees
- Interpret business policies to customers/clients
- Explain the nature of positive customer/client relations
- Handle customer inquiries
- Address people properly

Online Action!

For more information and DECA Prep practice, go to *marketingessentials.glencoe.com/32/DECA*

MARKETING INTERNSHIP

A SIMULATED DECA PRODUCT AND SERVICE MANAGEMENT EVENT

Create a New Exciting Food Product

BASIC BACKGROUND

Mainstream Foods wants to create healthy food for people on the go. Its competitors have already flooded the market with meal replacement products and low-carbohydrate alternatives to their existing foods.

Who Is Doing What? Unilever has a low-carb product line called Carb Options®, which includes salad dressings, peanut butter, iced tea, steak sauce, and a chocolate chip brownie bar. Keto carries an even broader line of low-carb foods, including spaghetti, elbow macaroni, pizza dough, macaroni and cheese, tortilla chips, cereal, ice cream, and ketchup. Russell Stover has low-carb candies and DeBoles offers low-carb spaghetti. Manufacturers have developed meal replacement bars such as Balance®, Atkins®, and Zone® bars, which target adults, and milk and cereal bars which target children.

YOUR OBJECTIVE

You are on the team of research and development (R&D) scientists and marketing staff members. The team's role is to develop a new line of low-carb foods or meal replacement products. The clock is ticking: Mainstream Foods wants the new products introduced in six months because it wants to capitalize on the active-lifestyle and low-carbohydrate crazes and popular diets such as Atkins, South Beach, Zone, and 40-30-30.

ASSIGNMENT AND STRATEGY

- **Get the background** You will have to conduct an environmental scan to identify threats and opportunities for Mainstream Foods. Include the popular diets and products noted above and any food labeling laws or other relevant government regulations.

  Research what competitors have already done to capitalize on these trends. Do your research at a library or on the Internet, as well as in food stores and supermarkets. Trade publications that may be helpful include *Brandweek*, *Advertising Age*, and *Supermarket News*.

- **Develop the product concept** Use the steps for new product planning to design one or more products or product lines for Mainstream Foods.

Once your team has developed a new product or product line, conduct marketing research with the intended target market(s) to see if any changes should be made. Include the product concept, its packaging, and the other marketing mix strategies in your market research study.

- **What your project should include** Your ideas for your product and/or product line should include its name, packaging, labeling, warranty or guarantee, and other marketing mix strategies (place, price, promotion). Be sure to conclude with a strong argument as to why this new product or product line will be successful.

YOUR REPORT

Use a word processing program and presentation software to prepare a double-spaced report and an oral presentation for Mainstream Foods. See a suggested outline and key evaluation points at *marketingessentials.glencoe.com/internship*

BUILD YOUR PORTFOLIO

Option 1 Internship Report Once you have completed your Marketing Internship project and presentation, include your written report and a few printouts of key slides from your oral presentation in your Marketing Portfolio.

Option 2 Designing a New Product Develop a new product or service of your choice. Use the steps in product development to decide on a new product. Analyze current market and PEST (political, economic, socio-cultural, and technological) conditions. Prepare a comprehensive written report and an oral presentation noting the target market, product name, packaging, labeling, price, place, and promotion. See a suggested outline and key evaluation points at *marketingessentials.glencoe.com/portfolio*

Online Action!

Go to *marketingessentials.glencoe.com/Unit/10/DECA* to review product and service management concepts that relate to DECA events.

UNIT 11 Entrepreneurship

In this unit you will find

Marketing Plan

ANALYSIS
1
- SWOT
- Economic
- Socio-Cultural
- Technological
- Competitive

STRATEGY
2
- Promotion
- Place
- Price
- Product

IMPLEMENTATION
3
- Organization
- Management
- Staffing

BUDGET
4
- Cost of Sales
- Cost of Promotion
- Incomes and Expenses

CONTROL
5
- Evaluation
- Performance Measures
- Performance Analysis

ANALYZE THE AD

Mary Kay sells its cosmetics through more than 1.3 million independent representatives who earn commissions. What is this ad selling?

Market Talk Most cosmetics companies sell through department stores or drugstores. Mary Kay and the much larger Avon both depend on independent representatives. The direct sales method lets representatives grow their businesses as much as they want. This flexibility appeals to entrepreneurs.

Think and Write An entrepreneur can start a business, be an independent salesperson for a company, or open a franchise. Choose the most appealing scenario and list three reasons for your preference.

Go to *marketingessentials.glencoe.com/u11/ad* for an extended activity.

In this unit

Foundations of Marketing
- Business, Management, Entrepreneurship
- Economics

Functions of Marketing
- Financing

CHAPTER 33
Entrepreneurial Concepts

Chapter Objectives

After reading this chapter, you should be able to:

- Define entrepreneurship
- Detail the advantages of entrepreneurship
- Explain the risks and disadvantages of entrepreneurship
- List the characteristics and skills of entrepreneurs
- Understand the importance of small business in the U.S. and global economies
- Identify the forms of business ownership
- Name the legal steps to take in establishing a business

GUIDE TO THE PHOTO

Market Talk A child's lemonade stand is an example of entrepreneurship and free enterprise principles. Who will make the lemonade? How much should be made? What will a glass of lemonade cost? These are questions these children must answer before setting up their stand. Business owners ask similar questions.

Quick Think Name at least two other questions entrepreneurs (or lemonade-stand owners) must answer before starting a new business.

THE   CONNECTION

Performance indicators represent key skills and knowledge. Relating them to the concepts explained in this chapter is your key to success in DECA events. These acronyms represent DECA events that involve knowledge of concepts in this chapter.

AAAL	**FMAL**	**MMS***	**TMDM***
AAML*	**FMDM***	**QSRM***	**TSE***
ADC*	**FMML***	**RMAL**	**VPM**
BSM	**FSRM***	**RMML***	
EMDM*	**HMDM***	**SMDM***	

In all these DECA events you should be able to follow these performance indicators:

- Determine the relationship between government and business
- Explain the concept of private enterprise
- Determine factors affecting business risk
- Explain the role of business in society
- Explain types of business ownership
- Describe current business trends
- Describe legal issues affecting business
- Explain the nature of legally binding contracts

All the events with an asterisk (*) also include these performance indicators:

- Explain the nature of tax regulations on business

Some events include additional performance indicators. These are:

FMDM Explain the nature of regulations affecting the financial services industry

TMDM Explain the nature of regulations affecting the travel and tourism industry

HMDM Explain the nature of regulations affecting the hospitality industry

EMDM Describe legal considerations in e-commerce

DECA PREP

Check your understanding of DECA performance indicators with the DECA activity in this chapter's review. For more information and DECA Prep practice, go to *marketingessentials .glencoe.com/33/DECA*

SECTION 33.1

Entrepreneurship

OBJECTIVES

- **Define entrepreneurship**
- **Detail the advantages of entrepreneurship**
- **Explain the risks and disadvantages of entrepreneurship**
- **List the characteristics and skills of entrepreneurs**
- **Understand the importance of small business in the U.S. and global economies**

KEY TERMS

- **entrepreneurship**
- **entrepreneurs**

BEFORE YOU READ

Predict Do you know any successful entrepreneurs? Make a list of reasons for their success.

THE MAIN IDEA

Entrepreneurship has advantages and disadvantages. Although it involves accepting risks, it can lead to personal freedom and financial reward.

STUDY ORGANIZER

Draw a diagram like the one below and list the characteristics of entrepreneurship as you read this section.

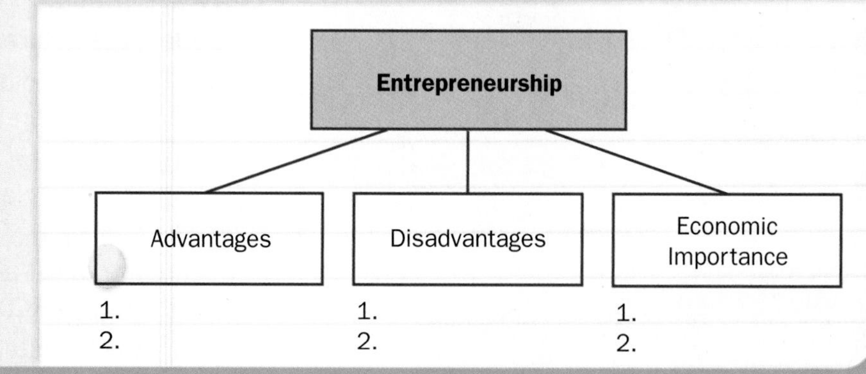

Connect Compare the characteristics of an entrepreneur to your own personality. Would you make a good entrepreneur?

What Is Entrepreneurship?

Entrepreneurship is the process of starting and operating your own business. **Entrepreneurs** are people who create, launch, organize, and manage a new business and take the risk of business ownership. You are an entrepreneur already if you have provided babysitting services or cut someone's lawn for pay.

Entrepreneurs make major contributions to our economy. Entrepreneurs often have an idea, or business concept, that drives their business. When an entrepreneur combines this vision with the means to manufacture the product (or provide the service) and market it, the contributions to the economy both within and outside the United States can be remarkable. The results of entrepreneurship can change our lives in other ways, too. Consider the following examples:

- Henry Ford introduced the mass production of automobiles, making them affordable to the average person. His entrepreneurship revolutionized transportation and transformed lifestyles.
- William Hewlett and David Packard started a small business in Packard's garage near Stanford University in California. They invented the three-and-a-half-inch floppy disk and the first pocket calculator. Their business grew into the giant Hewlett-Packard Corporation, which produces a vast array of computer products, including laser printers. These products changed the speed with which people process information.

These entrepreneurs became famous and wealthy as a result of starting their own businesses, but not all entrepreneurs achieve such success. Some start companies simply because they want to be their own bosses and make their own business decisions.

Advantages of Entrepreneurship

The advantages of entrepreneurship can include personal freedom, personal satisfaction, increased self-esteem, and increased income. Entrepreneurs set their own work schedules and make their own decisions. They are able to try out their own new ideas and direct their energies into business activities, take control of their businesses and their work settings.

Many business owners are willing to put in the extra effort to make their businesses succeed because of financial rewards. With

NET MARKETING

E-Training Anyone?

What do you need to do to earn second place on the *Fortune* Small Business 100 list? You need to be very good at providing technology-based products and services to pharmaceutical, biotechnological, medical device, and contract resource companies. eResearch Technology, Inc., sells centralized electrocardiographic (diagnostic) services as well as technology and services to streamline the clinical trial process.

Online Training for Customers

The company's Web site takes full advantage of the power of the Internet and Web marketing. One of its key e-commerce features is Web-based training through its eResearch Community's eHealth Education. This service lets customers access a series of sophisticated, interactive, Web-based training programs to learn clinical research processes and procedures.

THINK LIKE A MARKETER

If eResearch Technology, Inc., sells products and services, why does it bother with online training?

@ Online Action!

Go to *marketingessentials.glencoe.com/33/net* to find an activity about the Internet and entrepreneurship.

Case Study

Entrepreneur in the Kitchen

Housewife Estee Lauder began her cosmetics business in the 1930s, mixing up face creams in her New York kitchen and going into beauty salons to offer free demonstrations to women sitting under hair dryers. Her creams were high quality, and people who tried them usually bought them.

In 1948, Lauder persuaded a buyer at the prestigious retailer Saks Fifth Avenue to order her product. That first order sold out in two days.

Product Line Diversification

Over the years, Lauder developed a full line of cosmetics under her own name and sold it selectively through high-end department stores around the world. Her company also developed the Clinique, Aramis, Prescriptives, and Origins lines—each targeted to a slightly different market.

A Marketing Genius

Estee Lauder originated the "gift with purchase" concept, which has become very important in cosmetics sales. If a customer purchases one item, he or she receives a gift package containing many other items worth more than the amount spent. It is a creative way of developing customer loyalty. Lauder was the only woman in *Time* magazine's listing of the 20 most influential business geniuses of the twentieth century.

THINK STRATEGICALLY

How could it make sense to give away products worth more money than the item purchased? What qualities of an entrepreneur does that idea display?

@ Online Action! **Go to *marketingessentials.glencoe.com/33/case* to find an activity about entrepreneurship.**

success often comes money, and this potential motivates many entrepreneurs.

Disadvantages of Entrepreneurship

Being an entrepreneur has disadvantages, too. These include a high level of stress, possible setbacks, the risk of failure, potential loss of income, long and irregular hours, the need to handle multiple tasks, and the required strong self-discipline.

Most new businesses have a restricted cash flow because of start-up costs. As a result, an entrepreneur may not meet his or her personal financial needs during the first year of operation, or even longer. Increased income comes only when the business succeeds.

Entrepreneurs are not 40-hours-per-week people. To succeed, they must meet the needs of the marketplace, which often means long and irregular hours.

Running a business requires doing many tedious, time-consuming tasks. To save money, new business owners may do many of these jobs themselves. Among the tasks they may perform are time-consuming paperwork, such as accounts payable, accounts receivable, payroll, and government forms.

The Risks of Entrepreneurship

Starting a new business requires a major commitment of time, money, and effort. A new business owner must be a risk taker. It is often necessary to quit a job, work long hours, invest savings, and borrow money—all with no guarantee that the new business will succeed. Seven out of ten small-business owners started their businesses with less than $20,000, according to the 1998 report *The Wells Fargo/National Federation of Independent Business Series on Business Starts and Stops.* In fact, in 2002, 14 percent of *Inc.* magazine's 500 fast-growing companies started with less than $1,000.

The risk of failure with a new business is very real. Only two-thirds of new businesses survive at least two years, and about half survive at least four years. When a company fails, often much of the money invested in it is lost. Failure also means loss of employment.

Entrepreneurship as a Career Choice

Being an entrepreneur can be exciting and greatly rewarding, but it is not for everyone. Those who succeed have certain skills and personal characteristics that enable them to meet the challenges of business ownership.

First, entrepreneurs must have the skills necessary to run their business. Someone starting an online magazine should know how to write and have a good grasp of Internet technology. Beyond specific skills, most successful entrepreneurs share a number of characteristics.

Characteristics of Successful Entrepreneurs

- Determination
- Self-motivation
- Self-confidence
- Strong organizational skills
- Leadership ability
- Self-discipline
- Creativity
- Willingness to work hard
- Spirit of adventure
- Good social skills

Do You Have What It Takes?

You can answer this question by doing a self-evaluation—an assessment of your personal qualities, abilities, interests, and skills. The self-evaluation in Figure 33.1 on page 702 was developed by the Small Business Administration (SBA). Take a few minutes to answer each question and write your answers on a piece of paper. Think before you answer and be honest. Answering "yes" to most or all of these questions suggests that you may have the right characteristics for success.

Before you start a business, ask family members, friends, and other businesspeople who are in the same or a similar business about their experiences. Do research on the type of business you want to start. All this information should give you a good indication of whether you are ready to join the millions of small-business owners in the United States.

Marketing and Entrepreneurship

Although entrepreneurs may have the business and technical skills they need to produce and provide a quality product or service, they may overlook the importance of marketing. Entrepreneurs who possess a good understanding of marketing have an advantage over those who do not.

Many resources exist for entrepreneurs who need help with marketing. For example, The American Marketing Association has a special interest group devoted to helping entrepreneurs develop marketing skills, the Marketing & Entrepreneur Special Interest Group. The National Federation of Independent Businesses has an award-winning online library of business management information called the *Business Toolkit.*

Figure 33.1 Self-Evaluation

• **Know Yourself** Be honest as you answer each of these self-evaluation questions. Having a clear understanding of your personal strengths and skills will help you decide whether or not to become an entrepreneur.

What do your answers say about you?

The first seven questions relate to your personality characteristics.	**YES**	**NO**
1. Do you like to make your own decisions?	____	____
2. Do you enjoy competition?	____	____
3. Do you have willpower and self-determination?	____	____
4. Do you plan ahead?	____	____
5. Do you like to get things done on time?	____	____
6. Can you take advice from others?	____	____
7. Can you adapt to changing conditions?	____	____
The next series of questions relates to your physical, emotional, and financial well-being.		
8. Do you understand that owning your own business may entail working 12 to 16 hours a day, probably six days a week and maybe on holidays?	____	____
9. Do you have the physical stamina to handle a business?	____	____
10. Do you have the emotional strength to withstand the strain?	____	____
11. Are you prepared to lower your living standard for several months or years?	____	____
12. Are you prepared to lose your savings?	____	____
13. Do you know which skills and areas of expertise are critical to the success of your business?	____	____
14. Do you have these skills?	____	____
15. Does your idea for a business use these skills?	____	____
16. Can you find the people who have the expertise you lack?	____	____
17. Do you know why you are considering this business?	____	____
18. Will your business meet your career aspirations?	____	____

Online Action! Go to ***marketingessentials.glencoe.com/33/figure/1*** to find a project on self-evaluation.

The Role of Entrepreneurship in the Domestic and Global Economy

Entrepreneurs and small to medium businesses play a key role in the domestic and the global economy: They generate growth at a rate that is much faster than other larger and more established businesses. Eighty percent of the new jobs created annually come from businesses that are less than five years old.

The National Federation of Independent Businesses reported in its 2000 *Small Business Policy Guide* that more than 60 percent of all businesses in the United States employ four or fewer people. The Global Entrepreneurship Monitor (GEM) reports a strong correlation between national economic growth and the level of national entrepreneurial activity. Firms with fewer than 500 employees were responsible for 50 percent of the gross domestic product (GDP)—the measure of the goods and services produced using labor and property in the United States.

Small businesses benefit the economy and society in other ways, too. They offer consumers more choices of goods and services, and they help improve products and processes.

Entrepreneurship and the Global Economy

New businesses are a sign of an economy's vitality and readiness to find or invent new opportunities in a world market that has become more and more challenging.

The U.S. Small Business Administration (SBA) is finding new ways to help small businesses in the very competitive global economy. In 2004, SBA loaned more than $17 billion and trained two million small-business owners. A new SBA Web site provides business owners with helpful information. This includes access to government services, help with regulations, and applications for help, money, and training. The SBA is also providing more opportunities to work with government buyers and ways to compete in international markets.

Trends in Entrepreneurship

Entrepreneurship is on the rise. According to the SBA, the number of incorporated self-employed persons was 5.2 million in March 2004, up from an average of 4.4 million for the years 1999, 2000, and 2001. Several recent trends in the marketplace have fostered this growth:

- The availability of technology
- Increased global communication
- The rise of the Internet and e-commerce
- A society and a market that are more and more diversified

Smart entrepreneurs are always looking for business opportunities and trends that affect their business. They watch socio-economic and political trends such as dual-income families, changes in eating habits, and national and international security issues to get ideas.

33.1 AFTER YOU READ

Reviewing Key Terms and Concepts

1. How is being an entrepreneur different from being an employee?
2. Study the personal characteristics required of an entrepreneur and list the ones that describe you.
3. How do small businesses contribute to the U.S. economy?

Integrating Academic Skills

Math

4. There are 3,000 new business start-ups per year. How many business start-ups is this per week? Statistically, how many of these businesses will remain open at the end of four years?

Language

5. Etymology is the study of the origin and history of words. Use a dictionary to discover the etymology of the word *entrepreneur.* Look up the meaning of the prefix *en.* How are the words *entrepreneur* and *enterprise* related? Write a brief report on the history and meaning of the word *entrepreneur.*

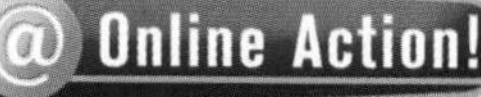

Check your answers at *marketingessentials.glencoe.com/33/read*

Logistics of Business Ownership

OBJECTIVES

- Identify the forms of business ownership
- Name the legal steps to take in establishing a business

KEY TERMS

- franchise
- sole proprietorship
- unlimited liability
- partnership
- general partnership
- limited partnership
- corporation
- stockholders
- limited liability
- foreign corporation
- limited liability company (LLC)
- Doing Business As (DBA)
- Articles of Incorporation

READ and STUDY

BEFORE YOU READ

Predict If you were to start a business, what would it be? What steps do you think you would have to take before opening the business?

THE MAIN IDEA

Going into business involves deciding how to enter business, determining the organizational form the business will take, and following the steps necessary to establish the business legally.

STUDY ORGANIZER

Think of yourself as an entrepreneur and write down the steps you need to take to establish your new business in a chart like the one below.

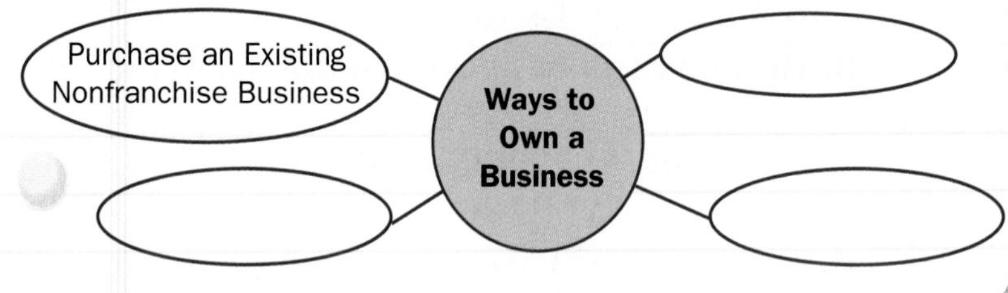

WHILE YOU READ

Analyze Compare the advantages and disadvantages of the four forms of business organization.

Business Ownership Opportunities

There are four ways to enter business: (1) purchase an existing nonfranchise business, (2) take over the family business, (3) start a new business, or (4) purchase a franchise business.

Purchase an Existing Nonfranchise Business

When an entrepreneur buys an existing nonfranchise business, there is usually little or no help from the previous owner. The prospective buyer must investigate the reasons for the

•STARTING YOUR OWN BUSINESS There are many different forms of business and various ways of organizing a company. This ad promotes a company that helps new owners through the incorporation process.

Why would an entrepreneur need assistance with setting up a business?

sale of the business. Likewise, business records, the condition of the property, and inventory must be carefully examined. The reputation of the business in the community must be considered as well. In some cases, the new owner may contract the services of the previous owner to assist with management during a transition period.

Take Over the Family Business

Many of the same considerations for purchasing an existing business apply to taking over a family business. The difference, in this case, is that the previous owner is a family member. Will this help or hinder the new owner in taking control? The new owner must explore potential conflicts and concerns with family members. Succession planning (transition to the next generation), managing growth, and family relations are some of the challenges of taking over and running a family business.

Start a New Business

Starting a new business gives an entrepreneur great freedom of choice. The new business owner can start the business of her choice and plan it from the ground up. She can decide where it is located, what it sells, and how it is organized. There are no old debts to settle and no bad reputation to overcome. On the other hand, it is up to the new owner to establish the business's reputation and build a customer base.

Purchase a Franchise Business

A **franchise** is a legal agreement to sell a parent company's product or services in a designated geographic area. McDonald's Corporation and Taco Bell are examples of companies that sell franchises. They are franchisors. The franchisee (the person buying the business) has to invest money to buy the franchise and also pays an annual fee and a share of the profits. In exchange, the franchisor provides a well-known name, a business plan, advertising, and the proven methods and products of the parent company.

In franchise businesses, new business owners have a lot of help. All the business planning is done by the franchisor. Planning generally includes management training, merchandising, and day-to-day operations.

One disadvantage of franchising is the initial cost. A significant amount of capital is needed to purchase most franchises. The franchisee must also pay high initial fees to begin operations. In addition, the franchisor is often very strict about how the business is run.

Forms of Business Organization

The choice of legal organization or structure a new business should have is a critical decision. It may make the difference between success and failure. It determines how fast business decisions are implemented and how well the business competes in the marketplace. There are four possible forms of business organization (see Figure 33.2):

- sole proprietorship
- partnership
- corporation
- limited liability company (LLC)

The choice depends on the financial and tax situation of the owner, the type of business, the number of employees who will be hired, and the level of risk involved in the new business. As a business grows, these factors may change and may require reorganization. A business could start out as a sole proprietorship, grow into a partnership, and ultimately wind up as a corporation.

Sole Proprietorship

A **sole proprietorship** is a business owned and operated by one person. This is the most common form of business ownership. Approximately 70 percent of all U.S. businesses are sole proprietorships. Sole proprietors usually have a special skill by which they can earn a living; for example, plumbers, contractors, and many entrepreneurs who start Web site businesses are often sole proprietors. The sole proprietor must provide the money and management skill to run the business. In return for all this responsibility, the sole proprietor is entitled to all the profits.

Advantages and Disadvantages of Sole Proprietorship

A sole proprietorship is easy to start. The sole proprietor provides the money to start the business. For instance, a plumber will spend money on tools, a truck, office space and supplies, and possibly advertising. The sole proprietorship is generally taxed less than other forms of business, and there is more freedom from government regulation. Because the owner is usually the only investor in the business, that person is entitled to all the profits. A sole proprietorship also gives a business owner great control over the business.

However, this also means that the owner is responsible for all business debts and legal judgments against the company. If the debts of a business exceed its assets, creditors can claim the owner's personal assets, such as a home, cars, and savings. This is called **unlimited liability**, which means that a business owner's financial liability is not limited to investments in the business, but extends to his or her total ability to make payments.

The Partnership

A **partnership** is a legal agreement between two or more people to be jointly responsible for the success or failure of a business. Partnerships represent about 10 percent of U.S. businesses. Common partnerships in your community may include real estate agencies, law offices, and medical offices.

Figure 33.2 Business Organization

• The Four Forms of Business Ownership The legal organization of a business is a key decision for an entrepreneur. It determines how fast business decisions can be made, how well the business will compete in the marketplace, and how quickly it can raise money.

Which form of business ownership is easiest to establish?

SOLE PROPRIETORSHIP

A sole proprietorship gives an entrepreneur the greatest control over business decisions and all the profits. It also exposes the owner to greater risks.

PARTNERSHIP

Partners share decision-making responsibility as well as the business's profits and losses. In a limited partnership, a limited partner is responsible for losses only to the level of his or her investment in the business. The general partner is fully responsible for losses.

LIMITED LIABILITY COMPANY

The limited liability company (LLC) is a cross between a partnership and a corporation. Its owners (called members) have only limited liability, and it has tax benefits over a corporation.

CORPORATION

Corporations are owned by stockholders, who may range in number from one to millions. Each stockholder owns a portion of the business and is responsible for losses only to the level of his or her investment. In a corporation, the owners may not be involved in the day-to-day decision making for the business. With this type of organization, the benefits and risks are shared among the stockholders. Corporations can raise money relatively easily, but the decision-making process can be slow.

Online Action! **Go to *marketingessentials.glencoe.com/33/figure/2* to find a project on entrepreneurship.**

A partnership is formed by a partnership agreement, usually prepared by an attorney, which specifies the responsibilities of each partner. Partners share the profits if the business is a success and the losses if it fails. Profits are usually divided according to the amount of time and money each partner invested. There are two kinds of partnerships: general and limited.

General Partnership

In a **general partnership**, each partner shares in the profits and losses. As in the sole proprietorship, each partner has unlimited liability for the company's debts. Also, each partner's share of the profits is taxed as personal income.

Limited Partnership

In a **limited partnership**, each limited partner is liable for any debts only up to the amount of his or her investment in the company. Every limited partnership, however, must have at least one general partner who has unlimited liability. In exchange for their limited liability, limited partners have no voice in the management of the partnership. The withdrawal of a limited partner does not dissolve the partnership.

Advantages and Disadvantages of Partnerships

There are several advantages to a partnership. It combines the skills of the owners. A partnership may make more capital (money)

GLOBAL MARKET

Promotion and Soccer

German electronics and engineering company Siemens is known in the United States for domestic appliances. However, its major businesses worldwide are transportation and communication systems and large power turbines.

Siemens deals mostly with governments and large corporations, not consumers. The company is huge, with almost $90 billion in sales in 190 countries.

Global Promotion Siemens is also a cell phone manufacturer in Europe. To compete with big names Nokia and Motorola, it needs to get the company name in the public eye.

The strategy Siemens has chosen is corporate sponsorship of sports, choosing teams that are extremely popular in its target markets of Europe, Latin America, and Asia. Siemens is the major sponsor of the Real Madrid Spanish soccer team. Soon after the Siemens deal, Real signed two soccer superstars, Brazilian Ronaldo and Englishman Beckham. Once the Siemens logo was on the jerseys of the team, Siemens's share of the cell phone market tripled in Latin America. The effect was strongest in Brazil.

What effects on its major engineering business could come from Siemens being more visible in consumer markets?

Online Action!

Go to *marketingessentials.glencoe.com/33/global* to find an activity about international entrepreneurship.

available, allowing easier operation and expansion. It gives each partner a voice in the management of the business. A partnership is taxed solely on the profits of the business and regulated less heavily than a corporation.

What are some of the disadvantages of partnerships? The owners may not always agree on business decisions, yet the actions of one partner are legally binding on the other partners. This means that all partners must assume their share of the business debt. They must also be responsible for the shares of any partners who cannot pay. Finally, the business is dissolved if one partner dies. It can be reorganized as a new partnership, but the process is time consuming and costly.

The Corporation

A **corporation** is a legal entity created by either a state or a federal statute authorizing individuals to operate an enterprise. In other words, a corporation is a business that is owned by several people but is considered to be just one person or entity under the law. A corporation has several unique features:

- **Legal permission to operate** To operate a business as a corporation, the owners must file an application with state officials for permission. Once the application is approved, this document becomes the corporation's charter.
- **Separate legal entity** A corporation is a separate legal entity that is created by law. A corporation can borrow money, sign contracts, buy or sell property, and sue and be sued in court.
- **Stockholders** The ownership of a corporation is divided into shares of stock. If the corporation sells stocks, it is one way to raise money. The owners of a corporation are the stockholders.
- **Board of directors** Stockholders own the corporation, but often they do not manage it. Instead, the stockholders elect a board of directors that is responsible for major decisions that affect the company.

Corporations offer owners limited liability. **Limited liability** means that the personal assets of the owners cannot be taken if the company does not meet its financial obligations or if it gets into legal trouble. Unlike a partnership, a corporation is not affected by the death, incapacity, or bankruptcy of an officer or a shareholder.

Types of Corporations

There are many types of corporations, but the two main categories are private and public corporations. A public corporation is a business entity created by the federal, state, or local government. This group can include incorporated cities as well as school, transit, and sanitation districts.

A private corporation is formed by private persons. This category is very broad and includes closely held corporations (or "close corporations") and publicly held corporations (sometimes these are called public corporations even though they are subject to different rules than the public corporations described above).

A closely held corporation is owned by a few persons or a family. Shares or stocks of a closely held corporation are not sold to the public. On the other hand, a publicly held corporation is one whose stock (shares) is owned by a large group of people. Selling stock helps a corporation raise capital. In the United States, stocks or shares of a publicly held corporation are usually sold on the New York Stock Exchange (NYSE), the American Stock Exchange (AMEX), or the National Association of Securities Dealers Automated Quotations (NASDAQ) system. Microsoft is an example of a publicly held corporation whose stock is traded on NASDAQ.

If a corporation succeeds, the value of the stock rises and stockholders benefit. Stockholders own their shares with limited liability. For example, if a stockholder purchased $1,000 worth of Dell Computers stock and the company failed, the investor would lose the investment amount but would not be responsible for the company's debt.

Forming a Corporation

Forming a corporation is a complicated process. An entrepreneur must determine the company's internal corporate structure, which is defined by its bylaws, and the processes for selecting a board of directors and electing officers (those who handle the day-to-day operations). In small corporations, members of the board of directors are frequently elected as the officers of the corporation.

An entrepreneur must also choose the state in which to incorporate (establish) the company. For small companies, it is generally best to do this in the state where the company will do business.

A **foreign corporation** is one that is incorporated under the laws of a state that differs from the one in which it does business. (*Foreign* here means another state, not another country.) Foreign corporations must register with each state in which they intend to do business.

Advantages and Disadvantages of Corporations

Why would an entrepreneur decide to incorporate his or her business? There are four main advantages of incorporation:

1. Each owner has limited liability.
2. It is easier to raise capital (money) with corporations than with other forms of business. Capital is often needed for expansion.
3. Owners can easily enter or exit the business simply by buying or selling stock.
4. Management is shared—each area of the business is handled by someone with expertise in that area.

Disadvantages include the following:

1. Complexity of formation
2. Increased government regulation
3. Corporate profits are taxed. Shareholders are taxed on dividends they earn as well as on profits made from the sale of a stock.
4. Intricate accounting and record keeping

The Limited Liability Company

The **limited liability company (LLC)** is a relatively new form of business organization. This business structure is a hybrid of a partnership and a corporation. Its owners (called members) are shielded from personal liability, and all profits and losses pass directly to the owners without taxation of the entity itself.

Legal Steps to Establishing a Business

Before an entrepreneur can officially open the doors of a new business, he or she must take specific steps to legally establish and protect the business. These steps vary depending on whether the business will be a sole proprietorship, partnership, corporation, or limited liability company.

Step 1: Find Help

New business owners may wish to consult an accountant, attorney, or other business advisor to determine the best organization for their new businesses. When a corporation is formed, the laws of many states require that an attorney be hired to guide the entrepreneur through the complicated process of incorporation. The entrepreneur must check the laws of the state in which she or he is incorporating.

Step 2: Register the Business

To form a sole proprietorship or partnership, a business owner must file for a DBA at the local county clerk's office. A **DBA (Doing Business As)** is the registration by which the county government officially recognizes that a new proprietorship or partnership exists.

A DBA also protects the name of the business for a certain number of years. This name protection applies only to the county where the business is registered. There is usually a filing fee for registration.

To form a corporation, an entrepreneur must file Articles of Incorporation with the corporation and securities bureau in the state department of commerce.

Articles of Incorporation identify the name and address of a new corporation, its purpose, the names of the initial directors, and the amount of stock that will be issued to each director.

There is a filing fee, but the business becomes protected and no other business may register under that business's name. The necessary forms, applications, and information on filing fees can be obtained from the state department of commerce.

An LLC is established by filing Articles of Organization with the state. This document describes the LLC and lists the names of its members and initial managers. Many states also require LLCs to have an operating agreement. For the company to have the tax advantage of an LLC, this document must show that the company is distinct from a corporation.

Step 3: Obtain Licenses

Depending on the type of business and where it is located, a new owner may have to obtain one or more licenses. Licenses establish minimum standards of education and training for people who practice in a particular profession. They also regulate where businesses can locate, and they protect neighborhoods and the environment.

Individual states license many businesses and occupations, such as doctors, accountants, cosmetologists, barbers, marriage counselors, and pharmacists.

Licensing is done to protect the public from unqualified people practicing in a business and to maintain the health and welfare of the citizens.

In addition to state licenses, the community may require special local licenses or permits to comply with zoning ordinances, building codes, and safety standards.

Local governments use licensing as a way to regulate people who plan to enter certain types of businesses. Most communities require a business owner to obtain a license before opening a hotel, restaurant, or movie theater.

33.2 AFTER YOU READ

Reviewing Key Terms and Concepts

1. List the four ways to become a business owner.
2. What are the four legal forms of business organization and which is the most common?
3. What is one advantage of a limited liability company?

Integrating Academic Skills

Mathematics

4. An entrepreneur works 11 hours a day, five days a week, 51 weeks a year. How many hours does this person work annually? To how many 40-hour workweeks is this equivalent?

Government

5. The U.S. government protects entrepreneurs by issuing trademarks, copyrights, and patents. Research each of these terms and write a description of the type of protection provided by each.

Check your answers at *marketingessentials.glencoe.com/33/read*

CAREERS IN MARKETING

JERMAINE GRIGGS
CEO AND FOUNDER, HEARANDPLAY.COM

What do you do at work?
In the beginning, I was head customer service representative, phone operator, fulfillment manager, and Web designer. As the business grew, the day-to-day operations began to be automated, allowing me to focus more on building and growing the business. I now focus on attracting joint-venture partners, building and cultivating relationships with affiliates, product development, and implementation of new strategies. Lastly, because of the power of the Internet to split-test different versions of a Web site, I am regularly testing and changing sales copy, advertisements, order form layouts, and other sections of our Web site to better improve conversion rates, visitor values, and overall sales.

What skills are most important to you?
A manager who has had wide success in the offline world is not necessarily guaranteed success on the Internet. If I had to rely totally on employees for Web design, e-mail marketing, search engine optimization, and other functions, I would truly be lost! To know at least the minimum rules of the game is essential. The ability to be aware of trends, consumer behaviors online, and audience interaction, and to be able to respond and alter strategic plans accordingly is vital. Also, patience and the ability to watch extraordinarily good days pass as well as all-time low days are definitely attributes of a net entrepreneur.

What is your key to success?
My eagerness to learn. I never stop learning.

Aptitudes, Abilities, and Skills

Creativity, knowledge of the Internet and the product/ service being offered

Education and Training

Many net entrepreneurs have no degrees at all, although business degrees can definitely be useful and provide valuable skills.

Career Path

Web entrepreneurs come from all walks of life—this has historically been a field in which people can succeed, if they have the right idea and the willingness to follow through.

THINKING CRITICALLY

Why is it a good idea for net entrepreneurs to perform many of the tasks that might ordinarily fall to employees?

Online Action!

Go to *marketingessentials.glencoe.com/ 33/careers* to find a career-related activity.

CHAPTER 33 REVIEW

FOCUS on KEY POINTS

SECTION 33.1

- Being an entrepreneur involves risk taking, but it can bring both personal and financial rewards.
- Advantages of entrepreneurship include being your own boss and earning a high income if the business succeeds. Entrepreneurs can try out their own ideas, set their own work schedules, and make their own business decisions. Disadvantages of entrepreneurship include the risk of failure, long working hours, and the potential loss of income.
- Entrepreneurship is important to our economy. It creates jobs, which provide income to individuals and communities.

SECTION 33.2

- The four ways to become a business owner are (1) purchase an existing business, (2) take over the family business, (3) start a new business, and (4) purchase a franchise business.
- The four forms of business organization are (1) sole proprietorship, (2) partnership, (3) corporation, and (4) limited liability company.

REVIEW VOCABULARY

Work with your classmates as part of a team. Your teacher will call out the terms below. The team that correctly defines the term first gets a point. The team with the most points wins.

1. entrepreneurship (p. 698)
2. entrepreneur (p. 698)
3. franchise (p. 706)
4. sole proprietorship (p. 706)
5. unlimited liability (p. 706)
6. partnership (p. 706)
7. general partnership (p. 708)
8. limited partnership (p. 708)
9. corporation (p. 709)
10. stockholders (p. 709)
11. limited liability (p. 709)
12. foreign corporation (p. 710)
13. limited liability company (LLC) (p. 710)
14. Doing Business As (DBA) (p. 710)
15. Articles of Incorporation (p. 710)

REVIEW FACTS and IDEAS

16. Define entrepreneurship. (33.1)
17. What risks are involved in being an entrepreneur? (33.1)
18. What are the advantages of being an entrepreneur? (33.1)
19. List the personal characteristics and skills needed to be a successful business owner. (33.2)
20. Why are small businesses important to the U.S. economy? (33.2)
21. List four opportunities for becoming a business owner. (33.2)

BUILD SKILLS

22. **Workplace Skills**

Human Relations A very good friend of yours wants to start a bicycle rental shop. Both of you are bicycle enthusiasts, and you decide to explore this possibility together. What important factors should you consider so that becoming business partners does not destroy your friendship?

23. **Technology Applications**

Filing a DBA Continue to explore the business opportunity described in the previous exercise. Create a name for your new business. Using the Internet, research the procedures and fees for filing for a DBA at your county clerk's office. Also determine whether another business is using this business name. Use a word processing program to write a report of your findings.

24. **Math Practice**

Business Numbers Your company had sales revenue of $2,000,000 last year. Profit was $90,000. Of that you decide to allocate 15 percent of that profit to new equipment. How much is left after you have bought the equipment you need?

DEVELOP CRITICAL THINKING

25. **Innovation and Entrepreneurship**

Why is entrepreneurship associated with innovation? List three reasons and three examples of companies that have been innovators. Explain briefly why each company you have selected is an example of innovation.

26. **Opening Your Own Restaurant**

Imagine that you have a talent for cooking Italian food and that you would like to open an Italian restaurant in your neighborhood. Consider the following questions:

- What kind of research would you do to finalize your decision?
- How would you go about choosing which type of organization your business would be?

List the research steps you would take to answer each question and the reasons for your final decision.

APPLY CONCEPTS

27. Investigating Small Business

Use the Internet or the periodicals section of your library to find an article about the rising number of women entrepreneurs.

Activity Summarize the article and print your summary to share with your classmates.

28. Buying a Franchise

Interview the owner of a local franchise. Learn how he or she decided to purchase this particular franchise, what kind of support he receives from the company, what his job is like, and advice he would give to someone considering purchasing a franchise.

Activity Use presentation software to create a report of what you learned.

NET SAVVY

29. Spotting Hot New Market Trends

Entrepreneurs often look into the future to find new market possibilities. Using the publication *The Futurist,* research a new market trend in your field of interest (go to *www.marketingessentials.glencoe.com/33/resources* and look for a link to the World Future Society Web site or find the publication in your library). Write an essay about what you find and describe how your skills would help you to enter this field.

THE DECA CONNECTION

An Association of Marketing Students

Role Play: Entrepreneurial Concepts

Situation You are to assume the role of experienced employee of a local nursery and garden center. You have focused your studies in that direction and worked at the nursery to gain experience. You want to own a nursery and feel the time is right to do so. The owner of the nursery you work at is retiring and plans to sell the business. You have several options. You could purchase the nursery you work at, you could start a new nursery business, or you could purchase a franchise nursery business.

Activity You are to explain each of the options to your banker (judge) who will be offering you advice about your decision.

Evaluation You will be evaluated on how well you meet the following performance indicators:

- Explain the types of business ownership
- Explain the concept of private enterprise
- Describe legal issues affecting businesses
- Explain the types of business risk
- Address people properly

@ Online Action!

For more information and DECA Prep practice, go to *marketingessentials.glencoe.com/33/DECA*

CHAPTER 34
Risk Management

Chapter Objectives

After reading this chapter, you should be able to:

- Explain the nature and scope of risk management
- Identify the various types of business risks
- Explain effective security and safety precautions, policies, and procedures
- Describe the various ways businesses can manage risk
- Explain the concept of insurance

GUIDE TO THE PHOTO

Market Talk Risk is part of doing business, and managing risk must be part of every business owner's planning process. Learning to prevent those risks that can be avoided and to minimize those that are beyond your control is what risk management is all about. Even in the case of hurricanes or tornadoes, there are ways of ensuring that after such a storm, your business can rebuild and continue.

Quick Think What kinds of risks should businesses prepare for?

THE DECA CONNECTION

Performance indicators represent key skills and knowledge. Relating them to the concepts explained in this chapter is your key to success in DECA events. These acronyms represent DECA events that involve knowledge of concepts in this chapter.

AAAL	**FMAL**	**MMS***	**TMDM***
AAML*	**FMDM***	**QSRM***	**TSE***
ADC*	**FMML***	**RMAL**	**VPM**
BSM	**FSRM***	**RMML***	
EMDM*	**HMDM***	**SMDM***	

In all these DECA events you should be able to follow these performance indicators:

- Determine factors affecting business risk
- Explain types of business risk
- Describe the concept of insurance
- Explain routine security precautions
- Follow safety precautions
- Explain procedures for handling accidents
- Explain procedures for dealing with workplace threats

Events with an asterisk (*) include these indicators:

- Correct hazardous conditions
- Establish a fire-prevention program
- Establish safety policies and procedures
- Establish policies/procedures for preventing internal theft
- Develop policies and procedures for preventing vendor theft

SMDM Describe risk management for event planning

EMDM Identify strategies for Web site and customer transaction protection

DECA PREP

Check your understanding of DECA performance indicators with the DECA activity in this chapter's review. For more information and DECA Prep practice, go to *marketingessentials .glencoe.com/34/DECA*

SECTION 34.1

Risk Management for Business

OBJECTIVES

- Explain the nature and scope of risk management
- Identify the various types of business risks

KEY TERMS

- business risk
- risk management
- economic risks
- natural risks
- human risks

BEFORE YOU READ

Predict What are some kinds of business risks?

THE MAIN IDEA

Risk is part of doing business. Businesses must manage risks in ways that accommodate public interest, human safety, the environment, and state and federal laws.

STUDY ORGANIZER

In a chart like the one below, note the main kinds of risks and some examples of each kind of risk.

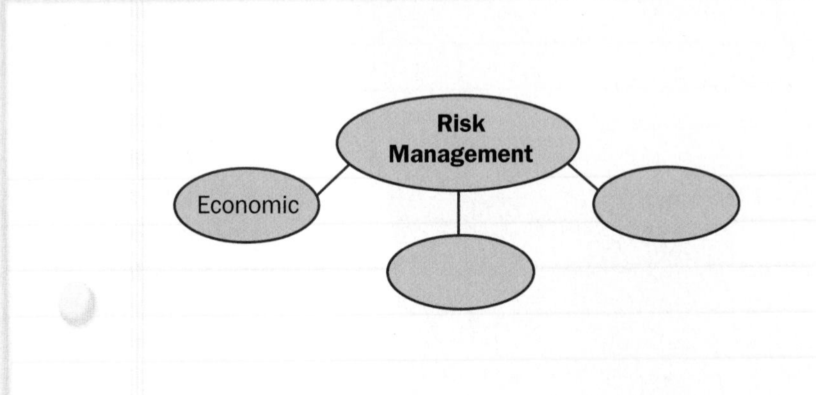

What Is Risk Management?

Question Is it possible for a business to eliminate risks completely?

To achieve our goals, all of us make decisions each day that involve taking risks. The possibility of financial loss is what is known as **business risk**. Business risks are situations that can lead to financial gain, loss, or failure.

A business cannot eliminate all risk, but marketers can reduce and manage their risks. According to the American Risk and Insurance Association, **risk management** is the systematic process of managing an organization's risks to achieve objectives in a manner consistent with public interest, human safety, environmental needs, and the law. Risks are managed by using the best available marketing information, analyzing opportunities, and making wise decisions.

Types of Business Risks

Economic, natural, and human risks are among the types of risks that a business may experience. (See figure 34.1)

Economic Risks

Economic risks are risks that result from changes in overall business conditions. These changes can include the level or type of competition, changing consumer lifestyles, population changes, limited usefulness or style of some products, product obsolescence, government regulation, inflation, or recession.

Businesses that fail to change their products when competitors offer more features and benefits lose sales and experience economic risk. Foreign competition is also an economic risk for many U.S. companies, because foreign products can often be produced and sold for less than similar domestic products.

Consumer lifestyles and population changes are other economic risks facing modern businesses if they fail to adapt products or services to meet customers' changing interests and needs.

The limited usefulness or style of some products is another potential economic risk. Prices are frequently reduced on products to sell them at the end of the season. Every price reduction reduces both revenue and profits.

Some products inevitably become obsolete or outdated. Known as product obsolescence, this type of economic risk frequently impacts businesses that depend on the latest trends to market goods and services. Obsolescence occurs because new products are constantly being developed.

Changes in the general business environment caused by inflation or recession can present economic risks. For example, businesses in an area experiencing high unemployment will suffer through reduced product sales.

Government Regulations

Government laws and regulations can also result in economic risks. Laws that require businesses to pay for such things as special licenses or permits, street and sewer improvements, environmental clean-ups, parking, and general upkeep will reduce profits.

Product recalls, or even the threat of recalls, by government agencies can affect sales and profits. Companies that have to recall products often face high legal costs in addition to expensive repairs and replacements. In 2003, a Texas court ordered the tire company Bridgestone/Firestone to pay $70 million to replace tires, $41 million to manufacture new tires, $15.5 million on a consumer education campaign, and $19 million in legal fees for 14.4 million tires recalled in 2000. The company incurred costly expenditures because it had to notify all owners by mail, provide free replacements, and then pay the legal settlement costs.

Natural Risks

Natural risks are risks that are caused by natural occurrences. They can result in loss or damage of property and may cause a business to be shut down for any length of time. Common natural risks can include catastrophes such as floods, tornadoes, hurricanes, fires, lightning, droughts, and earthquakes. Some risks that are caused by people are also called natural risks: power outages, civil unrest, oil spills, arson, terrorism, and even war are classified as natural risks. Businesses can insure against unexpected losses from some natural risks, but not all. For example, a typical business insurance policy may not cover damage caused by acts of war or riots; special insurance may be required to cover regional threats such as earthquakes or floods.

Weather is an example of a natural risk. Some businesses and products depend on predictable weather conditions for success.

Figure 34.1 Types of Business Risk

• Preparing and Coping There are three main categories of business risk.

How do businesses manage risks?

ECONOMIC RISKS

These include overestimating demand for merchandise. This store bought more summer styles than its customers wanted and now has to sell them at prices near cost to make room for the fall lines. Better planning could help manage this risk.

NATURAL RISKS

These include unexpected weather conditions as well as catastrophes, such as hurricanes. Earthquakes and fires are other natural risks to businesses. Both prevention and risk transfer are important in managing this kind of risk.

HUMAN RISKS

These include risks related to on-the-job safety as well as employee dishonesty and error. Training in the use of potentially dangerous machinery is an important part of managing safety risks.

@ Online Action! **Go to *marketingessentials.glencoe.com/34/figure/1* to find a project on handling business risks.**

A mild winter season or below-normal snowfall represents lost revenues and a natural risk for ski resorts.

Protecting your business property against the risk of loss by fire is a direct way to manage risk. Installing smoke detectors, portable fire extinguishers, and automatic sprinklers, for example, will help to protect your staff, property, and revenue.

Human Risks

Human risks are risks caused by human mistakes or dishonesty, or other risks that can be controlled by humans. They range from the financial impact of robbery or embezzlement to job-related injury or illness.

Customer Dishonesty

Loss caused by customer theft, fraudulent payment, or nonpayment is a human risk. In 2001, the National Retail Federation determined that shoplifting cost retailers $10.2 billion that year. This loss is passed on to all of us in the form of higher prices for every product to cover inventory shortages, pay for security personnel, and install theft prevention systems. Additional examples of customer dishonesty include the nonpayment of accounts or paying for goods and services with fraudulent checks or credit cards.

Employee Risks

Employees represent another human risk for business. For example, members of management at the energy trading giant Enron Corporation and its accounting firm, Arthur Andersen LLP, used questionable accounting techniques that inflated profits and hid losses. These fraudulent practices resulted in the company declaring bankruptcy in 2001—which was, at that time, the largest bankruptcy in U.S. history. Thousands of Enron employees lost their jobs, and many people lost savings they had invested in Enron stock. In addition, Arthur Andersen LLP, previously one of the top five accounting firms in the United States, lost its auditing license and sold its assets to competitors.

A MATTER OF ETHICS

A Difficult Choice

Herring's Auto Supply has been in business for twenty years, but a new discount store opened nearby six months ago, and sales have been off ever since. Herring's has had four low sales months in a row. Bills from vendors are piling up, and Mr. Herring is concerned that if he pays all the bills, there will not be enough cash on hand to pay all his employees when payday comes around at the end of next week. This situation has never happened in all his years of business.

Mr. Herring asks the store's manager what she thinks they should do. The manager thinks it is more important to pay the employees than to pay the vendors. After all, they work for Mr. Herring. Mr. Herring points out that the vendors have employees they need to pay, too.

THINKING ETHICALLY

What is the ethical thing for Mr. Herring to do in this situation? Explain your reasoning.

@ Online Action!

Go to *marketingessentials.glencoe.com/34/ethics* to find a project on ethics and risk management.

Skills and Working Environment

In a restaurant, failing to properly cook or handle food can lead to customers becoming ill or hospitalized. To reduce risks of this type, many companies have instituted safety programs that stress the importance of proper food handling.

The business environment or work setting itself often becomes a risk. Customer or employee accidents are potential human risks. Commercial airlines, for example, prepare crews for emergencies not only caused by mechanical problems but also by human factors. A passenger might fall in a crowded aisle, break an arm, and sue the airline. Employees could also be overcome by toxic fumes or sickened by other environmental hazards. Another type of risk sometimes faced by employers is the threat of sexual harassment or physical violence in the workplace.

Computer-Related Crime

Over the past decade, computer-related crime has emerged as a significant new human risk for businesses. Malicious programs called computer worms or viruses can be downloaded inadvertently by employees and can wreak havoc on internal computer networks and communications systems. Individuals may also penetrate the security of computer systems to gain access or information for mischievous or criminal purposes, including industrial espionage such as stealing proprietary company information or client lists.

Computer crime is committed by many different kinds of people, from current or past employees to professional cyberthieves. Protecting a business from computer crime requires securing the computer network using passwords, encoded firewall programs, and virus detectors. It also requires being vigilant about scanning for operational or human security risks that affect technology and keeping up to date on security alerts released by software producers. Training employees on privacy policies and the proper handling of confidential information related to voice mail, e-mail and Internet use is necessary to minimize risk of computer intrusion or information theft.

34.1 AFTER YOU READ

Reviewing Key Terms and Concepts

1. Why does product obsolescence pose an economic risk?
2. What are three examples of natural risks?
3. What causes human risks for businesses?

Integrating Academic Skills

Math

4. It is estimated that three to four percent is added to the price of a product to cover shoplifting losses. Calculate the price of a $29.99 skateboard without the four percent "hidden tax" due to shoplifting losses.

Social Studies/Language Arts

5. Perform an Internet search or library research on recent bankruptcies. Choose one company and write a short paper on the causes and effects of that company's bankruptcy.

Check your answers at *marketingessentials.glencoe.com/34/read*

SECTION 34.2

Handling Business Risks

READ and STUDY

BEFORE YOU READ

Predict A business faces many risks to earn a profit. What methods do you think a business might use to handle its risks?

THE MAIN IDEA

Businesses use certain strategies to help prevent, avoid, and protect against accidents, injuries, fires, thefts, defective products, and environmental and other disasters.

STUDY ORGANIZER

Copy the chart below. As you read, fill in the boxes with the different methods of handling risk.

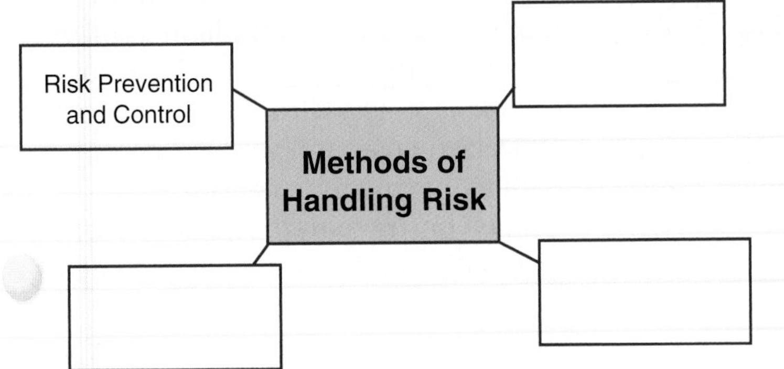

OBJECTIVES

- Explain effective security and safety precautions, policies, and procedures
- Describe the various ways businesses can manage risk
- Explain the concept of insurance

KEY TERMS

- insurance policy
- extended coverage
- fidelity bonds
- performance bonds

Question Which method of handling risks do you think is most important for a business?

Ways of Handling Business Risks

There are four basic ways that businesses can handle risks: risk prevention and control, risk transfer, risk retention, and risk avoidance. An effective risk prevention program for a business should use a combination of all these methods.

• **DETERRING THEFT** Closed-circuit television systems can help to deter both employee and customer theft.

What other systems do retailers use to help prevent theft?

Risk Prevention and Control

Business risks can be handled through prevention and control. Many common types of risks can be controlled and minimized by screening and training employees, providing safe working conditions and sufficient safety instruction, preventing external theft, and deterring employee theft.

Screening and Training Employees

The best way to prevent the human risk of employee carelessness and incompetence is through effective employee screening, orientation, and training. Background screening on all job applications, checking references, and requiring driver licenses are often used to assist in new employee selection. Many employers also use pre-employment tests for basic and technical skills to find the right people. Larger companies and some smaller ones now require prospective employees to undergo testing for illegal drugs before being hired. Drug abuse can lead to increased human risk by making employees careless and more likely to ignore or forget safety rules.

When employees begin a new job, some form of orientation, training, and instruction is normally provided. The training may be brief verbal instruction or extensive training that lasts several weeks or months. Workers should be trained in rules and regulations relating to safety.

Providing Safe Conditions and Safety Instruction

According to the National Safety Council, in 2002 there were 4,900 workplace deaths in the United States due to unintentional injuries. Another 3.7 million workers suffered disabling injuries. The financial impact of workplace accidents leading to wage loss, medical expense, and workers' compensation disability payments is staggering.

Based on these numbers alone, safety and health information must be provided to all employees. When employees receive safety instruction and have safe working conditions, the potential for on-the-job accidents is greatly reduced.

To manage such risks, businesses can design all employee work zones and customer selling areas for efficient foot traffic and storage. They can also provide training on proper ways to safely lift and store merchandise.

Many companies address workplace safety by developing accident management programs, which include:

- Creating a health and safety committee to check for hazards
- Correcting hazards before accidents occur
- Complying with all state and federal health and safety regulations
- Investigating and recording all workplace incidents and accidents
- Providing employees with protective clothing and equipment
- Placing first aid kits near workstations
- Posting the address and phone number of nearby healthcare facilities
- Offering employee classes in first aid and CPR
- Tracking how many workdays were missed due to accidents or injuries
- Scheduling regular safety meetings and training
- Preparing and distributing written safety and health plans

Case Study

Some Risks Pay Off

Cirque du Soleil is not your average circus. You will not see lion tamers, but you will see world-class acrobats and dancers performing amazing feats combined with fantastic sets, lighting, and music. Each Cirque show has a theme, and the company introduces one new show each year, after three years of development.

The company was started in 1984 by 23-year-old fire eaters Guy Laliberté and Daniel Gauthier. They persuaded the Quebec government to fund a show by street performers in a Montreal festival. Success led to well-received shows across Canada.

Taking a Gamble

Production companies offered to take Cirque on the road with traveling companies. Despite the temptation of having the shows in different locations with different casts to bring in more revenue faster, Cirque's managers decided that each show should only have one cast to maintain the highest level of performance. This allowed Cirque to raise ticket prices significantly. Forgoing immediate profits was a risk that paid off.

THINK STRATEGICALLY

What kinds of business risks do you see associated with Cirque du Soleil's business, including transporting people and sets around the world? How would you manage such risks?

Online Action! **Go to *marketingessentials.glencoe.com/34/case* to find an activity on business risks.**

- Offering incentives such as prizes or bonuses for improved safety records
- Addressing workplace threats such as sexual harassment or violence

Preventing Theft

One of the largest and most costly forms of human risk is theft by employees and customers. Internal theft by employees and external theft by customers in retail stores is high. The 2004 National Retail Security Survey estimated that inventory theft from retail stores costs the American public over $33 billion every year.

Shoplifting is external theft that involves stealing merchandise from a business. Shoplifting is one of the fastest-growing crimes against property in the country. While shoplifting losses vary by store type, it is estimated that one-third of lost inventory is caused by shoplifting.

There are many ways to deter shoplifting. Businesses can educate store employees about shoplifting prevention guidelines. Adequately lighting store layouts, storing expensive items in locked display cases, or tagging products with electronic anti-theft devices can cut down on shoplifting. Many stores use security personnel and security devices such as high-zoom digital recorders, electronic gates, closed-circuit television, and wall or ceiling mirrors to cut down on the risk of theft.

Apprehending shoplifters is a significant risk. Merchants can be sued for allegations of false arrest, false imprisonment, malicious prosecution, excessive use of force, or physical assault. To limit their liability, retailers must know acceptable shoplifter detention policies and be sure that employees are trained in these practices.

Robbery is stealing of money or merchandise by violence or threat. Many local police departments provide instruction on how to prevent and handle robberies. Businesses can lower their risk from robberies by:

- Limiting the amount of money that is kept on hand
- Handling bank deposits discreetly
- Installing video cameras to help identify robbers
- Hiring extra employees to assure double coverage
- Hiring security guards
- Installing bulletproof glass in cashier cubicles
- Opening back doors only for freight or trash
- Installing switches that allow employees to lock outside doors
- Increasing lighting inside and outside of the establishment
- Making sure doors are locked and alarms are set at night

Controlling Employee Theft

Employee theft represents 48 percent (compared to shoplifting's 31 percent) of all business losses due to theft. Most employee theft occurs at the point-of-sale (POS) terminal, or cash register. To protect against employee theft, many businesses have installed closed-circuit television systems and POS terminals that generate computerized reports.

POS computerized reports monitor void transfers, cash discrepancies, sales reports, refunds by employees, employees' discounts, and cash register transactions. By carefully analyzing these data, businesses improve the chances of apprehending dishonest employees.

Closed-circuit television systems used in conjunction with POS terminals also lower the risk of employee theft. Closed-circuit systems include cameras concealed in mannequins, ceilings, or walls. Usually operated by security personnel in a control room, they are backed up with a video recorder.

Internal business standards regarding policies to prosecute dishonest employees must be established. Open discussion about employee honesty and company policies keep all employees aware of expectations. Another prevention technique is pre-employment psychological testing to detect attitudes about honesty.

• TRANSFERRING RISK Insurance policies are a way of transferring risk from the business owner to an insurance company. How much you pay for such insurance depends on how high the risk of loss appears to the insurer.

How can an insurer help a business determine its insurance needs?

Risk Transfer

Some business risks can be handled by transferring the risk of loss to another business or to another party. Risk transfer methods include purchasing insurance, establishing product and service warranty periods, and contractual risk transfer.

Purchasing Insurance

A business can insure property and people against potential loss by purchasing insurance policies. An **insurance policy** is a contract between a business and an insurance company to cover a specific business risk. A business can buy an insurance package that combines two or more types of insurable risks of loss.

Insurance companies estimate the probability of loss due to natural risks such as fire, lightning, and wind damage, and human risks such as theft and vandalism. The insurance company then looks at the business's location, past experience, limits, and type of business to determine an insurance rate.

One of the most common forms of business insurance is property insurance. Property insurance covers the loss of or damage to buildings, equipment, machinery, merchandise, furniture, and fixtures. Coverage can be

•MANAGING RISKS There are different kinds of insurance for different kinds of risks.

Why might a business have different providers for property insurance and life insurance?

purchased for up to the full replacement value of the building, inventory, or other values.

In addition, property insurance may be extended to cover off-premise property, valuable papers and records, fire department service charges, and personal property of others, including theft. Property insurance typically includes the following features:

- **Replacement Cost Coverage** This will reimburse the business owner for the replacement cost of buildings and other personal property. A co-insurance penalty may apply if the insured business purchases less than the reconstruction value of property. This means, for example, that the insurance company might pay 80 percent of the covered items and the insured pays the balance.
- **Automatic Increase Protection** This policy feature automatically adjusts the coverage to compensate for inflation on both the building and contents.
- **Business Interruption** This feature compensates a business for loss of income during the time that repairs are being made to a building after a natural disaster. This coverage will also reimburse other expenses that continue during the repair period, such as interest on loans, taxes, rent, advertising, and salaries.

Property insurance policies can be purchased with an extended coverage endorsement. An

extended coverage endorsement provides protection against types of loss that may not be covered under a basic property insurance policy. Water leakage or sewer back-up are typical examples.

Liability Insurance

Business liability insurance protects a business against damages for which it may be held legally liable, such as an injury to a customer or damage to property of others. Primary business liability insurance is usually provided for claims up to $1 million. This type of insurance may be extended to cover business premises, company operations, customer medical expenses, and product and advertising liability claims.

Product liability insurance protects against business losses resulting from personal injury or property damage caused by products manufactured or sold by a business. Many businesses purchase product liability insurance to protect against potential customer claims even though private laboratories and government agencies may have tested the products extensively.

Fidelity bonds protect a business from employee dishonesty. Businesses usually require employees who handle money, such as bank tellers and cashiers, to be bonded. If a bonded employee steals money or merchandise, the bonding company pays the loss. Individuals who are to be bonded are subject to background checks before a bond is issued.

Performance bonds, also called surety bonds, provide financial protection for losses that might occur when a construction project is not finished due to the contractor's impaired financial condition.

Life insurance is often purchased to protect the owners or managers of a business. A sole proprietor (individual business owner) is usually required to have life insurance in order to borrow money. The policy will guarantee that there will be money to pay off the sole proprietor's debts and obligations if he or she dies.

MARKET TECH

Power Paper

Have you ever opened up a greeting card and heard it play *Happy Birthday to You*? Ultra-thin silicon technology makes the generation of music possible, but where does it get its power? Power Paper is an Israeli company that makes batteries as thin as a piece of paper to power such cards, among hundreds of other uses.

Work and Play

One powerful application of Power Paper technology is PowerID, which integrates radio frequency identification (RFID) with the company's power source. Merchandise tagged with PowerID can be tracked from manufacturer to retailer, even if stored in boxes or around materials that interfere with radio transmission. The labels can be read from as far as 40 feet away. This helps all members of a supply chain manage the risks of theft and other losses, as well as keep better track of the level of inventory on hand.

For the retail market, Power Paper has created products that incorporate printed clocks, simple games, or calculators into the covers of notebooks. Hasbro, the toy company, has incorporated Power Paper batteries into products such as thin LCD watches and touch-activated musical-instrument-shaped stickers that play tunes.

THINK LIKE A MARKETER

What other products can you think of that could be improved with batteries as thin as a piece of paper?

Online Action!

Go to *marketingessentials.glencoe.com/34/tech* to find an activity on technology and risk management.

Purchasing life insurance on a partner can provide the money needed for other partners to continue the business when the partners are named as beneficiaries and receive the money from the policy.

Credit insurance protects a business from losses on credit extended to customers. Credit life insurance pays off the balance due for loans granted by banks, credit unions, and other financial institutions in the event the borrower dies.

Workers' compensation insurance covers employees who suffer job-related injuries and illness and protects employers from lawsuits filed by an employee injured on the job. All states require employers that regularly employ a predetermined minimum number of employees for prescribed time periods to purchase workers' compensation insurance coverage.

Product and Service Warranties

Warranties are promises made by the manufacturer or distributor with respect to the performance and quality of a product.

Transferring Risks Through Business Ownership

In a sole proprietorship, the individual owner assumes all risks. Partnerships enable the partners to share in the business risks.

• AVOIDING RISK Many companies that provide businesses with insurance are also involved in helping them create effective risk management plans.

Why might an insurance company want its clients to minimize risks?

Corporations allow the stockholders, as owners, to share the business risks. The corporate form of ownership offers the most protection from losses.

Risk Retention

In some cases, it is impossible for businesses to prevent or transfer certain types of risks, so they retain or assume financial responsibility for the consequences of loss. This process is called risk retention. A business has to assume the loss—or retain the risk—if customer trends change and merchandise remains unsold. Most retail shops assume the loss of a certain percentage of goods due to damage or theft.

It is possible to underestimate the risk, such as when merchandise is purchased in anticipation of high demand but weather, fashion trends, or customers' purchasing habits change. A business may attempt to generate a profit by taking a risk, such as purchasing land for future development or sale through subdivision.

Risk Avoidance

Certain risks may be anticipated in advance. Risk avoidance means that a business refuses to engage in a particularly hazardous activity. Market research can lead businesses to conclude that investment in a product or service is not worth the risk. All business decisions should be made with the consideration of both potential benefits and potential risks. Avoiding unacceptable business risks should be a key consideration in any marketing decision.

34.2 AFTER YOU READ

Reviewing Key Terms and Concepts

1. What are the four basic ways to handle business risks?
2. What strategies can be used by businesses for risk prevention and control?
3. Identify three different ways that a business can transfer risks.

Integrating Academic Skills

Math

4. The total cost of theft from retail stores in 2004 was estimated at $33 billion. Calculate the individual costs of internal and external theft if internal theft represented 48 percent and shoplifting represented 31 percent.

Language Arts

5. Perform library research on the topic of shoplifting. Write a 100-word article abstract on the topic of shoplifting. In your article abstract identify the name of the article, its publication date and name of publication, and summarize the article.

Check your answers at *marketingessentials.glencoe.com/34/read*

CAREERS IN MARKETING

Billy Hardison
Independent Talent Buyer and Concert Promoter

What do you do at work?

As an independent talent buyer in a secondary market, marketing is just one of the necessary skills for survival. At the micro level every concert promoter negotiates as fiscally responsible a deal as possible with every artist on a case-by-case basis. Advertising the upcoming event is an obvious next step. Marketing, however, exists at the macro level. Marketing not only influences advertising decisions, it also affects the buying of the talent itself. Branding must be consistent. Shows that are bought, choice of sponsors (if any), use of mass media and to what degree, visibility to the common public, ideology, religion and eating habits are all factors that must be addressed when defining the brand.

What skills are most important to you?

The intangibles are the ability to communicate to the audience, even if it is not your audience, humility, diplomacy, foresight, street smarts, blue-collar skills and work ethic. The tangibles are the ability to communicate through all mediums, computer skills, an appreciation of the arts, a college degree.

What is your key to success?

This is a hard nut to crack. Drive is the most important quality, regardless of the formal training. We have a saying in the "biz": "This is the hardest business to get into and the hardest business to get out of."

Aptitudes, Abilities, and Skills

Strong interpersonal and people skills, versatility, sales aptitude, ability to manage several projects

Education and Training

A bachelor's degree can be helpful, although the exact nature of the degree is often not important.

Career Path

Many concert promoters start small, organizing local shows with friends; opportunities also exist within larger entertainment firms.

THINKING CRITICALLY

What type of business risks do you think this type of work include?

Online Action!

Go to *marketingessentials.glencoe.com/34/careers* to find a career-related activity.

CHAPTER 34 REVIEW

FOCUS on KEY POINTS

SECTION 34.1

- Business risks are situations that can lead to financial gain, loss, or failure. Risk management is the process of managing risk in an ethical way.
- Business risks fall into three categories: economic, natural, and human. Economic risks such as recession or population changes result from changes in overall business conditions. Natural risks such as floods or arson result from natural or sometimes human occurrences. Human risks are caused by human mistakes or things that can be controlled by humans, such as the working environment.

SECTION 34.2

- There are various ways that businesses can manage risks of financial loss, including loss prevention, control, transfer, retention, and avoidance. Establishing and maintaining safe conditions and controlling external and internal theft can reduce financial loss.
- Insurance is a common way to transfer risks. You can also transfer risk through warranties or business ownership changes.

REVIEW VOCABULARY

Define each of the following terms in a short sentence.

1. business risk (p. 718)
2. risk management (p. 718)
3. economic risks (p. 719)
4. natural risks (p. 719)
5. human risks (p. 721)
6. insurance policy (p. 727)
7. extended coverage (p. 729)
8. fidelity bonds (p. 729)
9. performance bonds (p. 729)

REVIEW FACTS and IDEAS

10. What is risk management, and why is it an important marketing function? (34.1)
11. What are the different types of business risk? Give an example of each type. (34.1)
12. How do safety and security policies reduce risks for businesses? (34.2)
13. Describe at least two ways businesses can manage risks. (34.2)
14. What is the purpose of an insurance policy? (34.2)
15. Name two types of bonds and the purpose of each. (34.2)

BUILD SKILLS

16. Workplace Skills

Interpersonal Communication Suppose you are the manager of a sandwich shop. Prepare a memo to your staff of food workers on the importance of hygiene and other good practices in the workplace. Explain the kinds of risks that both employees and others may face.

17. Technology Applications

Creating Charts Using the Internet or other resources, research the top five most costly natural disasters in your state's history. Use a spreadsheet or graphic design program to create a chart listing the five disasters and their costs.

18. Math Practice

Counting the Losses Calculate the amount of net sales lost to an apparel specialty store with annual sales of $1,234,000 and a shoplifting rate of 2.4 percent.

DEVELOP CRITICAL THINKING

19. Selecting Insurance

Different companies have different needs. Choose a company or a type of business that interests you. Research the type of risks your chosen business typically encounters.

As you research and find out facts about the business type you selected, try to answer the following questions:

- Are there any risk factors that the company you selected should not have to consider?
- What factors should this business consider when selecting an insurance company?

Explain your answers.

20. Extended Warranties

Why does a company sell extended warranties to its customers if its advertising stresses the product's quality and durability? Does this imply that the company's products are likely to malfunction? Explain your answers and give two product examples.

APPLY CONCEPTS

21. Improving Workplace Safety

Perform Internet or library research about workplace safety laws or regulations. Select a particular aspect of employment laws affecting workplace safety. Take notes about the law, including its name, date it went into effect, and protections found in the law.

Activity Review the information and use presentation software to prepare an oral report on one aspect of workplace safety.

22. Understand Insurance

Locate an insurance provider using the Internet or other sources. Select a provider that lists details such as type and length of coverage.

Activity Using presentation software, describe the nature and scope of the insurance company from the materials reviewed.

NET SAVVY

23. Business and the Environment

Find the Web site for the U.S. Environmental Protection Agency (EPA). The EPA plays a significant role in preventing, correcting, and eliminating potential environmental problems. Write a one-page summary about a recent situation involving a business and what actions were taken by the EPA to protect the public interest.

THE DECA CONNECTION

An Association of Marketing Students

Role Play: Assistant Manager

Situation You are to assume the role of an assistant manager for a 24-hour self-service gas station and convenience store. Your store has been experiencing an increasing number of drive-offs. Drive-offs happen when individuals leave the station without paying. Your store manager has asked you to design a procedure for handling external theft (shoplifting). Your procedure must avoid annoying regular customers.

Activity You are to prepare an oral presentation explaining your plan for reducing external theft without jeopardizing customer goodwill and employee safety.

Evaluation You will be evaluated on how well you meet the following performance indicators:

- Explain routine security precautions
- Explain procedures for handling shoplifting
- Follow safety precautions
- Demonstrate problem-solving skills
- Demonstrate effective oral presentation skills

@ Online Action!

For more information and DECA Prep practice, go to *marketingessentials.glencoe.com/34/DECA*

CHAPTER 35

Developing a Business Plan

Chapter Objectives

After reading this chapter, you should be able to:

- Explain the purpose and importance of a business plan
- Identify external planning considerations
- Develop a business's organization plan
- Construct a marketing plan
- Identify the financial elements of a business plan
- Describe financing sources for businesses

GUIDE TO THE PHOTO

Market Talk By the time a business opens its doors, it should have a business plan and a marketing plan in place. While the marketing plan outlines market analysis and marketing strategies, the business plan defines the larger picture and includes a mission statement and a detailed financial plan for all functions of the business. Entrepreneurs must look at all available sources of funding and opportunities to raise capital.

Quick Think Why must a small business entrepreneur make creative funding decisions when planning a new business or expanding an existing one?

THE DECA CONNECTION

Performance indicators represent key skills and knowledge. Relating them to the concepts explained in this chapter is your key to success in DECA events.

These acronyms represent DECA events that involve knowledge of concepts in this chapter.

AAAL	**FSRM***	**TSE***	**FMAL**
FMML*	**VPM**	**TMDM***	**RMAL**
RMML*	**SMDM***	**BSM**	**FMDM***
HMDM*	**ADC***	**QSRM***	
AAML*	**MMS***	**EMDM***	

In all these DECA events you should be able to follow these performance indicators:

- Conduct an environmental scan to obtain marketing information
- Explain the nature and scope of financing
- Assess personal interests and skills needed for success in business

Events with an asterisk (*) also include:

- Explain the nature of business plans
- Develop company objectives (for a strategic business unit)
- Develop strategies to achieve company goals/objectives
- Explain external planning considerations
- Develop business plan

Some events include one additional indicator: Conduct location feasibility study. These events are:

AAML	**FMDM**
FMML	**HMDM**
QSRM	**SMDM**
RMML	**TMDM**

DECA PREP

Check your understanding of DECA performance indicators with the DECA activity in this chapter's review. For more information and DECA Prep practice, go to *marketingessentials.glencoe.com/35/DECA*

SECTION 35.1

The Business Plan

OBJECTIVES

- Explain the purpose and importance of a business plan
- Identify external planning considerations

KEY TERMS

- business plan
- business philosophy
- trading area
- buying behavior

READ and STUDY

BEFORE YOU READ

Predict What do you think would happen if you started a business without planning first?

THE MAIN IDEA

A business plan helps an entrepreneur develop business goals, determine necessary resources, and identify how the new business will operate. This plan also helps potential lenders or investors assess if the business is a good financial risk.

STUDY ORGANIZER

In a chart like the one below, identify the elements in the first component of a business plan.

Description and Analysis

WHILE YOU READ

Connect Suppose you want to launch a business. List three questions a lender would ask you before loaning you funds.

Developing the Business Plan

If you want to establish your own business, you will probably need financial assistance. A business plan will help you secure that assistance. A **business plan** is a proposal that outlines a strategy to turn a business idea into a reality. It describes a business opportunity, such as a new business or plans to expand an existing one, to potential investors and lenders. They will review the business plan before granting you credit or start-up capital.

In addition to helping you obtain financing, a business plan will guide you as you open the business and plan for its management.

Your business plan should convince investors and lenders that your business idea is profitable, identify procedures necessary to legally establish the business, and work as a management tool to identify the month-to-month steps necessary to operate a profitable business. A business plan must be well organized and easy to read. It should contain three main components:

- Description and analysis of the proposed business
- Organizational and marketing plan
- Financial plan

Although the formats of business plans vary, the outline in Figure 35.1 on page 740 is an excellent model.

Description and Analysis of the Proposed Business

The description and analysis section introduces the proposed business concept. This section should clearly identify the products and services the business will sell. It includes your personal business philosophy, as well as a self-analysis that describes your business experience, education, and training. This section of your business plan also includes a trading area analysis, a market segment analysis, and an analysis of potential locations.

When preparing your plan, be as factual as possible. Where can you get up-to-date information online and off? For regional and national business information, consult recent issues of *BusinessWeek, Entrepreneur, Fortune, Money,* the *Wall Street Journal,* and other business publications. Trade and professional associations as well as industry groups can also be a source of data. Tap into research conducted by local and state economic advisory boards, councils, and government agencies. The U.S. Small Business Administration and the Senior Core of Retired Executives (SCORE) can also refer you to potential sources of information and classes for aspiring entrepreneurs.

Business Philosophy and Products

Begin your plan with a description of the type of business you want to open. In this section, you will present marketing research data and review significant trends that will influence the success of your business. Explain how a current or changing situation has created an opportunity for the business to fulfill consumer demand.

Business Philosophy

Next, state your **business philosophy**, which explores how you think the business should be run and demonstrates your understanding of your business's role in the marketplace. It reveals your attitude toward your customers, employees, and competitors. Your business philosophy will help you attract new customers and maintain existing customers once you start a business.

Wal-Mart's business philosophy is that it will not be undersold, and the return policy is that customers can always return merchandise if they are dissatisfied with it.

Type of Product or Service

After identifying your business philosophy, describe the product or service you will offer. Explain the potential consumer benefits and why your product or service will be successful. Include as many facts, trends, and statistics as you can, and be thorough in your research and documentation. Speculation and statements of belief do not convince investors and lenders to lend you money.

Self-Analysis

The next part of your business plan includes a self-analysis, a description of your personal education, training, strengths, and weaknesses, and a plan for personal development.

Experiences, Skills, and Plans

In this part of the business plan, you need to highlight your strengths and skills in your chosen area. You should also describe how you will acquire the skills you lack through additional training or by hiring other professionals.

Figure 35.1 Outline for a Business Plan

- **Business Plan Outline** Developing a business plan is like outlining a strategy for turning your business idea into a reality.

Why should a business plan be a continuing work-in-progress?

BUSINESS PLAN OUTLINE

1

Section 1 describes the general concept of the proposed business, outlines the entrepreneur's special skills, and analyzes the potential market.

I. Description and analysis of the proposed business situation

A. Type of business
B. Business philosophy
C. Description of good or service
D. Self-analysis
  1. Education and training
  2. Strengths and weaknesses
  3. Plan for personal development
E. Trading area analysis
  1. Geographic, demographic, and economic data
  2. Competition
F. Market segment analysis
  1. Target market
  2. Customer buying behavior
G. Analysis of potential location

2

Section 2 discusses how the business will be organized, describes the product or service to be offered, and details the marketing plan.

II. Organization and marketing plan

A. Proposed organization
  1. Type of ownership
  2. Steps in establishing business
  3. Personnel needs
B. Proposed good/service
  1. Manufacturing plans and inventory policies
  2. Suppliers
C. Proposed marketing plan
  1. Pricing policies
  2. Promotional activities

III. Financial plan

A. Sources of capital
  1. Personal sources
  2. External sources
B. Projected income and expenses
  1. Personal financial statement
  2. Projected start-up costs
  3. Projected personal needs
  4. Projected business income
  5. Projected business expenses
  6. Projected income statement(s)
  7. Projected balance sheet
  8. Projected cash flow

3

Section 3 identifies the sources of capital and projects income and expenses.

@ Online Action!

Go to *marketingessentials.glencoe.com/35/figure/1* to find a project on business plans.

Indicate the education and training you have had so far to prepare you for operating your new business. Your educational and work experience shows potential lenders that you can understand the industry and have the required skills for running a successful business.

Licenses

Some businesses require applying for a special license. In this section, you should explain if you already have this license or are in the application process.

Personal Traits

Finally, include the special personal traits and work habits you possess that will help you to operate the proposed business. Examples of past leadership activities, personal initiatives, and willingness to work hard all add strength to your business plan.

Trading Area Analysis

Following an explanation of your personal strengths and skills, define your trading area. A **trading area** is the geographical area from which a business draws its customers. Before going into business, you must analyze the trading area to become familiar with geographic, demographic, and economic data, as well as with the competition.

Information about the population in your trading area is available from your local chamber of commerce or state department of commerce. You can also consult the most recent local U.S. census data in your library or on the Internet.

Geographic, Demographic, and Economic Data

Geographic data include population distribution figures: how many people live in a certain area. Demographics are identifiable and measurable population statistics such as age, gender, marital status, and race/ethnicity. Knowing the demographics of your trading area will help you identify market trends that may have a direct impact on your business.

Prevailing economic conditions are among the major factors affecting a business. Economic factors include economic growth projections, trends in employment, interest rates, business mergers, and governmental regulations. Tax increases or decreases levied by the local, state, and federal governments will affect consumer buying power.

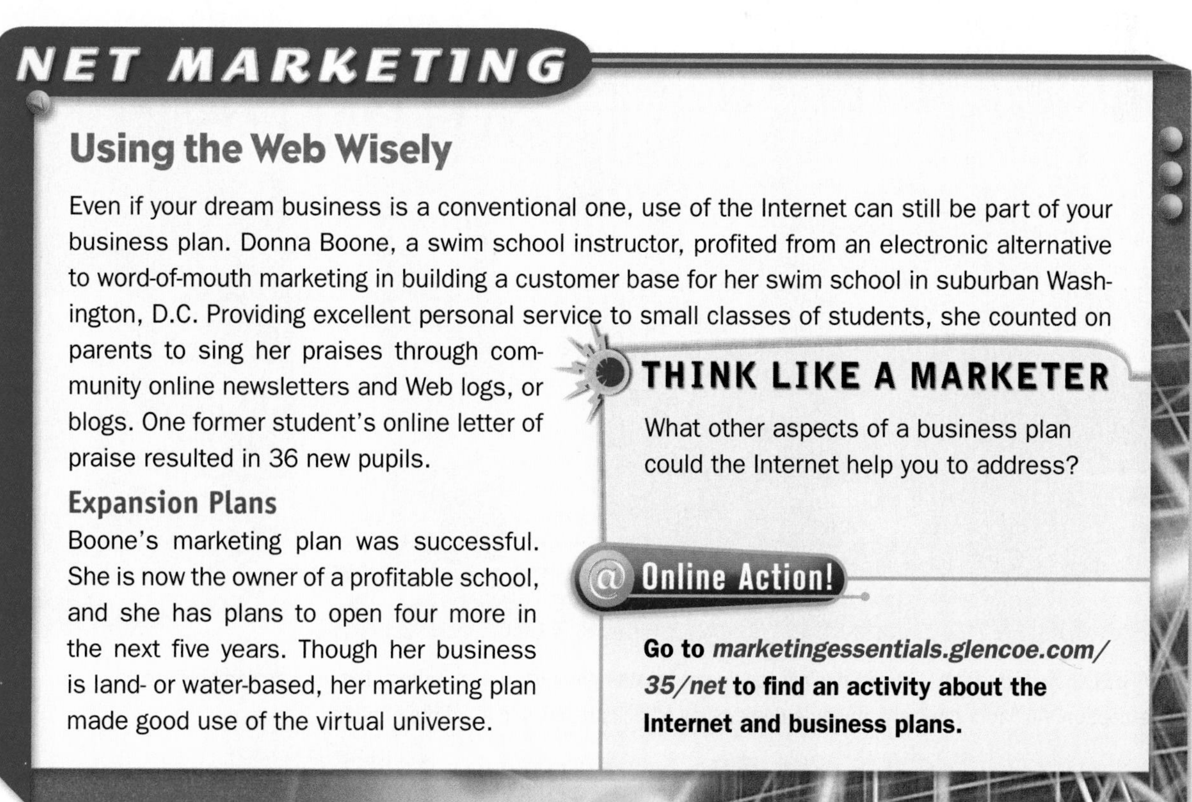

NET MARKETING

Using the Web Wisely

Even if your dream business is a conventional one, use of the Internet can still be part of your business plan. Donna Boone, a swim school instructor, profited from an electronic alternative to word-of-mouth marketing in building a customer base for her swim school in suburban Washington, D.C. Providing excellent personal service to small classes of students, she counted on parents to sing her praises through community online newsletters and Web logs, or blogs. One former student's online letter of praise resulted in 36 new pupils.

Expansion Plans

Boone's marketing plan was successful. She is now the owner of a profitable school, and she has plans to open four more in the next five years. Though her business is land- or water-based, her marketing plan made good use of the virtual universe.

THINK LIKE A MARKETER

What other aspects of a business plan could the Internet help you to address?

Online Action!

Go to *marketingessentials.glencoe.com/35/net* to find an activity about the Internet and business plans.

It is important to include how much disposable income the potential consumers in your trading area have. This is the personal income remaining from wages after all taxes are taken out. Disposable income is also referred to as buying income.

A special measurement called a buying power index (BPI) has been developed to help new business owners determine the buying power for a given target market. The BPI index factors total population, total income, and total retail sales figures to determine an overall indicator of an area's sales potential. A market can be a state, region, county, or metropolitan statistical area (MSA). These factors are then expressed as a percentage of total potential U.S. sales. You can find more information on buying power indexes in *Demographics USA* (formerly known as the *Survey of Buying Power Index*), which is published annually by Trade Dimensions International.

A good source of information on local economic conditions is your local bank. Bank officials often have business projections for major geographical areas and for most types of businesses located in their immediate area. In addition, the Small Business Administration (SBA) has funded over 1,100 small business development centers (SBDCs) to provide counseling, training, and technical assistance to small businesses and new entrepreneurs. Since 1980, over nine million rural and urban entrepreneurs have received services from SBDCs. Other good sources of information are related business publications available at schools, public libraries, colleges, and universities, or on the Internet.

Competition

As a new business owner, you must analyze your competition. List all the competitors in your trading area: products, prices, locations, general quality of products, and strengths and weaknesses. Try to estimate your competitors' sales volume and identify how they promote and sell their products. You should be able to use these factors to demonstrate how your business will be superior to the competition.

•**A BIG EXCEPTION** Usually, businesses do not locate right next to competitors, but auto dealerships are an exception. An "auto row" with multiple dealerships lets customers see all of their options.

What kind of location do auto dealerships prefer?

Some good sources of information about your competitors can be found through annual reports, the local chamber of commerce, trade associations, the Yellow Pages, the Internet, business publications, and reports such as those published by Dun & Bradstreet.

Market Segment Analysis

The next part of your business plan should contain a market segment analysis, a description of your target market, and the buying behavior of your potential customers.

Target Market

As you know, your target market is the specific group of people you want to reach. You can identify your target market by common geographic characteristics such as region, county size, size of city, density of population, and climate of the area. You can also categorize it by demographic characteristics such as age, gender, marital status, family size, income, occupation, education, religion, culture, or ethnic background.

You must carefully identify your target market so that you will know the needs and wants of different markets for your goods and services. Your task as an entrepreneur is to decide which market to target and how to do it.

Customer Buying Behavior

After you have identified your target market, you will need to explain how the market's buying behavior will be good for your business. **Buying behavior** is the process individuals use to decide what they will buy, where they will buy it, and from whom they will buy it.

Analysis of Potential Locations

The decision where to locate your store is vital to your success. You can select your location after you have analyzed your trading area and your market segment, including your target market and your competition. You need to consider several additional factors.

Buy, Lease, or Build?

Should you buy, lease, or build your facility? The advantages of leasing outweigh the other options for most new businesses. With leasing, you avoid a large initial outlay of cash, your risk is reduced by the shorter commitment, and your lease expenses are tax deductible. The process of buying or building is more complex and almost always requires major financing.

Regardless of whether you buy, lease, or build, you need to compare certain terms of each potential method of financing your property. Those terms include monthly rent or payments and the length of commitment. You will also need to find out who is responsible for insurance.

You should have an attorney review any lease or contract before you sign it. He or she will help you fully understand your obligations and negotiate the best possible terms before completing the deal.

Competing and Complementary Businesses

Before you decide, consider the number and size of potential competitors in the area. If your business is similar in size and merchandise to its competitors, you may want to locate near them. This can encourage comparison shopping. On the other hand, a larger business that offers more variety than the competition should be able to generate its own customers and therefore can be situated away from the competition.

A complementary business is one that would help generate store traffic. A shoe or accessories store located next to a clothing store is one example of a complementary business.

Hours of Operation

The nature of your business will dictate if you locate your business in a mall, neighborhood shopping center, freestanding location, or online. That location, in turn, will determine your hours of operation and the number of customers who will see and patronize your business.

Visibility

Restaurants and other businesses that rely on high visibility or prime locations may spend the extra money to locate in a high-traffic location. Such a site may not be a priority or profitable for all businesses.

Safety

Customer safety should be a consideration when choosing a business location. Research the community's crime rate. You do not want to open your operation in an area where customers feel uncomfortable or are reluctant to visit. Find out whether the fire department is a volunteer or municipal one; contact them to inquire about safety codes, if any, that apply to your business.

Customer Accessibility

Make sure your customers can get to your location easily. Identify the highways, streets, and public transportation options that they would have to use in getting to your site. Will traffic be an obstacle? Will they find sufficient parking easily and for a reasonable charge? Are the location, route, and parking wheelchair accessible?

Zoning and Other Regulations

Now, you are ready to find a specific site. Your first step should be to learn about any local ordinances or laws that may affect your business. Research any restrictions that might prevent you from locating in a particular area. Plans to build or renovate will require the necessary building permits. Operating a regulated business, such as a service station, will call for the necessary local zoning approvals and state licenses.

35.1 AFTER YOU READ

Reviewing Key Terms and Concepts

1. Why is it important to develop a business plan?
2. Identify the three major parts of a business plan.
3. What is a trading area?

Integrating Academic Skills

Math

4. Compute the buying power index for city A, given the following formula and information

   Buying Power Index =
   .5 × Area's Percentage for U.S. Effective Buying Power
   + .3 × Area's Percentage of U.S. Retail Sales
   + .2 × Area's Percentage of U.S. Population
   City A Percentage of U.S. Effective Buying Power = .0103
   City A Percentage of U.S. Retail Sales = .0099
   City A Percentage of U.S. Population = .008

Economics

5. Investigate what economic and demographic data are available for your community by consulting with your local chamber of commerce, the city government, the U.S. Census Bureau, or the Internet. Include such factors as employment levels, major industries, income, education, etc. Summarize your findings in a one-page written report.

@ Online Action! Check your answers at *marketingessentials.glencoe.com/35/read*

SECTION 35.2

The Marketing and Financial Plans

OBJECTIVES

- Develop a business's organization plan
- Construct a marketing plan
- Identify the financial elements of a business plan
- Describe financing sources for businesses

KEY TERMS

- job descriptions
- organization chart
- equity capital
- debt capital
- collateral
- credit union

READ and STUDY

BEFORE YOU READ

Predict What do you think a lender would be looking for in the marketing plan section of a business plan?

THE MAIN IDEA

The marketing plan section of the business plan outlines how you intend to organize the business. It also explains how you will use advertising and promotional activities to help your business grow and prosper in the competitive marketplace.

STUDY ORGANIZER

Complete a chart like the one below and describe the three components of a business plan.

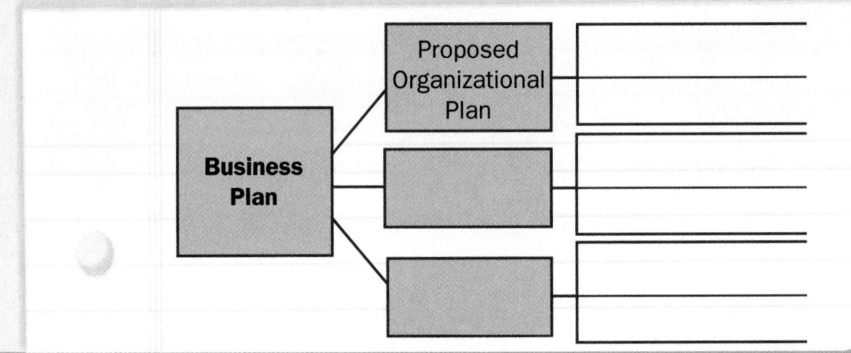

Connect Think of a business you know or have heard about and list facts it might use in its marketing plan.

Organizing the Plan

The second section of the business plan explains how you will organize the new business. It describes your current and anticipated staffing needs. It also reviews how you plan to sell your product and how you intend to reach and satisfy customers. The details of your proposed product are explained along with your potential suppliers, manufacturing or selling

Case Study

Design Is About More Than Looks!

The designers of Apple's first computer mouse and the first laptop computer formed IDEO in 1991. Throughout the 1990s, the company was a design leader in the tech field, focusing on making products user-friendly. Adding capabilities in psychology and architecture, it has become well-known for designing environments and processes, in addition to products and services. IDEO's innovative approach to design and solving problems has resulted in rave reviews from its clients, who range from Amtrak to clothing designer Prada.

The New Office

The popular comic strip Dilbert focuses on the challenges of working in a typical office cubicle. Scott Adams, Dilbert's creator, worked with IDEO to create a cubicle that would answer people's complaints about lack of privacy, space, tools, and control of the cubicle environment.

The walls of Dilbert's Ultimate Cubicle are snap-in modular blocks, some hollow for storage. Workers can choose from a catalog of different floor and wall modules and furnishings, including a hammock that snaps out of sight, an aquarium, or a hamster wheel. Floor modules flip over to reveal different textures and colors. Extra storage is found in hollow floor blocks, and seating folds down from the cubicle wall.

The cubicle is playful, but also efficient and comfortable. Rather than building expensive new space, IDEO redesigns spaces to be more pleasant, often saving companies money while enhancing the working environment for everyone.

THINK STRATEGICALLY

How would a design consulting firm like IDEO fit into a business plan for a neighborhood coffee shop?

@ Online Action! **Go to *marketingessentials.glencoe.com/35/case* to find an activity about business plans.**

methods, and inventory policies. Finally, it includes your marketing plan. Your marketing plan details your pricing strategies and promotional plans.

Proposed Organization

The organizational section of your business plan is a blueprint or a foundation for the structure of your proposed business. You must construct a clear, solid foundation around which to build the rest of your business.

Types of Ownership

There are three main types of business ownership structures: sole proprietorships, partnerships, and corporations. In this part of the business plan, you will identify which structure you have chosen and why. The structure you choose for your business will impact the remainder of the plan.

Steps in Establishing Your Business

Next, you will outline the steps you plan to take to establish your business. The specific

steps you will take depend on how you organize your business.

Staffing

You need to demonstrate to potential investors and lenders that you know how to staff the business so that it operates efficiently and successfully. List your personnel needs in your business plan and identify the people who will perform those jobs. For example, if you are opening a small coffee shop, what staffing needs will you have?

Many new businesses begin as one-person operations. It is not unusual for an entrepreneur to handle everything from management to financial oversight to advertising and promotion.

Job Descriptions

Prepare job descriptions for your partners, employees, and yourself. **Job descriptions** are written statements listing the requirements of a particular job and the skills needed to fulfill those requirements. Each job description includes the purpose of the job, qualifications and skills needed, duties to be performed, equipment to be used, and expected working conditions. Detailed job descriptions help employees know exactly what is expected of them and help you measure their performance against those expectations.

Organization Chart

Once you have completed the job descriptions, develop an organization chart to establish the chain of command within your business. An **organization chart** is a diagram of the company's departments and jobs with lines of authority clearly shown. Your organization chart tells employees to whom they report and to whom they can turn with problems or questions. It also establishes department responsibilities.

Outside Experts

Trained professionals will help you avoid mistakes that could damage your prospects for success. If you decide to use outside professionals, identify them and their responsibilities on your organization chart. Professionals who can help include accountants, attorneys, bankers, and insurance agents.

You can also use technical assistance to identify employment practices in your state or locality. State agencies such as state departments of civil rights, commerce, labor, licensing, and regulation publish many inexpensive or free publications and offer technical assistance to help new entrepreneurs understand various employment laws, rules, and regulations.

Proposed Product or Service

One part of your business plan should include information on the types of products and services you will offer, as well as your potential suppliers, manufacturing plans, and inventory policies. Your investors or lenders will also want to know what the associated costs will be.

If you are selling a product, you will need to develop a plan that details all of the purchasing or manufacturing requirements as well as your inventory policy and the anticipated costs. You need to show how you will manage the products you purchase or manufacture. How much, for example, will you keep on hand? How will you keep track of what to order and what has been sold? Where will you store the products that you have in stock?

Your inventory system depends on the size and scope of your proposed business. Trade associations and many suppliers can give you suggestions for the best inventory control system for your business.

For a service business, you need to develop a plan that addresses who will provide the service to your customers and how and when that will happen. In your plan, state the services provided by your competitors. Then describe the additional or distinct services you will provide and estimate their costs. Point out your edge over the competition.

Proposed Marketing Plan

You are now ready to develop your marketing policies, that is, the way you will price, promote, and distribute your product. Marketing mix strategies are vital to the success of your business (see Figure 35.2).

Pricing Policies

Your business plan must outline your pricing policies. As you learned in Unit 8, you must be able to set a price high enough to cover your costs and make a profit, but competitive enough to attract customers.

Reread Chapters 25, 26, and 27 to review the important factors in pricing.

Promotional Activities

Once pricing policies have been established, you need to describe your promotional activities. Identify how to reach the greatest number of potential customers in your target market in the most efficient and effective way.

You will need visibility, too. That comes from the promotional mix. A firm's promotional mix encompasses advertising, public relations, promotions, and personal selling. Your business plan will outline the mix that will be most effective in persuading prospects (wholesalers, retailers, and consumers) to do business with you. The plan will explain why you have selected this mix and what costs you anticipate. Specify an annual budget for each activity.

Financial Section of the Business Plan

In the financial section of a business plan, lenders and investors can see what monies are needed to start and operate the business. They will also review the entrepreneur's statements of personal and external sources of capital. In addition, the financial section contains statements of projected income and expenses for at least the first year of operation.

Sources of Capital

Capital is the funding needed to finance the operation of a business. It includes all goods used to produce other goods. In business, capital may include owned property and cash resources. In this chapter, the term *capital* refers to anything that can be converted into money.

Equity Capital

Raising money from within your company or by selling part of the interest in the business is called using **equity capital**. The advantage of using equity capital is that you do not need to repay the money or pay interest. However, the investor becomes a co-owner in your business. The larger the share of your business that you sell, the more control you relinquish to your investors. Equity capital sources include personal savings, partners, and shareholders.

Personal Savings

The most common method of financing a business is using personal savings. Although you may not prefer this option, you probably cannot avoid investing part of your savings. As you know, starting any new business involves risk. Your prospective investors and lenders will expect you to share in that risk.

Partners

Having partners is another way to raise capital for your business. Partners may bring in their own money and have access to other sources. As with equity investors, you may have to share control of the business when you bring in a partner.

Shareholders

You may sell stock to shareholders as a way of raising capital. You will need to form a corporation first (see Chapter 33). Shareholders have some influence over general corporate policy decisions, but as long as you hold a majority of the shares, you control the corporation's daily activities.

Debt Capital

Debt capital is a term used to describe borrowed funds that must be repaid. Some debt capital sources are banks, credit unions, the Small Business Administration, friends, relatives, suppliers, and previous business owners.

Debt capital can work to your advantage when you finance a new business because borrowing money and repaying it on a timely basis builds a good credit standing. In turn, a

Figure 35.2 Organization and Marketing

• **How It Will Work** **The second part of a business plan describes the organization of the company and outlines the marketing efforts that will be used to promote the company's products and services. Below are the three aspects of a business summarized in this part.**

What factors affect a company's organization?

ORGANIZATION

These three entrepreneurs have decided to become partners in an Internet café, and are signing partnership agreements that set out their responsibilities. They have already identified the perfect location and are negotiating a lease. Their business plan calls for the three partners to be the sole employees until the business becomes profitable, and they are willing to work 70–80 hours a week to make the café a success.

PRODUCTS AND SERVICES

This partner is arranging for Internet service. In the meantime, another is negotiating with coffee wholesalers and equipment suppliers, while the third is working with designers to choose furnishings and fixtures.

MARKETING

The partners' business plan calls for low pricing early on to build a customer base. The owners have confidence that the great pastries and coffee drinks will keep people coming in after the price for online service is increased. Another planned marketing move is putting a sandwich board ad in front of the café.

@ Online Action!

Go to *marketingessentials.glencoe.com/35/figure/2* to find a project on planning a business's organization and marketing.

good credit standing makes it easier for you to borrow additional money. Although interest must be paid with the loan, that interest becomes a tax-deductible business expense. In addition, by financing with debt capital, you do not share control of the business with lenders.

There is a major disadvantage to debt capital, however. If you cannot pay back your debt, you could be forced into bankruptcy. That does not always mean the business must close, but creditors might take control of the company away from the owner.

Banks

Commercial banks are one of the most common sources of business financing. They know their local areas and economies well and offer a number of different loans and services on competitive and government-regulated terms.

To evaluate a business owner's credit-worthiness, banks rely on the following criteria, called the six Cs of credit: capital, collateral, capability, character, coverage, and circumstances.

- How much of your own money, or capital, is to be invested in your new business? Banks, like other potential investors, will want to know how much capital you are willing to invest into your new venture.
- What assets (anything of value that you own) can be used as collateral for a loan? **Collateral** is something of value that you pledge as payment for a loan in case of default. Lenders will usually require that the value of the collateral be greater than the amount of the loan. Some businesses may use accounts receivable, which is the sum of money owed to a

GLOBAL MARKET

Targeting the Market

Cellular and long-distance phone companies know that marketing to the Hispanic population is good business. Hispanic Americans use cell phones 10 percent more than the national average.

Immigrants from Mexico and Central and South America tend to call their families back home more than other Americans call these areas. Plans that offer inexpensive rates for calls to countries in Latin America compete for the Hispanic phone dollar. Plans that allow unlimited calling between family members in the States are also more popular with Hispanic customers. And the lack of computers and scarcity of e-mail in many Central American countries means that the phone gets more use by people doing business with vendors in those countries.

Phone companies have learned it is important to distinguish between different segments of the Hispanic market. People whose first language is English have different phone needs than those whose first language is Spanish. It is important for phone companies to target their marketing campaigns to the right customer base, or they will be unsuccessful.

In creating a marketing campaign targeted to an ethnic group, what factors would you want to know about the group?

Online Action!

Go to *marketingessentials.glencoe.com/35/global* to find an activity about business plans and international business.

business by its customers, as collateral. Banks want to know that your loan will be repaid, even if your business fails.

- A résumé of your previous training and related work experience, including professional and personal references, will answer questions about your capability and character. Your personal credit history will also be reviewed to see if you regularly pay your bills on time.
- Banks will want to know the amount of insurance coverage that you carry and the general circumstances of your business. This is outlined in the description and analysis section of your business plan.

Credit Unions

A **credit union** is a cooperative association formed by labor unions or groups of employees for the benefit of its members. Credit unions often charge lower interest rates on loans than banks do. To borrow money from a credit union, however, you must be a member. Check with your parents, guardians, and relatives to determine your eligibility, since credit unions often accept memberships for relatives. Credit unions also use the six Cs of credit to decide whether they will accept your loan application.

Financial Statements

After you have identified your source or sources of capital, the last part of your business plan is to develop your financial statements. Your financial statements display your business's projected income and expenses and help persuade investors to lend you money. (See Chapter 36.)

35.2 AFTER YOU READ

Reviewing Key Terms and Concepts

1. What are the three major parts in the organization and marketing section of the business plan?
2. How is an organization chart used in a business?
3. What are the six Cs of credit?

Integrating Academic Skills

Math

4. A relative decides to lend you $12,500 at a simple 4.5 percent interest rate, payable one year after the start of your new business. How much will you owe at the end of the year?

Economics

5. Investigate a five-year balloon loan from a local lending institution in your community. Find out the rate of interest on a five-year balloon loan of $25,000. Identify the lending source, your monthly loan payment, and the total amount of interest that you would be charged over the five-year period.

@ Online Action!

Check your answers at *marketingessentials.glencoe.com/35/read*

CAREERS IN MARKETING

BARBARA DAY, M.S., R.D., C.N.
PUBLISHER
KENTUCKIANA HEALTH FITNESS MAGAZINE

What do you do at work?
As a publisher, assignments editor, marketing specialist, writer, operations manager, proofreader, radio talk show host, and television guest, my normal working day is very diverse. I juggle many tasks during the course of my workday and I really thrive in that type of environment. My workday starts at 6:00 A.M. answering e-mails and writing columns. Working seven days a week is not unusual.

What skills are most important to you?
Flexibility, organization, and good communication skills are essential as an entrepreneurial business person. To be a publisher, I have had to learn as I go. I am the only full-time person in my organization, so if a job needs to be done, I generally have to do it myself or contract the work out. Having a business background is essential for balancing the budget. I have an undergraduate degree in dietetics and institution administration and a master's degree in community nutrition with an emphasis on exercise science. Every type of job I have had since I graduated from college has been laced with program development—I have developed quite the entrepreneurial spirit—from self-publishing books to starting health promotion programs for the Department of Defense to local programs.

What is your key to success?
Believing in your product and yourself. When I hit an obstacle or roadblock, instead of accepting the situation, I regroup and go in another direction.

Aptitudes, Abilities, and Skills

Organization, strong communication skills, sales ability, and an outgoing personality

Education and Training

General business degrees are helpful with running the behind-the-scenes aspects of the business, although many niche publishers are entirely self-taught.

Career Path

Niche publications can be started by anyone, at any time—but to ensure success, study both the topic and the marketplace to see if they are a good fit. Larger alternative weeklies make good training grounds for this career.

THINKING CRITICALLY

What are some of the benefits of running a one-person company? What might be some of the down-sides?

Online Action!

Go to *marketingessentials.glencoe.com/35/careers* to find a career-related activity.

CHAPTER 35 REVIEW

FOCUS on KEY POINTS

SECTION 35.1

- The three components of a business plan are description and analysis of the proposed business; organizational and marketing plan; and financial plan.
- The description and analysis should include: type of business; business philosophy; product or service; self-analysis; trading area analysis; market segment analysis; and location analysis.

SECTION 35.2

- The organization and marketing plan outlines how the business will be organized and how it will be promoted.
- Most entrepreneurs need to borrow money to start a business. Investors and lenders want to see financial information about a business before they commit to making an investment.
- The financial plan should include sources of capital for the business and its projected income and expenses.

REVIEW VOCABULARY

Review the definitions for the following vocabulary terms with a classmate.

1. business plan (p. 738)
2. business philosophy (p. 739)
3. trading area (p. 741)
4. buying behavior (p. 743)
5. job descriptions (p. 747)
6. organization chart (p. 747)
7. equity capital (p. 748)
8. debt capital (p. 748)
9. collateral (p. 750)
10. credit union (p. 751)

REVIEW FACTS and IDEAS

11. Why should aspiring entrepreneurs conduct a self-analysis as part of a business plan? (35.1)
12. Why is it important to know the disposable income of potential customers? (35.1)
13. What sources can an entrepreneur access to research the competition for a proposed product or service? (35.1)
14. Why should personnel needs be identified in a business plan? (35.2)
15. What is the best way to promote a new business? (35.2)
16. What are debt capital and equity capital? (35.2)
17. What is the most common method of financing a business? (35.2)

BUILD SKILLS

18. **Workplace Skills**

Legal Some businesses and their employees must be licensed before they can open or perform their duties. Prepare a 250-word paper on the reasons that government agencies often require a license for certain business owners and their employees.

19. **Technology Applications**

Finding Resources Research on the Internet all the sources of business information that may be useful to an entrepreneur. List your findings and organize the information and URLs into broad categories such as government resources, trade organizations, and so on.

20. **Math Practice**

Number Crunching Given the facts below, determine the buying power indexes for the cities of Jonesville and Leadville. Which city would be a more favorable location for a new business?

Buying Power Index = .5 × Area's Percentage for U.S. Effective Buying Power
+ .3 × Area's Percentage of U.S. Retail Sales
+ .2 × Area's Percentage of U.S. Population

Jonesville Percentage of U.S. Effective Buying Power = .0271
Jonesville Percentage of U.S. Retail Sales = .0194
Jonesville Percentage of U.S. Population = .017

Leadville Percentage of U.S. Effective Buying Power = .0151
Leadville Percentage of U.S. Retail Sales = .013
Leadville Percentage of U.S. Population = .0143

DEVELOP CRITICAL THINKING

21. **Researching Small Business Services**

The Senior Corps of Retired Executives (SCORE) is a voluntary group of counselors who help America's small businesses. SCORE provides many resources to help individuals write business plans. Locate the SCORE Web site and find the address of the SCORE office nearest to your school. List at least three resources available from SCORE to help you develop a comprehensive business plan. Explain why and how these resources will help.

22. **Decide for Yourself**

"While debt capital can work to your advantage when establishing a business, there are many disadvantages if you cannot pay back your debt. Bankruptcy is one of these disadvantages, however it may not be the worst one." Explain what this statement means and decide whether you agree or disagree.

APPLY CONCEPTS

23. Describing and Analyzing a Business Situation

Begin developing a business plan using information in this chapter, from your instructor, or from DECA Entrepreneurship Event guidelines. Describe the type of business, the product/service involved, factors that make the business appealing, and the factors you think will make it successful. Describe your aspirations and career objectives, education, and related work experiences. Finally, make a chart of your potential advantages over your competitor(s).

Activity Use a word processing program to prepare your project. Be ready to present it to your class.

24. Developing an Organization and Marketing Plan

Continue the business plan that you created in the previous activity. Create an organization chart for your proposed business. The plan should contain a budget, pricing policies, and a method to evaluate its effectiveness. List special promotional events for each month of the year for your business.

Activity Using a word processing program and a spreadsheet program, organize a presentation for your classmates as if they were potential lenders.

NET SAVVY

25. Finding Small Business Resources

Find the U.S. Small Business Administration (SBA) Web site. Summarize at least five resources that are available through the SBA for new business start-ups in a one- to two-page written report.

THE DECA CONNECTION

Role Play: Developing a Business Plan

Situation You are to assume the role of loan officer for a community bank. You are having a chat with a friend (judge) you have known for several years who has been working as assistant manager of a local restaurant for the past three years. Your friend (judge) has decided to purchase and operate a coffee shop and is informally discussing the possibility of applying for a loan from your bank. Your friend (judge) has several questions about completing a business plan.

Activity You are to explain to your friend (judge) the importance of each of the three sections of a good business plan.

Evaluation You will be evaluated on how well you meet the following performance indicators:

- Explain the nature of business plans
- Develop company objectives
- Explain the nature and scope of financing
- Develop a business plan
- Explain loan evaluation criteria used by lending institutions

Online Action!

For more information and DECA Prep practice, go to *marketingessentials.glencoe.com/35/DECA*

CHAPTER 36

Financing the Business

Chapter Objectives

After reading this chapter, you should be able to:

- Explain the purpose of financial documents
- Develop a personal financial statement
- Determine start-up costs for a business
- Estimate business income and expenses
- Prepare an income statement
- Create a balance sheet
- Interpret a cash flow statement

GUIDE TO THE PHOTO

Market Talk Starting a business requires more than a good idea and a good market analysis. Seed money is necessary for that idea to grow. That money, the capital, often has to be borrowed from commercial bankers, investors, and other lenders. To convince them to lend you money, you need a good financial plan.

Quick Think What do you think it takes to convince a lender to provide capital?

THE DECA CONNECTION

Performance indicators represent key skills and knowledge. Relating them to the concepts explained in this chapter is your key to success in DECA events. These acronyms represent DECA events that involve knowledge of concepts in this chapter.

AAAL	**FMAL**	**MMS***	**TMDM***
AAML*	**FMDM***	**QSRM***	**TSE***
ADC*	**FMML***	**RMAL**	**VPM**
BSM	**FSRM***	**RMML***	
EMDM*	**HMDM***	**SMDM***	

In all these DECA events you should be able to follow these performance indicators:

- Explain the nature of overhead/operating costs
- Explain an employee's role in expense control
- Explain the concept of accounting
- Calculate net sales
- Describe the nature of cash flow statements
- Explain the nature of balance sheets
- Describe the nature of profit and loss statements
- Describe the nature of business records
- Describe the nature of budgets

All the events with an asterisk (*) also include these performance indicators:

- Analyze cash flow patterns
- Calculate financial ratios
- Interpret financial statements
- Analyze operating results in relation to budget/industry
- Prepare financial statements for audit
- Develop expense-control plans
- Develop a company's budget

DECA PREP

Check your understanding of DECA performance indicators with the DECA activity in this chapter's review. For more information and DECA Prep practice, go to *marketingessentials.glencoe.com/36/DECA*

SECTION 36.1

Preparing Financial Documents

OBJECTIVES

- **Explain the purpose of financial documents**
- **Develop a personal financial statement**
- **Determine start-up costs for a business**

KEY TERMS

- **personal financial statement**
- **asset**
- **liability**
- **net worth**
- **start-up costs**

READ and STUDY

BEFORE YOU READ

Predict Why would you need to include financial documents in a new business plan?

THE MAIN IDEA

The most common reason for writing a business plan is to obtain financing for a business. To get the money you need to start your business, you will need to prepare many financial statements.

STUDY ORGANIZER

In a chart like the one below, outline the steps in the preparation of a financial statement.

Organized Financing

1. Prepare financial documents.
2. ____________
3. ____________

Connect Why do you think it is necessary to develop personal and start-up financial statements?

The Financial Part of a Business Plan

Financial information is a major component of a business plan. In your business plan, you will include financial documents that describe your personal finances as well as the financial needs of your business. By preparing financial statements, you will be able to determine the amount of money needed to operate the business as well as the amount that must be borrowed, if any.

When you borrow money, the lender will want to see proof that you are able to repay a loan. The lender will examine your credit history, collateral (items you own that can be sold to pay off the loan), and prospects for business success. The financial documents you include in your business plan will help show that you will be able to pay off your loan.

The five important financial documents in a business plan are the personal financial statement, the start-up cost estimate, the income statement, the balance sheet, and the cash flow statement. In this section, you will learn about the first two.

The Personal Financial Statement

The **personal financial statement** is a summary of your current personal financial condition—a snapshot of your finances. It is an important part of any loan application for a new business. It measures your financial progress to date and shows how well you have met your personal financial obligations in the past. It compares your assets and liabilities at a particular point in time. An **asset** is anything of monetary value that you own, such as cash, checking and savings accounts, real estate, or stocks. A **liability** is a debt that you owe to others, such as credit card debt, school loans, car payments, or taxes.

Assets

To develop a personal financial statement, you first list your assets. Be realistic about the current value of your assets. For example, if you have a car worth $11,700, do not round it up to $12,000. Be sure to list all your cash assets (checking and savings accounts), any investments (stocks, bonds, mutual funds, and retirement funds), and personal assets (furniture, cars, clothes, and home). You will need to estimate the present value of each item. A lender will look for assets that you can sell to

•THE LENDER'S POINT of VIEW This ad is for a national legal firm that handles high-level financial transactions. It facilitates deals and advises lenders and borrowers.

Why would an entrepreneur need such financial and legal guidance?

A MATTER OF ETHICS

Borrowing From Parents

Serena, Frank, and Dominick are three friends who are going into business together. They plan to open a small sunglasses shop in a large mall. They have a clear business plan and are certain the shop will be a success if they can get the financing they need. In preparation for meeting with a bank loan officer, each of them has prepared a personal financial statement. Being young, they do not have a lot of assets, and they are concerned the bank will not consider them good risks for a loan.

Inflating Assets

Dominick asked his parents if they would add his name to the title of their house, just until the start-up financing comes in. They agreed, so Dominick has listed the family home as an asset. That has increased his net worth by $200,000. He feels the bank will look more favorably on the loan application as a result.

THINKING ETHICALLY

If you were one of his partners, what would you say to Dominick about this arrangement?

@ Online Action!

Go to *marketingessentials.glencoe.com/36/ethics* to find an activity on ethics and capital loans.

pay off the business loan if your business does not do as well as expected. Provide a total value for each asset and a grand total for all assets.

Debts

Next, list your debts, including your charge accounts, mortgage balance, and school and automobile loans. Calculate a total for each type of debt and a grand total for all debts.

Net Worth

Next, calculate your personal net worth. Your **net worth** is the difference between your assets and your liabilities. To find a business's net worth, subtract its debts from its assets. For corporations, net worth is called stockholders' equity; for partnerships and sole proprietorships, it is called owner's equity.

Your personal financial statement is one way to determine whether you and your business are good credit risks. A lender will require a copy of your personal tax returns to see how you have earned money in the past. A lender will also request a credit report to determine how well you have paid past debts. If you plan to continue working at another job, the lender will be interested in whether that income can cover your personal expenses until your new business becomes profitable.

PRACTICE 1

1. You have assets of $15,000 (car), $5,000 (savings), $1,000 (cash value of life insurance), $1,700 (cash), and personal property worth $2,500. What are your total assets?
2. You have liabilities of $10,000 (car loan), $5,000 (student loan), and $1,500 (credit card balances). What are your total liabilities?
3. What is your net worth?

Note: Answers to all practice sets at *marketingessentials.glencoe.com*

Estimating Start-Up Costs

Before starting your business, you need to know how much it will cost. **Start-up costs** are projections of how much money you will need for your first year of operation (see Figure 36.1). You also need an estimate of the long-term operating costs that you anticipate after the first year.

By assessing these start-up costs prior to getting involved in a project, you are protecting

Start-Up Cost Worksheet

• Estimating Costs The SBA provides many forms and worksheets to help new business owners project monthly expenses.

Why is a start-up worksheet helpful to a new entrepreneur?

ESTIMATED MONTHLY EXPENSES			
Item	**Your estimate of monthly expenses based on sales of $________ per year**	**Your estimate of how much cash you need to start your business (See column 3)**	**What to put in column 2. (These figures are typical for one kind of business. You will have to decide how many months to allow for your business.)**
	Column 1	Column 2	Column 3
Salary of owner	$	$	2 times column 1
All other salaries and wages			3 times column 1
Rent			3 times column 1
Advertising			3 times column 1
Delivery expenses			3 times column 1
Supplies			3 times column 1
Telephone and Internet			3 times column 1
Other utilities			3 times column 1
Insurance			Payment required by insurance company
Taxes, including Social Security			4 times column 1
Interest			3 times column 1
Maintenance			3 times column 1
Legal and other professional fees			3 times column 1
Miscellaneous			3 times column 1
STARTING COSTS YOU ONLY HAVE TO PAY ONCE			Leave column 2 blank
Fixtures and equipment			See separate worksheet
Decorating and remodeling			Talk it over with a contractor
Installation of fixtures and equipment			Talk to suppliers from whom you buy these
Starting inventory			Supplies will probably help you estimate this
Deposits with public utilities			Find out from utility companies
Legal and other professional fees			Lawyer, accountant, and so on
Licenses and permits			Find out from city offices what you need
Advertising and promotion			Estimate what you'll use for opening
Accounts receivable			What you need to buy more stock until credit customers pay
Cash			For unexpected expenses or losses, special purchases, etc.
Other			Make a separate list and enter total
TOTAL ESTIMATED CASH YOU NEED TO START	$	$	Add up all the numbers in column 2

Go to *marketingessentials.glencoe.com/36/figure/1* to find a project on start-up costs.

Figure 36.2 Financing Sources

• **Finding Funding** There are several funding sources for new businesses.

What is the difference between a primary and a secondary source of financing?

Primary Sources		Secondary Sources	
Long-term financing	***Short-term financing***	***Long-term financing***	***Short-term financing***
• Personal financing • Family and friends • Private investors • Equity financing • Leasing • Credit unions • SBA LowDoc	• Personal financing • Family and friends • Credit cards • Credit unions • Trade credit • Banks • SBA Microloans • SBA LowDoc	• Business alliances • SBA regular 7(a) program • Venture capital • SBICs • State and local public financing • Franchising • Asset-based financing	• SBA CAPLines • Consumer finance companies • Commercial finance companies • State and local public financing

@ Online Action! **Go to *marketingessentials.glencoe.com/36/figure/2* to find a project on financing a business.**

yourself and helping to ensure the viability of the business. You will need to spend money on goods and services ranging from furniture to advertising. The costs vary depending on the type of business.

Although start-up costs vary, they are based on factors such as:

- **The nature of your proposed business** Manufacturing, wholesale, and retail businesses all have different needs and requirements.
- **The size of your business** Small businesses usually do not require as much money to start as big ones.
- **The amount and kind of inventory needed** For example, it is much more costly to purchase inventory for a large supermarket than for a neighborhood convenience store.
- **The estimated time between starting the business and earning income from the first sales.**
- **The operating expenses** Expenses must be paid before cash is received from sales.

Business start-up costs may be one-time costs or continuing costs.

- **One-time costs** are expenses that will not be repeated after you begin the business. Examples of one-time costs are licenses and permits; deposits for telephone installation; and charges for installation of equipment, fixtures, and machinery.
- **Continuing costs** are operating expenses you will pay throughout the life of the business. Examples of continuing costs are payroll, monthly rent, advertising, supplies, insurance, repairs, maintenance, and taxes. Most businesses are not profitable immediately, so include at least three months of continuing costs when estimating the amount of cash you will need to get started.

You can get information from several sources to help you plan your financial needs. The Small Business Administration (SBA) provides information to people who want to start a new business. The SBA offers a wide variety of loan programs. These programs help small businesses borrow money at reasonable interest rates from traditional lenders. The SBA has developed a worksheet for estimating start-up costs and operating expenses for new businesses.

You can also get estimates of start-up costs from people who are already in a similar business or from a trade association. State and local government agencies, such as your state department of commerce and local chamber of commerce, are valuable sources of cost information (see Figure 36.2).

PRACTICE 2

1. Your business has one-time costs of $25,000 and average monthly costs of $3,600. What are your total costs for the first quarter of operation? Using the same average monthly costs, what are your total costs for the year?

Personal Costs

Unless you are starting your new business while still working at another job, you will need money to live on during the start-up phase. Your personal costs are those expenses that are necessary for you to live. You will need to project your monthly living expenses and household cash needs for at least the first year of business. When starting a new business, you may be able to meet your personal expenses by working at another job or by relying on income from your parents or a spouse.

You may choose not to work outside your business or seek any other income, but you must plan to have enough cash on hand to pay your personal expenses. Some experts suggest you have enough start-up capital to pay for up to six months of living expenses.

Set aside the money for living expenses in a savings account or another account from which you can withdraw money without penalty. Do not use the money for any other purpose. This fund will help you get through the start-up period. The amount should cover living expenses such as regular monthly payments, household operating expenses, food expenses, personal expenses, and tax expenses.

36.1 AFTER YOU READ

Reviewing Key Terms and Concepts

1. What is a personal financial statement?
2. Define asset, liability, and net worth.
3. How are one-time costs different from continuing costs?

Integrating Academic Skills

Math

4. Calculate the total start-up costs for an online business by using the Starting Cost Calculator on the U.S. Small Business Administration Web site and the following data:
   - Initial expenses: legal: $500; office supplies: $300; office equipment: $1,500; design: $150; brochures: $150; Web site: $500; other: $700.
   - Money needed for reserve for a total of six months: monthly payroll: $2,500; monthly rent: $750; and monthly expenses: $550.
   - Start-up inventory: $2,000.

   What are the total start-up costs for a six-month period?

Economics

5. Perform an Internet or library search on the factors that are considered by new business start-ups when locating in a particular state. Summarize the results of your research in a one-page paper.

Check your answers at *marketingessentials.glencoe.com/36/read*

SECTION 36.2

Financial Aspect of a Business Plan

OBJECTIVES

- Estimate business income and expenses
- Prepare an income statement
- Create a balance sheet
- Interpret a cash flow statement

KEY TERMS

- income statement
- gross sales
- net sales
- net income
- interest
- principal
- balance sheet
- cash flow statement

READ and STUDY

BEFORE YOU READ

Predict Why do you think so many new businesses fail?

THE MAIN IDEA

Financial institutions and investors will want to know why you need their money, how you are going to use it, and how you plan to repay them. The financial section of a business plan provides this information to prospective lenders.

STUDY ORGANIZER

In a chart like the one below, create an outline that lists key information about financial documents.

Organized Financing *(continued)*

1. Prepare an income statement.
2. ______________________
3. ______________________

WHILE YOU READ

Connect Suppose you want to start your own company. List the specific financial needs you would have as you read this section.

Estimating Business Income and Expenses

After you estimate your start-up costs and personal living expenses, the next step is to estimate the money you expect to earn and to spend while operating your business. Many small businesses fail because they do not bring in enough revenue to pay their costs and expenses. Estimating your business income and expenses is a key part of your business plan. Lenders will want to see your estimates to help them decide whether to lend you money.

If you are buying an existing business, you will have previous operating results to use as a guide. If you are starting a new business, you will need to estimate your potential revenue and the costs and expenses of operating the business.

The Income Statement

The financial document used to calculate revenue, costs, and expenses is the income statement. The **income statement** is a summary of income and expenses during a specific period such as a month, a quarter, or a year. This statement is often called a profit and loss statement.

The income statement for an existing business shows the previous year's income, costs, and expenses. The income statement for a new or planned business estimates earnings and expenses for the first few months (or the first year) of operation. Figure 36.3 shows a sample projected quarterly income statement. Refer to this figure as you read about the different parts of the income statement.

Income statements have several major parts: total and net sales, cost of goods sold, gross profit, expenses of operating the business, net income from operations, other income or expenses, net profit before income taxes, and net profit after income taxes. Each item on the income statement is added to or subtracted from total sales to find the amount of net profit or loss.

	Total Sales
−	Returns and Allowances
=	Net Sales
−	Cost of Goods Sold
=	Gross Profit
−	Operating Expenses
=	Net Income from Operations
−	Other Expenses (Interest)
=	Net Profit (Loss) Before Taxes
−	Taxes
=	Net Profit (Loss) After Taxes

Now we will see how to calculate the amounts for each part of the income statement.

Estimating Total Sales

The income generated by a business depends on the yearly volume of sales. Most new businesses grow slowly in the beginning, so you should be conservative in estimating your first-year sales.

Most people who start a new business have some idea about where they will sell their products. You may already have discussed your new product with potential buyers. You may even have a contract to produce a certain number of items. Suppose you are starting a new T-shirt printing business. You have a contract for 2,000 shirts, which you will sell at $8 each wholesale. Your estimated total sales will be $16,000. You would estimate your total sales at $160,000 if you think you can produce and sell ten times that amount during your first year.

It is important to calculate a reasonable estimated sales volume. You must verify your estimated sales volume by comparing it with projected industry figures for your size of business and location. Trade associations, bankers, and industry publications can help you make sales and income estimates.

The accuracy of your sales estimates will also depend on the quality of your market analysis. Losses rather than profits are common during the first year of business. In your business plan, you will need to show how you will cover any losses by investing more capital or reducing your operating expenses.

Calculating Net Sales

The total of all sales for any period of time is called **gross sales**. Your gross sales will simply be the total of all cash sales if your company sells only on a cash basis. When your company accepts credit and charge cards, sells gift certificates, or offers merchandise on account, then all of these different types of sales transactions must be totaled to arrive at gross sales.

Most businesses have some customer returns and allowances (credit granted to customers for damaged or defective goods kept by the customer); therefore, the gross sales figure does not reflect the actual income from sales.

Figure 36.3 Projected Quarterly Income Statement

• **Financial Statement** An income statement summarizes a business's income and expenses for a specific period of time. It gives a snapshot of the business's health, showing profits or losses. This is often used to attract investors or to show lenders. Because a new business doesn't have a business history, it develops a projected income statement that estimates expected income and expenses for a period of time.

How might a new business gather the information needed to project income and expenses?

	Month 1	Month 2	Month 3	TOTAL
Sales	30,900	34,000	36,400	101,300
Less Returns & Allowances	900	1,000	1,400	3,300
NET SALES	30,000	33,000	35,000	98,000
Cost of Goods Sold	19,500	21,000	22,750	63,250
GROSS PROFIT	10,500	12,000	12,250	34,750
Operating Expenses				
Variable Expenses				
Advertising	300	350	350	1,000
Automobile	450	400	525	1,375
Dues and Subscriptions	15	20	18	53
Legal and Accounting	300	400	350	1,050
Miscellaneous Expenses	360	480	420	1,260
Office Supplies	120	160	140	420
Security	300	400	350	1,050
Telephone	90	120	105	315
Utilities	90	120	105	315
Total Variable Expenses	2,025	2,450	2,363	6,838
Fixed Expenses				
Depreciation	180	180	180	540
Insurance	300	300	300	900
Rent	800	800	800	2,400
Salaries and Payroll Taxes	5,600	5,600	5,600	16,800
Total Fixed Expenses	6,880	6,880	6,880	20,640
TOTAL EXPENSES	8,905	9,330	9,243	27,478
NET INCOME FROM OPERATIONS	1,595	2,670	3,007	7,272
Other Income	0	0	0	0
Other Expenses (Interest)	300	300	300	900
NET PROFIT (LOSS) BEFORE TAXES	1,295	2,370	2,707	6,372
Taxes	325	590	680	1,595
NET PROFIT (LOSS) AFTER TAXES	970	1,780	2,027	4,777

Net Sales is determined by subtracting returns and allowances from total sales.

Gross Profit is the difference between net sales and the cost of goods sold.

Operating Expenses are the costs of operating a business. They are divided into variable and fixed expenses.

Total Expenses is determined by adding the total variable expenses to the total fixed expenses.

Net Income From Operations is found by subtracting total expenses from gross profit.

Net Profit Before Taxes is calculated by adding other income to net income from operations, then subtracting interest expense.

Net Profit After Taxes is found by subtracting taxes from net profit before taxes. This amount represents the actual profit after income taxes are paid from operating the business for a certain period of time.

Go to *marketingessentials.glencoe.com/36/figure/3* to find a project on personal finance.

The total of all sales returns, discounts, and allowances is subtracted from gross sales to get **net sales**. The net sales figure is the amount left after gross sales have been adjusted for returns and allowances. Look at Figure 36.3 to find the net sales for each month.

Cost of Goods Sold

The total amount spent to produce or to purchase the goods that are sold is called the cost of goods sold. To calculate cost of goods sold, add goods purchased during the period to the beginning inventory value. Then subtract the amount of the ending inventory.

  Beginning Inventory
+ Net Purchases, or Production Costs
− Ending Inventory
= Cost of Goods Sold

As you learned in Chapter 24, you count the stock on hand and calculate its value to determine beginning and ending inventory amounts.

Most service businesses do not provide goods to their customers. Therefore, they do not have to determine the cost of goods sold. Their gross profit is the same as net sales. Other businesses that produce or purchase products to sell must calculate the cost of goods sold.

Determining Gross Profit

Gross profit or gross margin on sales is the difference between the net sales and the cost of goods sold.

The formula for calculating gross profit is:

  Net Sales
− Cost of Goods Sold
= Gross Profit

Once you know the cost of goods sold, you can calculate your gross profit by subtracting the cost of goods sold from net sales.

Suppose you are employed by Downhill Racers, a company that sold $115,765 worth of mountain bikes last year. The company books show a total of $3,220 in sales returns and allowances. When you subtract the sales returns and allowances from total (gross) sales, you get net sales of $112,545. The cost of goods sold for last year totals $69,459; therefore, your gross profit is: $112,545 − $69,459 = $43,086.

Projecting Business Expenses

The next major part of the income statement is the operating expenses—the costs of operating the business, including variable and fixed expenses.

Calculating Variable Expenses

Variable expenses change from one month to the next. Variable costs can fluctuate depending upon the sales volume of the business. Variable expenses include items such as advertising, office supplies, telephone bills, and utilities.

Variable expenses are often calculated as a percentage of some baseline amount. Advertising expenses, for example, may average 5 percent of total sales.

Calculating Fixed Expenses

Fixed expenses are costs that remain the same for a period of time. These types of expenses stay fixed for months regardless of sales volume. Depreciation, insurance, rent, salaries, and payroll taxes are examples of fixed expenses.

Depreciation is a complicated fixed expense. Depreciation represents the amount by which an asset's value has fallen because of age, wear, or deterioration in a given period of time. IRS laws and rules govern the time period over which you can depreciate assets. An accountant can help you determine the asset depreciation schedule and amounts to use in listing assets on your income tax return.

Projecting other fixed expenses usually is easier because you simply add all your fixed costs, such as rent or insurance. Employee wages may be a significant part of your business expenses. Let's look at how to calculate payroll costs.

Calculating Payroll Expenses

To calculate payroll expenses, you must first estimate the number of employees you need to operate your business. Then, research typical salaries in your area for the work the employees will perform. You can get help on salary information by consulting your state employment security agency (SESA) office and by reviewing the help-wanted ads in the newspaper for similar jobs. You can also use the minimum wage as a starting point and decide how much more to pay for more skilled workers, recognizing that a skilled worker should have a higher salary than an unskilled one.

When setting up your business, you need to give careful attention to your payroll records. Payroll records are important to your employees and to your company. They are also used to prepare income tax returns, so the federal and state governments are also concerned with their accuracy.

Your bank, your accountant, a bookkeeping service, or a computer software program can help you set up a system to calculate and record payroll and cut checks.

Case Study

Two Men and a Truck

The sons of Mary Ellen Sheets started a local moving service when they were in high school. They used an old pickup to transport people's belongings around Lansing, Michigan, after school. In 1985, the boys' mother bought the company's first truck to keep the business going while the boys were away in college. In 1988, Two Men and a Truck became the first local moving company in the United States to offer franchises. By 2003, there were 125 local franchises in 25 states with revenues of $122 million. Sheets's sons, Brig and Jon Sorber, are still part of management.

Advice on Starting a Business

Sheets has advice for people starting a new business: Get your finances in order and keep accurate accounts. For years, she kept company receipts in a shoebox under her desk. As the company grew and annual audits were required, auditors would groan as they searched through boxes of paper receipts.

What stopped Sheets from getting accounting help was her idea that it was too expensive. When she finally hired an accountant, however, the errors he found in his first month on the job saved the company enough money to pay his first year's salary. Her advice to new businesses is: Either learn about finance or hire financial professionals.

THINK STRATEGICALLY

Why is it necessary for a business to keep good financial records?

Online Action!

Go to *marketingessentials.glencoe.com/36/case* to find an activity on financials and starting a business.

Your payroll records may be part of the cash disbursements journal where you keep records of all cash payments. You may prefer to keep your payroll records in a separate payroll journal. When using a separate journal for payroll records, use a separate record for each employee. Each record will show one employee's pay period, hours worked, earnings, deductions, and net pay.

The amount earned by an employee is that person's gross pay. Net pay is what the employee receives after deductions for taxes and insurance, and voluntary deductions. Nancy Baker earns $11 an hour and worked 40 hours during the week; therefore, her gross pay is $440 ($11 × 40 hours).

Nancy's deductions total $125.66, so you would calculate her net pay by subtracting the deductions from her gross pay:

$440 − $125.66 = $314.34 (net pay)

Tax tables are available for calculating the amount to be deducted from each employee's pay for local, state, and federal income tax. The percentage of gross pay to be deducted for FICA (Social Security and Medicare taxes) changes frequently. Get the latest information from your local Social Security office.

Example: Find the net pay for Rosarita Romerez, who worked a total of 44 hours during a week at $13 per hour. She is paid time-and-a-half for overtime (hours worked beyond 40 hours in a week). Her deductions totaled $105.25 for the week.

STEP 1 Calculate the gross pay.

$520.00 ($13 × 40 hours)
+ 78.00 ($13 × 4 hours × 1.5)
$598.00 (gross pay)

STEP 2 Subtract deductions.

$598.00 (gross pay)
− 105.25 (total deductions)
$492.75

In estimating your total payroll expenses, you will need to use current tax rates for local, state, and federal income taxes. Remember that as the employer, you will also pay FICA and unemployment payroll taxes on your employees' earnings. You will need to include those amounts in your total payroll expense estimate.

Calculating Total Expenses

Once you have calculated all your operating (variable and fixed) expenses, you are ready to total your expenses. To calculate total expenses, add the variable expenses to the fixed expenses.

Total Variable Expenses
+ Total Fixed Expenses
= Total Expenses

Net Income From Operations

After calculating your total expenses, the next step is to calculate net income from operations. **Net income** is the amount left after the total expenses are subtracted from gross profit.

The formula for calculating net income from operations is:

Gross Profit on Sales
− Total Expenses
= Net Income From Operations

Suppose you own the "I Can Do That" Home Remodeling Company, which had gross profit on sales of $153,156 during the year. Your total operating expenses for the year were $88,991, so your net income from operations was:

$153,156 − $88,991 = $64,165

During the first years of operation, a business may have a net loss from operations. A net loss results when total expenses are larger than the gross profit on sales. The financial plan should address how the business intends to pay its debts in the short term, especially if a loss is probable during the first months of operation.

Calculating Other Income

In the Net Income From Operations section of the income statement, list money earned from sources other than sales. You may earn dividends on stocks or interest on your savings or checking accounts. **Interest** is the money paid for the use of money borrowed or invested.

To estimate your interest earnings, check with local banks and find the current interest rate paid on similar accounts. It is likely that you will use some of this money during the year, so you will need to calculate interest only on the amount actually on deposit. Unless the interest income you expect to earn is significant, you may want to list this amount as zero in your business plan.

Calculating Other Expenses

You will pay interest on any money that you borrow to start your business. The amount you borrowed is called the **principal**. Interest is expressed as a percentage of the principal and is called the rate of interest.

For example, if you borrow $100 at 6 percent, the principal is $100 and the rate of interest is 6 percent. To find the amount of interest for one year, multiply the principal (p) times the rate of interest (r) times the length of time (t). This formula is stated as:

$$i = prt$$
$$(\$100 \times .06 \times 1 = \$6).$$

You would pay $6 in interest for the example above.

The units in the rate of interest and time must agree. That is, if the rate of interest is expressed in years, then the time must be expressed in years as well. Both may be expressed in months. Check this before you do your math so that your answers will be correct. If the rate is given without reference to a time period, you can assume that it is for one year.

Suppose you are quoted a yearly rate and need to convert it to a monthly rate. There are 12 months in a year, so you would divide the yearly rate by 12 to get the monthly rate. When you are quoted a monthly rate and want to convert it to a yearly rate, multiply the monthly rate by 12.

Once you decide how much money you will need to borrow and how long it will take you to repay the loan, you can calculate your total annual (or monthly) interest. This amount is listed on the financial statement as Other Expenses (Interest).

Net Profit or Loss Before Taxes

Net profit or net loss before taxes is calculated by adding other income to net income from operations and then subtracting other expenses from the total.

Net Income From Operations
\+ Other Income
− Other Expenses
= Net Profit (or Loss) Before Taxes

Net Profit or Loss After Taxes

Net profit (or loss) after taxes is the amount of money left over after federal, state, and local taxes are subtracted. This amount represents the actual profit from operating the business for a certain period of time.

The projected income statement should be done on a monthly basis for new businesses. After the first year, projected income statements can be prepared on a quarterly basis.

The steps that follow are a summary of how to prepare a monthly projected income statement.

STEP 1 Estimate total sales.

STEP 2 Subtract sales discounts, returns, and allowances from total sales to calculate net sales.

STEP 3 List the estimated cost of goods sold.

STEP 4 Subtract the cost of goods sold from net sales to find gross profit on sales.

STEP 5 List each monthly operating expense, categorizing each as a variable or fixed expense.

STEP 6 Total the monthly operating expenses.

STEP 7 Subtract total operating expenses from gross profit on sales to find net income from operations. Put parentheses around any projected losses; for example, a projected loss of $1,000 would be identified as ($1,000).

STEP 8 Add other income such as interest on bank deposits and subtract other expenses, such as interest expense, from net income from operations. The result is net profit (or loss) before income taxes.

STEP 9 Estimate total taxes on the net income and subtract that amount from net profit. The result is net profit (or loss) after taxes.

Practice 3

Using the income statement shown below, answer the following questions:

1. How much did Mountain Air pay for the bikes it sold?
2. How much was the gross profit for the year?
3. How much were total operating expenses?
4. Which operating expense was the most costly?
5. How much net income was earned during the year?

Mountain Air Bikes
Income Statement for the Year Ended December 31, 20--

Net Sales	$202,736
Cost of Goods Sold	$124,375
Gross Profit	$?
Operating Expenses	
Salaries	$ 28,022
Rent	$ 14,211
Utilities	$ 5,214
Advertising	$ 3,422
Total Operating Expenses	$?
Net Income From Operations	$?

MARKET TECH

Creating Loyalty

Encouraging customer loyalty has always been a goal of marketers. Marketing technology has pioneered many ways of getting customers to come back again and again. "New marketing" targets individuals rather than groups, because the software behind it collects specific information about each person.

Targeted Rewards

Harrah's, an entertainment, resort, and casino company, asks each customer to sign up for its Total Rewards loyalty program. Customers use their rewards cards whenever they make a purchase at the resort.

Harrah's tracks the results and offers special deals and privileges to consumers who return often even if they do not spend a lot of money on their visits.

The rewards offered are related to what the consumer has purchased in the past—free concert tickets to music lovers, for example.

The company tracked an increase of 20 percent in customer loyalty after the program's first year.

THINK LIKE A MARKETER

Where would you list on an income statement the expenses for the software necessary to track customer purchasing?

Online Action!

Go to *marketingessentials.glencoe.com/36/tech* to find an activity on technology and starting a business.

The Balance Sheet

A **balance sheet** is a summary of a business's assets, liabilities, and owner's equity.

Assets

Assets are anything of monetary value that you own. They are classified as either current or fixed.

- Current assets are cash and anything of value that can be converted into cash in a year. Examples of current assets are cash in the bank, accounts receivable (money owed to you by your customers), and inventory.
- Fixed assets are used over a period of years to operate your business. Fixed assets cannot be changed into cash within a year. Examples of fixed assets include land, buildings, equipment, furniture, and fixtures. The assets of the business are important because they are needed to operate the business. When borrowing money to start a business, assets are also often used as collateral for the loan.

Liabilities

Liabilities are listed in another section of the balance sheet. Liabilities are the amounts that the business owes—for example, money owed for merchandise purchased. Liabilities are classified as either current or long-term.

- Current liabilities are the debts the business must pay during the upcoming business year. Examples of current liabilities are accounts payable (money owed to suppliers), notes payable (money owed to a bank), taxes payable, and money owed to employees for salaries.
- Long-term liabilities are debts that are due after 12 months. Some examples are mortgages and long-term loans.

Equity

Equity, or net worth, is the third section of the balance sheet. When you start a new business, you will most likely invest some savings in the business. The amount of the savings is your equity, or ownership interest, in the business. The money invested will be used to buy assets and to operate the business. The assets owned by the business and the debts the business owes impact your equity. Remember, net worth is the difference between the assets of a business and its liabilities: Assets − Liabilities = Net Worth (Equity).

Analysis of Financial Statements

Lenders use ratio analysis to determine how a business is performing as compared to other businesses in the industry. Ratios indicate whether a business has too much debt, is carrying too much inventory, or is not making enough gross profit. Information on the balance sheet and the income statement may be used to calculate these ratios. Lenders use ratio analysis to determine whether your business would be a good investment risk and whether it could repay a loan.

Figures on the balance sheet will show you the amount of your ownership interest (owner's or stockholders' equity) and the financial strength of a business on a given date. The data on the income statement can give you an idea of how well the business is operating over a period of time. Sometimes you will need information from both statements to calculate the ratios.

The following are some of the most basic operating ratios and how they may be used to analyze or interpret financial statements. A number of sources and directories exist to help you determine the common business ratios for your type of business. These include *Financial Studies of Small Business* published by the Financial Research Associates, *Industry Norms and Key Business Ratios* by Dun & Bradstreet, and *Almanac of Business and Industrial Financial Ratios* by Leo Troy.

Liquidity Ratios

Liquidity ratios are used to analyze the ability of a firm to meet its current debts. One liquidity ratio is current ratio. Its formula is current assets divided by current liabilities. In this case, it is better to have a high ratio.

The acid test, or quick ratio, is used to see if the company can meet its short-term cash needs. Its formula is cash plus marketable securities plus accounts receivables divided by current liabilities.

Activity Ratios

Activity ratios are used to determine how quickly assets can be turned into cash. One such ratio is called accounts receivable turnover, which indicates the number of days it takes to collect the money owed by customers. To calculate this ratio, divide net sales by average trade receivables. In this case, it is better to have a lower ratio.

The stock turnover ratio measures how many days it takes to turn over, or sell, the inventory. Excessive inventory ties up cash that a company can use to grow its business. The basic formula for this ratio is cost of goods sold divided by average inventory.

Profitability Ratios

Profitability ratios measure how well the company has operated during the past year. One ratio is profit margin on sales, which shows the rate of profit in percentages. This information is found on the income statement. Its formula is net income divided by net sales. Another profitability ratio is the rate of return on assets, which shows how well you are doing when compared to other companies. The formula for this ratio is net income divided by average total assets.

PRACTICE 4

Using the balance sheet shown below, answer the following questions:

1. How much are the total assets for Mountain Air Bikes?
2. How much are the total liabilities?
3. What is Mountain Air's net worth?

Mountain Air Bikes

Balance Sheet December 31, 20--

Current Assets	
Cash	$ 10,000
Accounts Receivable	15,000
Inventory	68,000
Fixed Assets	
Building	120,000
Equipment	80,000
Vehicles	30,000
Total Assets	$?
Current Liabilities	
Notes Payable	$ 3,000
Accounts Payable	12,000
Salaries Payable	5,000
Taxes Payable	1,000
Long-Term Liabilities	
Notes Payable	90,000
Total Liabilities	$?
Net Worth	$?

Cash Flow Statement

A **cash flow statement** is a monthly plan that tracks when you anticipate that cash will come into the business and when you expect to pay out cash. A cash flow statement helps you determine whether you will have enough money to pay your bills on time.

Businesses need cash to pay bills and their employees, and to use for unexpected expenses. The cash flow statement itemizes how much cash you started with, what your projected cash expenditures are, and how and when you plan to receive cash. It also shows when you will need to find additional funds and when you will have cash remaining. Most lenders will require you to estimate cash flow for the first year of operation.

Cash Payments

When operating a business, one of your largest payments of cash will be for your merchandise. You will most likely have to pay for part of the merchandise in cash and part on credit.

When estimating sales for the income statement, you include both cash and credit sales. In contrast, the cash flow statement shows only the amount you expect to receive in cash (for cash sales and payments for credit sales) during the month.

You may receive payment for most of your credit sales 30 days after the sales. You will also need to calculate your monthly costs for operating the business.

How to Prepare a Cash Flow Statement

Use the following steps to prepare a cash flow statement.

STEP 1 Add the total cash on hand (in bank accounts) and money received from any loans to find your total start-up money.

STEP 2 Subtract the start-up costs to determine the amount of cash left for operation.

STEP 3 Enter the estimated cash you expect to receive from cash sales and credit sales for each month during the first year. Enter the amount of any income from business investments or additional loans.

STEP 4 Add all sources of cash receipts to find the total cash income for the month.

STEP 5 List the cost of goods that you will buy for your inventory. This cost should be separated into purchases for which you will pay cash and purchases on credit, which you will pay for the next month.

For example, the cash flow statement shows goods bought on credit in Month 1.

This is a payment for items bought on credit prior to the opening of the business. Add the cash and credit purchases to find the total cost of inventory purchases.

STEP 6 List the expenses you expect to pay during the month. These amounts are the same as those listed on the income statement, except for the depreciation expense.

Depreciation is a means of spreading the cost of an asset over a period of years. The amount of depreciation is not an actual payment made by the business, so it is not listed on the cash flow statement.

STEP 7 Total all expenses for the month.

STEP 8 List amounts that will be paid out for capital expenditures. A capital expenditure is money paid for an asset used to operate the business. The purchase of a delivery truck would be a capital expenditure.

STEP 9 List any other payments that will be made, such as repayment of the principal and interest for the loan.

STEP 10 Add all the cash expenditures (cost of inventory purchased, expenses, capital expenditures, and other payments).

Subtract the total cash payments from the total cash received during the month to determine net cash flow.

The amount of any cash payments that are higher than cash receipts should be placed in parentheses to show a loss.

STEP 11 Add the beginning cash balance from the start-up column to the net cash flow for the month.

The result is the cash surplus for the month. When the costs of operating the business are higher than income added to the beginning of the cash balance, the business will have a deficit rather than a surplus.

In that case, the business will need additional cash for its operations. The amount is listed on the Cash Needs line.

The income statement does not take into account how long it may take a business to collect the cash from sales made on credit.

Loans

What can you do if your cash flow statement indicates you will need additional money during the year? You should be able to borrow money if your business has potential and your balance sheet shows enough assets to serve as collateral.

A loan can help you keep the business going during the start-up period and during slow sales months. When your cash flow projections indicate that you need to borrow money to meet monthly expenses, you will want to include monthly payments on the loan as a part of your cash needs for the rest of the year.

PRACTICE 5

1. You have total cash of $23,000 to start your business and start-up costs of $12,000.
   What amount of cash is available for operating the business?
2. Suppose cash income for the first three months is $100, $750, and $980. Total expenses for these same months are $4,800, $3,400, and $2,700.
   What is the cash flow for each month?
3. What is the cumulative amount of cash available at the end of each month?

36.2 AFTER YOU READ

Reviewing Key Terms and Concepts

1. How is gross profit calculated on an income statement?
2. What is the difference between variable and fixed expenses on an income statement?
3. What is a balance sheet?

Integrating Academic Skills

Math

4. Total first-quarter sales for the Bad Frog Beverage Company were $315,000. Goods returned by customers amounted to $6,100. The cost of goods sold to customers was $212,000. The company's total fixed and variable expenses were $94,500. Calculate the following amounts: net sales, gross profit, net income from operations.

Reading and Language Arts

5. Investigate the concept and purpose of cash flow statements. Write a one-page paper on how a business owner could improve cash flow.

Check your answers at *marketingessentials.glencoe.com/36/read*

CAREERS IN MARKETING

JAMES KAISER
FINANCIAL MANAGER
AMERICAN GREETINGS CORP.

What do you do at work?
I gather specific financial information related to an investment (expected investment versus expected return) and develop financial performance goals, then structure the terms of the relationship in a manner that is most beneficial to American Greetings, while coaching the executive management team in developing customer-oriented strategies.

What skills are most important to you?
The most valuable technical skill important to success is in-depth knowledge and understanding of corporate finance, including profitability analysis (discounted cash flows, internal rate of return, net present value, return on net capital employed). The most valuable soft skill important to success is a broad knowledge of marketing, including product position/differentiation and product life cycle (what competitive advantages the product offers over competition, where the product is in its life cycle, and how these attributes affect product profitability).

What is your key to success?
There are two keys to be successful as a financial manager that recommends corporate profitability strategies to executive management teams. The first is financial knowledge, the ability to correctly and accurately analyze financial information. The second is presentation, the ability to market and defend your finding/results to a broad audience in a manner that achieves your objectives.

Aptitudes, Abilities, and Skills

Knowledge of finance and marketing, attention to detail, and presentation and communication skills

Education and Training

Degrees in marketing and general business; advanced degrees in finance and business administration are especially important.

Career Path

Finance careers often begin with entry-level positions in accounting, bookkeeping or similar departments.

THINKING CRITICALLY

How important is a thorough understanding of the workings of corporate finance in this career?

Online Action!

Go to *marketingessentials.glencoe.com/36/careers* to find a career-related activity.

CHAPTER 36 REVIEW

FOCUS on KEY POINTS

SECTION 36.1

- Five important financial documents are the personal financial statement, the start-up cost estimate, the income statement, the balance sheet, and the cash flow statement. The personal financial statement is a summary of your current personal financial condition. Start-up costs are a projection of how much initial money you will need for your first and continuing years of operation. You also need an estimate of your personal living expenses.

SECTION 36.2

- The next step is to estimate the money you expect to earn and to spend operating your business. The financial document that is used to calculate a business's revenue, costs, and expenses is the income statement. A balance sheet is a summary of a business's assets, liabilities, and owner's equity. A cash flow statement is a monthly plan that indicates when you anticipate cash coming into the business and when you expect to pay out cash. A cash flow statement shows whether you will have enough money to pay your bills.

REVIEW VOCABULARY

Use each of the following terms in a sentence.

1. personal financial statement (p. 759)
2. asset (p. 759)
3. liability (p. 759)
4. net worth (p. 760)
5. start-up costs (p. 760)
6. income statement (p. 765)
7. gross sales (p. 765)
8. net sales (p. 767)
9. net income (p. 769)
10. interest (p. 770)
11. principal (p. 770)
12. balance sheet (p. 772)
13. cash flow statement (p. 773)

REVIEW FACTS and IDEAS

14. What financial information should be included as part of a business plan? (36.1)
15. What factors determine start-up costs for a new business? (36.1)
16. How do start-up costs differ from personal costs? (36.1)
17. What are the major categories that are calculated on the income statement? (36.2)
18. How is a cash flow statement used? (36.2)
19. What is the purpose of a balance sheet? (36.2)
20. What is an asset? (36.2)
21. What does net worth tell a business owner? (36.2)
22. What kinds of financial information are presented on an income statement, a balance sheet, and a cash flow statement? (36.2)

BUILD SKILLS

23. Workplace Skills

Human Relations After high school, a friend has decided to open a landscaping business for cottage owners who live around a small inland lake. He believes that he will not need extra capital for personal living costs because the business will generate enough revenue to cover this. Should your friend be concerned about his personal living costs? If so, discuss the reasons why your friend should be concerned.

24. Technology Applications

Cash Requirement Worksheets Perform an Internet search for initial cash requirements worksheets. Use one of these templates to estimate expenses and calculate the total amount of cash needed to start a new business.

25. Math Practice

Develop a Budget Suppose that you are renting an apartment and earn a yearly salary of $24,000. Develop a cost-of-living budget. Be sure to include all regular monthly payments, household operating costs, food, and personal expenses. How might you help pay for your expenses?

DEVELOP CRITICAL THINKING

26. Business Ratios

Select an industry that interests you. Research several companies and contact the person in charge of finances at one or two companies. Interview each person to find out about three business ratios that have proven helpful to him or her in running the business.

Identify each ratio and write a one-paragraph summary on why each ratio was important.

27. Economic Development Loans

Many states and the federal government have economic development programs devoted to the needs of small businesses. Research such programs available in your state. Also look into business loans available from local and national banks. Why do a majority of economic development loans originate from banks rather than from the state or federal agencies?

APPLY CONCEPTS

28. Investigating Start-Up Costs

Select a business and investigate its start-up costs for the financial section of a business plan. Use the following resources to find the information: people in the business, suppliers, trade associations, Service Corps of Retired Executives (SCORE), Small Business Administration, local chambers of commerce, and business start-up guides and magazines.

Activity Develop a start-up worksheet for the business and be ready to present your project in class.

29. Cash Flow Statement and Income Statement

Locate the Microsoft Office Downloads Online Web site. Under "Templates," find the link for preparing a cash flow statement. Then, find the link for preparing an income statement.

Activity Develop a 12-month cash flow statement for the business that you selected for the financial section of the business plan. Develop a 12-month profit and loss projection based on the business that you selected for the financial section of the business plan.

NET SAVVY

30. Research Franchise Opportunities

Locate the International Franchise Association Web site on the Internet. Find an existing franchise opportunity to investigate. Use a word processing program to write a report describing the franchise opportunity, including the type of franchise, primary product or service, potential for growth, and other pertinent facts about it.

THE  CONNECTION

Role Play: Financing the Business

Situation You are to assume the role of branch manager for a large regional bank. You have a great deal of experience with business loan applications. You have been asked to make a presentation to a group of students (judge) enrolled in an entrepreneurship class. Your presentation is to focus on the financial part of a business plan. You are to prepare an outline of the information you plan to present.

Activity You are to make your presentation to the entrepreneurship students (judge).

Evaluation You will be evaluated on how well you meet the following performance indicators:

- Determine financing needed to start a business
- Determine financing needed for business operations
- Describe the nature of cash-flow statements
- Describe sources of financing for businesses
- Make oral presentations

@ Online Action!

For more information and DECA Prep practice, go to *marketingessentials.glencoe.com/36/DECA*

MARKETING INTERNSHIP

A SIMULATED DECA ENTREPRENEURSHIP PARTICIPATING EVENT

Start a Bicycle Business

BASIC BACKGROUND

Your firm has a new client, a cycling enthusiast, who wants to open a bicycle shop. As former vice president of marketing for a small manufacturer, she took early retirement with a $200,000 severance package, which she is willing to invest in this new venture.

Picking Up Speed Your client believes there's a growing interest in cycling because of Lance Armstrong's influence, and she says baby boomers are looking for exercise that is easier on the joints than running. That, combined with the client's passion for the sport of cycling, her business experience, and her capital resources, can mean potential success for your firm. Now all she needs is a good business plan to obtain the financing to begin her second career as a bicycle shop owner.

YOUR OBJECTIVE

Your objective is to prepare a complete business plan for a new cycling shop for our client. A detailed financial section is important because this plan will be used to secure a loan and/or to interest investors in this new business venture.

ASSIGNMENT AND STRATEGY

- **Get the background** Conduct research on the sport of cycling, as well as on different types of bicycles and accessories. Research suppliers of these items.

  Conduct a SWOT analysis and an assessment of the competition in your area. Study the geographic, demographic, and economic factors that could influence where the store is located. Consider what economic, socio-cultural, and technological factors might affect this business. Look for ways your client can differentiate her business from her competitors.
- **Figure out startup costs** Research the costs of opening the store, such as renovation of a local retail space that is available for lease or purchase, buying the initial inventory, and promotions, as well as fixed expenses to operate the business for the first year.

  Investigate ways of obtaining needed financial resources.

- **Develop the business plan** Prepare a business plan that includes an introduction, an analysis of the business situation, proposed organization (such as the type of ownership and needed staffing), proposed marketing mix decisions, and a complete financial analysis and plan.
- **What your project should include** To make your project complete, include a suggested store layout, sample promotional materials, and detailed projected financial statements, such as a projected income statement, cash flow statement, and balance sheet.

YOUR REPORT

Use a word processing program and presentation software to prepare a double-spaced report and an oral presentation for your client. See a suggested outline and key evaluation points at *marketingessentials.glencoe.com/internship*

BUILD YOUR PORTFOLIO

Option 1 Internship Report Once you have completed your Marketing Internship project and presentation, include your written report and a few printouts of key slides from your oral presentation in your Marketing Portfolio.

Option 2 Start Your Own Independent or Franchised Business Assuming you had $100,000 to start a new business, what type of business would you open? Select a business (independent or franchise) you would like to open some day and write a complete business plan for it. Assume this plan will be used to obtain additional financing. Prepare your written report using a word processing program and use presentation software for your oral presentation. See a suggested outline and key evaluation points at *marketingessentials.glencoe.com/portfolio*

@ Online Action!

Go to *marketingessentials.glencoe.com/Unit/11/DECA* to review entrepreneurship concepts that relate to DECA events.

UNIT 12 Employability &

In this unit you will find

- **Chapter 37** Identifying Career Opportunities
- **Chapter 38** Finding and Applying for a Job

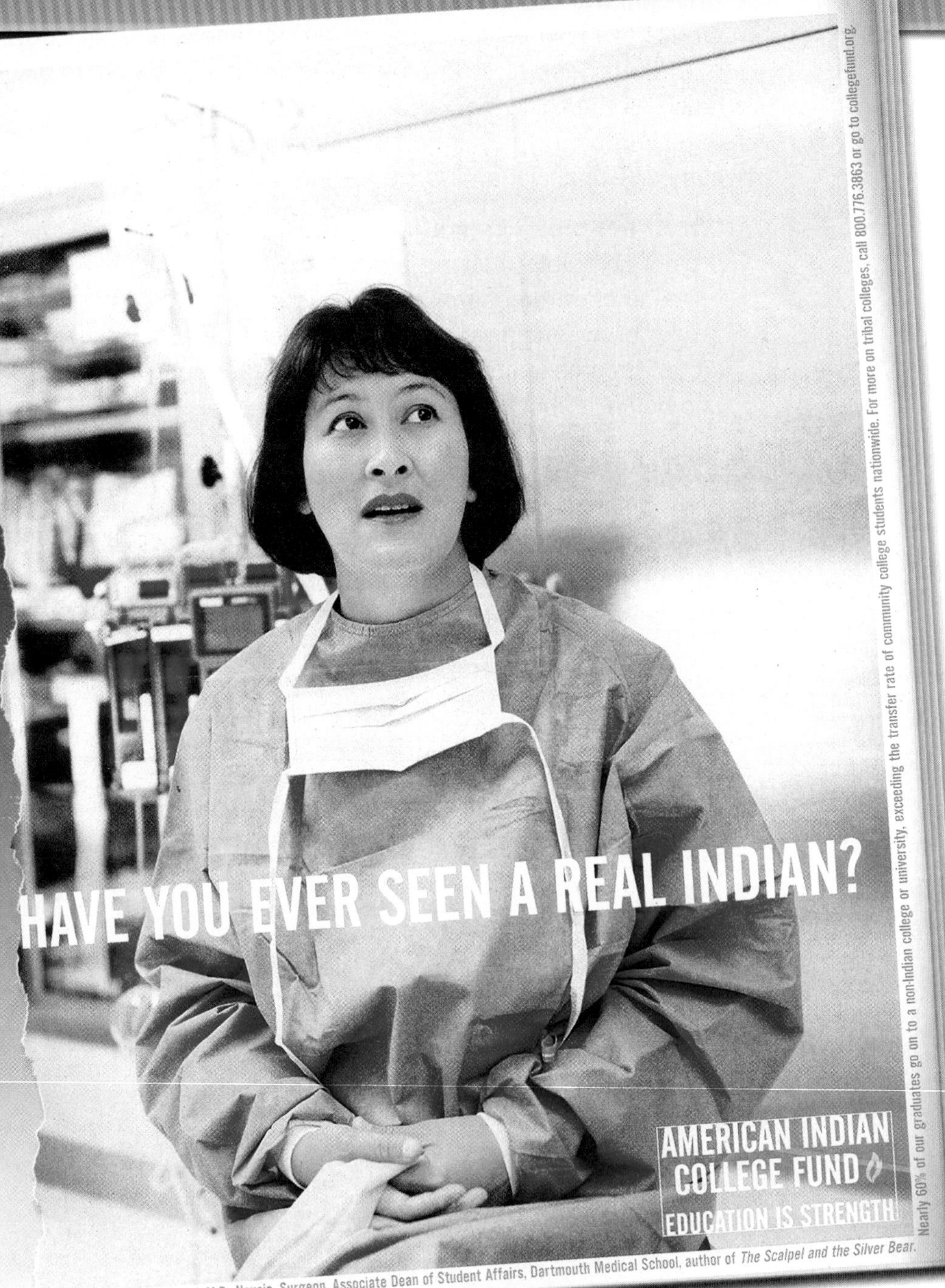

Career Development

ANALYZE THE AD

This ad promotes a nonprofit organization that supports education for American Indian youth. How does this ad relate to finding and pursuing a career path?

Market Talk Nonprofit and community-action organizations can use the power of marketing to help their causes. The nonprofit American Indian College Fund supports 34 tribal colleges and grants scholarships. What is the most powerful component of this ad?

Think and Write Many organizations help students with their educational and career goals. Look through Web sites and magazine and newspaper articles on education to find sources of support that could help you. Choose the most suitable or most promising options for you. Write out step-by-step plans for contacting the top three organizations on your list.

@ Online Action! **Go to *marketingessentials.glencoe.com/u12/ad* for an extended activity.**

Marketing Plan

1 **ANALYSIS**
SWOT
Economic
Socio-Cultural
Technological
Competitive

2 **STRATEGY**
Promotion
Place
Price
Product

3 **IMPLEMENTATION**
Organization
Management
Staffing

4 **BUDGET**
Cost of Sales
Cost of Promotion
Incomes and Expenses

5 **CONTROL**
Evaluation
Performance Measures
Performance Analysis

In this unit

Foundations of Marketing
- Communication, Interpersonal Skills
- Professional Development

CHAPTER 37

Identifying Career Opportunities

Chapter Objectives

After reading this chapter, you should be able to:

- Assess your goals, values, interests, skills, and aptitudes
- Appraise your personality
- Complete a career assessment
- Locate career research resources
- Develop a plan to reach your career goals
- Explain the importance of marketing careers to the U.S. economy

GUIDE TO THE PHOTO

Market Talk According to the American Marketing Association, there are over 750,000 marketing professionals working in the United States and Canada. A vast array of opportunities awaits you. You may want to work with the public, spend your days in a quiet office with a computer, or be outdoors coordinating a promotional event for a customer. Jobs in marketing are found in varied environments throughout the United States and around the world.

Quick Think Now is the time to start narrowing your choices down to find the career that will satisfy you the most. How will you begin?

THE DECA CONNECTION

Performance indicators represent key skills and knowledge. Relating them to the concepts explained in this chapter is your key to success in DECA events.

These acronyms represent DECA events that involve knowledge of concepts in this chapter.

AAAL*	**FMAL***	**MMS**	**TMDM***
AAML*	**FMDM***	**QSRM***	**TSE***
ADC*	**FMML***	**RMAL***	**VPM***
BSM	**FSRM***	**RMML***	
EMDM*	**HMDM***	**SMDM***	

In all these DECA events you should be able to follow these performance indicators:

- Assess personal interests and skills needed for success in business
- Use feedback for personal growth
- Make decisions
- Set personal goals
- Analyze employer expectations in the business environment
- Identify sources of career information
- Identify tentative occupational interest
- Explain employment opportunities in marketing
- Explain employment opportunities in business
- Describe techniques for obtaining work experience
- Explain the need for ongoing education as a worker
- Explain possible advancement patterns for job
- Identify skills needed to enhance career progression

All the events with an asterisk (*) also include this performance indicator:

- Describe/Explain career/employment opportunities in (that respective industry)

DECA PREP

Check your understanding of DECA performance indicators with the DECA activity in this chapter's review. For more information and DECA Prep practice, go to *marketingessentials .glencoe.com/37/DECA*

Define Goals

OBJECTIVES

- Assess your goals, values, interests, skills, and aptitudes
- Appraise your personality
- Complete a career assessment
- Locate career research resources
- Develop a plan to reach your career goals

KEY TERMS

- lifestyle
- values
- aptitude
- *Occupational Outlook Handbook (OOH)*
- career outlook
- O*NET
- internship
- planning goals
- specific goal
- realistic goal

READ and STUDY

BEFORE YOU READ

Predict Are you interested in the careers of any of your family members or neighbors? Why or why not?

THE MAIN IDEA

Understanding yourself is the first step in finding a career you will enjoy. You need to know yourself well in order to select the most satisfying career. This section will help you begin to assess your attributes so you can match them to the right career for you. Then you will compare your needs to the opportunities for careers you have identified and researched.

STUDY ORGANIZER

Use a chart like the one below to note key aspects of the six steps in the self-assessment process.

The Self-Assessment Process	
What do I do well?	

WHILE YOU READ

Compare Which of the six self-assessment areas will have the greatest effect on your career choice?

Choosing a Career

Your career is the work you will do to earn a living over a period of years, perhaps a lifetime. A career often includes a series of progressively more responsible jobs in one field or in related fields. Choosing a career requires careful thought and preparation. This six-step process for decision making can help guide you in making important career choices:

1. Define your lifestyle goals.
2. Conduct a self-assessment.
3. Identify possible career choices and gather information on each.
4. Evaluate your choices.
5. Make your decision.
6. Plan how you will reach your goal.

In this section, we will explore how to define lifestyle goals, conduct a self-assessment, and identify possible career choices by gathering information.

Define Your Lifestyle Goals

The first step in choosing a career requires that you do a bit of reflecting. You need to think about what kind of life you would like to live—your **lifestyle**. What type of lifestyle do you want? How do you want to spend your time, energy, and money? The answers to these questions will help you set lifestyle goals to make possible the life you want to have in the future.

Your career has a great effect on lifestyle. Some careers will fit your lifestyle goals better than others. If spending time with your family is important to you, then you probably will not want a career that requires a lot of travel. Similarly, if you cherish weekends for religious or leisure activities, you probably will not look for a job that requires working weekends. Knowing your lifestyle goals will help you find a career that enhances your lifestyle.

As a student, your life revolves around school, friends, and family. As an adult, your lifestyle will be influenced by:

- where you live (city, suburbs, or rural area)
- the type of housing in which you live
- the cultural environment in which you live, including the kinds of shopping and leisure activities you enjoy
- your mode of transportation
- your relationships with your family and friends
- the work you do to earn a living

Your career is the key to your lifestyle because it will provide the earnings needed to support your lifestyle. Before you can determine how compatible a career will be with lifestyle goals, you need to assess what your goals are.

Conduct a Self-Assessment

Be prepared to record your findings in a notebook. Label the notebook *Self-Assessment File*. Summarize your various assessments in paragraph form or, where appropriate, by using a rating scale.

Your Values

Values are beliefs that guide the way we live. Just as people have different abilities and personalities, they also have different values. Defining your system of values is essential in choosing a career.

•CITY or COUNTRY? Living in the city can be exciting yet demanding. A rural setting offers a quieter, more relaxed lifestyle.

In which setting would you feel most comfortable, urban or rural?

Identify your values by focusing on the beliefs and actions that are important to you. If you are willing to work very hard to succeed, you value achievement. Another possible value is the opportunity to express yourself.

Your Interests

Most people spend between 30 and 40 years working, so it makes sense to choose work that interests you. When you can clearly define your interests, you can gain a clearer picture of a career that will be fulfilling to you.

To evaluate your interests, write down the things you like to do. Include leisure activities, school activities, favorite classes, sports, and social activities.

Another way to find out about your interests is to take a career interest survey. Such surveys are similar to tests, but there are no right or wrong answers. You are given a long list of activities, and you decide how much you would like doing each of them. Then you score the survey yourself to learn which careers best match your interests. Your school counselor or marketing teacher can probably arrange for you to take one of these surveys.

Your Skills and Aptitudes

To be successful in any career, you will need specific skills and aptitudes.

An **aptitude** may be an ability or natural talent, or it may be the potential to learn a certain skill. Pursuing a career without having an aptitude for the required skills may be a struggle instead of a pleasure, and real success will be hard to achieve. Once you know what skills are required to perform a job, you can determine if you have the aptitude to acquire those skills.

You may have already developed skills that will be useful in a career that interests you. Do you find it easy to sell cookies, candy bars, or other items to raise funds for your DECA chapter? Are you good at organizing committees and getting others to do their jobs? Is math easy for you? Have you won any prizes for your creative efforts? List your skills and aptitudes on a separate sheet of paper in your self-assessment file, and update your list as you develop new skills.

Your Personality

Your personality is the combination of all of the unique qualities that make you who you are. Understanding your personality characteristics will help you to determine what types of work situations will best suit you. Personality tests, available through your guidance counselor, can help you identify your personality type. Think about how you respond to stress. Do you find it an enjoyable challenge, or do you avoid it? As you perform this exercise, remember that there is no right or wrong kind of personality. There are only different kinds of people.

Your Work Environment Preferences

Your work environment refers to where you work—the place and its working conditions. Working conditions include sights, sounds, and smells.

You do not have to know all your preferences about working conditions now, but you should start thinking about them. For example, do you prefer to work indoors or outdoors? Sitting down or standing up?

Your Relationship Preferences

All jobs require working with information and ideas, people, or objects—alone or in some combination. These categories can form the basis for describing different kinds of careers. Since any career you choose will likely involve an overlap of these categories, think about which interests you most. Do you like working with others, or do you prefer to work alone? Are you comfortable handling interpersonal conflicts at work? The answers to these questions, too, can help you understand your relationship preferences.

Identify Possible Career Choices and Gather Information

To research careers, you will need to gather information from a variety of sources. You will find current information at libraries or on the Internet. You can also learn a great deal through informational interviews, professional and trade organizations, and actual work experience.

Case Study

The Career of Stan Ovshinsky

One secret to a successful career is being open to change and willing to explore new possibilities. Stanley Ovshinsky has done just that. Born over 80 years ago, he has made discoveries and inventions in the world of physics and chemistry since 1960 that have had commercial uses in everything from cell phones to space stations.

Hero of the Planet

Time magazine named Ovshinsky a Hero of the Planet in 1999 for his development of small-scale solar electric systems that allow even remote villages to have electricity.

Ovshinsky's physics discoveries led to the development of the rechargeable, "green," NiMH battery. This technology powers not only millions of cell phones, digital cameras, and other small electronic devices but also the first consumer electric vehicle, the EV-1. His work on phase-change optical memory has been applied in rewritable DVD and CD products.

In recent years, Ovshinsky, together with Toyota, has built a prototype hydrogen hybrid car that produces no exhaust emissions and goes from 0 to 74 mph in 6 seconds. His goal is to have a commercially viable solid hydrogen system ready to fuel a zero-emission vehicle for the automotive industry by 2010. As he moves towards his 90th birthday, Ovshinsky shows no signs of resting on his laurels.

THINK STRATEGICALLY

Ovshinsky started out running a machine shop, and he was always interested in metals and their properties. What interests do you have that could lead to a successful career?

@ Online Action! **Go to *marketingessentials.glencoe.com/37/case* to find an activity on career development.**

Libraries

A publication you will find in the library is the ***Occupational Outlook Handbook* (*OOH*)**. The U.S. Department of Labor publishes a revised edition of the *OOH* every two years and the *OOH Quarterly* four times each year. The *OOH* describes what workers do on the job, working conditions, the training and education needed, earnings, and expected job prospects in a wide range of occupations. These publications will give you valuable information on the number and types of jobs available in any field, known as the **career outlook**.

Professional and Trade Associations

Professional and trade associations serve individuals and businesses with common interests. These are excellent sources for current information about careers in many professions.

Members are usually people working in or associated with the same industry. Some associations serve individuals in particular careers, such as the American Marketing Association or the Direct Marketing Association.

These associations promote pooling of resources, technology cooperation, common standards, and marketing strategies. Information is disseminated in newsletters, journals, and reports.

The Internet

Much of the information previously available in print at libraries is now available online.

O*NET, the Occupational Information Network, has replaced the *Dictionary of Occupational Titles,* which was the primary source of occupational information for fifty years. The O*NET database includes information on skills, abilities, knowledge, work activities, and interests associated with occupations. The O*NET site provides information on how to use the O*NET database. The *Occupational Outlook Handbook (OOH),* described previously in the section on libraries, is also available online. Directions for locating career information are given on the *OOH* site.

You can also find a wealth of resources for research from America's Career InfoNet Web site. The College Board has a section on its Web site devoted to helping you research careers.

Informational Interviews

You may want to set up an informational interview with a professional who works in a career that interests you. You can learn about the demands and opportunities of a career by talking with someone who has experience. You also get the opportunity to learn about the day-to-day realities of a job. Those who have met the challenges of a career are usually happy to talk about it.

Ask both your teacher and your counselor for suggestions about whom you should interview. They may have lists of people in the community who enjoy talking with young people about their work. Family members and friends of the family can also sometimes give you leads.

If you do not get some good suggestions from these sources, contact the public affairs

NET MARKETING

College While You Work

If your career goal is a high-level job in any area of marketing, you will want to continue your education past high school into college, and probably beyond a bachelor's degree to an MBA or other graduate degree. What if you have already begun your career path, and do not feel able to take time off for college or an advanced study? An online degree program could be the solution.

There are many fully accredited universities offering degrees in a variety of business areas to students who want to do some or most of their degree work in an online environment. Many online students are already working in fields related to their studies. Bachelor's, master's, and doctoral programs are all available online. Studying online means that students download lectures at their own pace and on their own schedules. Students receive and submit assignments and get instructor feedback by e-mail. They have access to online research libraries as well as to other students with whom they can discuss course content. The market for these services might include you.

THINK LIKE A MARKETER

List three pros and three cons of an online degree program.

Online Action!

Go to *marketingessentials.glencoe.com/37/net* to find an activity about online degrees.

•INTERVIEW for SUCCESS An interview with a prospective employer offers you an opportunity to collect information about a job or career.

What other opportunities does the interview offer the interviewer and the interviewee? Do you think an interview is a good resource in gathering information about a career of interest to you? Why or why not?

or public relations officer at a professional association. Ask if the organization sponsors career nights or other opportunities where you can speak with people who are currently working in the field.

Before any interview, prepare a list of questions that you want to ask. Here are some suggestions:

- How do you spend most of your time on the job?
- Which work activities do you like most?
- What skills will I need to do this type of work?
- What skills will I need to advance?
- What education and training will I need?
- Can I complete some of the training after I begin working?
- How much time do you spend working with ideas and information? With people? With objects?
- Will there be an increase in job opportunities in this field over the next several years? What impact will automation and new technology have on job opportunities in the next few years?

On-the-Job Experience

Many students work part-time after school, on weekends, or during the summer months. If you have an idea of a career you might be interested in pursuing, an entry-level position in that field will offer you great experience.

On-the-job experience offers you many benefits. You can:

- try out some of the work activities in your career field and decide how much you like doing them;
- experience the work environment associated with that career;
- develop work habits that will help you succeed in your career;
- broaden your understanding of the world of work and smooth the transition from school to work;
- make career contacts who can serve as mentors or assist you when you are searching for a job later; and
- build up your résumé, which will grow as you gain more working experience.

You may also look into an internship program at a company or organization that interests you. An **internship** offers students direct work experience and exposure to various aspects of a career, either with or without pay.

The value of an internship is in the experience and the contacts that you make. Employers seriously consider internship experience when reviewing candidates for new positions.

Figure 37.1 Personal Career Profile

• **Is It a Match?** A personal career profile helps you compare your self-assessment with a particular career assessment.

Based on this career profile, how does Joan Smith's personal information match the information about a teaching career? Rank each category from 1 to 5, with 5 being the best match.

Name Joan Smith **Date** September 4, 20--

Personal Information	Career Information	Match (1–5, with 5 being the best match)
Your Values: The value scales I took showed that I like to help other people (humanitarianism). I like to be a leader. Doing creative things is fun, too.	**Values:** As a teacher I would have a chance to help others—that's what it's all about. Teachers certainly have plenty of opportunities to be leaders, too. Teachers also need to be creative!	
Your Interests: My hobby interests have always been photography, reading, and theater. My career interest survey showed that I might like a career in leading/influencing, selling, the arts, or maybe a humanitarian career.	**Career Duties and Responsibilities:** As a teacher, I would present information, and direct student discussions and activities in class. I would help each student individually, too. (Maybe I could teach marketing or general business.) A teacher's working conditions would be good in most schools. (Summers off!)	
Your Personality: I like people, and I have a good attitude toward learning. I have an open mind. I'm enthusiastic, too. However, I don't have the energy and drive that some people have. I don't know if I could work night after night.	**Type of Personality Needed:** A teacher must like kids, even when they aren't very likeable. I would have to prepare my lessons every day—couldn't just forget about them. Teachers need to be organized, too.	
Data-People-Things Preferences: I think I like working with people most of all. I wouldn't want to be stuck in an office all day with only "data" to talk to. I also wouldn't like working only with things. Some data would be all right, though.	**Data-People-Things Relationships:** Teachers work mostly with people—their students, the principal, parents. They work with data (information), too, though. I don't think they work much with things.	
Skills and Aptitudes: I may have some natural teaching skills—the kids at the YMCA always come to me for help. I helped several kids in Miss Moore's class. Business classes are easy for me.	**Skills and Aptitudes Needed:** Being able to present information so students can understand it is a very important skill. Of course, you must know your subject. An appetite for learning new approaches to teaching is important, too.	
Education/Training Acceptable: I sure never thought I would go to college—I never even liked doing the homework in high school. However, here I am a senior with no real prospects of a good job. Maybe college is the answer.	**Education/Training Required:** Four years of college (it sounds like forever, but I guess it does go fast) are required before you can begin teaching in most states. Some states require course work beyond that.	

@ Online Action! Go to ***marketingessentials.glencoe.com/37/figure/1*** to find a project on career assessment.

GLOBAL MARKET

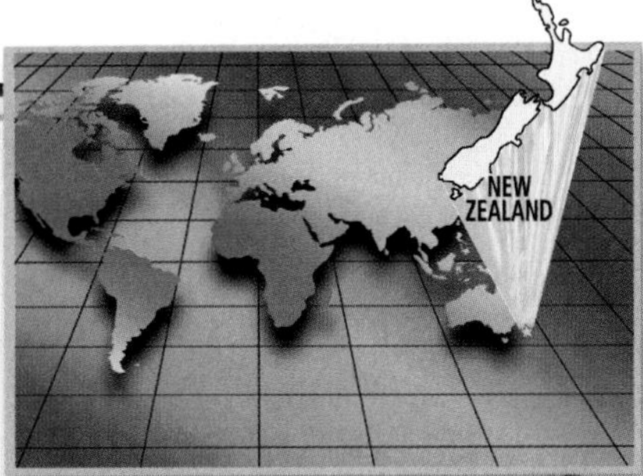

Marketing Yourself Globally

Have you ever thought about living in another country? Imagine you spot the information below on a Web site dedicated to working abroad.

- The New Zealand government will grant up to 500 young citizens of the United States of America (USA) work visas for a working holiday annually.
- Visas allow a working holiday of 12 months.

To be eligible **you must:**

- be a citizen or resident of the USA
- prove that your main reason for coming to New Zealand is to visit
- have a valid American passport
- hold a return ticket or sufficient funds to purchase such a ticket
- have a minimum of NZ$4,200 in available funds to meet your living costs while in New Zealand
- hold medical and comprehensive hospitalization insurance for the length of your stay

CRITICAL THINKING

How would working in a foreign country help your long-term career plan?

@ Online Action!

Go to *marketingessentials.glencoe.com/37/global* to find an activity on technology and career planning.

It demonstrates high interest and a willingness to put in time to gain valuable experience.

Evaluate Your Choices

Once you identify one or even several interesting careers, it is time to compare and contrast that potential career with your self-assessment. In this way, you can determine if a career that seems of interest is really a good match for you.

Organize your task before you begin for better efficiency. Gather all of your self-assessment notes and research on different careers. It is helpful to begin this matching process on paper. Create a personal career profile, using an evaluation format that allows you to compare your self-assessment side-by-side with a particular career assessment (see Figure 37.1).

On the left side of the profile, write down the information about yourself. Then make several photocopies of this form—one for each career that you researched and that interests you. Using these copies, fill in the career information on the right by referring to your notes. After you complete each profile, reread all the information carefully. The following questions will guide you as you evaluate your choices.

- Do the work values in this field match my values?
- Will this career support my lifestyle goals?

- Do the responsibilities match my skills and aptitudes?
- How suited is the job to my personality?
- Does the work environment match my needs?
- Does the career offer the work relationships I am seeking?

Develop an Action Plan and Reach Your Goal

A plan does not guarantee success, but outlining the steps that you need to follow to reach your ultimate goal will provide a path.

Formulate Planning Goals

The small steps you take to get from where you are now to where you want to be are **planning goals**. They give your life a sense of direction and move you steadily toward your ultimate career goal. Every time you reach a goal, you gain confidence to move on to the next one (see Figure 37.2).

Be Specific

The best way to make progress toward your ultimate goal is to make your planning goals specific. A **specific goal** is stated in exact terms and includes some details. The goal statement "I want to become a success" is not specific. "I want to complete my class in marketing this semester and earn at least a B" is specific. It is the type of planning goal that moves you forward. The more specific you are about your career goals, the more likely you are to formulate a plan to reach those goals.

Be Realistic

Planning goals must also be realistic. A **realistic goal** is one that you have a reasonable chance of achieving. Think about all of the different skills and aptitudes that you possess. They will guide you in identifying both your ultimate career goal and your planning goals.

Work Backward

When you set your planning goals, begin with your ultimate career goal. Then decide what objectives you must reach along the way to achieve your ultimate goal. Work backward, starting with your most distant, long-term goal, and move toward the present to determine the necessary medium- and short-term goals.

For example, suppose your ultimate career goal is to become a chef. A long-term goal may be to study with a world-class chef. To earn the credentials you need to get such an opportunity, you may set a medium-term goal of earning a degree from a culinary institute. Another medium-term goal may be to get a job at a well-respected restaurant in your town or city. To prepare for that opportunity, you may set a short-term goal to work in a local kitchen to gain practical experience. Another short-term goal may be to investigate what type of training you will need. So, you may subscribe to a cooking magazine or keep up-to-date with new cookbooks.

Having a progressive series of goals allows you to test your ultimate career goal and make corrections along the way. While progressing toward your career goal, your experiences may reinforce your career decision or lead to your changing your career goal. You may discover another career that you find more interesting. On the basis of work experience in a kitchen, you may discover that you would rather own a restaurant than be a chef. At any point along the way, you can adjust your path and your ultimate goal.

Professional Development

Whatever your career choice, you will need a plan of action to reach your goal. Your plan must include the concepts and strategies needed for personal and professional growth.

Choosing education is much like choosing a career. Follow the complete decision-making process to select the best program and the best school for you. Your school counselor is a good place to start. Your school and public libraries are likely to have useful information. You can also search the Internet and visit the Web sites of those schools that interest you.

Due to the continuing changes brought about by technology and the competition of a global economy, all professionals must

Figure 37.2 Developing a Career Plan

• **Steps to Take** After you have completed a self-evaluation to determine your personal strengths and weaknesses and researched possible career paths, you should be ready to write a career plan and begin to act on it.

What is your plan?

STEP 1: SET CAREER GOALS

You need a road map to get from where you are to your final destination. The specific, realistic, short- and medium-term goals you set are the mile markers on your map. Achieving each one takes you that much closer to your final career goal.

STEP 2: DEVELOP AN EDUCATION/ PROFESSIONAL DEVELOPMENT PLAN

Choosing how much and what kind of education or training you need for your career is one of the most important decisions you will make. Develop short- and long-term education and training goals, including internships with employers in the fields that attract you.

STEP 3: DRAW UP A PLAN OF ACTION

Create your plan, including both the work experience goals and the educational goals you will need to reach your ultimate career. Be realistic about the timing of each step of your plan. Know that you will likely revise it as time goes on and circumstances change.

Online Action!

Go to *marketingessentials.glencoe.com/37/figure/2* to find a project on career planning.

upgrade their existing skills and acquire new ones. It is no surprise, then, that lifelong learning is key to any successful career.

If you are planning for education and training beyond high school, consider the following questions:

- What is my ultimate career goal?
- What course can I take now that will help me to reach that career goal?
- What education and training beyond high school is required to reach my career goal?
- How much of this education and training must I complete before I enter this career?
- Where can I get this education and training?
- How much will this education and training cost, and how will I get the money?
- How much education and training can I get on the job?

Outlining Your Plan

After you have answered these questions, begin writing your personal plan of action. Write down all of your goals, the date that you plan to begin working toward each one, and the date you expect to reach each goal. Identify the skills you will need to enhance progression in your career. This will help keep you on track toward your ultimate career goal—the one that turns your dream lifestyle into reality.

37.1 AFTER YOU READ

Reviewing Key Terms and Concepts

1. What are the first two basic steps in choosing a career?
2. List three considerations that will help you formulate planning goals.
3. List six areas to explore when conducting a self-assessment.

Integrating Academic Skills

Math

4. Assume that you will work for 40 years before you retire. You invest \$5,000 in a retirement fund at the end of your first year. It compounds at a 7 percent annual rate of return for the next 39 years. How much will be in the account when you retire? Use the following equation to find the amount that will be in the account: Amount $= \$5000 \times (1.07)^{39}$ where $(1.07)^{39}$ is 13.9948204.

Language Arts

5. Use your library, school career center, local bookstore, or online bookstore to obtain two books on choosing a career. Browse through each book and read the chapters devoted to self-assessment. Then, make a chart comparing the information both books give about the steps to self-assessment.

Check your answers at ***marketingessentials.glencoe.com/37/read***

Careers in Marketing

OBJECTIVES

- Explain the importance of marketing careers to the U.S. economy

KEY TERMS

- occupational area

READ and STUDY

BEFORE YOU READ

Predict What do you already know about careers in marketing?

THE MAIN IDEA

If you are considering a career in marketing, you will need to learn about the requirements, opportunities, rewards, and trends in this exciting field. The more career information you have, the easier it will be to reach a career decision.

STUDY ORGANIZER

In a chart such as the one below write in the benefits, trends, and job levels of marketing careers.

Questions About a Marketing Career

1. ______________________
2. Are there many jobs available?
3. ______________________

Is Marketing a Career for You?

As you study marketing, you have the opportunity to evaluate marketing as a potential career. Even if you decide that marketing is not for you, the skills and knowledge you gain from your study will help you in school and on the job. These skills include writing, researching, communication, and analytical skills, among others.

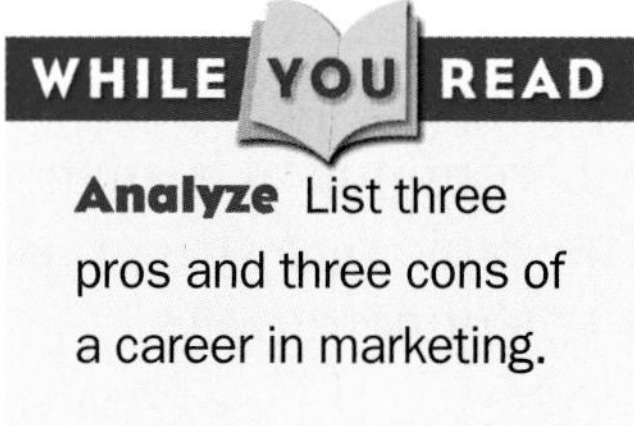

An Overview of Marketing Careers

Marketing provides perhaps the greatest diversity of opportunities of any career field—from purchasing merchandise, to selling, to designing ads, to steering the company as president. About 33 million Americans earn a living in marketing. Careers in marketing span an array of activities required to develop, promote, and distribute goods and services to consumers. When considered in this broad sense, marketing activities account for about one in every three American jobs.

Benefits of a Marketing Career

The most obvious benefit of a career in marketing is the opportunity to make an above-average income. Even in an entry-level job, it is nice to know that potential earnings in marketing are excellent.

There are usually more opportunities to advance in a marketing career than in almost any other area of business. This is because of the high visibility that many marketing positions have.

People who work in marketing frequently present and shape their ideas in meetings with company managers and executives. People who work in sales get constant feedback on their efforts in the form of sales figures that are regularly reviewed by upper-level management. People who work in advertising may develop ad campaigns that win critical acclaim from professional associations. In terms of a job, this means winning promotions faster in marketing than in many other careers.

A career in marketing can be stressful, however, because there are pressures to succeed, and results of one's efforts are highly visible.

Employment Trends in Marketing

The Bureau of Labor Statistics (BLS) projects that employment in marketing and sales will continue at a high level through 2012. The rapid growth of e-commerce provides many opportunities.

Department of Labor projections indicate that managerial jobs in marketing-related fields will continue to be plentiful, regardless of the industry.

Changes in the marketplace have created the need for more rather than fewer marketing professionals. The rise in the number of single-person households, changing preferences in recreational activities, and the increase in foreign competition must all be monitored through market research and marketing information systems. To track these and other quickly developing trends, companies are expanding their marketing programs and staffs.

Marketing Occupational Areas

An **occupational area** is a category of jobs that involve similar interests and skills. Focusing on one or two areas makes it much easier to find information about the career area that most interests you. Listed below are the 21 generally accepted areas or career applications within the field of marketing.

- Advertising
- Customer Service
- E-Commerce
- Entrepreneur
- Fashion Merchandising
- Financial Services
- Food Marketing
- Hospitality Marketing
- Importing/Exporting
- International Marketing
- Marketing Research
- Pharmaceutical/Medical Marketing
- Product Management
- Professional Sales
- Public Relations
- Real Estate
- Restaurant Management
- Retail Management
- Sales Management
- Service Marketing
- Sports Marketing
- Travel/Tourism/Hospitality Marketing

Job Levels in Marketing

Many jobs exist within each of the occupational areas, or career applications, of marketing. Jobs in each marketing area can be categorized according to five skill levels.

- **Entry-level jobs** usually require no prior experience and involve limited decision-making skills.
- **Career-sustaining jobs** require a higher level of skill and more decision making than entry-level jobs.
- **Marketing specialist employees** must show leadership ability and make many decisions on a daily basis. Being a marketing specialist is a long-term career goal for many in marketing.
- **Marketing supervisors** must have good management skills, the ability to make many decisions on a daily basis, and excellent marketing skills. This is the highest career level to which many people aspire. The prestige and income are generally quite high, and there is less risk involved than at the top management level.
- **Managers and CEOs/owners** are at the top level. People at this level are capable of running an entire company or a significant part of it. They must be highly skilled in a number of areas. They are responsible for the final success of the enterprise.

37.2 AFTER YOU READ

Reviewing Key Terms and Concepts

1. What are three benefits of a career in marketing?
2. There are ten major areas you should consider when investigating careers. Rank them by importance level, with number 1 being your highest priority and number 10 being your lowest.
3. Name five resources for researching careers.

Integrating Academic Skills

Math

4. Use the *Occupational Outlook Handbook* in the library or online to find the current annual salaries for two marketing jobs of interest to you. What is the difference between these two salaries? Assume that in two years, the salary for each job increases by 12 percent. What will be the new salary for each job?

Government and Economics

5. Government agencies and the policies they implement have a strong effect on our market economy. Select one of the following agencies to research: Federal Communications Commission, Federal Reserve Board, Federal Trade Commission, Food and Drug Administration, or Internal Revenue Service. Write a one-page report on the agency and what it does. Explain how the agency impacts the economy.

Check your answers at *marketingessentials.glencoe.com/37/read*

CAREERS IN MARKETING

NICK CORCODILOS
PRESIDENT, NORTH BRIDGE GROUP, INC. ASKTHEHEADHUNTER.COM

What do you do at work?

Companies turn to me to find great talent to do jobs that impact the bottom line positively. Finding great people does not involve running ads or searching for résumés on online job boards. A good headhunter serves as a hub of insider information in the industry he or she services. In other words, my job is to know the best people in the field I service, and to help those people meet one another and stay in touch. In essence, a good headhunter helps useful but sensitive information flow among the people who make an industry click.

What skills are most important to you?

Street smarts (the most useful form of intelligence), self-motivation, persistence, and enthusiasm are the keys to success as a headhunter. My most important skill is the ability to see connections where others do not. You cannot learn the business from a book, a course, or a workshop. You must work closely with a good headhunter who can teach you the business, and who you can observe closely at work. I think it is imperative to have a college degree.

What is your key to success?

Doing nice things for others for free. For every placement I make to earn a fee, I probably wind up helping 30 people make connections that somehow pay off for them. I have a lot of friends as a result.

Aptitudes, Abilities, and Skills

Outgoing personality, strong social and interpersonal skills, ability to make connections and think creatively

Education and Training

General business and marketing degrees are common; degrees in psychology can also be useful. Apprenticeships and internships are crucial.

Career Path

Industry contacts are crucial, so aspiring headhunters often begin their careers at established agencies.

THINKING CRITICALLY

Why is it sometimes beneficial to do work at no charge? What are some instances you can think of in which this might be valuable?

Online Action!

Go to *marketingessentials.glencoe.com/37/careers* to find a career-related activity.

CHAPTER 37 REVIEW

FOCUS on KEY POINTS

SECTION 37.1

- Good career choices are based on a comprehensive self-assessment of values, interests, skills, aptitudes, personality, and lifestyle preferences.
- Career planning includes looking at work values, lifestyle fit, and the education and training required. It also includes learning about the duties and skills required, and at helpful personality traits, work environment, and work relationships.
- Your plan of action to reach your career goal requires setting specific and realistic short- and medium-range planning goals.

SECTION 37.2

- Consider the benefits, employment trends, occupational areas, and job levels in marketing.

REVIEW VOCABULARY

Use these vocabulary terms in a paragraph on career research.

1. lifestyle (p. 787)
2. values (p. 787)
3. aptitude (p. 788)
4. *Occupational Outlook Handbook (OOH)* (p. 789)
5. career outlook (p. 789)
6. O*NET (p. 790)
7. internship (p. 791)
8. planning goals (p. 795)
9. specific goal (p. 795)
10. realistic goal (p. 795)
11. occupational area (p. 798)

REVIEW FACTS and IDEAS

12. Define values, lifestyle goals, interests, and aptitudes. Why is it important to assess these when choosing a career? (37.1)
13. What are two methods for appraising your personality? (37.1)
14. What is a work environment? What three categories are involved in relationship preferences? (37.1)
15. What areas should be investigated when completing a career assessment? (37.1)
16. Name two online career research resources. What resources are available at libraries? Name three other possible resources. (37.2)
17. What purpose does a personal career profile serve? (37.2)
18. What are three occupational areas in marketing? (37.2)

BUILD SKILLS

19. Workplace Skills

Human Relations Use a search engine on the Internet to do a search on personality tests. Find a site that will let you take a personality test for free. Print out the result of your test. Then write a brief paragraph explaining how this information might help you relate to others.

20. Technology Applications

Research Salary Ranges A possible career choice might be some type of research in marketing. You have considered your lifestyle goal and know that you want to have a comfortable lifestyle. Use the Internet to find the salary ranges of some specific jobs in marketing research. Name one or more specific jobs that meet your criteria. Then consider job opportunities in four marketing-related careers: computer technology, finance, business management, and economics. Go to the O*NET site to explore the outlook for job opportunities in these careers.

21. Math Practice

Calculating a Wage If the average national wage for an employee with a high school diploma is $26,000 while the average wage for an employee with a four-year degree is $40,000, how much more does the second employee earn? (Provide your answer in dollars and in percentage.)

DEVELOP CRITICAL THINKING

22. Preview Careers

Log on to the O*NET site (use a search engine to find the URL) and use the following steps:

- Click on the Skills Search and follow the directions.
- Once you have selected the skills you have or skills you wish to obtain, click on GO. (This search will identify occupations that use the skills you chose.)
- Prepare a list of the skills you selected and the occupations that were identified.

23. Assess Your Values

How do you think your values were formed? What effects do you think your personal values will have on the career you choose?

APPLY CONCEPTS

24. Long-Range Goals

One of your strong interests is plants and flowers. You have decided that your long-range career goal is to own a retail garden shop. You have an opportunity to work in a local garden shop as soon as you graduate, get on-the-job training, work your way up, and eventually buy into the business. Your parents want you to go to college first. Do some research into horticultural (gardening) programs offered at two- or four-year colleges. Use this information to formulate your decision.

Activity Write a brief plan of action for achieving your career goal. Present this plan to your parents.

25. Prepare for an Interview

Select a career that interests you. Prepare a list of six or more questions that you would like to ask someone who works in that field. Locate and arrange to interview such a person.

Activity Use a word processing program to write up your questions and the answers that you received. Share this information with your classmates.

NET SAVVY

26. Job Search

Access a job listing site on the Web and key in a search for the job of your dreams. Analyze the results of your search and develop a plan of action to obtain your favorite job on the list.

THE 

CONNECTION

Role Play: Career Opportunities

Situation You are to assume the role of high school junior. You plan to attend college upon graduation. You feel that you should explore some career areas that interest you. You know that you are interested in business and want to explore career opportunities in that field. You have decided to begin your career exploration at the library and on the Internet.

Activity You are to prepare an outline of your career exploration findings. You will discuss your findings with your parents (judge).

Evaluation You will be evaluated on how well you meet the following performance indicators:

- Assess personal interests and skills needed for success in business
- Analyze employer expectations
- Identify sources of career information
- Identify tentative occupational interest
- Explain employment opportunities in business

Online Action!

For more information and DECA Prep practice, go to *marketingessentials.glencoe.com/37/DECA*

CHAPTER 38

Finding and Applying for a Job

Chapter Objectives

After reading this chapter, you should be able to:

- Identify a variety of sources for job leads
- Describe the best ways to develop job leads
- Name the legal document necessary to begin working
- Write a letter of application and complete an application form
- Write a résumé and a cover letter
- Prepare for an interview

GUIDE TO THE PHOTO

Market Talk Finding job leads, attending job fairs, going through the application process, and getting interviews is a job in itself. Newspaper ads, networking, the Internet, and direct contacts are among the many sources for job leads. You will want to fuel your job search with those that are most effective for you.

Quick Think The time and effort you spend on your job search have a direct effect on the results. How many hours per week are you willing to spend looking for the right job?

THE DECA CONNECTION

Performance indicators represent key skills and knowledge. Relating them to the concepts explained in this chapter is your key to success in DECA events. These acronyms represent DECA events that involve knowledge of concepts in this chapter.

AAAL	**FMAL**	**MMS**	**TMDM***
AAML	**FMDM**	**QSRM**	**TSE***
ADC*	**FMML**	**RMAL**	**VPM**
BSM*	**FSRM**	**RMML**	
EMDM	**HMDM***	**SMDM***	

In all these DECA events you should be able to follow these performance indicators:

- Assess personal interests and skills needed for success in business
- Analyze employer expectations in the business environment
- Utilize job-search strategies
- Complete a job application
- Interview for a job
- Write a follow-up letter after job interview
- Write a letter of application
- Prepare a résumé
- Utilize resources that can contribute to professional development
- Use networking techniques for professional growth
- Identify skills needed to enhance career progression

All the events with an asterisk (*) also include this performance indicator:

- Assess the services provided by professional organizations in (that industry)

DECA PREP

Check your understanding of DECA performance indicators with the DECA activity in this chapter's review. For more information and DECA Prep practice, go to *marketingessentials.glencoe.com/38/DECA*

Finding a Job

OBJECTIVES

- Identify a variety of sources for job leads
- Describe the best ways to develop job leads

KEY TERMS

- job lead
- networking
- public employment agencies
- private employment agencies
- staffing/temporary agencies

BEFORE YOU READ

Predict How did your family members and friends find their jobs? What job-hunting techniques can you learn from them?

THE MAIN IDEA

This section will help you learn how to locate job leads to find the job that will start you on your way to success in your chosen career.

STUDY ORGANIZER

In a chart like the one below, write in seven types of sources of job leads.

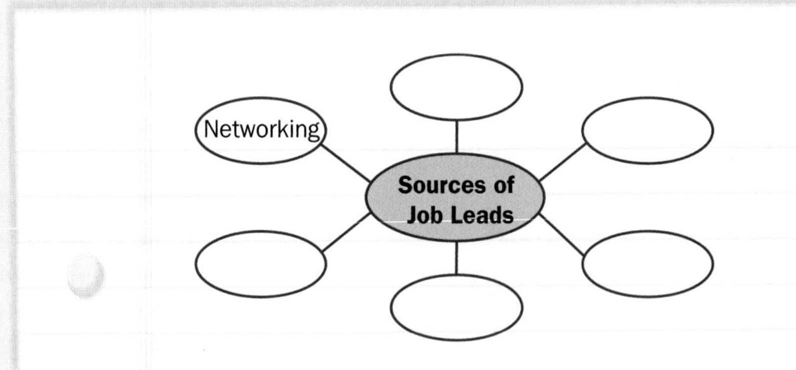

Compare Think about which sources for job leads would be most productive for you.

Finding Job Openings

Developing effective job search and interview skills will help you make the most of your time and effort when looking for a job. How do you uncover job opportunities?

The best way to start is by contacting all of the sources available to you that might produce a job lead. A **job lead** is information about a job opening. Sometimes you may have to act like a detective, following up skimpy leads and researching information about a company to plan the best approach. Finding the right job requires getting as many leads as possible and following up on them.

Networking

Often, the best source for job leads will be people you know—family, friends, schoolmates and their families, former employers, professionals, teachers or professors, local business owners, coaches, members of a religious or community group to which you belong, and even acquaintances. These people form your network.

Networking is the art of building alliances. Finding contacts among those in your network is, without a doubt, the most effective way to find a job. Most businesses welcome applications from friends of employees because they trust their employees' opinions. Make a list of all your contacts, including addresses, phone numbers, and e-mail addresses. Keep this list current and add to it as your career and education progress.

Let your contacts know you are seeking employment, the type of work you are suited for, what you have to offer, and the types of companies or careers that interest you.

Politely ask them if they would be comfortable letting you know if they hear of any openings that might suit you or meet your requirements. They may not immediately know of the perfect job for you, but they can keep you in mind and even ask their friends and coworkers about openings.

Networking is a mutual exchange, so be prepared to help them when they ask or when the need is apparent. Always let them know when you have responded to one of their leads and thank them for helping you.

School Counselor

When you are building your network, remember to include your school guidance counselor. Local retail stores and other businesses frequently call school counselors for names of qualified students for part-time or temporary jobs.

Professional People In Your Personal Life

You probably have occasional contact with professional people in your personal life—doctors, businesspeople, dentists, or lawyers. If you have established a good relationship with these people, they will probably be happy to help you in your job search. Since they are part of your network, you can ask them for names of people to contact or for advice about job prospects or the career you are pursuing.

Former Employers

Even if they were temporary or part-time jobs, your former employers may be good sources of job leads. It is likely that they will want to help you find a job if they were pleased with your work.

Cooperative Education and Work Experience Programs

Cooperative education teachers have contacts in the business community because they place and supervise students in part-time jobs. Students enrolled in cooperative work experience programs receive course credit and are sometimes paid, as well.

Newspaper and Magazine Ads

For many years, the Help Wanted section of the local newspaper, especially the Sunday edition, was perhaps the best place to find job openings. However, do not overlook your daily local newspaper. Look in the employment sections every day. Most papers organize listings of job openings by type.

These Help Wanted sections also teach you about the local job market. You will learn the qualifications required for different types of jobs. You may find information about salaries and benefits as well.

Follow up immediately on every ad that might lead to the job you want. Be aware, however, if an ad requires you to pay money or enroll in a course, it may be a disguised attempt to sell something rather than a genuine job offer.

In business newspapers and magazines, you can look for information about local and regional companies that are expanding, opening a new office, entering a new market, winning a bid for new business, or introducing a new product. These are the types of companies who are hiring.

Many professionals depend on their association's magazine to alert them to job openings. Some may be available in your library or a local college library. If not, you may be able to access them online.

Employment Agencies

Employment and temporary staffing agencies match workers with jobs. Most cities have several types of employment agencies—public, private, and staffing/temporary agencies. **Public employment agencies** are supported by state or federal taxes and offer free services to both job applicants and employers. **Private employment agencies** and **staffing/temporary agencies**, which are not supported by taxes, must earn a profit to stay in business. They charge a fee for their services, which is paid by either the job applicant or the employer.

Public employment agencies are identified by the names of the states in which they are located. The Texas Employment Commission and the California Employment Development Department are examples. In some cities, the state employment service is the only one available. When you fill out an application form at the public employment agency near you, you will be interviewed to determine your qualifications and interests. The agency will call you if they find a job that is a good match. You will be told about the company and the duties of the job, then referred for an interview if you are interested.

Many times, private employment agencies have job leads that are not listed with public agencies. Remember, however, that private agencies charge a fee if they place you on a job. Make sure you know who is expected to pay the fee—it might be you. This will be stated in a contract you will be asked to sign. The employer often pays the fee for matching workers with higher-level jobs. The employee usually pays the placement fee for an entry-level job. The fee is usually a percentage of salary for the first several months or even the first full year of employment.

Staffing services or temporary help agencies will test you, interview you, and match you with jobs that last from one day to several months. You will be assigned to a company, but the staffing service is your employer. Do your best work, because temporary assignments can lead to permanent positions for the right candidate.

Company Personnel Offices

In large companies, the personnel office (often known as Human Resources, or HR) handles employment matters, including the hiring of new workers. If you have a networking contact within a large company whom you can ask about job openings, that is great. If not, visit the organization's Web site and click on the "Jobs," "Careers," or "Join Us" links to see what positions are available. While you are visiting the company's Web site, try to find the name of the head of the department in which you are interested in working. Many sites include the names of key employees and their contact information. Although some companies welcome phone inquiries about job openings, most do not. Be sure to ask a contact if a phone call or drop-in visit to inquire about openings is acceptable. A few large companies and most government agencies such as the United States Postal Service may post job openings on public bulletin boards.

Searching the Internet

Employers are using the Internet extensively, and millions of jobs are posted at any given time. In addition to searching company Web sites for openings, search for opportunities at employment portals such as Hotjobs .com, Monster.com, or America's Job Bank. For jobs in marketing, also check MarketingJobs .com and many of the professional associations that serve the field, such as the American Marketing Association, the Direct Marketing Association, the Public Relations Society of America, and the International Association of Business Communicators. Check the listings on their local chapter sites, too.

Case Study

It's a Monster!

Monster.com is the world's largest job search firm. The company's roots go back more than 30 years. It began as a Yellow Pages advertising sales company. The now familiar online Monster was created in 1994, and in 2003, it had 24 million résumés posted online, more than Yahoo's HotJobs and CareerBuilder.com combined. In 2004, a subscriber could search more than 800,000 available jobs. The company has sites in 20 different languages to serve job seekers and employers worldwide.

An estimated 80 percent of human resources managers now look for potential employees by searching online résumés, and an estimated 96 percent of those seeking jobs post their résumés online. For a fee, potential employers can post jobs, search Monster's résumé bank, or screen and track job candidates. More than 30 percent of Monster's 2003 revenue came from its résumé service alone. Job seekers pay to subscribe, search through postings, and apply for jobs online using the site. They can also get career advice and information about everything from résumés to typical salaries to relocation.

In 2000, Monster started Monstermoving.com, a companion site offering its own services related to relocating, as well as a portal to such businesses as real estate and moving companies around the country.

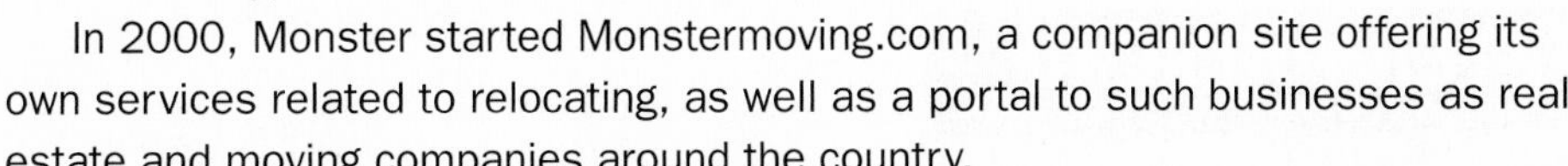

THINK STRATEGICALLY

Why would job seekers pay for Monster's service?

Online Action!

Go to *marketingessentials.glencoe.com/38/case* to find an activity on job searches.

On employment portals, search for up-to-date listings—nothing more than a month old. Many job search engines and portals enable you to search by location, job type, industry, date of posting, and even salary. Some enable you to subscribe to an e-mail alert to notify you when positions are posted. Check to see if there is a charge for this service. It is a great way to learn about opportunities as soon as they become available.

Contacting Your Job Leads

A letter of inquiry and a polished résumé will help you contact the company by regular mail or via e-mail.

If you call for an appointment, it is usually best not to discuss the job on the telephone. You will probably get more consideration by inquiring about the job after you arrive in person. If you are not sure about the best contact strategy, place a quick call to the personnel or human resources department to inquire what the company prefers. You will be better prepared if you have conducted your research about the organization. If the company sells consumer products, you should familiarize yourself with its products by studying the products and those of its competitors in stores.

As you research the company, make a note of key words used in the ad. You will learn below how these can be helpful in preparing your job application.

The goal is to be fully prepared—as if you are going to an actual interview—whenever you contact a company in any manner. Bring your résumé even if you expect just to fill out an application.

Letters of Inquiry

As you are learning, the Internet is a valuable research tool for any job search. In most situations, you can learn about openings on a company's Web site, through networking contacts, and via direct contact. If these activities do not yield the information you need about potential openings, you can write a letter of inquiry.

Before writing a letter of inquiry, you should have conducted your research about the company and found the name and contact details of the person to whom you should address your correspondence. Now you are ready to write a letter of inquiry. Include your résumé with your letter of inquiry. That is being proactive.

38.1 AFTER YOU READ

Reviewing Key Terms and Concepts

1. What is a job lead?
2. What is the most effective way to find a job?
3. List nine possible sources of job leads.

Integrating Academic Skills

Math

4. Your employer is encouraging workers to ride the bus to work by providing bus passes at the reduced rate of $8.00 per week. If you drive to work, your travel costs per week include $7.25 for gas, $12 for parking, and $10.00 for toll fares. Assuming you work 48 weeks per year, how much will you save if you ride the bus?

Government

5. Employers often state in their employment ads that they are equal opportunity employers. Research the various equal opportunity federal employment laws. Write a brief summary of the kinds of discrimination that are prohibited by these laws.

Check your answers at *marketingessentials.glencoe.com/38/read*

SECTION 38.2

Applying for a Job

OBJECTIVES

- **Name the legal document necessary to begin working**
- **Write a letter of application and complete an application form**
- **Write a résumé and a cover letter**
- **Prepare for an interview**

KEY TERMS

- **standard English**
- **references**
- **cover letter**
- **résumé**

READ and STUDY

BEFORE YOU READ

Predict Ask several of your networking contacts how they have applied for jobs. What experiences do they have in common?

THE MAIN IDEA

You have assembled some job leads and found a few jobs that interest you; your next step is to apply for them. This is done by completing application forms, writing letters of application, and preparing your own résumé.

STUDY ORGANIZER

In a chart like the one below, list ideas about how you would go about applying for a job.

Applying for a Job

1. Get a work permit.
2. ______
3. ______
4. ______

WHILE YOU READ

Analyze Study both the application form and résumé in this text, so that you will be familiar with their form and content.

Getting a Work Permit

A work permit establishes that it is legal for a young worker to do the type of work offered. In some states, work permits must specify the exact duties and hours of work. In these cases, both the employer and the worker fill out sections of an application for the permit. The employer, worker, and the worker's parent or guardian must sign the application before a work permit is issued.

Ask your marketing teacher or counselor whether you will need a work permit and, if so, where you can get one. A designated school official usually issues work permits. Check on this now so you can avoid possible delays when you are ready to go to work.

Applying for a Job

Companies are looking for the most qualified people to fill their jobs. The decision to hire is based on three criteria:

1. How well can you do the job?
2. How willing are you to do the job?
3. How well will you fit in?

The decision about whether to hire you will depend on information you provide in your résumé or application form and during the interview. The way you present the information and yourself are also very important.

Many employers ask job applicants to fill out an application form. Some request additional documents, such as a separate letter of application or a résumé. Throughout this course, you have been building your employment portfolio including examples of some of your best marketing-related efforts. You will want to add a copy of your résumé to your portfolio. Many employers administer one or more employment tests to applicants. Most companies today do background checks for any criminal activity and also do some type of drug testing.

Using Standard English

Everything you write and say to a prospective employer should be in standard English. **Standard English** is the formal style of writing and speaking that you have learned in school. It is standard because it means the same thing to everyone.

Standard English employs correct grammar, spelling, pronunciation, and usage. The repeated use in conversation of the interjections *you know* or *like* is also not advisable. Nonstandard pronunciations are another common lapse. An accent, however, either regional or foreign, is considered acceptable.

Employers will have several opportunities to evaluate your communication skills. Your letter of application or résumé will indicate your writing skills. Finally, when you are interviewed, the employer will evaluate your verbal communication skills and your ability to listen and interact in a businesslike manner.

Filling Out Application Forms

Most application forms are short (from one to four pages) and ask similar questions. More and more companies are asking applicants to complete online forms. Companies usually design their own application forms, so you may find differences among various applications.

The application form provides information about your qualifications so company personnel can decide whether to interview you. The first rule of filling out an application form is to complete the form neatly. Spell all words correctly. Complete the form at the place of employment, use a pen with blue or black ink. Do not use colored inks.

Answer every question that applies to you. Write "NA" for those questions that are not applicable. This shows that you did not overlook the item.

Use your full name, not a nickname, on the form. On most applications, your first name, middle initial, and last name are requested. Provide your complete address, including your zip code.

List a specific job title if asked about your job preference; do not write "anything" as an answer. Employers expect you to know what type of work you can and want to do.

Most application forms include a section on education. Write the names of all the schools you have attended and the dates of attendance. There will also be a section on previous work experience. You may not have had much work experience, but you can include short-term or unpaid jobs. Fill out this section in reverse chronological order—begin with your current or most recent job and end with your first job.

Be prepared to list several references. **References** are people who know your work habits and personal traits well and will recommend you for the job. Make sure you ask permission of your references before listing them on an application form. Try to use professional references, such as your teachers, friends established in business, or former employers. Do not list classmates, relatives, or personal friends. Sign your name using your first name, middle initial, and last name. Your signature should be written, never typed or printed.

Writing Cover Letters

Writing a **cover letter** is like writing a sales pitch about yourself. You must convince an employer that you are the best person to fill a specific job opening. Your cover letter should reflect your understanding of the company and how you may be able to meet its needs. Cover letters can be submitted via mail, e-mail, or fax. They usually accompany a résumé. A cover letter should be personalized for each position and addressed to an individual.

Tell why you are interested in the position and describe your special qualifications for it.

Write a first draft to get down most of the main points. Next, revise your letter until you are pleased with the end result. Ask a teacher, parent or guardian, or friend in business to read and critique your letter. Then put the final touches on it and print out a copy.

Describe how you learned about the job opening in the first sentence.

The second paragraph should contain a description of how your education and experience qualify you for the job. Emphasize facts that make you especially well qualified for the job. Do not repeat the information in the résumé; instead, demonstrate how that experience or education qualifies you for this position. If you have a lot to say about both your education and job experience, use a separate paragraph for each. Mention classes you have taken that are related to the job.

Finally, in your last paragraph, ask for an interview at the employer's convenience. State when you will be available, and provide your telephone number and e-mail address.

Many companies receive dozens of cover letters with résumés every week. Businesses that advertise jobs in the newspaper may receive hundreds of letters. Businesses interview only a small portion of those who write—those who qualify for the position and make an effective written presentation. Your cover letter can give you a big advantage over other applicants. Take the time to develop an effective letter of which you are really proud. Once you write a letter, you can adapt it for other jobs, personalizing the details to each position.

As with any sales pitch, a good first impression counts. Use the spell-check function of your word processing program to eliminate any spelling errors. Before you send your letter, make sure you have read it over for accuracy.

Your letter must not only be neat and clear but also follow the rules outlined in this section. Be sure to include all the elements of a business letter. In particular, use the salutation and a formal closing, as shown.

Print your cover letter with black ink on white or off-white paper; use paper that matches the kind you use for your résumé. Keep in mind that colored paper does not fax well. For electronic submission, be sure to apply the formatting suggestions that are discussed in the next section to your electronic cover letter.

Preparing Résumés

A cover letter and a résumé convey your qualifications in writing and sell your abilities. You can see an example of a traditional printed résumé in Figure 38.1. A **résumé** is a summary of personal information, education, skills, work experience, and activities. A résumé organizes the facts about you that are

MARKET TECH

Tomorrow's Office

Innovations in office technology have been coming at lightning speed since the middle of the 1980s. The office of tomorrow is likely to be as unrecognizable to us as today's office full of computers and fax machines would be to your grandparents.

Technology on the Go

The next wave of new office technologies will simplify complex tasks, interact with their users, and allow people to take their work with them wherever they go. The driving force is increasing productivity.

Wireless Connections

Wireless connections make it possible to set up an electronic office anywhere wireless networks are available.

Turning tabletops into plasma computer screens makes it possible for everyone at a meeting to see a presentation on the table in front of him or her, or for people at a restaurant to order from electronic menus. Microsoft is developing software that allows e-mail or voice messages to arrive at the nearest computer.

THINK LIKE A MARKETER

As a potential employee in a marketing-related business, how could keeping informed about new technologies help you get a job?

@ Online Action!

Go to *marketingessentials.glencoe.com/38/tech* to find an activity on job searches and office technology.

related to the job, which saves the employer time before and during an interview.

Your résumé outlines your qualifications for a particular job. When you send an employer a résumé, include a cover letter. The résumé makes filling out job applications a simpler process because you have already organized all the information. Many people prepare a résumé as the first step in the job application process. Even if you are not hired, many employers will keep your résumé on file for a certain period of time. If they have an opening for which you qualify in the future, they may call you.

Electronic Résumés

If you are applying for a position online, you may be required to submit an electronic résumé. First, compose your electronic résumé using a word processing program.

Electronic Formatting Issues

The format of your electronic résumé should be text only. Save your résumé as a text file; this is the easiest way to transmit and read electronic files. Avoid bold type, italics, and underlining, which do not transmit well and make your résumé difficult to read. Stick to a commonly used traditional font, such as Times New Roman, and keep the font size between 12 and 14 points. Do not use tabs; use the space bar instead.

Using Key Words

Companies that accept résumés electronically will usually search for job qualifications by looking for key words. It is very likely that a computer program, not a person, will first scan your résumé. In the scanning process, the computer searches for key words and phrases, and the résumé is summarized and ranked among other qualified candidates.

Because of this, it is important to use key words to describe what you can do. What are key words? Key words consist primarily of nouns and are usually divided into three categories: job title, industry, and personal traits. If you have done your preliminary research about the company, industry, and job—using methods such as the Internet, publications, or

Figure 38.1 Résumé

• **What Information Should You Include?** Your résumé should show off your education, skills, and experience in the best way possible—and do it in one page.

What are some tips for writing a résumé?

1 Objective Your objective statement should indicate the type of job you want. Change this item if you use the same résumé to apply for a different job.

2 Identification Include your name, address, telephone number, and e-mail address.

Frank Johnson
1235 East Tenth Avenue
Ventura, CA 93003
(805) 555-6264
frankjohnson@yourname.com

Objective:
A marketing analyst position that would complement my academic and work experience.

3 Experience List experience related to the specific job for which you are applying, including volunteer work.

Experience:
9/04-present Assistant Marketing Analyst
Ventura Volvo
6580 Leland Street
Ventura, CA 93003

Used computer to estimate sales by model and make recommendations for inventory. Accessed databases using computer terminal to study inventory in relation to buying estimates. Studied historical applications, including media ads, price and color changes, and impact of season.

9/03-9/04 Marketing Assistant
KVEN Radio
Ventura, CA 93003

Assisted Communications Manager in publishing articles and ads, sales presentations, vendor contracts, and trade shows. Contacted vendors for advertising needs (charts, overheads, banners).

4 Education List schools attended from high school on, the dates of attendance, and diplomas or degrees earned. It is fine to emphasize the courses that are related to the job you are applying for.

Education:
2002-2004 Ventura College. AA in Marketing. Dean's Honor Roll two semesters.

Courses included:
Marketing I and II
Marketing Information Systems
Advertising
Economics I and II
Computer Science

1999-2002 Ventura High School, Graduated in upper 10 percent of class. Served as Vice President of DECA two years.

5 Activities and Awards List school clubs or sports awards, and any recognition you received at work, school, or extracurricular settings.

Personal:
Hobbies include writing computer programs, tennis, and photography.

6 References Include up to three references on a short résumé. Or, indicate that they are available. Always ask people ahead of time if they are willing to be listed as references for you.

References:
Available upon request.

@ Online Action!

Go to *marketingessentials.glencoe.com/38/figure/1* to find a project on résumés.

networking—you will have developed a list of key words or phrases that are mentioned.

It is important to include industry-specific jargon, as many employers will search by industry language. Be sure to spell out all acronyms—mention your membership in the Distributive Education Clubs of America (DECA), not just DECA. You may not be considered for a job for which you are qualified if key words do not appear on your résumé.

Confidentiality is an issue when you post your résumé on the Internet. Remember that once posted on a career Web site, your résumé is a public document that is out of your control. When you give information so that a potential employer can contact you, you have the option of limiting your personal information by including only an e-mail address or post office box. Since most employers prefer to contact applicants by telephone or e-mail, make sure your answering machine message is professional, and check your messages and e-mails daily so you can respond promptly.

Before e-mailing your résumé to employers, e-mail a copy to yourself so that you can review the message.

How to Submit Your Résumé

When you have completed your cover letter and résumé, you can submit them as part of an e-mail. It is best to "cut and paste" the résumé into the body of an e-mail message rather than including it as an attached file. Attached files can be difficult to read if the file is created in a word processing program different from the one used by the employer. Also, some employers may be hesitant to open file attachments because of the risk of computer viruses. Some companies will specify what type of electronic form they prefer; read online submission directions carefully to avoid having your résumé rejected.

Traditional/Print Résumés

In addition to your electronic résumé, prepare a print résumé for positions that require a cover letter and résumé to be mailed or faxed. If you print your own résumé, use black ink on white or off-white paper; ideally, the paper should match the kind you use for your cover letter. Some applicants use local printing companies to print their résumés. If you have your résumé printed in this manner, inquire about prices and ask to look at samples of actual résumés. Shop around—some printing companies offer package deals that include matching paper for your cover letters, as well as envelopes.

Print Formatting Issues

As you can see in Figure 38.1, your printed résumé has formatting that helps organize the material and enables the reader to find the information easily. To review additional styles and formatting options for printed résumés, look at the many résumé sample books that can be found in your library or bookstore. Many online job search sites also feature samples and free advice about preparing résumés and cover letters. Enter "resume samples" on your favorite search engine to be directed to many sites where you can view résumés. Many sites are free, but some do charge.

Some students hire writers to help them develop their résumés. You can find these experts in your local Yellow Pages. Online résumé writing services can also be a resource. Prices, quality, and turnaround time vary; again, shop around.

What happens during an interview is usually what determines an employer's choice of one applicant over another. It is critical to prepare yourself carefully. Your plan should include three steps: preparing for the interview, conducting yourself properly during the interview, and following up the interview.

Preparing for an Interview

The employer's first impression of you will impact his or her hiring decision. Appropriate grooming and dress, body language that shows confidence, and use of standard English all combine to make a good first impression.

Dress and Grooming

Recently, employees in many stores and offices have adopted a dress code known as

•THE INTERVIEW There are a few common sense basics to remember when interviewing for a job: Look at the interviewer, pay attention, do not hesitate to ask questions, and answer questions as precisely as you can.

Why is it a good idea to prepare a few questions before the interview?

corporate casual. This does not mean, however, that you should dress casually for an interview. It is better to make the extra effort to make a good impression by dressing in a more formal way.

Your clothes should be neat, clean, and wrinkle-free for every interview. In some cases, appropriate interview dress depends on the job. In sales, for example, people dress formally and conservatively to make a good impression on customers.

Regardless of its style, your hair should be clean and neat. Remember, the interviewer will be looking to see how well you will fit in, so a conservative hairstyle is usually most appropriate.

Employers will notice whether your hands are clean and your nails are neatly trimmed. Wearing a great deal of jewelry, for both men and women, can be distracting in an interview. Too much makeup on women can also distract the interviewer. Also, it is a good idea not to wear any perfume or cologne to an interview. Strong scents can be overwhelming and distracting, and some people are allergic to them.

Things to Know

Once you call for an interview appointment, write down the date and time and ask for the interviewer's name. Check the spelling and make sure you can pronounce it correctly. Ask the receptionist how to pronounce the name if it is unfamiliar to you.

Before your interview, carefully review your résumé. Be ready to answer any questions about your education, work experience, or other qualifications.

The research you have conducted about a company will once again come in handy in an interview situation. Your knowledge will help you make a better impression because you will be able to talk intelligently about the company's products and operations. It will show that you are interested in the firm.

The following questions are often asked of job applicants during interviews. Write the answers to these questions, then practice answering them. Ask a family member, teacher, or friend to help you by asking the questions and giving you feedback on your reply.

- Why do you want to work for this company?
- Do you want permanent or temporary work?
- Why do you think you can do this job?
- What jobs have you had? Why did you leave?
- What classes do you like best in school?
- In what school activities have you participated?
- What do you want to be doing five years from now?
- Do you prefer working alone or with others?
- What is your main strength?
- What salary do you expect?
- What grades have you received in school?
- How do you feel about working overtime?
- How many days were you absent from school last year?
- Why should I hire you?
- When can you begin work?

Under federal law, employers cannot make employment decisions on the basis of race or ethnicity, gender, religion, marital status, age, country of origin, sexual preference, and physical and/or mental status. Questions should address only the factors that bear on the ability of a job applicant to carry the work required. Therefore, questions about these topics should not be asked. If asked such a question, you have three choices (The latter is usually the best way to handle such questions.):

1. You can answer truthfully if you feel your answer will not harm you.
2. You can mention to the interviewer that the question is inappropriate because

• **ABILITY** Federal law makes it illegal to discriminate in hiring decisions based on disabilities, unless it would cause the employer significant hardship.

According to this ad, what qualities do many disabled people have that would make them good employees?

of laws against discrimination in hiring—but this will likely end any chance of getting the job.

3. You can sidestep the question and base your answer on the requirements of the job and your ability to perform it.

Conducting Yourself Properly During an Interview

Always go alone for a job interview. If someone must accompany you on the day of the interview, ask that person to wait for you outside in a public location. Plan to arrive for your interview five to ten minutes early. Always allow some extra time in case you run into delays. Do not be too early, though. Waiting outside the interviewer's door for half an hour is not comfortable for you or the employer.

Before you meet the interviewer, you may meet a receptionist, administrative assistant, or other employee. Be courteous and polite to anyone you meet; these people might be your future coworkers.

If you have not already completed an application form, you may be asked to do so before or after the interview. Be prepared by bringing a good pen or two with black or blue ink. You may also need to supply your social security number and your references. Bring along two copies of your résumé to the interview, one to leave with your interviewer if he or she wants it and one to help you fill out an application form.

Remain standing until you are asked to sit down. When you do sit down, lean forward slightly toward the interviewer to show your interest. Relax and focus on your purpose: to make the best possible impression.

Place your purse or briefcase on the floor by your chair. Never put anything on the interviewer's desk, even if there is room. This may appear disrespectful or too casual.

It is normal to feel a little nervous at the beginning of an interview. You will relax as the interview progresses. Keep your hands in your lap, and try to keep them still. Never place your hands on the interviewer's desk. Look the interviewer in the eye most of the time and listen to him or her carefully. Be confident and be yourself. The employer has taken the time to interview you because he or she has confidence that you are a qualified candidate.

What to Say in an Interview

Most interviewers begin by asking specific questions. Answer each question honestly. If you do not know the answer to a particular question, say so. The interviewer will probably realize it if you try to fake an answer. Keep your answers short and to the point.

Two particular questions often cause problems for young job applicants. These questions are, "What type of work would you like to do?" and "What wage (or salary) do you expect?" You can answer the first question by giving the name of the specific job you want. The question about expected wage or salary is a little more difficult if you do not have a specific wage or salary in mind or if you are unsure of what the typical pay bracket is for the job. The best answer is something like, "What do you usually pay for this type of work?" Try to turn the question back to the interviewer. If you must answer, offer a pay range.

Wages and benefits are usually discussed toward the end of an interview. If your interviewer does not mention pay, wait until the interview is almost over; then ask how much the job pays. If you know that there will be a second interview before the job is offered, you may wait until then to ask about salary. You also may want to ask about benefits if you are applying for a full-time, permanent job. Benefits may include a paid vacation and insurance coverage.

The interviewer will expect you to ask some questions. Specific questions show the interviewer that you have done your research and are interested in learning more. Job applicants often ask questions like those listed below:

- Why is the position vacant?
- What are the typical responsibilities for this position?
- Would I work individually or with a team?
- With what other areas of the company would I interact on a regular basis?
- What type of training or orientation would I receive?

A MATTER OF ETHICS

Keeping One's Word?

Kendall worked for five years at Genaro's Music, a store selling recorded music and some DVDs. He learned a great deal from Genaro, his boss, and over the years did everything from stocking shelves to keeping track of sales. In exchange for teaching Kendall the business, Genaro asked Kendall to agree that, if he went into business himself, he would not compete directly with Genaro's.

Kendall feels ready to start his own business. He is thinking of focusing on world music, selling CDs and tapes, DVDs of concerts, and also unusual musical instruments from around the world. Genaro's does not have a big world music section, so Kendall does not feel he is competing directly with Genaro. When he tells Genaro about his plans, his boss disagrees and says that starting the business would violate the agreement not to compete.

THINKING ETHICALLY

Is it ethical for Kendall to start the new store? If the store turns out to take business away from Genaro's, what should Kendall do? Explain the reasons for your answers.

Online Action!

Go to *marketingessentials.glencoe.com/38/ethics* to find an activity on ethical conduct in the workplace.

- What are some of the issues the person hired will need to address immediately?
- Please tell me about the department in which I would work.
- What is the typical career path for someone starting in this position? What are the opportunities for advancement?
- Will I have regular evaluations or reviews?
- How are the company and the department structured?
- To whom would I report?
- Will I need to take any tests as part of the interview process?
- What is the dress code?
- What are the hours of work?
- Would I be expected to work on the weekend?
- Does the position require any travel?
- Is overtime common on this job?
- What benefits do you offer?
- When do you expect to be making your hiring decision?

Closing the Interview

At the close of the interview, one of several things can happen. You may be offered the job, or you may be told that you will not be hired. More likely, however, you will be told that a decision will be made later. You may be asked to a second interview with someone else in the company, such as a department head. This usually means you have made a good impression in your first interview, and your chances of being offered the job are good.

If you are interested in the position, let the interviewer know. You can ask for the job or ask for the next interview if another interview is required. Be a good salesperson and say something like, "I am very impressed with what I've seen and heard here today, and I am confident that I could do an excellent job in the position you've described to me. When might you be in a position to make an offer?"

If an offer is extended, accept it only if you are ready. If you are sure that you want it, accept it on the spot. If you want some time to think it over, be courteous and tactful in asking for that time. It is not unreasonable to want to think about this decision before making a commitment. Set a definite date when you can provide an answer (usually no more than 24 to 48 hours).

You will be able to sense when the interview is almost over. Then you should stand, smile, and thank your interviewer for his or

her time and consideration. Shake hands and go. Be sure to thank the receptionist or administrative assistant on your way out.

Following Up After an Interview

A thank-you letter is an appropriate way to follow up most interviews. Simply thank the employer for the time given you and reaffirm your interest in the job.

Include any information that you may have forgotten to mention during the interview that will help qualify you for the position. Your letter may be either handwritten or typed, but it must be neat.

Many employers check references and call your school for a recommendation. This may take several days. Unless you were told not to call, it is all right to telephone the employer five or six days after the interview. Ask to speak with the person who interviewed you. Then give your name and ask if he or she has made a decision on the job. This will let the employer know that you are still interested.

After You Are Hired

After you begin a new job, there are several steps you can take to enhance your career growth and future job searches:

- Thank all those who interviewed you.
- Make a list of your accomplishments and awards you may have received individually or as part of a team or department.
- Keep samples of your work, unless the material is confidential.
- Save copies of reviews and evaluations.
- Take advantage of any opportunity to learn new skills or receive training.
- Continue to build your networking contacts.
- Volunteer for committee responsibilities that are outside the scope of your job. These opportunities help you stand out in the company and may uncover the next step in your career path.
- Be a team player and work to the best of your ability.

38.2 AFTER YOU READ

Reviewing Key Terms and Concepts

1. List the basic information categories you would list in a résumé.
2. What three steps can you take to help you achieve a successful interview?
3. Describe how you can learn about a company in order to prepare for an interview.

Integrating Academic Skills

Math

4. You have been offered a job at $12.00 per hour for 40 hours plus an additional 5 hours per week at time-and-a-half. You will work 50 weeks per year. If the combined withholding of taxes on your pay is 22 percent, what will your total annual net pay?

History

5. Research gender pay equity issues in the United States. Write a one-page report on the history of this issue and on current developments in this area.

Check your answers at *marketingessentials.glencoe.com/38/read*

CAREERS IN MARKETING

KAREN BATTOE
PRESIDENT AND FOUNDER PERSONAL SUCCESS SYSTEMS, INC.

What do you do at work?
I am a certified professional coach and president and founder of Personal Success Systems, Inc., a corporate and individual coaching and consulting firm in Orlando, Florida. I work with managers and executives who are stuck, and want to learn a more creative approach to being successful in the job market. I coach clients through the exploration and self-discovery process, partner with them on all aspects of the job search, and continue to coach them through their first 60 days on the job.

What skills are most important to you?
Listening, observation, objectivity, the ability to ask thought-provoking questions, the ability to think outside of the box, creativity, and innovation. I recommend that anyone who wants to be a coach should experience working with a coach. Enroll in one of the coaching schools. Get your certifications. Once you learn the coaching process, then you can choose your specialty. If you want to specialize in career management, make sure you choose a coach who specializes in that area.

What is your key to success?
Over 20 years in the employment field. Before founding Personal Success Systems, Inc., I was an executive for several multinational corporations. I also am very intuitive when it comes to people, and have spent years building my credibility.

Aptitudes, Abilities, and Skills

Outgoing personality, ability to think creatively and ask unusual questions, strong interpersonal skills

Education and Training

Degrees in psychology, business, marketing, or management are useful.

Career Path

Coaching schools provide access to certifications necessary for this career; once certified, students can find entry-level work within the human resources department at large corporations, or can attempt to freelance.

THINKING CRITICALLY

Why is creativity so important in this career?

@ Online Action!

Go to *marketingessentials.glencoe.com/38/careers* to find a career-related activity.

CHAPTER 38 REVIEW

FOCUS on KEY POINTS

SECTION 38.1

- You can find job leads through many sources, and you should make use of most of them. Among the best are networking contacts, newspaper and magazine ads, employment and temporary staffing agencies, and the Internet.

SECTION 38.2

- You may apply for a job by filling out an application form or by submitting a résumé with a cover letter.
- The decision to hire is almost always made during or following the interview. Therefore, it is very important to be well prepared.
- For each job interview, conduct yourself properly during the interview, and follow up after each interview.

REVIEW VOCABULARY

Use the following vocabulary terms in a paragraph describing an effective job search.

1. job lead (p. 806)
2. networking (p. 807)
3. public employment agencies (p. 808)
4. private employment agencies (p. 808)
5. staffing/temporary agencies (p. 808)
6. standard English (p. 812)
7. references (p. 813)
8. cover letter (p. 813)
9. résumé (p. 813)

REVIEW FACTS and IDEAS

10. What will most likely be your best source of job leads? (38.1)
11. Name two methods of contacting job leads and describe one advantage of each method. (38.1)
12. What is one technique of expanding your list of job leads? (38.1)
13. What is a work permit, and what purpose does it serve? (38.2)
14. What information does a résumé contain? (38.2)
15. What should you do to make a good first impression at a job interview? (38.2)
16. What are some rules of conduct to follow during the interview? (38.2)
17. What are appropriate ways to follow up after an interview? (38.2)

BUILD SKILLS

18. Workplace Skills

Human Relations You are scheduled for a job interview. You arrive at the receptionist's desk about ten minutes before the interview. The receptionist checks her schedule and says she does not have your name on her list for today. A further check shows that she has you scheduled for tomorrow at the same time. You are certain that you wrote the appointment correctly on your calendar. What should you say?

19. Technology Applications

Preparing for an Interview Conduct a search on the Internet to learn more about job interviewing. Look for examples of tough questions that an interviewer might ask. Using a word processing program, list three of these questions. Write the answer you would give for each one if you were asked such a question during an interview.

20. Math Practice

Calculate a Pay Rate You work full time for a local retailer as a floor manager. For three days a week, you work a standard nine-to-five shift. For two days a week, you work a split shift. Your pay is $14.00 per hour. However, on the two days you work a split shift, you receive a 12 percent pay differential, which makes your pay $15.68 per hour for those two 8-hour days. What is your average rate of pay for the 40-hour week?

DEVELOP CRITICAL THINKING

21. Interview Question

Give an example of an interview question that might be difficult to answer, and explain how it could be handled.

22. To Call or Not to Call?

Suppose you spot an ad in an online listing. You think this is the perfect job for you, so you e-mail your résumé and cover letter. The ad warns, "no phone calls, please." However, you have researched the company thoroughly and you are convinced you match the job description. Should you call the company's Human Resources department? Why or why not? What else could you do to stand out among the applicants?

APPLY CONCEPTS

23. Finding Jobs in Marketing

Locate an ad for a marketing job that interests you in the employment section of a newspaper. Make a copy of this ad. Then do some research in your library or on the Internet to learn more about cover letters. Read several examples of cover letters. Also, research the company that placed the ad and the type of position that is advertised. Use this information to target your writing.

Activity Using a word processing program, write your own cover letter in response to the newspaper ad you selected. Display your ad and letter in your classroom.

24. Creating a Networking System

Use a database or spread sheet program to create a file listing all the friends, family members, professionals, and former employers who might be able to help you find work. Your networking file should contain the following categories: names and titles, company associations, addresses, phone numbers, fax numbers, and e-mail addresses. You should also include a category for noting dates of contact and brief summaries of what was discussed.

Activity Use the information you have gathered to list the types of jobs for which you could apply and the areas of industry that are covered by your networking contacts.

NET SAVVY

25. Internet Job Search

Find job search Web sites and narrow your search to focus on advertising. Select several areas in the United States and review the jobs that are offered. Compare and contrast the job offerings.

THE 

CONNECTION

Role Play: Finding a Job

Situation You are to assume the role of high school junior. You are enrolled in a marketing class and want to find a part-time job that will enhance your experience in your marketing class. Part of your class work is an assignment to prepare an outline of the process for finding and then applying for a job that you will find interesting and do a good job for your employer.

Activity You are to prepare your job-seeking assignment and present it to your marketing teacher (judge).

Evaluation You will be evaluated on how well you meet the following performance indicators:

- Utilize job-search strategies
- Prepare a résumé
- Complete a job application
- Interview for a job
- Write a follow-up letter after job interviews

Online Action!

For more information and DECA Prep practice, go to *marketingessentials.glencoe .com/38/DECA*

MARKETING INTERNSHIP

A SIMULATED DECA MANAGEMENT TEAM DECISION MAKING EVENT

Design an Employment Test

BASIC BACKGROUND

On the hit reality show *The Apprentice,* contestants competed for a six-figure salary in a job with Donald Trump's organization. They were divided into teams and given tasks to perform to prove their skills. Some of the tasks included selling lemonade in New York City, designing an ad campaign for a jet rental company, buying and selling items from a flea market, and managing a restaurant.

From Reality Show to Real Life This show gave your firm the idea to give its clients training programs or interview tools that use real-life situations.

YOUR OBJECTIVE

Your objective is to develop a real-life training program or a real-life employment test for a specific position within a company. The company you select may be a manufacturer or retailer of apparel, food, toys, sports equipment, a fast-food or full-service restaurant chain, a bank, a hotel chain, an e-commerce company, a professional sports team, an amusement park, or any of the clients identified in Units 1–11. Your training program or employment test must be realistic, evaluate the skills required for that position, and be highly customized for that specific client.

ASSIGNMENT AND STRATEGY

- **Get the background** Research the job position for which you will develop the training program or employment test. What education, experience, skills, and aptitudes are required for this position?

  Learn as much as you can about the position's specific tasks, as well as the interpersonal and communication skills that are useful in the position. To get the inside scoop, you might interview someone or spend a few hours shadowing a person who holds that position.

- **Design the program** Prepare the actual scenario(s) that will be part of the training program or employment testing. Explain where each scenario will take place, what the task is, and how the trainee or applicant will be evaluated. If the program is for job training, provide follow-up activities to help new hires learn how to improve their skills.

- **What your project should include** In addition to writing the proposal to pitch the client, refer to Unit 5 to review how to make an effective sales presentation. Such preparation steps might include an analysis of competing companies that offer similar services. You should also consider preparing a feature-benefit chart. Think about what your potential customers' objectives and motives might be and what type of decision-making process they are likely to follow. Prepare sample materials for training or testing, and use presentation software for your oral presentation. Add any additional materials you will need to reach your goal, which is selling your proposal to the client.

YOUR REPORT

Use a word processing program and presentation software to prepare a double-spaced report and an oral presentation for the client. See a suggested outline and key evaluation points at *marketingessentials.glencoe.com/internship*

BUILD YOUR PORTFOLIO

Option 1 Internship Report
Once you have completed your Marketing Internship project and presentation, include your written report and a few printouts of key slides from your oral presentation in your Marketing Portfolio.

Option 2 Preparing for a Job Interview Select and research a job for which to apply. Prepare a cover letter, résumé, references, portfolio of your work, and a sample thank-you note you would send to the person who interviewed you. Prepare responses to ten common interview questions. Find another person to pretend to interview you for the job and videotape the session. Use the videotape to evaluate your performance. See a suggested outline and key evaluation points at *marketingessentials.glencoe.com/portfolio*

Online Action!

Go to *marketingessentials.glencoe.com/Unit/12/DECA* to review employment concepts that relate to DECA events.

GLOSSARY

A

accounting The discipline that keeps track of a company's financial situation.

Ad Council A nonprofit organization that helps produce public service advertising campaigns for government agencies and other qualified sponsors.

ad layout A sketch that shows the general arrangement and appearance of a finished ad.

adaptation Changing an existing product and/or promotion to better suit the characteristics of a targeted country or region.

adjacent colors Colors that are located next to each other on the color wheel and share the same undertones; also known as analogous colors.

advertising A form of nonpersonal promotion in which companies pay to promote ideas, goods, or services in a variety of media outlets.

advertising agencies Independent businesses that specialize in developing ad campaigns and crafting the ads for clients.

advertising campaign A group of advertisements, commercials, and related promotional materials and activities that are designed as a part of a coordinated advertising plan to meet the specific goals of a company.

advertising proof A representation of an ad that shows exactly how it will appear in print.

agents Intermediaries who bring buyers and sellers together and do not own the goods they sell.

agreement A specific commitment that each member makes to the group.

allowance A partial return of the sale price for merchandise that the customer has kept.

aptitude An ability or natural talent; the potential to learn a certain skill.

Articles of Incorporation A document filed with a state department of commerce that identifies the name and address of a new corporation, its purpose, the names of the initial directors, and the amount of stock that will be issued to each director.

aseptic packaging A food storage process that keeps foods fresh without refrigeration for up to six months.

assertiveness Standing up for what you believe.

asset Anything of monetary value that a person owns, such as cash, checking and savings accounts, real estate, or stocks.

attitude research A type of research designed to obtain information on how people feel about certain products, services, companies, or ideas; also known as opinion research.

B

balance of trade The difference in value between a nation's exports and its imports.

balance sheet A summary of a business's assets, liabilities, and owner's equity.

bar graph A drawing made up of parallel bars whose lengths are proportional to the qualities being measured.

barriers Obstacles that interfere with the understanding of a message.

basic stock list A list used for those staple items that should always be in stock.

Better Business Bureau (BBB) One of the oldest nonprofit organizations that establishes self-regulation among businesses.

blind check method The receiver of a delivery writes the description of the merchandise, counts the quantities received, and lists them on a blank form or dummy invoice.

blisterpack Packaging with preformed plastic molds surrounding individual items arranged on a cardboard backing.

bonded warehouses Public or private warehouses that store products requiring the payment of a federal tax.

boomerang method A selling method that converts a customer's objection into a selling point.

brand A name, term, design, symbol, or combination of these elements that identifies a business, product, or service and distinguishes it from its competitors.

brand extension A branding strategy that uses an existing brand name to promote a new or improved product in a company's product line.

brand label Label giving the brand name, trademark, or logo.

brand licensing A legal authorization by a trademarked brand owner to allow another company (the licensee) to use its brand, brand mark, or trade character for a fee.

brand mark A unique symbol, coloring, lettering, or other design elements.

brand name A word, group of words, letters, or numbers that represent a product or service; also known as a product brand.

break-even point The point at which sales revenue equals the costs and expenses of making and distributing a product.

brick-and-mortar retailers Traditional retailers that sell goods to customers from physical stores, rather than over the Internet.

broadcast media Radio and television.

budget accounts Accounts that allow the payment of a purchased item over a certain time period without a finance charge.

bundle pricing A pricing technique in which a company offers several complementary products in a package that is sold at a single price.

business cycle Recurring changes in economic activity, such as the expansion and contraction of an economy.

business philosophy Beliefs about how a business should be run that demonstrate an understanding of the business's role in the marketplace.

business plan A proposal that outlines a strategy to turn a business idea into a reality.

business risk The possibility of financial loss.

business-to-business selling Sales that take place in a manufacturer's or wholesaler's show room (inside sales) or in a customer's place of business (outside sales).

buying behavior The process individuals use to decide what they will buy, where they will buy it, and from whom they will buy it.

buying signals The things customers do or say to indicate a readiness to buy.

C

career outlook Valuable information on the number and types of jobs available in any field.

carload The minimum number of pounds of freight needed to fill a boxcar.

cash flow statement A monthly plan that tracks when a person anticipates that cash will come into their business and when they expect to pay out cash.

cash on delivery (COD) sale A transaction that occurs when a customer pays for merchandise at the time of delivery.

category management A process that involves managing product categories as individual business units.

cause packaging Packaging that is used by companies to promote social and political causes.

centralized buying Buying process for all branches in a chain store operation, usually done in a central location, such as company headquarters.

channel of distribution The path a product takes from its producer or manufacturer to the final user.

channels The avenues through which messages are delivered.

circle graph A pie-shaped geometric representation of the relative sizes of the parts of a whole; also called a pie chart.

clip art Images, stock drawings, and photographs used in print advertisements.

closing the sale The process of obtaining a positive agreement from the customer to buy.

co-branding A combination of one or more brands in the manufacture of a product or in the delivery of a service.

cold canvassing The process of locating as many potential customers as possible without checking out leads beforehand.

collateral Something of value that a person pledges as payment for a loan in case of default.

color wheel A circular illustration of the relationships between colors.

command economy An economic system in which the government decides what, when, and how much will be produced and distributed.

common carriers Trucking companies that provide transportation services to any business in their operating area for a fee.

communication The process of exchanging messages between a sender and a receiver.

communications programs Software applications that enable users to electronically communicate through computers with people around the world.

competition The struggle between companies to attract new customers, keep existing ones, and take away customers from other companies.

complementary colors Colors that are opposites on the color wheel and are used to create high contrast.

consensus A decision on which all members of a team agree.

consignment buying Paying for goods only after the final customer purchases them.

consultative selling Sales that provide solutions to customers' problems by finding products that meet their needs.

consumer market Consumers who purchase goods and services for personal use.

consumer price index (CPI) Measurement of the change in price over a period of time of approximately 400 retail goods and services used by the average urban household.

Consumer Product Safety Commission (CPSC) Federal agency responsible for overseeing the safety of all products except food, drugs, cosmetics, medical devices, tobacco products, firearms and ammunition, motor vehicles, pesticides, aircraft, boats, and fixed site amusement rides.

consumer promotions Sales strategies that encourage customers and prospects to buy a product or service.

contract carriers For-hire trucking companies that provide equipment and drivers for specific routes.

contract manufacturing The process of hiring a foreign manufacturer to make products according to certain specifications.

controlling The process of setting standards and evaluating performance.

cooperative advertising A cost-sharing arrangement whereby both a supplier and a local advertiser pay for advertising.

copy The selling message of a written advertisement.

copyright The exclusive right to reproduce or sell a work authored by an individual, such as writings, music, and artwork.

corporation A legal entity created by either a state or a federal statute authorizing individuals to operate an enterprise.

cost-plus pricing All costs and expenses are calculated, and then the desired profit is added to arrive at a price.

coupons Certificates that entitle customers to discounts on goods and services.

cover letter A letter written by an applicant to an employer describing why that applicant is the best person to fill a specific job opening.

credit The opportunity for businesses or individuals to obtain products or money in exchange for a promise to pay later.

credit union A cooperative association formed by labor unions or groups of employees for the benefit of its members.

cross-training A process that prepares a team member to do many different activities.

customer benefits The advantages or personal satisfaction a customer will get from a good or service.

customer profile A list of information about a target market, such as age, income level, ethnicity, occupation, attitudes, lifestyle, and geographic residence.

customer relationship management (CRM) Identifying and understanding customers to form a strong, long-lasting relationship.

customization The process of creating products or promotions for certain countries or regions.

cycle counts A small portion of the inventory is physically counted each day by stockkeeping units so that the entire inventory is accounted for on a regular basis.

D

data analysis The process of compiling, analyzing, and interpreting the results of primary and secondary data collection.

database A collection of related information about a specific topic.

database marketing A process of designing, creating, and managing customer lists that contain information about an individual's characteristics and transactions with a business; also known as customer relationship management (CRM).

database programs Software applications that store and organize information.

debt capital Borrowed funds that must be repaid.

decentralized buying Local chain store managers or their designated buyers who are authorized to make special purchases for their individual stores.

decimal number A fraction or mixed number whose denominator is a multiple of 10.

demand Consumer willingness and ability to buy products.

demand elasticity The degree to which demand for a product is affected by its price.

demographics Statistics that describe a population in terms of personal characteristics such as age, gender, income, marital status, ethnicity, education, and occupation.

denominator The bottom number in a fraction; it represents how many parts make up a whole.

depression A period of prolonged recession.

derived demand The demand for industrial goods based on the demand for consumer goods and services.

descriptive label A label that gives information about the product's use, construction, care, performance, and other features.

desktop publishing programs A software application that is part word processor and part graphics application, and enables users to edit and manipulate both text and graphics in one document.

digit The ten basic symbols that compose the numbering system: 0, 1, 2, 3, 4, 5, 6, 7, 8, and 9.

direct check method The merchandise is checked directly against the actual invoice or purchase order.

direct close A closing method in which a salesperson asks for the sale.

direct distribution Sales of goods or services directly to the customer, with no intermediaries.

direct marketing A type of advertising directed to a targeted group of prospects and customers rather than to a mass audience.

disclaimer A statement that contains exceptions to and exclusions from a warranty.

discretionary income The money left over from a consumer's income after paying for basic living necessities such as food, shelter, and clothing.

display The visual and artistic aspects of presenting a product to a target group of customers.

disposable income The money left over after taxes are taken out of a consumer's income.

distractions Things that compete with the message for the listener's attention.

distribution center A warehouse designed to speed delivery of goods and to minimize storage costs.

Doing Business As (DBA) registration The registration by which a county government officially recognizes that a new proprietorship or partnership exists.

dollar control The planning and monitoring of the total inventory investment that a business makes during a stated period of time.

domestic business A business that sells its products only in its own country.

drop shippers Businesses that own the goods they sell but do not physically handle the products.

E

economic risks Risks that result from changes in overall business conditions.

economy The organized way a nation provides for the needs and wants of its people.

e-marketplace The online shopping location where products are sold to customers and industrial buyers through the use of the Internet.

embargo A total ban on specific goods coming into and leaving a country.

emotional barriers Biases against the sender's opinions that prevent a listener from understanding.

emotional motive A feeling experienced by a customer through association with a product.

empathy An understanding of a person's situation or frame of mind.

employee discounts Discounts offered by employers to their workers.

empowerment Encouragement of team members to contribute and take responsibility for the management process.

endless chain method The process of asking previous customers for names of potential customers.

enterprise resource planning (ERP) Sophisticated software that integrates all parts of a company's business management.

entrepreneurs People who create, launch, organize, and manage a new business and take the risk of business ownership.

entrepreneurship The process of starting and operating your own business.

enumeration Listing items in order.

Environmental Protection Agency (EPA) Federal agency that protects human health and our environment.

environmental scan An analysis of outside influences that may have an impact on an organization.

Equal Employment Opportunity Commission (EEOC) Federal agency responsible for the fair and equitable treatment of employees with regard to hiring, firing, and promotions.

equity The concept of equal rights and opportunities for everyone.

equity capital The process of raising money from within your company or by selling part of the interest in the business.

e-tailing Retailers selling products over the Internet to the customer; also known as online retailing.

ethics Basic values and moral principles that guide the behavior of individuals and groups.

European Union (EU) European trading bloc.

everyday low prices (EDLP) Consistently low prices with no intention of raising them or offering discounts in the future.

exclusive distribution Sales involving protected territories for distribution of a product in a given geographic area.

excuses Reasons for not buying or not seeing the salesperson.

executive summary A brief overview of an entire marketing plan.

exempt carriers Trucking companies that are free from direct regulation of rates and operating procedures.

exit interview An interview arranged by the human resources department when an employee leaves a company.

expansion A time when the economy is flourishing; also called prosperity.

experimental method A research technique in which a researcher observes the results of changing one or more marketing variables while keeping certain other variables constant under controlled conditions.

exports Goods and services sold to other countries.

express warranty A warranty that is explicitly stated, in writing or verbally, to encourage a customer to make a purchase.

extended coverage An endorsement that provides protection against types of loss that may not be covered under a basic property insurance policy.

extensive decision making The process used when there has been little or no previous experience with an item.

F

factors of production Economic term for the four categories of resources: land, labor, capital, and entrepreneurship.

feature-benefit selling Sales that match the characteristics of a product to a customer's needs and wants.

Federal Trade Commission (FTC) Federal agency responsible for enforcing the principles of a free enterprise system and protecting consumers from unfair or deceptive business practices.
feedback A receiver's response to a message.
fidelity bonds A type of insurance that protects a business from employee dishonesty.
finance A business function that involves money management.
firewall Hardware or software that protects a computer from attacks by hackers.
fixtures The principal installations in a store; permanent or movable store furnishings that hold and display merchandise.
flexibility Behavior that allows you to adapt to changing circumstances.
flexible-price policy A price policy that lets customers bargain for merchandise.
flextime A program that allows workers to choose their work hours.
focal point An area in a display that attracts attention first, above all else.
Food and Drug Administration (FDA) Federal agency that regulates labeling and safety of food, drugs, and cosmetics sold in the United States.
forced-choice questions Questions that ask respondents to choose answers from possibilities given on a questionnaire.
foreign corporation A company that is incorporated under the laws of a state that differs from the one in which it does business.
foreign direct investment (FDI) Investments in factories, offices, and other facilities in another country that are used for a business's operations.
formal balance When a large item is placed on one side of a display, a similarly large item should be placed on the other side.
for-profit business A business that seeks to make a profit from its operations.
fractions Numbers used to describe or compare parts of a whole.
franchise A legal agreement to sell a parent company's product or services in a designated geographic area.
free enterprise system A system that encourages individuals to start and operate their own businesses in a competitive market, without government involvement.
free trade Commercial exchange between nations that is conducted on free market principles, without tariffs, import quotas, or other restrictive regulations.
free-on-board (FOB) The price for goods includes delivery at the seller's expense to a specified point and no further.
freight forwarders Private companies that combine less than carload or truckload shipments from several businesses and deliver them to their destinations.
full warranty A warranty that guarantees that if a product is found to be defective within the warranty period, it will be repaired or replaced at no cost to the purchaser.

G

general partnership A way to organize a business in which each partner shares in the profits and losses.
generalization A statement that is accepted as true by most people.
generic brands Products that do not carry a company identity.
geographical pricing A pricing technique that makes price adjustments because of the location of the customer for delivery of products.
geographics Segmentation of the market based on where people live.
global business A business that sells its products to more than one country.
globalization The process of selling the same product and using the same promotion methods in all countries.
goods Tangible items of monetary value that satisfy needs and wants.
grade label A label that states the quality of the product.
graphics and design programs Software applications for creating and modifying images.
green marketing Producing and promoting environmentally safe products.
greeting approach A way to approach a customer that focuses on welcoming the customer to the store.
gross domestic product (GDP) The output of goods and services produced by labor and property located within a nation.
gross national product (GNP) The total dollar value of goods and services produced by a nation.
gross profit The difference between sales revenue and the cost of goods sold.
gross sales The total of all sales for a given period of time.

H

headline The phrase or sentence that captures the readers' attention, arouses their interest, and entices them to read the rest of the ad.
home page The main page of a Web site that clearly and quickly lets people know what site they are visiting.
horizontal organization A structure where top management shares decision making with self-managing teams of workers who

set their own goals and make their own decisions.

human risks Risks that are triggered by errors or omissions as well as the unpredictability of customers or of working environments.

hypertext markup language (HTML) A detailed code used to write Web pages.

hypertext transfer protocol (HTTP) The global computer protocol used to identify and locate Web pages on the Internet.

I

illustration The photograph, drawing, or other graphic elements used in an advertisement.

implied warranty A warranty that takes effect automatically by state law whenever a purchase is made.

imports Goods and services purchased from other countries.

incentives Products earned or given away through contests, sweepstakes, and rebates.

income statement A summary of income and expenses during a specific period of time; also known as profit and loss statement.

indirect distribution Sales of goods or services to the customer through one or more intermediaries.

Industrial market Businesses that buy products to use in their operations; also called the business-to-business market (this can be abbreviated as B-to-B or B2B).

industry A group of establishments primarily engaged in producing or handling the same product or group of products or in rendering the same services.

inflation A period of rising prices.

informal balance The placement of several small items with one large item within a display.

infrastructure The physical development of a country, including its roads, ports, sanitation facilities, and utilities.

initiative The process of taking action and doing what needs to be done without being asked.

installment accounts Accounts that allow for payment over a period of time; also known as time payment accounts.

institutional advertising The process used to try to create a favorable image for a company and foster goodwill in the marketplace.

institutional promotion A promotion method used to create a favorable image for a business, help it advocate for change, or take a stand on trade or community issues.

insurance policy A contract between a business and an insurance company to cover a specific business risk.

integrated distribution A distribution system in which manufacturers act as wholesaler and retailer for their own products.

intensive distribution Sales involving the use of all suitable outlets to sell a product.

interest The money paid for the use of money borrowed or invested.

intermediaries Businesses involved in sales transactions that move products from the manufacturer to the final user; also known as middlemen.

Internet A worldwide network of computer networks, allowing a free flow of information.

Internet service providers (ISPs) Companies that provide Internet access for businesses, organizations, and individuals.

internship An opportunity that offers students direct work experience and exposure to various aspects of a career, either with or without pay.

inventory All the goods stored by a business before they are sold.

inventory management The process of buying and storing materials and products while controlling costs for ordering, shipping, handling, and storage.

inventory turnover The number of times the average inventory has been sold and replaced in a given period of time.

invoice An itemized list of goods that includes prices, terms of sales, total, taxes and fees, and amount due.

J

jargon Specialized vocabulary used by members of a particular group.

job descriptions Written statements listing the requirements of a particular job and the skills needed to fulfill those requirements.

job lead Information about a job opening.

joint venture A business enterprise that different companies set up together; often, the venture involves a domestic company and a foreign company.

just-in-time (JIT) inventory system An inventory system that controls the flow of parts and material into assembly and manufacturing plants.

K

kiosks Interactive point-of-purchase displays that are typically four feet high, have pedestal-mounted high-tech screens, and take up only a few square feet of floor space.

L

label An information tag, wrapper, seal, or imprinted message that is attached to a product or its package.

law of diminishing marginal utility An economic law stating that consumers will buy only so much of a given product, even though the price is low.

layaway A sales method that keeps merchandise in storage until the customer finishes paying for it.

layman's terms Words the average customer can understand.

liability A debt that a person owes to others, such as credit card debt, school loans, car payments, or taxes.

licensing The process of letting another company (licensee) use a trademark, patent, special formula, company name, or some other intellectual property for a fee or royalty.

lifestyle The kind of life a person lives.

limited decision making The process used when a person buys goods and services that he or she has purchased before but not regularly.

limited liability The personal assets of the owners cannot be taken if the company does not meet its financial obligations.

limited liability company (LLC) A relatively new form of business organization that is a hybrid of a partnership and corporation.

limited partnership A form of business organization in which each limited partner is liable for any debts only up to the amount of his or her investment in the company. The business's general partner is liable for all debts.

limited warranty A warranty that excludes certain parts of the product from coverage or requires the customer to bear some of the expense for repairs resulting from defects.

line graph A line that joins points representing changes in a variable quantity, usually over a period of time.

loss leader An item priced at or below cost to draw customers into a store.

M

maintained markup The difference between an item's final sale price and its cost.

management The business function of planning, organizing, and controlling all available resources to achieve company goals.

market People who share similar needs and wants and are capable of buying products.

market economy An economic system in which individuals and companies decide what will be produced, when, and how it will be distributed.

market intelligence Information about the size and location of a market, the competition, and the segmentation within the market for a particular product or service.

market segmentation The process of analyzing and classifying customers in a given market to create smaller, more precise target markets.

market share A company's percentage of total sales volume generated by all competition in a given market.

marketing The process of planning, pricing, promoting, selling, and distributing products to satisfy customers' needs and wants.

marketing concept Businesses should satisfy customers' needs and wants while making a profit.

marketing information system A set of procedures and methods that regularly generates, stores, analyzes, and distributes information for use in making marketing and other business decisions.

marketing mix The four basic marketing strategies, called the four Ps: product, place, price, and promotion.

marketing plan A formal written document communicating the goals, objectives, and strategies of a company.

marketing research The process and methods used to gather information, analyze it, and report findings related to marketing goods and services.

marketing strategy Identification of target markets and determination of marketing mix choices that focus on those markets.

markup pricing The process where resellers add a dollar amount (markup) to its cost to arrive at a price.

marquee An architectural canopy that extends over a store's entrance.

mass marketing Use of a single marketing plan to reach all customers.

media The avenues through which messages are delivered; also known as channels.

media planning The process of selecting the advertising media and deciding the time or space in which the ads should appear to accomplish a marketing objective.

media research A type of research focusing on the issues of media effectiveness, selection, frequency, and ratings; also known as advertising research.

memorandum buying A buying process in which the supplier agrees to take back any unsold goods by a certain pre-established date.

merchandise approach A way to approach a customer that focuses on making a comment or asking questions about a product in which the customer shows interest.

middle management Managers who implement the decisions of top management.

mini-nationals Midsize or smaller companies that have operations in multiple countries.

mission statement A brief paragraph or two that describes the ultimate goals of a company.

mixed brand A combination of manufacturer, private distributor, and generic brands as a strategy to sell products.

mixed bundling The practice of packaging different products and services together.

mixed number A whole number and a fraction written together.

model stock list An inventory monitoring plan used for merchandise that quickly goes out of fashion.

monopoly Exclusive control over a product or the means of producing it.

multinationals Large corporations that have operations in multiple countries.

N

national brands Brands that are owned and initiated by national manufacturers or service companies; also known as producer brands.

natural risks Risks that result from natural occurrences, such as an earthquake or bad weather.

negotiation The process of working with different parties to find a resolution to their conflict.

net income The amount left after the total expenses are subtracted from gross profit.

net sales The amount left after gross sales have been adjusted for returns and allowances.

net worth The difference between the assets of a business and its liabilities.

networking The art of building business contacts and alliances.

never-out list An inventory monitoring plan used for best-selling products that make up a large percentage of sales volume.

news release An announcement that is sent by a business or organization to media outlets.

nonprice competition Competition based on factors that are not related to price, such as product quality, service and financing, business location, and reputation.

nonprofit organization An organization that can function like a business but uses the money it makes to fund the cause identified in its charter.

nonverbal communication Expressing oneself without the use of words.

North American Free Trade Agreement (NAFTA) An international trade agreement among the United States, Canada, and Mexico.

numerator The top number in a fraction; it represents the number of parts being considered.

O

objection analysis sheet A document that lists common objections and possible responses to them.

objections Concerns, hesitations, doubts, or other honest reasons a customer has for not making a purchase.

observation method A research technique in which the actions of people are watched and recorded either by cameras or by observers.

occupational area A category of jobs that involve similar interests and skills.

Occupational Information Network (O*NET) An online database that includes information on skills, abilities, knowledge, work activities, and interests associated with occupations.

Occupational Outlook Handbook (OOH) A publication that describes what workers do on the job, working conditions, the training and education needed, earnings, and expected job prospects in a wide range of occupations.

Occupational Safety and Health Administration (OSHA) Federal agency that provides guidelines for workplace safety and enforces those regulations.

on-approval sale An agreement permitting a customer to take merchandise (usually clothing) home for further consideration.

one-price policy All customers are charged the same price for the goods and services offered for sale.

online advertising A form of advertising that uses either e-mail or the World Wide Web.

open-ended questions Questions that require respondents to construct their own answers.

opening cash fund A limited amount of money for the cash register provided by a manager or other designated person at the beginning of each business day.

open-to-buy (OTB) The amount of money left for buying goods after all purchases received and on order have been considered.

organization chart A diagram of a company's departments and jobs with lines of authority clearly shown.

organizational buyers Buyers who purchase goods for business purposes, usually in much greater quantities than the average consumer buys.

organizing Establishment of a time frame in which to achieve a goal, assigning employees to the project, and determining a method for approaching the work.

P

package The physical container or wrapping for a product.
paraphrase To restate something in a different way.
partnership A legal agreement between two or more people to be jointly responsible for the success or failure of a business.
patent A government-issued exclusive right to make, use, or sell an invention for up to 20 years.
penetration pricing A pricing policy that sets the initial price for a new product very low.
percentage A number expressed in parts per 100.
performance bonds A type of insurance that provides financial protection for losses that might occur when a construction project is not finished due to the contractor's impaired financial condition; also known as surety bonds.
performance standard An expectation of performance that reflects a company's goals and marketing plan objectives.
perpetual inventory system An inventory system that tracks the number of items in inventory on a constant basis.
personal financial statement A summary of a person's current personal financial condition.
personal selling Any form of direct contact between a salesperson and a customer.
persuade The process used to convince someone to change a perception in order to get them to do what you want.
physical distribution Activities to deliver the right amount of product to the right place at the right time.
physical inventory system An inventory system where every so often, stock is visually inspected or actually counted to determine the quantity on hand.
pie chart A pie-shaped geometric representation of the relative sizes of the parts of a whole; also called a circle graph.
planning The process of setting goals and determining how to reach them.
planning goal The small steps you take to get from where you are now to where you want to be.
planogram A computer-developed diagram that shows retailers how and where products within a category should be displayed on a shelf at individual stores.
point-of-purchase displays (POPs) A sales promotion device; manufactured units with bold graphics and signage that hold, display, or dispense products.
point-of-sale research A form of research that combines natural observation with personal interviews to get people to explain buying behavior.
point-of-sale system The process of combining a cash register with a computer, making it possible to capture information about the transaction at the time of sale, then applying it to different functions.
pre-approach The preparation for the face-to-face encounter with potential customers.
premiums Low-cost items given to consumers at a discount or for free.
presentation software Software application that produces slide shows or multimedia presentations.
prestige pricing A pricing technique that sets higher-than-average prices to suggest status and high quality to the consumer.
price The value (in money or its equivalent) placed on a product.
price bundling Two or more similar products are placed on sale for one package price.
price competition The sale price of a product; the assumption is that consumers will buy the product with the lowest price.
price discrimination Charging different prices to similar customers in similar situations.
price fixing When competitors agree on certain price ranges within which they can set their own prices.
price gouging Pricing products unreasonably high when there is a high demand resulting from a monopoly or a natural disaster.
price lining A special pricing technique that sets a limited number of prices for specific groups or lines of merchandise.
primary data Data obtained for the first time and used specifically for the particular problem or issue under study.
principal Money that is borrowed, sometimes to start a business.
print media Newspapers, magazines, direct mail, signs, and billboards used in advertising.
private carriers Trucking companies that transport goods for an individual business.
private distributor brands Brands that are developed and owned by wholesalers and retailers; also known as private brands, store brands, dealer brands, or private labels.
private employment agencies Employment agencies that are not supported by taxes and must earn a profit to stay in business.
private sector Businesses not associated with government agencies.
private warehouse A facility designed to meet the specific needs of its owner.
problem definition The process by which a business clearly identifies a problem and what is needed to solve it.
producer price index (PPI) Measurement of wholesale price levels in the economy.

product depth The number of items offered within each product line.

product features Basic, physical, or extended attributes of a product or purchase.

product item A specific model, brand, or size of a product within a product line.

product life cycle The stages that a product goes through during its life.

product line A group of closely related products manufactured or sold by a business.

product mix All the different products that a company makes or sells.

product mix pricing strategies Adjusting prices to maximize the profitability for a group of products rather than just one item.

product modification An alteration in a company's existing product.

product planning Making decisions about the features and services of a product or idea that will help sell that product.

product positioning The image a product projects that sets it apart from the competition.

product promotion A promotion method businesses use to convince consumers to select its products or services.

product research The evaluation of product design, package design, product usage, and consumer acceptance of new and existing products.

product width The number of different product lines a business manufactures or sells.

production The process of creating, expanding, manufacturing, or improving on goods and services.

productivity The output per worker hour that is measured over a defined period of time, such as a week, month, or year.

profit The money earned from conducting business after all costs and expenses have been paid.

promotion Decisions about advertising, personal selling, sales promotion, and publicity used to attract potential customers.

promotional advertising Advertising designed to increase sales.

promotional mix A combination of strategies and a cost effective allocation of resources.

promotional pricing A pricing technique in which prices are reduced for a short period of time, generally used in conjunction with sales promotions.

promotional tie-ins Sales promotional arrangements between one or more retailers or manufacturers; also known as cross-promotion and cross-selling campaigns.

proportion The relationship between and among objects in a display.

prospect A potential customer; also known as a lead.

protectionism A government's establishment of economic policies that restrict imports to protect domestic industries.

psychographics Studies of consumers based on social and psychological characteristics.

public employment agencies Employment agencies that are supported by state or federal taxes and offer free services to both job applicants and employers.

public relations (PR) Activities that help an organization influence a target audience

public sector Local, state, and federal government agencies and services, such as public libraries and state universities.

public warehouse Storage and handling facilities offered to any individual or company that will pay for its use.

publicity A tactic that public relations professionals use to bring information about an organization to the public's attention.

pull policy A process that directs promotion towards consumers.

purchase order (PO) A legal contract between a buyer and a supplier to purchase a specified number of products at a specified price.

push policy A manufacturer uses a mix of personal selling, advertising, and buying discounts to promote a product to large retailers that sell its products.

Q

qualitative research A type of research that focuses on smaller numbers of people (usually fewer than 100) and tries to answer why or how questions.

quality check method The merchandise is checked to determine whether the quality of goods received matches the quality of the products, which were ordered

quantitative research A type of research that answers questions that start with how many or how much.

quota A limit on either the quantity or monetary value of a product that may be imported.

R

rack jobbers Wholesalers that manage inventory and merchandising for retailers by counting stock, filling it in when needed, and maintaining store displays.

rational motive A conscious, logical reason for a purchase.

real-time inventory system An Internet technology that connects applications, data, and users in real time.

realistic goal A goal that a person has a reasonable chance of achieving.

receiving record Information recorded by businesses about the goods they receive.

recession A period of economic slowdown that lasts for two quarters, or six months.

recovery A period of renewed economic growth followed by a recession or depression.

references People who know a job applicant's work habits and personal traits well and will recommend that person for the job.

referrals The names of other people who might buy a product, given to salespeople by satisfied customers.

reliability When a research technique produces nearly identical results in repeated trials.

remedial action Using preventive discipline or corrective discipline to encourage appropriate workplace behavior.

resources All the things used in producing goods and services.

résumé A brief summary of personal information, education, skills, work experience, activities, and interests.

retailers Channel of distribution that buys goods from wholesalers or directly from manufacturers and resells them to the consumer.

return on investment (ROI) A calculation that is used to determine the relative profitability of a product.

revolving accounts Charge accounts where the retailer determines the credit limit and payment terms.

risk management The systematic process of managing an organization's risks to achieve objectives in a manner consistent with public interest, human safety, environmental needs, and the law.

routine decision making The process used when a person needs little information about a product to make a decision because he or she buys it regularly.

S

sales check A written record of a sales transaction that includes such information as the date of the transaction, items purchased, purchase prices, sales tax, and the total amount due.

sales forecasts The projection of probable future sales in units or dollars.

sales promotion All marketing activities--other than personal selling, advertising, and public relations--that are used to stimulate purchasing and sales.

sales quotas Dollar or unit sales goals set for the sales staff to achieve in a specified period of time.

sales tax A percentage fee placed by the government on the sale of goods and services.

sample A part of the target population that is assumed to represent the entire population.

scarcity The difference between what consumers want and need and what the available resources are.

secondary data Data that has already been collected for some purpose other than the current study.

Securities and Exchange Commission (SEC) Federal agency that regulates the sale of securities (stocks and bonds), licenses brokerage firms and financial advisers, and investigates dealings among corporations.

segmented pricing strategy A pricing strategy that uses two or more different prices for a product, even though there is no difference in the item's cost.

selective distribution A limited number of outlets in a given geographic area are used to sell the product.

service approach A way to approach a customer that focuses on asking the customer if he or she needs assistance.

service close A way to close a sale in which a salesperson explains services that overcome obstacles or problems.

services Intangible items of monetary value that satisfy needs and wants.

setting The circumstances under which communication takes place.

signature The distinctive identification for a business; also known as logotype or logo.

situation analysis The study of the internal and external factors that affect marketing strategies.

site map An outline of what can be found on each page within the Web site.

six-month merchandise plan The budget that estimates planned purchases for a six-month period.

skimming pricing A pricing policy that sets a very high price for a new product.

slogan A catchy phrase or words that identify a product or company.

sole proprietorship A business owned and operated by one person.

source marking The seller or manufacturer marks the price before delivering the merchandise to the retailer; the marking often uses a universal product code (UPC).

specialty media Relatively inexpensive, useful items featuring an advertiser's name or logo that are given away; also known as giveaways or advertising specialties.

spot check method The receiver of a delivery conducts a check of one carton in a shipment to see if the right kind and quantity of goods were delivered.

spreadsheet programs Software applications used to organize, calculate, and analyze numerical data.

staffing/temporary agencies Employment agencies that are not supported by taxes and must earn a profit to stay in business.

standard English The formal style of writing and speaking that is taught in school.

standing-room-only close A method of closing a sale that is used when a product is in short supply or when the price will be going up in the near future.

start-up costs Projections of how much money a new business owner will need for the business's first year in operation.

stockholders The owners of a corporation with limited liability.

stockkeeping unit (SKU) A unit or a group of related items in a unit control inventory system; the smallest unit used in inventory control.

storage A marketing function that refers to the holding of goods until they are sold.

store layout The ways that stores use floor space to facilitate and promote sales and serve customers.

storefront The exterior of a business that includes a store's sign or logo, marquee, outdoor lighting, banners, planters, awnings, windows, the exterior design, ambiance, landscaping, and lighting of the building.

substitution method A selling method that involves recommending a different product that would still satisfy the customer's needs.

suggestion selling A method of selling in which the salesperson recommends additional goods or services to the customer.

superior-point method A selling technique that permits the salesperson to acknowledge objections as valid yet still offset them with other features and benefits.

supervisory-level management Managers who supervise the activities of employees who carry out the tasks determined by middle and top management.

supply The amount of goods producers are willing to make and sell.

survey method A research technique in which information is gathered from people through the use of surveys or questionnaires.

SWOT analysis An assessment of a company's strengths and weaknesses and the opportunities and threats that surround it; SWOT: strengths, weaknesses, opportunities, threats.

T

target market A group of people identified as those most likely to become customers.

tariff A tax on imports; also known as a duty.

teamwork Work done by a group of people to achieve a common goal.

telecommuting A program that involves working at home, usually on a computer, with completed jobs transmitted by e-mail or mail-in disk.

telemarketing The process of selling over the phone.

terms for delivery The final delivery arrangement between the buyer and seller.

third-party method A selling method that involves using a previous customer or other neutral person who can give a testimonial about the product.

30-day accounts Accounts that enable customers to charge purchases during a month and pay the balance in full within 30 days after they are billed.

till The cash drawer of a cash register.

time management The process of budgeting time to accomplish tasks on a certain schedule.

ton-mile The movement of one ton (2,000 lbs) of freight one mile.

top management Managers who make decisions that affect the whole company.

trade character A specific type of brand mark, one with human form or characteristics.

trade name A phrase or symbol that identifies and promotes a company or a division of a particular corporation; also known as a corporate brand.

trade promotions Sales promotion activities designed to get support for a product from manufacturers, wholesalers, and retailers.

trademark A brand name, brand mark, trade name, trade character, or a combination of these elements that is given legal protection by the federal government.

trading area The geographical area from which a business draws its customers.

traditional economy Traditions and rituals that answer basic questions of what, how, and for whom.

transit advertising Advertising found on public transportation.

transportation The marketing function of moving a product from the place where it is made to the place where it is sold.

triadic colors Three colors that are equally spaced on the color wheel.

trial close An initial effort to close a sale.

U

uniform resource locator (URL) The address of a file that is available on the Internet, usually on the World Wide Web.

unit control A method of stock control that measures the quantities of merchandise that a business handles during a period of time.

unit pricing Including price information for a standard unit or measure so that consumers can compare prices more easily.

universal product code (UPC) A combination bar code and number used to identify a product and manufacturer.

unlimited liability A business owner's financial liability is not limited to investments in the business, but extends to his or her total ability to make payments.

utility An attribute of a product or service that makes it capable of satisfying consumers' wants and needs.

V

validity When questions asked on a questionnaire measure what was intended to be measured.

values Beliefs that guide the way people live.

vertical organization A hierarchical, up-and-down organizational structure in which the tasks and responsibilities of each level are clearly defined.

visual merchandising Coordinating the physical elements in a place of business to project the right image to customers.

W

want slips Customer requests for items that are not carried in the store.

warranty A promise or guarantee given to a customer that a product will meet certain standards.

warranty of fitness for a particular purpose A warranty used when the seller advises a customer that a product is suitable for a particular use, and the customer acts on that advice.

warranty of merchantability The seller's promise that the product sold is fit for its intended purpose.

which close A method of closing a sale that encourages a customer to make a decision between two items.

whistle-blowing Reporting an illegal action by one's employer.

wholesale and retail buyers Buyers who purchase goods for resale.

wholesalers Channel of distribution that obtains goods from manufacturers and resells them to industrial users, other wholesalers, and retailers.

Wi-Fi Technology that establishes a wireless fidelity Internet connection using radio frequencies.

word processing programs Software applications designed to create documents that are primarily text but may contain a few graphics.

World Trade Organization (WTO) A global coalition of more than 140 governments that makes rules governing international trade.

World Wide Web (www) A subset of the Internet that is a collection of interlinked electronic documents.

INDEX

A

B

INDEX

C

D

INDEX

INDEX

J

K

L

M

N

O

P

INDEX

Q

T

U

V

W

Y

Z

Photo Credits

© 2004 ACE Limited. ACE, ACE Group, Insuring Progress and the ACE logo are trademarks or registered trademarks of ACE Limited and/or its affiliates in the U.S. and/or other countries **728;** AFP/Getty Images **72–73;** © AirTran Airways. All rights reserved. Reprinted by permission **685;** Roger Allyn Lee/SuperStock **724;** © Almond Board of California. All rights reserved. Reprinted by permission **128;** © 2004 amazon.com, Inc. All rights reserve **28;** The 3-A-Day™ of Dairy logo is a mark owned by Dairy Management Inc™. © 2005 American Dairy Association® managed by Dairy Management Inc™. All rights reserved **5;** Courtesy/Apple Computer, Inc. **160,** AP/Wide World Photos **24–25, 122-123, 322(t);** Bill Aron/PhotoEdit **296(t), 817;** ASAP Ltd./Index Stock Imagery **470;** © Athleta. All rights reserved. Reprinted by permission **297, 486;** © AT&T All rights reserved. Reprinted by permission **545;** Sandra Baker/Photographer's Choice/Getty Images **462–463;** BananaStock/Age Fotostock **181(c), 364(bl);** © Barnes & Noble.com. Reprinted by permission **447;** Davis Barber/PhotoEdit **644;** Tom Bible/Alamy Images **78;** © Bingham McCutchen LLP. Reprinted by permission **759;** Sky Bonillo/PhotoEdit **17(tr), 707(tr);** © Boost Mobile. All rights reserved. Reprinted by permission **18;** Matthew Borkoski/Index Stock Imagery **v, 298;** © BP p.l.c. All rights reserved. Reprinted by permission **136;** Paula Bronstein/Getty Images Editorial **492;** Cleve Bryant/PhotoEdit **350,** William Thomas Cain/Getty Images Editorial **707(br);** Tom Carter/ PhotoEdit **17(bl);** Ken Cedeno/Corbis **598(tl);** Chapman/The Image Works, Inc. **749(br);** Flip Chalfant/Image Bank/Getty Images **466(br);** Stephen Chernin/Getty Images Editorial **267(t);** Steve Chenn/Corbis **vii, 101;** © Citicorp. All rights reserved. Reprinted by permission **404;** L. Clarke/Corbis **127(t);** © The Company corporation® 1993–2002. All rights reserved. Reprinted by permission. The Company Corporation is an incorporated service company ad does not offer legal or financial advice **705;** Comstock Images/Alamy Images **322(b);** Gary Conner/Index Stock Imagery **611(bl);** Corbis **315, 466(bl), 611(cr);** Corbis/Sygma **281;** Greig Cranna/Index Stock Imagery **442–443;** Jim Craigmyle/Corbis **749(tr);** Francisco Cruz/SuperStock **736–737;** Richard Cummins/Corbis **386(tl);** Bob Daemmrich Photography **286(b);** Bob Daemmrich/PhotoEdit **185, 804–805;** photo used with permission from DECA, 1908 Association Drive, Reston, Virginia 20191-1594 **23, 45, 71, 93, 121, 145, 175, 195, 215, 233, 253, 275, 291, 311, 331, 355, 379, 398, 419, 438, 461, 479, 499, 519, 541, 563, 585, 607, 627, 651, 671, 691, 715, 735, 755, 779, 803, 825;** © Dell Inc. All rights reserved. Reprinted by permission **549;** © 2004 DHL. All rights reserved. Reprinted by permission **29;** Digital Vision **286(t), 480–481, 557(l), 707(bl);** DiMaggio/Kalish/Corbis **534(br);** Reprinted by permission of The National Organization on Disability **246;** Tommy Dodson/Unicorn Stock Photos **404(br);** Dynamic Graphics Group / Creatas/Alamy Images **112;** David Epperson/Photographer's Choice/Getty Images **780;** Rachel Epstein/PhotoEdit **286(c);** Britt Erlanson/Image Bank/Getty Images **201;** ER Productions/Brand X Pictures/Alamy Images **181(t);** © ESPN All rights reserved. Reprinted by permission **413;** Amy Etra/PhotoEdit **720(tr);** Susan Van Etten/PhotoEdit **480–481, 534(l), 580;** Najlah Feanny/Corbis **742;** © 2003 FedEx. All rights reserved. Reprinted by permission **29;** Jon Feingersh/Corbis **238, 280;** Myrleen Ferguson Cate/PhotoEdit **164,** Fisher/Thatcher/Stone/Getty Images **216–217;** Florida's Natural Growers, a division of Citrus World, Inc., based in Lake Wales, FL © 2004 **445;** © Ford Motor Company. All rights reserved. Reprinted by permission **424;** Daniel Fort/Index Stock Imagery **386(cr);** Rob Gage/Taxi/Getty Images **xiv, 15(b);** © Garmin. All rights reserved. Reprinted by permission **364;** Mannie Garcia/Reuters/Landov **127(c);** Jane Garnes, photographer **iii;** © 2003 Genta Inc. All rights reserved. Reprinted by permission **266;** © General Motors corporation. All rights reserved. Reprinted by permission **638;** Getty Images **196–197;** Getty Images Editorial **15(t), 50–51, 391, 449;** Robert W. Ginn/PhotoEdit **322(cr);** Todd A. Gipstein/Corbis **104;** © GlaxoSmithKline. All rights reserved. Reprinted by permission **137;** Spencer Grant/PhotoEdit **129, 207(t), 276–277, 296(b), 575, 598(tr), 720(br);** Jeff Greenberg/Age Foto-stock **83, 296(c), 638(bl);** Jeff Greenberg/PhotoEdit **220, 398–399, 493(bl), 720(l);** Holly Harris/Taxi/Getty Images **564–565;** Will Hart/PhotoEdit **228(r);** John Henley/Corbis **181(b);** Noel Hendrickson/Masterfile **420–421;** Holos/Image Bank/Getty Images **179,** Jack Hollingsworth/Brand X Pictures/Alamy Images **267(b), 684;** Robert Holmes/Corbis **493(l);** Reprinted by permission of Operation HOPE **403;** Richard Hutchings/PhotoEdit **557(r);** © The Iams Company. All rights reserved. Reprinted by permission **636;** Reprinted by permission of Ideo **746;** © Independent Bank Corp. All rights reserved. Reprinted by permission **372;** © JCP Media, L.P., 2005. All rights reserved. Reprinted by permission **364, 371;** Ray Juno/Corbis **466(tr);** ® TM, © Kellogg NA Co. All rights reserved. Reprinted by permission **306;** Michael Keller/Corbis **156;** Kraus/f1online/Alamy Images **241(t);** Christian Lagereek/Stone/Getty Images **468;** Robert Landau/Corbis **542–543;** © Levi Strauss & Co. All rights reserved. Reprinted by permission **655;** Rob Lewine/Corbis **826;** All rights reserved. Reprinted with permission from Liberty Mutual Group, 2004 **727;** Robert Llewellyn/ImageState/Alamy Images **511;** Richard Lord/PhotoEdit **787;** Buck Lovell/Index Stock Imagery **xii, 466(tl), 602(tl);** LWA- JDC/Corbis **241(b);** Dennis MacDonald/Alamy Images **615;** Dennis MacDonald/PhotoEdit **ix, 385, 432;** Marketing Wheel copyright 2000, Marketing Education Resource Center, Columbus, Ohio. Used with permission **xxvii, 49, 97, 149, 257, 359, 441, 523, 589, 631, 695, 783;** © Marsh Inc. All rights reserved. Reprinted by permission **730;** Cesar® is a trademark of Mars, Incorporated and its affiliates. The trademark is used with permission. Mars, Incorporated is not associated with Glencoe/McGraw-Hill. Advertisement printed with permission of Mars, Incorporated. © Mars, Inc. 2005. **427;** Felicia Martinez/PhotoEdit **665;** James Marshall/The Image Works, Inc. **176–177;**Marianna Day Massey/Zuma Press **484;** © Marvel Enterprises. Reprinted by permission **xi, 87;** © McDonald's corporation. All rights reserved. Reprinted by permission **135;** Jim McGuire/Index Stock Imagery **505(tl);** Ryan McVay/PhotoDisc/Getty Images **312–313, 364(br);** Rob Melnychuk/PhotoDisc **386(bl);** Reprinted by permission of the Metal Roofing Alliance **677;** Frank Micelotta/Getty Images Editorial **572;** © Mitsubishi Motors. All rights reserved. Reprinted by permission **228;** © Monster Inc. All rights reserved. Reprinted by permission **809;** Gail Mooney/Masterfile **150–151;** Antonio Mo/Taxi/Getty Images **234–235;** Sven Nackstrand/AFP/Getty Images **390–391;** Michael Newman/PhotoEdit **386(br), 509, 598(br);** © The Northwestern Mutual financial Network® All rights reserved. Reprinted by permission **285;** Dennis O'Clair/Stone/Getty Images **505(tl);** Paul O Driscoll/Bloomberg News/Landov **500–501;** Patrick Olear/PhotoEdit **332–333;** © OnStar. All rights reserved. Reprinted by permission **31;** Jose Luis Pelaez, Inc./Corbis **247, 534(tr), 598(bl);** © PeopleSoft® All rights reserved. Reprinted by permission **200;** © 2003 Perdue Farms Incorporated. All rights reserved. Reprinted by permission **13;** Performance standards copyright 2000, Marketing Education Resource Center, Columbus, Ohio. Used with permission **3, 25, 51, 71, 73, 150, 176, 197, 217, 235, 259, 277, 293, 313, 333, 361, 381, 399, 421, 443, 463, 481, 501, 525, 543, 565, 591, 609, 633, 653, 673, 697, 717, 737, 757, 785, 805;** Bryan F. Peterson/Corbis **652–653;** PhotoDisc **222, 611(tr);** PhotoDisc/Getty Images **254;** Joseph Pobereskin/Stone/Getty Images **611(br);** © 2004 United States Postal Service. Eagle symbol is a registered trademark of the United States Postal Service. All rights reserved. Reprinted by permission **29;** Reprinted by permission of the United States Potato Board **621;** © Procter & Gamble. All rights reserved. Reprinted by permission **404;** © Procter & Gamble. All rights reserved. Reprinted by permission **426;** © QantasUSA. All rights reserved. Reprinted by permission **110;** David Raymer/Corbis **241(c);** Jon Feingersh/Masterfile **632–633;** Reuters/Corbis **316;** Jiri Rezac/Alamy Images **672–673;** Jim Richardson/Corbis **125;** Mark Richards/PhotoEdit **505(bl), 638(tl);** Elena Rooraid/PhotoEdit **749(l);** Sandisk and the SanDisk logo are registered trademarks and Cruzer is a trademark of Sandisk corporation. ©2003 SanDisk Corporation. All rights reserved **299;** Stefan Sauer/dpa/Landov **58;** Chuck Savage/Corbis **258–259, 628, 756–757;** Harvey Schwartz/Index Stock Imagery **130,** Mark Scott/Image Bank/Getty Images **505(br);** Mike Segar/Reuters/Landov **586;** © Sharman Networks 2002–2004. All rights reserved. Reprinted by permission **127;** © Sherwin-Williams. All rights reserved. Reprinted by permission **9;** Mike Simons/Getty Images Editorial **590–591;** © Sodexho USA. All rights reserved. Reprinted by permission **139;** Joe Sohm/Alamy Images **707(tl);** *www.spaininfo.com.* All rights reserved. Reprinted by permission **54;** Chris Stanford/Getty Images Editorial **46, 360–361;** Tom Stewart/Corbis **239, 784–785;** © Stonyfield Farm Inc., 2004. All rights reserved. Reprinted by permission **664;** SuperStock **270,** SuperStock/Age Fotostock **338;** SW Productions/PhotoDisc **696–697;** © Symantec Corporation. All rights reserved. Reprinted by permission **210;** Syracuse Newspapers/The Image Works, Inc. **203;** Syracuse Newspapers/The Image Works, Inc. **520;** Mario Tama/Getty Images Editorial **483;** © 2003 by Tempur-Pedic, Inc. All rights reserved. Reprinted by permission **303;** © The Territory Ahead. All rights reserved. Reprinted by permission **448;** Arthur Tilley/Taxi/Getty Images **98–99, 608–609;** Time Life Pictures/Getty Images **700;** © 2004 Toyota Motor Sales, U.S.A., Inc. All rights reserved. Reprinted by permission **103, 263;** © 2004 Tropicana Products, Inc. All rights reserved. Reprinted by permission **21;** Yoshikazu Tsuno/AFP/Getty Images **243;** Reprinted by permission of Two Men and a Truck® **768;** © 2002 Underwriters Laboratory Inc. All rights reserved. Reprinted by permission **680;** UPI Photo/Bill Greenblatt/Landov **676;** © Verizon Wireless. All rights reserved. Reprinted by permission **75;** Vote Photography/Alamy Images **vi, 53;** Peter Walton/Index Stock Imagery **474;** © Warner Books, a division of Little, Brown & Company. Reprinted by permission **223;** © WebEx. All rights reserved. Reprinted bypermission **318;** © Wendy's International, Inc. All rights reserved.Reprinted by permission **529;** WENN/Landov **493(tl);** Jim West/Alamy Images **94;** Jamal A. Wilson/AFP/Getty Images **716–717;** Marshall Williams/ImageState **xvi, 102;** Colin Young-Wolff/PhotoEdit **793(b), 793(t);** David Young-Wolff/PhotoEdit **207(b), 302, 322(cl), 384, 386(tr), 532, 547, 600, 611(tl), 692, 791;** David Young-Wolff/Stone/Getty Images **292–293;** How-Man Wong/Corbis **55;** © 2002 Woods & Poole Economics, Inc. Reprinted by permission **599;** Andrew Woodley/Alamy Images **2–3;** © 2002 Xerox corporation. All rights Reserved. Xerox®, The Document Company®, Phaser® and There's a new way to look at it™ are trademarks of Xerox Corporation **431;** Peter Yates/Zuma Press **789;** Barry Yee/Stone/Getty Images **267(c);** Image copyright-Zappos.com. All rights reserved. Reprinted by permission **113.**